Windows® 2000 Programming Secrets®

Windows® 2000 Programming Secrets®

Clayton Walnum

IDG Books Worldwide, Inc.
An International Data Group Company

Foster City, CA ♦ Chicago, IL ♦ Indianapolis, IN ♦ New York, NY

Windows® 2000 Programming Secrets®
Published by
IDG Books Worldwide, Inc.
An International Data Group Company
919 E. Hillsdale Blvd., Suite 400
Foster City, CA 94404
www.idgbooks.com (IDG Books Worldwide Web site)

Copyright © 2000 IDG Books Worldwide, Inc. All rights reserved. No part of this book, including interior design, cover design, and icons, may be reproduced or transmitted in any form, by any means (electronic, photocopying, recording, or otherwise) without the prior written permission of the publisher.

ISBN: 0-7645-4663-5

Printed in the United States of America

10 9 8 7 6 5 4 3 2 1

1B/RY/QX/QQ/FC

Distributed in the United States by IDG Books Worldwide, Inc.

Distributed by CDG Books Canada Inc. for Canada; by Transworld Publishers Limited in the United Kingdom; by IDG Norge Books for Norway; by IDG Sweden Books for Sweden; by IDG Books Australia Publishing Corporation Pty. Ltd. for Australia and New Zealand; by TransQuest Publishers Pte Ltd. for Singapore, Malaysia, Thailand, Indonesia, and Hong Kong; by Gotop Information Inc. for Taiwan; by ICG Muse, Inc. for Japan; by Intersoft for South Africa; by Eyrolles for France; by International Thomson Publishing for Germany, Austria, and Switzerland; by Distribuidora Cuspide for Argentina; by LR International for Brazil; by Galileo Libros for Chile; by Ediciones ZETA S.C.R. Ltda. for Peru; by WS Computer Publishing Corporation, Inc., for the Philippines; by Contemporanea de Ediciones for Venezuela; by Express Computer Distributors for the Caribbean and West Indies; by Micronesia Media Distributor, Inc. for Micronesia; by Chips Computadoras S.A. de C.V. for Mexico; by Editorial Norma de Panama S.A. for Panama; by American Bookshops for Finland.

For general information on IDG Books Worldwide's books in the U.S., please call our Consumer Customer Service department at 800-762-2974. For reseller information, including discounts and premium sales, please call our Reseller Customer Service department at 800-434-3422.

For information on where to purchase IDG Books Worldwide's books outside the U.S., please contact our International Sales department at 317-596-5530 or fax 317-572-4002.

For consumer information on foreign language translations, please contact our Customer Service department at 800-434-3422, fax 317-572-4002, or e-mail rights@idgbooks.com.

For information on licensing foreign or domestic rights, please phone +1-650-653-7098.

For sales inquiries and special prices for bulk quantities, please contact our Order Services department at 800-434-3422 or write to the address above.

For information on using IDG Books Worldwide's books in the classroom or for ordering examination copies, please contact our Educational Sales department at 800-434-2086 or fax 317-572-4005.

For press review copies, author interviews, or other publicity information, please contact our Public Relations department at 650-653-7000 or fax 650-653-7500.

For authorization to photocopy items for corporate, personal, or educational use, please contact Copyright Clearance Center, 222 Rosewood Drive, Danvers, MA 01923, or fax 978-750-4470.

Library of Congress Cataloging-in-Publication Data

Walnum, Clayton.
    Windows 2000 programming secrets / Clayton Walnum.
       p. cm.
    ISBN 0-7645-4663-5 (alk. paper)
    1. Microsoft Windows (Computer file) 2. Operating systems (Computers) I. Title.

QA76.76.063 W3592   2000
005.4'4769--dc21   00-032015

LIMIT OF LIABILITY/DISCLAIMER OF WARRANTY: THE PUBLISHER AND AUTHOR HAVE USED THEIR BEST EFFORTS IN PREPARING THIS BOOK. THE PUBLISHER AND AUTHOR MAKE NO REPRESENTATIONS OR WARRANTIES WITH RESPECT TO THE ACCURACY OR COMPLETENESS OF THE CONTENTS OF THIS BOOK AND SPECIFICALLY DISCLAIM ANY IMPLIED WARRANTIES OF MERCHANTABILITY OR FITNESS FOR A PARTICULAR PURPOSE. THERE ARE NO WARRANTIES WHICH EXTEND BEYOND THE DESCRIPTIONS CONTAINED IN THIS PARAGRAPH. NO WARRANTY MAY BE CREATED OR EXTENDED BY SALES REPRESENTATIVES OR WRITTEN SALES MATERIALS. THE ACCURACY AND COMPLETENESS OF THE INFORMATION PROVIDED HEREIN AND THE OPINIONS STATED HEREIN ARE NOT GUARANTEED OR WARRANTED TO PRODUCE ANY PARTICULAR RESULTS, AND THE ADVICE AND STRATEGIES CONTAINED HEREIN MAY NOT BE SUITABLE FOR EVERY INDIVIDUAL. NEITHER THE PUBLISHER NOR AUTHOR SHALL BE LIABLE FOR ANY LOSS OF PROFIT OR ANY OTHER COMMERCIAL DAMAGES, INCLUDING BUT NOT LIMITED TO SPECIAL, INCIDENTAL, CONSEQUENTIAL, OR OTHER DAMAGES.

Trademarks: All brand names and product names used in this book are trade names, service marks, trademarks, or registered trademarks of their respective owners. IDG Books Worldwide is not associated with any product or vendor mentioned in this book.

 is a registered trademark or trademark under exclusive license to IDG Books Worldwide, Inc. from International Data Group, Inc. in the United States and/or other countries.

 is a trademark of IDG Books Worldwide, Inc.

ABOUT IDG BOOKS WORLDWIDE

Welcome to the world of IDG Books Worldwide.

IDG Books Worldwide, Inc., is a subsidiary of International Data Group, the world's largest publisher of computer-related information and the leading global provider of information services on information technology. IDG was founded more than 30 years ago by Patrick J. McGovern and now employs more than 9,000 people worldwide. IDG publishes more than 290 computer publications in over 75 countries. More than 90 million people read one or more IDG publications each month.

Launched in 1990, IDG Books Worldwide is today the #1 publisher of best-selling computer books in the United States. We are proud to have received eight awards from the Computer Press Association in recognition of editorial excellence and three from Computer Currents' First Annual Readers' Choice Awards. Our best-selling ...*For Dummies*® series has more than 50 million copies in print with translations in 31 languages. IDG Books Worldwide, through a joint venture with IDG's Hi-Tech Beijing, became the first U.S. publisher to publish a computer book in the People's Republic of China. In record time, IDG Books Worldwide has become the first choice for millions of readers around the world who want to learn how to better manage their businesses.

Our mission is simple: Every one of our books is designed to bring extra value and skill-building instructions to the reader. Our books are written by experts who understand and care about our readers. The knowledge base of our editorial staff comes from years of experience in publishing, education, and journalism — experience we use to produce books to carry us into the new millennium. In short, we care about books, so we attract the best people. We devote special attention to details such as audience, interior design, use of icons, and illustrations. And because we use an efficient process of authoring, editing, and desktop publishing our books electronically, we can spend more time ensuring superior content and less time on the technicalities of making books.

You can count on our commitment to deliver high-quality books at competitive prices on topics you want to read about. At IDG Books Worldwide, we continue in the IDG tradition of delivering quality for more than 30 years. You'll find no better book on a subject than one from IDG Books Worldwide.

John Kilcullen
Chairman and CEO
IDG Books Worldwide, Inc.

Eighth Annual Computer Press Awards ≥1992

Ninth Annual Computer Press Awards ≥1993

Tenth Annual Computer Press Awards ≥1994

Eleventh Annual Computer Press Awards ≥1995

IDG is the world's leading IT media, research and exposition company. Founded in 1964, IDG had 1997 revenues of $2.05 billion and has more than 9,000 employees worldwide. IDG offers the widest range of media options that reach IT buyers in 75 countries representing 95% of worldwide IT spending. IDG's diverse product and services portfolio spans six key areas including print publishing, online publishing, expositions and conferences, market research, education and training, and global marketing services. More than 90 million people read one or more of IDG's 290 magazines and newspapers, including IDG's leading global brands — Computerworld, PC World, Network World, Macworld and the Channel World family of publications. IDG Books Worldwide is one of the fastest-growing computer book publishers in the world, with more than 700 titles in 36 languages. The "...For Dummies®" series alone has more than 50 million copies in print. IDG offers online users the largest network of technology-specific Web sites around the world through IDG.net (http://www.idg.net), which comprises more than 225 targeted Web sites in 55 countries worldwide. International Data Corporation (IDC) is the world's largest provider of information technology data, analysis and consulting, with research centers in over 41 countries and more than 400 research analysts worldwide. IDG World Expo is a leading producer of more than 168 globally branded conferences and expositions in 35 countries including E3 (Electronic Entertainment Expo), Macworld Expo, ComNet, Windows World Expo, ICE (Internet Commerce Expo), Agenda, DEMO, and Spotlight. IDG's training subsidiary, ExecuTrain, is the world's largest computer training company, with more than 230 locations worldwide and 785 training courses. IDG Marketing Services helps industry-leading IT companies build international brand recognition by developing global integrated marketing programs via IDG's print, online and exposition products worldwide. Further information about the company can be found at www.idg.com.
1/26/00

Credits

Acquisitions Editor
Greg Croy

Project Editor
Andy Marinkovich

Technical Editor
Greg Guntle

Copy Editors
Victoria Lee
Luann Rouff
Mildred Sanchez

Proof Editor
Neil Romanosky

Project Coordinators
Joe Shines
Danette Nurse

Media Development Manager
Stephen Noetzel

Graphics and Production Specialists
Robert Bilhmayer
Jude Levinson
Michael Lewis
Dina F Quan

Illustrator
Karl Brandt

Proofreading and Indexing
York Production Services

Design Specialists
Kurt Krames
Kippy Thomsen

About the Author

Award-winning author Clayton Walnum started programming computers in 1982, when he traded in an IBM Selectric typewriter to buy an Atari 400 computer (16K of RAM!). Clay soon learned to combine his interest in writing with his newly acquired programming skills and started selling programs and articles to computer magazines. In 1985, ANALOG Computing, a nationally distributed computer magazine, hired him as a technical editor, and, before leaving the magazine business in 1989 to become a freelance writer, Clay had worked his way up to executive editor. He has since acquired a degree in Computer Science, as well as written or co-written more than 40 books (translated into many languages) covering everything from computer gaming to 3D graphics programming. He has also written hundreds of magazine articles and software reviews, as well as countless programs. His recent books include *Standard C++ Bible* (written with Al Stevens), *C++ Master Reference*, and *The Complete Idiot's Guide to Visual Basic 6*. Clay's biggest disappointment in life is that he wasn't one of the Beatles. To compensate, he writes and records rock music in his home studio. You can reach Mr. Walnum at his home page, which is located at www.claytonwalnum.com, or visit his music page at www.mp3.com/claywalnum.

To Lynn

Preface

You may have heard that learning to program Windows 2000 is a lot like studying to build a spaceship, that there's so much to learn that only someone with an IQ of 180, and with 12 hours a day to study, could possibly master the techniques required. Of course, none of this is true, although, as with all exaggerations, there's an element of truth. Yes, learning to program Windows 2000 applications represents a big task. However, most people will be able to get the job done, and you don't have to dedicate your life to it either. A couple of hours a day will suffice.

Would-be Windows programmers, today, have a big advantage over those of a few years ago. Namely, the programming tools available to them are more sophisticated than ever. Not only can a basic Windows application be put together in minutes (as compared with hours the old-fashioned way), but extras such as toolbars, status bars, and dialog boxes are only a few button clicks away. In fact, with Visual C++ 6.0, you can create a Windows application by simply typing a program name and clicking the mouse five times. Pretty easy, eh?

Of course, creating a program like this isn't especially useful. Like a new house without electricity, plumbing, or furnishings, you still have to supply all the stuff that makes people want to visit. That's where this book comes in. In the pages that follow, you'll learn not only what makes a basic Windows 2000 program work, but also how to add everything beyond the basic essentials to your programs. You'll learn about event-driven programming, responding to Windows messages, creating custom dialog boxes, drawing a window's display, printing documents, displaying bitmaps, creating threads, and much more.

Along the way, you'll also get an introduction to some advanced technologies, including ActiveX, DirectX, and Internet programming with WinInet. ActiveX is Microsoft's name for what you may have known as OLE, a technology that enables applications to share not only data, but also program functionality. Using ActiveX, you can even create mini-applications, called ActiveX controls, which can be embedded into Web pages. DirectX, on the other hand, is a set of multimedia technologies used mostly for game programming, whereas WinInet is a set of classes that make creating Internet applications easier than you might believe possible.

Who Should Read This Book

This book is not a C++ tutorial. In order to understand the lessons here, you must already be fluent in C++ and understand object-oriented programming (OOP) concepts. If you're new to C++ and OOP, you should pick up a good general C++ programming book such as *Standard C++ Bible* by Al Stevens and Clayton Walnum, as well as a comprehensive Visual C++ book such as

Visual C++ Bible by Richard C. Leinecker and Paul Yao. Both books are published by IDG Books Worldwide. Once you've worked through those books (or some similar books), you can come back to this one.

Although this book assumes reasonable expertise with C++, it assumes no previous Windows programming knowledge. This book includes all the information you need to create most types of Windows applications. When you've completed this book, you'll have a solid grasp of Windows programming techniques and will be able to move on to more advanced books that concentrate on specific technologies, such as ActiveX or DirectX.

System Requirements

The system and software requirements for the programs and lessons in this book are essentially the same as the requirements for Visual C++ 6.0 running under Windows 2000:

- IBM-compatible with a 133MHz or higher Pentium processor
- Microsoft Windows 2000
- 32MB RAM (64MB recommended)
- 2GB hard disk with 650MB free
- CD-ROM drive
- VGA or better graphics (Super VGA recommended)
- Mouse
- Visual C++ 6.0

This Book's Overall Structure

This book covers a huge amount of Windows 2000 programming territory and, therefore, is divided into seven sections, each of which is described below.

Part I: Fundamental Windows 2000 Programming

This section covers the various types of Windows 2000 programs, before jumping into user-interface programming, including using the Windows' Graphics Device Interface (GDI), which enables applications to display data in their windows. You'll also study the various types of windows you can create, including frame windows, view windows, MDI windows, dialog boxes, property sheets, and wizards.

After presenting the basics, this section moves on to show how to manipulate text, create menu resources, and use standard and common controls. The standard controls include objects such as pushbuttons, edit boxes, checkboxes, radio buttons, list boxes, and combo boxes. The common controls include progress bars, status bars, sliders, spinners, list views, and tree views. After studying controls, you'll move on to printing documents under Windows 2000.

Part II: Advanced Windows 2000 Programming

This section includes information on managing and displaying device-dependent and device-independent bitmaps. You also get some advanced GDI training, as you learn about coordinate systems, mapping modes, rectangles, regions, paths, and metafiles. Other chapters in this section cover such advanced topics as the taskbar, the system tray, shortcuts, and the Registry, as well as creating an installation program for your application's end users.

Part III: OS Core Programming

By this point in the book, you'll already have accumulated most of the basic skills you need to create Windows applications, so here you'll dig into some more advanced topics, including memory management, process control, input devices, and file handling. You'll learn how to allocate and manage memory, as well as how to create multithreaded applications. As you study these topics, you'll understand about movable, discardable, and virtual memory, as well as process and thread priorities, user-interface and worker threads, and thread synchronization.

In this part of the book, you also get the skinny on handling the mouse and keyboard, as well as how to use Visual C++'s MFC classes to manage files and create persistent classes. Finally, you'll get lessons in implementing Clipboard support in your programs, including using standard, registered, private, and multiple data formats. You'll learn how to open the Clipboard, place data on the Clipboard, and copy data from the Clipboard.

Part IV: ActiveX Programming

The remainder of the book dedicates itself to the introduction of advanced technologies. In this part, you learn to create ActiveX applications with Visual C++'s tools. These applications include container applications (which can hold data objects from other applications), server applications (which supply data objects, as well as editing services for those objects), automation applications (which can control or be controlled by other applications in the system), and ActiveX controls.

As you learn about the ActiveX technologies, you'll work through hands-on projects that create functional ActiveX programs. Sample programs include container and server applications for sharing and editing data objects, automation clients and servers, and an ActiveX control. When you finish this section, you'll have a basic understanding of ActiveX technology and how it's supported by Visual C++ and the MFC libraries.

Part V: Multimedia Programming

This part of the book introduces you to Microsoft's DirectX multimedia technologies, which include DirectDraw, DirectSound, DirectInput, and

Direct3D. (DirectPlay is not covered here.) You learn to create animated displays using DirectDraw and how to play wave files using DirectSound. In the DirectInput chapter, you'll see how this advanced library can give input devices interesting new capabilities, without a lot of programming on your part. You'll even display and rotate a 3D model using Direct3D.

Part VI: Internet Programming

The Internet is becoming more and more important to computer operators everywhere. No Windows programming book would be complete without a look into programming Internet applications. MFC's WinInet libraries make it easy to create HTTP, FTP, and Gopher applications. In this section, you'll not only get an overview of these handy Internet programming classes, you'll also build an FTP application that can browse the directories on an FTP server and even download files.

Later in this section, you'll learn to use Internet Explorer's programmable objects to create your own sophisticated Internet applications. By exposing Internet Explorer's impressive capabilities via ActiveX, Microsoft made it reasonably easy for you to add even Web browsing capabilities to any application, a good example of Microsoft's ActiveX vision coming of age.

Icons Used in This Book

As you read this book, you'll notice several types of icons designed to draw your attention to important notes and tips. The following list describes the icons used in this book:

This icon marks programs and files that you can find on this book's CD-ROM.

This icon marks additional information about the current topic.

This icon marks tips that make programming tasks easier.

This icon directs you to additional or related material elsewhere in the book.

This icon highlights potential pitfalls you might encounter as you learn the material in the book.

Moving On

As you can see, this book covers a lot of territory. Seems to me that you have a lot of reading to do. And now just might be the perfect time to turn the page and get to work. I'll meet you there.

–Clayton Walnum

`www.claytonwalnum.com`

Acknowledgments

I would like to thank the many people whose hard work made this book as good as it could be. Special thanks go to Greg Croy for placing this important project in my care, to Andy Marinkovich for keeping things rolling, to Valerie Perry, Luann Rouff, Mildred Sanchez, Victoria Lee for polishing up the words, and to Greg Guntle for checking all the facts. As always, thanks goes to my family: Lynn, Christopher, Justin, Stephen, and Caitlynn.

Contents at a Glance

Preface ix
Acknowledgments xv

Part I: Fundamental Windows 2000 Programming 1

Chapter 1: Application Fundamentals 3
Chapter 2: Graphical Device Interface Basics 23
Chapter 3: Windows and Dialog Boxes 53
Chapter 4: Text 113
Chapter 5: Menus 139
Chapter 6: Standard Controls 163
Chapter 7: Common Controls 225
Chapter 8: Printing 295

Part II: Advanced Windows 2000 Programming 333

Chapter 9: Bitmaps 335
Chapter 10: Advanced GDI 397
Chapter 11: Programming the Windows User Interface 443
Chapter 12: The Registry 467
Chapter 13: Installing User Applications 485

Part III: OS Core Programming 511

Chapter 14: Process Control 513
Chapter 15: Input Devices: The Mouse and the Keyboard 547
Chapter 16: File Handling 571
Chapter 17: The Clipboard 593

Part IV: ActiveX Programming 621

Chapter 18: Introduction to ActiveX 623
Chapter 19: Containers 635
Chapter 20: Servers 651
Chapter 21: Automation 671
Chapter 22: ActiveX Controls 695

Part V: Multimedia Programming 711

Chapter 23: DirectDraw 713
Chapter 24: DirectSound 741
Chapter 25: DirectInput 761
Chapter 26: Direct3D 779

Part VI: Internet Programming 817
Chapter 27: WinInet 819
Chapter 28: Internet Explorer 849

Appendix: About the CD-ROM 885

Index 889

End-User License Agreement 926

CD-ROM Installation Instructions 930

Contents

Preface ix

Acknowledgments xv

Part I: Fundamental Windows 2000 Programming 1

Chapter 1: Application Fundamentals 3
Win32 Applications 3
    Traditional Win32 Applications 3
    Win32 Console Applications 4
    Dynamic-Link Libraries 5
    ActiveX Controls 6
Programming Windows the Hard Way 7
MFC versus C 15
    Initializing the Application 15
    MFC Message Handling 15

Chapter 2: Graphical Device Interface Basics 23
Introducing the GDI 23
Device Contexts 24
The Paint Device Context 27
    The Client-Area Device Context 29
    The Metafile Device Context 35
Device Capabilities 39
The CPen Class 42
The CBrush Class 45

Chapter 3: Windows and Dialog Boxes 53
The MFC Window Base Classes 54
    The CObject Class 54
    The CCmdTarget Class 55
    The CWnd Class 55
Frame and View Windows 58
    The CFrameWnd Class 58
    The CView Class 59
Window Basics: Creating an Application Without AppWizard 60
    Creating the BasicApp Application 61
    Understanding the BasicApp Application 66

Window Styles 69
    Changing Window Styles 71
    Window Styles in Non-MFC Programs 73
MDI Windows 77
Dialog Boxes 79
    Custom Dialog Boxes 80
Common Dialog Boxes 86
    The File Dialog Box 86
    The Font Dialog Box 91
    The Color Dialog Box 93
    The Common Dialog Application 95
Property Sheets 100
    Creating Property Pages and Sheets 101
    Programming the Property Sheet 104
    The PropSheet Application 106
Wizards 107
    Creating a Wizard 107
    Setting a Wizard's Buttons 107
    The WizardApp Application 110

Chapter 4: Text 113

Displaying Text 113
Setting Text Color 114
Setting Character Spacing 118
Setting Text Alignment 119
    Horizontal Text Alignment 120
    Vertical Text Alignment 123
Getting Text Metrics 128
Creating Fonts 131

Chapter 5: Menus 139

Creating Menu Resources 139
Creating Message-Response Functions 144
Understanding Menu UI Functions 147
    Creating Update Command UI Functions 148
    Marking Menu Items with Checks 149
    Bulleting Menu Items 150
    Enabling and Disabling Menu Items 151
    Changing Menu Item Text 152
The MenuApp Sample Application 154
    Using the MenuApp Sample Application 155
    Understanding the MenuApp Sample Application 156

Chapter 6: Standard Controls 163

Introducing the Standard Controls 163
Placing Controls in Non-Dialog Box Windows 164
Running the ControlApp2 Sample Application 165
Creating and Programming Standard Controls 170
    Static Controls 170

Edit Controls 174
Pushbuttons 181
Checkboxes 184
Radio Buttons 185
List Boxes 187
Combo Boxes 193
Changing a Control's Color 197
Manipulating Controls in Dialog Boxes 202
Creating the Application Skeleton 203
Creating the New Dialog Box 206
Adding Source Code to the View Class 212
Adding Source Code to the Dialog Box Class 214
Running DialogControlsApp 220
Understanding DialogControlsApp 221

Chapter 7: Common Controls 225

Introducing the Common Controls 225
Basic Common Controls 227
The CommonControlsApp Sample Application 227
Understanding the OnCreate() Function 228
The Progress Bar Control 229
The Slider Control 233
The Spinner Control 245
The Image List Control 249
Advanced Common Controls 255
The CommonControlsApp2 Sample Application 256
Understanding the OnCreate() Function 260
The List View Control 261
The Tree View Control 279

Chapter 8: Printing 295

An Overview of Printing in Windows 295
The Six Steps to Printing a Document 295
The BasicPrintApp Sample Program 298
Printing Text in an MFC Application 302
The PrintApp Sample Application 303
MFC Member Functions for Printing 304
Printing Graphics in an MFC Application 316
The PrintCircleApp Sample Application 316
Scaling Between the Screen and Printer 317
The OnCreate() Function 320
The OnDraw() Function 321
The OnPreparePrinting() Function 323

Part II: Advanced Windows 2000 Programming 333

Chapter 9: Bitmaps 335

Introducing DDBs and DIBs 335

Programming with Device-Dependent Bitmaps 336
    Creating and Initializing a Bitmap Object 336
    Creating the Memory DC 338
    Selecting the Bitmap into the Memory DC 339
    Drawing on the Bitmap 340
    Copying the Bitmap to the Display 341
    Copying a Bitmap Without Changing its Size 342
    Copying a Bitmap and Changing its Size 343
    Creating the BitmapApp Application 345
    Running the BitmapApp Application 351
Programming with Device-Independent Bitmaps 352
    Loading a DIB File 353
    The Custom CDib Class 358
    Displaying a DIB 363
    Managing Palettes 364
    Creating the BitmapApp2 Application 368
    Customizing the Application's Resources 370
    Adding Source Code 375
    Running the BitmapApp2 Application 380

Chapter 10: Advanced GDI 397

Physical and Logical Coordinates 397
Mapping Modes 399
    Experimenting with Window and Viewport Origins 400
    The MM_TEXT Mode 403
    Mapping with a Physical Unit of Measurement 406
    Scaling Logical Units to Arbitrary Coordinates 409
Raster Operations 416
    Bitmap Raster Operations 416
    Line Drawing Modes 421
Using Regions 428
    Creating and Drawing a Region 429
    Combining Regions 430
Using Paths 435
    Creating a Path 436
    Rendering a Path 436
    Defining Subpaths 437
    The PathApp Sample Program 437

Chapter 11: Programming the Windows User Interface 443

Using Drag-and-Drop 443
    Registering as a Drag-and-Drop Application 444
    Handling the WM_DROPFILES Message 445
    Getting the Dropped File Names 445
    Ending a Drag-and-Drop Operation 446
    The DragDrop2 Application 446
Manipulating Shortcuts 447
    Initializing COM 447
    Creating an IShellLink Object 448

Getting an IPersistFile Interface Pointer 449
Initializing the New Shortcut 449
Saving a Shortcut 450
Releasing Pointers and Uninitializing COM 451
The Shortcut Example Application 451
Manipulating Icons in the System Tray 452
Adding an Icon to the Tray 453
Responding to Icon Events 454
Removing an Icon from the Tray 455
The TrayApp Example Application 455
The Shell Namespace 458
Enumerating the Contents of a Folder 458
The NamespaceApp Application 459
Advanced Windows 2000 Features 464
DNA 464
Active Directory 465
MTS 465

Chapter 12: The Registry 467

Overview of the Registry 467
How the Registry Is Organized 468
Manipulating the Registry 471
Using the Registry Editor 471
Using the Registry Files 472
Using the Registry API 473
The RegistryApp Sample Program 474
Writing User Preferences to the Registry 475
Reading User Preferences from the Registry 480

Chapter 13: Installing User Applications 485

Product Packaging 485
Using InstallShield 486
Determining the Files to Package 486
Creating an Application to Install 487
Starting an InstallShield Project 488
Completing Component Setup 494
Completing File Group Setup 499
Creating the Media 502

Part III: OS Core Programming 511

Chapter 14: Process Control 513

Processes, Threads, and Priorities 513
Priority Settings for Processes and Threads 514
Worker Threads and User Interface Threads 516
Creating a Worker Thread 516
Creating a UI Thread 519

Thread Synchronization 524
    Using Event Objects 524
    Using Critical Sections 533
    Using Mutexes 536
    Using Semaphores 541

Chapter 15: Input Devices: The Mouse and the Keyboard 547

Input Events and Messages 547
Handling the Mouse 548
    Client-Area Mouse Messages 548
    Nonclient-Area Mouse Messages 549
    The Mouse Sample Application 552
Handling the Keyboard 559
    Keyboard Messages 559
    The Keys Sample Application 560
    Examining the Keys Application 561
    The KeyDown Sample Application 562
    Examining the KeyDown Application 566

Chapter 16: File Handling 571

The Document/View Architecture 571
    Step 1: Create a Skeleton Application 572
    Step 2: Declare the Document's Data Objects 573
    Step 3: Complete the OnNewDocument() Function 573
    Step 4: Override the DeleteContents() Function 574
    Step 5: Complete the Serialize() Function 574
    Step 6: Complete the OnDraw() Function 576
    Step 7: Add Editing Code 577
Persistent Objects 578
File Handling with the CFile Class 588

Chapter 17: The Clipboard 593

Standard Formats 594
    A Clipboard Example Application 595
    Copying a Bitmap to the Clipboard 596
    Pasting a Bitmap from the Clipboard 600
Registered and Private Clipboard Formats 603
    Registering a Private Format 605
Multiple Clipboard Data Formats 609
    Multiple Formats in Action 610
    Copying CircleApp Data in Multiple Formats 612
    Pasting CircleApp Data in Multiple Formats 615

Part IV: ActiveX Programming 621

Chapter 18: Introduction to ActiveX 623
OLE 1.0 623
OLE 2.0 626
Component Object Model (COM) 628
    Distributed Component Object Model (DCOM) 628
ActiveX 628
COM+ 629
ActiveX Applications and Components 629
    ActiveX Container Applications 629
    ActiveX Server Applications 630
    ActiveX Automation Applications 632
    ActiveX Controls 633
    ActiveX Documents 633

Chapter 19: Containers 635
Creating a Skeleton Container Application 635
Managing Embedded Object Size and Position 639
Using the Mouse to Select Items..641

Chapter 20: Servers 651
Creating a Skeleton Server Application 652
Customizing the Application's Resources 655
Completing the Application's Document Class 659
Completing the Server Item's Class 661
Completing the View Class 662
Running the Server Application 663
    Running ServerApp as a Stand-Alone Application 663
    Running ServerApp as an In-Place Editor 665
    Running ServerApp as an Editor for a Linked Item 666

Chapter 21: Automation 671
The Automation Server Application 671
    Creating a Skeleton Automation Server 672
    Customizing the Automation Server's Resources.......................................673
    Completing the Automation Server's Document Class 676
    Completing the Automation Server's View Class 677
    Defining the Server's Properties and Methods 678
The Automation Client Application 683
    Creating the Automation Client Skeleton..683
    Customizing the Client Application's Resources 684
    Completing the Client Application's View Class 685
    Initializing ActiveX in the Client Application...689
Controlling the Server from the Client..689

Chapter 22: ActiveX Controls 695
Creating a Skeleton ActiveX Control 695
Creating the ActiveX Control's User Interface 697
Creating Properties and Methods 702
Responding to the Control's Button 705
Testing the ActiveX Control 706

Part V: Multimedia Programming 711

Chapter 23: DirectDraw 713
Creating a DirectDraw Program 714
Adding DirectDraw Files to Your Visual C++ Project 715
    Adding the ddraw.h Header File to Your Program 715
    Adding the ddraw.lib File to Your Program 716
Creating a DirectDraw Object 717
Setting the Screen Access Level 717
Setting the Display Mode 718
Creating the Primary DirectDraw Surface 718
Creating Offscreen Surfaces 720
Creating DirectDraw Palettes 720
Exploring the DirectDrawApp Sample Application 721
    DirectDrawApp's OnInitialUpdate() Function 722
    DirectDrawApp's InitMemberVariables() Function 723
    DirectDrawApp's InitDirectDraw() Function 724
    DirectDrawApp's CreateDDrawSurfaces() Function 725
    DirectDrawApp's ClearDDrawSurface() Function 726
    DirectDrawApp's CreateOffScreenSurface() Function 727
    DirectDrawApp's InitImages() Function 728
    DirectDrawApp's CreateDDrawPal() Function 729
    DirectDrawApp's DibToSurface() Function 730
    DirectDrawApp's OnTimer() Function 732
    DirectDrawApp's OnKeyDown() Function 734
    DirectDrawApp's OnDestroy() Function 734

Chapter 24: DirectSound 741
Creating a DirectSound Program 741
Adding DirectSound Files to Your Visual C++ Project 742
    Adding the dsound.h Header File 742
    Adding the dsound.lib File 743
Creating a DirectSound Object 744
Setting the Sound-Hardware Access Level 744
    Creating the Secondary DirectSound Buffer 745
Exploring the DirectSoundApp Application 746
    DirectSoundApp's View-Class Constructor 746
    DirectSoundApp's OnInitialUpdate() Function 747
    DirectSoundApp's InitDirectSound() Function 748
    DirectSoundApp's CreateSoundBuffer() Function 749
    The CWave Class 750

DirectSoundApp's LoadWaveData() Function 753
DirectSoundApp's OnLButtonDown() Function 754
DirectSoundApp's OnDestroy() Function 754

Chapter 25: DirectInput 761

Creating a DirectInput Program 762
Adding DirectInput Files to Your Visual C++ Project...763
    Adding the dinput.h Header File 763
    Adding the dinput.lib and dxguid.lib Files 763
Creating a DirectInput Object 764
Creating a DirectInput Device 765
Setting the Data Format 766
Setting the Device Access Level 766
Acquiring the Device..766
Exploring the DirectInputApp Application..767
    DirectInputApp's View-Class Constructor 768
    DirectInputApp's OnInitialUpdate() Function 769
    DirectInputApp's OnTimer() Function 770
    DirectInputApp's OnDraw() Function 771
    DirectInputApp's OnDestroy() Function 772

Chapter 26: Direct3D 779

Creating a Direct3D Program 780
Creating a Direct3D Main Object 781
Creating a Clipper Object 781
Creating a Direct3D Device 782
Creating the Root Frame..784
Creating Meshes for Objects 785
Creating Frames for Meshes 785
The Viewport..786
    Creating the Viewport Frame 786
    Creating the Viewport 787
Adding Lights 788
    Creating the Light Object 788
    Creating the Light's Child Frame...789
The Direct3DApp Sample Application 790
    Building a New Direct3D Application 790
    Running Direct3DApp...794
    Writing an AppWizardless MFC Application...795

Part VI: Internet Programming 817

Chapter 27: WinInet 819

Introducing WinInet...819
    The CInternetSession Class 820
    The CInternetConnection Class 821
    The CHttpConnection Class..822
    The CFtpConnection Class..822

The CInternetFile Class 823
The CHttpFile Class 824
The CFileFind Class 824
The CFtpFileFind Class 825
The CInternetException Class 826
Writing an HTTP Application 826
Starting an Internet Session 827
Opening the Connection to an HTTP Server 827
Reading a File from an HTTP Server 828
Closing the Connection and Session 829
Creating an HTTP Session 829
Writing an FTP Application 830
Opening an FTP Connection 830
Getting the Root Directory 831
Reading a Directory 831
Closing the Connection and Session 832
Running the FTPAccessApp Application 832
Creating the FTPAccessApp Sample Application 835
Examining the Member Variables 835
Creating the OnDraw() Function 837
Creating the OnFtpConnect() Function 839
Creating the OpenFTPDirectory() Function 840
Creating the ReadFileNames() Function 841
Creating the OnLButtonDblClk() Function 841
Creating the OnRButtonDown() Function 843
Creating the DownloadFile() Function 843
Creating the MoveToPreviousDirectory() Function 845
Creating the DisplayStatusMessage() Function 846
Creating the InitSelection() Function 846

Chapter 28: Internet Explorer 849

The Internet Explorer Components 850
Creating a Skeleton Browser Application 851
Compiling MyBrowser 854
Configuring the WebBrowser Control 855
Navigating with the WebBrowser Component 856
Using HTML Dialog Boxes 862
Including an HTML Resource 866
Working in the Dialog Box 867
Using Dynamic HTML 868
Introducing the DHTML Object Model 868
Accessing the Document Interface 871
Using the Object Model 872
Extending the DHTML Object Model 873
Distributing the Browser Control 877
Determining Versions with the Registry 878
Determining Versions with shdocvw.dll 879
Using the Minimum Installation 880
Warning Users about Uninstalling IE 5.0 880
Running MyBrowser 881

Appendix: About the CD-ROM 885

Index 889

End-User License Agreement 926

CD-ROM Installation Instructions 930

Part I
Fundamental Windows 2000 Programming

Chapter 1: Application Fundamentals

Chapter 2: Graphical Device Interface Basics

Chapter 3: Windows and Dialog Boxes

Chapter 4: Text

Chapter 5: Menus

Chapter 6: Standard Controls

Chapter 7: Common Controls

Chapter 8: Printing

Chapter 1
Application Fundamentals

In This Chapter

- Examining different types of Windows applications
- Taking a look at traditional C Windows programming
- Discovering the differences between MFC and C

Love it or hate it, Windows has become the operating system of choice for a majority of computer users. Besides making Bill Gates rich beyond comprehension, Windows has managed to establish the closest thing to an operating-system standard since the DOS command line popped up on computers the world over. There are, however, several different kinds of Windows programs and many ways to program them. This chapter introduces you to the different kinds of Windows 2000 programs. You also examine how traditional C programs and Visual C++ MFC programs compare.

Win32 Applications

There are many types of Win32 applications, from traditional programs to console applications and dynamic-link libraries (DLLs). You even can include *ActiveX* controls, which are programmable components that you can add to applications, Web pages, and even the Active Desktop. In the following sections, you examine several types of these Win32 applications.

Traditional Win32 Applications

A traditional Windows application has all the features you might expect in a full-fledged application, including a frame window, menu bar, toolbar, and status bar. Most of the applications that you use every day, and most of the applications you create with Visual C++, fall into this category. Figure 1-1, for example, shows Microsoft *WordPad*—a traditional Win32 application familiar to most Windows users.

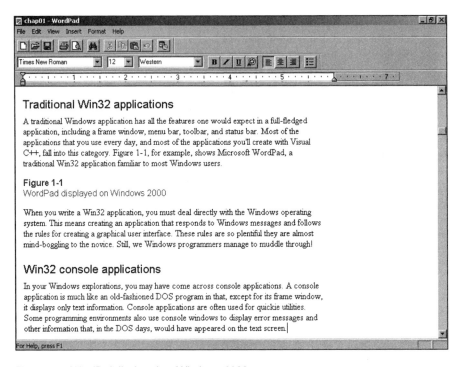

Figure 1-1: WordPad displayed on Windows 2000

When you write a Win32 application, you must deal directly with the Windows operating system. This means creating an application that responds to Windows messages and follows the rules for creating a graphical user interface. These rules are so plentiful they are almost mind-boggling to the novice. Still, we Windows programmers manage to muddle through!

Win32 Console Applications

In your Windows explorations, you may have come across console applications. A *console application* is much like an old-fashioned DOS program in that, except for its frame window, it displays only text information. Console applications often are used for quickie utilities. Some programming environments also use *console windows* to display error messages and other information that, in DOS days, would have appeared on the text screen.

Figure 1-2 shows a running console application. The code that created the application looks like this:

```
#include <stdio.h>

int main()
{
```

```
        printf("This is a console application.\n\n");
        return 0;
}
```

As you can see, you write a console application just as you wrote C applications in the good old days. This bit of simplicity—not having to deal with all the extra baggage Windows throws at you—makes console applications perfect for simple tasks in which you don't want to create window classes, manage message maps, and draw to device contexts.

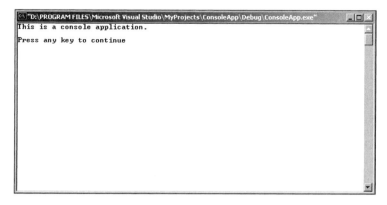

Figure 1-2: A Win32 console application displaying only text information

Dynamic-Link Libraries

A *dynamic-link library,* or *DLL* as it's more commonly called, is not a complete program or even an executable file. Instead, a DLL is a library of functions that can be called from other modules in the system. Because a DLL is not an application per se, it rarely has a visible presence and doesn't receive Windows messages. A DLL isn't even loaded into memory until some other module, such as an application, either explicitly loads the DLL or calls one of the DLL's functions. The "dynamic" portion of the name comes from the fact that the library is not linked to other modules at compile time, but rather is linked at run time.

For example, a Windows programmer writes a DLL that contains image-editing functions for a paint program. When the paint program runs, the user gets busy drawing an image. Because the program doesn't need the functions defined in the DLL yet, the DLL is not loaded into memory yet. After working for a while, though, the user decides to reduce the image by 50 percent. It just so happens that the functions the program must call to perform the reduction reside in the DLL. When the paint program calls these functions, Windows loads the DLL and dynamically (on the fly, so to speak) links the library with the paint program.

The big advantage of using a DLL is that many modules can share the same library without the modules having to be linked to the library at compile time. This saves the user disk space. In fact, DLLs can be shared among completely different applications, which can save not only disk space, but also RAM. Windows itself is an excellent example of DLLs in action. Virtually all of Windows is implemented in DLLs that are loaded as needed. If you look in your Windows 2000 system folder, you see many files with the .DLL file extension (as shown in Figure 1-3). Most of these files came with Windows; applications you installed may have placed the others.

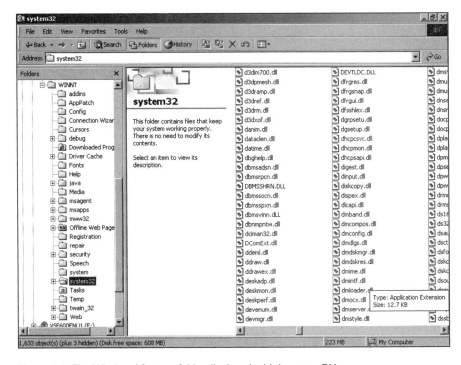

Figure 1-3: The Windows\System folder displayed with its many DLLs

ActiveX Controls

ActiveX controls are kind of like mini-applications that can be embedded into some type of container object. The container usually is an application's frame window or an HTML document. In any case, an ActiveX control is not an executable file. That is, you cannot run it as a stand-alone application.

ActiveX controls enable programmers to add functionality to programs easily. For example, Figure 1-4 shows Microsoft's `Calendar` ActiveX control loaded into Visual C++'s ActiveX Control Test Container application. If you write an application that needs to display a calendar, you can opt to use the `Calendar`

ActiveX control rather than write your own code to display and manage a calendar. This way, you save a lot of time without having to compromise the final product.

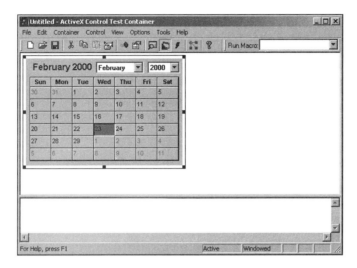

Figure 1-4: The Calendar ActiveX control embedded in an application window

ActiveX controls have a programmable interface made up of properties and methods. The application or Web page containing the ActiveX control can determine how the control looks and acts by setting properties and calling methods. For example, an ActiveX control that implements a table can have properties that determine the number of rows and columns in the table. The control also can have methods that enable the container to add elements to the table and sort the table entries in various ways.

You can download ActiveX controls from the Web, buy them from third-party vendors, or program your own using Visual C++. For more information on creating ActiveX controls, see Chapter 22.

Programming Windows the Hard Way

When Windows first became popular, sophisticated programming tools were as scarce as flies in a Raid factory. Programmers wrote Windows applications in straight C (no C++) and compiled them under DOS, strange as that sounds. There weren't any C compilers that ran under Windows, even though you could program Windows applications with the compilers. These days, complex libraries such as Microsoft Foundation Classes (MFC) take a lot of the drudgery out of writing Windows applications — but such advantages come with a price. MFC, which is a set of classes that encapsulates the Windows API, itself has a steep learning curve. Moreover, if you don't understand how a conventional

Windows program works, learning MFC is even harder. In this section, you learn to write basic Windows programs like the old timers did (and as many programmers still do). This experience can help you better appreciate MFC's capabilities.

Listing 1-1 is a simple Windows application called BasicApp that is written in C. Figure 1-5 shows BasicApp when you click in its window, which causes a message box to appear. It sure looks different from an MFC program, doesn't it (assuming that you've seen an MFC program before)? That's because an MFC program hides many of the details of programming Windows. However, MFC isn't magical. In order to get a Windows application up on the screen, an MFC application must perform exactly the same chores as a straight C program.

Figure 1-5: After you click in the Basic Application window, this message box appears.

Name: `basicapp.c`
Location: `WinPrgS\Chap01\basicapp`

Listing 1-1: A basic Win32 application

```
/************************************************************
 * BASICAPP.C: A basic Windows application.
 ************************************************************/

#include <windows.h>

LRESULT CALLBACK WndProc(HWND hWnd, UINT message,
    WPARAM wParam, LPARAM lParam);

int WINAPI WinMain(HINSTANCE hCurrentInst,
    HINSTANCE hPrevInstance, PSTR lpszCmdLine,
    int nCmdShow)
{
    WNDCLASS wndClass;
    HWND hWnd;
    MSG msg;
    UINT width;
```

```
    UINT height;

    wndClass.style = CS_HREDRAW | CS_VREDRAW;
    wndClass.lpfnWndProc = WndProc;
    wndClass.cbClsExtra = 0;
    wndClass.cbWndExtra = 0;
    wndClass.hInstance = hCurrentInst;
    wndClass.hIcon = LoadIcon(NULL, IDI_APPLICATION);
    wndClass.hCursor = LoadCursor(NULL, IDC_ARROW);
    wndClass.hbrBackground = GetStockObject(WHITE_BRUSH);
    wndClass.lpszMenuName = NULL;
    wndClass.lpszClassName = "BasicApp";

    RegisterClass(&wndClass);

    width = GetSystemMetrics(SM_CXSCREEN) / 2;
    height = GetSystemMetrics(SM_CYSCREEN) / 2;

    hWnd = CreateWindow(
       "BasicApp",            /* Window class's name.    */
       "Basic Application",   /* Title bar text.         */
       WS_OVERLAPPEDWINDOW,   /* The window's style.     */
       10,                    /* X position.             */
       10,                    /* Y position.             */
       width,                 /* Width.                  */
       height,                /* Height.                 */
       NULL,                  /* Parent window's handle. */
       NULL,                  /* Menu handle.            */
       hCurrentInst,          /* Instance handle.        */
       NULL);                 /* No additional data.     */

    ShowWindow(hWnd, nCmdShow);
    UpdateWindow(hWnd);

    while (GetMessage(&msg, NULL, 0, 0))
    {
        TranslateMessage(&msg);
        DispatchMessage(&msg);
    }

    return msg.wParam;
}
LRESULT CALLBACK WndProc(HWND hWnd, UINT message,
    WPARAM wParam, LPARAM lParam)
{
    HDC hDC;
    PAINTSTRUCT paintStruct;

    switch(message)
    {
        case WM_PAINT:
            hDC = BeginPaint(hWnd, &paintStruct);
```

```
            TextOut(hDC, 10, 10, "This is a test.", 15);
            EndPaint(hWnd, &paintStruct);
            return 0;
        case WM_LBUTTONDOWN:
            MessageBox(hWnd, "Got mouse click!",
                "Basic Application",
                MB_ICONEXCLAMATION | MB_OK);
            return 0;

        case WM_DESTROY:
            PostQuitMessage(0);
            return 0;
    }

    return DefWindowProc(hWnd, message, wParam, lParam);
}
```

The first thing to notice in Listing 1-1 is the line

```
#include <windows.h>
```

near the top of the listing. The `windows.h` file contains many declarations that all Windows programs require. All Windows programs include this header file.

The next thing to notice is the `WinMain()` function, whose signature looks like this:

```
int WINAPI WinMain(HINSTANCE hCurrentInst,
    HINSTANCE hPrevInstance, PSTR lpszCmdLine,
    int nCmdShow)
```

`WinMain()` is the entry point for all Windows programs in the same way that `main()` is the entry point for DOS C programs. `WinMain()`'s four parameters are as follows:

hCurrentInst	The handle of this instance of the program
hPrevInstance	The handle of the previous instance
lpszCmdLine	A pointer to the command line used to run the program
nCmdShow	A set of flags that determine how the application's window should be displayed

A handle is one type of data you don't see very often in an MFC program because MFC's classes manage handles internally. A *handle* is nothing more than a value that identifies a window or some other object. In a traditional C Windows program, you almost always refer to a window by its handle; most Windows API functions that manipulate windows require a handle as their first argument.

An instance of an application is much the same as an instance of a class in object-oriented programming. For example (in most cases), the user can run the same Windows application multiple times, having several separate but identical windows on the screen. Each window represents an instance of the program. In 16-bit Windows programming, all application instances shared the same memory space. By checking the handle to the previous instance, programmers could prevent multiple instances. If `hPrevInstance` was `NULL`, there was no previous instance. If `hPrevInstance` was not `NULL`, then the application already ran and the programmer could display the already existing window rather than create a new instance of the application.

Under Windows 2000, however, every application gets its own block of virtual memory. For this reason, the `hPrevInstance` handle in Windows 2000 programs is always `NULL`. There are still ways to determine whether an application has run already, but it's a more complicated process that requires searching running processes for a specific Windows name.

Getting back to the program, the `WinMain()` function must create a class for its window. First, register the class with Windows, and then display the window. Windows defines a structure for holding the values that make up a window class. `WinMain()` declares an instance of this structure like this:

```
WNDCLASS wndClass;
```

`WinMain()` also initializes this structure to the values required for the window class, as shown here:

```
wndClass.style = CS_HREDRAW | CS_VREDRAW;
wndClass.lpfnWndProc = WndProc;
wndClass.cbClsExtra = 0;
wndClass.cbWndExtra = 0;
wndClass.hInstance = hCurrentInst;
wndClass.hIcon = LoadIcon(NULL, IDI_APPLICATION);
wndClass.hCursor = LoadCursor(NULL, IDC_ARROW);
wndClass.hbrBackground = GetStockObject(WHITE_BRUSH);
wndClass.lpszMenuName = NULL;
wndClass.lpszClassName = "BasicApp";
```

The `WNDCLASS` structure defines the window's style, as well as specifies the window's icons, cursor, background color, and menu. Because most programs in this book are written using MFC, fully describing the `WNDCLASS` structure (and all the values that are appropriate for the structure's members) is beyond the scope of this book. However, you can find plenty of details in your Visual C++ online documentation or in your favorite Windows programming manual. The important thing to know here is that every Windows application must create an instance of this structure and register it with Windows.

`WinMain()` registers the new window class with Windows by calling `RegisterClass()` like this:

```
RegisterClass(&wndClass);
```

`RegisterClass()`'s single argument is the address of the initialized `WNDCLASS` structure.

Often in a Windows program, you need to know the size of the screen, fonts, and other objects. In the case of BasicApp, the application gets the size of the screen by calling `GetSystemMetrics()`. The program then divides the screen width and height by two in order to determine the initial size of the application's window:

```
width = GetSystemMetrics(SM_CXSCREEN) / 2;
height = GetSystemMetrics(SM_CYSCREEN) / 2;
```

Your online documentation describes the many other flags that you can use with `GetSystemMetrics()`. Using the appropriate flags as the function's single argument, you can determine the size of just about any part of the window or screen.

After determining the window's initial size, `WinMain()` creates an instance of the window class, as shown here:

```
hWnd = CreateWindow(
    "BasicApp",             /* Window class's name.     */
    "Basic Application",    /* Title bar text.          */
    WS_OVERLAPPEDWINDOW,    /* The window's style.      */
    10,                     /* X position.              */
    10,                     /* Y position.              */
    width,                  /* Width.                   */
    height,                 /* Height.                  */
    NULL,                   /* Parent window's handle.  */
    NULL,                   /* Menu handle.             */
    hCurrentInst,           /* Instance handle.         */
    NULL);                  /* No additional data.      */
```

The comments in the listing describe `CreateWindow()`'s arguments.

At this point, the application has defined a window class and has created an instance of that window class. But, so far, there is nothing on the screen. To display the new window, `WinMain()` calls the Windows API function `ShowWindow()`:

```
ShowWindow(hWnd, nCmdShow);
```

Finally, to ensure that the window updates its display, the program calls the Windows API function `UpdateWindow()`:

```
UpdateWindow(hWnd);
```

Notice how both of these functions — like most other window-manipulation functions — take a window handle as their first argument.

Now that the window is up on the screen, it can start to process the many messages that Windows sends it. The program does this by setting up a message loop, which looks like this:

```
while (GetMessage(&msg, NULL, 0, 0))
{
    TranslateMessage(&msg);
    DispatchMessage(&msg);
}
```

The `GetMessage()` Windows API function retrieves a message from the window's message queue. As long as `GetMessage()` returns a nonzero value, the message loop continues. In fact, you can say that a Windows program does nothing more than gather and respond to messages. The message loop continues until the user exits the application, at which point `GetMessage()` returns zero and the message loop ends.

Inside the loop, the call to `TranslateMessage()` handles *virtual-key messages* (messages that represent keystrokes), translating them into character messages that go back into the message queue. The `DispatchMessage()` function sends the message off to the application's window procedure.

What's a window procedure? When you defined BasicApp's window class in the `WNDCLASS` structure, you specified the function to which Windows messages should be directed:

```
wndClass.lpfnWndProc = WndProc;
```

When the program registered the window class, Windows made note of the window procedure passed in the `lpfnWndProc` structure member. So, calls to `DispatchMessage()` result in Windows sending the message to `WndProc()`. There the messages are handled by the application or sent back to Windows for default processing.

In BasicApp, `WndProc()`'s signature looks like this:

```
LRESULT CALLBACK WndProc(HWND hWnd, UINT message,
    WPARAM wParam, LPARAM lParam)
```

The function's four parameters are as follows:

hWnd	The handle of the window to which the message is directed
message	The message ID (for example, WM_CREATE)
wParam	A 32-bit message parameter
lParam	A 32-bit message parameter

The values of the two 32-bit parameters depend on the type of message. For example, when the user selects a menu item from an application's menu bar, the application gets a `WM_COMMAND` message with the menu item's ID in the low word of the `wParam` parameter.

`WndProc()`'s job is to determine whether the application needs to handle the message or pass it back to Windows for default processing. (All messages must be dealt with in one of these ways.) In most Windows procedures, the programmer sets up a `switch` statement with `case` clauses for the messages the application should handle. BasicApp handles only three Windows messages. Its `switch` statement looks like this:

```
switch(message)
{
    case WM_PAINT:
        hDC = BeginPaint(hWnd, &paintStruct);
        TextOut(hDC, 10, 10, "This is a test.", 15);
        EndPaint(hWnd, &paintStruct);
        return 0;

    case WM_LBUTTONDOWN:
        MessageBox(hWnd, "Got mouse click!",
            "Basic Application",
            MB_ICONEXCLAMATION | MB_OK);
        return 0;

    case WM_DESTROY:
        PostQuitMessage(0);
        return 0;
}
```

`WndProc()` handles the following three Windows messages:

WM_PAINT	The window must redraw its display. Any Windows application with a visible display must handle WM_PAINT.
WM_LBUTTONDOWN	The user clicked the left mouse button inside the window's client area.
WM_DESTROY	The user wants to close the application. All Windows applications must handle WM_DESTROY.

Notice that, after handling a message, the function returns a value of zero. Messages that are not handled in the `switch` statement must be passed back to Windows. Failure to do this can result in the application's incapability to respond to the user. To pass a message back to Windows, the application calls `DefWindowProc()`:

```
return DefWindowProc(hWnd, message, wParam, lParam);
```

The function's arguments are the same as the parameters passed to the window procedure. Notice that `WndProc()` returns `DefWindowProc()`'s return value.

Now that you have a general idea of how a "handwritten" Windows application works, you can better appreciate what a class library such as MFC does for you. In the next section, you see how MFC deals with the tasks you must handle yourself in BasicApp.

MFC versus C

As previously stated, there's nothing magical about MFC. An MFC program must perform all the same start-up procedures as any other Windows program. It also must receive and process Windows messages. In this section, you get an overview of how MFC performs these important tasks.

Initializing the Application

When you create an MFC application with AppWizard, the generated source code — and the MFC classes on which that source code relies — takes care of many details, such as creating and registering the window class. MFC initializes a `WNDCLASS` structure for your application, registers the window class via the `RegisterClass()` function, and displays the window. This doesn't mean, however, that you have no control over the window's styles. Various class member functions enable you to intercept MFC's default processing and change it to suit your needs. See the "Problems & Solutions" section in this chapter for some MFC programming techniques that give you more control over your application's window.

Every MFC program has an application object, which is instantiated from a class derived from `CWinApp`. This application object contains the required `WinMain()` function, as well as the application's message loop. You don't have to do anything to get the message loop going; it's automatic.

The application class also provides the `InitApplication()` and `InitInstance()` member functions so that you can perform your own custom application initialization. However, `InitApplication()` is useful only under 16-bit Windows, which allows multiple instances of a single application. For 32-bit applications, you should ignore `InitApplication()` and use `InitInstance()` instead.

MFC Message Handling

When it comes to message handling in an MFC program, you must tell MFC what messages your application handles and where those message are handled. You do this by creating a message map in the class that accepts the messages. (Of course, if you use AppWizard and ClassWizard, you don't have to create message maps by hand; AppWizard creates the basic message maps for you, and ClassWizard adds new entries to the message maps as needed.) To create a message map, perform the following steps:

1. Declare the message map in the class's header file.
2. Declare message-response functions in the class's header file.
3. Define the message map in the class's implementation file.
4. Define the message-response functions in the class's implementation file.

Declaring a message map is as easy as including the `DECLARE_MESSAGE_MAP()` macro in your class's header file. You declare message-response functions in much the same way as you declare any other class member function. However, MFC provides a special prefix, `afx_msg`, which marks a function as a message-response function. This prefix goes right before the function's return type, as shown here:

```
afx_msg void OnLButtonDown(UINT nFlags, CPoint point);
```

In the class's implementation file, you create the actual message map. This message map is made up of the `BEGIN_MESSAGE_MAP()` and `END_MESSAGE_MAP()` macros, between which are other macros that define each entry in the message map. For example, look at this message map:

```
BEGIN_MESSAGE_MAP(CCircleAppView, CView)
ON_WM_LBUTTONDOWN()
ON_COMMAND(ID_CIRCLE_CHANGECOLOR, OnCircleChangecolor)
ON_COMMAND(ID_CIRCLE_CHANGEDIAMETER,
    OnCircleChangediameter)
END_MESSAGE_MAP()
```

The first line starts the message map. The `BEGIN_MESSAGE_MAP()` macro's two arguments are the name of the class in which the map is located and the name of the base class. The first argument tells MFC where to direct the messages. The second argument tells MFC where to direct the messages if the current class doesn't handle them. In this way, MFC can pass messages all the way up a class hierarchy until a class handles the message or MFC passes the message back to Windows for default processing.

After the `BEGIN_MESSAGE_MAP()` macro comes the message map entries, which tell MFC which function to associate with which message. MFC defines many macros for the different types of messages a class handles in its message map. The most common are the macros that represent standard Windows messages. The names for these macros are derived from the message name.

For example, the message map macro for the `WM_LBUTTONDOWN` message is `ON_WM_LBUTTONDOWN()`. By prefixing the message name with `ON_` and adding parentheses to the end, you form the macro name. The message-response functions for standard Windows messages also are named using a strict naming convention. To determine the name for a message, drop the `WM_` from the message, lowercase all letters except for those that start a word, and add `On` to the front of the name. Then the message-response function for `WM_LBUTTONDOWN` is `OnLButtonDown()`, whereas the message-response function for `WM_CREATE` is `OnCreate()`.

Another common message-map macro is `ON_COMMAND`, which usually associates menu commands with the functions that handle them. Unlike the standard Windows message macros, the `ON_COMMAND` macro requires two arguments: the message ID and the name of the function that handles the message.

When MFC receives a standard Windows message, it "cracks" the parameters into more easily usable data types. For example, the `WM_LBUTTONDOWN` message stores the mouse position in `lParam`, with the X coordinate in the low word and the Y coordinate in the high word. MFC extracts these values from `lParam` and stores them in a `CPoint` object, which it passes as an argument to the `OnLButtonDown()` message-response function.

This message cracking means that MFC message-response functions all have different signatures, depending on how MFC decides to crack the message parameters. When you use ClassWizard to add message handling to your application, you don't need to worry about the parameters because ClassWizard creates the function for you. However, if you want to add message-response functions by hand, you need to look up the function signatures for the messages you want to handle.

PROBLEMS & SOLUTIONS

Finding Message-Response Function Signatures

PROBLEM: *When I'm not using ClassWizard, how can I easily define a message-response function for a Windows message? Each function's signature is different from the next. It's enough to drive me crazy!*

SOLUTION: Your Visual C++ online documentation can provide more than enough information. It also provides snippets of source code that you can paste right into your programs. For example, suppose you want to respond to the `WM_CREATE` Windows message in a window class. You already know from the Visual C++ naming conventions that the name of the message-response function is `OnCreate()`. Type `OnCreate()` into your code window, place the text cursor on the function name, and then press F1. The documentation for the function, including the function's signature, appears in the window (as shown in Figure 1-6). Use your mouse to highlight the function's signature, press Ctrl+C to copy the signature to the clipboard, return to your source code, and press Ctrl+V to paste the signature into your code.

Continued

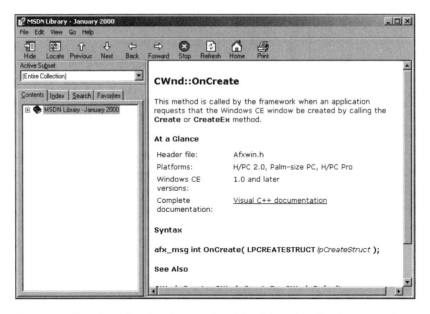

Figure 1-6: Obtaining a function signature from Visual C++'s online documentation

Problems & Solutions

Sizing MFC Windows

PROBLEM: *How can I specify the size and position of a frame window in an MFC program?*

SOLUTION: In your frame window class, usually called `CMainFrame`, find the `PreCreateWindow()` function. `CMainFrame`, and every other MFC window class, inherits `PreCreateWindow()` from `CWnd`. MFC calls this function just before it creates the window; by placing your custom code in `PreCreateWindow()`, you can modify the way your window looks and acts.

Continued

Chapter 1: Application Fundamentals

`PreCreateWindow()` receives a reference to a `CREATESTRUCT` structure as a single parameter. The `CREATESTRUCT` structure contains four members that determine the window's size and position. These members are `cx`, `cy`, `x`, and `y`. To change the windows starting width and height, set `cx` and `cy` respectively. To change the window's starting location, set `x` and `y`. Here is the code required to set a window's starting size and position:

```
BOOL CMainFrame::PreCreateWindow(CREATESTRUCT& cs)
{
    // TODO: Modify the Window class or styles
    //   here by modifying
    //   the CREATESTRUCT cs

    cs.cx = 400;
    cs.cy = 300;
    cs.x = 100;
    cs.y = 50;

    return CMDIFrameWnd::PreCreateWindow(cs);
```

Note that the members of the `CREATESTRUCT` structure are the same values that you pass to the `CreateWindow()` function in a standard C Windows program.

PROBLEMS & SOLUTIONS

Modifying MFC Window Styles

PROBLEM: *How can I remove control buttons, such as the Maximize and Restore buttons, from a window's title bar?*

SOLUTION: Again, the answer lies in the `PreCreateWindow()` function. The `CREATESTRUCT` structure passed to the class contains a member, called `style`, which holds the window's style flags. By changing the style flags, you can change the way the window looks and acts. The following code, for example, creates a window that has only a Close button. In addition, the window has a border that you cannot use to resize the window. This combination of styles creates a window that the user cannot resize:

```
BOOL CMainFrame::PreCreateWindow(CREATESTRUCT& cs)
{
    // TODO: Modify the Window class or styles
    //   here by modifying
    //   the CREATESTRUCT cs
```

Continued

```
        cs.style = WS_OVERLAPPED | WS_SYSMENU | WS_BORDER;

        return CMDIFrameWnd::PreCreateWindow(cs);
}
```

Figure 1-7 shows the window created by this example.

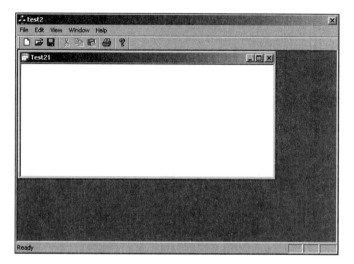

Figure 1-7: After changing this window's style flags, you cannot resize it.

Summary

Old-fashioned C Windows programs and modern MFC programs both have to perform the same tasks to get a window up on the screen. MFC, however, does a lot of the work that you would have to accomplish on your own; which enables you to concentrate on the implementation details of your specific application, rather than get bogged down in the minutiae of Windows programming.

Also discussed in this chapter:

▶ Windows applications come in several forms, including traditional GUI applications, console applications, DLLs, and ActiveX controls.

▶ Before fancy tools such as Visual C++ were available, Windows programs were written in C and compiled from the DOS command line.

▶ Every Windows application with a visible display must declare and register a window class. The application then creates its windows based on the registered classes.

- To provide custom initialization for an MFC application, you override the application object's `InitInstance()` function.
- Windows programs written in C contain a message loop that receives and dispatches a Windows message. MFC programs also have a message loop, which is hidden from the programmer, along with the other overhead required to get a Windows application going.
- Whereas Windows programs written in C usually use a complex `switch` statement to route Windows messages to the appropriate functions, MFC uses a message map.

Chapter 2

Graphical Device Interface Basics

In This Chapter

▶ Introducing the Graphical Device Interface
▶ Understanding device contexts
▶ Determining device capabilities
▶ Working with pens
▶ Using brushes to fill shapes

Windows is a graphical operating system, which means that it displays everything on the screen as an image. The system even draws text as an image. For this reason, you shouldn't be surprised to discover that Windows has a library of functions that enables applications to handle graphics in various ways. Whether you want to print a line of text on the screen or draw a 3-D background for a computer game, you have to deal with Window's Graphical Device Interface (GDI). In this chapter, you learn the basic skills required to create a Windows screen display. (In Chapter 10, you learn more about the GDI.)

Introducing the GDI

The *GDI (Graphical Device Interface)* is an extensive set of functions that you call whenever you draw or manage graphics from within a Windows application. Because everything seen on a Windows screen is graphical in nature, you must call a GDI function every time you display something in your application's window.

Besides the functions that perform display operations, the GDI also features a set of objects that programs use to render a display. These objects include the following:

Device context   A set of attributes that describes the surface on which images are displayed and the objects used to display those images

Pen	A GDI object that draws lines
Brush	A GDI object that fills onscreen shapes with color
Font	A GDI object that determines the style of the characters used to draw text on the screen
Bitmap	A GDI object that stores an image
Palette	A set of colors that you can use when an application draws on the screen

All these objects work together to create the displays you see in an application's window. In the following sections, you examine device contexts, pens, and brushes in greater detail. For information on fonts, refer to Chapter 4; for information on bitmaps and palettes, check out Chapter 9.

Device Contexts

As covered in the previous section, a *device context (DC)* is a set of attributes that determines how to display graphics in an application's window. Before you can draw anything in a window, you must acquire a DC for the area of the window in which you want to draw. You then route all graphics calls to the GDI, which carries out your commands as is appropriate for the DC.

You don't need to concern yourself with many of these attributes because when you acquire a DC, Windows initializes a complete set of attributes and objects that you use to render a display. You can, however, change the attributes and objects in order to create your application's specific display.

For example, the default DC includes a black pen. Any lines you draw — including those that outline shapes such as rectangles and circles — are black. Obviously, you may want to draw lines in another color. In this case, you must replace the default pen with a pen of the required color, which you create in your program and pass to the device context. In Windows programming jargon, the act of giving a new object to a DC is called *selecting* the object into the DC.

A device context doesn't represent a screen display always. It also can represent the attributes of a printer or some other graphical device. That is, when you print a document from a Windows application, the application obtains a printer device context to which the program directs the data to print.

Keep in mind that a DC must have a complete set of tools always. This means that you cannot remove tools from the DC. Instead, you replace one tool with another. When your program is ready to destroy custom GDI objects you select into a DC, you must replace those objects with the old, default GDI objects.

A DC also represents the area in which you can draw. If you try to draw outside of this area, Windows clips the drawing to the edges of the valid area. This is one way Windows forces your display to stay within the confines of the application's window. More precisely, Windows usually restricts your drawing operations to the window's client area. Normally, you can't draw on the window's title bar or controls.

Visual C++'s MFC library encapsulates the GDI into a number of classes that simplify handling DCs and GDI objects such as pens, brushes, fonts, and palettes. The biggest of these classes is the `CDC` class, which represents a general DC from which the library derives specific types of DCs. Table 2-1 lists some of the more useful functions of the `CDC` class.

Table 2-1 Some Useful Functions of the CDC Class

Message	Description
`Arc()`	Draws an elliptical arc
`BitBlt()`	Copies a bitmap from one DC to another
`Draw3dRect()`	Draws a three-dimensional rectangle
`DrawDragRect()`	Draws a rectangle that the mouse drags
`DrawEdge()`	Draws the edges of a rectangle
`DrawIcon()`	Draws an icon
`Ellipse()`	Draws an ellipse
`FillRect()`	Fills a rectangle with the color of the given brush
`FillRgn()`	Fills a region with the color of the given brush
`FillSolidRect()`	Fills a rectangle with the given color
`FloodFill()`	Fills an area with the color of the current brush
`FrameRect()`	Draws a rectangle border
`FrameRgn()`	Draws a region border
`GetBkColor()`	Gets the background color
`GetCurrentBitmap()`	Gets a pointer to the selected bitmap
`GetCurrentBrush()`	Gets a pointer to the selected brush
`GetCurrentFont()`	Gets a pointer to the selected font
`GetCurrentPalette()`	Gets a pointer to the selected palette
`GetCurrentPen()`	Gets a pointer to the selected pen
`GetCurrentPosition()`	Gets the pen's current position

Continued

Table 2-1 *(continued)*

Message	Description
GetDeviceCaps()	Gets information about the display device's capabilities
GetMapMode()	Gets the currently set mapping mode
GetPixel()	Gets an RGB color value for the given pixel
GetPolyFillMode()	Gets the polygon-filling mode
GetTextColor()	Gets the text color
GetTextExtent()	Gets the width and height of a text line
GetTextMetrics()	Gets information about the current font
GetWindow()	Gets a pointer to the DC's window
GrayString()	Draws grayed text
LineTo()	Draws a line
MoveTo()	Sets the current pen position
Pie()	Draws a pie slice
Polygon()	Draws a polygon
Polyline()	Draws a set of lines
RealizePalette()	Maps the logical palette to the system palette
Rectangle()	Draws a rectangle
RoundRect()	Draws a rectangle with rounded corners
SelectObject()	Selects a GDI drawing object
SelectPalette()	Selects the logical palette
SelectStockObject()	Selects a predefined stock drawing object
SetBkColor()	Sets the background color
SetMapMode()	Sets the mapping mode
SetPixel()	Sets a pixel to a given color
SetTextColor()	Sets the text color
StretchBlt()	Copies a bitmap from one DC to another, stretching or compressing the bitmap as needed
TextOut()	Draws a text string

The MFC library derives several specific device-context classes from the general `CDC` class. These classes are as follows:

`CClientDC`	A device context that provides drawing access to a window's client area. Use this type of DC when you want to draw in a window, except in response to a `WM_PAINT` Windows message.
`CMetaFileDC`	A device context that represents a Windows *metafile*, which is a file that holds a list of commands for reproducing an image. Use this type of DC when you want to create a device-independent file that you can play back to create an image.
`CPaintDC`	A device context that MFC creates in response to a Windows `WM_PAINT` message. Your application uses this DC to update the window's display, usually in an MFC application's `OnDraw()` function.
`CWindowDC`	A device context that provides drawing access to an entire window, rather than just the client area.

In the following sections, you examine the first three device-context classes in more detail. I do not discuss the `CWindowDC` class, as it rarely is used in applications.

As you learn to use the device-context classes, remember that each of the classes inherits dozens of member functions from the `CDC` class. Only the `CMetaFileDC` class defines member functions specific to the class, in addition to those inherited from `CDC`.

The Paint Device Context

As you learned in Chapter 1, when a window needs to redraw its display, Windows sends a `WM_PAINT` message. In C Windows programs, you handle this message in the window's message loop like this:

```
switch(message)
{
    case WM_PAINT:
        hDC = BeginPaint(hWnd, &paintStruct);

        // Draw window display here.

        EndPaint(hWnd, &paintStruct);
        return 0;

    // Handle other messages here.
}
```

To get the DC, you call the Windows `BeginPaint()` function, after which you call GDI functions to draw the window's display. After drawing the display, you call `EndPaint()`. Chapter 1 explains this process.

In an MFC program, handling a paint DC is much easier because MFC handles the details of calling `BeginPaint()` and `EndPaint()` for you. MFC even creates the DC for you and passes it to the view class's `OnDraw()` function, which is the function in which you draw the window's display. A simple `OnDraw()` function can look like this:

```
void CPaintDCAppView::OnDraw(CDC* pDC)
{
    CPaintDCAppDoc* pDoc = GetDocument();
    ASSERT_VALID(pDoc);

    // TODO: add draw code for native data here

    pDC->Rectangle(20, 20, 300, 200);
}
```

As you can see, in an MFC program, you call GDI functions through an instance of a `CDC`-derived class. In the `OnDraw()` example, pDC is a pointer to an instance of the `CPaintDC` class, whose base class is `CDC`. The `OnDraw()` function draws a rectangle in the window's client area, as shown in Figure 2-1, by calling the `CDC Rectangle()` function through the pDC pointer.

Figure 2-1: An MFC application that draws a rectangle in response to a WM_PAINT message

Chapter 2: Graphical Device Interface Basics

MFC not only takes care of calling `BeginPaint()` and `EndPaint()`, it also deletes the DC object when the view class is through with it. You never have to create an instance of `CPaintDC` yourself; MFC handles this special type of DC object completely. All you need to do is call GDI functions through the supplied pointer in order to create the window's display.

The Client-Area Device Context

You don't have to wait for `WM_PAINT` messages in order to draw in a window. You can create a DC for the window's client area and then use this DC to call GDI functions. In a C Windows program, this involves calling the Windows API functions `GetDC()` and `ReleaseDC()`. `GetDC()` acquires a handle to a DC for the window's client area; `ReleaseDC()` releases the DC, which you must ensure happens in order not to tie up this important system resource.

Listing 2-1 shows `BasicDCApp`, a Windows program written in C that creates a client-area device context in response to a left mouse-button click. When the user clicks in the window's client area, the word "Click" appears at the click location, as shown in Figure 2-2.

CD

Name: `BasicDCApp.c`
Location: `WinPrgS\Chap02\BasicDCApp`

Listing 2-1: A basic Windows program that creates a client-area device context

```c
#include <windows.h>

LRESULT CALLBACK WndProc(HWND hWnd, UINT message,
    WPARAM wParam, LPARAM lParam);

int WINAPI WinMain(HINSTANCE hCurrentInst,
    HINSTANCE hPrevInstance, PSTR lpszCmdLine,
    int nCmdShow)
{
    WNDCLASS wndClass;
    HWND hWnd;
    MSG msg;
    UINT width;
    UINT height;

    wndClass.style = CS_HREDRAW | CS_VREDRAW;
    wndClass.lpfnWndProc = WndProc;
    wndClass.cbClsExtra = 0;
    wndClass.cbWndExtra = 0;
    wndClass.hInstance = hCurrentInst;
    wndClass.hIcon = LoadIcon(NULL, IDI_APPLICATION);
    wndClass.hCursor = LoadCursor(NULL, IDC_ARROW);
    wndClass.hbrBackground = GetStockObject(WHITE_BRUSH);
    wndClass.lpszMenuName = NULL;
    wndClass.lpszClassName = "BasicDCApp";
```

```
    RegisterClass(&wndClass);

    width = GetSystemMetrics(SM_CXSCREEN) / 2;
    height = GetSystemMetrics(SM_CYSCREEN) / 2;

    hWnd = CreateWindow(
        "BasicDCApp",          /* Window class's name.    */
        "Basic DC Application", /* Title bar text.         */
        WS_OVERLAPPEDWINDOW,   /* The window's style.     */
        10,                    /* X position.             */
        10,                    /* Y position.             */
        width,                 /* Width.                  */
        height,                /* Height.                 */
        NULL,                  /* Parent window's handle. */
        NULL,                  /* Menu handle.            */
        hCurrentInst,          /* Instance handle.        */
        NULL);                 /* No additional data.     */

    ShowWindow(hWnd, nCmdShow);
    UpdateWindow(hWnd);

    while (GetMessage(&msg, NULL, 0, 0))
    {
        TranslateMessage(&msg);
        DispatchMessage(&msg);
    }

    return msg.wParam;
}

LRESULT CALLBACK WndProc(HWND hWnd, UINT message,
    WPARAM wParam, LPARAM lParam)
{
    HDC hDC;
    int xPos, yPos;

    switch(message)
    {
        case WM_LBUTTONDOWN:
            hDC = GetDC(hWnd);
            xPos = LOWORD(lParam);
            yPos = HIWORD(lParam);
            TextOut(hDC, xPos, yPos, "Click", 5);
            ReleaseDC(hWnd, hDC);
            return 0;

        case WM_DESTROY:
            PostQuitMessage(0);
            return 0;
    }

    return DefWindowProc(hWnd, message, wParam, lParam);
}
```

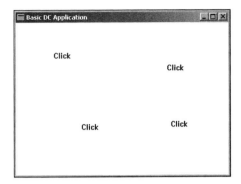

Figure 2-2: The BasicDCApp Windows application draws text in the window's client area.

If you like to do things the long way, you can create a client-area device context in an MFC program in almost exactly the same way that BasicDCApp does, by calling GetDC() and ReleaseDC(). For example, the following example shows the MFC version of responding to the WM_LBUTTONDOWN message to draw the word "Click" in the window:

```
void CClientDCAppView::OnLButtonDown(UINT nFlags,
    CPoint point)
{
    // TODO: Add your message handler code here
    //  and/or call default

    CWnd* pWnd = AfxGetMainWnd();
    HWND hWnd = pWnd->m_hWnd;
    HDC hDC = ::GetDC(hWnd);
    ::TextOut(hDC, point.x, point.y, "Click", 5);
    ::ReleaseDC(hWnd, hDC);

    CView::OnLButtonDown(nFlags, point);
}
```

This version of OnLButtonDown() creates a DC and draws to the screen with the same function calls that BasicDCApp does. The only difference is that OnLButtonDown() must call AfxGetMainWnd() to get a pointer to the MFC window object, which holds the window handle.

MFC's CClientDC class makes handling client-area DCs much easier. You can create a local DC object without having to worry about calling GetDC() or ReleaseDC(). When you create the object, MFC calls GetDC() for you; when the DC object goes out of scope, MFC automatically calls ReleaseDC() on behalf of the DC object. You just create the DC and use it.

Listing 2-2 is the view class for a program called ClientDCApp, which contains a revised version of the OnLButtonDown() function. This function uses the MFC CClientDC class to create the client-area DC, rather than create the DC the standard Windows API way. Figure 2-3 shows the running application.

Part I: Fundamental Windows 2000 Programming

Just as with BasicDCApp, when the user clicks in the window, the word "Click" appears in the clicked location.

Name: `ClientDCAppView.cpp`
Location: `WinPrgS\Chap02\ClientDCApp`

Listing 2-2: Creating a CClientDC object

```cpp
// ClientDCAppView.cpp : implementation of the CClientDCAppView class
//

#include "stdafx.h"
#include "ClientDCApp.h"

#include "ClientDCAppDoc.h"
#include "ClientDCAppView.h"

#ifdef _DEBUG
#define new DEBUG_NEW
#undef THIS_FILE
static char THIS_FILE[] = __FILE__;
#endif

/////////////////////////////////////////////////////////////////////////////
// CClientDCAppView

IMPLEMENT_DYNCREATE(CClientDCAppView, CView)

BEGIN_MESSAGE_MAP(CClientDCAppView, CView)
    //{{AFX_MSG_MAP(CClientDCAppView)
    ON_WM_LBUTTONDOWN()
    //}}AFX_MSG_MAP
END_MESSAGE_MAP()

/////////////////////////////////////////////////////////////////////////////
// CClientDCAppView construction/destruction

CClientDCAppView::CClientDCAppView()
{
    // TODO: add construction code here

}

CClientDCAppView::~CClientDCAppView()
{
}

BOOL CClientDCAppView::PreCreateWindow(CREATESTRUCT& cs)
{
    // TODO: Modify the Window class or styles here by modifying
    //  the CREATESTRUCT cs
```

Chapter 2: Graphical Device Interface Basics

```cpp
    return CView::PreCreateWindow(cs);
}

/////////////////////////////////////////////////////////////////////
// CClientDCAppView drawing

void CClientDCAppView::OnDraw(CDC* pDC)
{
    CClientDCAppDoc* pDoc = GetDocument();
    ASSERT_VALID(pDoc);

    // TODO: add draw code for native data here
}

/////////////////////////////////////////////////////////////////////
// CClientDCAppView diagnostics

#ifdef _DEBUG
void CClientDCAppView::AssertValid() const
{
    CView::AssertValid();
}

void CClientDCAppView::Dump(CDumpContext& dc) const
{
    CView::Dump(dc);
}

CClientDCAppDoc* CClientDCAppView::GetDocument() // non-debug version
is inline
{
    ASSERT(m_pDocument->IsKindOf(RUNTIME_CLASS(CClientDCAppDoc)));
    return (CClientDCAppDoc*)m_pDocument;
}
#endif //_DEBUG

/////////////////////////////////////////////////////////////////////
// CClientDCAppView message handlers

void CClientDCAppView::OnLButtonDown(UINT nFlags, CPoint point)
{
    // TODO: Add your message handler code here and/or call default

    CClientDC* clientDC = new CClientDC(this);
    clientDC->TextOut(point.x, point.y, "Click");
    delete clientDC;

    CView::OnLButtonDown(nFlags, point);
}
```

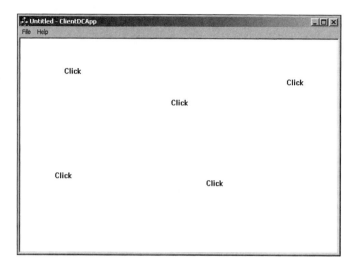

Figure 2-3: The MFC ClientDCApp application responds to clicks just as the BasicDCApp does.

You create a `CClientDC` object by calling the class's constructor. You can create the DC object on the stack or on the heap (as with most other MFC objects). Creating the DC object on the stack is easiest because you don't need to explicitly delete it; the system deletes the DC object when it goes out of scope. You create a `CClientDC` object on the stack like this:

```
CClientDC clientDC(this);
```

The constructor's single argument is a pointer to the window with which the DC is associated. The view class's `this` pointer fits the bill nicely.

You create the `CClientDC` object on the heap like this:

```
CClientDC* clientDC = new CClientDC(this);
```

You now have a pointer to the DC object. When you're finished with the object, you must delete it. This deletes the C++ object from memory, which forces the object's destructor to be called; this, in turn, causes `ReleaseDC()` to be called on behalf of the object.

The Metafile Device Context

Although the third device context's name sounds fancy, a metafile is nothing more than a list of drawing commands. You use a metafile when you want to create a graphical object that can be redrawn again and again. For example, a drawing program can use metafiles to store the objects that make up the current drawing. By defining each object separately, the user can select the object to draw and place it anywhere on the screen. Most drawing programs even enable the user to select objects and move them around the screen.

You create a metafile DC in much the same way you create any other type of DC. The difference is that when you call GDI functions to draw on the metafile DC, the DC stores the drawing commands in the metafile rather than have them appear onscreen. You then later play the metafile back, which displays the drawing on the screen.

As you probably already suspect, Visual C++'s MFC library features a class that encapsulates the metafile DC object. This class, called CMetaFileDC, works a little differently than the other DC classes. To create and use the metafile DC, follow these steps:

1. Create an object of the CMetaFileDC class.
2. Call the CMetaFileDC object's Create() member function to create the device context.
3. Call the CMetaFileDC's drawing commands (inherited from CDC) to draw the image that is stored in the metafile.
4. Call the CMetaFileDC's Close() member function, saving the metafile handle returned from the function.
5. Call the window's active DC's PlayMetaFile() function to draw the shape represented by it.
6. Call the Windows API function DeleteMetaFile() to delete the metafile when finished with the metafile.

Location: WinPrgS\Chap02\MetafileDCApp

In the Chap02\MetafileDCApp folder of this book's CD-ROM, you can find the MetafileDCApp program, which demonstrates how to create and draw a metafile using MFC's CMetaFileDC class. When you run the program, you see a blank window. Click in the window, and the application draws the shape it created as a metafile, as shown in Figure 2-4.

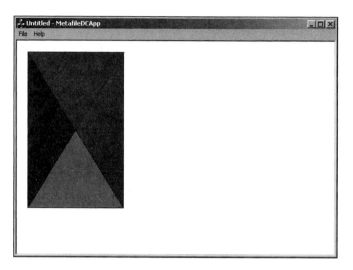

Figure 2-4: MetafileDCApp draws a shape stored in a metafile.

Now, take a look at the source code to see how the `MetafileDCApp` application works. The program creates its metafile in the `OnCreate()` member function of the view class. The `OnCreate()` function responds to the `WM_CREATE` message, which Windows sends to the application after the window is created but before the window is displayed. In an MFC program, you can think of `OnCreate()` as a counterpart to the class's constructor. Whereas the constructor initializes data for the C++ class, `OnCreate()` initializes data that requires the creation of the window element. Following is the `OnCreate()` function:

```
int CMetafileDCAppView::OnCreate
    (LPCREATESTRUCT lpCreateStruct)
{
    if (CView::OnCreate(lpCreateStruct) == -1)
        return -1;

    // TODO: Add your specialized creation code here

    CMetaFileDC metaFileDC;
    metaFileDC.Create(NULL);

    metaFileDC.Rectangle(20, 20, 200, 300);
    metaFileDC.MoveTo(20, 20);
    metaFileDC.LineTo(200, 300);
    metaFileDC.MoveTo(200, 20);
    metaFileDC.LineTo(20, 300);

    CBrush redBrush(RGB(255,0,0));
    CBrush* oldBrush =
        metaFileDC.SelectObject(&redBrush);
    metaFileDC.FloodFill(100, 50, RGB(0,0,0));
```

```
    CBrush greenBrush(RGB(0,255,0));
    metaFileDC.SelectObject(&greenBrush);
    metaFileDC.FloodFill(100, 250, RGB(0,0,0));

    CBrush blueBrush(RGB(0,0,255));
    metaFileDC.SelectObject(&blueBrush);
    metaFileDC.FloodFill(50, 150, RGB(0,0,0));

    CBrush purpleBrush(RGB(190,0,190));
    metaFileDC.SelectObject(&purpleBrush);
    metaFileDC.FloodFill(150, 150, RGB(0,0,0));

    metaFileDC.SelectObject(oldBrush);
    m_hMetaFile = metaFileDC.Close();

    return 0;
}
```

`OnCreate()` starts off by creating the metafile DC object:

```
CMetaFileDC metaFileDC;
metaFileDC.Create(NULL);
```

The `CMetaFileDC Create()` member function takes a single parameter, which is the file name where you should store the metafile. If you provide `NULL` for this argument, MFC creates an in-memory metafile.

After creating the metafile DC, the program draws the shape on the DC. It starts by drawing a rectangle with lines connecting its corners:

```
metaFileDC.Rectangle(20, 20, 200, 300);
metaFileDC.MoveTo(20, 20);
metaFileDC.LineTo(200, 300);
metaFileDC.MoveTo(200, 20);
metaFileDC.LineTo(20, 300);
```

The `Rectangle()` method's arguments are the coordinates for the rectangle's upper-left corner and lower-right corner. The `MoveTo()` function positions the DC's pen at the given coordinates, and the `LineTo()` command draws a line from the pen's current position to the coordinates given as the function's arguments.

`Rectangle()` and `LineTo()` are only two of the many DC functions you can use to draw shapes in a window's client area. You also can call `Draw3dRect()`, `Ellipse()`, `Arc()`, `Pie()`, `Polygon()`, `Polyline()`, `RoundRect()`, and other functions that the `CDC` class defines. Most of these functions are MFC versions of the Windows API functions of the same name.

The function then fills each triangle in the image with a color, starting with the top rectangle, which gets filled with red:

```
CBrush redBrush(RGB(255,0,0));
CBrush* oldBrush =
    metaFileDC.SelectObject(&redBrush);
metaFileDC.FloodFill(100, 50, RGB(0,0,0));
```

These lines create a new brush, select the brush into the DC, and then fill the rectangle section with the brush's color. You read about brushes a little later in this chapter. The `FloodFill()` function takes three arguments: the two coordinates at which to start filling and the color that acts as the fill's border. That is, the given color acts as a wall that contains the fill color. `OnCreate()` fills the other sections of the rectangle with color in the same way, but it uses brushes of a different color.

After the function completes the drawing, it restores the old brush to the DC and closes the metafile:

```
metaFileDC.SelectObject(oldBrush);
m_hMetaFile = metaFileDC.Close();
```

At this point, the program has a handle stored in the `m_hMetaFile` data member that it can use to access the metafile whenever it wants to draw the shape defined in the metafile. The program draws the shape in response to a user mouse click. This happens in the view class's `OnLButtonDown()` function, as shown here:

```
void CMetafileDCAppView::OnLButtonDown(UINT nFlags,
    CPoint point)
{
    // TODO: Add your message handler code here
    //    and/or call default

    CClientDC clientDC(this);
    clientDC.PlayMetaFile(m_hMetaFile);

    CView::OnLButtonDown(nFlags, point);
}
```

`OnLButtonDown()` creates a client DC for the window and then calls the client DC's `PlayMetaFile()` function to draw the shape defined in the metafile. `PlayMetaFile()`'s single argument is the metafile's handle.

When the user quits the program, MFC calls the `OnDestroy()` function, which responds to the Windows message `WM_DESTROY`. Windows sends the `WM_DESTROY` message when the window is removed from the screen and about to be destroyed. `OnDestroy()` is the counterpart to `OnCreate()`. Just as `OnCreate()` acts as a constructor for a window element, `OnDestroy()` acts as the destructor. That is, you do cleanup for the C++ object in the class's destructor, and you do window cleanup in the `OnDestroy()` function. In the MetafileDCApp application, `OnDestroy()` looks like this:

```
void CMetafileDCAppView::OnDestroy()
{
    CView::OnDestroy();

    // TODO: Add your message handler code here

    ::DeleteMetaFile(m_hMetaFile);
}
```

Here, `OnDestroy()` calls the Windows API function `DeleteMetaFile()` to delete the metafile from memory. The function's single argument is the metafile's handle. If you specify a file name when you create the metafile, you also may want to delete the resultant file in `OnDestroy()`. You can do this by calling MFC's `Remove()` function, which is a static member of the `CFile` class:

```
CFile::Remove(pFileName);
```

`Remove()`'s single argument is the path and file name of the file to remove.

Device Capabilities

Now that you've seen how a device context can represent any graphical device, you're ready to learn how to determine device capabilities. Most full-featured Windows programs wouldn't get too far if they weren't capable of discovering information about the devices on which they display data. For this reason, the Windows API includes a function called `GetDeviceCaps()` that can obtain most information you need to know about a device whether it is a screen, a printer, or something else.

The `CDC` class, from which MFC derives all device context classes, defines its own version of `GetDeviceCaps()` as a member function of the class. Once you have a DC object, you can call `GetDeviceCaps()` to obtain whatever information you need about the display device. For example, do this if you want to get the resolution of the screen:

```
CClientDC clientDC(this);
int horRes = clientDC.GetDeviceCaps(HORZRES);
int verRes = clientDC.GetDeviceCaps(VERTRES);
```

The `GetDeviceCaps()` function takes a single argument, which is the device capability that you want to obtain. Windows defines a set of constants that represent the available device capabilities. Table 2-2 lists these constants and their meanings. If you don't understand what some of the device capabilities mean, don't panic. You don't need to use most of them for a while. And by the time you need them, you'll know what they are!

Table 2-2 Some Useful Device Capabilities

Constant	Description
ASPECTX	Relative width of a pixel
ASPECTXY	Diagonal width of a pixel
ASPECTY	Relative height of a pixel
BITSPIXEL	Number of color bits per pixel

Continued

Table 2-2 (continued)

Constant	Description
CLIPCAPS	Device's clipping capabilities
COLORRES	Device's color resolution
HORZRES	Display width in pixels
HORZSIZE	Display width in millimeters
LOGPIXELSX	Number of horizontal pixels per inch
LOGPIXELSY	Number of vertical pixels per inch
NUMBRUSHES	Number of brushes
NUMCOLORS	Number of colors in the color table
NUMFONTS	Number of fonts
NUMPENS	Number of pens
NUMRESERVED	Number of reserved colors in the system palette
PLANES	Number of color planes
RASTERCAPS	Device's raster capabilities
SIZEPALETTE	Number of colors in the system palette
VERTRES	Display height in pixels
VERTSIZE	Display height in millimeters

CD

Location: `WinPrgS\Chap02\DeviceCapsApp`

In the `\Chap02\DeviceCapsApp` folder of this book's CD-ROM, you can find the DeviceCapsApp program. This program displays some of the system's device capabilities by calling `GetDeviceCaps()`. When you run the program, you see seven capabilities listed in the window (as shown in Figure 2-5).

In Figure 2-5, the application shows the device capabilities for a system that's set to 256 colors (8-bit color) and 800x600 resolution. The number of colors is shown as 20 because the Windows system reserves only 20 colors for its own use. In the configuration, an application that creates a palette should be capable of displaying 256 colors. (When you run the program on a system set to True Color, you see -1 for the number of colors because True Color displays don't use a color palette.) Following is the code that creates DeviceCapsApp's display. The `wsprintf()` function is a Windows API function that works similarly to the C `sprintf()` function.

Chapter 2: Graphical Device Interface Basics

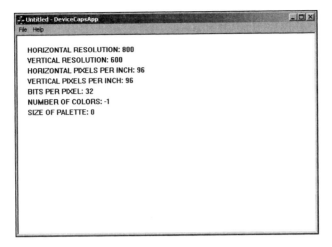

Figure 2-5: DeviceCapsApp displays capabilities for the current device.

```cpp
void CDeviceCapsAppView::OnDraw(CDC* pDC)
{
    CDeviceCapsAppDoc* pDoc = GetDocument();
    ASSERT_VALID(pDoc);

    // TODO: add draw code for native data here

    int horRes = pDC->GetDeviceCaps(HORZRES);
    int verRes = pDC->GetDeviceCaps(VERTRES);
    int logPixelsX = pDC->GetDeviceCaps(LOGPIXELSX);
    int logPixelsY = pDC->GetDeviceCaps(LOGPIXELSY);
    int bitsPixel = pDC->GetDeviceCaps(BITSPIXEL);
    int numColors = pDC->GetDeviceCaps(NUMCOLORS);
    int sizePalette = pDC->GetDeviceCaps(SIZEPALETTE);

    char s[81];
    wsprintf(s, "HORIZONTAL RESOLUTION: %d", horRes);
    pDC->TextOut(20, 20, s);
    wsprintf(s, "VERTICAL RESOLUTION: %d", verRes);
    pDC->TextOut(20, 40, s);
    wsprintf(s, "HORIZONTAL PIXELS PER INCH: %d",
        logPixelsX);
    pDC->TextOut(20, 60, s);
    wsprintf(s, "VERTICAL PIXELS PER INCH: %d",
        logPixelsY);
    pDC->TextOut(20, 80, s);
    wsprintf(s, "BITS PER PIXEL: %d", bitsPixel);
    pDC->TextOut(20, 100, s);
    wsprintf(s, "NUMBER OF COLORS: %d", numColors);
    pDC->TextOut(20, 120, s);
    wsprintf(s, "SIZE OF PALETTE: %d", sizePalette);
    pDC->TextOut(20, 140, s);
}
```

The CPen Class

In order to enable your application to draw different types of lines, you create your own pens and select them into the DC. Pens are the most basic drawing tools that you use with a DC. They draw all lines in a display, including the lines that border shapes such as rectangles and circles. Once you select your pen into the DC, the DC automatically uses it for its line-drawing operations.

MFC's CPen class represents GDI pens. Creating a new pen is just a matter of calling the CPen class's constructor, whose signature looks like this:

```
CPen(int style, int width, COLORREF color);
```

The CPen constructor's arguments are as follows:

- ***style*** The pen's drawing style, which is PS_SOLID, PS_DASH, PS_DOT, PS_DASHDOT, PS_DASHDOTDOT, PS_NULL, or PS_INSIDEFRAME. Most of these styles specify a pattern. The PS_NULL style is an invisible pen; PS_INSIDEFRAME is a pen that draws shape borders within the shape, rather than outside the shape.
- ***width*** The pen's width in pixels.
- ***color*** The pen's color as an RGB value.

Location: **WinPrgS\Chap02\PenApp**

In the \Chap02\PenApp folder of this book's CD-ROM, you can find the PenApp program. This program demonstrates drawing with pens using MFC's CPen class. When you run the program, you see the window shown in Figure 2-6.

All the drawing occurs in the view class's OnDraw() function. The following lines show the OnDraw() function, which creates a different pen for each line displayed in the window:

```
void CPenAppView::OnDraw(CDC* pDC)
{
    CPenAppDoc* pDoc = GetDocument();
    ASSERT_VALID(pDoc);

    // TODO: add draw code for native data here

    int red = 0;
    int green = 0;
    int blue = 0;
    int width = 2;
    int row = 20;

    for (int x=0; x<8; ++x)
    {
        int color = RGB(red,green,blue);
        CPen newPen(PS_SOLID, width, color);
        CPen* oldPen = pDC->SelectObject(&newPen);
```

```
            pDC->MoveTo(20, row);
            pDC->LineTo(300, row);
            pDC->SelectObject(oldPen);

            red += 32;
            green += 16;
            blue += 8;
            width += 2;
            row += 30;
        }
    }
```

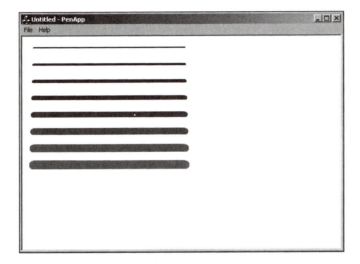

Figure 2-6: PenApp draws with pens of different sizes and colors.

Within the for loop, the function creates a pen, selects the pen into the DC, draws a line, and then restores the old pen to the DC.

Restoring the old pen is important because the newly created pen goes out of scope in each iteration of the loop, causing the deletion of the pen object. Never delete a pen that's selected into a DC. Selecting the old pen back into the DC before each loop iteration ends prevents the new pen from being deleted while it's still selected into the DC.

Location: WinPrgS\Chap02\PenApp2

If you want to see pen styles in action, check out the program in the Chap02\PenApp2 folder of this book's CD-ROM. This program draws lines in the five different line styles shown in Figure 2-7. The following source code (taken from PenApp2) shows the view class's OnDraw() function, which works similarly to the previous version except that it changes pen drawing styles rather than widths and colors.

```
void CPenApp2View::OnDraw(CDC* pDC)
{
    CPenApp2Doc* pDoc = GetDocument();
    ASSERT_VALID(pDoc);

    // TODO: add draw code for native data here

    int styles[] =
        {PS_SOLID, PS_DASH, PS_DOT,
         PS_DASHDOT, PS_DASHDOTDOT};

    int row = 20;

    for (int x=0; x<5; ++x)
    {
        int color = RGB(0,0,0);
        CPen newPen(styles[x], 1, color);
        CPen* oldPen = pDC->SelectObject(&newPen);
        pDC->MoveTo(20, row);
        pDC->LineTo(300, row);
        pDC->SelectObject(oldPen);

        row += 30;
    }
}
```

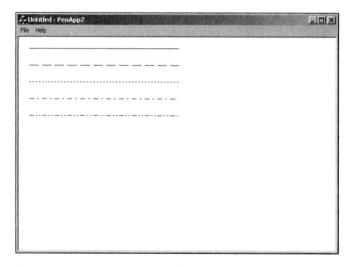

Figure 2-7: PenApp2 draws with different pen styles.

The CBrush Class

Whenever a program fills a shape with color, it uses the DC's current brush. A DC's default brush is white, which is why rectangles drawn in windows with white backgrounds don't look filled. If you draw two overlapping rectangles, as shown in Figure 2-8, however, you can see that the rectangles aren't as empty as they appear; the fill color is indeed white.

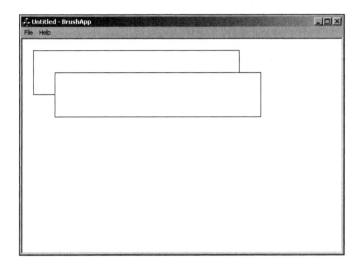

Figure 2-8: A DC's default brush is white, as shown by these overlapping rectangles.

Just as with pens, you can create your own brushes and so control the way the DC draws and fills shapes. MFC features the CBrush class, which represents GDI brush objects. To create a new brush, you just call the class's constructor, whose signature looks like this:

```
CBrush(COLORREF color);
```

The constructor's single argument is the brush's color, specified as a COLORREF value. After creating the brush, you select it into the DC; then all fill operations use the new brush. When you're finished with the brush, you reselect the old brush back into the DC.

Location: **WinPrgS\Chap02\BrushApp**

In the \Chap02\BrushApp folder of this book's CD-ROM, you can find the BrushApp program. This program demonstrates drawing with brushes using MFC's CBrush class. When you run the program, you see the window shown in Figure 2-9.

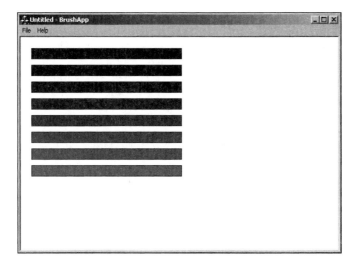

Figure 2-9: BrushApp draws with different brush colors.

The following source code example shows BrushApp's `OnDraw()` function, which is where the application draws the filled rectangles in its display:

```
void CBrushAppView::OnDraw(CDC* pDC)
{
    CBrushAppDoc* pDoc = GetDocument();
    ASSERT_VALID(pDoc);

    // TODO: add draw code for native data here

    int red = 0;
    int green = 0;
    int blue = 0;
    int row = 20;

    for (int x=0; x<8; ++x)
    {
        int color = RGB(red,green,blue);
        CBrush newBrush(color);
        CBrush* oldBrush = pDC->SelectObject(&newBrush);
        pDC->Rectangle(20, row, 300, row+20);
        pDC->SelectObject(oldBrush);

        red += 32;
        green += 16;
        blue += 8;
        row += 30;
    }
}
```

Within the `for` loop, the function creates a brush, selects the brush into the DC, draws a rectangle, and then restores the old brush to the DC. As with the pens in PenApp and PenApp2, restoring the old brush is important because the newly created brush goes out of scope in each iteration of the loop, causing the deletion of the brush object.

Like many MFC classes, the `CBrush` class overloads its constructor to give you several ways to create a brush. One constructor enables you to specify a fill pattern for your brush. That constructor's signature looks like this:

```
CBrush(int style, COLORREF color);
```

Here, `style` is one of the brush styles defined by Windows, which are HS_BDIAGONAL, HS_CROSS, HS_DIAGCROSS, HS_FDIAGONAL, HS_HORIZONTAL, and HS_VERTICAL.

Location: **WinPrgS\Chap02\PatternBrushApp**

In the \Chap02\PatternBrushApp folder of this book's CD-ROM, you can find the PatternBrushApp program that demonstrates drawing with different brush styles. When you run the program, you see the window shown in Figure 2-10. Here is the revised OnDraw() function that creates the display:

```
void CPatternBrushAppView::OnDraw(CDC* pDC)
{
    CPatternBrushAppDoc* pDoc = GetDocument();
    ASSERT_VALID(pDoc);

    // TODO: add draw code for native data here

    int styles[] = {HS_BDIAGONAL, HS_CROSS, HS_DIAGCROSS,
        HS_FDIAGONAL, HS_HORIZONTAL, HS_VERTICAL};
    int row = 20;

    for (int x=0; x<6; ++x)
    {
        CBrush newBrush(styles[x], RGB(255,0,0));
        CBrush* oldBrush = pDC->SelectObject(&newBrush);
        pDC->Rectangle(20, row, 300, row+30);
        pDC->SelectObject(oldBrush);
        row += 40;
    }
}
```

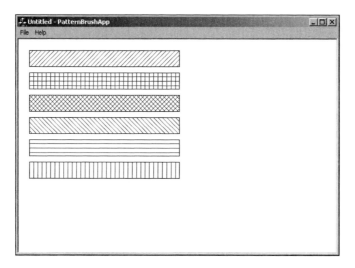

Figure 2-10: PatternBrushApp draws with different fill patterns.

   PROBLEMS & SOLUTIONS

Bitmapped Brushes

PROBLEM: *It's great that Windows enables me to choose from many types of pattern fills, but what if none of the standard fill patterns works for me? Can I create my own?*

SOLUTION: If you need a custom fill pattern for a brush, you can create a bitmap that holds the required pattern and use it as a brush. Although the process requires that you know a little something about bitmaps, you easily can modify the sample provided here for your own purposes. When you're ready to learn more about this subject, turn to Chapter 9.

First, you create a memory DC to hold the bitmap. A *memory DC* is like any other DC, except it remains hidden in memory and is never displayed on the screen. You can think of a memory DC as a buffer for holding off-screen graphics. To create a memory DC, you must have a valid display DC already. You then create the memory DC based on the settings in the display DC. The whole process looks like this:

```
CClientDC clientDC(this);
CDC memoryDC;
memoryDC.CreateCompatibleDC(&clientDC);
```

Here, an object of the `CDC` class represents the memory DC. The call to the object's `CreateCompatibleDC()` function creates a device context with the same attributes as `clientDC` and attaches the DC to the `memoryDC` object.

Continued

Chapter 2: Graphical Device Interface Basics

Next, you create a bitmap object and select it into the memory DC:

```
CBitmap* pBitmap = new CBitmap();
pBitmap->CreateCompatibleBitmap(&memoryDC, 8, 8);
CBitmap* pOldBitmap =
    memoryDC.SelectObject(pBitmap);
```

The `CBitmap` object's `CreateCompatibleBitmap()` function creates a bitmap and attaches it to the `CBitmap` object. The function's three arguments are the DC with which the bitmap must be compatible and the width and height of the bitmap. The smallest bitmap that you can use with a brush is 8x8 pixels, which is the size of the bitmap created here.

When you select the bitmap into the memory DC, the bitmap becomes the DC's drawing surface. All the drawing commands that you direct to the memory DC are rendered on the bitmap. Usually, the first thing you do is clear the bitmap to a single color:

```
CBrush whiteBrush(RGB(255,255,255));
memoryDC.FillRect(CRect(0,0,799,599),
    &whiteBrush);
```

Clearing the bitmap is important because, before you draw on it, the bitmap contains values that were in memory before the bitmap was created.

With the bitmap cleared, you can draw whatever pattern you like on its surface. Once you draw the bitmap, use it to create a new brush and then select the brush into the display DC like this:

```
CBrush brush(pBitmap);
CBrush* pOldBrush = clientDC.SelectObject(&brush);
```

Now, any shapes that use a brush are filled with the pattern you created.

Location: **WinPrgS\Chap02\BitmapBrushApp**

Check out the `Chap02\BitmapBrushApp` folder of this book's CD-ROM. There you can find the BitmapBrushApp application, which draws a rectangle filled with a custom brush pattern (as shown in Figure 2-11). Following is the function that creates the display:

```
void CBitmapBrushAppView::OnDraw(CDC* pDC)
{
    CBitmapBrushAppDoc* pDoc = GetDocument();
    ASSERT_VALID(pDoc);

    // TODO: add draw code for native data here

    CDC memoryDC;
    memoryDC.CreateCompatibleDC(pDC);

    CBitmap* pBitmap = new CBitmap();
    pBitmap->CreateCompatibleBitmap(&memoryDC, 8, 8);
    CBitmap* pOldBitmap =
        memoryDC.SelectObject(pBitmap);
```

Continued

```
CBrush whiteBrush(RGB(255,255,255));
    memoryDC.FillRect(CRect(0,0,799,599),
        &whiteBrush);
    memoryDC.Rectangle(2, 2, 6, 6);
    CBrush brush(pBitmap);
    CBrush* pOldBrush = pDC->SelectObject(&brush);
    pDC->Rectangle(20, 20, 200, 200);

    pDC->SelectObject(pOldBrush);
    memoryDC.SelectObject(pOldBitmap);
}
```

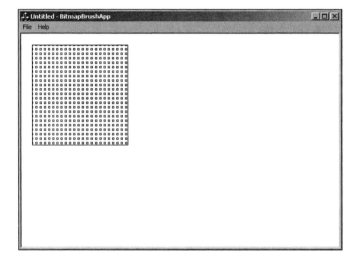

Figure 2-11: The BitmapBrushApp application displays a rectangle filled with a custom brush.

Summary

Device contexts are important to all Windows programmers because without them no application can display data in its window. By calling the many GDI functions, an application can draw anything from a simple line of text to commercial-quality images. Customizable GDI objects, such as pens and brushes, enable you to fine-tune the DC's attributes in order to create the exact graphics you need.

Also discussed in this chapter:

▶ The GDI is a huge library of graphics functions.

▶ A device context represents the attributes for a display device.

- Every DC is associated with a set of GDI objects, including a pen, a brush, and a font.
- A paint DC enables an application to update a window in response to a `WM_PAINT` message.
- A client DC enables an application to draw in a window's client area.
- A metafile DC enables an application to store drawing commands that the application can play back later.
- A GDI pen can have a pattern, a width, and a color.
- A GDI brush can fill shapes with a solid color or with patterns.

Chapter 3

Windows and Dialog Boxes

In This Chapter

▶ Exploring the MFC window classes

▶ Using frame and view windows

▶ Creating a basic window without AppWizard

▶ Understanding window styles

▶ Understanding multiple-document interface application windows

▶ Creating custom and common dialog boxes

▶ Using property sheets

▶ Creating and adding wizards to a program

If there's one thing the Windows platform has, it's plenty of windows. There are application windows, pop-up windows, wizard windows, dialog box windows, message box windows, SDI windows, MDI windows, property sheet windows and . . . well . . . you get the point. Let's just say that Windows definitely comes by its name well. The truth is that Windows is filled with objects — buttons, list boxes, and toolbars — that don't even look like windows. In fact, they are just other types of windows.

And just in case you feel you don't have enough windows to work with, Visual C++ and its MFC library break the window types down into even more categories, including frame, view, edit, MDI frame, MDI child, OLE, splitter, and database form windows, just to name a few. MFC also features classes for dialog boxes, property sheets, wizards, toolbars, status bars, and more, all of which are classes that represent — you guessed it — windows.

In its simplest form, a *window* is just a rectangular area on the screen that usually represents a running process. The window often displays, and enables the user to edit, whatever types of data are native to the application. Of course, nothing is ever that simple. These days, windows also sport controls, menu bars, toolbars, status bars, and other adornments that users have come to expect and which programmers must supply.

Windows also are the objects to which Windows 2000 sends messages. An application can have a main window and several child windows, with specific messages routed to each window. In fact, even controls in a window can and do receive messages; controls are, after all, windows themselves. Because Windows' messages enable the interactivity between a user and an application, it's clear that windows are the engines that drive all applications.

MFC applications, however, handle Windows messages much differently than straight C applications do. If you want to see the difference, refer to Chapter 1, which demonstrates programming Windows 2000 with C versus programming Windows 2000 with MFC. In that chapter, you can see the difference between C and MFC message handling. However, although MFC programs seem to handle messages differently, way down in the innards of the MFC libraries, it's business as usual; the application frameworks receive and respond to messages at the same level C programs do.

In this chapter, because C Windows programming is falling out of fashion, you examine window objects from the MFC point of view. Along the way, you learn the relationship between frame and view windows, as well as gain experience with *multiple-document interface (MDI)* windows. I also introduce dialog boxes, property sheets, and wizards here.

The MFC Window Base Classes

As you've probably figured out by now, MFC represents a complicated hierarchy of classes. Most classes that you use in your Visual C++ programs have a long ancestry, and the window classes are no exception. A frame window, for example, traces its ancestry from CFrameWnd back through CWnd to CCmdTarget and finally to CObject. Each one of these base classes provides important functionality to the window, as you learn in the following sections.

The CObject Class

The granddaddy of almost all MFC classes, CObject provides support for *serialization* (object persistence), debugging information, and run-time class information. The only MFC classes that can't trace their ancestry back to CObject are support classes such as the value-type classes (CPoint, CRect, CSize, CString, CTime, and CTimeSpan) and Internet server classes (CHtmlStream, CHttpFilter, CHttpFilterContext, CHttpServer, and CHttpServerContext), as well as various other support classes and wrapper classes. The CObject member functions and their descriptions are:

AssertValid()	Checks the validity of the object
Dump()	Prints the contents of the object

GetRuntimeClass	Returns a pointer to the object's CRuntimeClass structure, which contains information about the class from which the object was instantiated
IsKindOf()	Compares the object to a given class
IsSerializable()	Returns a nonzero value if the object can be serialized
Serialize()	Serializes (saves or loads) the object

Three of the CObject member functions—AssertValid(), Dump(), and Serialize()—must be overridden in your custom class in order to be useful.

The CCmdTarget Class

CCmdTarget is the class that gives other MFC classes the capability to implement message maps to respond to Windows messages. Any MFC class that processes messages—including windows, dialog boxes, control bars, and controls—has CCmdTarget in its ancestry. Most of CCmdTarget's functionality can be included in your MFC program with little additional effort on your part. In fact, the class has only a few member functions; the most useful ones are listed here:

BeginWaitCursor()	Displays the hourglass cursor
EnableAutomation()	Enables OLE automation for the object
EndWaitCursor()	Changes the hourglass cursor back to the arrow
RestoreWaitCursor()	Restores the hourglass cursor after another object, such as a dialog box, changes the cursor to an arrow

The CWnd Class

All window classes—including frame windows, control bars, dialog boxes, views, property sheets, and controls—have CWnd in their ancestry. This immense class makes a window a window by providing member functions that enable a program to manipulate a window in various ways.

Your programs can create windows directly from the CWnd class, but more often they derive custom windows from one of the more specific window classes, such as CFrameWnd or CMDIFrameWnd. Table 3-1 lists some of the most useful CWnd member functions.

Table 3-1 Some Useful CWnd Member Functions

Function	Description
`CenterWindow()`	Centers a window within its parent window
`Create()`	Creates a child window
`DestroyWindow()`	Destroys the window element
`EnableWindow()`	Enables or disables the window's mouse and keyboard input
`GetActiveWindow()`	Gets a pointer to the active window
`GetCapture()`	Retrieves a pointer to the window that captures the mouse
`GetClientRect()`	Gets the dimensions of the window's client area
`GetDlgItem()`	Gets a pointer to a dialog box control
`GetFocus()`	Gets a pointer to the window that has the input focus
`GetFont()`	Gets a pointer to the window's font
`GetIcon()`	Gets the handle to the window's icon
`GetMenu()`	Gets a pointer to a menu
`GetParent()`	Gets a pointer to the window's parent window
`GetParentFrame()`	Gets a pointer to the window's parent frame window
`GetParentOwner()`	Gets a pointer to a child window's parent window
`GetSafeHwnd()`	Returns a window's handle
`GetStyle()`	Gets the window's style
`GetSystemMenu()`	Gets a pointer to the window's system menu
`GetWindowRect()`	Gets the window's screen coordinates
`GetWindowText()`	Gets the window's caption text
`Invalidate()`	Invalidates a window's entire client area
`InvalidateRect()`	Invalidates a rectangle within a window's client area
`IsIconic()`	Returns TRUE if the window is minimized
`IsWindowEnabled()`	Returns TRUE if the window can receive mouse and keyboard input
`IsWindowVisible()`	Returns TRUE if the window is visible
`IsZoomed()`	Returns TRUE if the window is maximized
`KillTimer()`	Kills a system timer
`MessageBox()`	Displays a message box

Chapter 3: Windows and Dialog Boxes

Function	Description
ModifyStyle()	Changes the window's style
MoveWindow()	Changes the window's position and dimensions
OpenClipboard()	Opens the clipboard
PostMessage()	Sends a message to a window and returns immediately, without waiting for the message to be processed
PreCreateWindow()	Enables programs to change a window's style before the window is displayed
SendMessage()	Sends a message to a window, returning only after the window processes the message
SetActiveWindow()	Activates a window
SetCapture()	Forces all mouse messages to be sent to the window
SetFocus()	Gives the window the input focus
SetFont()	Sets the window's font
SetIcon()	Sets the window's icon
SetMenu()	Sets the window's menu
SetTimer()	Starts a system timer
SetWindowText()	Sets the window's caption text
ShowWindow()	Shows or hides the window
UpdateData()	Transfers data to and from a dialog box

The functions listed in Table 3-1 display only a small sampling of what's available in the CWnd class; they should give you some idea of how much power the class gives you over window elements. When you become more familiar with Visual C++ and MFC, you may want to examine the window classes more closely, which you can do by looking up the classes in your Visual C++ online documentation.

Tip

To quickly locate information about an MFC class, place the text cursor on the class name in the source code window and press F1.

Most conspicuously absent from Table 3-1 are the message-response functions that the CWnd class defines for standard Windows messages. These functions definitely are useful, but are so numerous that they would make the table too big. Just know that the CWnd class defines the functions that enable MFC windows to respond to Windows messages. These functions include OnLButtonDown() (which responds to WM_LBUTTONDOWN), OnCreate() (which responds to WM_CREATE), OnDestroy() (which responds to WM_DESTROY), OnChar() (which responds to WM_CHAR), and dozens of others.

Frame and View Windows

Now that you are familiar with MFC's base window classes, you're ready to learn about the many types of windows you can create in your programs. A *frame window,* which is represented by MFC's CFrameWnd window class, is an application's main window that contains the title bar, window controls, and menu bar. When programming a straight C Windows application, the main window also holds the area in which the application displays its document data. This document-display portion of the window is called the *client area.*

With MFC, however, the application framework separates a document from the way the user views the document. This document/view architecture relies upon three main objects: the document, frame window, and view window. (For more information on the document/view architecture, please refer to Chapter 16.) The frame window is much like the main window in a C Windows program. However, rather than drawing the document's data directly on the frame window's client area, the frame window's client area contains a view window.

The *view window* has no title bar, controls, or even a border. It basically is an invisible window that positions itself exactly over the frame window's client area. An MFC application then displays its document in the view window's client area, rather than in the frame window's client area.

This is a powerful programming technique because you quickly can change the way the user views and edits a document just by switching to a new view window. A document can be associated with any number of view windows.

Note

Not all MFC applications implement the document/view architecture. If you write an MFC program from scratch (that is, without using AppWizard to generate a skeleton application), you can create a frame window that displays data directly in its client area. However, if you use AppWizard to start a program, the resultant application usually uses the document/view architecture.

The CFrameWnd Class

As previously discussed, an MFC application's main window is represented by the CFrameWnd class, which the framework derives from CWnd. CFrameWnd has a rich ancestry, inheriting member variables and functions from CObject, CCmdTarget, and CWnd. In addition, CFrameWnd adds its own set of member functions; Table 3-2 lists the most useful ones.

Table 3-2 The Most Useful CFrameWnd Member Functions

Function	Description
ActivateFrame()	Makes the window visible and available
Create()	Creates the Windows window associated with the CFrameWnd object

Function	Description
`DockControlBar()`	Docks a control bar
`EnableDocking()`	Enables control bar docking
`FloatControlBar()`	Floats a control bar
`GetActiveDocument()`	Gets a pointer to the document object
`GetActiveFrame()`	Gets a pointer to the active `CFrameWnd` object
`GetActiveView()`	Gets a pointer to the active view object
`GetControlBar()`	Gets a pointer to the toolbar
`GetDockState()`	Gets a frame window's dock state
`GetMessageBar()`	Gets a pointer to a frame window's status bar
`LoadAccelTable()`	Loads an accelerator table
`LoadBarState()`	Restores toolbar settings
`SaveBarState()`	Saves toolbar settings
`SetActiveView()`	Sets the active view object
`SetMessageText()`	Sets the status bar's text
`ShowControlBar()`	Shows the toolbar

The CView Class

The `CView` class represents a document view in an MFC program. A document can have multiple views, but a view can be associated with only a single document. MFC programs implementing the document/view architecture always derive a custom view class from the `CView` base class, which then overrides member functions in the `CView` class to provide the functionality needed by the view object. Table 3-3 lists important `CView` member functions.

Table 3-3 The Most Useful CView Member Functions

Function	Description
`DoPreparePrinting()`	Displays the Print dialog box and creates a printer device context
`GetDocument()`	Gets a pointer to the document associated with the view
`OnActivateFrame()`	Called by MFC when the view's frame window becomes activated or deactivated
`OnActivateView()`	Called by MFC when a view is activated

Continued

Table 3-3 *(continued)*

Function	Description
`OnBeginPrinting()`	Called by MFC when printing begins
`OnDraw()`	Called by MFC to draw the document in the view window or on the printer
`OnEndPrinting()`	Called by MFC when printing ends
`OnEndPrintPreview()`	Called by MFC when preview mode is closed
`OnInitialUpdate()`	Called by MFC after a view is associated with its document
`OnPrepareDC()`	Called by MFC before `OnDraw()` renders the document or before `OnPrint()` starts printing or starts the print preview
`OnPreparePrinting()`	Called by MFC to give a view window the chance to set up the Print dialog box
`OnPrint()`	Called by MFC in order to print one page of the document
`OnUpdate()`	Called by MFC when the associated document is modified

All the entries in Table 3-3 whose descriptions begin with "Called by MFC" are functions that you can override in your own view class in order to implement some extra functionality in the class. For example, you almost always override `OnDraw()` in order to display the application's current document in the view window. The `CView` base class's `OnDraw()` function does nothing on its own.

Some of the base class functions do, however, perform useful services for your view class even if you don't override the functions in your class. `OnUpdate()`, for example, makes sure that the view window gets updated whenever the document changes. You can override `OnUpdate()` to perform additional tasks before the view window gets updated.

Window Basics: Creating an Application Without AppWizard

One of the big problems with AppWizard is that it creates such sophisticated source code it obscures much of what happens behind the scenes in an MFC program. To understand MFC window basics, you really need to see an MFC application that leaves out all the fancy stuff and performs the basic functions, which involves creating a window and responding to Windows messages.

Creating the BasicApp Application

Although most programmers don't bother, you easily can create a basic MFC application without cranking up AppWizard. The source code for such an application reveals much about the ways MFC windows perform. Listing 3-1 shows the source code for BasicApp, which is this type of MFC application. To create a project for this application, as well as compile and link the application, complete the following steps:

1. From Visual C++'s File menu, select the New command (see Figure 3-1). The New dialog box appears.

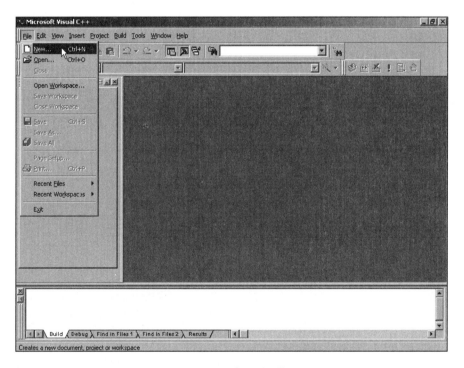

Figure 3-1: To start a new project, select New from the File menu.

2. Select the Projects tab. In the left pane, select the Win32 application project type, type **BasicApp** into the Project Name dialog box, and select the destination directory in the Location dialog box (as shown in Figure 3-2).

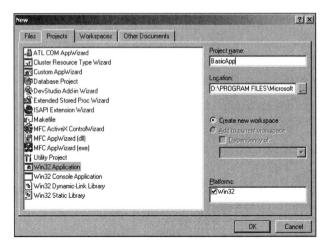

Figure 3-2: The New dialog box is displayed with the new project's parameters.

3. Click OK in the New dialog box, and Visual C++ displays the Win32 application—Step 1 of 1 dialog box. Make sure the An Empty Project option is selected and click Finish. Click OK on the dialog box that appears, and Visual C++ creates and opens the new project.

4. Select the File menu's New command a second time. The New dialog box reappears, this time with the Files tab selected.

5. In the left pane, select the C++ Source File type. In the File Name dialog box, type **BasicApp.cpp** (as shown in Figure 3-3).

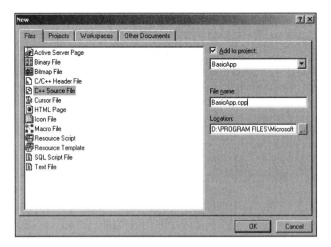

Figure 3-3: The New dialog box is displayed with parameters to add a source code file to the project.

Chapter 3: Windows and Dialog Boxes

6. Make sure the Add to Project checkbox is selected and click OK. Visual C++ creates the new empty file and displays it in the text editor.

7. Type the contents of Listing 3-1 into the new source code window, or copy the source code into the window from this book's CD-ROM.

Name: `BasicApp.cpp`
Location: `WinPrgS\Chap03\BasicApp`

Listing 3-1: Source code for the BasicApp application

```
// Header file for all MFC classes.
#include <afxwin.h>

////////////////////////////////////////
// Application class's declaration.
////////////////////////////////////////

class CBasicApp : public CWinApp
{
public:
    CBasicApp();
    ~CBasicApp();
    BOOL InitInstance();
};

////////////////////////////////////////
// Frame window class's declaration.
////////////////////////////////////////

class CSimpleFrame : public CFrameWnd
{
public:
    CSimpleFrame();
    ~CSimpleFrame();

    afx_msg void OnLButtonDown(UINT nFlags, CPoint point);

    DECLARE_MESSAGE_MAP()
};

////////////////////////////////////////
// Application class's implementation.
////////////////////////////////////////

// Global application object.
CBasicApp app;

CBasicApp::CBasicApp()
{
}
```

```
CBasicApp::~CBasicApp()
{
}

CBasicApp::InitInstance()
{
    m_pMainWnd = new CSimpleFrame();
    m_pMainWnd->ShowWindow(m_nCmdShow);

    return TRUE;
}

/////////////////////////////////////////////
// Frame window class's implementation.
/////////////////////////////////////////////

BEGIN_MESSAGE_MAP(CSimpleFrame, CFrameWnd)
    ON_WM_LBUTTONDOWN()
END_MESSAGE_MAP()

CSimpleFrame::CSimpleFrame()
{
    Create(NULL, "Basic MFC Application");
}

CSimpleFrame::~CSimpleFrame()
{
}

void CSimpleFrame::OnLButtonDown(UINT nFlags,
    CPoint point)
{
    CClientDC clientDC(this);
    clientDC.TextOut(20, 20, "Hello from BasicApp!");
}
```

8. Select the Project menu's Settings command (see Figure 3-4). The Project Settings property sheet appears.

9. In the Settings For dialog box, select All Configurations. In the Microsoft Foundation Classes drop-down list, select Use MFC in a Static Library (as shown in Figure 3-5). Click OK to finalize your choices.

10. Click the Build button on the toolbar, or press F7, to compile and link your new application.

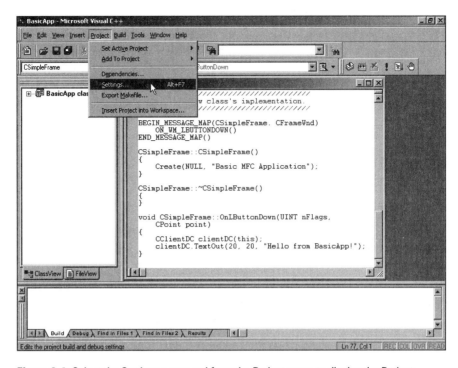

Figure 3-4: Select the Settings command from the Project menu to display the Project Settings property sheet.

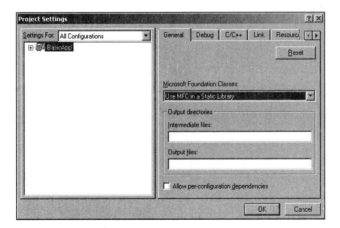

Figure 3-5: The Project Settings property sheet, specifying that the project should use the static MFC library

When you run BasicApp, you can see a fairly plain frame window. This window has the basic window controls but no extra adornments such as a menu bar, toolbar, or status bar. Still, it's a fully functioning window that can respond to Windows messages. To prove this, click inside the window's client area. When you do, the message "Hello from BasicApp!" appears in the upper-left corner (as shown in Figure 3-6).

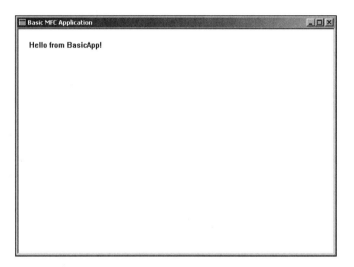

Figure 3-6: BasicApp responding to a mouse click

Understanding the BasicApp Application

In this section, you get a look at how MFC works by examining the application you just created, as well as touching on a few additional subjects.

The afxwin.h header file

First, BasicApp's source code includes the `afxwin.h` header file like this:

```
#include <afxwin.h>
```

The `afxwin.h` file includes in your program all the header files for the many MFC classes. Any program that uses MFC must include this header file.

The application class

Every MFC program must have an application object derived from `CWinApp`. In the BasicApp application, the application class is called `CBasicApp` and includes a constructor and a destructor. The class also overrides `CWinApp`'s `InitInstance()`, which is where the application creates its main window. The class's declaration looks like this:

```
class CBasicApp : public CWinApp
{
```

```
public:
    CBasicApp();
    ~CBasicApp();
    BOOL InitInstance();
};
```

Because the application object must exist at program startup and must continue to exist while the application is running, every MFC program creates a global application object from its application class:

```
CBasicApp app;
```

As the MFC application starts up, MFC calls the application object's InitInstance() member function. In CBasicApp, you've overridden InitInstance() in order to create the application's frame window:

```
CBasicApp::InitInstance()
{
    m_pMainWnd = new CSimpleFrame();
    m_pMainWnd->ShowWindow(m_nCmdShow);

    return TRUE;
}
```

The application class has a data member called m_pMainWnd that holds a pointer to the application's frame window. In InitInstance(), CBasicApp creates a CSimpleFrame frame window object and assigns its pointer to m_pMainWnd. CSimpleFrame is the application's frame window class, which, as you soon see, is derived from MFC's CFrameWnd.

The application class also inherits the m_nCmdShow data member from CWinApp. This variable contains the flags that normally are passed to a Windows application's WinMain() function. This value determines how the window initially appears, and usually is set to SW_SHOW. (For more information, please refer to Chapter 1.) CBasicApp's InitInstance() function passes this value to the frame window when it calls the frame window's ShowWindow() member function, which displays the window on the screen.

The frame window class

BasicApp's frame window class, CSimpleFrame, represents the application's main window and is derived from MFC's CFrameWnd. The class includes a constructor and a destructor, as well as the OnLButtonDown() message-response function. The class also declares a message map, as you can see in the class's declaration:

```
class CSimpleFrame : public CFrameWnd
{
public:
    CSimpleFrame();
    ~CSimpleFrame();

    afx_msg void OnLButtonDown(UINT nFlags,
```

```
        CPoint point);

    DECLARE_MESSAGE_MAP()
};
```

There's not much to say about CSimpleFrame's declaration that I haven't covered already in this book. For information on message maps and message-response functions, please refer to Chapter 1.

In the frame window's implementation, the class first defines its message map:

```
BEGIN_MESSAGE_MAP(CSimpleFrame, CFrameWnd)
    ON_WM_LBUTTONDOWN()
END_MESSAGE_MAP()
```

You immediately can tell from the message map that this window handles only the WM_LBUTTONDOWN Windows message.

In the constructor, the class calls Create() for the window:

```
CSimpleFrame::CSimpleFrame()
{
    Create(NULL, "Basic MFC Application");
}
```

The Create() member function creates the actual Windows window and attaches it to the MFC window class. If you don't call Create(), you will have no window to display. Although the call to Create() in the class's constructor has only two arguments, Create() actually takes eight arguments, all of which — except the first two — have default values. Create()'s signature looks like this:

```
BOOL Create(
    LPCTSTR lpszClassName,
    LPCTSTR lpszWindowName,
    DWORD dwStyle = WS_OVERLAPPEDWINDOW,
    const RECT& rect = rectDefault,
    CWnd* pParentWnd = NULL,
    LPCTSTR lpszMenuName = NULL,
    DWORD dwExStyle = 0,
    CCreateContext* pContext = NULL);
```

Table 3-4 lists the function's arguments.

Table 3-4 Create() Member Function Arguments

Argument	Description
lpszClassName	The window class's name, or NULL to accept CFrameWnd's default class name
lpszWindowName	The text for the window's title bar

Argument	Description
dwStyle	The window's style flags
rect	The size and position of the window
pParentWnd	The window's parent window, or NULL if there is no parent window
lpszMenuName	The name of the window's menu resource
dwExStyle	The window's extended styles
pContext	A pointer to a CCreateContext structure or NULL

The only other function of interest is OnLButtonDown(), which responds to the Windows message WM_ONLBUTTONDOWN:

```
void CSimpleFrame::OnLButtonDown(UINT nFlags,
    CPoint point)
{
    CClientDC clientDC(this);
    clientDC.TextOut(20, 20, "Hello from BasicApp!");
}
```

This function first creates a DC (device context) object for the window's client area and then displays the text "Hello from BasicApp!" in the window. Simply put, a device context is a set of attributes that the window needs in order to draw on the screen. If you want more information on device contexts, refer to Chapter 2.

Window Styles

You now know how to create an application that displays a basic window. What you haven't learned is how a window's style settings affect what you see on the screen. If every application window looked and acted exactly the same, what a boring world it would be (at least for those of us with IBM-compatible computers). Luckily, when Microsoft designed Windows, it knew that programmers would want to be able to control the way their windows look and act. To accommodate this desire, Windows defines a set of window styles that enable a window to be anything from an invisible rectangle to a full-frame window.

These window styles are represented by a set of constants that you can combine in various ways to create the style of window you need for your application. Table 3-5 lists the window styles defined by Windows. As you can see, there are a lot of choices, making the creation of a window style as much an art as a science.

Table 3-5 Window Style Constants

Constant	Description
WS_BORDER	Creates a window with a border
WS_CAPTION	Creates a window with a title bar
WS_CHILD	Creates a child window
WS_CLIPCHILDREN	Prevents the application from drawing over child windows when it draws in the parent window's client area
WS_CLIPSIBLINGS	Prevents the application from drawing over child windows when it draws inside a child window that's overlapped by other child windows
WS_DISABLED	Creates a disabled window
WS_DLGFRAME	Creates a window with a double border and no title
WS_GROUP	Specifies the first control of a control group
WS_HSCROLL	Creates a window with a horizontal scroll bar
WS_MAXIMIZE	Creates a maximized window
WS_MAXIMIZEBOX	Creates a window with a Maximize button
WS_MINIMIZE	Creates a minimized window
WS_MINIMIZEBOX	Creates a window with a Minimize button
WS_OVERLAPPED	Creates a window with a caption and a border
WS_OVERLAPPEDWINDOW	Combines the WS_OVERLAPPED, WS_CAPTION, WS_SYSMENU, WS_THICKFRAME, WS_MINIMIZEBOX, and WS_MAXIMIZEBOX styles
WS_POPUP	Creates a pop-up window
WS_POPUPWINDOW	Combines the WS_BORDER, WS_POPUP, and WS_SYSMENU styles
WS_SYSMENU	Creates a window with a control menu
WS_TABSTOP	Specifies a control that you can select with the Tab key
WS_THICKFRAME	Creates a window with a sizing frame
WS_VISIBLE	Creates a visible window
WS_VSCROLL	Creates a window with a vertical scroll bar

Table 3-5 shows that not all the styles apply to all types of windows. In fact, some of the window styles apply only to certain types of windows, including dialog boxes and controls. Moreover, while you can combine many styles as WS_OVERLAPPEDWINDOW does, not all styles get along. For example, you can't have a system menu on a window that has no title bar. The title bar is, after all, where the system menu goes.

If you were programming Windows applications in straight C — that is, without the help of a sophisticated applications framework like MFC — you'd have a lot of flexibility in the type of windows your application creates. MFC, however, predetermines the basic look of a window, leaving you with only a few acceptable style modifications.

This makes sense when you think about it. The CFrameWnd class, for example, creates a frame window. In order to exist as a frame window, the window requires certain characteristics. MFC enables you to do things such as remove the Minimize and Maximize buttons, but it won't let you remove the title bar.

Changing Window Styles

In an MFC program, you can change a window's style in the frame window class's PreCreateWindow() function, which MFC calls just before creating the window. To do this, override PreCreateWindow() in the class you derive from CFrameWnd. For example, in the BasicApp application of the previous section, you can add a PreCreateWindow() function that changes the window's style, as well as sizes and positions the window. Listing 3-2 shows just such a PreCreateWindow() function. Figure 3-7 shows the resultant window.

Listing 3-2: The PreCreateWindow() function

```
BOOL CSimpleFrame::PreCreateWindow(CREATESTRUCT& cs)
{
    // Set window's size.
    cs.cx = 500;
    cs.cy = 400;

    // Set window's position.
    cs.x = 100;
    cs.y = 50;

    // Set window's style.
    cs.style = WS_OVERLAPPED | WS_SYSMENU;

    return CFrameWnd::PreCreateWindow(cs);
}
```

Figure 3-7: The BasicApp window displayed after a style-change notice that the window's Minimize and Maximize buttons are removed

The PreCreateWindow() has a single parameter, which is a reference to a CREATESTRUCT structure. This structure contains information that Windows needs in order to create the window. Windows defines the structure, as shown in Listing 3-3:

Listing 3-3: The CREATESTRUCT structure

```
typedef struct tagCREATESTRUCT {
    LPVOID    lpCreateParams;
    HANDLE    hInstance;
    HMENU     hMenu;
    HWND      hwndParent;
    int       cy;
    int       cx;
    int       y;
    int       x;
    LONG      style;
    LPCSTR    lpszName;
    LPCSTR    lpszClass;
    DWORD     dwExStyle;
} CREATESTRUCT;
```

The window's style is in the structure's style member, but you can manipulate many of the CREATESTRUCT members in order to change the way the window looks. For example, the previous PreCreateWindow() example sets the window's size and position by changing the values in the cy, cx, x, and y members. The PreCreateWindow() example also sets the window's style to WS_OVERLAPPED | WS_SYSMENU.

Because the WS_MINIMIZEBOX and WS_MAXIMIZEBOX styles aren't included, the resultant window has no Minimize, Maximize, or Restore buttons.

Similarly, because the WS_THICKFRAME style is missing, the window has no sizing border and so the user can't resize it. Even the system menu reflects these changes, as shown in Figure 3-8. Notice how the Restore, Size, Minimize, and Maximize commands are disabled in the system menu.

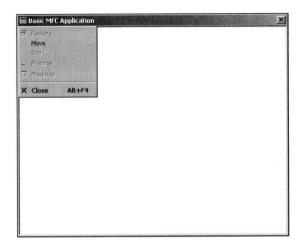

Figure 3-8: The application's system menu after its Restore, Size, Minimize, and Maximize commands are disabled

Window Styles in Non-MFC Programs

As I mentioned previously, MFC must insist on the presence of certain window styles in order to create windows associated with classes such as CFrameWnd. Setting inappropriate window styles for these types of windows may lead to unpredictable behavior. However, if you really want to mess with window styles, write a C windows program and leave MFC out of the picture completely.

Listing 3-4, for example, shows the source code for BasicApp2, a C Windows application whose window only has the style WS_POPUP.

Name: BasicApp2.c
Location: WinPrgS\Chap03\BasicApp2

Listing 3-4: Source code for the BasicApp2 application

```
#include <windows.h>

LRESULT CALLBACK WndProc(HWND hWnd, UINT message,
    WPARAM wParam, LPARAM lParam);

int WINAPI WinMain(HINSTANCE hCurrentInst,
    HINSTANCE hPrevInstance, PSTR lpszCmdLine,
    int nCmdShow)
```

```c
{
    WNDCLASS wndClass;
    HWND hWnd;
    MSG msg;
    UINT width;
    UINT height;

    wndClass.style = CS_HREDRAW | CS_VREDRAW;
    wndClass.lpfnWndProc = WndProc;
    wndClass.cbClsExtra = 0;
    wndClass.cbWndExtra = 0;
    wndClass.hInstance = hCurrentInst;
    wndClass.hIcon = LoadIcon(NULL, IDI_APPLICATION);
    wndClass.hCursor = LoadCursor(NULL, IDC_ARROW);
    wndClass.hbrBackground = GetStockObject(WHITE_BRUSH);
    wndClass.lpszMenuName = NULL;
    wndClass.lpszClassName = "BasicApp2";

    RegisterClass(&wndClass);

    width = GetSystemMetrics(SM_CXSCREEN) / 2;
    height = GetSystemMetrics(SM_CYSCREEN) / 2;

    hWnd = CreateWindow(
        "BasicApp2",         /* Window class's name.     */
        "Basic Application", /* Title bar text.          */
        WS_POPUP,            /* The window's style.      */
        100,                 /* X position.              */
        100,                 /* Y position.              */
        width,               /* Width.                   */
        height,              /* Height.                  */
        NULL,                /* Parent window's handle.  */
        NULL,                /* Menu handle.             */
        hCurrentInst,        /* Instance handle.         */
        NULL);               /* No additional data.      */

    ShowWindow(hWnd, nCmdShow);
    UpdateWindow(hWnd);

    while (GetMessage(&msg, NULL, 0, 0))
    {
        TranslateMessage(&msg);
        DispatchMessage(&msg);
    }

    return msg.wParam;
}
```

```
LRESULT CALLBACK WndProc(HWND hWnd, UINT message,
    WPARAM wParam, LPARAM lParam)
{
    HDC hDC;
    PAINTSTRUCT paintStruct;

    switch(message)
    {
        case WM_PAINT:
            hDC = BeginPaint(hWnd, &paintStruct);
            TextOut(hDC, 20, 20,
                "This is a plain pop-up window.", 29);
            EndPaint(hWnd, &paintStruct);
            return 0;

        case WM_LBUTTONDOWN:
            PostMessage(hWnd, WM_DESTROY, 0, 0);
            return 0;

        case WM_DESTROY:
            PostQuitMessage(0);
            return 0;
    }

    return DefWindowProc(hWnd, message, wParam, lParam);
}
```

Providing only the WS_POPUP style causes the window to display the white rectangle shown in Figure 3-9. Yep, that rectangle is a window. Although completely unadorned, the window still functions as a window. It can, for example, display data and even respond to Windows messages. To prove this, click inside the window. The window receives a WM_LBUTTONDOWN message, to which the program responds in its WndProc() function. The program responds by sending its own window a WM_DESTROY message, which closes down the application.

You can get some really bizarre windows if you monkey with the styles and colors. For example, Figure 3-10 shows BasicApp2 when you set its background color to the NULL_BRUSH (no color) rather than the WHITE_BRUSH. Now all that appears on the screen is the text.

When you use AppWizard to create a skeleton application, you can set window styles for the frame window from the MFC AppWizard - Step 4 of 6 dialog box. To do this, click the Advanced button, select the Window Styles tab of the Advanced Options property sheet, and click the checkboxes for the styles you want to add or remove.

Part I: Fundamental Windows 2000 Programming

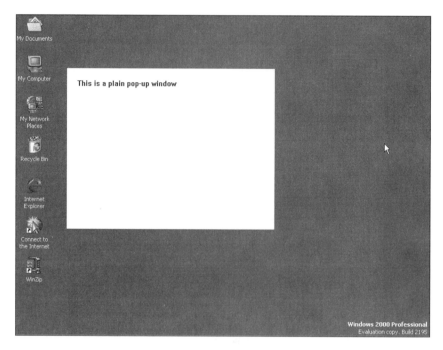

Figure 3-9: The BasicApp2 application window displayed with only the WS_POPUP style

Figure 3-10: The BasicApp2 window displayed without a background color

MDI Windows

All the preceding applications in this book, such as the BasicApp2 application just created, are *single-document interface (SDI)* applications. This type of application window can display only a single document at a time, which is sufficient for most applications. MDI, or multiple-document interface applications, can display more than one document at a time.

MDI windows are falling out of favor quickly. Microsoft's programming guidelines suggest opening another instance of an application for each document, rather than displaying several child document windows inside an MDI window.

An MDI frame window is much like a mini-desktop on which the user can arrange several document windows (called *MDI child windows*). You can reduce document windows in an MDI application to icons inside the frame window, much like you can reduce applications to icons on Windows' taskbar.

AppWizard enables you to create MDI applications with little fuss. In fact, MDI applications are the default type in the MFC AppWizard - Step 1 dialog box. Figure 3-11 shows the MFC AppWizard - Step 1 dialog box. Notice the options — Single document, Multiple documents, and Dialog based — you can select at the top of the dialog box. To create an MDI application, select the Multiple documents option.

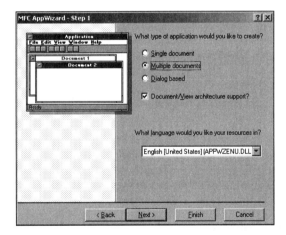

Figure 3-11: The MFC AppWizard - Step 1 dialog box, displayed with the parameters to create an MDI application

The other options in the remaining AppWizard dialog boxes are unaffected by the Multiple documents selection. If you leave those options set to their default values, you get the application shown in Figure 3-12. As you can see, when the application runs, it displays two windows: the frame window and a child window. The child window represents a document in the application.

As such, the child window's client area contains the view window for the document.

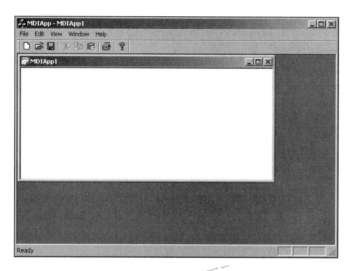

Figure 3-12: A basic MDI application displayed with its child and frame windows

An MFC MDI application derives some of its classes from different base classes than does an SDI application. Specifically, an MDI frame window is derived from the CMDIFrameWnd class, which is derived from CFrameWnd. This derivation should tell you that a CMDIFrameWnd window is just a frame window with some extra features. Those features include the capability to manage multiple documents.

The child window is represented by the CChildFrame class, which is derived from CMDIChildWnd. The child window is a frame window that appears inside an MDI frame window. Also, an MDI child frame window doesn't have a menu bar. Instead, it places menu commands in the MDI frame window's menu bar. MDI child windows can never leave the MDI frame window's client area.

Figure 3-13 shows an MDI application with several open document windows. Notice how the MDIApp1:3 child window is positioned so it doesn't fit entirely inside the MDI frame window. Rather than extend onto the window's desktop though, the portion of the child window that doesn't fit is not visible at all. This resembles what happens on the Windows 2000 desktop if you try to move an application window beyond the limits of the screen.

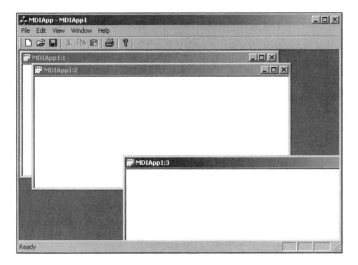

Figure 3-13: If you do not position a child window entirely within its frame window, the extended section is not visible.

AppWizard never creates a child window class for an SDI application because SDI applications rarely display child windows, with the exception of windows such as dialog boxes and message boxes. Child document windows are, in fact, the main difference between SDI and MDI applications.

MDI applications are mostly out of vogue these days. Rather than trying to juggle multiple documents within a single frame window, Microsoft suggests that it's easier and more practical to run multiple instances of an application in order to accommodate multiple-document manipulation. For this reason, I do not cover the hairy details of programming MDI applications in this book. You can find additional information on MDI applications in your Visual C++ online documentation.

Dialog Boxes

Dialog boxes are everywhere in Windows programs. Virtually every time a program communicates with its user, a dialog box is involved. They don't call them dialog boxes for nothing! Your programs can incorporate two types of dialog boxes into the application. The first type is a *custom dialog box* that you create yourself using the dialog box editor and creating a class to represent the dialog box in the program. The second type is the so-called *common dialog box,* which is part of the Windows operating system and for which MFC provides classes.

Custom Dialog Boxes

Probably more often than not, the dialog boxes you display in your application are custom dialog boxes that you design and create using Visual C++'s dialog box editor. Creating a custom dialog box requires the following steps:

1. Start a new dialog box resource by selecting the Insert menu's Resource command. When the Insert Resource dialog box appears, select Dialog in the Resource Type box (see Figure 3-14) and click New.

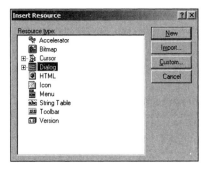

Figure 3-14: To create a new dialog box, choose Dialog as your resource type.

2. Use the dialog box editor to add the necessary controls and to set the controls' and dialog box's attributes (see Figure 3-15).

3. Double-click the dialog box and create a class for it by following the instructions in the dialog boxes that appear (see Figure 3-16).

4. From ClassWizard, add member variables to the class for the controls that you need to transfer data to and from (as shown in Figure 3-17).

5. In the source code file that uses the dialog box, include the dialog box class's header file, such as the following:

    ```
    #include "MyDialog.h"
    ```

6. To display the dialog box, first create an object of the dialog class:

    ```
    CMyDialog dialog;
    ```

7. Set the dialog box's member variables to the values that you want to appear in the dialog box's controls; for example:

    ```
    dialog.m_info = "Default text";
    ```

8. Call the dialog box class's `DoModal()` function to display the dialog box and enable the user to manipulate the controls; for example:

    ```
    int result = dialog.DoModal();
    ```

Chapter 3: Windows and Dialog Boxes

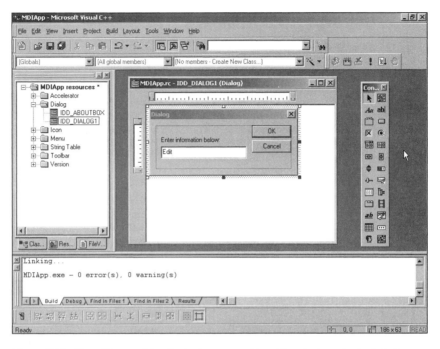

Figure 3-15: The editor provides the tools you need to add controls and set attributes.

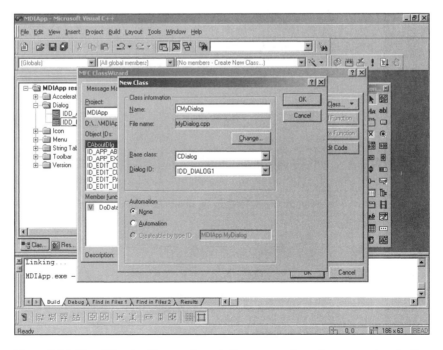

Figure 3-16: ClassWizard guides you through the process of creating a new class for the dialog box.

Part I: Fundamental Windows 2000 Programming

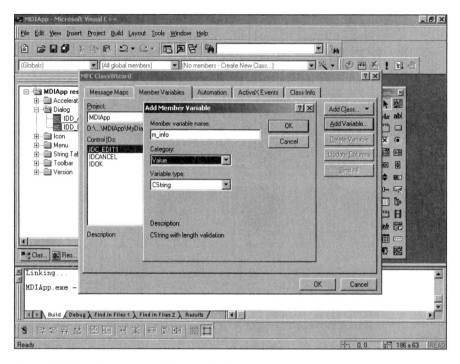

Figure 3-17: To add member variables to the dialog box class, choose a member variable name, category, and variable type.

9. If the return value from DoModal() is IDOK, extract data from the dialog box's controls; for example:

```
if (result == IDOK)
{
    m_info = dialog.m_info;
}
```

When it's all put together, a function that displays the custom dialog box and extracts information from its controls may look like the one in Listing 3-5.

Listing 3-5: A function that initializes, displays, and handles a custom dialog box

```
void CDialogAppView::OnTestDialog()
{
    // TODO: Add your command handler code here

    CMyDialog dialog;
    dialog.m_info = "Default text";

    int result = dialog.DoModal();
```

```
        if (result == IDOK)
        {
            m_info = dialog.m_info;
        }
}
```

When the user exits a dialog box by clicking the Cancel button, `DoModal()`'s return value is `IDCANCEL`.

PROBLEMS & SOLUTIONS

Dialog Box: OK and Cancel Buttons

PROBLEM: *In my application, I have to know when the user clicks my dialog box's OK or Cancel button. How can I modify my dialog class to manage these buttons directly?*

SOLUTION: MFC defines message-response functions for both the OK and Cancel buttons. All you have to do is override the functions called `OnOK()` and `OnCancel()` in your dialog box's class. Here's an `OnOK()` function that displays a message box when the user clicks the OK button:

```
void CTestDialog::OnOK()
{
    MessageBox("You clicked OK.");

    CDialog::OnOK();
}
```

Of course, normally in `OnOK()`, you don't display a message box; you do something more useful, such as validate the user's entries in the dialog box. Notice the call to the base class's version of `OnOK()`. If you don't call `CDialog::OnOK()`, the dialog box stays on the screen, which might be what you want if the user enters some invalid data. Sooner or later, though, you have to call `CDialog::OnOK()` in order to close the dialog box when the user clicks OK.

The `OnCancel()` message-response function works similarly, as shown here:

```
void CTestDialog::OnCancel()
{
    MessageBox("You clicked Cancel.");

    CDialog::OnCancel();
}
```

As with `OnOK()`, a call to the base class's version of the function is required in order to retain the button's standard behavior.

PROBLEMS & SOLUTIONS

Creating Modeless Dialog Boxes

PROBLEM: *How can I create a dialog box that enables the application's user to switch back and forth between the dialog box and the application's window?*

SOLUTION: A dialog box that doesn't force the user to exit it before going back to the application's window is called a *modeless dialog box.* Other dialog boxes that you work with — the ones that you must dismiss before you can get back to the application window — are called *modal dialog boxes.*

Modeless dialog boxes are useful when the user needs to update values continually in the dialog box while working in the application's main window. The classic example of a modeless dialog box is the Find and Replace dialog box. Creating and managing modeless dialog boxes, however, is a bit of a pain. You have to decide yourself whether it's worth the effort.

You create a modeless dialog box's resource the same way you do any other dialog box. The main difference between modal and modeless dialog boxes is the way you display them. You display a modeless dialog box by calling its `Create()` and `ShowWindow()` functions, rather than calling `DoModal()`.

The first step is to declare a pointer to the dialog box as a member variable of the class that displays the dialog box. Such a declaration might look like this:

```
CTestDialog* m_pDialog;
```

When you're ready to display the dialog box, first create the dialog box object with the new operator and then initialize the dialog box controls. Finally, call the dialog box's `Create()` function and, if the dialog box doesn't have its Visible attribute set, also call `ShowWindow()` like this:

```
m_pDialog = new CTestDialog(this);
m_pDialog->m_name = m_name;
m_pDialog->Create(IDD_DIALOG1);
m_pDialog->ShowWindow(SW_SHOW);
```

The `Create()` and `ShowWindow()` functions return immediately, rather than waiting for the user to click a button as `DoModal()` does. This means you have the dialog box on the screen, but you need some way to communicate to the main program when the user clicks a button. You do this by overriding the dialog box class's `OnOK()` and `OnCancel()` functions and sending a Windows message to the application's window when the user clicks a button.

To implement this messaging system, you define custom Windows messages in which you can do something like this:

```
const WM_OKPRESSED = WM_USER + 100;
const WM_CANCELPRESSED = WM_USER + 101;
```

Continued

Chapter 3: Windows and Dialog Boxes

You then can use the `PostMessage()` function to send these messages to the application from the dialog box object. For example, your dialog box's `OnOK()` function might look like this:

```
void CTestDialog::OnOK()
{
    UpdateData(TRUE);
    m_pViewWnd->PostMessage(WM_OKPRESSED, 0, 0);
}
```

First, `OnOK()` calls `UpdateData()`, which causes MFC to transfer the contents of the dialog box controls to the appropriate member variables. Then the function calls the parent window's `PostMessage()` function to notify the program that the user clicked the OK button. In this version of `OnOK()`, you do not call the base class's `OnOK()` function. If you do, MFC muddles everything up for you.

The dialog box's `OnCancel()` function looks similar, except it doesn't call `UpdateData()` because the user wants to abandon any changes made to the dialog box's controls:

```
void CTestDialog::OnCancel()
{
    m_pViewWnd->PostMessage(WM_CANCELPRESSED, 0, 0);
}
```

In the parent window class, you use the `ON_MESSAGE` macro to define message-map entries for the custom messages:

```
BEGIN_MESSAGE_MAP(CDialogAppView, CView)
    ON_MESSAGE(WM_OKPRESSED, DialogOnOK)
    ON_MESSAGE(WM_CANCELPRESSED, DialogOnCancel)
END_MESSAGE_MAP()
```

With this message map in place, MFC calls the window's `DialogOnOK()` function when the dialog box posts the `WM_OKPRESSED` message. The function might look like this:

```
LONG CDialogAppView::DialogOnOK(UINT wParam, LONG lParam)
{
    m_name = m_pDialog->m_name;
    m_pDialog->DestroyWindow();
    delete m_pDialog;
    m_pDialog = NULL;

    return 0;
}
```

This function transfers the contents of the dialog box's member variables to the window's member variables, destroys the dialog box window, and deletes the dialog box object.

The `DialogOnCancel()` function, which MFC calls when the dialog box posts the `WM_CANCELPRESSED` message, might look like this:

```
LONG CDialogAppView::DialogOnCancel(UINT wParam,
    LONG lParam)
{
```

Continued

```
m_pDialog->DestroyWindow();
delete m_pDialog;
m_pDialog = NULL;

return 0;
}
```

Location: `WinPrgS\Chap07\DialogApp`

If you want to experiment with a working modeless dialog box, look in the `Chap07\DialogApp` folder of this book's CD-ROM. There you can find the DialogApp application, which enables you to display and manipulate a modeless dialog box. All of the source code shown in this section is taken from that application.

Common Dialog Boxes

Some tasks are common to so many applications that it's silly for programmers to write source code to accomplish them. Such tasks include getting file names, colors, and fonts. So common are these tasks that Microsoft decided to build dialog boxes into Windows 2000 to handle them. Appropriately enough, we refer to these dialog boxes as the common dialog boxes. In this section, you learn how to program common dialog boxes into your applications. The common dialog boxes are as follows:

Color Dialog Box	Enables the user to select a color
File Dialog Box	Enables the user to select file names
Find-Replace Dialog Box	Enables the user to search and replace words in a document
Font Dialog Box	Enables the user to select a font and font attributes
Page Setup Dialog Box	Enables the user to select page options
Print Dialog Box	Enables the user to select printing options

The File Dialog Box

The vast majority of Windows applications (and most other applications, for that matter) require the user to load and save files. To help programmers with this ubiquitous task, Windows 2000 features the File dialog box, which is represented in MFC by the `CFileDialog` class. In its simplest form, the File dialog box is criminally easy to display.

First, you must include the afxdlgs.h file in your source code (as you must do for any of the common dialog boxes):

```
#include "afxdlgs.h"
```

Then create an object of the CFileDialog class:

```
CFileDialog fileDlg(TRUE);
```

A value of TRUE for the constructor's single argument specifies an Open dialog box; a value of FALSE specifies a Save As dialog box.

Then call the dialog box object's DoModal() member function, just as you do for any dialog box:

```
int result = fileDlg.DoModal();
```

The File dialog box appears, and the user locates and selects a file. If the user clicks the Open button to exit the dialog box, you can get the selected file name by calling the dialog box object's GetFileName() function like this:

```
if (result == IDOK)
{
    m_openFileName = fileDlg.GetFileName();
}
```

Figure 3-18 shows the dialog box created by the previous example. Notice how the dialog box lacks some features that a professional application offers. For example, there are no file types listed in the Files of Type box, nor does a default filter appear in the File Name box.

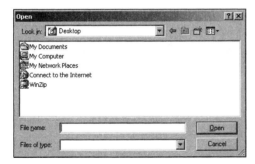

Figure 3-18: The Open dialog box is one of the common file dialog boxes.

In the previous example, the CFileDialog constructor receives only a single argument: a BOOL value that specifies whether the dialog box should be a Save As or Open box. The constructor actually has six arguments, all of which (except the first) have default values. The constructor's full signature looks like this:

```
CFileDialog(
    BOOL bOpenFileDialog,
```

```
LPCTSTR lpszDefExt = NULL,
LPCTSTR lpszFileName = NULL,
DWORD dwFlags = OFN_HIDEREADONLY |
    OFN_OVERWRITEPROMPT,
LPCTSTR lpszFilter = NULL,
CWnd* pParentWnd = NULL);
```

You use the six arguments as follows:

bOpenFileDialog	A BOOL value specifying an Open (TRUE) or Save (FALSE) dialog box
lpszDefExt	The file extension that you should add to file names that have no extension
lpszFileName	The file name that should be initially selected
dwFlags	Customization flags
lpszFilter	The file filters for the Files of Type box
pParentWnd	A pointer to the dialog box's parent window

To create a full Open dialog box, you use the lpszFileName argument to specify a file filter for the File Name box. In addition, you use the lpszFilter argument to specify file filters for the Files of Type box. These *file filters* consist of two strings separated by an OR symbol (|). For example, one complete file filter looks like this:

```
Test Files (*.tst)|*.tst
```

The string on the left appears in the Files of Type box. The string on the right specifies the actual filter. You can string together as many of the filters as you need. For example, you always want to include the All Files filter, as well as the filters associated with your application's documents, like this:

```
char filters[] =
    "Test Files (*.tst)|*.tst|All Files (*.*)|*.*|";
```

The following lines create and display the dialog box shown in Figure 3-19:

```
char filters[] =
    "Test Files (*.tst)|*.tst|All Files (*.*)|*.*|";
CFileDialog fileDlg(TRUE, NULL, "*.tst",
    NULL, filters, NULL);
int result = fileDlg.DoModal();
```

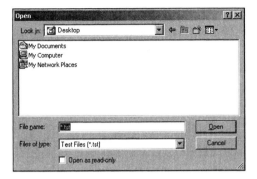

Figure 3-19: A complete Open dialog box created by the previous example lines

The Save As dialog box works much like the Open dialog box. The main difference lies in the arguments you pass to the `CFileDialog` constructor. Normally, you set the arguments as follows:

bOpenFileDialog	Set to FALSE to specify the Save dialog box
lpszDefExt	Set to the file extension associated with the application's documents
lpszFileName	Set to the currently loaded document's file name; if the document is not named yet, set to a default file name
dwFlags	Set to OFN_HIDEREADONLY | OFN_OVERWRITEPROMPT in order to hide read-only files and to prompt before overwriting existing files
lpszFilter	Set to the file filters for the Files of Type box
pParentWnd	Set to NULL

Considering these values, the lines that create and display a Save dialog box might look like those in Listing 3-6. Figure 3-20 shows the resultant dialog box.

Listing 3-6: Creating and displaying a Save dialog box

```
CString fileName;

char filters[] =
    "Test Files (*.tst)|*.tst|All Files (*.*)|*.*|";

if (m_saveFileName == "")
    fileName = "default.tst";
else
```

```
        fileName = m_saveFileName;

CFileDialog fileDlg(FALSE, "*.tst", fileName,
    OFN_HIDEREADONLY | OFN_OVERWRITEPROMPT,
    filters, NULL);

int result = fileDlg.DoModal();
```

Figure 3-20: The complete Save As dialog box created by the previous example's code lines

If the user selects a file that already exists on the disk, the Save As dialog box displays the warning in Figure 3-21. As you can see, this warning box gives users a chance to change their minds before overwriting valuable data.

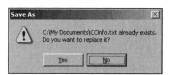

Figure 3-21: A Save As dialog box warning appears when you attempt to save with the name of an existing file.

As with the Open dialog box, you call the GetFileName() function to retrieve the file name the user selects. The CFileDialog class has many other member functions that you can call, the most useful of which Table 3-6 lists.

Table 3-6 The Most Useful CFileDialog Member Functions

Function	Description
DoModal()	Displays the dialog box
GetFileExt()	Gets the selected file's extension
GetFileName()	Gets the selected file's name

Function	Description
`GetFileTitle()`	Gets the selected file's title
`GetPathName()`	Gets the selected file's path
`GetReadOnlyPref()`	Gets the selected file's read-only attribute
`OnFileNameOK()`	Called by MFC to validate the selected file name; overridable in a derived class
`OnShareViolation()`	Called by MFC in the event of a share violation; overridable in a derived class

The Font Dialog Box

While the File dialog boxes are common to most Windows 2000 applications, the Font dialog box operates only with text-based applications. When using an application on Windows 2000, the user usually expects to be able to select fonts and font sizes, as well as character attributes such as bold and underlining. To accommodate these needs, Windows 2000 features the Font dialog box. This dialog box enables the user to select any font on the system and apply text attributes as needed.

The MFC `CFontDialog` class represents the Font dialog box. Creating a Font dialog box is even easier than creating a File dialog box because the `CFontDialog` class's constructor requires no arguments:

```
CFontDialog fontDialog;
```

After creating the dialog box object, you display it by calling the `DoModal()` member function:

```
int result = fontDialog.DoModal();
```

These two lines result in the dialog box shown in Figure 3-22. Notice how the default Font dialog box enables the user to select not only a font, but also font styles, size, attributes, and color. That's a lot of power for only two lines of source code.

If the user clicks OK to exit the Font dialog box, `DoModal()` returns `IDOK`. In this case, you can get the selected font by calling the `CFontDialog` member function `GetCurrentFont()`:

```
LOGFONT logFont;
fontDialog.GetCurrentFont(&logFont);
```

`GetCurrentFont()`'s single argument is the address of a `LOGFONT` structure, into which `GetCurrentFont()` stores the values that define the selected font.

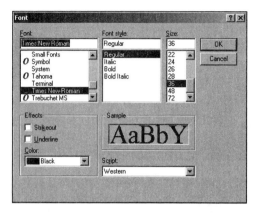

Figure 3-22: The default Font dialog box, which is created with only two lines of source code, enables users to select many font options.

After retrieving the LOGFONT structure, you create a CFont object and call that object's CreateFontIndirect() function to actually create the font:

```
CFont font;
font.CreateFontIndirect(&logFont);
```

You then can use the font by selecting it into the current device context. For more information on LOGFONT structures and the CFont class, please refer to Chapter 4. To learn more about device contexts, please refer to Chapter 2. Although the CFontDialog constructor requires no arguments, it defines four that all have default values. The constructor's full signature looks like this:

```
CFontDialog(
    LPLOGFONT lplfInitial = NULL,
    DWORD dwFlags = CF_EFFECTS | CF_SCREENFONTS,
    CDC* pdcPrinter = NULL,
    CWnd* pParentWnd = NULL);
```

You use the arguments as follows:

lplfInitial	A pointer to a LOGFONT structure
dwFlags	Font dialog box flags
pdcPrinter	A pointer to a printer device context
pParentWnd	A pointer to the dialog box's parent window

Because the default Font dialog box works fine in most cases, this chapter doesn't get into the details of modifying the dialog box's flags and attributes.

If you want more control over the Font dialog box, look up the `CFontDialog` class in your Visual C++ online documentation. Table 3-7 lists the most useful `CFontDialog` member functions.

Tip

If you want the currently active font to be selected in the Font dialog box when it appears, pass a pointer to the font's `LOGFONT` structure as the `CFontDialog` constructor's first argument, like this: `CFontDialog fontDialog(logFont)`.

Table 3-7   The Most Useful CFontDialog Member Functions

Function	Description
DoModal()	Displays the dialog box
GetColor()	Gets the selected font's color
GetCurrentFont()	Gets the selected font's name
GetFaceName()	Gets the selected font's face name
GetSize()	Gets the selected font's point size
GetStyleName()	Gets the selected font's style name
GetWeight()	Gets the selected font's weight
IsBold()	Returns TRUE if the font is bold
IsItalic()	Returns TRUE if the font is italic
IsStrikeOut()	Returns TRUE if the font is struck through
IsUnderline()	Returns TRUE if the font is underlined

The Color Dialog Box

Although not as common a task as selecting files and fonts, the ability to select colors is often important in applications. As you probably figured out, Windows 2000 features a dialog box called the Color dialog box that makes selecting colors easy. Using the Color dialog box, the user also can create custom colors.

The MFC `CColorDialog` class represents the Color dialog box. Because `CColorDialog`'s constructor requires no arguments, you can create and display a Color dialog box object easily:

```
CColorDialog colorDialog;
int result = colorDialog.DoModal();
```

These two lines result in the dialog box shown in Figure 3-23. Notice how the user can select from already defined colors or from a palette of custom colors. When the dialog box first appears, the custom color palette is empty.

The user can fill the custom palette by clicking the Define Custom Colors button and selecting the color in the color window, as shown in Figure 3-24.

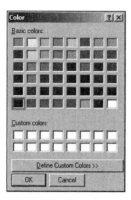

Figure 3-23: The default Color dialog box, which is created with only two lines of source code, enables users to choose from different color options.

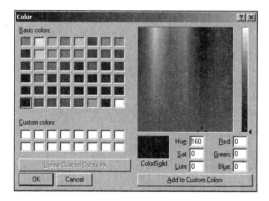

Figure 3-24: You can define custom colors with the default Color dialog box.

If the user clicks OK to exit the Color dialog box, `DoModal()` returns `IDOK`. In this case, you can get the selected color by calling the `CColorDialog` member function `GetColor()`:

```
COLORREF m_color = colorDialog.GetColor();
```

What you do with the selected color depends upon your application. You might, for example, use the color to create a custom pen or brush for the window's device context. For more information on device contexts, please refer to Chapter 2.

Although the `CColorDialog` constructor requires no arguments, it defines three that all have default values. The constructor's full signature looks like this:

```
CColorDialog(
    COLORREF clrInit = 0,
    DWORD dwFlags = 0,
    CWnd* pParentWnd = NULL);
```

You use the arguments as follows:

`clrInit`	The color that should be initially selected
`dwFlags`	Color dialog box flags
`pParentWnd`	A pointer to the dialog box's parent window

Because the default Color dialog box works fine in most cases, this chapter doesn't get into the details of modifying the dialog box's flags and attributes. If you want more control over the Color dialog box, look up the `CColorDialog` class in your Visual C++ online documentation. `CColorDialog`'s member functions include:

`DoModal()`	Displays a color dialog box
`GetColor()`	Returns a `COLORREF` representing the selected color
`GetSavedCustomColors()`	Gets the user's custom colors
`SetCurrentColor()`	Sets the current color selection
`OnColorOK()`	Called by MFC when the user selects the OK button; overridable in a derived class

The Common Dialog Application

Location: `WinPrgS\Chap03\CommonDlgApp`

In the `CommonDlgApp` folder of this book's CD-ROM, you can find the Common Dialog application, which demonstrates programming common dialog boxes in the context of a full application. When you run the application, you see the application's main window. The Dialogs menu contains four commands — Open File Dialog, Save File Dialog, Font Dialog, and Color Dialog — that enable you to display and manipulate Open, Save, Font, and Color dialog boxes respectively. The choices you make in the dialog boxes are reflected in the window's display (as shown in Figure 3-25).

Figure 3-25: The Common Dialog application's window reflects the choices you make in your dialog boxes.

If you read this chapter carefully, the source code for the Common Dialog application should be easy to understand. The application is created using AppWizard and ClassWizard, so it is made up of source code files for application, main window, document, and view classes. However, all of the program's dialog boxes are managed in the view class. In this section, you quickly examine each of the view class's member functions that are relevant to common dialog boxes.

When you select the Open File Dialog command from the Dialogs menu, MFC calls the `OnDialogsOpenfiledialog()` message-response function. Listing 3-7 shows the function. A brief description of the function follows the source code.

Listing 3-7: Handling the Open File dialog box

```
void CCommonDlgAppView::OnDialogsOpenfiledialog()
{
    // TODO: Add your command handler code here

    char filters[] =
        "Test Files (*.tst)|*.tst|All Files (*.*)|*.*|";
    CFileDialog fileDlg(TRUE, NULL, "*.tst",
        NULL, filters, NULL);

    int result = fileDlg.DoModal();

    if (result == IDOK)
    {
        m_openFileName = fileDlg.GetFileName();
```

```
        Invalidate();
    }
}
```

This function performs the following tasks:

- Creates an array of file filters
- Creates a `CFileDialog` object that represents an Open File dialog box
- Displays the dialog box to the user
- Extracts the selected file name
- Calls `Invalidate()` in order to force the window to repaint

When you select the Save File Dialog command from the Dialogs menu, MFC calls the `OnDialogsSavefiledialog()` message-response function. Listing 3-8 shows the function. A brief description of the function follows the source code.

Listing 3-8: Handling the Save File dialog box

```
void CCommonDlgAppView::OnDialogsSavefiledialog()
{
    // TODO: Add your command handler code here

    CString fileName;

    char filters[] =
        "Test Files (*.tst)|*.tst|All Files (*.*)|*.*|";

    if (m_saveFileName == "NO FILE NAME SELECTED")
        fileName = "default.tst";
    else
        fileName = m_saveFileName;

    CFileDialog fileDlg(FALSE, "*.tst", fileName,
        OFN_HIDEREADONLY | OFN_OVERWRITEPROMPT,
        filters, NULL);

    int result = fileDlg.DoModal();

    if (result == IDOK)
    {
        m_saveFileName = fileDlg.GetFileName();
        Invalidate();
    }
}
```

This function performs the following tasks:

- Creates a string object (`fileName`) for storing the current file name
- Creates an array of file filter strings

- Determines whether to use the default or a selected file name
- Creates a `CFileDialog` object that represents a Save File dialog box
- Displays the dialog box to the user
- Deletes the old font and creates the selected font
- Calls `Invalidate()` in order to force the window to repaint

When you select the Font Dialog command from the Dialogs menu, MFC calls the `OnDialogsFontdialog()` message-response function. Listing 3-9 shows the function, and, as you probably can guess, a brief description of the function follows the source code.

Listing 3-9: Handling the Font dialog box

```
void CCommonDlgAppView::OnDialogsFontdialog()
{
    // TODO: Add your command handler code here

    CFontDialog fontDialog(&m_logFont);

    int result = fontDialog.DoModal();

    if (result == IDOK)
    {
        delete m_pFont;
        m_pFont = new CFont;
        m_pFont->CreateFontIndirect(&m_logFont);
        Invalidate();
    }
}
```

This function performs the following tasks:

- Creates a `CFontDialog` object that represents a Font dialog box
- Displays the dialog box to the user
- Extracts the selected file name
- Calls `Invalidate()` in order to force the window to repaint

Selecting the Color Dialog command from the Dialogs menu causes MFC to call the `OnDialogsColordialog()` message-response function. Listing 3-10 shows this function's source code, after which is a brief description of the function.

Listing 3-10: Handling the Color dialog box

```
void CCommonDlgAppView::OnDialogsColordialog()
{
    // TODO: Add your command handler code here

    CColorDialog colorDialog(m_color);
```

```
        int result = colorDialog.DoModal();

        if (result == IDOK)
        {
            m_color = colorDialog.GetColor();
            Invalidate();
        }
    }
```

This function performs the following tasks:

- Creates a `CColorDialog` object that represents a Color dialog box
- Displays the dialog box to the user
- Extracts the selected color
- Calls `Invalidate()` in order to force the window to repaint

Each of the functions that display a common dialog box calls the `Invalidate()` function, which causes the program to repaint its window with the new values the user selects. The view class's `OnDraw()` function handles the repainting tasks, as shown in Listing 3-11. Once again, a brief description of the function follows the source code.

Listing 3-11: Rendering the new display

```
void CCommonDlgAppView::OnDraw(CDC* pDC)
{
    CCommonDlgAppDoc* pDoc = GetDocument();
    ASSERT_VALID(pDoc);

    // TODO: add draw code for native data here

    pDC->TextOut(20, 20, m_openFileName);
    pDC->TextOut(20, 40, m_saveFileName);

    CString fontName = m_logFont.lfFaceName;
    CFont* oldFont = (CFont*)pDC->SelectObject(m_pFont);
    pDC->TextOut(20, 60, fontName);
    pDC->SelectObject(oldFont);

    CBrush brush(m_color);
    CBrush* oldBrush =
        (CBrush*)pDC->SelectObject(&brush);
    pDC->Rectangle(20, 150, 120, 250);
    pDC->SelectObject(oldBrush);
}
```

This function performs the following tasks:

- Displays the selected file names
- Selects the selected font into the device context
- Displays a string in the selected font

- Restores the original font to the device context
- Creates a `CBrush` object from the selected color
- Selects the new brush into the device context
- Draws a rectangle in the selected color
- Restores the original brush to the device context

Property Sheets

A property sheet is a special type of dialog box suitable for organizing many options. A *property sheet* organizes options into a series of tabbed pages, each page (called a *property page*) of which holds a set of related settings. Figure 3-26, for example, shows the property sheet Windows 2000 uses to enable the user to set the system's display properties. Each tab at the top of a property sheet is associated with a different page of properties. If you click the Appearance tab, you see the property page shown in Figure 3-27.

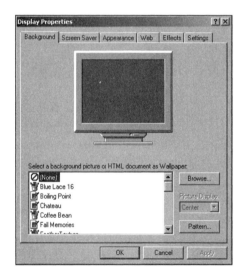

Figure 3-26: This Windows 2000 property sheet enables users to set their systems' background display.

You can create your own property sheets fairly easily using Visual C++'s dialog box editor. Each property page in the property sheet actually is a dialog box resource associated with MFC's `CPropertyPage` class. The property sheet itself, which contains the property pages, is an object of the `CPropertySheet` class.

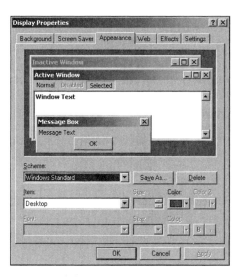

Figure 3-27: The Appearance property page enables you to change the way windows look. The message box is the part of the graphic that shows what the current window settings look like.

Creating Property Pages and Sheets

The following steps illustrate how to create a property page resource and how to derive your own classes from CPropertyPage and CPropertySheet. These steps assume that you've created a skeleton application with AppWizard.

1. Select the Resource command from Visual C++'s Insert menu and double-click Dialog in the Insert Resource dialog box, as shown in Figure 3-28.

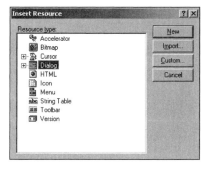

Figure 3-28: Selecting Dialog in the Insert Resource dialog box starts your creation of a property page resource.

2. When the new dialog box appears, press Enter to display its Dialog Properties property sheet. In the General page, change the ID and the Caption properties to appropriate values. For example, you can set the ID to `IDD_TEXTOPTIONS` and set the caption to Text Options, as shown in Figure 3-29. The caption appears in the property page's tab.

Figure 3-29: Set the dialog box's properties in the General tab.

3. In the Dialog Properties property sheet, click the Styles tab in order to switch to the Styles page. Set the Style box to Child, set the Border box to Thin, and turn off the System menu option, as shown in Figure 3-30. A property page requires these window styles.

Figure 3-30: Set the dialog box's styles in the Styles tab.

4. Remove the OK and Cancel buttons from the dialog box and add the controls you need for the property page. Figure 3-31 shows an example of an assembled property page in Visual C++'s dialog box editor.

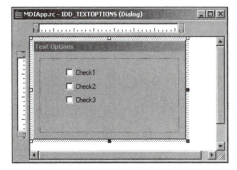

Figure 3-31: A complete property page is much like a dialog box.

5. With the property page selected, press Ctrl+W to display ClassWizard. The Adding a Class dialog box appears. Click OK to create a new class. The New Class dialog box appears.

6. Type the name of your property page class into the Name box and select `CPropertyPage` in the Base class box, as shown in Figure 3-32. Click OK to create the class.

Figure 3-32: Defining a class for the property page occurs in the New Class dialog box.

7. In the ClassWizard's Add Member Variable page, create member variables for the controls with which your application must communicate (see Figure 3-33).

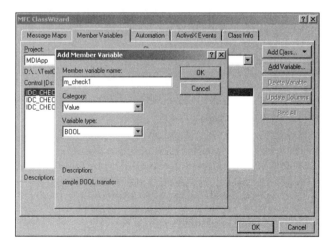

Figure 3-33: ClassWizard enables you to define member variables for the property page.

8. Repeat Steps 1 through 7 for each property page you want to display in your property sheet.

9. Click ClassWizard's Add Class button and select New from the pop-up menu. The New Class dialog box appears.

10. Type a name for your property sheet class into the Name box and select `CPropertySheet` in the Base class box. Click OK to create the class and then dismiss ClassWizard by clicking its OK button.

Programming the Property Sheet

Now that you have your property page resources defined and your property page and property sheet classes derived from `CPropertyPage` and `CPropertySheet`, you're ready to write the source code that displays and manipulates the property sheet.

The first step is to include the property page header files in the property sheet class:

```
#include "TextOptionsPage.h"
#include "ColorOptionsPage.h"
```

Now that your property sheet class has access to your property page classes, you can create the property page objects as member variables of the property sheet class:

```
CColorOptionsPage m_colorPage;
CTextOptionsPage m_textPage;
```

I mentioned before that the property sheet class contains property pages. In order to enable you to add property pages, `CPropertySheet` offers the `AddPage()` member function. You should add your property pages to the property sheet in the property sheet's constructor:

```
CMyPropertySheet::CMyPropertySheet(
    LPCTSTR pszCaption, CWnd* pParentWnd,
    UINT iSelectPage):CPropertySheet(pszCaption,
    pParentWnd, iSelectPage)
{
    AddPage(&m_textPage);
    AddPage(&m_colorPage);
}
```

That's the minimum you need to do to finish up the property sheet class. Next, you must include the property sheet class in the source file that displays the property sheet. Often, in an AppWizard-generated application, this is the view class. So, you can place a line such as the following near the top of the view class's implementation file:

```
#include "MyPropertySheet.h"
```

Chapter 3: Windows and Dialog Boxes

Finally, displaying the property sheet is no different from displaying a dialog box. Just define a property sheet object and call its `DoModal()` member function:

```
CMyPropertySheet propertySheet("My Property Sheet");
int result = propertySheet.DoModal();
```

When creating the property sheet, the constructor requires one argument: the title that appears in the property sheet's title bar.

Transferring values between your program and the property sheet works just as it does for dialog boxes. That is, to place data in a property sheet's controls before displaying the sheet, you initialize the property page classes' member variables. Conversely, you extract information from the property pages by copying the values of the property page's member variables into variables you define in the main program. Listing 3-12 shows a message-response function that initializes and displays a property sheet. If the user clicks OK to exit the property sheet, the program extracts the data entered by the user into the property pages.

Listing 3-12: Managing a property sheet

```
void CPropSheetView::OnTestPropertysheet()
{
    // TODO: Add your command handler code here

    CMyPropertySheet propertySheet("My Property Sheet");

    propertySheet.m_textPage.m_check1 = m_check1;
    propertySheet.m_textPage.m_check2 = m_check2;
    propertySheet.m_textPage.m_check3 = m_check3;

    propertySheet.m_colorPage.m_backgrnd = m_backgrnd;
    propertySheet.m_colorPage.m_red = m_red;
    propertySheet.m_colorPage.m_green = m_green;
    propertySheet.m_colorPage.m_blue = m_blue;

    int result = propertySheet.DoModal();

    if (result == IDOK)
    {
        m_check1 = propertySheet.m_textPage.m_check1;
        m_check2 = propertySheet.m_textPage.m_check2;
        m_check3 = propertySheet.m_textPage.m_check3;

        m_backgrnd =
            propertySheet.m_colorPage.m_backgrnd;
        m_red = propertySheet.m_colorPage.m_red;
        m_green = propertySheet.m_colorPage.m_green;
        m_blue = propertySheet.m_colorPage.m_blue;

        Invalidate();
    }
}
```

The PropSheet Application

Location: `WinPrgS\Chap03\PropSheet`

The function in Listing 3-12 is taken from a program called PropSheet that you can find on this book's CD-ROM. This simple application gives you a chance to experiment with property sheets in the context of a running program. When you run the program, you see the window shown in Figure 3-34. Select the Test menu's Property Sheet command to display the property sheet.

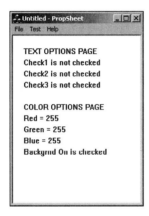

Figure 3-34: The PropSheet application window displayed

Figure 3-35 shows the property sheet's first page; Figure 3-36 shows the second page. Change the values of the controls any way you like. When you click OK to exit the property sheet, the application's window displays your choices.

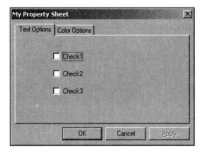

Figure 3-35: The property sheet's Text Options page displayed

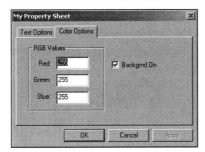

Figure 3-36: The property sheet's Color Options page displayed

Wizards

Wizards are special dialog boxes that guide a user step by step through complex tasks. You already have a lot of experience with at least one wizard—Visual C++'s AppWizard. A wizard is a close cousin of the property sheet. The main differences are that a wizard uses buttons rather than tabs to move from page to page and the user must view the pages consecutively rather than jump to any page as with a property sheet.

Creating a Wizard

So similar are wizards to property sheets that you construct your wizard pages exactly as you do property pages. You even associate the dialog box resource for a page with the CPropertyPage class. The wizard itself is an object of the CPropertySheet class. What turns the property sheet into a wizard is a call to the property sheet object's SetWizardMode() member function. You can call SetWizardMode() right after you construct the object. So, you create and display a wizard with code something like this:

```
CMyWizard wizard("My Wizard");
wizard.SetWizardMode();
int result = wizard.DoModal();
```

Setting a Wizard's Buttons

One thing you have to do differently with a wizard's pages is to override the CPropertyPage class's OnSetActive() member function. MFC calls OnSetActive() for a property (and wizard) page when the page is displayed. This gives the wizard a chance to perform any needed initialization.

One bit of initialization that the wizard must perform is the enabling of buttons. A wizard has three important buttons: Back, Next, and Finish. The Back button brings the user back to the previous wizard page. The Next button brings the user to the next wizard page. And the Finish button closes the wizard.

Obviously, if the user is viewing the first wizard page, only the Next button should be enabled. Similarly, on the wizard's last page, only the Back and Finish buttons usually are enabled. You can have a Finish button on every page if you like, assuming that you provide default settings for any wizard options the user doesn't set explicitly.

To enable the correct wizard buttons, each wizard page calls the wizard's SetWizardButtons() function, which is a member function of the CPropertySheet class (as shown in Listing 3-13).

Listing 3-13: Setting the wizard buttons

```
BOOL CWizardPage1::OnSetActive()
{
    // TODO: Add your specialized code here
    //  and/or call the base class

    CPropertySheet* pParentSheet =
        (CPropertySheet*)GetParent();
    pParentSheet->SetWizardButtons(PSWIZB_NEXT);

    return CPropertyPage::OnSetActive();
}
```

Notice how the function first gets a pointer to the CPropertySheet object that is the wizard page's parent. Then the program calls SetWizard Buttons() through the pointer. Notice also SetWizardButtons()'s single argument. There are several constants you can use for this argument:

PSWIZB_NEXT	Enables the Next button
PSWIZB_BACK	Enables the Back button
PSWIZB_FINISH	Enables the Finish button
PSWIZB_DISABLEDFINISH	Disables the Finish button

You OR together the button constants in order to select which buttons to enable. For example, Listing 3-14 shows the OnSetActive() function for a second wizard page, which ORs together the PSWIZB_BACK and PSWIZB_NEXT constants.

Listing 3-14: Setting the wizard buttons for a second wizard page

```
BOOL CWizardPage2::OnSetActive()
{
    // TODO: Add your specialized code here
    //  and/or call the base class
```

Chapter 3: Windows and Dialog Boxes

```
    CPropertySheet* pParentSheet =
        (CPropertySheet*)GetParent();
    pParentSheet->
        SetWizardButtons(PSWIZB_BACK | PSWIZB_NEXT);

    return CPropertyPage::OnSetActive();
}
```

The last wizard page, which usually needs the Back and Finish buttons, can set its buttons like this:

```
CPropertySheet* pParentSheet =
    (CPropertySheet*)GetParent();
pParentSheet->
    SetWizardButtons(PSWIZB_BACK | PSWIZB_FINISH);
```

PROBLEMS & SOLUTIONS

Responding to Wizard Buttons

PROBLEM: *I need to know when the user clicks a wizard button so that I can ensure none of the options on a wizard page are left blank. How can I do this?*

SOLUTION: Often, you need to know when the user clicks the Back, Next, or Finish buttons. For example, you may want to validate the information the user enters into the current wizard page. The `CPropertyPage` class provides several button-response functions that you can override in your own class:

`OnWizardBack()`	Called when the user clicks the Back button
`OnWizardNext()`	Called when the user clicks the Next button
`OnWizardFinish()`	Called when the user clicks the Finish button

Listing 3-15 shows overridden `OnWizardBack()` and `OnWizardFinish()` functions. Neither function does anything fancy — they just display a message box — but they demonstrate how these helpful button-response functions work.

Listing 3-15: Responding to wizard buttons

```
LRESULT CWizardPage3::OnWizardBack()
{
    // TODO: Add your specialized code here
```

Continued

```
    //     and/or call the base class

    MessageBox("You just clicked Back.",
        "Wizard Message");

    return CPropertyPage::OnWizardBack();
}

BOOL CWizardPage3::OnWizardFinish()
{
    // TODO: Add your specialized code here
    //     and/or call the base class

    MessageBox("Thanks for using MyWizard.",
        "Wizard Message");

    return CPropertyPage::OnWizardFinish();
}
```

The WizardApp Application

Location: WinPrgS\Chap03\WizardApp

This book's CD-ROM provides the WizardApp application, which demonstrates displaying and handling a wizard. When you run the program, select the Test menu's Wizard command. When you do, the application's sample wizard appears (see Figure 3-37). Experiment with the wizard's buttons to get a feel for how the wizard works.

Figure 3-37: The WizardApp application's wizard, displaying its first of three steps

Summary

Windows 2000 features more kinds of windows than you can shake an icon at. These windows include not only application windows, but also dialog boxes, property sheets, and wizards. Even controls such as buttons and text boxes are windows at heart.

Also discussed in this chapter:

- MFC window classes are part of a complex hierarchy of classes.
- A frame window acts as an application's main window.
- View windows display the data that makes up a document.
- Windows defines a set of styles that determines how a window looks and acts.
- MDI windows enable the user to open and edit more than one document at a time.
- Most dialog boxes are custom dialog boxes that you design using Visual C++'s dialog box editor.
- Windows 2000 features common dialog boxes for selecting files, fonts, and colors.
- Property sheets are dialog boxes with tabbed pages.
- Wizards are similar to property sheets, except that they have buttons instead of tabs.

Chapter 4
Text

In This Chapter
- Displaying text
- Setting text color
- Setting character spacing
- Setting text alignment
- Getting text metrics
- Creating fonts

Windows can display many kinds of data. But even in a graphical OS such as Windows, text remains the main way a program communicates with the user. Unfortunately, because text is displayed as an image in a window, creating text displays under Windows is a bit more complicated than it is under a character-oriented OS such as DOS. At the very least, you must deal with a device context (DC). You also may have to handle fonts, which are complex critters under Windows.

Displaying Text

In previous programs in this book, you got an introduction to displaying text. Chapter 2, for example, discusses how you must have a device context in order to display text on the screen. You then call the `TextOut()` function to display a line of text:

```
CClientDC clientDC(this);
clientDC.TextOut(20, 20, "This is a line of text.");
```

- The MFC `TextOut()` function's three arguments, in order, are:
    - The X coordinate at which to print the text
    - The Y coordinate at which to print the text
    - The text to print

`TextOut()` is an MFC version of a Windows API function of the same name. The Windows version's signature looks like this:

```
BOOL TextOut(
    HDC hdc,
    int X,
    int Y,
    LPCTSTR string,
    int numChars);
```

The function's arguments, in order, are as follows:

hdc	A handle to the device context
X	The horizontal position at which to display the text
Y	The vertical position at which to display the text
string	The text to display
numChars	The number of characters in the string to display

Setting Text Color

Normally, Windows draws black text; you can change the text color by calling the `SetTextColor()` function. In an MFC program, this is a member function of the `CDC` class, and so it is inherited by the other DC classes. A call to `SetTextColor()` might look like this:

```
CClientDC clientDC(this);
clientDC.SetTextColor(RGB(255,0,0));
```

`SetTextColor()`'s single argument is a `COLORREF` value that specifies the text color. In this example, `SetTextColor()` sets the text color to red.

You can retrieve the current text color by calling the `GetTextColor()` function:

```
COLORREF color = clientDC.GetTextColor();
```

You also can set the background color, which is the color that appears behind the text, by calling `SetBkColor()`:

```
clientDC.SetBkColor(color);
```

This function's single argument is a `COLORREF` value specifying the new background color.

You can obtain the current background color by calling the `GetBkColor()` function:

```
COLORREF backColor = clientDC.GetBkColor();
```

Windows displays all text with a background color (the default is white) unless you change the background color mode. By changing the mode, you can tell Windows to ignore the background color and display only the text itself. To do this, you call the SetBkMode() function:

clientDC.SetBkMode(TRANSPARENT);

SetBkMode()'s single argument is one of two values: TRANSPARENT or OPAQUE. If you set the background mode to TRANSPARENT, Windows ignores the background color.

You can obtain the current background mode by calling GetBkMode():

int backMode = clientDC.GetBkMode();

When your program gets a DC, the DC's text attributes remain set to their default values. This means the functions that obtain text attributes, such as GetTextColor() and GetBkMode(), are useful only if you already changed the DC's default attributes.

Location: **WinPrgS\Chap04\ColorTextApp**

On this book's CD-ROM, you can find the ColorTextApp application that demonstrates setting text color, background color, and background mode. When you run the application, you see a color version of the window shown in Figure 4-1. Notice how the program displays the text in color with a black background.

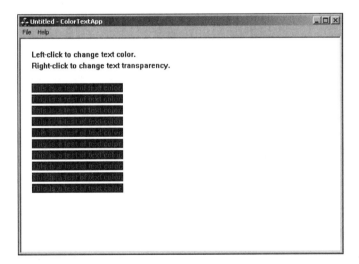

Figure 4-1: ColorTextApp displays text in color.

To change the text color, click in the window. You also can change the text background mode by right-clicking the window. When you do, the background mode toggles between OPAQUE (which is the Windows default) and TRANSPARENT. Figure 4-2 shows the application with a transparent background.

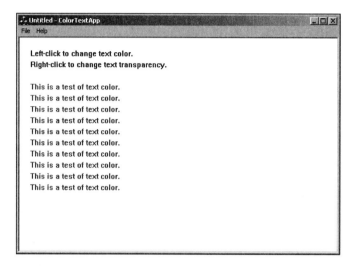

Figure 4-2: ColorTextApp can display transparent, as well as opaque, text backgrounds.

ColorTextApp's view class declares two data members for keeping track of the currently selected text color and background mode:

```
BOOL m_transparent;
COLORREF m_textColor;
```

The class's constructor sets these data members to their default values when the program starts:

```
CColorTextAppView::CColorTextAppView()
{
    // TODO: add construction code here

    m_textColor = RGB(255,0,0);
    m_transparent = FALSE;
}
```

The view class's OnDraw() function uses these values when it draws the application's display, as shown here:

```
void CColorTextAppView::OnDraw(CDC* pDC)
{
    CColorTextAppDoc* pDoc = GetDocument();
    ASSERT_VALID(pDoc);
```

```
    // TODO: add draw code for native data here

    pDC->TextOut(20, 20,
        "Left-click to change text color.");
    pDC->TextOut(20, 40,
        "Right-click to change text transparency.");

    pDC->SetTextColor(m_textColor);
    pDC->SetBkColor(RGB(0,0,0));
    if (m_transparent)
        pDC->SetBkMode(TRANSPARENT);
    else
        pDC->SetBkMode(OPAQUE);

    for (int x=0; x<10; ++x)
        pDC->TextOut(20, 80+x*20,
            "This is a test of text color.");
}
```

The `OnDraw()` function performs the following tasks:

- Displays instructions for using the program. This text output uses the DC's default settings.
- Sets the text and background colors as selected by the user.
- Sets the currently selected background mode.
- Displays ten lines of text using the new attributes.

When the user clicks the application's window, MFC calls the `OnLButtonDown()` function to change the currently selected text color. Following is the source code for `OnLButtonDown()`:

```
void CColorTextAppView::OnLButtonDown(UINT nFlags,
    CPoint point)
{
    // TODO: Add your message handler code here
    //    and/or call default

    COLORREF red = RGB(255,0,0);
    COLORREF green = RGB(0,255,0);
    COLORREF blue = RGB(0,0,255);

    if (m_textColor == red)
        m_textColor = green;
    else if (m_textColor == green)
        m_textColor = blue;
    else
        m_textColor = red;
```

```
        Invalidate();

        CView::OnLButtonDown(nFlags, point);
}
```

Finally, when the user right-clicks the window, MFC calls the view class's OnRButtonDown() function to toggle the background mode. Here is the OnRButtonDown() function:

```
void CColorTextAppView::OnRButtonDown(UINT nFlags,
    CPoint point)
{
    // TODO: Add your message handler code here
    //       and/or call default

    m_transparent = !m_transparent;
    Invalidate();

    CView::OnRButtonDown(nFlags, point);
}
```

Setting Character Spacing

Another attribute you can set is the spacing between the characters of text. You do this by calling SetTextCharacterExtra():

```
clientDC.SetTextCharacterExtra(space);
```

Here, space is the number of pixels of extra space you want between text characters. You can obtain the current character spacing by calling the GetTextCharacterExtra() function:

```
int space = clientDC.GetTextCharacterExtra();
```

Location: **WinPrgS\Chap04\CharSpaceApp**

On this book's CD-ROM, you can find the CharSpaceApp application that demonstrates character spacing. When you run the application, you see the window shown in Figure 4-3. Notice how each line of text has more space between the characters than the previous line. The first line is displayed with a spacing of 0, which is the Windows default.

There's not much to examine in CharSpaceApp. All the action happens in the OnDraw() method, as shown here:

```
void CCharSpaceAppView::OnDraw(CDC* pDC)
{
    CCharSpaceAppDoc* pDoc = GetDocument();
    ASSERT_VALID(pDoc);
```

```
    // TODO: add draw code for native data here

    for (int x=0; x<15; ++x)
    {
        pDC->SetTextCharacterExtra(x);
        pDC->TextOut(20, 20+x*20,
            "A test of character spacing.");
    }
}
```

Here, the OnDraw() function sets up a for loop that displays 15 lines of text. Each time through the loop, the program sets the character spacing to the value of the loop variable x, which adds a pixel of space between characters for each text line. That is, the first line starts with a spacing of 0, which increases by 1 until the program displays the last line of text with a spacing of 14.

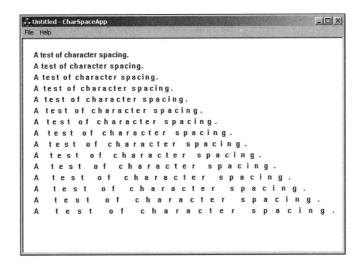

Figure 4-3: CharSpaceApp displays text with different character spacing.

Setting Text Alignment

Sometimes, you may need to align your application's text output in different ways. For example, you may want a paragraph of text centered in the window rather than displayed flush left. Other times, you may want text to be flush right. The CDC class provides functions for setting not only horizontal alignment, but also vertical alignment, which causes text to be displayed higher or lower than usual. In the following sections, you learn to manage text alignment in your programs.

Horizontal Text Alignment

Horizontal text alignment enables you to specify the horizontal position of text in a window. The type of horizontal alignment you choose determines how Windows interprets the coordinates you supply when displaying text. For example, when displaying a table of values, you may find it handy to display text left- or center-aligned. Windows can handle this type of horizontal alignment for you. All you need to do is call SetTextAlign():

```
clientDC.SetTextAlign(alignment);
```

Here, alignment is one of three values: TA_LEFT, TA_CENTER, or TA_RIGHT. The TA_LEFT constant represents Windows' default left text alignment. With this setting, Windows starts the left end of the text at the coordinate given as TextOut()'s first argument. With the TA_CENTER setting, Windows interprets the first TextOut() argument to be the point around which the string should be centered. Finally, with the TA_RIGHT setting, Windows interprets TextOut()'s first argument as the coordinate for the right end of the text string.

CD

Location: **WinPrgS\Chap04\HorizontalAlignApp**

On this book's CD-ROM, you can find the HorizontalAlignApp application that demonstrates horizontal text alignment. When you run the application, you see the window shown in Figure 4-4 that displays the text with left alignment.

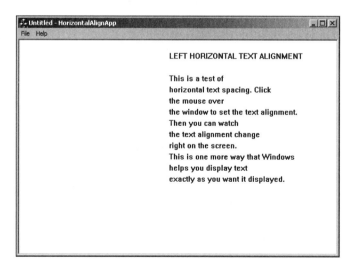

Figure 4-4: HorizontalAlignApp displaying left-aligned text

Click the window, and the text alignment switches to center alignment, as shown in Figure 4-5.

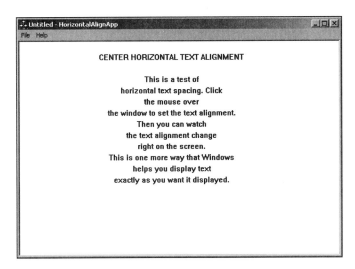

Figure 4-5: HorizontalAlignApp displaying center-aligned text

Finally, click again and you get right-aligned text, as shown in Figure 4-6. Continue clicking to cycle through the alignments as many times as you like.

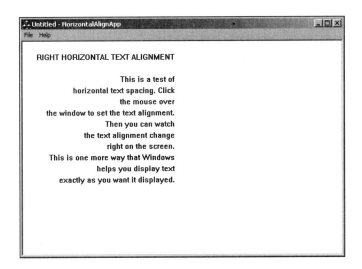

Figure 4-6: HorizontalAlignApp displaying right-aligned text

HorizontalAlignApp creates its display in the view class's `OnDraw()` function, which is shown here:

```
void CHorizontalAlignAppView::OnDraw(CDC* pDC)
{
    CHorizontalAlignAppDoc* pDoc = GetDocument();
    ASSERT_VALID(pDoc);

    // TODO: add draw code for native data here

    pDC->SetTextAlign(m_currentHAlign);

    CString string;
    if (m_currentHAlign == TA_LEFT)
        string = "LEFT HORIZONTAL TEXT ALIGNMENT";
    else if (m_currentHAlign == TA_CENTER)
        string = "CENTER HORIZONTAL TEXT ALIGNMENT";
    else
        string = "RIGHT HORIZONTAL TEXT ALIGNMENT";

    pDC->TextOut(280, 20, string);
    pDC->TextOut(280, 60, "This is a test of");
    pDC->TextOut(280, 80,
        "horizontal text spacing. Click");
    pDC->TextOut(280, 100, "the mouse over");
    pDC->TextOut(280, 120,
        "the window to set the text alignment.");
    pDC->TextOut(280, 140, "Then you can watch");
    pDC->TextOut(280, 160, "the text alignment change");
    pDC->TextOut(280, 180, "right on the screen.");
    pDC->TextOut(280, 200,
        "This is one more way that Windows");
    pDC->TextOut(280, 220, "helps you display text");
    pDC->TextOut(280, 240,
        "exactly as you want it displayed.");
}
```

Before drawing the text lines, `OnDraw()` calls `SetTextAlign()` to set the currently selected text alignment. Windows then automatically aligns the text as it's displayed.

When the user clicks the application's window, the text alignment changes. The view class's `OnLButtonDown()` function handles this task, as shown here:

```
void CHorizontalAlignAppView::OnLButtonDown(UINT nFlags,
    CPoint point)
{
    // TODO: Add your message handler code here
    //    and/or call default

    if (m_currentHAlign == TA_LEFT)
        m_currentHAlign = TA_CENTER;
```

```
    else if (m_currentHAlign == TA_CENTER)
        m_currentHAlign = TA_RIGHT;
    else
        m_currentHAlign = TA_LEFT;

    Invalidate();

    CView::OnLButtonDown(nFlags, point);
}
```

Vertical Text Alignment

You also can set the text's vertical alignment, which controls how Windows interprets TextOut()'s second parameter—the vertical coordinate at which to place text. To set vertical alignment, you call SetTextAlign() with one of three values: TA_TOP, TA_BOTTOM, or TA_BASELINE. With TA_TOP, the default vertical alignment, Windows positions text with the top of the characters located at TextOut()'s second argument. TA_BOTTOM is just the opposite, with the text positioned above TextOut()'s vertical coordinate. Finally, TA_BASELINE specifies that a character's *baseline* (the bottom of a character, not including extenders) sits at TextOut()'s vertical coordinate.

Location: **WinPrgS\Chap04\VerticalAlignApp**

On this book's CD-ROM, you can find the VerticalAlignApp application that demonstrates vertical text alignment. When you run the application, you see the window shown in Figure 4-7, which displays the text with the default TA_TOP alignment.

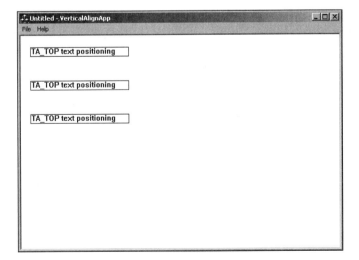

Figure 4-7: VerticalAlignApp displaying top-aligned text

Click the window, and the text alignment in the second two lines of text switches to TA_BOTTOM and TA_BASELINE alignment, as shown in Figure 4-8. The rectangles drawn around the text lines show the position for the default TA_TOP alignment.

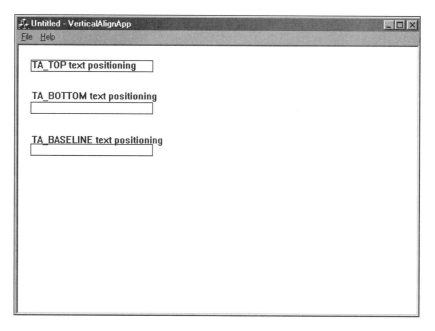

Figure 4-8: VerticalAlignApp displaying top-, bottom-, and baseline-aligned text

VerticalAlignApp, like HorizontalAlignApp, creates its display in the view class's OnDraw() function, as shown here:

```
void CVerticalAlignAppView::OnDraw(CDC* pDC)
{
    CVerticalAlignAppDoc* pDoc = GetDocument();
    ASSERT_VALID(pDoc);

    // TODO: add draw code for native data here

    CBrush* oldBrush =
        (CBrush*)pDC->SelectStockObject(NULL_BRUSH);

    if (m_showAllAlignments)
    {
        pDC->SetTextAlign(TA_TOP);
        pDC->TextOut(20, 20, "TA_TOP text positioning");
        pDC->Rectangle(18, 21, 200, 38);
```

```
            pDC->SetTextAlign(TA_BOTTOM);
            pDC->TextOut(20, 80,
                "TA_BOTTOM text positioning");
            pDC->Rectangle(18, 81, 200, 98);

            pDC->SetTextAlign(TA_BASELINE);
            pDC->TextOut(20, 140,
                "TA_BASELINE text positioning");
            pDC->Rectangle(18, 141, 200, 158);
    }
    else
    {
            pDC->SetTextAlign(TA_TOP);
            pDC->TextOut(20, 20, "TA_TOP text positioning");
            pDC->Rectangle(18, 21, 200, 38);

            pDC->TextOut(20, 80, "TA_TOP text positioning");
            pDC->Rectangle(18, 81, 200, 98);

            pDC->TextOut(20, 140, "TA_TOP text positioning");
            pDC->Rectangle(18, 141, 200, 158);
    }

    pDC->SelectObject(oldBrush);
}
```

The m_showAllAlignments flag determines whether OnDraw() displays text lines with TA_TOP alignment or with all three alignments.

When the user clicks the application's window, the vertical text alignment of the second and third text lines changes. The view class's OnLButtonDown() function handles this task, as shown here:

```
void CVerticalAlignAppView::OnLButtonDown(UINT nFlags,
    CPoint point)
{
    // TODO: Add your message handler code here
    //    and/or call default

    m_showAllAlignments = !m_showAllAlignments;

    Invalidate();

    CView::OnLButtonDown(nFlags, point);
}
```

Here, OnLButtonDown() reverses the value of the m_showAllAlignments flag. The call to Invalidate() then forces the window to redraw its display.

Problems & Solutions

Displaying Tabbed Text

PROBLEM: *I have a table that I want to display in my application's window. How can I use tabs to position the table elements, rather than having to fool with a lot of special text alignments?*

SOLUTION: Sounds like a job for the `TabbedTextOut()` function, which is a member of the CDC class. `TabbedTextOut()` enables you to display text strings that contain tab characters. To use the function, perform these steps:

1. Create an array of integers that holds the tab positions you need.
2. Create the text strings you want to display, embedding tab characters (\t) as appropriate.
3. Call `TabbedTextOut()` to display each line of tabbed text.

`TabbedTextOut()` is a complicated function that requires several more arguments than the regular `TextOut()` function. Its signature looks like this:

```
TabbedTextOut(
    int x,
    int y,
    Const CString& str,
    int numTabs,
    LPINT tabs,
    int tabOrigin);
```

`TabbedTextOut()`'s arguments, in order, are as follows:

x	The horizontal position at which to display the string
y	The vertical position at which to display the string
str	The string to display, which also can be the address of a char array
numTabs	The number of tabs in the tab array
tabs	The address of the tab array
tabOrigin	The horizontal position at which tab measurement begins

Location: WinPrgS\Chap04\TabTextApp

Continued

To see `TabbedTextOut()` do its stuff, take a look at the TabTextApp application on this book's CD-ROM. This application displays a multicolumn table that uses tabs to space the columns. Figure 4-9 shows the application's display, created by this `OnDraw()` function:

```
void CTabTextAppView::OnDraw(CDC* pDC)
{
    CTabTextAppDoc* pDoc = GetDocument();
    ASSERT_VALID(pDoc);

    // TODO: add draw code for native data here

    int tabs[] = {150, 260, 340};
    CString header =
        "LAST NAME\tFIRST NAME\tAGE\tOCCUPATION";
    CString row1 = "Wilson\tAlphonso\t32\tFarmer";
    CString row2 = "Richards\tMarcy\t25\tLawyer";
    CString row3 = "Harrison\tLarence\t64\tRetired";
    CString row4 = "Billingsly\tThomas\t41\tDentist";
    CString row5 = "Kelly\tSusan\t35\tNurse";
    CString row6 =
        "Underwood\tSamantha\t47\tPolice officer";

    pDC->TabbedTextOut(20, 20, header, 3, tabs, 20);
    pDC->TabbedTextOut(20, 60, row1, 3, tabs, 20);
    pDC->TabbedTextOut(20, 80, row2, 3, tabs, 20);
    pDC->TabbedTextOut(20, 100, row3, 3, tabs, 20);
    pDC->TabbedTextOut(20, 120, row4, 3, tabs, 20);
    pDC->TabbedTextOut(20, 140, row5, 3, tabs, 20);
    pDC->TabbedTextOut(20, 160, row6, 3, tabs, 20);
}
```

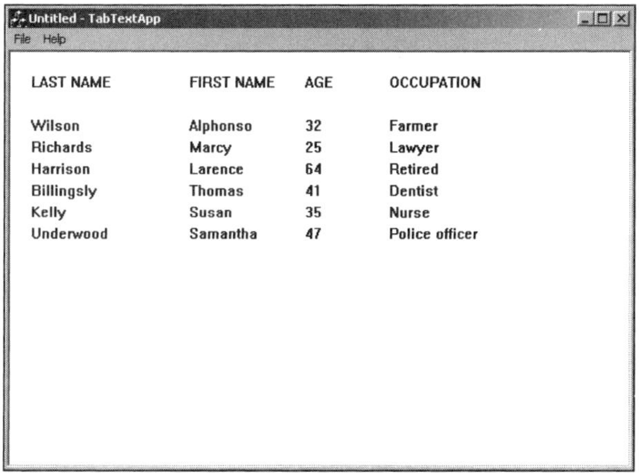

Figure 4-9: TabTextApp displays tabbed text.

Getting Text Metrics

Until now, this book's programs have displayed text using hard-coded coordinates in the TextOut() function. This isn't the safest way to space text because you can't always be sure of the current font's size. When you display multiple lines of text, first determine the size of the font the application's using. Then, you easily can calculate the appropriate line spacing for the text the application displays.

To get information about the currently selected font, you call the GetTextMetrics() function:

```
TEXTMETRIC textMetric;
pDC->GetTextMetrics(&textMetric);
```

GetTextMetrics() single argument is the address of a TEXTMETRIC structure. Windows defines the structure like this:

```
typedef struct tagTEXTMETRIC {   /* tm */
    int    tmHeight;
    int    tmAscent;
    int    tmDescent;
    int    tmInternalLeading;
    int    tmExternalLeading;
    int    tmAveCharWidth;
    int    tmMaxCharWidth;
    int    tmWeight;
    BYTE   tmItalic;
    BYTE   tmUnderlined;
    BYTE   tmStruckOut;
    BYTE   tmFirstChar;
    BYTE   tmLastChar;
    BYTE   tmDefaultChar;
    BYTE   tmBreakChar;
    BYTE   tmPitchAndFamily;
    BYTE   tmCharSet;
    int    tmOverhang;
    int    tmDigitizedAspectX;
    int    tmDigitizedAspectY;
} TEXTMETRIC;
```

Table 4-1 describes each of the structure's members. Unless you know a bit about typography, some of the terms used in the table may be new to you. In most cases, however, you don't need to deal with the more esoteric members of the TEXTMETRIC structure.

Table 4-1 Members of the TEXTMETRIC Structure

Member	Description
tmAscent	Character *ascent* (the height above the baseline)
tmAveCharWidth	Average character width
tmBreakChar	Break character for text justification
tmCharSet	Font's character set
tmDefaultChar	Character that is substituted for those not included in the font
tmDescent	Character *descent* (the height below the baseline)
tmDigitizedAspectX	Horizontal element of the aspect ratio
tmDigitizedAspectY	Vertical element of the aspect ratio
tmExternalLeading	*External leading* (space between lines of text)
tmFirstChar	Value of the font's first character
tmHeight	Character height
tmInternalLeading	*Internal leading* (space used for adding marks such as accents)
tmItalic	Value indicating italic (0=no italic; nonzero=italic)
tmLastChar	Value of the font's last character
tmMaxCharWidth	Width of the widest character
tmOverhang	Extra width that may be increased in order to add attributes, such as bold or italic, to characters
tmPitchAndFamily	Pitch, technology, and family of a physical font
tmStruckOut	Value indicating strikeout (0=no strikeout; nonzero=strikeout)
tmUnderlined	Value indicating an underline (0=no underline; nonzero=underlined)
tmWeight	Font weight (amount of "boldness")

Location: **WinPrgS\Chap04\TextMetricsApp**

On this book's CD-ROM, you can find the TextMetricsApp application that demonstrates vertical text spacing. When you run the application, you see the window shown in Figure 4-10, which displays text using a character height obtained through the `GetTextMetrics()` function. The `OnDraw()` function, in which the application determines the text height and displays several lines of text, looks like this:

```
void CTextMetricsAppView::OnDraw(CDC* pDC)
{
    CTextMetricsAppDoc* pDoc = GetDocument();
    ASSERT_VALID(pDoc);

    // TODO: add draw code for native data here

    TEXTMETRIC textMetric;
    pDC->GetTextMetrics(&textMetric);
    int charHeight = textMetric.tmHeight;

    char* s[] = {
        "This is a test of line spacing",
        "using the text height returned",
        "in a TEXTMETRIC structure.",
        "This is a safer way to display",
        "text than using hard-coded",
        "values that may not be appropriate",
        "for the currently selected font.",
        "By checking the tmHeight member of",
        "the TEXTMETRIC structure, you can",
        "always be sure of the character",
        "height with which your application",
        "must work."};

    for (int x=0; x<12; ++x)
        pDC->TextOut(20, 20+x*charHeight, s[x]);
}
```

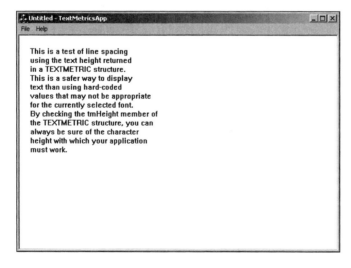

Figure 4-10: TextMetricsApp displaying lines of text

Creating Fonts

When you write simple applications, you don't have to deal much with fonts. The system font usually works fine for most purposes. However, if you need a specific font, you can create your own by creating an object of MFC's `CFont` class. To create a font, you first initialize an instance of the `LOGFONT` structure, which holds the information Windows needs to create the font. You then pass the structure to your `CFont` object in order to create the actual font. The process looks something like this:

```
LOGFONT logFont;
logFont.lfHeight = 24;
logFont.lfWidth = 0;
logFont.lfEscapement = 0;
logFont.lfOrientation = 0;
logFont.lfWeight = FW_NORMAL;
logFont.lfItalic = 0;
logFont.lfUnderline = 0;
logFont.lfStrikeOut = 0;
logFont.lfCharSet = ANSI_CHARSET;
logFont.lfOutPrecision = OUT_DEFAULT_PRECIS;
logFont.lfClipPrecision = CLIP_DEFAULT_PRECIS;
logFont.lfQuality = PROOF_QUALITY;
logFont.lfPitchAndFamily = VARIABLE_PITCH | FF_ROMAN;
strcpy(logFont.lfFaceName, "Times New Roman");

CFont font;
font.CreateFontIndirect(&logFont);
```

Before creating a font, you have to understand the `LOGFONT` structure, which Windows defines. It looks like this:

```
typedef struct tagLOGFONT { // lf
    LONG  lfHeight;
    LONG  lfWidth;
    LONG  lfEscapement;
    LONG  lfOrientation;
    LONG  lfWeight;
    BYTE  lfItalic;
    BYTE  lfUnderline;
    BYTE  lfStrikeOut;
    BYTE  lfCharSet;
    BYTE  lfOutPrecision;
    BYTE  lfClipPrecision;
    BYTE  lfQuality;
    BYTE  lfPitchAndFamily;
    TCHAR lfFaceName[LF_FACESIZE];
} LOGFONT;
```

Table 4-2 describes each of the `LOGFONT` members. Unfortunately, a complete discussion of fonts can take up an entire book. So if some of the descriptions in Table 4-2 make your head spin, know that you're in good company. As luck would have it, most of the `LOGFONT` members have default values (see the

FontApp application's source code later in this chapter) that you can plug in. This leaves you to concentrate on more useful aspects of the font such as height and width, as well as attributes such as bold and underline. For more information on the LOGFONT structure, check your Visual C++ online documentation.

Table 4-2 Members of the LOGFONT Structure

Member	Description
lfCharSet	Font's character set. Can be ANSI_CHARSET, DEFAULT_CHARSET, SYMBOL_CHARSET, SHIFTJIS_CHARSET, GB2312_CHARSET, HANGEUL_CHARSET, CHINESEBIG5_CHARSET, OEM_CHARSET, JOHAB_CHARSET, HEBREW_CHARSET, ARABIC_CHARSET, GREEK_ CHARSET, TURKISH_CHARSET, THAI_CHARSET, EASTEUROPE_CHARSET, RUSSIAN_CHARSET, MAC_CHARSET, or BALTIC_CHARSET.
lfClipPrecision	Font's clipping precision, which specifies how to clip characters that fall partially outside the clipping region. Can be CLIP_DEFAULT_ PRECIS, CLIP_CHARACTER_PRECIS, CLIP_STROKE_PRECIS, CLIP_MASK, CLIP_EMBEDDED, CLIP_LH_ANGLES, or CLIP_TT_ ALWAYS.
lfEscapement	Font angle.
lfFaceName	Font's typeface name.
lfHeight	Font height.
lfItalic	Font's italic attribute. A nonzero value turns on the attribute.
lfOrientation	Font angle.
lfPitchAndFamily	Font's pitch and family. Can be DEFAULT_PITCH, FIXED_PITCH, or VARIABLE_PITCH using the OR operator with one of the following: FF_DECORATIVE, FF_DONTCARE, FF_MODERN, FF_ROMAN, FF_SCRIPT, or FF_SWISS.
lfQuality	Font's *output quality,* which is how well the GDI matches the logical-font attributes to those of a physical font. Can be DEFAULT_QUALITY, DRAFT_QUALITY, or PROOF_QUALITY.
lfStrikeOut	Font's strikeout attribute. A nonzero value turns on the attribute.
lfUnderline	Font's underline attribute. A nonzero value turns on the attribute.
lfWeight	Font weight (degree of boldness). Can be FW_DONTCARE, FW_THIN, FW_EXTRALIGHT, FW_ULTRALIGHT, FW_LIGHT, FW_NORMAL, FW_REGULAR, FW_MEDIUM, FW_SEMIBOLD, FW_DEMIBOLD, FW_BOLD, FW_EXTRABOLD, FW_ULTRABOLD, FW_HEAVY, FW_BLACK, or any value between 0 and 1,000.
lfWidth	Font width.

Chapter 4: Text   **133**

CD

Location: `WinPrgS\Chap04\FontApp`

On this book's CD-ROM, you can find the FontApp application that demonstrates creating fonts. When you run the application, you see the window shown in Figure 4-11.

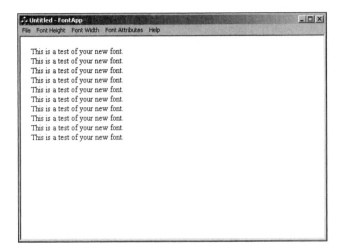

Figure 4-11: FontApp displays ten lines of text using its own font.

You can change the size and look of the displayed font from the application's menus. Figure 4-12 shows the application after the user increased the font height to 36.

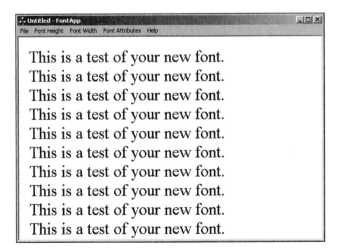

Figure 4-12: FontApp after the user enlarged the font

Figure 4-13 shows the font with a larger width and its italics attribute selected.

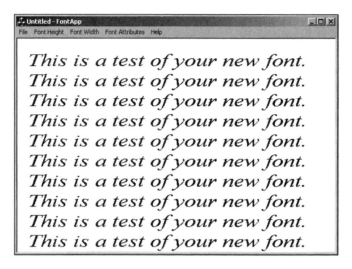

Figure 4-13: FontApp after the user selected the wide and italics attributes

FontApp seems to do quite a bit of work, but all this application does is change the values of a few variables and create a new font based on the newly selected values. These values are members of the application's view class and are initialized in the class's constructor, as shown here:

```
CFontAppView::CFontAppView()
{
    // TODO: add construction code here

    m_height = 12;
    m_width = 0;
    m_italic = 0;
    m_underline = 0;
    m_strikeout = 0;
    m_weight = FW_NORMAL;
}
```

When FontApp must update its window, MFC calls the view class's `OnDraw()` function, which looks like this:

```
void CFontAppView::OnDraw(CDC* pDC)
{
    CFontAppDoc* pDoc = GetDocument();
    ASSERT_VALID(pDoc);

    // TODO: add draw code for native data here

    LOGFONT logFont;
    logFont.lfHeight = m_height;
```

```
        logFont.lfWidth = m_width;
        logFont.lfEscapement = 0;
        logFont.lfOrientation = 0;
        logFont.lfWeight = m_weight;
        logFont.lfItalic = m_italic;
        logFont.lfUnderline = m_underline;
        logFont.lfStrikeOut = m_strikeout;
        logFont.lfCharSet = ANSI_CHARSET;
        logFont.lfOutPrecision = OUT_DEFAULT_PRECIS;
        logFont.lfClipPrecision = CLIP_DEFAULT_PRECIS;
        logFont.lfQuality = PROOF_QUALITY;
        logFont.lfPitchAndFamily = VARIABLE_PITCH | FF_ROMAN;
        strcpy(logFont.lfFaceName, "Times New Roman");

        CFont font;
        font.CreateFontIndirect(&logFont);

        CFont* pOldFont = pDC->SelectObject(&font);

        for (int x=0; x<10; ++x)
            pDC->TextOut(20, 20+x*logFont.lfHeight,
                "This is a test of your new font.");

        pDC->SelectObject(pOldFont);
}
```

In `OnDraw()`, the program creates a new font based on the user's selections, selects the font into the DC, and displays text with the new font. `OnDraw()` spaces the text in the window by using the font's height (as stored in the `LOGFONT` structure) to calculate the vertical position for each line.

PROBLEMS & SOLUTIONS

The Size of a Text Line

PROBLEM: *Most Windows fonts use proportionate character spacing, making it difficult to determine the actual size of a line of text. This problem is multiplied by the fact that in the application I'm writing, the user can select a different font, which changes the size of the text string. How can my application accurately determine the size of a text string on the screen?*

SOLUTION: Proportionate fonts sure make life interesting. They look great on the screen, but because every character is a different width, you can't find the length of a string as easily as you can with a proportionate font.

Continued

Or can you? Windows has just the function to solve this dilemma. With the impressive name `GetTextExtentPoint32()`, this function returns the height and width of a text string based on the currently active font. This Windows API function's signature looks like this:

```
::GetTextExtentPoint32(
    HDC hDC,
    LPCTSTR pText,
    int numChars,
    LPSIZE pSize);
```

`GetTextExtentPoint32()`'s arguments, in order, are as follows:

hDC	A handle to the current device context
pText	The address of the text for which you want the size
numChars	The number of characters in the text string
pSize	The address of a `SIZE` structure

`GetTextExtentPoint32()` stores the size of the string in a `SIZE` structure—a pointer to which you supply the function's fourth argument. Windows defines the `SIZE` structure like this:

```
typedef struct tagSIZE {
    LONG cx;
    LONG cy;
} SIZE;
```

The width of the string ends up in the `cx` member and the height in the `cy` member. You can use these values to determine other coordinates based on the size of the string.

Location: **WinPrgS\Chap04\FontApp2**

For example, on this book's CD-ROM, you can find a new version of the FontApp application. This version works much like the previous version, enabling you to select font sizes and attributes for the text on the screen. However, this new version draws a rectangle around each string, calculating the rectangle's width from the string size returned by a call to `GetTextExtentPoint32()`. Figure 4-14 shows the program running. The program's `OnDraw()` function looks like this:

```
void CFontAppView::OnDraw(CDC* pDC)
{
    CFontAppDoc* pDoc = GetDocument();
    ASSERT_VALID(pDoc);
```

Continued

Chapter 4: Text

```cpp
// TODO: add draw code for native data here

    LOGFONT logFont;
    logFont.lfHeight = m_height;
    logFont.lfWidth = m_width;
    logFont.lfEscapement = 0;
    logFont.lfOrientation = 0;
    logFont.lfWeight = m_weight;
    logFont.lfItalic = m_italic;
    logFont.lfUnderline = m_underline;
    logFont.lfStrikeOut = m_strikeout;
    logFont.lfCharSet = ANSI_CHARSET;
    logFont.lfOutPrecision = OUT_DEFAULT_PRECIS;
    logFont.lfClipPrecision = CLIP_DEFAULT_PRECIS;
    logFont.lfQuality = PROOF_QUALITY;
    logFont.lfPitchAndFamily = VARIABLE_PITCH | FF_ROMAN;
    strcpy(logFont.lfFaceName, "Times New Roman");

    CFont font;
    font.CreateFontIndirect(&logFont);

    CFont* pOldFont = pDC->SelectObject(&font);
    CBrush* pOldBrush =
        (CBrush*)pDC->SelectStockObject(NULL_BRUSH);

    SIZE size;
    ::GetTextExtentPoint32(pDC->m_hDC,
        "This is a test of your new font.", 32, &size);

    for (int x=0; x<10; ++x)
    {
        pDC->TextOut(20, 20+x*logFont.lfHeight,
            "This is a test of your new font.");

        int top = 20+x*logFont.lfHeight;
        int right = 20+size.cx;
        int bottom = 20+x*logFont.lfHeight +
            logFont.lfHeight;
        pDC->Rectangle(20, top, right, bottom);
    }

    pDC->SelectObject(pOldFont);
    pDC->SelectObject(pOldBrush);
}
```

Continued

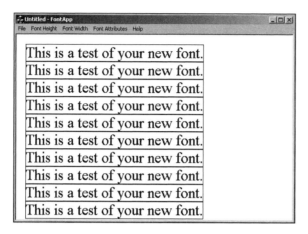

Figure 4-14: This version of FontApp calculates the size of each string in the display, regardless of the string's attributes.

Summary

Most applications display text in one form or another. Unfortunately, due to Windows' graphical nature, creating the perfect text display can be a chore. Proportional fonts of different sizes with different attributes complicate matters by making it tricky to determine the right line spacing. Although there's a lot to know about displaying text and handling fonts, Windows provides all the tools you need to generate your application's display. In this chapter, you got an overview of the most useful techniques for displaying text.

Also discussed in this chapter:

- The TextOut() function displays text easily — if you're not too fussy about the outcome.
- An application can set the text color, as well as the background color.
- An application can change the character spacing in a line of text.
- An application can use left, center, or right horizontal alignment with text.
- An application can display text with top, bottom, or baseline vertical alignment.
- The TabbedTextOut() function displays text containing embedded tabs.
- The GetTextMetrics() function acquires information about a font.
- An application can create its own fonts using MFC's CFont class.

Chapter 5

Menus

In This Chapter

- Creating menu resources
- Creating message-response functions
- Understanding menu UI functions
- Marking menu items with checks
- Using and understanding the MenuApp sample application

Windows 2000 applications that do not contain menu bars are few and far between. It is, after all, the menu bar that gives the user access to the commands that control the application. Luckily, creating menus for your application is a simple task when programming with MFC. Although some menu programming techniques require that you roll up your sleeves and write a few lines of code from scratch, ClassWizard can help with most conventional menu coding tasks. In this chapter, you get the inside scoop on programming professional-looking menus.

Creating Menu Resources

The first thing you must do to add menus to your Visual C++ application is create your menus' resources with the Menu Editor, as shown in Figure 5-1. The Menu Editor not only enables you to create new menus and add menu items, but it also enables you to set the attributes for the menus. These attributes include whether each menu item should be checked or enabled initially. Following is an overview of the steps required to define a new menu.

1. Double-click the menu ID (located within the Menu folder) in the ResourceView pane of the Project Workspace window, as shown in Figure 5-1. The menu appears in the Menu Editor.

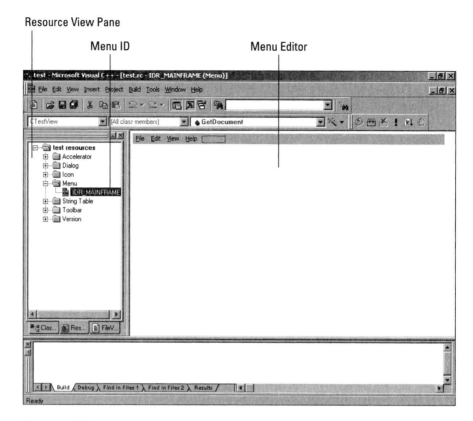

Figure 5-1: When you double-click a menu ID, the menu appears in the editor.

2. Select the blank menu in the menu bar and press Enter. The Menu Item Properties property sheet appears, as shown in Figure 5-2.

Chapter 5: Menus 141

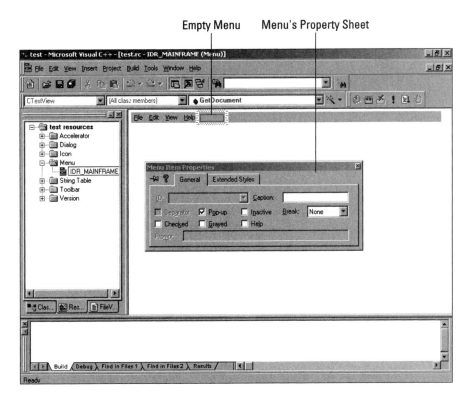

Figure 5-2: The blank menu represents a new pop-up menu.

3. Type the menu's name into the Caption box, using an ampersand (&) to indicate the menu's hot key (as shown in Figure 5-3).

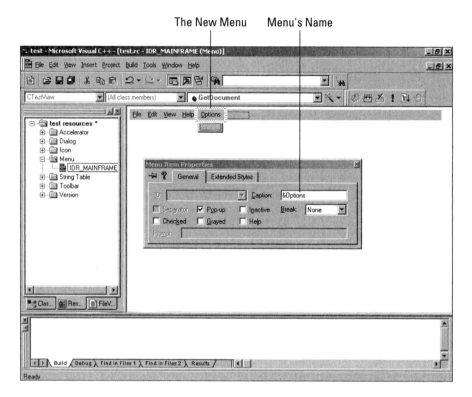

Figure 5-3: The menu's name appears in the menu bar.

4. Double-click the first empty menu item in the new menu. The Menu Item Properties property sheet reappears, as shown in Figure 5-4.

Chapter 5: Menus **143**

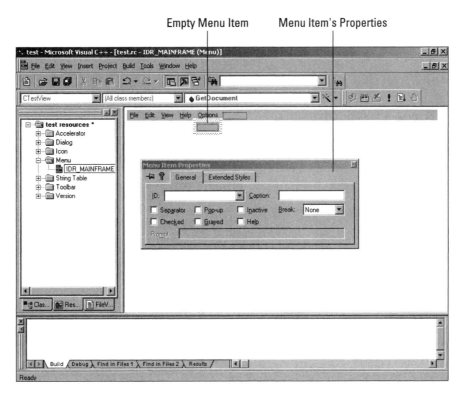

Figure 5-4: The property sheet appears for menu items, as well as for pop-up menus.

5. Type the menu item's command ID into the ID box and type an ampersand followed by the command's caption into the Caption box, as shown in Figure 5-5.

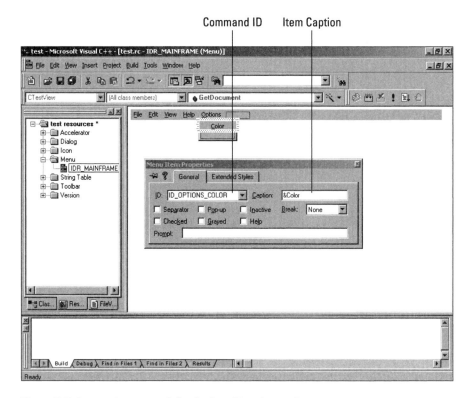

Figure 5-5: A menu item must define both an ID and a caption.

6. Repeat steps 4 and 5 for each menu item in the menu.

Creating Message-Response Functions

Once you create the menu resource, you must associate each menu item with a message-response function. This enables MFC to call the associated function when the user selects a menu item. The program then can process the user's request with the associated function. Creating message-response functions is a snap with ClassWizard, as shown in Figure 5-6. You simply follow these steps:

1. Select the class in which you want the message-response function defined.
2. Select the menu ID associated with the function.
3. Add the function to the program.

ClassWizard enables you to perform these tasks with a few mouse clicks.

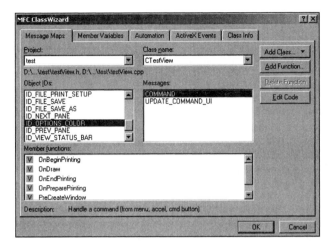

Figure 5-6: ClassWizard makes it easy to add message-response functions to your application.

When ClassWizard adds a message-response function to a class, it first declares the new function in the class's header file:

```
afx_msg void OnOptionsTime();
```

The `afx_msg` prefix simply marks the line as a message-response function. The prefix isn't required, but it should appear to differentiate message-response functions from other class member functions.

After declaring the function in the class's header file, ClassWizard adds the function to the class's message map:

```
BEGIN_MESSAGE_MAP(CMenuAppView, CView)
    //{{AFX_MSG_MAP(CMenuAppView)
    ON_COMMAND(ID_OPTIONS_TIME, OnOptionsTime)
    //}}AFX_MSG_MAP
END_MESSAGE_MAP()
```

The message map associates a message ID with a message-response function. That is, the preceding message map tells MFC that when the application receives a command with ID_OPTIONS_TIME ID, it should call the OnOptionsTime() message-response function.

Finally, after adding the function to the message map, MFC defines the function's skeleton in the class's implementation file:

```
void CTestView::OnOptionsTime()
{
    // TODO: Add your command handler code here

}
```

MFC defines an empty message-response function. (MFC, after all, doesn't have a clue what you want to do with the menu item that the function represents.) You must write the function's body yourself, providing the source code that handles the request represented by the menu item.

Problems & Solutions

Handling a Range of Menu Items

PROBLEM: *My application's menus have several related commands that I want to manage in one message-response function. Is this possible, or must I have a separate message-response function for every menu item?*

SOLUTION: You can manage several, related menu items in a single message-response function. The problem with this technique is that you have to write the code by hand, without ClassWizard's help. Still, it's a simple enough process.

The trick is to use the ON_COMMAND_RANGE macro in your message map, rather than the usual ON_COMMAND macro:

```
BEGIN_MESSAGE_MAP(CTestView, CView)
    ON_COMMAND_RANGE(ID_COLORS_RED,
        ID_COLORS_BLUE, OnColors)
END_MESSAGE_MAP()
```

The ON_COMMAND_RANGE macro's three arguments are the first ID in the range, the last ID in the range, and the name of the message-response function that handles the range. In order for this macro to work, all the command IDs in the range must be consecutive. For example, the preceding example sets up a range of command IDs that includes ID_COLORS_RED, ID_COLORS_GREEN, and ID_COLORS_BLUE, in that order. The IDs are defined like this:

```
#define ID_COLORS_RED 32771
#define ID_COLORS_GREEN 32772
#define ID_COLORS_BLUE 32773
```

As you can see, the IDs are numbered consecutively—a requirement for the ON_COMMAND_RANGE macro.

Next, you must declare the message-response function in the class's header file. The declaration looks something like this:

```
afx_msg void OnColors(UINT commandID);
```

A message-response function associated with an ON_COMMAND_RANGE macro must accept a single UINT argument, which is the ID of the command on whose behalf MFC calls the function. You use commandID to determine which command the user selects and how you should respond to it.

Continued

Finally, you must define the message-response function that handles the command range. Such a function might look like this:

```
void CTestView::OnColors(UINT commandID)
{
    if (commandID == ID_COLORS_RED)
        m_color = RED;
    else if (commandID == ID_COLORS_GREEN)
        m_color = GREEN;
    else
        m_color = BLUE;
}
```

The function checks to see which command results in a call to the function, and acts accordingly. The preceding function replaces the three functions shown here:

```
void CTestView::OnColorsRed()
{
    // TODO: Add your command handler code here

    m_color = RED;
}

void CTestView::OnColorsGreen()
{
    // TODO: Add your command handler code here

    m_color = GREEN;
}

void CTestView::OnColorsBlue()
{
    // TODO: Add your command handler code here

    m_color = BLUE;
}
```

Although ClassWizard can generate these three functions for you (except for the body of the function, of course), you have to write your own code from scratch when using command ranges.

Understanding Menu UI Functions

Your application must maintain the appearance of menu items. For example, the application may have menu items that must be checked or disabled depending upon the current settings of the program's options. MFC provides a mechanism for keeping menu items properly updated. Each time a menu item is about to be displayed, MFC checks whether the program defines an update command UI function for the menu item. If so, MFC runs the update command UI function immediately before it displays the menu item, giving the application a chance to add checkmarks, disable options, change a menu item's text, and so on.

Creating Update Command UI Functions

You add update command UI functions to a program in exactly the same way that you add message-response functions. Call up ClassWizard and select a menu command ID in the Object IDs box. When you do, you see COMMAND and UPDATE_COMMAND_UI function types in the Messages pane. Double-click UPDATE_COMMAND_UI, and ClassWizard displays the Add Member Function dialog box containing a suggested name for the new update command UI function, as shown in Figure 5-7. Accept the name by clicking OK, and MFC adds the function to the application.

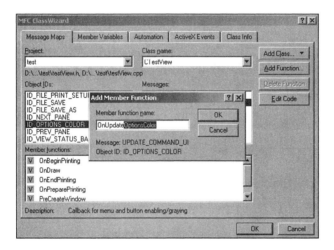

Figure 5-7: ClassWizard can add update command UI functions to your application.

Just adding the function to the application, however, is not enough. Once you have the update command UI function, you must complete the function. Exactly how you do this depends upon what you want to do with the menu item before MFC displays it. In any case, you set the menu item's attributes by calling member functions of the CCmdUI class — an object that is passed to the update command UI function as its single parameter. In the following sections, you discover how to manipulate the CCmdUI object.

Marking Menu Items with Checks

One way you can manipulate a `CCmdUI` object is to set checks on menu items. When you create menu items that represent *option toggles* — commands that turn an option on and off — you usually use checkmarks to notify the user that a particular option is on. For example, you may have an option that turns on and off the application's toolbar. When the attribute is on, the application places a checkmark next to the menu item (as shown in Figure 5-8).

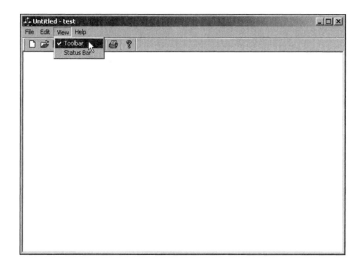

Figure 5-8: Checkmarks indicate whether an application option is selected.

An update command UI function that handles the checkmark might look like this:

```
void CTestView::OnUpdateViewToolbar(CCmdUI* pCmdUI)
{
    // TODO: Add your command update UI handler code here

    pCmdUI->SetCheck(m_toolbar);
}
```

As you can see, the update command UI function receives a pointer to a `CCmdUI` object as its single parameter. To set a checkmark on the menu item, the program calls the `CCmdUI` object's `SetCheck()` member function. The function's single argument is a Boolean value: A value of `TRUE` turns on the checkmark; a value of `FALSE` turns off the checkmark. In the toolbar example, the `m_toolbar` member variable holds the current state of the option. That is, `m_toolbar` is either `TRUE` or `FALSE` depending on whether the user has the toolbar turned on or off.

When the user opens the View menu, MFC calls `OnUpdateViewToolbar()` in order to set the Toolbar command's checkmark. This occurs right before MFC displays the menu, so the user never sees the process of turning the checkmark on or off. When the menu appears, all the menu items' update command UI functions already are called and the menu items' attributes already are set.

Bulleting Menu Items

Another way you can manipulate a `CCmdUI` object is to set bullets on menu items. Some menu option settings are mutually exclusive. That is, you can select only one of the options at a time. These mutually exclusive items display bullets next to current settings. An example of this is a set of commands for selecting colors. Because the user can draw with only one color in a given moment, the user can select only one color at a time. In this case, the application's menu can use a bullet to indicate the currently selected color, as shown in Figure 5-9.

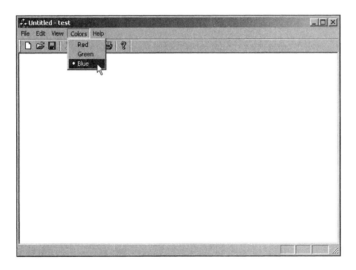

Figure 5-9: A bullet indicates the current selection in a set of mutually exclusive options.

The update command UI function for a color menu item might look like this:

```
void CTestView::OnUpdateColorsRed(CCmdUI* pCmdUI)
{
    // TODO: Add your command update UI handler code here

    pCmdUI->SetRadio(m_color == RED);
}
```

The `CCmdUI` member function `SetRadio()` adds or removes bullets from menu items. The function's single argument is a Boolean value that indicates whether the bullet should or should not be visible. In this case, the Boolean expression `m_color == RED` evaluates to either `TRUE` or `FALSE`. The `m_color` member variable holds the current color setting.

You may wonder why `SetRadio()` isn't called `SetBullet()`. The function gets its name from *radio buttons,* which are Windows buttons that represent mutually exclusive selections. This concept comes from the buttons you have on your car radio, which also represent mutually exclusive settings. You sure wouldn't want to listen to more than one radio station at a time!

Enabling and Disabling Menu Items

`CCmdUI` objects also can enable or disable menu items. The state of an application, as well as the currently selected options, often dictates which menu items are selectable. For example, before you load a document into a word processor, the word processor disables all editing commands in its Edit menu (as shown in Figure 5-10). You can't, after all, edit text that doesn't exist yet in the application's window.

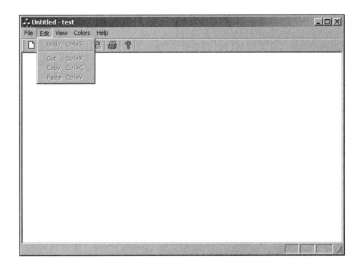

Figure 5-10: An application disables menu items that currently are invalid.

In an MFC program, you enable and disable a menu item in the item's update command UI function by calling the `CCmdUI` object's `Enable()` member function, as shown here:

```
void CTestView::OnUpdateEditCut(CCmdUI* pCmdUI)
{
    // TODO: Add your command update UI handler code here

    pCmdUI->Enable(m_cut);
}
```

The `Enable()` member function requires a single argument — a Boolean value indicating whether the item should be enabled (`TRUE`) or disabled (`FALSE`).

Changing Menu Item Text

When you create a menu item, you define the item's *caption* — the text that appears in the menu. Although the text of most menu items remains unchanged throughout the application's run, some do change based on the program's state or the currently selected options. As an example, reconsider the option toggle commands in the earlier section on menu checkmarks. Another way to handle such options is to change the menu text to reflect the current settings, rather than checkmark the options. For example, a command that toggles the toolbar can change its text from Show Toolbar to Hide Toolbar, depending on whether the toolbar currently is visible.

You handle this text change in the menu item's update command UI function:

```
void CTestView::OnUpdateViewToolbar(CCmdUI* pCmdUI)
{
    // TODO: Add your command update UI handler code here

    if (m_toolbar)
        pCmdUI->SetText("&Hide Toolbar");
    else
        pCmdUI->SetText("&Show Toolbar");
}
```

To change the menu item's text, you call the `CCmdUI` object's `SetText()` member function, which takes the new text as its single argument.

PROBLEMS & SOLUTIONS

Update Command UI Functions and Menu Item Ranges

PROBLEM: *Now that I know I can use the* `ON_COMMAND_RANGE` *macro to handle a range of related commands in a single message-response function, what about the update command UI functions for that same ID range?*

SOLUTION: As you may have guessed, MFC also provides a mechanism for creating a single update command UI function for a group of related menu items. In fact, the programming works much like it does for creating a command-range message-response function.

Continued

The trick this time is to use the ON_UPDATE_COMMAND_UI_RANGE macro in your message map, rather than the usual ON_UPDATE_COMMAND_UI macro:

```
BEGIN_MESSAGE_MAP(CTestView, CView)
    ON_COMMAND_RANGE(ID_COLORS_RED,
        ID_COLORS_BLUE, OnColors)
    ON_UPDATE_COMMAND_UI_RANGE(ID_COLORS_RED,
        ID_COLORS_BLUE, OnUpdateColors)
END_MESSAGE_MAP()
```

The ON_UPDATE_COMMAND_UI_RANGE macro's three arguments are the first ID in the range, the last ID in the range, and the name of the update command UI function that handles the range. In order for this macro to work (as with ON_COMMAND_RANGE), all the command IDs in the range must be consecutive:

```
#define ID_COLORS_RED 32771
#define ID_COLORS_GREEN 32772
#define ID_COLORS_BLUE 32773
```

Next, you declare the update command UI function in the class's header file. The declaration looks something like this:

```
afx_msg void OnUpdateColors(CCmdUI* pCmdUI);
```

Notice that this declaration looks like any other update command UI function declaration receiving a pointer to a CCmdUI object as its single parameter.

Finally, you must define the update command UI function that handles the command range. Such a function might look like this:

```
void CTestView::OnUpdateColors(CCmdUI* pCmdUI)
{
    // TODO: Add your command update UI handler code here

    if (pCmdUI->m_nID == ID_COLORS_RED)
        pCmdUI->SetRadio(m_color == RED);
    else if (pCmdUI->m_nID == ID_COLORS_GREEN)
        pCmdUI->SetRadio(m_color == GREEN);
    else
        pCmdUI->SetRadio(m_color == BLUE);
}
```

The function determines the command that results in the function call by examining the CCmdUI object's m_nID member variable. With the ID in hand, the function can determine what action to take. The preceding function replaces the three functions shown here:

```
void CTestView::OnUpdateColorsBlue(CCmdUI* pCmdUI)
{
    // TODO: Add your command update UI handler code here

    pCmdUI->SetRadio(m_color == BLUE);
}
```

Continued

```
void CTestView::OnUpdateColorsGreen(CCmdUI* pCmdUI)
{
    // TODO: Add your command update UI handler code here

    pCmdUI->SetRadio(m_color == GREEN);
}
void CTestView::OnUpdateColorsRed(CCmdUI* pCmdUI)
{
    // TODO: Add your command update UI handler code here

    pCmdUI->SetRadio(m_color == RED);
}
```

Although ClassWizard can generate the three preceding functions for you (except for the body of the function), you have to write your own code from scratch when using command ranges. You encounter the same disadvantage with message-response functions for ranges.

The MenuApp Sample Application

Location: `WinPrgS\Chap05\MenuApp`

On this book's CD-ROM, you can find the MenuApp application that demonstrates all the techniques discussed in this chapter. When you run the application, you see the window shown in Figure 5-11. Besides the usual File and Help menus, MenuApp has On/Off, Options 1, and Options 2 menus; each menu demonstrates various types of menu items.

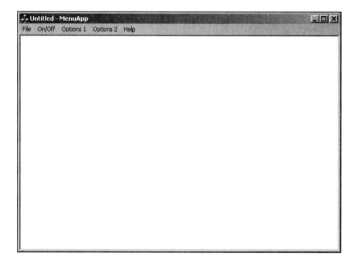

Figure 5-11: The MenuApp application displays a set of sample menus.

Using the MenuApp Sample Application

Now you use the application to demonstrate some of the information discussed in this chapter. First, select the On command in the On/Off menu. When you do, the On command changes to Off, and the other items in the menu become enabled (as shown in Figure 5-12). This menu demonstrates changing a menu item's text, as well as enabling and disabling menu items.

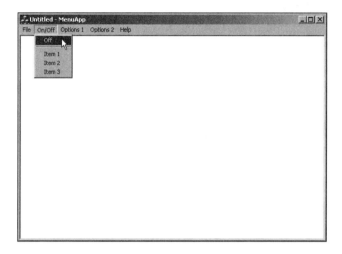

Figure 5-12: The On/Off menu demonstrates enabling and disabling menu items.

Next, check out the Options 1 menu. When you select an item on this menu, it becomes checkmarked (as shown in Figure 5-13). You can checkmark any or all of the menu items.

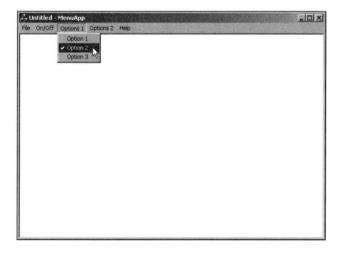

Figure 5-13: The Options 1 menu demonstrates checkmarking menu items.

Finally, the Options 2 menu shows how bullets work. In this menu, you can select any option — but only one option at a time — as shown in Figure 5-14. These options work like radio button controls, enabling the user to select from among mutually exclusive options.

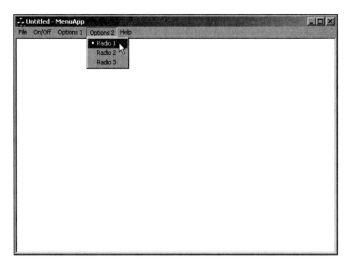

Figure 5-14: The Options 2 menu demonstrates mutually exclusive options.

Understanding the MenuApp Sample Application

The MenuApp application's view class defines both message-response and update command UI functions. ClassWizard created the skeleton functions, and I added the source code lines that make the functions do what they're designed to do. The following code shows how the functions are declared in the view class's header file. (The member variables that hold the status of the program's options also are declared in this example.)

```
// Generated message map functions
protected:
    int m_radio;
    boolean m_option3;
    boolean m_option2;
    boolean m_option1;
    boolean m_onOff;

    //{{AFX_MSG(CMenuAppView)
    afx_msg void OnOnoffOn();
    afx_msg void OnUpdateOnoffOn(CCmdUI* pCmdUI);
    afx_msg void OnOnoffItem1();
    afx_msg void OnUpdateOnoffItem1(CCmdUI* pCmdUI);
```

```
afx_msg void OnOnoffItem2();
afx_msg void OnUpdateOnoffItem2(CCmdUI* pCmdUI);
afx_msg void OnOnoffItem3();
afx_msg void OnUpdateOnoffItem3(CCmdUI* pCmdUI);
afx_msg void OnOptions1Option1();
afx_msg void OnUpdateOptions1Option1(CCmdUI* pCmdUI);
afx_msg void OnOptions1Option2();
afx_msg void OnUpdateOptions1Option2(CCmdUI* pCmdUI);
afx_msg void OnOptions1Option3();
afx_msg void OnUpdateOptions1Option3(CCmdUI* pCmdUI);
afx_msg void OnOptions2Radio1();
afx_msg void OnUpdateOptions2Radio1(CCmdUI* pCmdUI);
afx_msg void OnOptions2Radio2();
afx_msg void OnUpdateOptions2Radio2(CCmdUI* pCmdUI);
afx_msg void OnOptions2Radio3();
afx_msg void OnUpdateOptions2Radio3(CCmdUI* pCmdUI);
//}}AFX_MSG
```

Notice how each of the function declarations starts with the `afx_msg` prefix. Also notice the naming convention that ClassWizard uses to name the functions. The message-response functions all start with the word "On" followed by the name of the menu and the menu item, whereas all the update command UI functions start with "OnUpdate."

Here is the message map that ClassWizard created for the functions:

```
BEGIN_MESSAGE_MAP(CMenuAppView, CView)
    //{{AFX_MSG_MAP(CMenuAppView)
    ON_COMMAND(ID_ONOFF_ON, OnOnoffOn)
    ON_UPDATE_COMMAND_UI(ID_ONOFF_ON, OnUpdateOnoffOn)
    ON_COMMAND(ID_ONOFF_ITEM1, OnOnoffItem1)
    ON_UPDATE_COMMAND_UI(ID_ONOFF_ITEM1,
      OnUpdateOnoffItem1)
    ON_COMMAND(ID_ONOFF_ITEM2, OnOnoffItem2)
    ON_UPDATE_COMMAND_UI(ID_ONOFF_ITEM2,
      OnUpdateOnoffItem2)
    ON_COMMAND(ID_ONOFF_ITEM3, OnOnoffItem3)
    ON_UPDATE_COMMAND_UI(ID_ONOFF_ITEM3,
      OnUpdateOnoffItem3)
    ON_COMMAND(ID_OPTIONS1_OPTION1, OnOptions1Option1)
    ON_UPDATE_COMMAND_UI(ID_OPTIONS1_OPTION1,
      OnUpdateOptions1Option1)
    ON_COMMAND(ID_OPTIONS1_OPTION2, OnOptions1Option2)
    ON_UPDATE_COMMAND_UI(ID_OPTIONS1_OPTION2,
      OnUpdateOptions1Option2)
    ON_COMMAND(ID_OPTIONS1_OPTION3, OnOptions1Option3)
    ON_UPDATE_COMMAND_UI(ID_OPTIONS1_OPTION3,
      OnUpdateOptions1Option3)
    ON_COMMAND(ID_OPTIONS2_RADIO1, OnOptions2Radio1)
    ON_UPDATE_COMMAND_UI(ID_OPTIONS2_RADIO1,
      OnUpdateOptions2Radio1)
    ON_COMMAND(ID_OPTIONS2_RADIO2, OnOptions2Radio2)
    ON_UPDATE_COMMAND_UI(ID_OPTIONS2_RADIO2,
```

```
        OnUpdateOptions2Radio2)
    ON_COMMAND(ID_OPTIONS2_RADIO3, OnOptions2Radio3)
    ON_UPDATE_COMMAND_UI(ID_OPTIONS2_RADIO3,
        OnUpdateOptions2Radio3)
    //}}AFX_MSG_MAP
END_MESSAGE_MAP()
```

The message map function entries use the `ON_COMMAND` macro to associate the command ID with the function, whereas the update command UI functions use the `ON_UPDATE_COMMAND_UI` macro for the same purpose.

The message-response functions respond to the user's command by performing some action in the application. In MenuApp, that action is changing the value of an option. The options start off with the settings they get in the view class's constructor, as shown here:

```
CMenuAppView::CMenuAppView()
{
    // TODO: add construction code here

    m_onOff = false;
    m_option1 = false;
    m_option2 = false;
    m_option3 = false;
    m_radio = 1;
}
```

When the user selects a menu item, the program assigns a new value to the appropriate member variable. For example, if the user selects the Option 1 command from the Options 1 menu, the program toggles the Boolean value assigned to the `m_option1` member variable. The menu item's update command UI function uses this value to determine whether or not to display a checkmark next to the menu item. Here are the message-response functions defined in the application's view class:

```
void CMenuAppView::OnOnoffOn()
{
    // TODO: Add your command handler code here

    m_onOff = !m_onOff;
}


void CMenuAppView::OnOnoffItem1()
{
    // TODO: Add your command handler code here

    MessageBox("Item 1");
}

void CMenuAppView::OnOnoffItem2()
{
    // TODO: Add your command handler code here
```

```cpp
    MessageBox("Item 2");
}

void CMenuAppView::OnOnoffItem3()
{
    // TODO: Add your command handler code here

    MessageBox("Item 3");
}

void CMenuAppView::OnOptions1Option1()
{
    // TODO: Add your command handler code here

    m_option1 = !m_option1;
}

void CMenuAppView::OnOptions1Option2()
{
    // TODO: Add your command handler code here

    m_option2 = !m_option2;
}

void CMenuAppView::OnOptions1Option3()
{
    // TODO: Add your command handler code here

    m_option3 = !m_option3;
}

void CMenuAppView::OnOptions2Radio1()
{
    // TODO: Add your command handler code here

    m_radio = 1;
}

void CMenuAppView::OnOptions2Radio2()
{
    // TODO: Add your command handler code here

    m_radio = 2;
}

void CMenuAppView::OnOptions2Radio3()
{
    // TODO: Add your command handler code here

    m_radio = 3;
}
```

MFC calls the update command UI functions just before displaying menu items so that the menu items are displayed properly when the menu appears. As you now know, the application can display menu items in several ways, including disabled, checkmarked, and bulleted. MenuApp's update command UI functions look like this:

```
void CMenuAppView::OnUpdateOnoffOn(CCmdUI* pCmdUI)
{
    // TODO: Add your command update UI handler code here

    if (m_onOff)
        pCmdUI->SetText("&Off");
    else
        pCmdUI->SetText("&On");
}

void CMenuAppView::OnUpdateOnoffItem1(CCmdUI* pCmdUI)
{
    // TODO: Add your command update UI handler code here

    pCmdUI->Enable(m_onOff);
}

void CMenuAppView::OnUpdateOnoffItem2(CCmdUI* pCmdUI)
{
    // TODO: Add your command update UI handler code here

    pCmdUI->Enable(m_onOff);
}

void CMenuAppView::OnUpdateOnoffItem3(CCmdUI* pCmdUI)
{
    // TODO: Add your command update UI handler code here

    pCmdUI->Enable(m_onOff);
}

void CMenuAppView::OnUpdateOptions1Option1
    (CCmdUI* pCmdUI)
{
    // TODO: Add your command update UI handler code here

    pCmdUI->SetCheck(m_option1);
}

void CMenuAppView::OnUpdateOptions1Option2
    (CCmdUI* pCmdUI)
{
    // TODO: Add your command update UI handler code here

    pCmdUI->SetCheck(m_option2);
}
```

```cpp
void CMenuAppView::OnUpdateOptions1Option3
    (CCmdUI* pCmdUI)
{
    // TODO: Add your command update UI handler code here

    pCmdUI->SetCheck(m_option3);
}

void CMenuAppView::OnUpdateOptions2Radio1(CCmdUI* pCmdUI)
{
    // TODO: Add your command update UI handler code here

    pCmdUI->SetRadio(m_radio == 1);
}

void CMenuAppView::OnUpdateOptions2Radio2(CCmdUI* pCmdUI)
{
    // TODO: Add your command update UI handler code here

    pCmdUI->SetRadio(m_radio == 2);
}

void CMenuAppView::OnUpdateOptions2Radio3(CCmdUI* pCmdUI)
{
    // TODO: Add your command update UI handler code here

    pCmdUI->SetRadio(m_radio == 3);
}
```

Summary

Menus are an important part of most Windows 2000 applications. In fact, almost every application has a menu bar that contains the commands the user needs to manipulate the program. Visual C++ features powerful and easy-to-use tools for creating and programming your application's menus.

Also discussed in this chapter:

- An application defines its menus in the application's resources.
- MFC programs contain message-response functions that handle menu commands.
- MFC programs also frequently contain update command UI functions, which add attributes such as checkmarks and bullets to menu items.
- Applications usually checkmark menu items that represent selected options.
- Mutually exclusive options display a bullet next to the current setting.
- Besides checkmarking and bulleting menu items, an application also can change a menu item's text.

Chapter 6

Standard Controls

In This Chapter

▶ Introducing the standard controls
▶ Placing controls in non-dialog box windows
▶ Creating and programming standard controls
▶ Changing a control's color
▶ Manipulating controls in dialog boxes

If you took away its controls, Windows would be a crippled operating system. The system's interactivity is based almost completely upon Windows controls, whether the user clicks a button to issue a command, types in an edit box to give data to a program, or selects a file from a dialog box. Without these objects that Windows users take so much for granted, applications would be about as useful as a car without pedals and a steering wheel. The bottom line is that if you want to be a Windows programmer, you have to know about controls. In this chapter, you learn the basic programming techniques required to add the standard controls to your applications. In the following chapter, you learn about Windows 2000's common controls.

Introducing the Standard Controls

If you've used Windows for a while, you know the operating system's standard controls. *Standard controls* are interactive objects, which appear mostly in dialog boxes but also can appear in main windows and even in toolbars. The standard controls enable a Windows application to receive information from, and pass information to, the user. Table 6-1 lists the most common Windows controls and their descriptions.

Table 6-1 The Most Common Windows Controls

Control	Description
Static Text	A string of text that you cannot edit. Static text controls usually are used to label other components in a dialog box.
Edit Box	A box in which you can enter text. You can edit, as well as copy and paste, text in the edit box via the Windows clipboard.
Pushbutton	A control that triggers a command when clicked. Pushbuttons usually contain a text label and often are animated so they appear pressed down when clicked.
Radio Button	A button usually used in groups; you can select only one button at a time. When you select a radio button, the previously selected button turns off.
Checkbox	A button used to turn options on and off. Unlike radio buttons, checkboxes traditionally function to enable you to choose any or all of the selections in the group simultaneously.
List Box	A list of items. You can use the mouse to select one or more items from the list. When there are more items in the list box than can fit, the list box displays a scroll bar that enables the user to view items not shown currently in the box.
Combo Box	A list of items combined with an edit box. You can click the combo box's arrow to display a list of choices or type a selection into the associated edit box.
Group Box	Used to group other controls. For example, a group box often serves to group a set of radio buttons. The box includes a caption that describes the contents of the box.

Some controls are more complex than other ones. Combo boxes, for example, require that the application fill the control with a list of items from which the user can select. A pushbutton, on the other hand, is ready to go as soon as the application creates it. In the sections that follow, you learn to add the standard controls to your applications as well as how to manage the controls and respond to the messages they generate. I present the controls in the order of their increasing complexity.

Placing Controls in Non-Dialog Box Windows

Most often, you find standard controls such as edit boxes and pushbuttons in dialog boxes. However, there's no reason you can't place these controls in any type of window. For example, an application can display and manipulate standard controls in its main window. This flexibility enables developers to create a variety of user interfaces.

To place, and respond to, controls in a non-dialog box window, you must perform the following steps:

1. Create an object of the appropriate MFC class. For example, if you want to display a list box in the window, create an object of the CListBox class.

2. Call the control object's Create() member function to create the control element and associate it with the class. For example, after creating an object of the CListBox class called listBox, call listBox.Create().

3. Add the appropriate messages to the application's message map. For a list box, you might add the ON_LBN_DBLCLK() macro so that the application can respond to selections in the list box.

4. Implement the message-response functions associated with the message-map macros you add in Step 3.

You can create objects of MFC's various control classes on the stack by creating them as member variables of a window class; you also can create them on the heap by using the new operator. Once you create the objects, you must call their Create() member functions. You can't, however, call Create() in a window class's constructor because the window element is not created at that point. Instead, you override the window class's OnCreate() function, which MFC calls in response to the Windows WM_CREATE message just before the window is displayed.

In the following sections, you examine a sample program that illustrates how to create and manage standard controls in a non-dialog box window.

Running the ControlApp2 Sample Application

Location: WinPrgS\Chap06\ControlApp2

On this book's CD-ROM, you can find the ControlApp2 application that demonstrates using standard controls in a non-dialog box window. (Many of the techniques used to program controls in a non-dialog box window are the same for dialog boxes.) Run the program and perform the following steps to experiment with the various controls:

1. Type text into the first edit control. The second edit control mirrors your typing, as shown in Figure 6-1. Every time you type a character, Windows sends a message to the application that copies the text from the first control to the second.

Part I: Fundamental Windows 2000 Programming

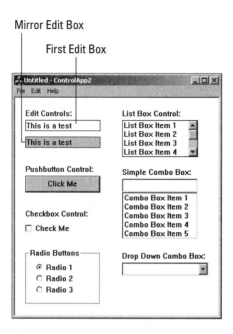

Figure 6-1: The second edit box mirrors the contents of the first edit box.

2. Click the Click Me button. When you do, a message box appears in response to the message Windows sends to the application (as shown in Figure 6-2).

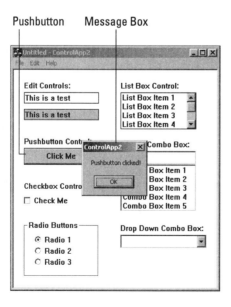

Figure 6-2: Clicking the pushbutton causes a message box to appear.

3. Click the Check Me checkbox. A check appears in the box, and a message box pops up telling you whether the box is checked or unchecked. The message box, shown in Figure 6-3, appears in response to the message Windows sends the application when the checkbox gets clicked. You can turn the checkmark off by clicking the checkbox again.

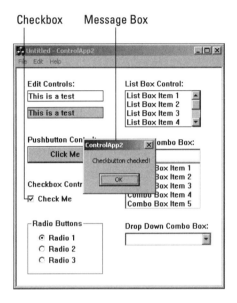

Figure 6-3: Clicking the checkbox turns its checkmark on and off.

4. Click a radio button in the Radio Buttons group. The new button becomes selected, while the old button becomes deselected. At the same time, Windows sends a message to the application, prompting a message box with the radio button's name to appear (as seen in Figure 6-4).

5. Double-click a selection in the List Box Control box. When you do, Windows sends a message to the application, which copies the selected item from the list box and displays the item in a message box (as shown in Figure 6-5).

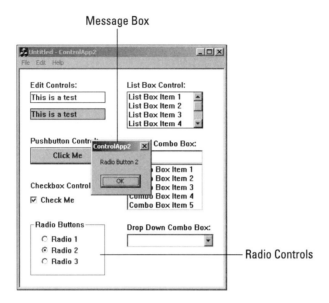

Figure 6-4: Clicking a radio button deselects the previous radio button.

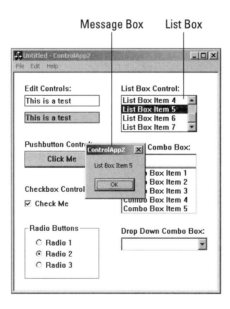

Figure 6-5: A message box displays the selected list-box item's name.

6. Double-click a selection in the Simple Combo Box. Windows sends a message to the application, which copies the selected item from the combo box and displays the item's name in a message box (as shown in Figure 6-6).

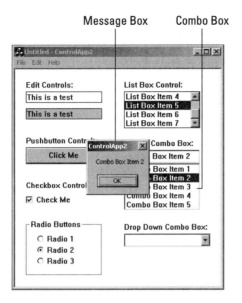

Figure 6-6: A message box displays the simple combo box's selected item name.

7. Click the arrow on the Drop Down Combo Box. The box's drop-down list appears. Select an item from the list, and a message box containing the selected item's name appears in response to the Windows message. Figure 6-7 shows the combo box with its drop-down list displayed.

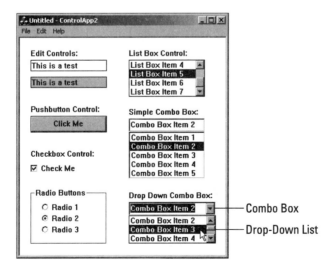

Figure 6-7: The Drop Down Combo Box stores its items in a drop-down list.

Creating and Programming Standard Controls

The basic techniques used to create and manipulate the various standard controls are similar. That is, in every case, you first create an object of the appropriate control class and then call the object's Create() function. However, each control has its own set of style flags and member functions. In this section, you explore each type of standard control and see what makes it tick.

Static Controls

One type of control that you didn't do much with in the preceding section is the static text control. Figure 6-8 shows static controls used in a typical dialog box. Most often, static controls display text; they also can display icons, bitmaps, and other types of images.

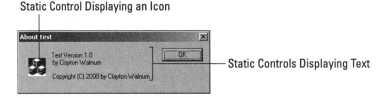

Figure 6-8: A dialog box displaying static controls

All of the text labels in ControlApp2's window are static text controls, which can display text and images. ControlApp2 declares the static text controls, which are objects of the MFC CStatic class, in the view class's header files as follows:

```
CStatic m_editStatic;
CStatic m_buttonStatic;
CStatic m_checkStatic;
CStatic m_listStatic;
CStatic m_comboStatic;
CStatic m_comboStatic2;
```

Each of these static controls represents the descriptive label on one of the other controls. For example, m_editStatic is the edit box's descriptive label, whereas m_buttonStatic is the pushbutton control's descriptive label.

As you already know, all controls that you want to appear in a window must be created in the window class's OnCreate() function. This is true of the static text control as well. Here is the `OnCreate()` function from ControlApp2's view class:

```
int CControlApp2View::OnCreate
   (LPCREATESTRUCT lpCreateStruct)
{
    if (CView::OnCreate(lpCreateStruct) == -1)
        return -1;

    // TODO: Add your specialized creation code here

    CreateStaticText();
    CreateEditBoxes();
    CreatePushbutton();
    CreateCheckbox();
    CreateRadioButtons();
    CreateListBox();
    CreateComboBoxes();

    m_whiteBrush.CreateSolidBrush(RGB(255,255,255));

    return 0;
}
```

As you can see, `OnCreate()` calls several member functions—each of which creates a specific type of control. `OnCreate()` calls `CreateStaticText()` to create the window's static text controls. As the following code shows, `CreateStaticText()` calls each static text object's `Create()` function to create the control element and associate it with the `CStatic` object:

```
void CControlApp2View::CreateStaticText()
{
    m_editStatic.Create("Edit Controls:",
        WS_CHILD | WS_VISIBLE,
        CRect(20, 20, 220, 40), this, 0);

    m_buttonStatic.Create("Pushbutton Control:",
        WS_CHILD | WS_VISIBLE,
        CRect(20, 120, 220, 140), this, 0);

    m_checkStatic.Create("Checkbox Control:",
        WS_CHILD | WS_VISIBLE,
        CRect(20, 200, 220, 220), this, 0);

    m_listStatic.Create("List Box Control:",
        WS_CHILD | WS_VISIBLE,
        CRect(200, 20, 320, 40), this, 0);

    m_comboStatic.Create("Simple Combo Box:",
        WS_CHILD | WS_VISIBLE,
        CRect(200, 125, 350, 145), this, 0);
```

```
    m_comboStatic2.Create("Drop Down Combo Box:",
        WS_CHILD | WS_VISIBLE,
        CRect(200, 275, 390, 295), this, 0);
}
```

The CStatic class's Create() function has the following signature (I list the arguments' descriptions in order after the signature):

```
BOOL Create(
    LPCTSTR lpszText,
    DWORD dwStyle,
    const RECT& rect,
    CWnd* pParentWnd,
    UINT nID = 0xffff);
```

lpszText	The address of the text to display in the control
dwStyle	The control's style flags
rect	A RECT or CRect object that specifies the control's size and position
pParentWnd	A pointer to the control's parent window
nID	The control's ID

Because the ControlApp2 application doesn't need to access the static controls, the program gives all the static controls an ID of 0. You also can leave the ID argument off, and so accept the Create() function's default ID of 0xffff.

Most of the function's arguments are described fully in the previous list. The control's dwStyle argument, however, specifies the window and control flags that determine the way the control looks and acts. You combine these flags, using the OR operator, into a single DWORD value. You at least should specify the WS_VISIBLE and WS_CHILD window styles. You also may want to use one or more of the flags defined specifically for a static control. Table 6-2 lists these style flags and their descriptions.

Table 6-2   Static Control Styles

Style Flag	Description
SS_BLACKFRAME	Draws the control's frame with the same color as the window frame, usually black
SS_BLACKRECT	Fills the control's rectangle with the same color as the window frame, usually black
SS_CENTER	Centers text in the control

Style Flag	Description
SS_GRAYFRAME	Draws the control's frame with the same color as the desktop background, usually gray
SS_GRAYRECT	Draws the control's rectangle with the same color as the desktop background, usually gray
SS_ICON	Specifies that the control holds an icon
SS_LEFT	Left-aligns text in the control
SS_LEFTNOWORDWRAP	Disables word wrapping
SS_NOPREFIX	Prevents Windows from interpreting an ampersand in the control's text as a hot key indicator
SS_RIGHT	Right-aligns text in the control
SS_SIMPLE	Specifies a simple, single-line control
SS_USERITEM	Specifies a user-defined control
SS_WHITEFRAME	Draws the control's frame with the same color used to draw the window's background, usually white
SS_WHITERECT	Draws the control's rectangle with the same color used for the window's background, usually white

Most controls require unique IDs that you can use to access the control. Visual C++ offers a quick and easy way to define these IDs. Select the View menu's Resource Symbols command. When the Resource Symbols dialog box appears, click the New button. Enter the new ID's name and click OK. (Visual C++ suggests a unique value for the ID, so you don't even need to keep track of all the used ID numbers.) Visual C++ places all the defined IDs in the resource.h file.

In most cases, you don't need to manipulate a CStatic control once it is created. However, the CStatic class does define a number of member functions in addition to those it inherits from its base classes. Table 6-3 lists those functions and their descriptions.

Table 6-3 CStatic Member Functions

Function	Description
Create()	Creates the control element and associates it with the CStatic object
GetBitmap()	Gets a handle to the control's bitmap
GetCursor()	Gets a handle to the control's cursor

Continued

Table 6-3 *(continued)*

Function	Description
GetEnhMetaFile()	Gets a handle to the control's metafile
GetIcon()	Gets a handle to the control's icon
SetBitmap()	Specifies the bitmap that the control should display
SetCursor()	Specifies the cursor that the control should display
SetEnhMetaFile()	Specifies the metafile that the control should display
SetIcon()	Specifies the icon that the control should display

Edit Controls

Edit controls, represented in MFC by the CEdit class, are the main objects used to obtain text responses from an application's user. These handy controls not only enable the user to type text, but also to edit the text in various ways. In addition, the user can cut and paste text between the control and Windows' clipboard. The edit control is so powerful, you can use it to create a mini word-processing application similar to Windows' Notepad. Figure 6-9 shows a dialog box containing several edit controls, including a multiline edit control.

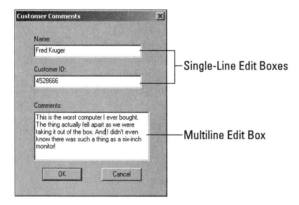

Figure 6-9: A dialog box displayed with both single-line and multiline edit boxes

In most cases, you find edit controls in their single-line incarnation. In this form (although they retain many editing features), they can display only a single line of text at a time. This is the type of edit control displayed in

ControlApp2's window. ControlApp2's edit control objects are declared like this in the view class's header file:

```
CEdit m_edit;
CEdit m_edit2;
```

As with the static controls, the program creates the edit controls in the view class's `OnCreate()` function. This function calls the local `CreateEditBoxes()` function to accomplish the task. `CreateEditBoxes()` looks like this:

```
void CControlApp2View::CreateEditBoxes()
{
    m_edit.Create(ES_AUTOHSCROLL | WS_CHILD | WS_VISIBLE
        | WS_BORDER, CRect(20, 40, 160, 60),
        this, IDC_EDIT);

    m_edit2.Create(ES_READONLY | WS_CHILD | WS_VISIBLE
        | WS_BORDER, CRect(20, 70, 160, 90), this, 0);
}
```

This function creates two edit controls: the control in which the user can type and the control that mirrors the user's typing. This second control is *read-only,* meaning that the user cannot change the text this control displays.

The `CEdit` class's `Create()` function has the following signature (I list the arguments' descriptions in order after the signature):

```
BOOL Create(
    DWORD dwStyle,
    const RECT& rect,
    CWnd* pParentWnd,
    UINT nID);
```

dwStyle	The control's style flags
rect	A RECT or CRect object that specifies the control's size and position
pParentWnd	A pointer to the control's parent window
nID	The control's ID

As with the `CStatic` control, the edit control's `dwStyle` argument specifies the window and control flags that determine the way the control looks and acts. You combine these flags, using the `OR` operator, into a single `DWORD` value. You at least should specify the `WS_VISIBLE` and `WS_CHILD` window styles. You also may want to use one or more of the flags defined specifically for an edit control. Table 6-4 lists these style flags and their descriptions.

Table 6-4   Edit Control Styles

Style Flag	Description
ES_AUTOHSCROLL	Selects automatic horizontal scrolling
ES_AUTOVSCROLL	Selects automatic vertical scrolling
ES_CENTER	Selects center text alignment in a multiline control
ES_LEFT	Selects left text alignment
ES_LOWERCASE	Forces all text to lowercase
ES_MULTILINE	Specifies that the control should allow multiple text lines
ES_NOHIDESEL	Forces selected text to remain highlighted even when the control no longer has the input focus
ES_OEMCONVERT	Converts ANSI text entered in the edit control to OEM text and back to ANSI
ES_PASSWORD	Replaces all typed text with the current password character, usually an asterisk (*)
ES_RIGHT	Selects right text alignment in a multiline control
ES_UPPERCASE	Forces all text to uppercase
ES_READONLY	Locks the control from user editing
ES_WANTRETURN	Specifies that the control should insert a return character when the user presses Enter

When the user manipulates the text in an edit control, Windows sends a series of notification messages to the parent window. The types of messages Windows sends depend on the type of edit control you create, which itself depends on the flags you specify in the call to Create(). For example, a single-line control receives a more limited set of messages than a multiline control does.

In order to respond to the user's action, the application must respond to the edit messages it receives. You set up this mechanism by adding entries to the window class's message map, which associates message-response functions with the notification messages. MFC defines a number of macros for the various edit messages. ControlApp2, for example, responds to the EN_CHANGE notification message — which Windows sends whenever the user changes the text in the control. To add this notification to the message map, you use the ON_EN_CHANGE macro:

```
ON_EN_CHANGE(IDC_EDIT, OnEditChange)
```

The macro's two arguments are the control's ID and the name of the function associated with the notification. ControlApp2's `OnEditChange()` function appears as follows:

```
void CControlApp2View::OnEditChange()
{
    char str[81];
    m_edit.GetWindowText(str, 80);
    m_edit2.SetWindowText(str);
}
```

Thanks to the new message-map entry, MFC calls `OnEditChange()` when the user changes the text in the control. In that function, the program calls the control's `GetWindowText()` member function to obtain the text in the control. The function then calls the second edit control's `SetWindowText()` member function, setting the second control's text to that of the first.

The `EN_CHANGE` notification is one of many messages an edit control generates. Table 6-5 lists the entire set of edit control notifications, along with their descriptions.

Table 6-5   Edit Control Notifications

Notification	Description
EN_CHANGE	Signals a change in the control's text (This notification comes after ON_EN_UPDATE.)
EN_ERRSPACE	Signals a lack of memory
EN_HSCROLL	Signals when the user changes the horizontal scroll bar
EN_KILLFOCUS	Signals when the control loses the input focus
EN_MAXTEXT	Signals when the user attempts to enter more text than the control can hold
EN_SETFOCUS	Signals when the control receives the input focus
EN_UPDATE	Signals that the control is about to display changed text (This notification comes before ON_EN_CHANGE.)
EN_VSCROLL	Signals when the user changes the vertical scroll bar

To get the name of a macro for a control notification, add `ON_` to the front of the notification name. For example, the message-map macro for the `EN_HSCROLL` notification is `ON_EN_HSCROLL`.

In ControlApp2's `OnEditChange()` function, you saw how to use two of the `CEdit` class's many member functions. Table 6-6 lists all the member functions, along with their descriptions. As you can see from the list, you can do a lot with an edit control — even build a simple word processing application.

Table 6-6 CEdit Member Functions

Function	Description
CanUndo()	Returns TRUE if an edit operation can be undone
CharFromPos()	Gets the character and line indexes for the given position
Clear()	Clears the current selection
Copy()	Copies the current selection to the clipboard
Create()	Creates the edit control element and associates it with the CEdit object
Cut()	Cuts the current selection to the clipboard
EmptyUndoBuffer()	Clears the control's undo flag
FmtLines()	Toggles soft line-break characters in a multiline control
GetFirstVisibleLine()	Gets the index of the visible line at the top of the control
GetHandle()	Gets a handle to the control's contents
GetLimitText()	Gets the control's maximum capacity
GetLine()	Gets a text line from the control
GetLineCount()	Gets the number of text lines in the control
GetMargins()	Gets the control's left and right margins
GetModify()	Returns TRUE if the control's contents have been modified
GetPasswordChar()	Gets the control's password character
GetRect()	Gets the control's formatting rectangle
GetSel()	Gets the current selection's starting and ending indexes
GetWindowText()	Gets the contents of a single-line control
LimitText()	Limits the length of the text that the user may enter into an edit control
LineFromChar()	Gets the index of the line containing the given character index
LineIndex()	Gets the character index of the beginning of a text line
LineLength()	Gets the control's line length
LineScroll()	Scrolls a multiline control's text
Paste()	Pastes text from the clipboard into the control

Function	Description
PosFromChar()	Gets the coordinates of a character, given its index
ReplaceSel()	Replaces a selection with the given text
SetHandle()	Sets the handle to the control's contents
SetLimitText()	Sets the control's maximum capacity
SetMargins()	Sets the control's left and right margins
SetModify()	Toggles the control's modification flag
SetPasswordChar()	Sets the control's password character
SetReadOnly()	Sets the control's read-only state
SetRect()	Sets a multiline control's formatting rectangle
SetRectNP()	Sets a multiline control's formatting rectangle without redrawing the control
SetSel()	Selects a range of characters in the control
SetTabStops()	Sets a multiline control's tab stops
Undo()	Undoes the most recent edit

PROBLEMS & SOLUTIONS

Using the Tab Key in Non-Dialog Box Windows

PROBLEM: *When I place controls in a dialog box, I can use the Tab key to move from one control to another. But when I place controls in a non-dialog box window, the Tab key doesn't seem to work. How can I fix this?*

SOLUTION: A non-dialog box window processes keystrokes differently than a dialog box does. However, you can get that Tab key back by overriding the window's PreTranslate Message() function and adding a couple of lines of code.

The steps to this process are as follows:

1. Call up ClassWizard.
2. Select your window's class (the class that acts as a parent to the controls) in the Class Name box.
3. Select PreTranslateMessage in the Messages box.
4. Click the Add Function button.

Continued

ClassWizard then adds the function to the class. Figure 6-10 shows ClassWizard after the programmer overrides the `PreTranslateMessage()` function.

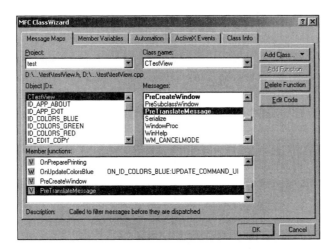

Figure 6-10: Use ClassWizard to override the window's PreTranslateMessage() function.

After overriding `PreTranslateMessage()`, add the following lines to the function:

```
BOOL dlgMsg = IsDialogMessage(pMsg);

if(dlgMsg)
    return TRUE;
else
    return CView::PreTranslateMessage(pMsg);
```

The call to `IsDialogMessage()` determines whether the message is intended for a dialog box. If so, the function handles the message and returns `TRUE`. In this case, you should return `TRUE` from `PreTranslateMessage()`, which tells MFC not to continue processing the message. If the message is not intended for a dialog box, `IsDialogMessage()` returns `FALSE`. In this case, you should call the base class's `PreTranslateMessage()` and return its return value.

Finally, a control must be created with the `WS_TABSTOP` style flag in order for it to respond to the Tab key. For example, the following lines create a combo box to which the user can tab:

```
m_comboBox.Create(CBS_SIMPLE | CBS_SORT |
    WS_TABSTOP | WS_CHILD | WS_VISIBLE | WS_GROUP,
    CRect(200, 145, 340, 255), this, IDC_COMBOBOX);
```

Don't add the `WS_TABSTOP` style to static controls or group boxes because the user can never select those controls and so can never tab to them.

Pushbuttons

Clicking a button is one of the simplest ways a user can issue a command to a Windows application. For this reason, pushbutton objects appear everywhere in Windows — most conspicuously in dialog boxes and toolbars. MFC's `CButton` class represents pushbuttons and several other types of buttons, including checkboxes and radio buttons. In the window shown in Figure 6-11, both the toolbar and the dialog box contain pushbutton controls.

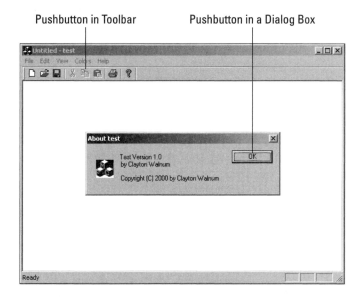

Figure 6-11: Windows applications often use pushbuttons in toolbars and dialog boxes.

In ControlApp2, the program declares its single pushbutton in the view class's header file as follows:

```
CButton m_button;
```

The application creates the button element in the `OnCreate()` function by calling the `CreatePushbutton()` member function, which looks like this:

```
void CControlApp2View::CreatePushbutton()
{
    m_button.Create("Click Me", BS_PUSHBUTTON |
        WS_BORDER | WS_CHILD | WS_VISIBLE,
        CRect(20, 140, 160, 170), this, IDC_PUSHBUTTON);
}
```

The `CButton` class's `Create()` function has the following signature (I list the arguments' descriptions in order after the signature):

```
BOOL Create(
    LPCTSTR lpszCaption,
```

```
DWORD dwStyle,
const RECT& rect,
CWnd* pParentWnd,
```

lpszCaption	The button's caption
dwStyle	The button's style flags
rect	A RECT or CRect object that specifies the button's size and position
pParentWnd	A pointer to the button's parent window
nID	The button's ID

The button control's dwStyle argument specifies the window and control flags that determine the way the control looks and acts. You combine these flags, using the OR operator, into a single DWORD value. You at least should specify the WS_VISIBLE and WS_CHILD window styles. You also should use one or more of the flags defined specifically for a button control. Table 6-7 lists these style flags and their descriptions.

Table 6-7   Button Control Styles

Style Flag	*Description*
BS_3STATE	Creates a three-state checkbox
BS_AUTO3STATE	Selects an automatic three-state checkbox
BS_AUTOCHECKBOX	Selects automatic checkmarks in a checkbox
BS_AUTORADIOBUTTON	Selects automatic radio buttons
BS_CHECKBOX	Creates a checkbox style button
BS_DEFPUSHBUTTON	Specifies that the button should have a thick border
BS_GROUPBOX	Creates a group box object
BS_LEFTTEXT	Selects left-hand text for a checkbox or radio button
BS_OWNERDRAW	Creates an owner-drawn style button
BS_PUSHBUTTON	Creates a pushbutton-style button
BS_RADIOBUTTON	Creates a radio button-style button

When the user clicks the button, Windows sends a notification message to the parent window. This message is BN_CLICKED for a single click and BN_DOUBLECLICKED for a double-click. In order to respond to the user's action, the application must respond to the button messages it receives. MFC defines the `ON_BN_CLICKED` and `ON_BN_DOUBLECLICKED` macros for adding button messages to your application's message map. ControlApp2 responds to the `BN_CLICKED` notification, and so defines the following message-map entry:

```
ON_BN_CLICKED(IDC_PUSHBUTTON, OnPushbuttonClicked)
```

The macro's two arguments are the control's ID and the name of the function associated with the notification. ControlApp2's `OnPushbuttonClicked()` function, which only displays a message box in response to the `BN_CLICKED` notification, looks like this:

```
void CControlApp2View::OnPushbuttonClicked()
{
    MessageBox("Pushbutton clicked!");
}
```

Although pushbuttons tend to work without your program having to call `CButton` member functions, `CButton` does define a set of member functions that are useful for manipulating the other types of buttons. Later in this chapter, you see how to manage these other types of buttons. For now, Table 6-8 lists the `CButton` class's member functions.

Table 6-8   CButton Member Functions

Function	Description
Create()	Creates a button element and associates it with the CButton object
DrawItem()	Draws an owner-drawn CButton object
GetBitmap()	Gets a handle to the button's bitmap
GetButtonStyle()	Gets the button's style info
GetCheck()	Gets the control's checked state
GetCursor()	Gets a handle to the button's cursor
GetIcon()	Gets a handle to the button's icon
GetState()	Gets state information from the control
SetBitmap()	Sets the button's bitmap
SetButtonStyle()	Sets the button's style
SetCheck()	Sets the button's checked state
SetCursor()	Sets the button's cursor
SetIcon()	Sets the button's icon
SetState()	Sets the button's highlight state

Checkboxes

In the previous section, you got a close look at the CButton class and discovered the types of notification messages your program receives from button objects. A checkbox is another type of button that you can create from the CButton class. Checkboxes usually enable the user to turn options on and off. If the checkbox is checked, the associated option is on; otherwise, the option is off. Figure 6-12 shows a dialog box that contains several checkboxes.

Figure 6-12: Checkboxes usually represent program options.

ControlApp2 displays a single checkbox that you can checkmark by clicking with your mouse. Although this button doesn't represent a program option, it does demonstrate all the programming techniques you need to know to use checkboxes. The program declares the checkbox button object like this in the view class's header file:

```
CButton m_checkButton;
```

The view class's OnCreate() function calls CreateCheckbox(), which creates the checkbox object. CreateCheckbox() looks as follows:

```
void CControlApp2View::CreateCheckbox()
{
    m_checkButton.Create("Check Me",
        BS_AUTOCHECKBOX | WS_CHILD | WS_VISIBLE,
        CRect(20, 215, 140, 255), this, IDC_CHECKBUTTON);
}
```

Notice that this call to CButton's Create() function uses the BS_AUTOCHECKBOX style, which tells MFC to create a checkbox that the program doesn't need to check or uncheck. Instead, the button automatically toggles its checkmark when the user clicks it.

The program handles the checkbox in much the same way it handles the pushbutton—by responding to the BN_CLICKED notification. The message-map entry that associates the notification with a message-response function looks like this:

```
ON_BN_CLICKED(IDC_CHECKBUTTON, OnCheckboxClicked)
```

Now whenever the user clicks the checkbox, MFC calls the `OnCheckbox Clicked()` function, which displays a message box. The function uses a `CButton` member function, `GetCheck()`, to determine whether the checkbox currently is checked and then displays the result in the message box. Windows defines the `BST_CHECKED` and `BST_UNCHECKED` constants; they represent the button's checked or unchecked state, respectively. The `OnCheckboxClicked()` function looks like this:

```
void CControlApp2View::OnCheckboxClicked()
{
    int checked = m_checkButton.GetCheck();

    if (checked == BST_CHECKED)
        MessageBox("Checkbutton checked!");
    else if (checked == BST_UNCHECKED)
        MessageBox("Checkbutton unchecked!");
}
```

Radio Buttons

Another object you can create with the `CButton` class is a radio button, which represents a selection from a mutually exclusive set of options. That is, radio buttons usually come in sets of two or more with only one button selected at a time. ControlApp2 displays three radio buttons in a group box. Strangely, the group box is another object of the `CButton` class. Figure 6-13 shows a dialog box containing a set of radio buttons organized by a group box.

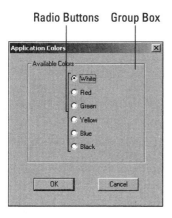

Figure 6-13: Radio buttons represent mutually exclusive selections.

ControlApp2 declares these button objects like this in the view class's header file:

```
CButton m_radioGroup;
CButton m_radioButton1;
CButton m_radioButton2;
CButton m_radioButton3;
```

The view class's `OnCreate()` function calls `CreateRadioButtons()`, which creates the group box and radio button objects. Here is the `CreateRadioButtons()` function:

```
void CControlApp2View::CreateRadioButtons()
{
    m_radioGroup.Create("Radio Buttons",
        BS_GROUPBOX | WS_CHILD | WS_VISIBLE,
        CRect(20, 270, 160, 370), this, 0);

    m_radioButton1.Create("Radio 1",
        BS_AUTORADIOBUTTON | WS_CHILD | WS_VISIBLE |
        WS_GROUP, CRect(40, 295, 110, 315),
        this, IDC_RADIOBUTTON1);

    m_radioButton1.SetCheck(BST_CHECKED);

    m_radioButton2.Create("Radio 2",
        BS_AUTORADIOBUTTON | WS_CHILD | WS_VISIBLE,
        CRect(40, 315, 110, 335), this,
        IDC_RADIOBUTTON2);

    m_radioButton3.Create("Radio 3",
        BS_AUTORADIOBUTTON | WS_CHILD | WS_VISIBLE,
        CRect(40, 335, 110, 355), this,
        IDC_RADIOBUTTON3);
}
```

Notice that the first call to `CButton`'s `Create()` function specifies the `BS_GROUPBOX` style, which tells MFC to create a *group box*. The group box really isn't much of a button at all; instead, it is just a rectangular frame with a caption used to organize a set of controls. Unlike other buttons, a group box is a non-interactive object. The user cannot manipulate the control, nor does the control generate notification messages.

The second call to `Create()` specifies the `BS_AUTORADIOBUTTON` and `WS_GROUP` styles. The former style tells MFC to create a radio button that handles its own selection tasks. (When the user clicks the button, it automatically turns on its check and turns off the check on the previously selected control.) The latter style tells Windows that this radio button is the first of the group. Because the remaining radio buttons don't specify the `WS_GROUP` style, Windows adds them to the group starting with the first radio button. The next control created after the last radio button in the group also should specify the `WS_GROUP` style. That way, Windows knows that the radio button group has ended and a new group has started.

Why must you tell Windows which radio buttons belong together in a group? Remember that you can select only a single radio button in a group at a time. With automatic radio buttons, Windows handles the checking and unchecking of the buttons. Obviously, Windows can't ensure that only a single button is selected at a time if it doesn't know which buttons belong to the group.

The program handles radio buttons in much the same way it handles the pushbutton—by responding to the BN_CLICKED notification. The message-map entries that associate the notifications with message-response functions for each button look like this:

```
ON_BN_CLICKED(IDC_RADIOBUTTON1, OnRadio1Clicked)
ON_BN_CLICKED(IDC_RADIOBUTTON2, OnRadio2Clicked)
ON_BN_CLICKED(IDC_RADIOBUTTON3, OnRadio3Clicked)
```

Now whenever the user clicks a radio button, MFC calls the appropriate message-response function. This function displays a message box telling you which button was clicked. Here are the OnRadio1Clicked(), OnRadio2Clicked(), and OnRadio3Clicked() functions:

```
void CControlApp2View::OnRadio1Clicked()
{
    MessageBox("Radio Button 1");
}

void CControlApp2View::OnRadio2Clicked()
{
    MessageBox("Radio Button 2");
}

void CControlApp2View::OnRadio3Clicked()
{
    MessageBox("Radio Button 3");
}
```

List Boxes

Often, programs need to present the user with a list of items from which the user can select. Windows provides two types of controls to handle this task: list boxes and combo boxes. List boxes, represented in MFC by the CListBox class, are the simpler of these two controls; they amount to little more than a rectangular border containing a list of items. Figure 6-14 shows a list box displayed in an application's window.

ControlApp2 displays a list box that contains seven data items. The program declares its list box like this in the view class's header file:

```
CListBox m_listBox;
```

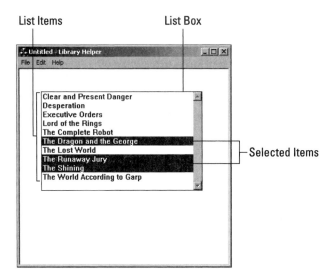

Figure 6-14: List boxes enable the user to select one or more items from a list.

The view class's OnCreate() function calls CreateListBox(), which creates the list box object. The CreateListBox() function looks like this:

```
void CControlApp2View::CreateListBox()
{
    m_listBox.Create(LBS_STANDARD | WS_CHILD |
        WS_VISIBLE | WS_GROUP,
        CRect(200, 40, 340, 120), this, IDC_LIST);

    m_listBox.AddString("List Box Item 1");
    m_listBox.AddString("List Box Item 2");
    m_listBox.AddString("List Box Item 3");
    m_listBox.AddString("List Box Item 4");
    m_listBox.AddString("List Box Item 5");
    m_listBox.AddString("List Box Item 6");
    m_listBox.AddString("List Box Item 7");
}
```

The CListBox class's Create() function has the following signature (I list the arguments' descriptions in order after the signature):

```
BOOL Create(
    DWORD dwStyle,
    const RECT& rect,
    CWnd* pParentWnd,
    UINT nID);
```

`dwStyle`	The list box's style flags
`rect`	A `RECT` or `CRect` object that specifies the list box's size and position
`pParentWnd`	A pointer to the list box's parent window
`nID`	The list box's ID

The list box control's `dwStyle` argument specifies the window and control flags that determine the way the list box looks and acts. You combine these flags, using the `OR` operator, into a single `DWORD` value. You at least should specify the `WS_VISIBLE` and `WS_CHILD` window styles. You also should use one or more of the flags defined specifically for a list box control. Table 6-9 lists these style flags and their descriptions.

Table 6-9 List Box Control Styles

Style Flag	Description
`LBS_DISABLENOSCROLL`	Specifies that the scroll bar should remain visible even when not needed
`LBS_EXTENDEDSEL`	Specifies that the user can extend the selection of multiple items by using the Shift key and the mouse
`LBS_HASSTRINGS`	Specifies that the control is an owner-drawn list box containing string items
`LBS_MULTICOLUMN`	Specifies a multicolumn list box that you can horizontally scroll
`LBS_MULTIPLESEL`	Specifies that the user can select multiple items by clicking each item with the mouse
`LBS_NOINTEGRALHEIGHT`	Specifies that the list box should exactly match the size given, rather than automatically adjust to an even line height
`LBS_NOREDRAW`	Specifies that the list-box display should not be updated when changes are made
`LBS_NOTIFY`	Specifies that the parent window should receive notifications when the user clicks an item
`LBS_OWNERDRAWFIXED`	Specifies that the list box's owner draws the list box's contents, with each item of the same height

Continued

Table 6-9 *(continued)*

Style Flag	Description
LBS_OWNERDRAWVARIABLE	Specifies that the list box's owner draws the list box's contents; each item can be a different height
LBS_SORT	Specifies that the list box's contents should be sorted alphabetically
LBS_STANDARD	Combines the WS_BORDER, WS_VSCROLL, LBS_NOTIFY, and LBS_SORT styles
LBS_USETABSTOPS	Specifies that the list box should expand tab characters in its item strings
LBS_WANTKEYBOARDINPUT	Specifies that the list box's owner should receive WM_VKEYTOITEM or WM_CHARTOITEM messages when the user types in the list box

When the user clicks an item in the list box, Windows sends a notification message to the parent window. This message can be LBN_SELCHANGE for a single click or LBN_DBLCLK for a double-click. In order to respond to the user's action, the application must respond to the list box messages it receives. MFC defines macros you can use to add notifications to the window's message map. ControlApp2 responds to the LBN_DBLCLK notification, and so defines the following message-map entry:

```
ON_LBN_DBLCLK(IDC_LIST, OnListItemDblClk)
```

The OnListItemDblClk() message-response function gets the current selection and displays it in a message box. The source code looks like this:

```
void CControlApp2View::OnListItemDblClk()
{
    int selection = m_listBox.GetCurSel();
    char str[81];
    m_listBox.GetText(selection, str);
    MessageBox(str);
}
```

Here the program first calls the list box's GetCurSel() member function, which returns the zero-based index of the currently selected item. Then the program calls the list box's GetText() member function to get the text of the selected item, finally displaying the text in a message box.

The LBN_DBLCLK notification is one of several messages a list box generates. Table 6-10 lists the entire set of list box control notifications along with their descriptions.

Table 6-10   List Box Notifications

Notification	Description
LBN_DBLCLK	Signals when the user double-clicks an item in the list box
LBN_ERRSPACE	Signals when the list box can't allocate memory
LBN_KILLFOCUS	Signals when the list box loses the input focus
LBN_SELCANCEL	Signals when the current selection is canceled
LBN_SELCHANGE	Signals when the list box selection changes
LBN_SETFOCUS	Signals when the list box receives the input focus

Besides the member functions CListBox inherits from its base classes, CListBox defines many of its own functions. Table 6-11 lists those functions along with their descriptions.

Table 6-11   CListBox Member Functions

Function	Description
AddString()	Adds a string to the list box
CharToItem()	Handles WM_CHAR messages for owner-drawn list boxes without strings
CompareItem()	Called by MFC to get an item's position in a sorted owner-drawn list box
Create()	Creates a list box element and associates it with the CListBox object
DeleteItem()	Called by MFC when the user deletes an item from an owner-drawn list box
DeleteString()	Deletes a string from the list box
Dir()	Adds file names to the list box
DrawItem()	Called by MFC when an element of an owner-drawn list box must be redrawn
FindString()	Finds a string in the list box
FindStringExact()	Finds the first matching string
GetAnchorIndex()	Gets the current anchor's index
GetCaretIndex()	Gets the index of the item with the focus rectangle
GetCount()	Gets the number of strings in the list box

Continued

Table 6-11 *(continued)*

Function	Description
GetCurSel()	Gets the selected item's index
GetHorizontalExtent()	Gets the list box's horizontally scrollable width
GetItemData()	Gets the 32-bit value associated with a given item in the list box
GetItemDataPtr()	Gets a pointer to a given item in the list box
GetItemHeight()	Gets the list box's item height
GetItemRect()	Gets an item's bounding rectangle
GetLocale()	Gets the list box's locale identifier
GetSel()	Gets an item's selection state
GetSelCount()	Gets the number of selected strings
GetSelItems()	Gets the indexes of the selected strings
GetText()	Gets a list-box item
GetTextLen()	Gets an item's length in bytes
GetTopIndex()	Gets the index of the list box's first visible string
InitStorage()	Allocates memory for list-box items
InsertString()	Inserts a string into the list box
ItemFromPoint()	Gets the index of the item nearest the given point
MeasureItem()	Called by MFC to determine list-box dimensions
ResetContent()	Removes all items from the list box
SelectString()	Selects a string in the list box
SelItemRange()	Toggles the selected range of strings
SetAnchorIndex()	Sets the extended selection anchor
SetCaretIndex()	Sets the index of the item with the focus rectangle
SetColumnWidth()	Sets the list box's column width
SetCurSel()	Selects a string in a list box
SetHorizontalExtent()	Sets the list box's horizontally scrollable width
SetItemData()	Sets the 32-bit value associated with a given item in the list box
SetItemDataPtr()	Sets a pointer to a given item in the list box
SetItemHeight()	Sets the list box's item height
SetLocale()	Sets the list box's locale identifier

Function	Description
SetSel()	Toggles an item's selection state
SetTabStops()	Sets the list box's tab positions
SetTopIndex()	Sets the index of the list box's first visible string
VKeyToItem()	Handles WM_KEYDOWN messages for list boxes with the LBS_WANTKEYBOARDINPUT style

Combo Boxes

Combo boxes are a lot like list boxes; the main difference is that a combo box has both a list and an *edit box,* which holds the current selection from the list. Moreover, the user can type a selection into the edit box, rather than select it from the list. Combo boxes are great for places where you don't want to take up a lot of space with a long list because you can create the combo box with a drop-down list. This way, the list doesn't appear until the user requests it by clicking an arrow next to the edit box. Figure 6-15 shows a combo box in an application's main window.

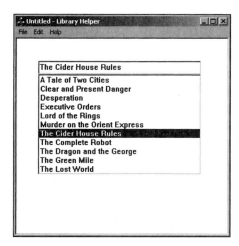

Figure 6-15: Combo boxes combine a list box and an edit box.

ControlApp2 displays two combo boxes: one simple box that always shows its list and one with a drop-down list. The program declares its combo boxes in the view class's header file like this:

```
CComboBox m_comboBox;
CComboBox m_comboBox2;
```

As you can see, the MFC CComboBox class represents Windows combo box controls.

Part I: Fundamental Windows 2000 Programming

The view class's `OnCreate()` function calls `CreateComboBoxes()`, which creates the combo box objects:

```
void CControlApp2View::CreateComboBoxes()
{
    m_comboBox.Create(CBS_SIMPLE | CBS_SORT |
        WS_CHILD | WS_VISIBLE | WS_GROUP,
        CRect(200, 145, 340, 255), this, IDC_COMBOBOX);

    m_comboBox.AddString("Combo Box Item 1");
    m_comboBox.AddString("Combo Box Item 2");
    m_comboBox.AddString("Combo Box Item 3");
    m_comboBox.AddString("Combo Box Item 4");
    m_comboBox.AddString("Combo Box Item 5");
    m_comboBox.AddString("Combo Box Item 6");
    m_comboBox.AddString("Combo Box Item 7");

    m_comboBox2.Create(CBS_DROPDOWN | CBS_SORT |
        WS_CHILD | WS_VISIBLE | WS_VSCROLL,
        CRect(200, 295, 360, 375), this, IDC_COMBOBOX2);

    m_comboBox2.AddString("Combo Box Item 1");
    m_comboBox2.AddString("Combo Box Item 2");
    m_comboBox2.AddString("Combo Box Item 3");
    m_comboBox2.AddString("Combo Box Item 4");
    m_comboBox2.AddString("Combo Box Item 5");
    m_comboBox2.AddString("Combo Box Item 6");
    m_comboBox2.AddString("Combo Box Item 7");
}
```

In `CreateComboBoxes()`, the program creates two combo boxes and populates the boxes with items by calling their `AddString()` member functions. Each call to `AddString()` adds one item to the combo boxes. When the combo boxes appear on the screen, these items are in their lists.

The `CComboBox` class's `Create()` function has the following signature (I list the arguments' descriptions in order after the signature):

```
BOOL Create(
    DWORD dwStyle,
    const RECT& rect,
    CWnd* pParentWnd,
    UINT nID);
```

dwStyle	The combo box's style flags
rect	A `RECT` or `CRect` object that specifies the combo box's size and position
pParentWnd	A pointer to the combo box's parent window
nID	The combo box's ID

The combo box control's `dwStyle` argument specifies the window and control flags that determine the way the combo box looks and acts. You at least should specify the `WS_VISIBLE` and `WS_CHILD` window styles. You also should use one or more of the flags defined specifically for a combo box control. Table 6-12 lists these style flags and their descriptions.

Table 6-12 Combo Box Control Styles

Style Flag	Description
CBS_AUTOHSCROLL	Specifies automatic horizontal scrolling in the combo box's edit control
CBS_DROPDOWN	Specifies a drop-down list
CBS_DROPDOWNLIST	Specifies a combo box with a drop-down list and a static text control in place of the edit box
CBS_HASSTRINGS	Specifies an owner-drawn combo box containing string items
CBS_OEMCONVERT	Specifies that text entered in the combo-box edit control should be converted from ANSI characters to OEM characters and back to ANSI
CBS_OWNERDRAWFIXED	Specifies that the combo box's owner should draw the combo box's contents, with each item of the same height
CBS_OWNERDRAWVARIABLE	Specifies that the combo box's owner should draw the combo box's contents; each item can vary in height
CBS_SIMPLE	Specifies that the combo box's list should be visible always
CBS_SORT	Specifies that the combo box's contents should be sorted alphabetically
CBS_DISABLENOSCROLL	Specifies that the scroll bar should be visible even when not needed
CBS_NOINTEGRALHEIGHT	Specifies that the combo box should exactly match the size given, rather than automatically adjust to an even line height

When the user manipulates the combo box, Windows sends a notification message to the parent window. Because a combo box contains an edit box as well as a list, it can receive more types of notifications than a list box. Clicking an item in the list, however, results in similar notifications: `CBN_SELCHANGE` (or `CBN_SELENDOK`) for a single click and `CBN_DBLCLK` for a double-click. A combo box also receives notifications when the user changes the text in the text box, or when the combo box displays or closes its drop-down list.

In order to respond to the user's action, the application must respond to the combo box messages it receives. MFC defines macros you can use to add notifications to the window's message map. ControlApp2 responds to the CBN_DBLCLK notification for the first combo box (the one without the drop-down list) and responds to CBN_SELENDOK for the second combo box (the one with the drop-down list). In order to respond to these notifications, the program defines the following message-map entries:

```
ON_CBN_DBLCLK(IDC_COMBOBOX, OnComboItemDblClk)
ON_CBN_SELENDOK(IDC_COMBOBOX2, OnComboSelEndOk)
```

In either case, the message-response functions OnComboItemDblClk() and OnComboSelEndOk() call the GetCurSel() member function to get the index of the selected item. Then they call the GetLBText() member function to get the actual item, displaying the text in a message box. The OnComboItem DblClk() and OnComboSelEndOk() functions look like this:

```
void CControlApp2View::OnComboItemDblClk()
{
    int selection = m_comboBox.GetCurSel();
    char str[81];
    m_comboBox.GetLBText(selection, str);
    MessageBox(str);
}

void CControlApp2View::OnComboSelEndOk()
{
    int selection = m_comboBox2.GetCurSel();
    char str[81];
    m_comboBox2.GetLBText(selection, str);
    MessageBox(str);
}
```

Table 6-13 lists the many types of notification messages that combo boxes can generate. These notifications represent not only selections by the user, but also other events that occur in the edit box and list components.

Table 6-13 Combo Box Notifications

Notification	Description
CBN_CLOSEUP	Signals when the combo box's list closes
CBN_DBLCLK	Signals when the user double-clicks an item in the combo box
CBN_DROPDOWN	Signals when the combo box's list drops down
CBN_EDITCHANGE	Signals when the user changes the text in the combo box's edit control (sent after CBN_EDITUPDATE)
CBN_EDITUPDATE	Signals when the user changes the text in the combo box's edit control, but before the change appears on the screen (sent before CBN_EDITCHANGE)

Notification	Description
CBN_ERRSPACE	Signals that the combo box cannot allocate memory
CBN_KILLFOCUS	Signals when the combo box loses the input focus
CBN_SELCHANGE	Signals when the combo box's current selection changes
CBN_SELENDCANCEL	Signals that the combo box's current selection should be canceled
CBN_SELENDOK	Signals that the combo box's current selection is valid, rather than canceled
CBN_SETFOCUS	Signals when the combo box receives the input focus

Changing a Control's Color

If you just throw a bunch of controls into a window, you may be surprised at what you get (see Figure 6-16). Notice that the controls' background colors don't match the window's white background. If you place these controls in a dialog box, which normally has a gray background, they fit right in. But when you place the controls in a non-dialog box window, you have to deal with color.

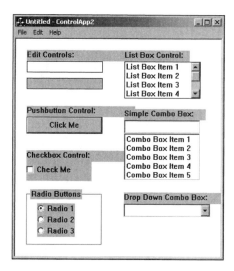

Figure 6-16: The controls' background colors don't match the window's background color.

Unfortunately, setting a control's background color isn't as easy as you might think. You don't find anything like a SetBackgroundColor() member function in the control classes. Instead, you must respond to the WM_CTLCOLOR message, which Windows sends just before it draws a control. To add this message to your window's message map, use the `ON_WM_CTLCOLOR` macro:

```
ON_WM_CTLCOLOR()
```

As you can see, this macro requires no arguments. If you include the macro in your message map, you also must implement the `OnCtlColor()` function. MFC calls this function when it receives the `WM_CTLCOLOR` message. That function's signature and a description of its arguments follow:

```
HBRUSH CControlApp2View::OnCtlColor(
    CDC* pDC,
    CWnd* pWnd,
    UINT nCtrlColor);
```

pDC	A pointer to the device context used to draw the control
pWnd	A pointer to the control
nID	The type of WM_CTLCOLOR message

The third argument requires a little extra explanation. There are actually several types of `WM_CTLCOLOR` messages, each with their own IDs. The message types represent the type of control that generates the `WM_CTLCOLOR` message. Table 6-14 lists these IDs along with their descriptions.

Table 6-14 Types of WM_CTLCOLOR Messages

Message ID	Description
CTLCOLOR_BTN	Message generated by a button control
CTLCOLOR_DLG	Message generated by a dialog box
CTLCOLOR_EDIT	Message generated by an edit control
CTLCOLOR_LISTBOX	Message generated by a list box
CTLCOLOR_MSGBOX	Message generated by a message box
CTLCOLOR_SCROLLBAR	Message generated by a scroll bar
CTLCOLOR_STATIC	Message generated by a static control, as well as by checkboxes, radio buttons, group boxes, and disabled edit boxes

In ControlApp2, the `OnCtlColor()` function looks like this:

```
HBRUSH CControlApp2View::OnCtlColor
    (CDC* pDC, CWnd* pWnd, UINT nCtrlColor)
{
    if ((nCtrlColor == CTLCOLOR_STATIC) &&
        (pWnd->m_hWnd != m_edit2.m_hWnd))
        return (HBRUSH)m_whiteBrush;

    return CView::OnCtlColor(pDC, pWnd, nCtrlColor);
}
```

Here, `OnCtlColor()` first checks whether it receives a `CTLCOLOR_STATIC` type of `WM_CTLCOLOR` message. The function also checks that the control generating the message isn't the read-only edit control because the program needs to retain that edit control's gray background color. If the message is one the function is waiting for, it returns a white brush from the function. Windows then uses the brush to paint the control's background, rather than use the default gray brush.

If you want to change the text color in `OnCtlColor()`, you can call the device context's `SetTextColor()` function. If you want to change the text background color, you can call the DC's `SetBkColor()` function. Those function calls might look like this:

```
pDC->SetTextColor(RGB(255,255,255));
pDC->SetBkColor(RGB(0,0,255));
```

These lines set the text color to white and the text background color to blue.

Problems & Solutions

Dialog Boxes as Main Windows

PROBLEM: *I want my application's main window to contain a number of controls, but I don't want to go through all the hassle of creating and positioning the controls in the window class. Isn't there an easier way?*

SOLUTION: One technique you can try is creating your application using a dialog box as its main window. You can accomplish this handy trick easily through MFC and AppWizard. The big bonus is, because the main window holds a dialog box, you can define the controls using Visual C++'s dialog box editor.

First, create a new AppWizard application. When the Step 1 dialog box appears, select the Dialog based option (as shown in Figure 6-17).

Continued

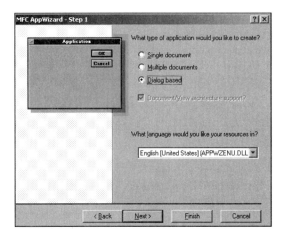

Figure 6-17: In AppWizard's Step 1 dialog box, you can select a dialog box as a main window.

This selection changes the remaining AppWizard steps. For example, Figure 6-18 shows the Step 2 dialog box, which now displays options that apply only to dialog box-based windows. You do not see options for a regular frame window.

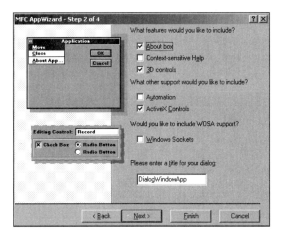

Figure 6-18: AppWizard provides different options for dialog box-based windows.

When you finish selecting your application's options, AppWizard creates the skeleton application. Now, however, the program consists of as few as two classes: the application class and the dialog box class that represents the window's display. (You also may have a `CAboutDlg` class if you opted to include an About dialog box in the program.)

Continued

To create your window's user interface, first switch to the ResourceView page of the project workspace window. There, you find a dialog box with an ID created from your application's name. For example, if you call the project MyApp, the dialog box ID is ID_MYAPP_DIALOG. This is the dialog box resource that represents your application's user interface. Double-click the ID to open the dialog box into the editor, as shown in Figure 6-19.

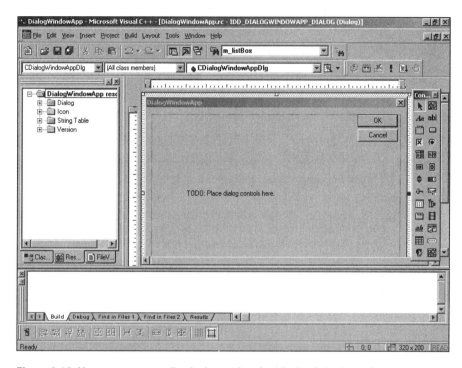

Figure 6-19: You create your application's user interface in the dialog box editor.

All the controls you place in the dialog box appear in your application's main window. Moreover, the main window is the same size as the dialog box resource. As an example, suppose that you leave the dialog box in its default state (as shown in Figure 6-19). When you compile and run the application, you see the window shown in Figure 6-20.

You can respond to the dialog box's controls within the dialog box class by handling notification messages. In fact, in every way, the dialog box class that represents the application's user interface works just like a normal dialog box. You can apply everything you know about dialog boxes to the construction of your application's dialog box-based window.

Continued

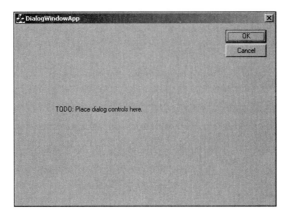

Figure 6-20: The application as it appears with the default dialog box resource

The application creates and displays the dialog box in the application class's InitInstance() function. Here is the code that accomplishes this task:

```
CMyAppDlg dlg;
m_pMainWnd = &dlg;
int nResponse = dlg.DoModal();
if (nResponse == IDOK)
{
    // TODO: Place code here to handle
    //   when the dialog is
    //   dismissed with OK
}
else if (nResponse == IDCANCEL)
{
    // TODO: Place code here to handle
    //   when the dialog is
    //   dismissed with Cancel
}
```

Notice the comments that indicate where you process dialog box data when the user dismisses the dialog box with the OK or Cancel button.

Manipulating Controls in Dialog Boxes

Most often, you see the standard controls used in dialog boxes. The controls you place in the dialog box handle themselves, although you may have to initialize some controls such as list boxes and combo boxes. If you haven't worked much with MFC dialog boxes, you may find managing controls other than edit boxes and buttons in a dialog box a little tricky. In this section, you see how to create a new dialog box and add source code to the classes.

Creating the Application Skeleton

Location: `WinPrgS\Chap06\DialogControlsApp`

To better understand how to manipulate controls in dialog boxes, you create the DialogControlsApp application. This application also appears on this book's CD-ROM. To create the first part of DialogControlsApp, you need to perform the following steps:

1. Start a new AppWizard project called DialogControlsApp, as shown in Figure 6-21.

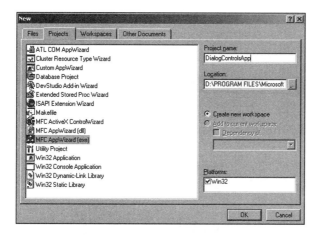

Figure 6-21: MFC's New dialog box is displayed when you create the DialogControlsApp project.

2. In the Step 1 dialog box, select the Single document option (as shown in Figure 6-22).

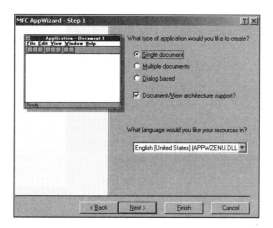

Figure 6-22: DialogControlsApp uses a single document window.

3. In the Step 2 dialog box, keep the database support setting to None—its default option (as shown in Figure 6-23).

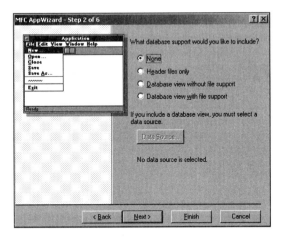

Figure 6-23: DialogControlsApp needs no database support.

4. In the Step 3 dialog box, turn off the ActiveX Controls option (as shown in Figure 6-24).

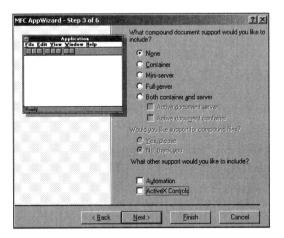

Figure 6-24: DialogControlsApp needs no ActiveX support.

5. In the Step 4 dialog box, turn off all options except 3D controls, as shown in Figure 6-25.

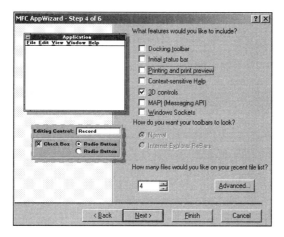

Figure 6-25: DialogControlsApp doesn't have a toolbar, a status bar, printing capabilities, or context-sensitive help support.

6. In the Step 5 dialog box, select the option to include MFC as a statically linked library (as shown in Figure 6-26).

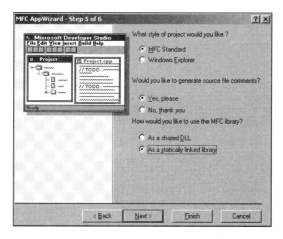

Figure 6-26: Linking this project to MFC's static library

7. In the Step 6 dialog box (see Figure 6-27), click Finish to accept the suggested classes. When the New Project Information dialog box appears, click OK to create the skeleton application.

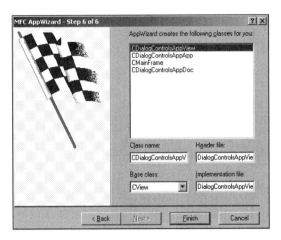

Figure 6-27: AppWizard suggests the final classes for the application.

At this point, you've created the basic application. You can compile and run the program if you like. You at least should save your work before moving on to the next section where you create the dialog box resource.

Creating the New Dialog Box

Now that you have the basic application created, it's time to put together the dialog box resource and its associated class. Perform the following steps to complete this task:

1. Select the Resource command from Visual C++'s Insert menu. The Insert Resource dialog box appears, as shown in Figure 6-28.

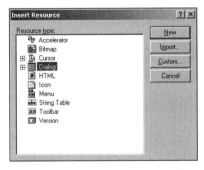

Figure 6-28: You can add resource objects from the Insert Resource dialog box.

2. Double-click Dialog in the Resource type box. A new dialog box appears in Visual C++'s dialog box editor (see Figure 6-29).

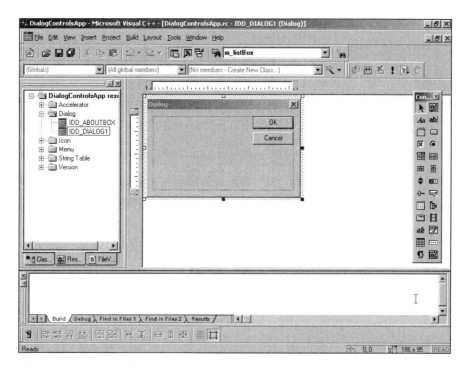

Figure 6-29: The new dialog box appears in the editor window.

3. Enlarge the box and add the list box shown in Figure 6-30.

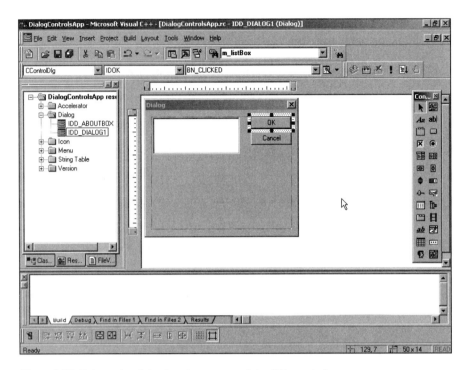

Figure 6-30: Enlarge the dialog box to accommodate all its controls.

4. Add a pushbutton control to the dialog box, setting its label to "Click Me" (see Figure 6-31).

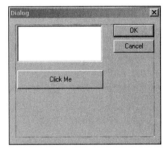

Figure 6-31: The dialog box gets a new button.

5. Add two edit controls to the dialog box, as shown in Figure 6-32.

Chapter 6: Standard Controls   **209**

Figure 6-32: The dialog box displayed with its two new edit controls

6. Change the second edit box's style to read-only, as shown in Figure 6-33.

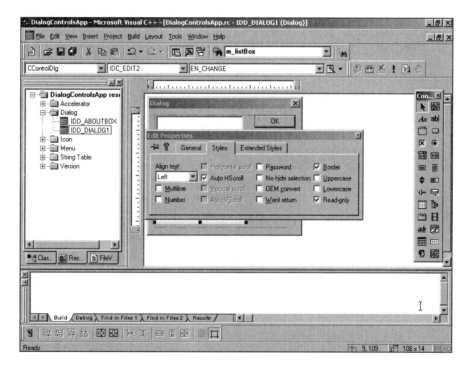

Figure 6-33: Here is the Edit Properties dialog box displayed over the dialog box you're creating. Notice that the read-only style grays out the edit box's background.

7. Double-click the dialog box. The Adding a Class dialog box appears, as shown in Figure 6-34.

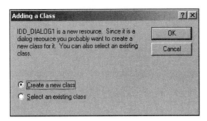

Figure 6-34: You need to create a class for the new dialog box.

8. Make sure the Create a new class option is selected and click OK. The New Class dialog box appears.

9. Type `CControlDlg` into the Name box (see Figure 6-35). This is the new dialog box class's name.

Figure 6-35: The dialog box class gets a name.

10. Click OK to dismiss the New Class dialog box, revealing the ClassWizard property sheet. Select the Member Variables page, as shown in Figure 6-36.

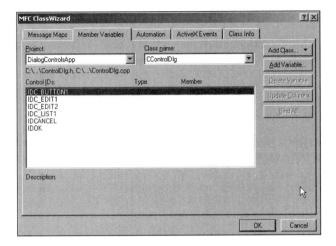

Figure 6-36: On the Member Variables page, you can add variables to the new class.

11. Double-click `IDC_LIST1` in the Control IDs box. The Add Member Variable dialog box appears. Name the new variable `m_listStr`, as shown in Figure 6-37.

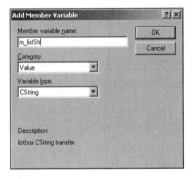

Figure 6-37: The m_listStr variable holds the list box's selection.

12. Click OK to dismiss the Add Member Variable dialog box. Then click OK to dismiss ClassWizard.

Now you've created the dialog box and the class that represents the dialog box in the application. The final step is to add the source code needed to complete the application, which you do in the next section.

Adding Source Code to the View Class

At this point, the application doesn't do much. For example, although you've created a new dialog box, you have no way of displaying it on the screen. Moreover, the program doesn't add items to the list box in the dialog box. An empty list box isn't too useful. In this section, you add the program lines that enable the application to display the dialog box. Perform the following steps to add this functionality:

1. Load the `DialogControlsAppView.cpp` file and add the following line near the top of the file, after the line `#include DialogControls AppView.h`:

   `#include "ControlDlg.h"`

2. Press Ctrl+W to bring up ClassWizard. Add a message-response function for the `WM_LBUTTONDOWN` message, as shown in Figure 6-38. (Make sure you have `CDialogControlsAppView` selected in the Class name box.)

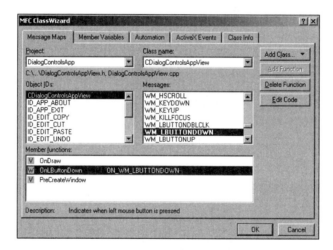

Figure 6-38: ClassWizard adding the OnLButtonDown() message-response function

3. Click the Edit Code button to bring the new function up in the editor (see Figure 6-39).

Chapter 6: Standard Controls   213

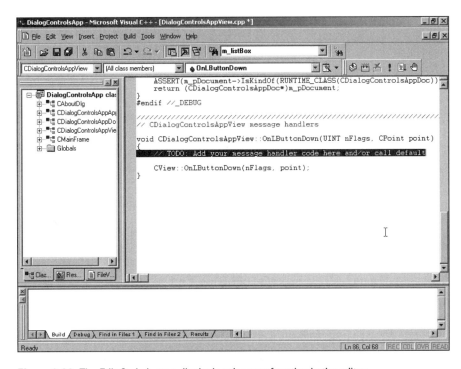

Figure 6-39: The Edit Code button displaying the new function in the editor

4. Add the following lines to the `OnLButtonDown()` function, right after the `// TODO: Add your message handler code here and/or call default` comment:

```
CControlDlg dlg(this);

int result = dlg.DoModal();

if (result == IDOK)
{
    CString str = dlg.m_listStr;
    if (str != "")
        MessageBox(str);
}
```

You've completed the application's view class. Press Ctrl+F5 to compile and run the program. When you do, the application's main window appears. Click the window, and your new dialog box appears, as shown in Figure 6-40. You can manipulate the dialog box's controls, but the program won't respond to your changes yet. You take care of that in the next section, where you complete the application.

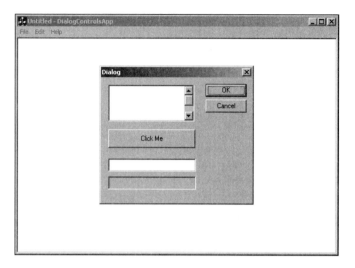

Figure 6-40: The application can display the dialog box now.

Adding Source Code to the Dialog Box Class

Now that you've created a new dialog box and finished the application's view class, you're ready to complete the dialog box class: CControlDlg. Along the way, you discover how to initialize controls in a dialog box and respond to the controls' notifications. Perform the following steps to complete the DialogControlsApp application:

1. In the ClassView page of the Project Window, right-click the CControlDlg class. The class's context menu appears (see Figure 6-41).

2. Select the context menu's Add Member Function command. The Add Member Function dialog box appears.

3. Type BOOL into the Function Type box, type OnInitDialog() into the Function Declaration box, and select the Protected access option (as shown in Figure 6-42).

4. Add the lines shown here to the new OnInitDialog() function:

```
CDialog::OnInitDialog();

CListBox* listBox = (CListBox*)GetDlgItem(IDC_LIST1);
listBox->AddString("List Box Item 1");
listBox->AddString("List Box Item 2");
listBox->AddString("List Box Item 3");
listBox->AddString("List Box Item 4");
listBox->AddString("List Box Item 5");
listBox->AddString("List Box Item 6");

return TRUE;
```

Chapter 6: Standard Controls 215

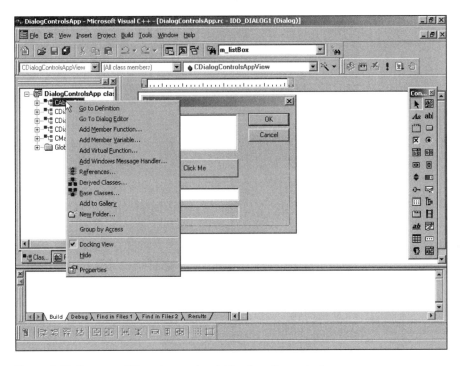

Figure 6-41: You can add functions and variables from the context menu.

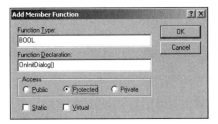

Figure 6-42: Use the Add Member Function dialog box to define the new function.

5. Press Ctrl+W to display ClassWizard. Make the following selections: CControlDlg from the drop-down list in the Class name box, IDC_LIST1 in the Object IDs box, and LBN_SELCHANGE in the Messages box (see Figure 6-43).

216 Part I: Fundamental Windows 2000 Programming

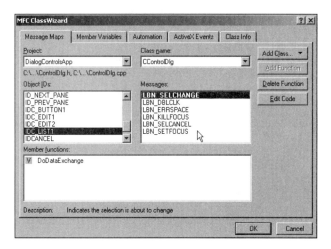

Figure 6-43: You can add notification response functions to a dialog box with ClassWizard.

6. Click the Add Function button. When the Add Member Function dialog box appears, click OK to accept the suggested function name. ClassWizard adds the function to the class.

7. Click the Edit Code button. The new `OnSelchangeList1()` function appears in the edit window. Add the following lines to the function:

```
CListBox* listBox = (CListBox*)GetDlgItem(IDC_LIST1);
int selection = listBox->GetCurSel();
listBox->GetText(selection, m_listStr);
```

8. Use ClassWizard to add the `OnButton1()` function to the dialog box class, as shown in Figure 6-44.

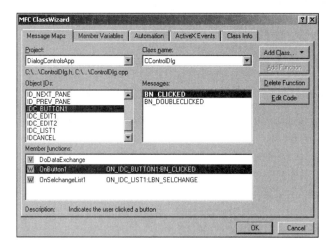

Figure 6-44: The OnButton1() function responds to button clicks.

9. Click the Edit Code button. The new `OnButton1()` function appears in the edit window. Add the following lines to the function:

   ```
   CButton* button = (CButton*)GetDlgItem(IDC_BUTTON1);
   CString str;
   button->GetWindowText(str);
   if (str == "Click Me")
       button->SetWindowText("I've Been Clicked!");
   else
       button->SetWindowText("Click Me");
   ```

10. Use ClassWizard to add the `OnChangeEdit1()` function to the dialog box class, as shown in Figure 6-45.

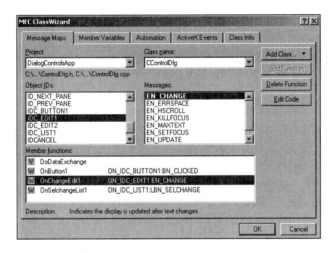

Figure 6-45: The OnChangeEdit1() function responds to changes in the first edit control.

11. Click the Edit Code button. The new `OnChangeEdit1()` function appears in the edit window. Add the following lines to the function:

    ```
    CEdit* edit1 = (CEdit*)GetDlgItem(IDC_EDIT1);
    CEdit* edit2 = (CEdit*)GetDlgItem(IDC_EDIT2);
    CString str;
    edit1->GetWindowText(str);
    edit2->SetWindowText(str);
    ```

The DialogControlsApp application is complete. You can compile and run the program by pressing Ctrl+F5 on your keyboard. Here are the completed `CControlDlg` class header and implementation files so that you can see the source code you added in the context of the entire class:

```
/////////////////////////////////////////////////////
// CControlDlg dialog

class CControlDlg : public CDialog
{
// Construction
```

```cpp
public:
    CControlDlg(CWnd* pParent = NULL);

// Dialog Data
    //{{AFX_DATA(CControlDlg)
    enum { IDD = IDD_DIALOG1 };
    CString    m_listStr;
    //}}AFX_DATA


// Overrides
    // ClassWizard generated virtual function overrides
    //{{AFX_VIRTUAL(CControlDlg)
    protected:
    // DDX/DDV support
    virtual void DoDataExchange(CDataExchange* pDX);
    //}}AFX_VIRTUAL

// Implementation
protected:
    BOOL OnInitDialog();

    // Generated message map functions
    //{{AFX_MSG(CControlDlg)
    afx_msg void OnSelchangeList1();
    afx_msg void OnButton1();
    afx_msg void OnChangeEdit1();
    //}}AFX_MSG
    DECLARE_MESSAGE_MAP()
};
```

Listing 6-11: The CControlDlg class's header file

```cpp
// ControlDlg.cpp : implementation file
//

#include "stdafx.h"
#include "DialogControlsApp.h"
#include "ControlDlg.h"

#ifdef _DEBUG
#define new DEBUG_NEW
#undef THIS_FILE
static char THIS_FILE[] = __FILE__;
#endif

/////////////////////////////////////////////////////////////////
// CControlDlg dialog


CControlDlg::CControlDlg(CWnd* pParent /*=NULL*/)
    : CDialog(CControlDlg::IDD, pParent)
{
    //{{AFX_DATA_INIT(CControlDlg)
    m_listStr = _T("");
```

```
        //}}AFX_DATA_INIT
}


void CControlDlg::DoDataExchange(CDataExchange* pDX)
{
    CDialog::DoDataExchange(pDX);
    //{{AFX_DATA_MAP(CControlDlg)
    DDX_LBString(pDX, IDC_LIST1, m_listStr);
    //}}AFX_DATA_MAP
}


BEGIN_MESSAGE_MAP(CControlDlg, CDialog)
    //{{AFX_MSG_MAP(CControlDlg)
    ON_LBN_SELCHANGE(IDC_LIST1, OnSelchangeList1)
    ON_BN_CLICKED(IDC_BUTTON1, OnButton1)
    ON_EN_CHANGE(IDC_EDIT1, OnChangeEdit1)
    //}}AFX_MSG_MAP
END_MESSAGE_MAP()

/////////////////////////////////////////////////////////
// CControlDlg message handlers

BOOL CControlDlg::OnInitDialog()
{
    CDialog::OnInitDialog();

    CListBox* listBox = (CListBox*)GetDlgItem(IDC_LIST1);
    listBox->AddString("List Box Item 1");
    listBox->AddString("List Box Item 2");
    listBox->AddString("List Box Item 3");
    listBox->AddString("List Box Item 4");
    listBox->AddString("List Box Item 5");
    listBox->AddString("List Box Item 6");

    return TRUE;
}

void CControlDlg::OnSelchangeList1()
{
    // TODO: Add your control notification
    //    handler code here

    CListBox* listBox = (CListBox*)GetDlgItem(IDC_LIST1);
    int selection = listBox->GetCurSel();
    listBox->GetText(selection, m_listStr);
}

void CControlDlg::OnButton1()
{
    // TODO: Add your control notification
```

```
    //    handler code here

    CButton* button = (CButton*)GetDlgItem(IDC_BUTTON1);
    CString str;
    button->GetWindowText(str);
    if (str == "Click Me")
        button->SetWindowText("I've Been Clicked!");
    else
        button->SetWindowText("Click Me");
}

void CControlDlg::OnChangeEdit1()
{
    // TODO: If this is a RICHEDIT control,
    //    the control will not
    //    send this notification unless you
    //    override the CDialog::OnInitDialog()
    //    function to send the EM_SETEVENTMASK
    //    message to the control
    //    with the ENM_CHANGE flag ORed into
    //    the lParam mask.

    // TODO: Add your control notification
    //    handler code here

    CEdit* edit1 = (CEdit*)GetDlgItem(IDC_EDIT1);
    CEdit* edit2 = (CEdit*)GetDlgItem(IDC_EDIT2);
    CString str;
    edit1->GetWindowText(str);
    edit2->SetWindowText(str);
}
```

Running DialogControlsApp

When you run DialogControlsApp, you see the application's main window. Note that the program's menu bar contains commands that you didn't implement in the previous steps. The only valid menu commands are the File menu's Exit command and the Help menu's About DialogControlsApp command. (AppWizard adds the other commands by default. Normally, you either implement the commands or remove them from the menus. Although the Open and Save commands display dialog boxes, they don't open or save anything.)

To display the program's dialog box, click the window. When the dialog box appears (see Figure 6-46), you can experiment with the controls. Click the button, and its caption changes. Type something into the edit control, and the read-only control displays the same text. Finally, select an item in the list box and click OK to dismiss the dialog box. When you do, a message box appears displaying the item you picked.

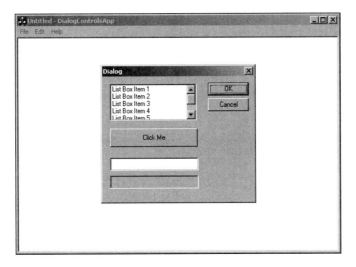

Figure 6-46: DialogControlsApp's dialog box illustrates how to manage standard controls.

Understanding DialogControlsApp

DialogControlsApp demonstrates some important techniques for manipulating controls in a dialog box. First, just as you can initialize window controls in a class's `OnCreate()` function, you also can initialize dialog box controls in the dialog class's `OnInitDialog()` function. This function responds to the `WM_INITDIALOG` window's message. MFC calls `OnInitDialog()` just before the dialog box is displayed, so it's a great place to do any last-minute processing for the dialog box. In the `CControlDlg` class's `OnInitDialog()` function, the program adds items to the list box.

The other controls in the dialog box don't require initializing in `OnInitDialog()`, but they all generate notification messages that the dialog box handles. When you click the pushbutton, for example, the control generates a `BN_CLICKED` notification. The dialog box class handles this notification in its `OnButton1()` member function. In that function, the program first gets a pointer to the pushbutton control:

```
CButton* button = (CButton*)GetDlgItem(IDC_BUTTON1);
```

`GetDlgItem()` takes one argument: the ID of the control for which you want a pointer. The function returns a `CWnd` pointer, so the returned value must be cast to a pointer of the correct type—which in this case is `CButton*`.

After getting a pointer to the button, the program retrieves the button's current text label:

```
CString str;
button->GetWindowText(str);
```

The program then compares the button's label to the original value and sets the label to the appropriate new value:

```
if (str == "Click Me")
    button->SetWindowText("I've Been Clicked!");
else
    button->SetWindowText("Click Me");
```

When you type in the edit control box, the control generates EN_CHANGE notifications that the OnChangeEdit1() message-response function handles. In that function, the program first gets pointers to the two edit controls:

```
CEdit* edit1 = (CEdit*)GetDlgItem(IDC_EDIT1);
CEdit* edit2 = (CEdit*)GetDlgItem(IDC_EDIT2);
```

The program then copies the text from the first control to the second, read-only control:

```
CString str;
edit1->GetWindowText(str);
edit2->SetWindowText(str);
```

The last control is the list box. When you make a selection in the list box, the control generates an LBN_SELCHANGE notification. The dialog box class handles this notification in its OnSelchangeList1() function. That function first gets a pointer to the list box control:

```
CListBox* listBox = (CListBox*)GetDlgItem(IDC_LIST1);
```

The function then gets the currently selected item's index:

```
int selection = listBox->GetCurSel();
```

Finally, the function copies the selected item's text into the dialog box class's member variable m_listStr, which holds the list box string so the view class can access it:

```
listBox->GetText(selection, m_listStr);
```

The view class creates and displays the dialog box in its OnLButtonDown() function. When the user dismisses the dialog box, OnLButtonDown() gets the selected string from the dialog box and displays it in a message box:

```
if (result == IDOK)
{
    CString str = dlg.m_listStr;
    if (str != "")
        MessageBox(str);
}
```

Summary

As you've learned in this chapter, you can add controls to both dialog boxes and non-dialog box windows. When adding controls to a dialog box, you use Visual C++'s dialog box editor to create the user interface. However, when adding controls to a non-dialog box window, you must create instances of the control classes and call the objects' Create() functions. The arguments you supply to Create() determine not only the control's position, but also the way the control looks and acts.

Also discussed in this chapter:

- Standard controls include static text, edit boxes, pushbuttons, checkboxes, radio buttons, list boxes, group boxes, and combo box controls.
- When placing controls in non-dialog box windows, you explicitly must specify the control's location and style flags when you call the control's Create() function.
- You respond to controls by creating message-response functions for the control's notifications.
- You can change a control's colors by implementing the MFC OnCtlColor() function.
- In a dialog box class, you override the OnInitDialog() function to initialize the dialog box's controls.
- When you place controls in a dialog box, you can respond to the controls' notifications to manage the user's interaction with the controls.

Chapter 7

Common Controls

In This Chapter

- ▶ Introducing the common controls
- ▶ Programming progress bars, sliders, and spinners
- ▶ Programming image list controls
- ▶ Programming list view and tree view controls
- ▶ Exploring sample applications

In the previous chapter, you learned to incorporate Windows' standard controls into your applications. While these basic controls are the building blocks of most user interfaces, they aren't anywhere near as sophisticated as the newer common controls. Windows 2000's common controls, which include list views and tree views, add sizzle to mundane applications while providing the user with a fully modern user interface. In this chapter, you discover how to create and manage these important elements of a modern Windows application.

Introducing the Common Controls

Windows 2000's common controls include some handy devices that you see often, not only in applications but also in Windows itself. In fact, many of Windows' utilities, such as Windows Explorer, rely on these advanced controls in order to present an elegant user interface. These extended controls, which were introduced with Windows 95, include the following:

Progress bar A *progress bar* shows the status of an ongoing operation by filling the control's display area with a colored bar. The bar displays an operation's degree of completion. For example, a progress bar can track the saving of a large file. When the file is half saved, the progress bar's display is half filled.

Slider	A *slider* (often called a trackbar) is a control for selecting a value from a range of values. The user drags the slider's thumb to select a value. When dragged, the thumb slides in the control's track (either horizontally or vertically) depending upon how you set up the control. Sliders also serve to select a range of values.
Spinner	A *spinner* (often called an up-down control) provides another way to select a value from a range of values. The spinner control is made up of two arrows, which enable the user to raise or lower a displayed value.
Image list	An *image list* control usually stores images for toolbar buttons or stores the images used to display a tree in a tree view control. An image list, however, can store images for any use. For example, you can use an image list to store a group of images that make up an animation sequence. The images are stored in memory and can't be seen on the screen until the program needs them.
List view	A *list view* control displays an organized group of items. How the items are displayed depends upon the list view's current setting. For instance, a list view control can display just a list of items or it can display the list in columns that include details about the items.
Tree view	A *tree view* control displays items in a hierarchy. Parent items (such as folders on a disk) can contain child items (such as subfolders or files on a disk). You can open and close parent items by clicking them with a mouse. Closing a parent item hides its child items.
Toolbar	A *toolbar* is a row of controls (usually buttons) that provides quick access to important commands. The buttons on a toolbar often mirror the commands found in the application's menus. However, a toolbar often features drop-down list boxes that enable you to select fonts, colors, and other document attributes.
Status bar	A *status bar* provides a place for an application to display command descriptions and status information, such as the state of the keyboard and the position of the text cursor. It usually sits at the bottom of an application's display.

Because the toolbar and status bar controls are integrated so fully into AppWizard applications, you don't spend any time here exploring their classes. However, there's a lot to learn about the other controls. In the remainder of this chapter, you not only learn to program the common controls (starting with the simplest and moving to the most complex), but you also get hands-on experience with applications that demonstrate the controls.

Basic Common Controls

Some common controls are easier to program than others. Specifically, you can add progress bar, slider, and spinner controls to your applications with little fuss. Tree view and list view controls, on the other hand, require a lot of initialization and handling. In this section, you examine the more basic progress bar, slider, and spinner controls, as well as learn how to add them to your applications. You also learn how to manage them once you create them.

The CommonControlsApp Sample Application

Location: `WinPrgS\Chap07\CommonControlsApp`

Before you look at how to create and program the progress bar, slider, and spinner controls, you should take some time out to see them in action. On this book's CD-ROM, find the CommonControlsApp application that lists and demonstrates the basic common controls. When you run the program, you see the window shown in Figure 7-1.

The image list control is not part of CommonControlsApp, as it is a nonvisual control that the user cannot manipulate.

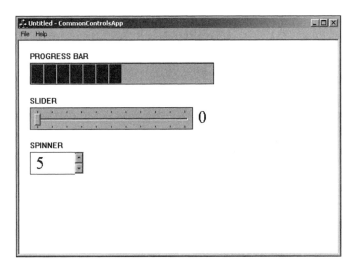

Figure 7-1: The CommonControlsApp application displays a progress bar, slider, and spinner in action.

To get the progress bar going, click the window. When you do, the progress bar starts to fill with colored blocks. In this case, the progress bar doesn't represent any ongoing process (except arriving timer events), but you can get an idea of how the control looks. To stop the progress bar, click the window again.

To try out the slider, use your mouse to move the slider's thumb. When you do, the number to the right of the control displays the slider's new current setting. The spinner control works similarly, except you change the value by clicking the arrows.

Understanding the OnCreate() Function

Creating each control in the view class is an almost identical process, so you now take a look at how the CommonControlsApp completes this task at once. The parts of the program that implement the controls are fairly simple. First, the program creates the controls in the view class's OnCreate() function, which responds to the Windows WM_CREATE message. OnCreate() looks like this:

```
int CCommonControlsAppView::OnCreate
    (LPCREATESTRUCT lpCreateStruct)
{
    if (CView::OnCreate(lpCreateStruct) == -1)
        return -1;

    // TODO: Add your specialized creation code here

    InitStaticText();
    InitProgressBar();
    InitSlider();
    InitSpinner();

    m_whiteBrush.CreateSolidBrush(RGB(255,255,255));

    return 0;
}
```

As you can see here, OnCreate() doesn't create the program's controls directly. Instead, it calls four member functions — InitStaticText(), InitProgressBar(), InitSlider(), and InitSpinner() — to handle the task. OnCreate() also creates a white brush that the program uses to draw the controls' backgrounds so that they match the window background. The program changes the background color in response to the WM_CTLCOLOR windows message, which is handled by the OnCtlColor() function:

```
HBRUSH CCommonControlsAppView::OnCtlColor
    (CDC* pDC, CWnd* pWnd, UINT nCtrlColor)
```

```
{
    if ((nCtrlColor == CTLCOLOR_STATIC) &&
        (pWnd->m_hWnd != m_slider.m_hWnd))
        return (HBRUSH)m_whiteBrush;

    return CView::OnCtlColor(pDC, pWnd, nCtrlColor);
}
```

You learn to modify control colors in Chapter 6, so please refer to that chapter if you don't understand how the OnCtlColor() message-response function works.

To take a closer look at how static controls function in this application, please take a look at the code in the CommonControlsApp folder in Chapter 7 of this book's CD-ROM. You also may be interested in looking at how the code is written to display text in a larger font.

The Progress Bar Control

As previously mentioned, the progress bar control graphically displays the status of an ongoing operation. It does this by filling the bar with colored blocks as the operation progresses. Represented in MFC by the CProgressCtrl class, the progress bar is the easiest to use of the common controls. You just display the control and increment its display at appropriate times during the operation that the bar represents. Figure 7-2 shows a progress bar control that indicates an operation about half completed.

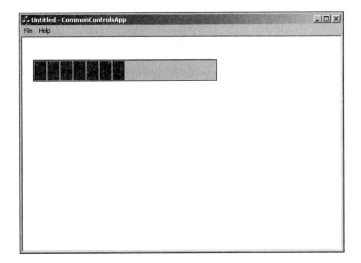

Figure 7-2: A progress bar fills with colored blocks as an operation progresses.

Creating and programming a progress bar control

To create a progress bar, you first define an object of the `CProgressCtrl` class:

```
CProgressCtrl m_progBar;
```

You then call the object's `Create()` member function, which creates the actual progress bar control and associates it with the `CProgressCtrl` object. The `CProgressCtrl` class's `Create()` function has the following signature. I list the arguments' descriptions in order after the signature.

```
BOOL Create(
    DWORD dwStyle,
    const RECT& rect,
    CWnd* pParentWnd,
    UINT nID);
```

dwStyle	The progress bar's style flags
rect	A `RECT` or `CRect` object that specifies the progress bar's size and position
pParentWnd	A pointer to the progress bar's parent window
nID	The progress bar's ID

A call to `Create()` might look something like this:

```
m_progBar.Create(WS_CHILD | WS_BORDER | WS_VISIBLE,
    CRect(20, 40, 360, 80), this, IDC_PROGBAR);
```

Notice that the progress bar's style flags are all standard window styles. (Windows doesn't define any special styles for a progress bar.) You at least should specify the `WS_CHILD` and `WS_VISIBLE` styles. You may find other window styles useful in specific circumstances. For example, the preceding progress bar specifies the `WS_BORDER` style so that the edges of the control stand out against the window's white background.

Once you create the progress bar, you can set its attributes — including the control's range, step size, and initial position. The *range* is the scope of values represented by the bar. For example, if you use the bar to represent a percentage, you can give the control a range of 0 to 100. The *step size* is the portion of the bar that fills when the application increments the control. In the case of a percentage progress bar, you can set the step size to 10; this means the control must be incremented ten times before its bar is filled. The *initial position* is the portion of the bar that's filled already when the application displays the control. Typically, you set this value to 0.

To set the control's range, step, and position, you call the `CProgressCtrl` class's `SetRange()`, `SetStep()`, and `SetPos()` member functions:

```
m_progBar.SetRange(1, 100);
m_progBar.SetStep(10);
m_progBar.SetPos(0);
```

The only thing left to do is increment the control as the task it represents progresses. You do this by calling the `StepIt()` member function:

```
m_progBar.StepIt();
```

The `StepIt()` function increments the control by its step value. In the case of a control with a range of 0 to 100 and a step value of 10, an application has to call `StepIt()` ten times to fill the control's bar. Table 7-1 lists all of the `CProgressCtrl` class's member functions along with their descriptions.

Table 7-1 CProgressCtrl Member Functions

Function	Description
Create()	Creates the progress bar element and associates it with the CProgressCtrl object
GetRange()	Gets the values of the controls lower and upper range
GetPos()	Gets the control's current position
OffsetPos()	Advances the progress bar's position by a given amount
SetPos()	Sets the progress bar's current position
SetRange()	Sets the progress bar's minimum and maximum range
SetRange32()	Sets the progress bar's minimum and maximum range as 32-bit values
SetStep()	Sets the progress bar's step increment
StepIt()	Advances the progress bar's position by the step increment

Understanding CommonControlsApp's progress bar

The application creates its progress bar in the `InitProgressBar()` function, just as described in the previous section. The `InitProgressBar()` function looks like this:

```
void CCommonControlsAppView::InitProgressBar()
{
    m_progBar.Create(WS_CHILD | WS_BORDER | WS_VISIBLE,
        CRect(20, 40, 360, 80), this, IDC_PROGBAR);
    m_progBar.SetRange(1, 100);
    m_progBar.SetStep(10);
    m_progBar.SetPos(50);
}
```

This progress bar has a range of 1 to 100 with a step value of 10, and it starts off at a position of 50. This means that the progress bar is half filled when it first appears. When the user clicks in the application's window, Windows sends a `WM_LBUTTONDOWN` message that the program handles in the `OnLButtonDown()` function shown here:

```
void CCommonControlsAppView::OnLButtonDown
    (UINT nFlags, CPoint point)
{
    // TODO: Add your message handler code here
    //    and/or call default

    if (m_timerSet)
    {
        KillTimer(1);
        m_timerSet = FALSE;
    }
    else
    {
        SetTimer(1, 250, NULL);
        m_timerSet = TRUE;
    }

    CView::OnLButtonDown(nFlags, point);
}
```

The `m_timerSet` variable is a member of the view class that acts as a timer flag. When `m_timerSet` equals `TRUE`, the timer is running; otherwise, the timer is off. `OnLButtonDown()` first checks the value of `m_timerSet`. If `m_timerSet` is `FALSE`, the program calls `SetTimer()` to start a Windows timer.

`SetTimer()`'s three arguments are the timer number, the number of milliseconds between timer events, and the address of a callback function. If the third argument is `FALSE` (no callback function), Windows places the timer messages on the Windows message queue. You'll see what happens to those messages soon.

If `m_timerSet` is `FALSE`, `OnLButtonDown()` stops the timer by calling the `KillTimer()` function. This function takes the timer number as its single argument. After the program calls `KillTimer()`, Windows stops sending timer messages.

When the timer starts running, Windows sends a `WM_TIMER` message to the window. By now, you should be MFC-savvy enough to realize that you can respond to these messages by adding the `ON_WM_TIMER()` macro to your window class's message map and implementing the `OnTimer()` message-response function:

```
void CCommonControlsAppView::OnTimer(UINT nIDEvent)
{
    // TODO: Add your message handler code here
    //    and/or call default
```

```
        m_progBar.StepIt();

        CView::OnTimer(nIDEvent);
}
```

Every time the application receives a WM_TIMER message, MFC calls OnTimer( ). In turn, OnTimer( ) calls the progress bar's StepIt( ) function. As long as the timer runs, the progress bar continues to cycle through its display.

The Slider Control

The slider control provides a snazzy way of getting input from the user when you want the input value constrained to a given range. For example, if you create a slider with a range of 0 to 100, the user can select only values (or ranges of values) from 0 to 100. Figure 7-3 shows a slider control displayed in a window. To select a value, the user moves the sliding thumb with the mouse (the user also can use arrow keys on the keyboard). The farther to the right the user drags the thumb, the higher the value selected up to the set maximum.

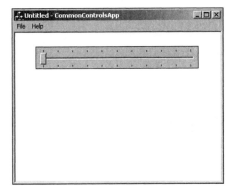

Figure 7-3: A slider represents a range of values from which a user can choose.

Creating and programming a slider control

To create a slider control, you first define an object of the CSliderCtrl class:

```
CSliderCtrl m_slider;
```

You then call the object's Create( ) member function, which creates the actual control and associates it with the CSliderCtrl object. The CSliderCtrl class's Create( ) function has the following signature. I list the arguments' descriptions in order after the signature.

```
BOOL Create(
    DWORD dwStyle,
```

```
const RECT& rect,
CWnd* pParentWnd,
UINT nID);
```

dwStyle	The slider's style flags
rect	A RECT or CRect object that specifies the slider's size and position
pParentWnd	A pointer to the slider's parent window
nID	The slider's ID

A call to Create() might look something like this:

```
m_slider.Create(WS_CHILD | WS_VISIBLE | WS_BORDER |
    TBS_BOTH | TBS_AUTOTICKS | TBS_HORZ,
    CRect(20, 120, 320, 160), this, IDC_SLIDER);
```

Notice that, unlike the progress bar, the slider does have styles of its own besides the standard window styles. For the window styles, you at least should specify the WS_CHILD and WS_VISIBLE styles. You may find other window styles useful in specific circumstances. For instance, like the previous progress bar example, the preceding slider specifies the WS_BORDER style so that the edges of the control stand out against the window's white background. The remaining styles are specific to slider controls. Table 7-2 lists all these styles along with their descriptions.

Table 7-2 Slider Control Styles

Style	Description
TBS_AUTOTICKS	Gives the slider the capability to draw tick marks
TBS_BOTH	Displays tick marks on both sides of the slider
TBS_BOTTOM	Displays tick marks on the bottom of a horizontal slider
TBS_ENABLESELRANGE	Enables the slider to show selection ranges
TBS_HORZ	Creates a horizontal slider
TBS_LEFT	Places tick marks on the left side of a vertical slider
TBS_NOTICKS	Creates a slider with no tick marks
TBS_RIGHT	Places tick marks on the right side of a vertical slider
TBS_TOP	Places tick marks on the top of a horizontal slider
TBS_VERT	Creates a vertical slider

Once you have a slider up on the screen, you need some way of knowing what the user is doing with it. When the user moves the control's thumb, the control generates WM_HSCROLL messages that you can respond to in the application. To do this, use ClassWizard to add the OnHScroll() message-response function to your application (as shown in Figure 7-4).

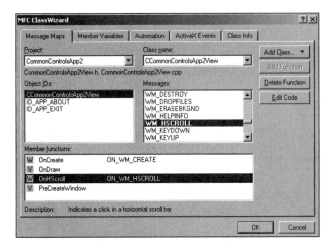

Figure 7-4: Sliders generate WM_HSCROLL messages to which your application can respond.

Here's what the OnHScroll() function might look like in an application:

```
void CCommonControlsAppView::OnHScroll
    (UINT nSBCode, UINT nPos, CScrollBar* pScrollBar)
{
    // TODO: Add your message handler code here
    //    and/or call default

    CSliderCtrl* s = (CSliderCtrl*)pScrollBar;
    int pos = s->GetPos();

    // Do something with the new position here.

    CView::OnHScroll(nSBCode, nPos, pScrollBar);
}
```

The OnHScroll() function receives three parameters: the scroll-bar code, the new scroll position, and a pointer to the scroller. (In this case, the *scroller* is the slider control.) For the most part, you don't need to concern yourself with the scroll-bar code. If you want to know more about the code's possible values, look up the OnHScroll() function in your Visual C++ online documentation.

In the `OnHScroll()` example, the program first casts the scroller pointer to a `CSliderCtrl` pointer. This pointer gives the function access to the slider object. The program then gets the slider's current position by calling the slider's `GetPos()` member function. The `CSliderCtrl` class defines many other member functions that you may find useful. Table 7-3 lists these functions along with their descriptions.

Table 7-3 CSliderCtrl Member Functions

Function	Description
ClearSel()	Clears the slider's current selection
ClearTics()	Erases the slider's tick marks
Create()	Creates the slider element and associates it with the `CSliderCtrl` object
GetBuddy()	Gets the handle of a slider's buddy control
GetChannelRect()	Gets the slider's channel size
GetLineSize()	Gets the slider's line size
GetNumTics()	Gets the slider's tick-mark count
GetPageSize()	Gets the slider's page size
GetPos()	Gets the slider's current position
GetRange()	Gets the slider's minimum and maximum positions
GetRangeMax()	Gets the slider's maximum position
GetRangeMin()	Gets the slider's minimum position
GetSelection()	Gets the current selection's range
GetThumbRect()	Gets the slider's thumb size
GetTic()	Gets a single tick-mark position
GetTicArray()	Gets the slider's tick-mark positions
GetTicPos()	Gets a single tick-mark position in client coordinates
GetToolTips()	Gets a handle to the slider's tooltip control
SetBuddy()	Sets the slider's buddy control
SetLineSize()	Sets the slider's line size
SetPageSize()	Sets the slider's page size
SetPos()	Sets the slider's current position
SetRange()	Sets the slider's minimum and maximum positions
SetRangeMax()	Sets the slider's maximum position
SetRangeMin()	Sets the slider's minimum position

Function	Description
SetSelection()	Sets the current selection's range
SetTic()	Sets a tick mark's position
SetTicFreq()	Sets the tick-mark frequency
SetTipSide()	Sets the position of a slider's tooltip control
SetToolTips()	Sets the slider's tooltip control
VerifyPos()	Verifies that a slider is between the minimum and maximum positions

Understanding CommonControlsApp's slider

The `InitSlider()` function gets the honor of creating and initializing the CommonControlsApp application's slider control. That function looks like this:

```
void CCommonControlsAppView::InitSlider()
{
    m_slider.Create(WS_CHILD | WS_VISIBLE | WS_BORDER |
        TBS_BOTH | TBS_AUTOTICKS | TBS_HORZ,
        CRect(20, 120, 320, 160), this, IDC_SLIDER);
    m_slider.SetRange(0, 100, TRUE);
    m_slider.SetTicFreq(10);
    m_slider.SetLineSize(1);
    m_slider.SetPageSize(10);
}
```

`InitSlider()` creates a horizontal slider with tick marks both above and below the slider track. The function then calls `SetRange()` to set the control's range to 0 through 100. The call to `SetTicFreq()` determines how many tick marks appear on the control.

Finally, the `SetLineSize()` and `SetPageSize()` function calls determine how far the slider moves when the user presses a key or clicks the mouse. The line size determines the increment value when the user uses the keyboard's up and down arrow keys. The page size determines the increment value when the user clicks the slider track with the mouse or presses the keyboard's Page Up and Page Down keys.

When the slider moves, it generates `WM_HSCROLL` messages to which the program responds in its `OnHScroll()` function shown here:

```
void CCommonControlsAppView::OnHScroll
    (UINT nSBCode, UINT nPos, CScrollBar* pScrollBar)
{
    // TODO: Add your message handler code here
    //    and/or call default

    CSliderCtrl* s = (CSliderCtrl*)pScrollBar;
    int pos = s->GetPos();
```

```
        char str[10];
        wsprintf(str, "%d   ", pos);
        m_sliderStatic2.SetWindowText(str);

        CView::OnHScroll(nSBCode, nPos, pScrollBar);
}
```

`OnHScroll()` gets the current value of the slider, converts the value to a string, and then displays the string in the `m_sliderStatic2` static text control. This control displays text in a large font.

Problems & Solutions

Enabling Slider Range Selection

PROBLEM: *From what I've seen and read, I should be able to set up a slider control so that the user can select not only a single value, but also a range of values. How can I get this feature to work?*

SOLUTION: It's easy to set a slider to display a range of values. Just include the `TBS_ENABLESELRANGE` style when you create the slider and call the slider's `SetSelection()` member function to set the desired range. A problem rears its ugly head, however, if you want the user to make the range selection. You can create a dialog box into which the user enters the minimum and maximum values of the range, and then you can apply the range to the slider — but that's not particularly elegant. What you really want is to give the slider control its own range-selection capability.

Customizing the slider control is easier than you may think. The first step is to create your own slider class based on the `CSliderCtrl` class. If you write an MFC program using AppWizard and ClassWizard, you can use ClassWizard to create the new class and add it to your project. To do this, follow these steps:

1. Press Ctrl+W to display ClassWizard. Click the Add Class button and select New from the drop-down selections, as shown in Figure 7-5.

2. In the New Class dialog box, type your new class's name (for example, `CMySlider`) into the Name box and select the `CSliderCtrl` class in the Base class box (see Figure 7-6).

3. Click the OK button to finalize your entries. ClassWizard creates the new class and adds it to your project.

Now that you have your new class created, you can start fiddling with the way a slider works. A common way of enabling the user to select a range of values is to use the Shift key combined with the mouse. With this method, the user drags the slider to the starting position. Then the

Continued

user holds down the Shift key, places the mouse pointer over the slider's thumb, clicks and holds the left mouse button, and drags the slider to the ending position. When the user releases the mouse button (while still holding down Shift), the range selection is complete.

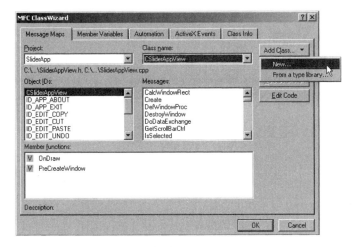

Figure 7-5: You can create new classes with ClassWizard.

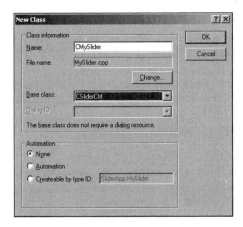

Figure 7-6: The New Class dialog box enables you to name your new class, as well as select a base class.

To add this functionality to your new slider class, add the `OnLButtonDown()` and `OnLButtonUp()` message-response functions to the slider class (as shown in Figures 7-7 and 7-8). You use these functions to track mouse movement when the Shift key is pressed. When the user clicks the slider's thumb, MFC calls `OnLButtonDown()`; when the user releases the mouse, MFC calls `OnLButtonUp()`.

Continued

In the `OnLButtonDown()` function, the slider has to initialize the range-selection operation. This means initializing some member variables. You need to add four member variables to the class's header file, as shown here:

```
BOOL m_rangeSelected;
int m_rangeStart;
int m_rangeEnd;
int m_rangeValue;
```

In `OnLButtonDown()`, you want to check for the Shift key. If it's pressed, you set the range's starting position to the slider's current position and set the range value (the difference between the start and end of the range) to zero. Here are the lines to add to `OnLButtonDown()`:

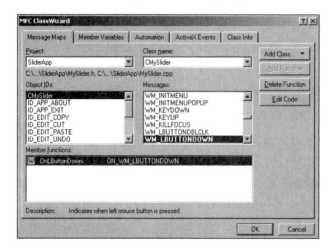

Figure 7-7: ClassWizard adding the OnLButtonDown() function

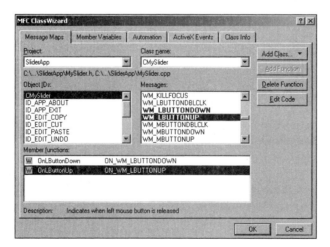

Figure 7-8: ClassWizard adding the OnLButtonUp() function

Continued

```
m_rangeSelected = FALSE;

if (nFlags & MK_SHIFT)
{
    m_rangeStart = GetPos();
    m_rangeValue = 0;
}
```

In `OnLButtonUp()`, you need to check whether the Shift key is held down still. If not, don't do anything further. If it is, you want to set the range's end to the slider's current position. Then you can calculate the range value by subtracting the start from the end. You also need to plan for the user dragging the control to the left rather than to the right. To do this, swap the starting and ending values. After all the calculations, you call the slider's `SetSelection()` member function to display the selected range in the control. Here's the code for the `OnLButtonUp()` function:

```
if (nFlags & MK_SHIFT)
{
    m_rangeSelected = TRUE;

    int pos = GetPos();
    if (pos < m_rangeStart)
    {
        m_rangeEnd = m_rangeStart;
        m_rangeStart = pos;
    }
    else
        m_rangeEnd = pos;

    SetSelection(m_rangeStart, m_rangeEnd);
    m_rangeValue = m_rangeEnd - m_rangeStart;
}
```

To complete the class, you should create member functions called `GetRangeStart()`, `GetRangeEnd()`, `GetRangeValue()`, and `IsRangeSelected()` so that the slider's parent object can obtain information about the slider. The first three functions should have public access and do nothing more than return the values of the `m_rangeStart`, `m_rangeEnd`, and `m_rangeValue` member variables. The `IsRangeSelected()` function should return the value of `m_rangeSelected`, which indicates whether a new range is ready to be read. `IsRangeSelected()` also should turn off the `m_rangeSelected` flag. Listing 7-1 is the new class's header file and the class's implementation file:

Listing 7-1: The CMySlider class's header file

```
// MySlider.h : header file
//
/////////////////////////////////////////////////////
// CMySlider window
class CMySlider : public CSliderCtrl
{
// Construction
```

```
public:
    CMySlider();
// Attributes
public:

// Operations
public:

// Overrides
    // ClassWizard generated virtual function overrides
    //{{AFX_VIRTUAL(CMySlider)
    //}}AFX_VIRTUAL

// Implementation
public:
    BOOL IsRangeSelected();
    int GetRangeValue();
    int GetRangeEnd();
    int GetRangeStart();
    virtual ~CMySlider();

    // Generated message map functions
protected:
    BOOL m_rangeSelected;
    int m_rangeValue;
    int m_rangeEnd;
    int m_rangeStart;
    //{{AFX_MSG(CMySlider)
    afx_msg void OnLButtonDown(UINT nFlags,
        CPoint point);
    afx_msg void OnLButtonUp(UINT nFlags, CPoint point);
    //}}AFX_MSG

    DECLARE_MESSAGE_MAP()
};
// MySlider.cpp : implementation file
//

#include "stdafx.h"
Continued
#include "SliderApp.h"
#include "MySlider.h"

#ifdef _DEBUG
#define new DEBUG_NEW
#undef THIS_FILE
static char THIS_FILE[] = __FILE__;
#endif
```

Continued

```
/////////////////////////////////////////////////////////
// CMySlider

CMySlider::CMySlider()
{
}

CMySlider::~CMySlider()
{
}


BEGIN_MESSAGE_MAP(CMySlider, CSliderCtrl)
    //{{AFX_MSG_MAP(CMySlider)
    ON_WM_LBUTTONDOWN()
    ON_WM_LBUTTONUP()
    //}}AFX_MSG_MAP
END_MESSAGE_MAP()

/////////////////////////////////////////////////////////
// CMySlider message handlers

void CMySlider::OnLButtonDown(UINT nFlags, CPoint point)
{
    // TODO: Add your message handler code here
    //    and/or call default

    m_rangeSelected = FALSE;

    if (nFlags & MK_SHIFT)
    {
        m_rangeStart = GetPos();
        m_rangeValue = 0;
    }

    CSliderCtrl::OnLButtonDown(nFlags, point);
}

void CMySlider::OnLButtonUp(UINT nFlags, CPoint point)
{
    // TODO: Add your message handler code here
    //    and/or call default

    if (nFlags & MK_SHIFT)
    {
        m_rangeSelected = TRUE;
        int pos = GetPos();
        if (pos < m_rangeStart)
```

Continued

```
        {
            m_rangeEnd = m_rangeStart;
            m_rangeStart = pos;
        }
        else
            m_rangeEnd = pos;

        SetSelection(m_rangeStart, m_rangeEnd);
        m_rangeValue = m_rangeEnd - m_rangeStart;
    }

    CSliderCtrl::OnLButtonUp(nFlags, point);
}

int CMySlider::GetRangeStart()
{
    return m_rangeStart;
}

int CMySlider::GetRangeEnd()
{
    return m_rangeEnd;
}

int CMySlider::GetRangeValue()
{
    return m_rangeValue;
}

BOOL CMySlider::IsRangeSelected()
{
    BOOL selected = m_rangeSelected;
    m_rangeSelected = FALSE;

    return selected;
}
```

Location: WinPrgS\Chap07\SliderApp

On this book's CD-ROM, you find the SliderApp application that demonstrates the custom slider control. When you run the program, select a range with the slider by dragging the slider's thumb while holding down the Shift key. Figure 7-9 shows the application after the user selects a range of values.

Continued

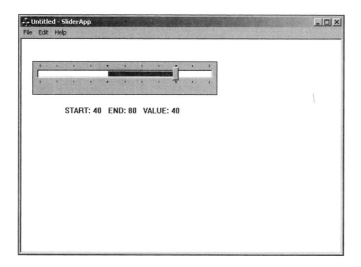

Figure 7-9: This custom slider enables a user to select a range of values.

The Spinner Control

The spinner control provides another way of getting input from the user when you want the input value constrained to a given range. But rather than moving a slider in a track, the user clicks onscreen arrows to change the control's value. Figure 7-10 shows a spinner control displayed in a window. To raise the control's value, the user clicks the up arrow. To lower the control's value, the user clicks the down arrow.

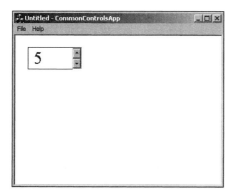

Figure 7-10: A spinner is another control that represents a range of values.

Creating and programming the spinner control

To create a spinner control, you first define an object of the `CSpinButtonCtrl` class:

```
CSpinButtonCtrl m_spin;
```

You then call the object's `Create()` member function, which creates the actual control and associates it with the `CSpinButtonCtrl` object. The `CSpinButtonCtrl` class's `Create()` function has the following signature. I list the arguments' descriptions in order after the signature.

```
BOOL Create(
    DWORD dwStyle,
    const RECT& rect,
    CWnd* pParentWnd,
    UINT nID);
```

dwStyle	The spinner's style flags
rect	A `RECT` or `CRect` object that specifies the spinner's size and position
pParentWnd	A pointer to the spinner's parent window
nID	The spinner's ID

A call to `Create()` might look something like this:

```
m_spinEdit.Create(WS_CHILD | WS_VISIBLE | WS_BORDER |
    UDS_ALIGNLEFT | UDS_WRAP,
    CRect(20, 200, 120, 240), this, IDC_SPINNER);
```

Besides the standard window styles, a spinner control defines styles of its own. Table 7-4 lists all these styles along with their descriptions. For the window styles, you at least should specify the `WS_CHILD` and `WS_VISIBLE` styles. You may find other window styles useful in specific circumstances.

Table 7-4   Spinner Control Styles

Style	Description
UDS_ALIGNLEFT	Places the spin button on the left of the buddy control
UDS_ALIGNRIGHT	Places the spin button on the right of the buddy control
UDS_ARROWKEYS	Enables the control to respond to the keyboard's up and down arrow keys
UDS_AUTOBUDDY	Automatically specifies the previous control as the buddy control
UDS_HORZ	Points the control's arrows left and right instead of up and down

Style	Description
UDS_NOTHOUSANDS	Stops the control from displaying thousands of separators (usually commas)
UDS_SETBUDDYINT	Sets the text of the buddy control when the user changes the spinner's position
UDS_WRAP	Creates a spinner that wraps around from its highest value to its lowest and vice versa

A spinner control is little more than a pair of arrows. If you want the control's value to be visible on the screen, you must associate the spinner with a buddy control. Then when the spinner's value changes, MFC automatically updates the buddy control. In most cases, the buddy control is a `CEdit` object. After creating the spinner control, create the buddy control and give it to the spinner by calling the spinner's `SetBuddy()` function:

```
m_edit.Create(WS_CHILD | WS_VISIBLE | WS_BORDER,
    CRect(20, 200, 120, 240), this, IDC_SPINNER);
m_spin.SetBuddy(&m_edit);
```

As with the slider control, you also need to set the spinner's range and position:

```
m_spin.SetRange(1, 10);
m_spin.SetPos(5);
```

`SetRange()` and `SetPos()` are only two of the `CSpinButtonCtrl` class's member functions. Table 7-5 lists all the member functions and their descriptions.

Table 7-5 CSpinButtonCtrl Member Functions

Function	Description
Create()	Creates a spin button element and associates it with the `CSpinButtonCtrl` object
GetAccel()	Gets the spinner's acceleration information
GetBase()	Gets the spinner's current base
GetBuddy()	Gets a pointer to the spinner's buddy control
GetPos()	Gets the spinner's current position
GetRange()	Gets the spinner's upper and lower limits
GetRange32()	Gets the spinner's 32-bit upper and lower limits
SetAccel()	Sets the spinner's acceleration
SetBase()	Sets the spinner's base

Continued

Table 7-5 *(continued)*

Function	Description
SetBuddy()	Sets the spinner's buddy control
SetPos()	Sets the spinner's current position
SetRange()	Sets the spinner's upper and lower limits
SetRange32()	Sets the spinner's upper and lower limits as 32-bit values

Understanding CommonControlsApp's spinner

The last common control demonstrated in CommonControlsApp is the spinner. The program creates this handy control in its InitSpinner() function. In InitSpinner(), the program first creates the spinner's buddy control:

```
m_spinEdit.Create(WS_CHILD | WS_VISIBLE | WS_BORDER,
    CRect(20, 200, 120, 240), this, IDC_SPINNER);
```

The program then creates a large font for displaying text in the buddy edit box. The following code shows how the program creates the font and gives it to the edit buddy control:

```
LOGFONT logFont;
logFont.lfHeight = 36;
logFont.lfWidth = 0;
logFont.lfEscapement = 0;
logFont.lfOrientation = 0;
logFont.lfWeight = FW_NORMAL;
logFont.lfItalic = 0;
logFont.lfUnderline = 0;
logFont.lfStrikeOut = 0;
logFont.lfCharSet = ANSI_CHARSET;
logFont.lfOutPrecision = OUT_DEFAULT_PRECIS;
logFont.lfClipPrecision = CLIP_DEFAULT_PRECIS;
logFont.lfQuality = PROOF_QUALITY;
logFont.lfPitchAndFamily = VARIABLE_PITCH | FF_ROMAN;
strcpy(logFont.lfFaceName, "Times New Roman");
m_spinEditFont.CreateFontIndirect(&logFont);
m_spinEdit.SetFont(&m_spinEditFont);
```

After getting the buddy control ready to go, the program creates the spinner control:

```
m_spin.Create(WS_CHILD | WS_VISIBLE | WS_BORDER |
    UDS_SETBUDDYINT | UDS_ALIGNRIGHT | UDS_ARROWKEYS,
    CRect(0, 0, 0, 0), this, 104);
```

The flags passed to the spinner's `Create()` function result in a spinner that automatically updates its buddy control, aligns the arrows to the right of the buddy control, and enables the user to manipulate the spinner with the keyboard's up and down arrow keys. The control's position and size are set to zero because the size and position of the buddy control determine these values.

After creating the spinner, the program gives it the buddy control and sets its range and initial position:

```
m_spin.SetBuddy(&m_spinEdit);
m_spin.SetRange(1, 10);
m_spin.SetPos(5);
```

The Image List Control

Image list controls differ greatly from the other types of controls you've learned about so far. They don't appear on the screen, and the user can't manipulate them. It is for these reasons that image list controls do not appear in any of this chapter's sample applications. Although they don't appear on the screen as part of your application's user interface, they nevertheless contribute to the construction of that interface. Using image controls, you can manage images for other types of controls. These controls include list view and tree view controls, which you learn about in the following section.

To create an image list control, you first define an object of the `CImageList` class:

`CImageList m_imageList;`

You then call the object's `Create()` member function, which creates the actual control and associates it with the `CImageList` object. The `CImageList` class's `Create()` function has the following signature. (Note that there are other `Create` functions with different arguments.) I list the arguments' descriptions in order after the signature.

```
BOOL Create(
    int cx,
    int cy,
    UINT nFlags,
    int nInitial,
    int nGrow);
```

cx	The width of each image in the list
cy	The height of each image in the list
nFlags	The list's color flags
nInitial	The initial number of images in the list
nGrow	The amount that the list should grow to accommodate additional images

A call to `Create()` might look something like this:

```
m_imageList.Create(16, 16, ILC_COLOR4, 6, 4);
```

This call to `Create()` results in an image list that holds 16x16 pixel images. The `ILC_COLOR4` flag specifies that the images are 4-bit (16-color) bitmaps; the last two arguments specify that the image list should start with six images and grow to accommodate four additional images whenever needed.

After creating the image list, you add your images by calling the object's `Add()` member function:

```
m_treeImages.Add(hIcon);
```

Here, the program adds an icon to the image list. In this case, the `Add()` function's single argument is the icon's handle. There are several versions of `Add()`, however, so you can add icons or bitmaps to the image list. The `CImageList` class defines many other member functions as well; Table 7-6 lists all of them. Although `CImageList` is a powerful class, you mostly just create your image list and hand it off to another control such as a tree view or list view control.

Table 7-6   CImageList Member Functions

Function	Description
Add()	Adds images to an image list
Attach()	Associates an image list with a `CImageList` object
BeginDrag()	Starts image dragging
Copy()	Copies a `CImageList` image
Create()	Creates an image list element and associates it with the `CImageList` object
DeleteImageList()	Deletes an image list

Function	Description
DeleteTempMap()	Deletes temporary `CImageList` objects created by FromHandle()
Detach()	Disassociates an image list element from a `CImageList` object
DragEnter()	Shows the drag image at the given position
DragLeave()	Erases the drag image
DragMove()	Moves the drag image
DragShowNolock()	Shows or erases the drag image without locking the window
Draw()	Draws the dragged image during a drag-and-drop operation
DrawIndirect()	Draws an image-list image
EndDrag()	Ends a drag operation
ExtractIcon()	Creates an icon from an image and mask
FromHandle()	Gets a pointer to a `CImageList` object from a device-context handle
FromHandlePermanent()	Gets a pointer to a `CImageList` object from an image-list handle
GetBkColor()	Gets the image list's background color
GetDragImage()	Gets the image list used for dragging
GetImageCount()	Gets the image list's image count
GetImageInfo()	Fills an `IMAGEINFO` structure with image list information
GetSafeHandle()	Gets the image list's handle
Read()	Reads an image list from an archive
Remove()	Removes an image from the image list
Replace()	Replaces an image in an image list
SetBkColor()	Sets the image list's background color
SetDragCursorImage()	Creates a new drag image
SetImageCount()	Sets the image list's image count
SetOverlayImage()	Sets an image as an overlay mask
Write()	Writes an image list to an archive

Problems & Solutions

Creating Composite Icons

PROBLEM: *I've noticed that many Windows 2000 objects require two types of icons: a small 16x16-pixel icon and a full-size 32x32-pixel icon. Isn't there some sort of object that simplifies the management of this pair of icons?*

SOLUTION: It's true that many Windows 2000 objects require a standard pair of large and small icons. For example, document and application icons that appear in Windows Explorer require large and small icons so that Explorer can display them properly regardless of the current view. In order to manage such icon pairs, Windows developed composite icons.

Composite icons are two icons — the standard 16x16 and 32x32 icons — stored in a single file. Although many icon editors don't support composite icons, Visual C++'s icon editor does. Once you create a composite icon, you have a single icon resource — with a single ID — that contains both icons.

To create a composite icon, first select the Resource command from Visual C++'s Insert command. The Insert Resource dialog box appears, as shown in Figure 7-11.

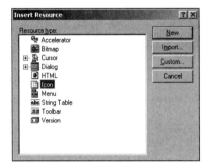

Figure 7-11: The Insert Resource dialog box enables you to add a new resource object to a project.

Double-click the icon resource, and Visual C++ opens the icon editor with a standard 32x32 icon displayed (see Figure 7-12). This will be the large image of your composite icon. Use the drawing tools to create the icon. Figure 7-13 shows the large icon you draw.

Now that you have the 32x32 image drawn, add the 16x16 image to the composite icon. To do this, click the New Device Image button (the small button to the right of the Device box). The New Icon Image dialog box appears, as seen in Figure 7-14.

Continued

Chapter 7: Common Controls 253

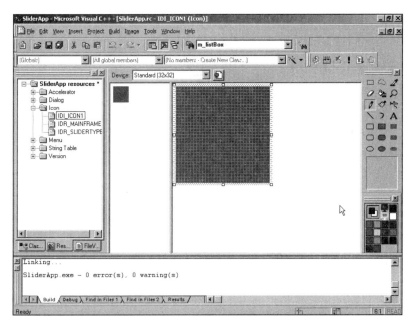

Figure 7-12: The icon editor opens to a new 32x32 icon.

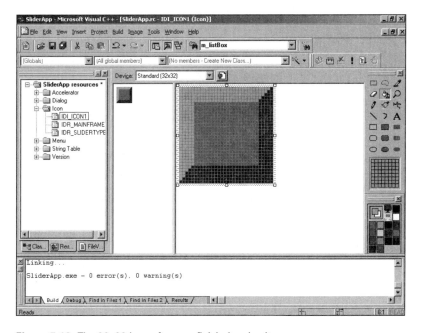

Figure 7-13: The 32x32 icon after you finish drawing it

Continued

254 Part I: Fundamental Windows 2000 Programming

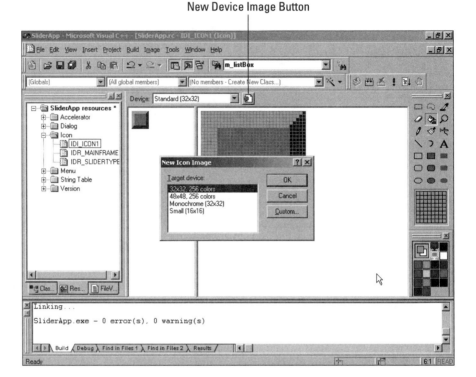

Figure 7-14: The New Icon Image dialog box enables you to add a second image to your composite icon.

Double-click the Small (16x16) entry in the dialog box. A 16x16 icon appears in the icon editor. Draw the 16x16 image (see Figure 7-15) to complete your composite icon.

When editing a composite icon, you can select the image on which to work from the Device box that lists both the 32x32 and 16x16 images. When you refer to the composite image in a program, you use the icon's single ID for either image. Windows automatically accesses the specific icon it needs.

Continued

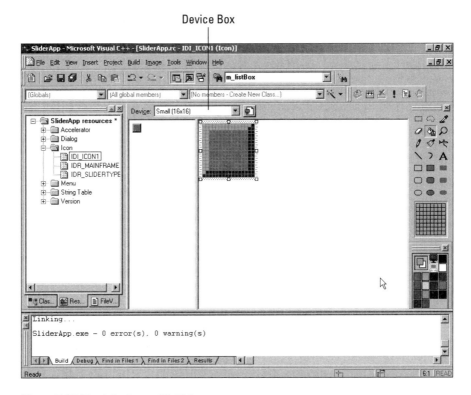

Figure 7-15: The fully drawn 16x16 image

Advanced Common Controls

Now things get really interesting. The list view and tree view controls are among the most complex controls available in Windows 2000. Although these controls aren't difficult to program, you do have to perform a number of often meticulous steps to get them up and running. These steps include setting styles, creating image lists, and defining columns and subitems. In the following sections, you see how to handle the list view and tree view controls.

The CommonControlsApp2 Sample Application

Location: `WinPrgS\Chap07\CommonControlsApp2`

Before examining how to create and program the more complex common controls, you should take some time out to see what they look like. On this book's CD-ROM, you can find the CommonControlsApp2 application, which demonstrates the list view and tree view controls in action. When you run the program, you see the window shown in Figure 7-16.

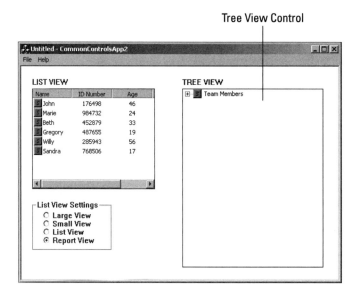

Figure 7-16: The CommonControlsApp2 application with its list view and tree view controls

Start by clicking a main item in the list view control. When you do, a message box appears showing the data associated with the chosen item (see Figure 7-17). Notice that the message box appears only when you click a main item. If you click a subitem, nothing happens.

The columns have a special capability that you may not be aware of yet. Place your mouse cursor over the line between the first and second columns. The cursor changes into a cross with a horizontal arrow. Hold down the left mouse button and drag to enlarge the first column, as shown in Figure 7-18.

Chapter 7: Common Controls

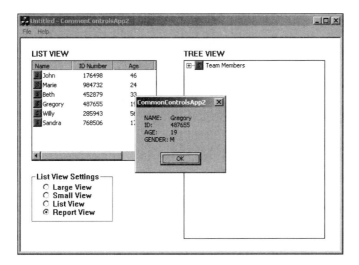

Figure 7-17: The message box displays data for a selected item.

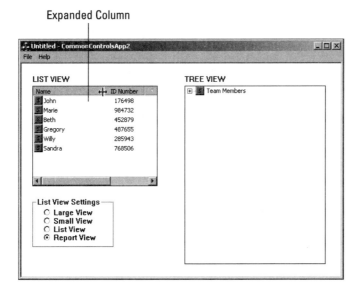

Figure 7-18: The list view's columns are adjustable.

Below the list view controls, you see a group of radio buttons. These buttons control the type of view displayed in the list view control. Currently, the list view control is in its report view. Click the radio buttons to see the other views. Figures 7-19, 7-20, and 7-21 show the large icon, small icon, and list views respectively.

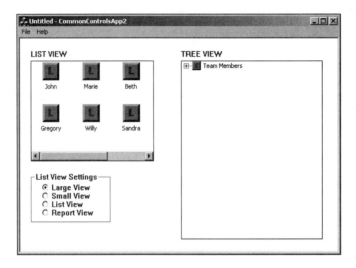

Figure 7-19: The list view control in large icon view

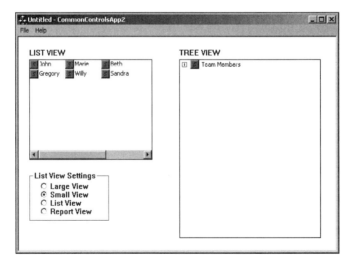

Figure 7-20: The list view control in small icon view

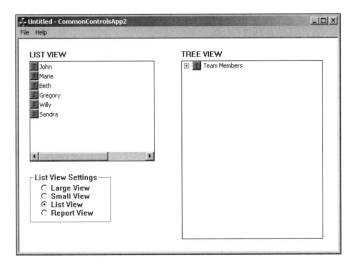

Figure 7-21: The list view control in list view

The tree view control contains the same data as the list view control, but the tree view's data is organized into a tree hierarchy. Click the plus sign next to an item to expand the item. Click the minus sign to collapse an item. Double-click any item to display a message box containing the item's text. Figure 7-22 shows the tree view control fully expanded. Notice that the items no longer fit in the control, so a scroll bar appears.

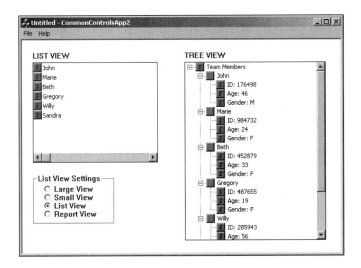

Figure 7-22: The tree view control with its items expanded

Understanding the OnCreate() Function

As you now know, the best place in an MFC program to create controls is in the window class's `OnCreate()` function, which responds to Windows' WM_CREATE message. Here is CommonControlsApp2's `OnCreate()` function:

```
int CCommonControlsApp2View::OnCreate
    (LPCREATESTRUCT lpCreateStruct)
{
    if (CView::OnCreate(lpCreateStruct) == -1)
        return -1;

    // TODO: Add your specialized creation code here

    InitStaticText();
    InitListView();
    InitRadioButtons();
    InitTreeView();

    m_whiteBrush.CreateSolidBrush(RGB(255,255,255));

    return 0;
}
```

From `OnCreate()`, the program calls the `InitStaticText()`, `InitListView()`, `InitRadioButtons()`, and `InitTreeView()` functions. `OnCreate()` also creates the white brush that the program uses for the static controls' backgrounds, which normally are colored gray.

The program changes the background color in response to the WM_CTLCOLOR windows message, which the `OnCtlColor()` function handles:

```
HBRUSH CCommonControlsApp2View::OnCtlColor
    (CDC * pDC, CWnd * pWnd, UINT nCtrlColor)
{
    if (nCtrlColor == CTLCOLOR_STATIC)
        return (HBRUSH)m_whiteBrush;

    return CView::OnCtlColor(pDC, pWnd, nCtrlColor);
}
```

The List View Control

In this section, you learn to incorporate list view controls into your programs. There are four types of list views—report view, small icon view, large icon view, and list view—as indexed below. Figures 7-23 through 7-26 show examples of all four.

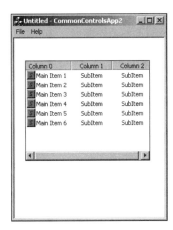

Figure 7-23: The list view control in its report view

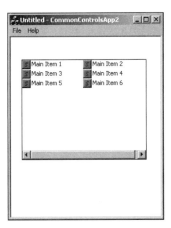

Figure 7-24: The list view control in its small icon view

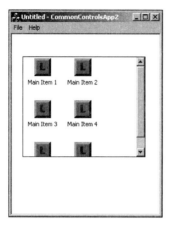

Figure 7-25: The list view control in its large icon view

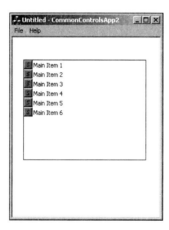

Figure 7-26: The list view control in its list view

Creating the list view control object

To create a list view control, you first define an object of the CListCtrl class:

```
CListCtrl m_listView;
```

You then call the object's Create() member function, which creates the actual control and associates it with the CListCtrl object. The CListCtrl class's Create() function has the following signature. I list the arguments' descriptions in order after the signature.

```
BOOL Create(
    DWORD dwStyle,
    const RECT& rect,
    CWnd* pParentWnd,
    UINT nID);
```

dwStyle	The list view's style flags
rect	A RECT or CRect object that specifies the list view's size and position
pParentWnd	A pointer to the list view's parent window
nID	The list view's ID

A call to Create() might look something like this:

```
m_listView.Create(WS_VISIBLE | WS_CHILD |
    WS_BORDER | LVS_REPORT | LVS_NOSORTHEADER,
    CRect(20, 40, 250, 220), this, IDC_LISTVIEW);
```

For the standard window styles, you at least should specify WS_CHILD and WS_VISIBLE. You may find other window styles useful in specific circumstances. For example, the preceding list view control specifies the WS_BORDER style so that the edges of the control stand out against the window's white background.

The CListCtrl class defines a set of styles specific to the list view control. Table 7-7 lists these styles and their descriptions. You use these styles to specify how the list view control should look and act. Probably the most important styles are LVS_ICON, LVS_SMALLICON, LVS_LIST, and LVS_REPORT. These styles determine the type of view the list view control displays.

Table 7-7   List View Control Styles

Style	Description
LVS_ALIGNLEFT	Left-aligns items in large and small icon view
LVS_ALIGNTOP	Top-aligns items in large and small icon view
LVS_AUTOARRANGE	Automatically arranges icons in large and small icon view
LVS_EDITLABELS	Enables text editing of items
LVS_ICON	Creates the list in large icon view
LVS_LIST	Creates the list in list view
LVS_NOCOLUMNHEADER	Hides column headers in report view

Continued

Table 7-7 *(continued)*

Style	Description
LVS_NOLABELWRAP	Disables text wrapping for item text
LVS_NOSCROLL	Disables list scrolling
LVS_NOSORTHEADER	Disables column header buttons
LVS_OWNERDRAWFIXED	Creates an owner-drawn list view control
LVS_REPORT	Creates the list in report view
LVS_SHAREIMAGELISTS	Enables multiple components to share the list view control's image list
LVS_SHOWSELALWAYS	Shows the current selection whether or not the list has the input focus
LVS_SINGLESEL	Enables the user to select only one item at a time
LVS_SMALLICON	Creates the list in small icon view
LVS_SORTASCENDING	Sorts items in ascending order
LVS_SORTDESCENDING	Sorts items in descending order

Setting the control's image lists

After creating the list view control, you set the control's image lists. You at least should specify small and large icons. You also can specify an icon for how an item looks when selected. You might, for example, want a folder icon to look closed when not selected and open when selected. You store the icons for your list view in image list controls. Specify the large and small icons like this:

```
m_listView.SetImageList(&smlImageList, LVSIL_SMALL);
m_listView.SetImageList(&lrgImageList, LVSIL_NORMAL);
```

The CListCtrl class's SetImageList() member function takes two arguments: a pointer to the image list and a flag indicating how the control should use the images in the list. You can specify LVSIL_SMALL (small icons), LVSIL_NORMAL (large icons), and LVSIL_STATE (state icons) for the second argument. (*State icons* enable the list item to change appearance when selected.)

Creating the control's columns

After setting the list view's icons, you can define the columns that the list displays in report view. To accomplish this task, you initialize an LV_COLUMN structure with the values that define a column and then call the CListCtrl's InsertColumn() member function to add the column to the control.

Windows defines the `LV_COLUMN` structure as follows. Descriptions of each of the structure's members appear in order after the structure declaration.

```
typedef struct _LV_COLUMN {
    UINT mask;
    int fmt;
    int cx;
    LPTSTR pszText;
    int cchTextMax;
    int iSubItem;
} LV_COLUMN;
```

mask	A flag that specifies which of the structure's members contain information. The flag can be a combination of any or all of the following: `LVCF_FMT`, `LVCF_SUBITEM`, `LVCF_TEXT`, and `LVCF_WIDTH`.
fmt	A flag that indicates the column's text alignment. Can be `LVCFMT_CENTER`, `LVCFMT_LEFT`, or `LVCFMT_RIGHT`.
cx	The column's width.
pszText	A pointer to the string used for the column's heading.
cchTextMax	The size of the `pszText` buffer (not used when setting columns).
iSubItem	The index of the item within the column.

You define the column's header using code something like this:

```
LV_COLUMN lvColumn;
lvColumn.mask = LVCF_WIDTH | LVCF_TEXT |
    LVCF_FMT | LVCF_SUBITEM;
lvColumn.fmt = LVCFMT_LEFT;
lvColumn.cx = 75;
lvColumn.iSubItem = 0;
lvColumn.pszText = "Column 0";
m_listView.InsertColumn(0, &lvColumn);
```

The `InsertColumn()` function requires two arguments: the column's index (the first column is 0, the second is 1, and so on) and a pointer to the `LV_COLUMN` structure containing the column information.

After defining the first column, you can define additional columns using the same `LV_COLUMN` structure by changing the appropriate values. For example, after creating the first column shown previously, you can create a second column with code something like this:

```
lvColumn.iSubItem = 1;
lvColumn.pszText = "Column 1";
m_listView.InsertColumn(1, &lvColumn);
```

Note: The first column of a list view control always uses left alignment. If you specify another type of alignment for the first column, the control ignores your request and still uses left alignment.

Adding main items to the control

Now that you have the columns created, you need to put items into the columns. List view controls hold two types of items. The first type is the main item that appears in the first column. In a directory list, for example, this item can be the name of a file. The second type of item is a subitem, which you can think of as a child to the main item. In the directory list, the subitems can be the file's size and date of creation.

To create a main item, you initialize an `LV_ITEM` structure with the values that define an item and then call `CListCtrl`'s `InsertItem()` member function to add the item to the control. Windows defines the `LV_ITEM` structure as follows. A description of each of the structure's members appears in order after the structure declaration.

```
typedef struct _LV_ITEM {
    UINT    mask;
    int     iItem;
    int     iSubItem;
    UINT    state;
    UINT    stateMask;
    LPTSTR  pszText;
    int     cchTextMax;
    int     iImage;
    LPARAM  lParam;
} LV_ITEM;
```

mask	A flag that specifies which of the structure's members contain information. The flag can be a combination of any or all of the following: `LVIF_TEXT`, `LVIF_IMAGE`, `LVIF_PARAM`, and `LVIF_STATE`.
iItem	The main item's index.
iSubItem	The subitem's index.
state	The item's state, which can be one or more of these: `LVIS_CUT` (marked for cut-and-paste), `LVIS_DROPHILITED` (highlighted as a drag-and-drop target), `LVIS_FOCUSED` (has the focus), and `LVIS_SELECTED` (selected).
stateMask	A flag that specifies which of the state member's bits contain information.
pszText	A pointer to the item's text.

cchTextMax	The size of the `pszText` buffer (not used when adding items).
iImage	The index of the item's image in the image lists for the small and large icons.
LParam	An application-specific, 32-bit value.

You define a main item using code something like this:

```
LV_ITEM lvItem;
lvItem.mask = LVIF_TEXT | LVIF_IMAGE | LVIF_STATE;
lvItem.state = 0;
lvItem.stateMask = 0;
lvItem.iImage = 0;
lvItem.iItem = 0;
lvItem.iSubItem = 0;
lvItem.pszText = "John";
m_listView.InsertItem(&lvItem);
```

Adding subitems to the control

Once you have a main item defined, you can add subitems. Considering all the details you need to know about columns and main items, you should be pleased to learn that adding a subitem requires only a single call to the list view's `SetItemText()` function. You can add as many subitems as you want:

```
m_listView.SetItemText(0, 1, "Subitem 1");
m_listView.SetItemText(0, 2, "Subitem 2");
m_listView.SetItemText(0, 3, "Subitem 3");
```

The `SetItemText()` function takes three arguments: the main item's index, the subitem's index (starting with 1), and the subitem's text.

Responding to user selections

Often, you use a list view control to do more than just display data to the user. You may want the user to be able to select items in the control. When the user double-clicks an item in the list view control, the control generates an `NM_DBLCLK` notification to which your application can respond. To accomplish this task, you first must add the notification to your window's message map:

```
ON_NOTIFY(NM_DBLCLK, IDC_LISTVIEW, OnListViewDblClk)
```

The `ON_NOTIFY` macro requires three arguments: the notification's ID, the control's ID, and the name of the message-response function.

In the message-response function, you can get the index of the selected item by calling the list view object's `GetNextItem()` member function:

```
int index = m_listView.GetNextItem(-1, LVNI_SELECTED);
```

The function's two arguments are the item index at which to start searching and the relationship of the requested item to the given item. To find the first item that matches the flag, use -1 for the first argument. You can use any one of the following flags for the second argument: `LVNI_ABOVE`, `LVNI_ALL`, `LVNI_BELOW`, `LVNI_TOLEFT`, `LVNI_TORIGHT`, `LVNI_DROPHILITED`, `LVNI_FOCUSED`, or `LVNI_SELECTED`. If you need more information about these flags, look up `GetNextItem()` in your Visual C++ online documentation.

If the value returned from `GetNextItem()` is -1, there is no selected item. If `GetNextItem()` returns a valid index, you can call `GetItemText()` to get the selected item's text:

```
CString str = m_listView.GetItemText(index, 0);
```

This function's two arguments are the index of the main item and the index of a subitem. If the subitem index is 0, `GetItemText()` returns the main item text; otherwise, it returns the subitem text. So to get the text for the subitems, you might make these calls to `GetItemText()`:

```
CString subItem1 = m_listView.GetItemText(index, 1);
CString subItem2 = m_listView.GetItemText(index, 2);
CString subItem3 = m_listView.GetItemText(index, 3);
```

The MFC list view shortcuts

You just learned the standard methods for constructing and initializing a list view control. Now that you know how the control works, I discuss a few MFC shortcuts that make it easier to create a list view control.

The `CListCtrl` class overloads its `InsertColumn()` and `InsertItem()` member functions with versions that don't require you to initialize `LV_COLUMN` and `LV_ITEM` structures in your program. You simply pass a few arguments to `InsertColumn()` and `InsertItem()`, and MFC fills in the structures for you. Following is the overloaded version of `InsertColumn()`. Descriptions of each of its arguments follow.

```
int InsertColumn(
    int nCol,
    LPCTSTR lpszColumnHeading,
    int nFormat = LVCFMT_LEFT,
    int nWidth = -1,
    int nSubItem = -1);
```

nCol	The zero-based column number
lpszColumnHeading	The text for the column heading
nFormat	The column's alignment
nWidth	The column's width
nSubItem	The subitem index

The shortcut version of InsertItem() looks like the following. I list the arguments' descriptions in order after the signature.

```
int InsertItem(
    int nItem,
    LPCTSTR lpszItem,
    int nImage);
```

nItem	The main item index
lpszItem	The main item's text
nImage	The index of the image-list image associated with the item

Using these alternative versions of InsertColumn() and InsertItem() simplifies the code needed to create and initialize a list view control. For example, here's the code required to create the list view control in Figure 7-27:

```
// Create the image list controls.
m_lrgImageList.Create(32, 32, ILC_COLOR4, 1, 0);
m_smlImageList.Create(16, 16, ILC_COLOR4, 1, 0);

// Add images to the image lists.
HICON hIcon = ::LoadIcon (AfxGetResourceHandle(),
    MAKEINTRESOURCE(IDI_ICON1));
m_lrgImageList.Add(hIcon);
hIcon = ::LoadIcon (AfxGetResourceHandle(),
    MAKEINTRESOURCE(IDI_ICON1));
m_smlImageList.Add(hIcon);

// Create the list view control.
m_listView.Create(WS_VISIBLE | WS_CHILD | WS_BORDER |
    LVS_REPORT | LVS_NOSORTHEADER,
    CRect(20, 40, 250, 220), this, IDC_LISTVIEW);
m_listView.SetImageList(&m_smlImageList,
    LVSIL_SMALL);
m_listView.SetImageList(&m_lrgImageList,
    LVSIL_NORMAL);

// Add the columns.
m_listView.InsertColumn(0, "Column 0",
    LVCFMT_LEFT, 75);
m_listView.InsertColumn(1, "Column 1",
    LVCFMT_CENTER, 75);
m_listView.InsertColumn(2, "Column 2",
    LVCFMT_LEFT, 75);

// Add the main items.
m_listView.InsertItem(0, "Main Item 1", 0);
m_listView.InsertItem(1, "Main Item 2", 0);
```

```
m_listView.InsertItem(2, "Main Item 3", 0);
m_listView.InsertItem(3, "Main Item 4", 0);
m_listView.InsertItem(4, "Main Item 5", 0);
m_listView.InsertItem(5, "Main Item 6", 0);

// Add the subitems to each main item.
m_listView.SetItemText(0, 1, "Subitem");
m_listView.SetItemText(0, 2, "Subitem");

m_listView.SetItemText(1, 1, "Subitem");
m_listView.SetItemText(1, 2, "Subitem");

m_listView.SetItemText(2, 1, "Subitem");
m_listView.SetItemText(2, 2, "Subitem");

m_listView.SetItemText(3, 1, "Subitem");
m_listView.SetItemText(3, 2, "Subitem");

m_listView.SetItemText(4, 1, "Subitem");
m_listView.SetItemText(4, 2, "Subitem");

m_listView.SetItemText(5, 1, "Subitem");
m_listView.SetItemText(5, 2, "Subitem");
```

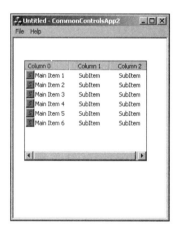

Figure 7-27: The list view control created by the preceding listing

The m_lrgImageList, m_smlImageList, and m_listView objects are all members of the window's class and are declared in the window class's header file.

The list view control's member functions

The CListCtrl class defines many more member functions than the few already mentioned. Table 7-8 lists some of these functions and their descriptions. As there are a multitude of member functions, supplying a complete description of them all is beyond the scope of this book. However, you should have little difficulty figuring out and using most of the functions in this table.

Table 7-8   CListCtrl Member Functions

Function	Description
`Arrange()`	Arranges items on a grid
`Create()`	Creates a list control element and associates it with the `CListCtrl` object
`CreateDragImage()`	Creates an item's drag image list
`DeleteAllItems()`	Deletes all items
`DeleteColumn()`	Deletes a column
`DeleteItem()`	Deletes individual items
`DrawItem()`	Called by MFC when an owner-drawn control must be redrawn
`EditLabel()`	Begins item text editing
`EnsureVisible()`	Ensures that a specified item is visible
`FindItem()`	Searches for a list-view item
`GetBkColor()`	Gets the list view's background color
`GetCallbackMask()`	Gets the list view's callback mask
`GetColumn()`	Gets a column's attributes
`GetColumnWidth()`	Gets a column's report- or list-view width
`GetCountPerPage()`	Determines how many items fit vertically in the list view
`GetEditControl()`	Gets the handle of an item's edit control
`GetImageList()`	Gets a handle to the list view's image list
`GetItem()`	Gets a list-view item's attributes
`GetItemCount()`	Gets the list view's item count
`GetItemData()`	Gets an item's application-specific value
`GetItemPosition()`	Gets a list-view item's position
`GetItemRect()`	Gets an item's bounding rectangle
`GetItemState()`	Gets an item's state
`GetItemText()`	Gets an item's text
`GetNextItem()`	Finds a list-view item

Continued

Table 7-8 *(continued)*

Function	Description
GetOrigin()	Gets the list view's view origin
GetSelectedCount()	Gets the list view's selected item count
GetStringWidth()	Gets the column width required to display a given string
GetTextBkColor()	Retrieves the list view's text background color
GetTextColor()	Gets the list view's text color
GetTopIndex()	Gets the index of the visible item at the top of the list view
GetViewRect()	Gets the bounding rectangle of all items
HitTest()	Returns the index of the item at a given position
InsertColumn()	Inserts a new column
InsertItem()	Inserts a new item
RedrawItems()	Repaints a range of items
Scroll()	Scrolls the list view's contents
SetBkColor()	Sets the list view's background color
SetCallbackMask()	Sets the list view's callback mask
SetColumn()	Sets a list-view column's attributes
SetColumnWidth()	Changes the report- or list-view column width
SetImageList()	Sets the list view's image list
SetItem()	Sets item attributes
SetItemCount()	Allocates resources to accommodate adding multiple items
SetItemData()	Sets the item's application-specific value
SetItemPosition()	Sets an item's position
SetItemState()	Sets an item's state
SetItemText()	Sets an item's text
SetTextBkColor()	Sets the list view's background color
SetTextColor()	Sets the list view's text color
SortItems()	Sorts list-view items
Update()	Repaints a specified item

Problems & Solutions

Enabling List-View Item Editing

PROBLEM: *When I click an item in some list view controls (such as those in Windows Explorer), the item text turns into an edit box. I then can edit the item text, changing it to anything I want. But when I create my own list view, the editing doesn't work. What's up?*

SOLUTION: A snazzy feature of list view controls enables you to edit item text. A good example of this is when you click a file in Windows Explorer and press F2. The file's name then becomes an edit box into which you can type a new file name. However, handy as this feature is for some list views, it doesn't come free. There are several things you must do to make it work.

First, when you create your list view control, you must include the `LVS_EDITLABELS` style:

```
m_listView.Create(WS_VISIBLE | WS_CHILD | WS_BORDER |
    LVS_REPORT | LVS_NOSORTHEADER | LVS_EDITLABELS,
    CRect(20, 40, 250, 220), this, IDC_LISTVIEW);
```

Now, when the user clicks a selected main item in the list view, the item's label changes to an edit control. The user can edit the item, but when the user presses Enter to end the editing, the label returns to its old text. This occurs because your application must accept the user's changes before they become permanent.

To manage user edits, you respond to two list-view notifications: `LVN_BEGINLABELEDIT` and `LVN_ENDLABELEDIT`. To do this, first use ClassWizard to override the `OnNotify()` member function in the window class (as shown in Figure 7-28). The `OnNotify()` message responds to `WM_NOTIFY` messages into which Windows packages the `LVN_BEGINLABELEDIT` and `LVN_ENDLABELEDIT` notifications.

Here is `OnNotify()`'s signature, followed by descriptions of each of its arguments:

```
virtual BOOL CWnd::OnNotify(
    WPARAM wParam,
    LPARAM lParam,
    LRESULT* pResult);
```

wParam	The WM_NOTIFY message's WPARAM value
lParam	The WM_NOTIFY message's LPARAM value
pResult	A pointer to a result code

Continued

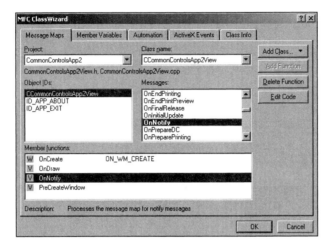

Figure 7-28: The OnNotify() function responds to Windows notifications.

How you interpret the three parameters received by `OnNotify()` depends on the type of message you process. In the case of a list view control, `wParam` holds the control's ID. The value of `lParam` depends also on the type of notification. With `LVN_BEGINLABELEDIT` and `LVN_ENDLABELEDIT`, `lParam` holds a pointer to an `LV_DISPINFO` structure; this structure contains the information you need to process the user's editing request.

In `OnNotify()`, the first step is to cast `lParam` to an `LV_DISPINFO` pointer:

```
LV_DISPINFO* pDispInfo = (LV_DISPINFO*)lParam;
```

With a pointer to the structure in hand, the program can get the notification code tucked away in the structure's `hdr.code` member:

```
UINT notificationID = pDispInfo->hdr.code;
```

If the notification ID is `LVN_BEGINLABELEDIT`, the program can do whatever it needs to do to process the request:

```
if (notificationID == LVN_BEGINLABELEDIT)
{
    // Perform pre-edit processing here.
}
```

If the notification ID is `LVN_ENDLABELEDIT`, you need to copy the new label from the edit control into the list-view item. The `item.iItem` member of the `LV_DISPINFO` structure holds the item's ID:

```
UINT itemIndex = pDispInfo->item.iItem;
```

You can get the new text from the structure's `item.pszText` member:

```
CString newText = pDispInfo->item.pszText;
```

Continued

Chapter 7: Common Controls

You must test for an empty string (or NULL, if you use a character array) because that's what the text will be if the user decides to exit the edit box by pressing Esc to cancel the editing operation.

If the new text is valid, you call the list view's `SetItemText()` function to complete the operation:

```
if (newText != "")
    m_listView.SetItemText(itemIndex, 0, newText);
```

Location: **WinPrgS\Chap07\EditControls**

On this book's CD-ROM, you can find an application named EditControls that demonstrates label editing in a list view control.

Understanding CommonControlsApp2's list view control

CommonControlsApp2 creates its list view control in the view-window class's `InitListView()` member function, which looks like this:

```
void CCommonControlsApp2View::InitListView()
{
    // Create the Image List controls.
    m_lrgImageList.Create(32, 32, ILC_COLOR4, 1, 0);
    m_smlImageList.Create(16, 16, ILC_COLOR4, 1, 0);

    HICON hIcon = ::LoadIcon (AfxGetResourceHandle(),
        MAKEINTRESOURCE(IDI_ICON1));
    m_lrgImageList.Add(hIcon);
    hIcon = ::LoadIcon (AfxGetResourceHandle(),
        MAKEINTRESOURCE(IDI_ICON1));
    m_smlImageList.Add(hIcon);

    // Create the List view control.
    m_listView.Create(WS_VISIBLE | WS_CHILD | WS_BORDER |
        LVS_REPORT | LVS_NOSORTHEADER,
        CRect(20, 40, 250, 220), this, IDC_LISTVIEW);
    m_listView.SetImageList(&m_smlImageList,
        LVSIL_SMALL);
    m_listView.SetImageList(&m_lrgImageList,
        LVSIL_NORMAL);

    CreateListColumns();
    AddListItems();
}
```

`InitListView()` begins by creating the list view's image lists. The function then creates the list view objects and assigns the image lists to the objects.

Finally, the function calls the `CreateListColumns()` and `AddListItems()` member functions to complete the list view control.

The `CreateListColumns()` function creates and adds columns to the list view control. That function looks like this:

```
void CCommonControlsApp2View::CreateListColumns()
{
    LV_COLUMN lvColumn;
    lvColumn.mask = LVCF_WIDTH | LVCF_TEXT |
        LVCF_FMT | LVCF_SUBITEM;
    lvColumn.fmt = LVCFMT_CENTER;
    lvColumn.cx = 75;
    lvColumn.iSubItem = 0;
    lvColumn.pszText = "Name";
    m_listView.InsertColumn(0, &lvColumn);

    lvColumn.iSubItem = 1;
    lvColumn.pszText = "ID Number";
    m_listView.InsertColumn(1, &lvColumn);

    lvColumn.iSubItem = 2;
    lvColumn.pszText = "Age";
    m_listView.InsertColumn(2, &lvColumn);

    lvColumn.iSubItem = 3;
    lvColumn.pszText = "Gender";
    m_listView.InsertColumn(3, &lvColumn);
}
```

The function first creates and initializes an `LV_COLUMN` structure. The program then uses the structure in several calls to the list view object's `InsertColumn()` member function to create the four columns.

The `AddListItems()` function adds the main items and subitems to the list view control. That function looks like this:

```
void CCommonControlsApp2View::AddListItems()
{
    LV_ITEM lvItem;
    lvItem.mask = LVIF_TEXT | LVIF_IMAGE | LVIF_STATE;
    lvItem.state = 0;
    lvItem.stateMask = 0;
    lvItem.iImage = 0;

    lvItem.iItem = 0;
    lvItem.iSubItem = 0;
    lvItem.pszText = "John";
    m_listView.InsertItem(&lvItem);
    m_listView.SetItemText(0, 1, "176498");
    m_listView.SetItemText(0, 2, "46");
    m_listView.SetItemText(0, 3, "M");
```

```
        lvItem.iItem = 1;
        lvItem.iSubItem = 0;
        lvItem.pszText = "Marie";
        m_listView.InsertItem(&lvItem);
        m_listView.SetItemText(1, 1, "984732");
        m_listView.SetItemText(1, 2, "24");
        m_listView.SetItemText(1, 3, "F");

        lvItem.iItem = 2;
        lvItem.iSubItem = 0;
        lvItem.pszText = "Beth";
        m_listView.InsertItem(&lvItem);
        m_listView.SetItemText(2, 1, "452879");
        m_listView.SetItemText(2, 2, "33");
        m_listView.SetItemText(2, 3, "F");

        lvItem.iItem = 3;
        lvItem.iSubItem = 0;
        lvItem.pszText = "Gregory";
        m_listView.InsertItem(&lvItem);
        m_listView.SetItemText(3, 1, "487655");
        m_listView.SetItemText(3, 2, "19");
        m_listView.SetItemText(3, 3, "M");

        lvItem.iItem = 4;
        lvItem.iSubItem = 0;
        lvItem.pszText = "Willy";
        m_listView.InsertItem(&lvItem);
        m_listView.SetItemText(4, 1, "285943");
        m_listView.SetItemText(4, 2, "56");
        m_listView.SetItemText(4, 3, "M");

        lvItem.iItem = 5;
        lvItem.iSubItem = 0;
        lvItem.pszText = "Sandra";
        m_listView.InsertItem(&lvItem);
        m_listView.SetItemText(5, 1, "768506");
        m_listView.SetItemText(5, 2, "17");
        m_listView.SetItemText(5, 3, "F");
}
```

The function creates the main items by setting up an `LV_ITEM` structure and using it in calls to the list view object's `InsertItem()` member function. The program adds the subitems by calling the `SetItemText()` member function.

A set of radio buttons controls the list view control's current view setting. The program creates the radio button group in the `InitRadioButtons()` function, as shown here:

```
void CCommonControlsApp2View::InitRadioButtons()
{
    m_radioGroup.Create("List View Settings",
        BS_GROUPBOX | WS_CHILD | WS_VISIBLE,
        CRect(20, 240, 170, 330), this, 0);
```

```
    m_radioLarge.Create("Large View",
        BS_AUTORADIOBUTTON | WS_CHILD | WS_VISIBLE |
        WS_GROUP, CRect(40, 260, 130, 275),
        this, IDC_RADIOLARGE);

    m_radioSmall.Create("Small View",
        BS_AUTORADIOBUTTON | WS_CHILD | WS_VISIBLE,
        CRect(40, 275, 130, 290),
        this, IDC_RADIOSMALL);

    m_radioList.Create("List View",
        BS_AUTORADIOBUTTON | WS_CHILD | WS_VISIBLE,
        CRect(40, 290, 130, 305), this,
        IDC_RADIOLIST);

    m_radioReport.Create("Report View",
        BS_AUTORADIOBUTTON | WS_CHILD | WS_VISIBLE,
        CRect(40, 305, 150, 320), this,
        IDC_RADIOREPORT);

    m_radioReport.SetCheck(BST_CHECKED);
}
```

You already should understand the way this function works. If you need a refresher on radio buttons, please refer to Chapter 6.

When the user clicks one of the radio button controls, the control generates a BN_CLICKED notification to which the program responds in the OnRadio LargeClicked(), OnRadioSmallClicked(), OnRadioListClicked(), or OnRadioReportClicked() function. These functions, shown in the following code, change the view type by modifying the list view control's style flags. They do this by calling the view window's SetWindowLong() function:

```
void CCommonControlsApp2View::OnRadioLargeClicked()
{
    SetWindowLong(m_listView.m_hWnd, GWL_STYLE,
        WS_VISIBLE | WS_CHILD | WS_BORDER |
        LVS_ICON);
}

void CCommonControlsApp2View::OnRadioSmallClicked()
{
    SetWindowLong(m_listView.m_hWnd, GWL_STYLE,
        WS_CHILD | WS_VISIBLE | WS_BORDER |
        LVS_SMALLICON);
}

void CCommonControlsApp2View::OnRadioListClicked()
{
    SetWindowLong(m_listView.m_hWnd, GWL_STYLE,
        WS_CHILD | WS_VISIBLE | WS_BORDER |
        LVS_LIST);
}
```

```
void CCommonControlsApp2View::OnRadioReportClicked()
{
    SetWindowLong(m_listView.m_hWnd, GWL_STYLE,
        WS_CHILD | WS_VISIBLE | WS_BORDER |
        LVS_REPORT);
}
```

SetWindowLong() takes three arguments: the handle of the window whose style you want to change, the index of the value to change, and the new value. The second argument can be one of the following values: GWL_EXSTYLE (changes the extended window style), GWL_STYLE (changes the window style), GWL_WNDPROC (changes the window procedure's address), GWL_HINSTANCE (changes the application instance handle), GWL_ID (changes the window identifier), or GWL_USERDATA (changes the window's application-specific, 32-bit value).

When the user double-clicks an item in the list view control, the control generates an NM_DBLCLK notification; the view window's OnListViewDblClk() function manages this notification:

```
void CCommonControlsApp2View::OnListViewDblClk
    (NMHDR* pNMHDR, LRESULT* pResult)
{
    int index =
        m_listView.GetNextItem(-1, LVNI_SELECTED);

    if (index != -1)
    {
        CString str = "NAME:\t" +
            m_listView.GetItemText(index, 0);
        str += "\nID:\t" +
            m_listView.GetItemText(index, 1);
        str += "\nAGE:\t"
            + m_listView.GetItemText(index, 2);
        str += "\nGENDER: "
            + m_listView.GetItemText(index, 3);

        MessageBox(str);
    }
}
```

The function first gets the index of the clicked item. It then gets the text for all the subitems, using the text to build a string that the program displays in a message box.

The Tree View Control

The tree view control is every bit as complex as the list view control because you must perform similar steps to get the tree view up and running. In this section, you learn to incorporate tree view controls into your programs. Figure 7-29 shows a simple tree view control displayed in a window. The program displays the control with only its root item visible. Because the root item is in its collapsed state, you can't see any of the child items in the control.

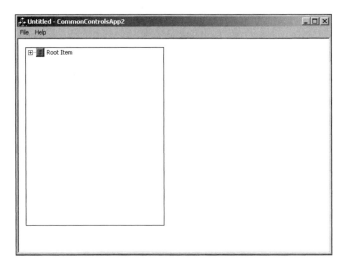

Figure 7-29: The tree view control with the root item in its collapsed state

To see the child items, you must click the plus sign next to the root item (or you can double-click the root item). When you do, the tree expands to show its next level (see Figure 7-30). As you can see in the figure, the child items also are marked with plus signs; this means that you can expand each to reveal another level of the tree. Figure 7-31 shows the tree completely expanded.

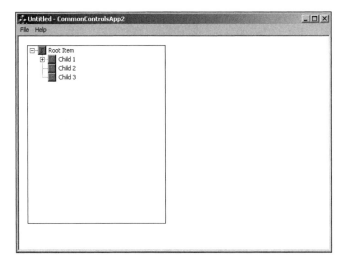

Figure 7-30: The tree view control with the first level of child items revealed

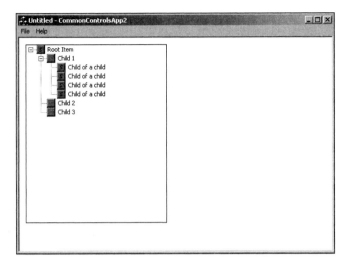

Figure 7-31: The tree view control with all child items revealed

Creating the tree view control object

To create a tree view control, you first define an object of the CTreeCtrl class:

CTreeCtrl m_treeView;

You then call the object's Create() member function, which creates the actual control and associates it with the CTreeCtrl object. The CTreeCtrl class's Create() function has the following signature. I list the arguments' descriptions in order after the signature.

```
BOOL Create(
    DWORD dwStyle,
    const RECT& rect,
    CWnd* pParentWnd,
    UINT nID);
```

dwStyle	The tree view's style flags
rect	A RECT or CRect object that specifies the tree view's size and position
pParentWnd	A pointer to the tree view's parent window
nID	The tree view's ID

A call to Create() might look something like this:

```
m_treeView.Create(WS_VISIBLE | WS_CHILD | WS_BORDER |
    TVS_HASLINES | TVS_LINESATROOT | TVS_HASBUTTONS,
    CRect(300, 40, 560, 360), this, IDC_TREEVIEW);
```

For the standard window styles, you at least should specify WS_CHILD and WS_VISIBLE. You may find other window styles useful in specific circumstances. For example, the preceding tree view control specifies the WS_BORDER style so that the edges of the control stand out against the window's white background.

The CTreeCtrl class defines a set of styles specific to the tree view control. The following list in Table 7-9 describes these styles, which you use to specify how the tree view control should look and act.

Table 7-9 CTreeCtrl Styles and Descriptions

Style	Description
TVS_DISABLEDRAGDROP	Prevents TVN_BEGINDRAG notifications
TVS_EDITLABELS	Enables the user to edit item labels
TVS_HASBUTTONS	Adds a button to the left of each parent item
TVS_HASLINES	Draws lines linking child and parent items
TVS_LINESATROOT	Draws lines linking child items to the root item
TVS_NOTOOLTIPS	Turns off the control's tooltips
TVS_SHOWSELALWAYS	Forces a selected item to stay highlighted whether or not the tree view has the input focus
TVS_SINGLEEXPAND	Allows only one item at a time to be expanded

Adding items to the tree view control

An empty tree view control doesn't do your application much good. So, after creating the control, you need to add the tree items. You do this by calling the tree view's InsertItem() member function. The first step in adding an item is to create and initialize a TV_ITEM structure. Windows defines the TV_ITEM structure as follows. A description of each of the structure's members appears in order after the structure declaration.

```
typedef struct _TV_ITEM {
    UINT mask;
    HTREEITEM hItem;
    UINT state;
    UINT stateMask;
    LPSTR pszText;
```

```
    int cchTextMax;
    int iImage;
    int iSelectedImage;
    int cChildren;
    LPARAM lParam;
} TV_ITEM, FAR *LPTV_ITEM;
```

mask	A flag that specifies which of the structure's members contain information. The flag can be a combination of any or all of the following: TVIF_CHILDREN, TVIF_HANDLE, TVIF_IMAGE, TVIF_PARAM, TVIF_SELECTEDIMAGE, TVIF_STATE, and TVIF_TEXT.
hItem	The item's handle.
state	The item's state.
stateMask	Flags that indicate the valid bits in the state member.
pszText	A pointer to the item text.
cchTextMax	The size of the buffer pointed to by pszText.
iImage	The image-list index of the item's image.
iSelectedImage	The image-list index of the item's selected image.
cChildren	A flag that specifies whether the item has child items.
Lparam	An application-specific, 32-bit value for the item.

To create a new root item, you can start with the following code that sets up the TV_ITEM structure:

```
TV_ITEM tvItem;
tvItem.mask =
    TVIF_TEXT | TVIF_IMAGE | TVIF_SELECTEDIMAGE;
tvItem.pszText = "Root Item";
tvItem.cchTextMax = 10;
tvItem.iImage = 0;
tvItem.iSelectedImage = 0;
```

Next, you need to set up a TV_INSERTSTRUCT structure. Windows defines the TV_INSERTSTRUCT structure as follows. A description of each of the structure's members appears in order after the structure declaration.

```
typedef struct _TV_INSERTSTRUCT {
    HTREEITEM hParent;
    HTREEITEM hInsertAfter;
    TV_ITEM   item;
} TV_INSERTSTRUCT, FAR *LPTV_INSERTSTRUCT;
```

hParent	The parent item's handle or TVI_ROOT
hInsertAfter	The handle of the item after which to place the new item or one of the following flags: TVI_FIRST (place at the start of the list), TVI_LAST (place at the end of the list), or TVI_SORT (place in alphabetical order)
item	The TV_ITEM structure that defines the new item

For the root item, you can write the following code to create and initialize the TV_INSERTSTRUCT structure:

```
TV_INSERTSTRUCT tvInsert;
tvInsert.hParent = TVI_ROOT;
tvInsert.hInsertAfter = TVI_FIRST;
tvInsert.item = tvItem;
```

Finally, you can add the item by calling InsertItem():

```
HTREEITEM hRoot = m_treeView.InsertItem(&tvInsert);
```

The InsertItem() function takes the address of a TV_INSERTSTRUCT structure as its single argument and returns the handle of the newly inserted item. You should save the handle because you need it to add child items to the tree's root.

To add child items to the root, you follow similar steps using slightly different flags, a different image, and the handle to the parent item. For example, the following lines add a child item to the previously created root item:

```
tvItem.pszText = "Child Item 1";
tvItem.cchTextMax = 13;
tvItem.iImage = 1;
tvItem.iSelectedImage = 1;
tvInsert.hParent = hRoot;
tvInsert.hInsertAfter = TVI_FIRST;
tvInsert.item = tvItem;
HTREEITEM hChild1 = m_treeView.InsertItem(&tvInsert);
```

To add a second child item on the same level (called a *sibling*), you change the hInsertAfter flag to TVI_LAST. This tells Windows to add the item at the end of the list:

```
tvItem.pszText = "Child Item 2";
tvItem.cchTextMax = 13;
tvItem.iImage = 1;
tvItem.iSelectedImage = 1;
tvInsert.hParent = hRoot;
tvInsert.hInsertAfter = TVI_LAST;
tvInsert.item = tvItem;
HTREEITEM hChild2 = m_treeView.InsertItem(&tvInsert);
```

To add a child item to another child item (that is, to create a third level to the tree), you use the first child's handle as the parent:

```
tvItem.pszText = "Child of a child";
tvItem.cchTextMax = 17;
tvItem.iImage = 2;
tvItem.iSelectedImage = 2;
tvInsert.hParent = hChild1;
tvInsert.hInsertAfter = TVI_FIRST;
tvInsert.item = tvItem;
HTREEITEM hChildChild1 =
    m_treeView.InsertItem(&tvInsert);
```

Responding to user selections

As with a list view control, often you use a tree view control to do more than just display data to the user. You may want the user to be able to select items in the control. When the user double-clicks an item in the tree view control, the control generates an NM_DBLCLK notification to which your application can respond. To accomplish this task, you first must add the notification to your window's message map:

```
ON_NOTIFY(NM_DBLCLK, IDC_TREEVIEW, OnTreeViewDblClk)
```

In the message-response function, you can get the handle of the selected item by calling the tree view object's GetSelectedItem() member function:

```
HTREEITEM hItem = m_treeView.GetSelectedItem();
```

If the value returned from GetSelectedItem() is NULL, there is no selected item. If GetNextItem() returns a valid handle, you can call GetItemText() to get the selected item's text:

```
CString str = m_treeView.GetItemText(hItem);
```

This function's single argument is the handle of the item for which you want the text.

PROBLEMS & SOLUTIONS

Enabling Tree-View Item Editing

PROBLEM: *Now that I have item editing working on my list view control, what about on tree view controls?*

SOLUTION: Enabling editing in a tree view control is very similar to enabling editing in a list view control. First, when you create your tree view control, you must include the TVS_EDITLABELS style:

Continued

```
m_treeView.Create(WS_VISIBLE | WS_CHILD | WS_BORDER |
    TVS_HASLINES | TVS_LINESATROOT | TVS_HASBUTTONS |
    TVS_EDITLABELS, CRect(300, 40, 560, 360),
    this, IDC_TREEVIEW);
```

Now, when the user clicks a selected item in the tree view, the item's label changes to an edit control. The user can edit the item, but when the user presses Enter to end the editing, the label returns to its old text. As you know from the list view control, this action occurs because your application must accept the user's changes before they become permanent.

To manage user edits, the application responds to two tree view notifications: TVN_BEGINLABELEDIT and TVN_ENDLABELEDIT. To do this, first use ClassWizard to override the OnNotify() member function in the window class. The OnNotify() message responds to WM_NOTIFY messages into which Windows packages the TVN_BEGINLABELEDIT and TVN_ENDLABELEDIT notifications.

Here is OnNotify()'s signature, followed by descriptions of each of its arguments:

```
virtual BOOL CWnd::OnNotify(
    WPARAM wParam,
    LPARAM lParam,
    LRESULT* pResult);
```

wParam	The WM_NOTIFY message's WPARAM value
lParam	The WM_NOTIFY message's LPARAM value
pResult	A pointer to a result code

How you interpret the three parameters received by OnNotify() depends on the type of message you process. In the case of a tree view control, wParam holds the control's ID. The value of lParam also depends on the type of notification. With TVN_BEGINLABELEDIT and TVN_ENDLABELEDIT, lParam holds a pointer to a TV_DISPINFO structure that contains the information you need to process the user's editing request.

In OnNotify(), the first step is to cast lParam to a TV_DISPINFO pointer like this:

```
TV_DISPINFO* pDispInfo = (TV_DISPINFO*)lParam;
```

With a pointer to the structure in hand, the program can get the notification code tucked away in the structure's hdr.code member:

```
UINT notificationID = pDispInfo->hdr.code;
```

If the notification ID is TVN_BEGINLABELEDIT, the program can do whatever it needs to do before the editing actually begins:

Continued

```
if (notificationID == TVN_BEGINLABELEDIT)
{
    // Perform pre-edit processing here.
}
```

If the notification ID is TVN_ENDLABELEDIT, you need to copy the new label from the edit control into the tree view item. The item.hItem member of the TV_DISPINFO structure holds the item's handle:

```
HTREEITEM hItem = pDispInfo->item.hItem;
```

You can get the new text from the structure's item.pszText member:

```
CString newText = pDispInfo->item.pszText;
```

You must test for an empty string (or NULL, if you use a character array) because that's what the text will be if the user decides to exit the edit box by pressing Esc to cancel the editing operation. If the new text is valid, you call the tree view's SetItemText() function to complete the operation:

```
if (newText != "")
    m_treeView.SetItemText(hItem, newText);
```

Location: **WinPrgS\Chap07\EditControls**

On this book's CD-ROM, you can find the EditControls application that demonstrates label editing in a tree view control.

The MFC tree view shortcuts

You just learned the standard methods for constructing and initializing a tree view control. Now that you know how the control works, you probably suspect that (as you discovered with the list view control) MFC features shortcuts that make it easier to create a tree view control.

The CTreeCtrl class overloads its InsertItem() member function with versions that don't require you to initialize TV_ITEM and TV_INSERTSTRUCT structures in your program. You simply pass a few arguments to InsertItem(), and MFC fills in the structures for you. Here is the signature of the handiest overloaded version of InsertItem(), followed by descriptions of its arguments:

```
HTREEITEM InsertItem(
    LPCTSTR lpszItem,
    int nImage,
    int nSelectedImage,
    HTREEITEM hParent = TVI_ROOT,
    HTREEITEM hInsertAfter = TVI_LAST);
```

lpszItem	The item's text
nImage	The image-list index of the item's image
nSelectedImage	The image-list index of the item's selected image
hParent	The parent item's handle or TVI_ROOT
hInsertAfter	The handle of the item after which to place the new item or one of the following flags: TVI_FIRST, TVI_LAST, or TVI_SORT

Using the alternate version of InsertItem( ) simplifies the code needed to create and initialize a tree view control. Here is the code required to create the tree view control shown in Figure 7-32:

```
// Create the tree view's image list
m_treeImages.Create(16, 16, ILC_COLOR4, 3, 0);
HICON hIcon = ::LoadIcon(AfxGetResourceHandle(),
    MAKEINTRESOURCE(IDI_ICON1));
m_treeImages.Add(hIcon);
hIcon = ::LoadIcon(AfxGetResourceHandle(),
    MAKEINTRESOURCE(IDI_ICON2));
m_treeImages.Add(hIcon);
hIcon = ::LoadIcon(AfxGetResourceHandle(),
    MAKEINTRESOURCE(IDI_ICON3));
m_treeImages.Add(hIcon);

// Create the Tree View control.
m_treeView.Create(WS_VISIBLE | WS_CHILD | WS_BORDER |
    TVS_HASLINES | TVS_LINESATROOT | TVS_HASBUTTONS,
    CRect(300, 40, 560, 360), this, 110);
m_treeView.SetImageList(&m_treeImages, TVSIL_NORMAL);

// Create the root item.
HTREEITEM hRoot = m_treeView.InsertItem("Root Item",
    0, 0, TVI_ROOT, TVI_FIRST);

// Create the first-level child items.
HTREEITEM hChild1 = m_treeView.InsertItem("Child 1",
        1, 1, hRoot, TVI_FIRST);
HTREEITEM hChild2 = m_treeView.InsertItem("Child 2",
    1, 1, hRoot, TVI_LAST);
HTREEITEM hChild3 = m_treeView.InsertItem("Child 3",
    1, 1, hRoot, TVI_LAST);

// Create the second-level child items.
m_treeView.InsertItem("Child of a child",
    2, 2, hChild1, TVI_FIRST);
m_treeView.InsertItem("Child of a child",
    2, 2, hChild1, TVI_LAST);
```

```
m_treeView.InsertItem("Child of a child",
    2, 2, hChild1, TVI_LAST);
m_treeView.InsertItem("Child of a child",
    2, 2, hChild1, TVI_LAST);
```

The `m_treeImages` and `m_treeView` objects are members of the window's class and are declared in the window class's header file.

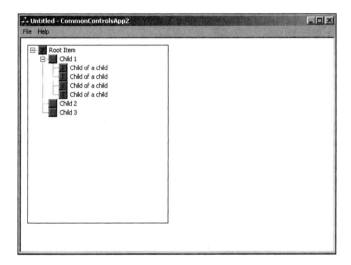

Figure 7-32: The tree view control created using the shortcut method

The tree view control's member functions

The `CTreeCtrl` class defines many more member functions than the few you've learned about so far. Table 7-10 lists some these functions and their descriptions. A complete description of all the member functions is beyond the scope of this book. However, you should have little difficulty figuring out and using most of the functions in this table.

Table 7-10 CTreeCtrl Member Functions

Function	Description
`Create()`	Creates a tree view element and associates it with the `CTreeCtrl` object
`CreateDragImage()`	Creates an item's dragging bitmap
`DeleteAllItems()`	Deletes all items
`DeleteItem()`	Deletes a new item

Continued

Table 7-10 *(continued)*

Function	Description
`EditLabel()`	Edits an item
`EnsureVisible()`	Ensures that an item is visible
`Expand()`	Expands or collapses child items
`GetChildItem()`	Gets an item's child
`GetCount()`	Gets the tree view's item count
`GetDropHilightItem()`	Gets the drag-and-drop target
`GetEditControl()`	Gets a handle to an item's edit control
`GetFirstVisibleItem()`	Gets the first visible item
`GetImageList()`	Gets a handle to the tree view's image list
`GetIndent()`	Gets the number of pixels an item is indented from its parent
`GetItem()`	Gets an item's attributes
`GetItemData()`	Gets an item's 32-bit, application-specific value
`GetItemImage()`	Gets an item's images
`GetItemRect()`	Gets an item's bounding rectangle
`GetItemState()`	Gets an item's state
`GetItemText()`	Gets an item's text
`GetNextItem()`	Gets the next tree view item
`GetNextSiblingItem()`	Gets an item's next sibling
`GetNextVisibleItem()`	Gets the next visible item
`GetParentItem()`	Gets an item's parent
`GetPrevSiblingItem()`	Gets an item's previous sibling
`GetPrevVisibleItem()`	Gets the previous visible item
`GetRootItem()`	Gets the root item
`GetSelectedItem()`	Gets the currently selected item
`GetVisibleCount()`	Gets tree view's visible-item count
`HitTest()`	Returns the index of the item at a given position
`InsertItem()`	Inserts an item
`ItemHasChildren()`	Determines whether an item has child items
`Select()`	Performs a selection, highlight, or scrolling action for an item

Function	Description
SelectDropTarget()	Redraws an item as a drag-and-drop target
SelectItem()	Selects an item
SelectSetFirstVisible()	Specifies the first visible item
SetImageList()	Sets the tree view's image list
SetIndent()	Sets an item's indent
SetItem()	Sets an item's attributes
SetItemData()	Sets an item's 32-bit, application-specific value
SetItemImage()	Sets an item's images
SetItemState()	Sets an item's state
SetItemText()	Sets an item's text
SortChildren()	Sorts the children of a parent item
SortChildrenCB()	Sorts the children of a parent item using a custom sort function

Understanding CommonControlsApp2's tree view control

CommonControlsApp2 creates its tree view control in the view window class's InitTreeView() member function, which looks like this:

```
void CCommonControlsApp2View::InitTreeView()
{
    // Create the Image List.
    m_treeImages.Create(16, 16, ILC_COLOR4, 3, 0);
    HICON hIcon = ::LoadIcon(AfxGetResourceHandle(),
        MAKEINTRESOURCE(IDI_ICON1));
    m_treeImages.Add(hIcon);
    hIcon = ::LoadIcon(AfxGetResourceHandle(),
        MAKEINTRESOURCE(IDI_ICON2));
    m_treeImages.Add(hIcon);
    hIcon = ::LoadIcon(AfxGetResourceHandle(),
        MAKEINTRESOURCE(IDI_ICON3));
    m_treeImages.Add(hIcon);

    // Create the Tree View control.
    m_treeView.Create(WS_VISIBLE | WS_CHILD | WS_BORDER |
        TVS_HASLINES | TVS_LINESATROOT | TVS_HASBUTTONS,
        CRect(300, 40, 560, 360), this, IDC_TREEVIEW);
    m_treeView.SetImageList(&m_treeImages, TVSIL_NORMAL);

    // Create the root item.
    HTREEITEM hRoot = AddTreeItem("Team Members",
        15, 0, 0, TVI_ROOT, TVI_FIRST);
```

```
    HTREEITEM hChildItem = AddTreeItem("John",
        12, 1, 1, hRoot, TVI_FIRST);
    AddTreeItem("ID: 176498", 12, 2, 2,
        hChildItem, TVI_FIRST);
    AddTreeItem("Age: 46", 12, 2, 2,
        hChildItem, TVI_LAST);
    AddTreeItem("Gender: M", 12, 2, 2,
        hChildItem, TVI_LAST);

    HTREEITEM hChildItem2 = AddTreeItem("Marie",
        12, 1, 1, hRoot, TVI_LAST);
    AddTreeItem("ID: 984732", 12, 2, 2,
        hChildItem2, TVI_FIRST);
    AddTreeItem("Age: 24", 12, 2, 2,
        hChildItem2, TVI_LAST);
    AddTreeItem("Gender: F", 12, 2, 2,
        hChildItem2, TVI_LAST);

    HTREEITEM hChildItem3 = AddTreeItem("Beth",
        12, 1, 1, hRoot, TVI_LAST);
    AddTreeItem("ID: 452879", 12, 2, 2,
        hChildItem3, TVI_FIRST);
    AddTreeItem("Age: 33", 12, 2, 2,
        hChildItem3, TVI_LAST);
    AddTreeItem("Gender: F", 12, 2, 2,
        hChildItem3, TVI_LAST);

    HTREEITEM hChildItem4 = AddTreeItem("Gregory",
        12, 1, 1, hRoot, TVI_LAST);
    AddTreeItem("ID: 487655", 12, 2, 2,
        hChildItem4, TVI_FIRST);
    AddTreeItem("Age: 19", 12, 2, 2,
        hChildItem4, TVI_LAST);
    AddTreeItem("Gender: F", 12, 2, 2,
        hChildItem4, TVI_LAST);

    HTREEITEM hChildItem5 = AddTreeItem("Willy",
        12, 1, 1, hRoot, TVI_LAST);
    AddTreeItem("ID: 285943", 12, 2, 2,
        hChildItem5, TVI_FIRST);
    AddTreeItem("Age: 56", 12, 2, 2,
        hChildItem5, TVI_LAST);
    AddTreeItem("Gender: M", 12, 2, 2,
        hChildItem5, TVI_LAST);

    HTREEITEM hChildItem6 = AddTreeItem("Sandra",
        12, 1, 1, hRoot, TVI_LAST);
    AddTreeItem("ID: 768506", 12, 2, 2,
        hChildItem6, TVI_FIRST);
    AddTreeItem("Age: 17", 12, 2, 2,
        hChildItem6, TVI_LAST);
    AddTreeItem("Gender: F", 12, 2, 2,
        hChildItem6, TVI_LAST);
}
```

`InitTreeView()` begins by creating the tree view's image lists. The function then creates the tree view object and assigns the image lists to the object. Finally, the function calls the `AddTreeItem()` member function for each item in the control.

`AddTreeItem()` is a member function of the view window's class. Its task is to take some of the hassle out of managing the `TV_ITEM` and `TV_INSERTSTRUCT` structures. The calling function supplies the data needed to create an item; `AddTreeItem()` initializes the structures with the data and creates the item, returning the item's handle. Here is the `AddTreeItem()` function:

```
HTREEITEM CCommonControlsApp2View::AddTreeItem
    (LPSTR pText, UINT max, UINT image, UINT selImage,
    HTREEITEM hParent, HTREEITEM hInsert)
{
    TV_ITEM tvItem;
    tvItem.mask =
        TVIF_TEXT | TVIF_IMAGE | TVIF_SELECTEDIMAGE;
    tvItem.pszText = pText;
    tvItem.cchTextMax = max;
    tvItem.iImage = image;
    tvItem.iSelectedImage = selImage;

    TV_INSERTSTRUCT tvInsert;
    tvInsert.hParent = hParent;
    tvInsert.hInsertAfter = hInsert;
    tvInsert.item = tvItem;
    HTREEITEM hItem =
        m_treeView.InsertItem(&tvInsert);

    return hItem;
}
```

Finally, when the user clicks an item in the tree view control, the control generates an `NM_DBLCLK` notification. The view window's `OnTreeViewDblClk()` function manages this notification. Here is `OnTreeViewDblClk()`:

```
void CCommonControlsApp2View::OnTreeViewDblClk
    (NMHDR* pNMHDR, LRESULT* pResult)
{
    HTREEITEM hItem =
        m_treeView.GetSelectedItem();

    if (hItem != NULL)
    {
        CString str = m_treeView.GetItemText(hItem);
        MessageBox(str);
    }
}
```

The function first gets the handle of the clicked item. It then gets the text for the item and displays it in a message box.

Summary

Windows 2000's common controls are great tools for putting together sophisticated user interfaces. Whether you need to retrieve a single value from the user or display a large data set in an organized way, the common controls can fit the bill. Unfortunately, this chapter isn't long enough to cover the myriad ways in which you can use the common controls. Therefore, you should take the time to explore the common control classes on your own in order to discover details not presented here.

Also discussed in this chapter:

- The progress bar control displays the status of an ongoing operation.
- The slider control enables the user to select a value from a given range.
- The spinner control also provides a method for obtaining values within a given range.
- Image list controls hold images that other controls need to complete their displays.
- A list view control enables applications to organize large amounts of data in a table-like format.
- A tree view control also organizes data, but it uses a hierarchical display rather than a table.

Chapter 8

Printing

In This Chapter

- Printing from a traditional Windows application
- Printing text in an MFC application
- Printing graphics in an MFC application

Handling printers under Windows was once a task that made even experienced programmers shudder. Nowadays, printing documents from a Windows application is easier — but Windows still requires that you handle many details. This complexity is due to the fact that you never can be sure exactly what printer is connected to the user's computer; this forces you to write code that adapts itself to the current printer's attributes. You do this by using variables in place of hard-coded values wherever the printer's attributes can affect the output. In this chapter, you discover the techniques you need to know to print text and graphics from a Windows application successfully.

An Overview of Printing in Windows

Most of this chapter covers printing documents from MFC programs. However, in order to understand what's going on behind the scenes in MFC, it helps to know how you print data from a traditional C Windows program. You tackle that topic in this section where you not only learn the traditional Windows printing process, but also study a small sample application that demonstrates the concepts.

The Six Steps to Printing a Document

Under Windows, the basic printing process involves six steps:

1. Call the `CreateDC()` function to acquire a printer DC.
2. Call the `StartDoc()` function to begin the document.
3. Call the `StartPage()` function to begin a page.

4. Render the document onto the printer DC.
5. Call the `EndPage()` function to end a page. (Repeat Steps 3 through 5 for each page in the document.)
6. Call the `EndDoc()` function to end the print job.

You call `CreateDC()` to create a printer device context first because—just as you need a device context to draw data in an application's window—you also need a DC to send data to a printer. To determine the type of printer connected to the system, the application must search the user's WIN.INI file or call the Windows API `EnumPrinters()` function. Calling `EnumPrinters()` is the easiest method. The `EnumPrinters()` function's signature looks like this:

```
BOOL EnumPrinters(
    DWORD Flags,
    LPTSTR Name,
    DWORD Level,
    LPBYTE pPrinterEnum,
    DWORD cbBuf,
    LPDWORD pcbNeeded,
    LPDWORD pcReturned,
);
```

The function's arguments are described, in order, as follows:

Flags	A flag indicating the type of printer needed
Name	The name of the printer object
Level	The type of printer info structure
pPrinterEnum	A pointer to the printer info structure
cbBuf	The size of the printer info array
pcbNeeded	A pointer to the variable that holds the number of bytes copied to the printer info array
pcReturned	A pointer to the variable that holds the number of print info structures copied to the array

Some of `EnumPrinters()`'s arguments have many different possible values depending upon how you want Windows to describe the printers available on the system. For the most part, however, concern yourself only with getting the default printer. (If you're interested in all the other hairy details, look up `EnumPrinters()` in your Visual C++ online documentation.) To program your application to ask Windows for the default printer, use the following code:

```
PRINTER_INFO_5 printerInfo5[3];
DWORD needed, returned;
```

```
EnumPrinters(PRINTER_ENUM_DEFAULT, NULL, 5,
    (LPBYTE)printerInfo5, sizeof(printerInfo5),
    &needed, &returned);
```

If the previous lines execute successfully, you have the name of the default printer in the first printer info structure's `pPrinterName` member. You can access that member like this:

```
printerInfo5[0].pPrinterName
```

The printer name is exactly what you need in order to create a DC for the printer. To get the DC, call `CreateDC()`:

```
HDC printDC;

printDC = CreateDC(NULL,
    printerInfo5[0].pPrinterName, NULL, NULL);
```

Here, you provide the printer's system name as the second argument. The remaining arguments should be `NULL`.

Once you have a DC for the user's printer, you can start printing the document. First call the Windows API function `StartDoc()`, which sets up Windows to begin spooling your document to the system print spooler. This process resembles how you call `BeginPaint()` in a C Windows program (see Chapter 1) to start displaying data in an application's window. If `StartDoc()` succeeds, it returns an ID for the print job; otherwise, it returns a value less than or equal to zero.

One of `StartDoc()`'s arguments is a pointer to a `DOCINFO` structure. You must initialize the members of the structure before calling `StartDoc()`. In most cases, you just place the size of the structure in the `cbSize` member and a pointer to the document's name in the `lpszDocName` member. The remaining members can be `NULL` or zero. The entire process looks something like this:

```
char docName[] = "RectangleDoc";
DOCINFO docInfo;
docInfo.cbSize = sizeof(docInfo);
docInfo.lpszDocName = docName;
docInfo.lpszOutput = NULL;
docInfo.lpszDatatype = NULL;
docInfo.fwType = 0;

result = StartDoc(printDC, &docInfo);

if (result <= 0)
{
    MessageBox(0, "StartDoc() failed",
        "Basic Print App", MB_OK | MB_ICONERROR );
    return;
}
```

If the call to `StartDoc()` succeeds, you can start your first page by calling `StartPage()`. The `StartPage()` function takes only a single argument, which is the printer DC. The function returns a value greater than zero if it succeeds; otherwise, it returns a value less than or equal to zero. The code to start a page looks similar to the following snippet:

```
result = StartPage(printDC);
if (result <= 0)
{
    MessageBox(0, "StartPage() failed",
        "Basic Print App", MB_OK | MB_ICONERROR );
    return;
}
```

Once you have the page started, sending data to the printer is just like sending data to an application's window. You just direct the output to the printer DC, rather than to a window DC. Of course, a printer isn't as versatile as a video display. For example, your printer probably can't display a bitmap the same way a window does. Also, the dots on the screen are a different size than the dots on most printers, so you often need to scale data destined for the printer.

After printing a page, you call the `EndPage()` function to end the current page. `EndPage()`, like `StartPage()`, requires the printer DC as its single argument. Also like `StartPage()`, `EndPage()` returns a value greater than zero if it succeeds and zero or less if it doesn't succeed. The code to end a page looks similar to the following snippet:

```
result = EndPage(printDC);
if (result <= 0)
{
    MessageBox(0, "EndPage() failed",
        "Basic Print App", MB_OK | MB_ICONERROR );
    return;
}
```

At this point, the application can call `StartPage()` again to begin another page. If there are no other pages to print, the application should call `EndDoc()` to end the print job:

```
EndDoc(printDC);
```

The BasicPrintApp Sample Program

Location: `WinPrgS\Chap08\BasicPrintApp`

Now that you've explored the basic process for printing a document under Windows, you can put all that knowledge to the test. Listing 8-1 shows BasicPrintApp—a short Windows program that prints a rectangle and a line of text on the default printer:

Listing 8-1: Printing from a standard Windows program

```c
#include <windows.h>

LRESULT CALLBACK WndProc(HWND hWnd, UINT message,
    WPARAM wParam, LPARAM lParam);
void PrintRectangle();

int WINAPI WinMain(HINSTANCE hCurrentInst,
    HINSTANCE hPrevInstance, PSTR lpszCmdLine,
    int nCmdShow)
{
    WNDCLASS wndClass;
    HWND hWnd;
    MSG msg;
    UINT width;
    UINT height;

    wndClass.style = CS_HREDRAW | CS_VREDRAW;
    wndClass.lpfnWndProc = WndProc;
    wndClass.cbClsExtra = 0;
    wndClass.cbWndExtra = 0;
    wndClass.hInstance = hCurrentInst;
    wndClass.hIcon = LoadIcon(NULL, IDI_APPLICATION);
    wndClass.hCursor = LoadCursor(NULL, IDC_ARROW);
    wndClass.hbrBackground = GetStockObject(WHITE_BRUSH);
    wndClass.lpszMenuName = NULL;
    wndClass.lpszClassName = "BasicPrintApp";

    RegisterClass(&wndClass);

    width = GetSystemMetrics(SM_CXSCREEN) / 2;
    height = GetSystemMetrics(SM_CYSCREEN) / 2;

    hWnd = CreateWindow(
        "BasicPrintApp",   /* Window class's name.  */
        "Basic Print App", /* Title bar text.       */
        WS_OVERLAPPEDWINDOW,/* The window's style.  */
        10,     /* X position.         */
        10,     /* Y position.         */
        width,  /* Width.              */
        height, /* Height.             */
        NULL,   /* Parent window's handle. */
        NULL,   /* Menu handle.        */
        hCurrentInst,   /* Instance handle.    */
        NULL);  /* No additional data. */

    ShowWindow(hWnd, nCmdShow);
    UpdateWindow(hWnd);

    while (GetMessage(&msg, NULL, 0, 0))
    {
        TranslateMessage(&msg);
```

```c
            DispatchMessage(&msg);
    }

    return msg.wParam;
}

LRESULT CALLBACK WndProc(HWND hWnd, UINT message,
    WPARAM wParam, LPARAM lParam)
{
    HDC hDC;
    PAINTSTRUCT paintStruct;

    switch(message)
    {
        case WM_PAINT:
            hDC = BeginPaint(hWnd, &paintStruct);
            TextOut(hDC, 10, 10,
                "Click in the window to print.", 29);
            EndPaint(hWnd, &paintStruct);
            return 0;

        case WM_LBUTTONDOWN:
            PrintRectangle();
            return 0;

        case WM_DESTROY:
            PostQuitMessage(0);
            return 0;
    }

    return DefWindowProc(hWnd, message, wParam, lParam);
}

void PrintRectangle()
{
    PRINTER_INFO_5 printerInfo5[3];
    DWORD needed, returned;
    HDC printDC;
    DOCINFO docInfo;
    char docName[] = "RectangleDoc";
    int result;

    // Step 1: Get a printer DC.
    EnumPrinters(PRINTER_ENUM_DEFAULT, NULL, 5,
        (LPBYTE)printerInfo5, sizeof(printerInfo5),
        &needed, &returned);
    printDC = CreateDC(NULL,
        printerInfo5[0].pPrinterName, NULL, NULL);

    // Step 2: Call StartDoc().
    docInfo.cbSize = sizeof(docInfo);
    docInfo.lpszDocName = docName;
    docInfo.lpszOutput = NULL;
```

```
            docInfo.lpszDatatype = NULL;
            docInfo.fwType = 0;
            result = StartDoc(printDC, &docInfo);
            if (result <= 0)
            {
                MessageBox(0, "StartDoc() failed",
                    "Basic Print App", MB_OK | MB_ICONERROR );
                return;
            }

            // Step 3: Call StartPage().
            result = StartPage(printDC);
            if (result <= 0)
            {
                MessageBox(0, "StartPage() failed",
                    "Basic Print App", MB_OK | MB_ICONERROR );
                return;
            }

            // Step 4: Print data.
            Rectangle(printDC, 20, 20, 1000, 200);
            TextOut(printDC, 100, 90,
                "Windows printing in action!", 27);

            // Step 5: Call EndPage().
            result = EndPage(printDC);
            if (result <= 0)
            {
                MessageBox(0, "EndPage() failed",
                    "Basic Print App", MB_OK | MB_ICONERROR );
                return;
            }

            // Step 6: Call EndDoc().
            EndDoc(printDC);
            MessageBox(0, "Document printed", "Basic Print App",
                MB_OK | MB_ICONINFORMATION);
}
```

When you run the application, you see the window shown in Figure 8-1. Just click in the window to send the rectangle data to your printer. If the printing process fails anywhere along the way, a message box appears indicating the location of the problem (see Figure 8-2).

BasicPrintApp handles all its printing chores in the `PrintRectangle()` function, using the same techniques you just learned. In that function, you can see how all the function calls work together to produce a complete (albeit simple) document. Each step of the six printing steps is marked with a comment, making it easier for you to decipher the code.

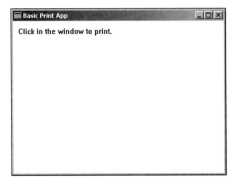

Figure 8-1: The BasicPrintApp application puts Windows printing to the test.

Figure 8-2: The application notifies you when the print job fails.

Printing Text in an MFC Application

If you use MFC AppWizard to put together your application, you can get basic printing and print preview functions very easily. To get this functionality, make sure that you select the *Printing and print preview* option in AppWizard's Step 4 of 6 dialog box (as shown in Figure 8-3). Such an AppWizard application handles all the details of getting the printer's name and acquiring the printer DC. You only need to refine the generated source code to produce an appropriate printout for the application.

When you use MFC's default printing functions, the application's document is displayed on the screen and sent to the printer in the OnDraw() function. The difference is that, in the case of screen display, the DC object sent to OnDraw() is for the client window; in the case of printing, the DC is for the current printer. This clever bit of DC switching enables one function to render output for both the screen and the printer, making it easier to produce *WYSIWYG (What You See Is What You Get)* output. The complication sets in when the coordinates used for screen display don't match those needed for printing. This is where the concept of scaling printer output enters.

Scaling the printer output so that it appears to be the correct size is just one of the printing details with which you must contend — depending on the type of document you print. You also may need to deal with pagination, headers and footers, fonts, and other tasks that Windows applications must complete to print professional-looking documents. Luckily, MFC takes much of the busywork out of printing documents by not only creating the printer context but also by providing member functions in the `CView` class that enable view windows to access the printing process at various stages. In the next section, you get a look at those functions and how they work. Along the way, you learn printing skills such as pagination and scaling.

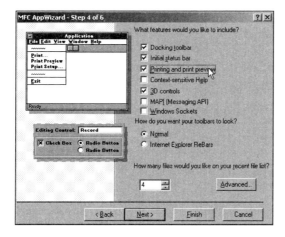

Figure 8-3: The AppWizard Printing and print preview option generates printing functions in your application.

The PrintApp Sample Application

CD

Location: `WinPrgS\Chap08\PrintApp`

Before examining how to print in an MFC application, you should take some time out to see what such an application can do. On this book's CD-ROM, you can find the PrintApp application. When you run the application, you see its main window. Although the window contains no scroll bars for displaying the full document, the application can hold any number of text lines. To increase the number of lines in the document, click in the window (see Figure 8-4). Right-click in the window to reduce the number of lines in the document. Use the File menu's Print Preview and Print commands to test the application's printing features, or select the Print command to print the document.

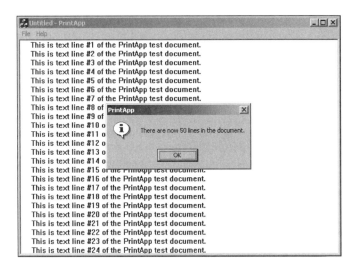

Figure 8-4: You add or remove lines to the display by clicking in the window.

MFC Member Functions for Printing

When you write an MFC program with printing features, you don't have to worry about getting the name of the current printer and creating the printer DC. You also don't have to worry about displaying the Print dialog box. In many cases, you don't even have to worry about sending the application's document to the printer. MFC handles all these details for you. Often, though, you need to refine the default MFC printing features for a specific application. The CView class, from which you derive your application's view window, defines five functions that enable you to take control of different phases of the printing process:

- OnPreparePrinting()
- OnBeginPrinting()
- OnPrepareDC()
- OnPrint()
- OnEndPrinting()

In the following sections, you examine these five functions in detail so you can use them to customize MFC's printing capabilities.

The OnPreparePrinting() function

OnPreparePrinting() is the first of the five special functions that MFC calls for a print or print preview job. You must override this function in the view window's class and call the DoPreparePrinting() function, which displays the Print dialog box and creates the printer DC. In OnPreparePrinting(), you can change some of the values displayed in the Print dialog box to set the minimum and maximum page count — if you can calculate the page count without the printer DC. When MFC calls OnPreparePrinting(), the printer DC is not created yet.

When you create your application with MFC AppWizard and select the Printing and print preview option for the application, AppWizard automatically overrides the OnPreparePrinting() function for you, as shown here:

```
BOOL CPrintAppView::OnPreparePrinting(CPrintInfo* pInfo)
{
    // default preparation
    return DoPreparePrinting(pInfo);
}
```

Notice that the OnPreparePrinting() override calls DoPreparePrinting(), which is where the Print dialog box gets displayed (see Figure 8-5). You can control the options displayed in the dialog box by initializing members of the CPrintInfo object passed to the function as its single parameter. For example, if you know that the document will be three pages, you can add calls to the CPrintInfo object's SetMinPage() and SetMaxPage() member functions as follows:

```
BOOL CPrintAppView::OnPreparePrinting(CPrintInfo* pInfo)
{
    // default preparation

    pInfo->SetMinPage(1);
    pInfo->SetMaxPage(3);

    return DoPreparePrinting(pInfo);
}
```

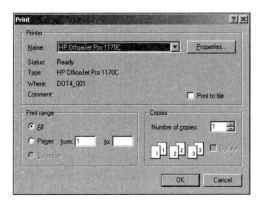

Figure 8-5: The DoPreparePrinting() function automatically displays the Print dialog box.

The `SetMinPage()` and `SetMaxPage()` functions not only tell MFC how many pages are to be printed, but they also determine the values shown in the Print dialog box's From and To boxes. If you don't call `SetMinPage()` and `SetMaxPage()`, the From box defaults to 1 and the To box remains empty (although MFC assumes only one page is to be printed).

If your document is a fixed size, as in the preceding example, you know in advance how many pages will print. This enables you to set the minimum and maximum pages in `OnPreparePrinting()`. The problem with `OnPreparePrinting()` is that the application does not have access to the printer DC yet, which limits how much information you can determine about the current document and printer. In many cases, you need the printer DC in order to determine how much of the document can fit on a page. If this is the case, you can modify the `OnBeginPrinting()` function.

The OnBeginPrinting() function

MFC calls the `OnBeginPrinting()` function after calling `OnPreparePrinting()`. The `CView` version does nothing, but if you override `OnBeginPrinting()` in your application's view window class, you can create GDI resources needed by the print job. Such resources include pens, brushes, and fonts. Also, because `OnBeginPrinting()` is the first place the view window has access to both the printer DC and the `CPrintInfo` structure, you can set page counts and other values here when those values depend upon the settings of the printer DC.

When you create your application with MFC AppWizard and select the Printing and print preview option for the application, AppWizard automatically overrides the `OnBeginPrinting()` function for you, as shown here:

```
void CPrintAppView::OnBeginPrinting(CDC* /*pDC*/,
    CPrintInfo* /*pInfo*/)
{
    // TODO: add extra initialization before printing
}
```

Presumably, to avoid compilation warnings about unreferenced variables, the AppWizard version of `OnBeginPrinting()` comments out the names of the printer DC and `CPrintInfo` objects. If you plan to access these parameters, you must remove the comments.

Many applications, especially those that must space lines of text properly, need to calculate different character sizes for the screen and printer. This is because screen and printer fonts are rarely the same size from a DPI point of view. For example, a 10-point font might be 20 pixels high on the screen but 50 dots high on the printer. If you try to use the same character height for the screen and the printer, the printer output almost certainly will overlap. Figure 8-6 shows an application displaying text, whereas Figure 8-7 shows the print preview window using the same character height for the same text.

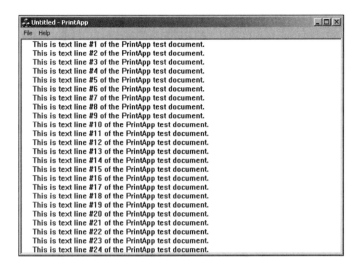

Figure 8-6: Text displayed on the screen uses screen font sizes.

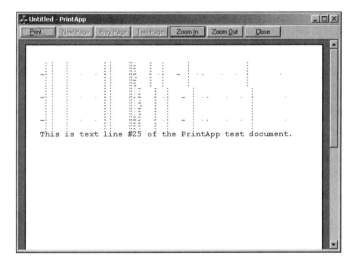

Figure 8-7: If an application uses the screen character size for printing, the text probably will overlap.

When you need to scale text output or calculate page sizes based on printer attributes, you override OnBeginPrinting() — the first place you have access to the printer DC. By calling printer DC member functions such as GetTextMetrics(), you can determine the correct character height for the printer as well as calculate the number of lines per page and the number of pages needed to display the entire document. Here's an example of the `OnBeginPrinting()` function calculating character sizes and page counts:

```
void CPrintAppView::OnBeginPrinting(CDC* pDC,
    CPrintInfo* pInfo)
{
    // TODO: add extra initialization before printing

    TEXTMETRIC textMetric;
    pDC->GetTextMetrics(&textMetric);
    m_printerCharHeight = textMetric.tmHeight +
        textMetric.tmExternalLeading;

    m_vertRes = pDC->GetDeviceCaps(VERTRES);
    m_linesPerPage = m_vertRes / m_printerCharHeight;
    int numPages = m_numLines / m_linesPerPage + 1;

    pInfo->SetMinPage(1);
    pInfo->SetMaxPage(numPages);
}
```

After setting the value of `m_printerCharHeight` (which you add as a member variable to the view class), you can use the value in the `OnDraw()` function to properly space the text. How can you determine whether MFC calls `OnDraw()` on behalf of the screen or the printer? The `CDC` object passed to the function defines a member function called `IsPrinting()` that returns TRUE if MFC calls the function to render data for the printer. The following code shows one way to write the `OnDraw()` function so that it displays text correctly on both the screen and the printer. Figure 8-8 shows the print preview window when the application uses this version of `OnDraw()`:

```
void CPrintAppView::OnDraw(CDC* pDC)
{
    CPrintAppDoc* pDoc = GetDocument();
    ASSERT_VALID(pDoc);

    // TODO: add draw code for native data here

    int charHeight;

    if (pDC->IsPrinting())
        charHeight = m_printerCharHeight;
    else
        charHeight = m_charHeight;

    for(int x=0; x<m_numLines; ++x)
    {
        char str[81];
        wsprintf(str, "This is text line #%d of \
the PrintApp test document.", x+1);
        pDC->TextOut(20, x*charHeight, str);
    }
}
```

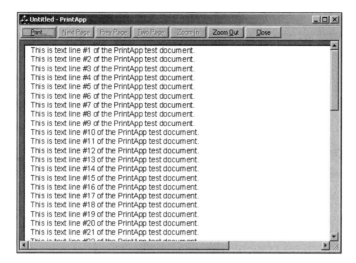

Figure 8-8: The print preview window now shows that the text spacing is correct for the printer.

This version of OnDraw() calls IsPrinting() to determine whether the output is going to the screen or the printer. If IsPrinting() returns TRUE, the data is about to be rendered on the printer, so OnDraw() sets charHeight to m_printerCharHeight—which got its value in OnBeginPrinting(). If IsPrinting() returns FALSE, the data is about to be rendered on the screen, so OnDraw() sets charHeight to m_charHeight—which holds the character height for the screen.

Where does m_charHeight come from? It's a member variable that you add to the view class. You then override the class's OnCreate() function, which responds to the Windows WM_CREATE message. MFC calls OnCreate() after the application's window is created but right before it displays the window on the screen. To initialize m_charHeight to the screen character size, you create a DC for the client window and call its GetTextMetrics() member function. The following code shows the entire process:

```
int CPrintAppView::OnCreate(LPCREATESTRUCT lpCreateStruct)
{
    if (CView::OnCreate(lpCreateStruct) == -1)
        return -1;

    // TODO: Add your specialized creation code here

    TEXTMETRIC textMetric;
    CClientDC clientDC(this);
    clientDC.GetTextMetrics(&textMetric);
    m_charHeight = textMetric.tmHeight +
        textMetric.tmExternalLeading;

    return 0;
}
```

Note

If you use OnBeginPrinting() to create GDI objects for a print job, don't select the new GDI objects into the printer DC right away. Instead, select them in the OnPrint() member function that gets called for each page. This rule applies because the DC is reinitialized for each page of the document. MFC calls OnBeginPrinting() only once for the entire document, but it calls OnPrint() for each page. That is, you can access information about the printer in OnBeginPrinting(), but you shouldn't modify the DC until OnPrint().

The OnPrepareDC() function

This brings you to the third function in the list: OnPrepareDC(). After MFC calls OnBeginPrinting(), it calls OnPrepareDC() for each page in the document right before the page prints. When you use OnDraw() to render data for both the screen and the printer, it's in OnPrepareDC() that your program can control exactly what portion of the document MFC outputs to the printer. So, you can override this function when the application must print multiple-page documents. You also can use OnPrepareDC() to set mapping modes and other attributes of the printer device context for each page of the document.

For example, in the previous section, you learned how to determine the character size for printer output. Using this character size when sending data to the printer ensures that the text lines get spaced properly. However, the document won't print correctly if its length exceeds one page. You get all the pages, but each page starts with the first text line and runs off the bottom of the page. This phenomenon occurs because for each page of the document, OnDraw() draws the entire document. To paginate properly, you need some way of telling OnDraw() to start printing further into the document as appropriate for each page. You do this by calling the printer DC's SetViewportOrg() function, as shown here:

```
void CPrintAppView::OnPrepareDC(CDC* pDC,
    CPrintInfo* pInfo)
{
    // TODO: Add your specialized code here
    //       and/or call the base class

    if (pDC->IsPrinting())
    {
        int start = (pInfo->m_nCurPage - 1) * m_vertRes;
        pDC->SetViewportOrg(0, -start);
    }

    CView::OnPrepareDC(pDC, pInfo);
}
```

You learn more about `SetViewportOrg()` in Chapter 10. For now, just know that `SetViewportOrg()` tells Windows that the document starts at a different point. The function's two arguments are the X and Y coordinates of the new origin (where the document starts). MFC calls `OnPrepareDC()` once for each page in the document.

The first time MFC calls `OnPrepareDC()` (for the first page), the function sets the document's origin to 0,0 — the real beginning of the document. The program sends the entire document to the page, starting at coordinate 0,0. The part of the document that doesn't fit on the page just runs off the bottom of the page and doesn't appear.

The second time MFC calls `OnPrepareDC()` (for the second page), the function sets the origin to the coordinate that marks the start of the second page. Again, the program sends the entire document to the page, but now the program thinks the document starts at the new origin. If the document is still too long for the second page, the remaining data runs off the bottom of the second page and doesn't appear.

This process continues for each page in the document, with `OnPrepareDC()` moving the document's origin forward a page at a time.

Notice that `OnPrepareDC()` calls the DC's `IsPrinting()` member function before doing anything. This function call is important because MFC calls `OnPrepareDC()` when displaying data on the screen, as well as on the printer. When displaying data on the screen, you may not want to fiddle with the origin.

You may think you've got this printing thing licked now that you're able to space and paginate the output. And for some printing tasks, this probably is enough. But a problem still remains. For many printers, the number of lines that fit on the printed page is not a whole number. For example, a printer with a vertical page resolution of 3,175 and a character height of 50 can display 63.5 lines per page. And that is exactly what you get when you print the document. For example, Figure 8-9 shows the print preview for the bottom of a document's first page, whereas Figure 8-10 shows the print preview for the top of a document's second page. As you can see, the printer splits line 64 between the two pages.

The application gets to the point where it no longer makes sense to let `OnDraw()` render the document both on the screen and the printer. To rectify this problem, you now need to move the printing tasks to the `OnPrint()` function, which you do in the next section.

When you create your application with AppWizard, AppWizard doesn't override `OnPrepareDC()` in your view window's class automatically. You must override `OnPrepareDC()` using ClassWizard (or add it by hand).

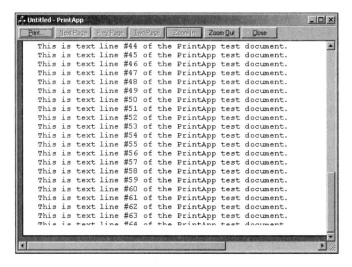

Figure 8-9: The print preview shows the bottom line running off the document's first page.

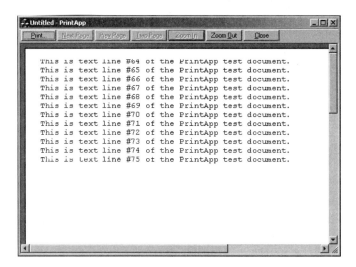

Figure 8-10: The second page then shows the rest of the line.

The OnPrint() function

After calling `OnPrepareDC()`, MFC calls `OnPrint()` for each page. Not only can you set the *viewport origin* (which controls what portion of the document is output for the page) in `OnPrepareDC()`, you also can set it in `OnPrint()`. Usually, though, you override `OnPrint()` when you want to output the document's data differently for the printer than for the screen. You also can use `OnPrint()` to output headers and footers before the `OnDraw()` function renders the document.

When you create your application with AppWizard, AppWizard doesn't override `OnPrint()` in your view window's class automatically. You must override `OnPrint()` using ClassWizard. When you do, make sure that you comment out the call to `CView::OnPrint()` because that's where MFC calls the `OnDraw()` function — something your application should not do when it performs all its printing in `OnPrint()`.

In the previous examples of text output, each document's page had its last line cut in half. To get pagination to work properly in this case, you completely separate the code that draws the screen display from the code that draws to the printer. Then the program can handle the entire printing task in one place rather than having to keep calling `IsPrinting()` and performing different tasks based on the result. Here is how `OnPrint()` might look for this section's text example:

```
void CPrintAppView::OnPrint(CDC* pDC, CPrintInfo* pInfo)
{
    // TODO: Add your specialized code here
    //    and/or call the base class

    int startLine = (pInfo->m_nCurPage - 1) *
        m_linesPerPage + 1;
    int endLine = startLine + m_linesPerPage - 1;
    if (endLine > m_numLines)
        endLine = m_numLines;

    int curLine = 0;
    for(int x=startLine; x<=endLine; ++x)
    {
        char str[81];
        wsprintf(str, "This is text line #%d of \
the PrintApp test document.", x);
        pDC->TextOut(20, curLine*m_printerCharHeight,
            str);
        ++ curLine;
    }
```

```
    //CView::OnPrint(pDC, pInfo);
}

void CPrintAppView::OnPrepareDC(CDC* pDC,
    CPrintInfo* pInfo)
{
    // TODO: Add your specialized code here
    //       and/or call the base class

    CView::OnPrepareDC(pDC, pInfo);
}

void CPrintAppView::OnDraw(CDC* pDC)
{
    CPrintAppDoc* pDoc = GetDocument();
    ASSERT_VALID(pDoc);

    // TODO: add draw code for native data here

    for(int x=0; x<m_numLines; ++x)
    {
        char str[81];
        wsprintf(str, "This is text line #%d of \
the PrintApp test document.", x+1);
        pDC->TextOut(20, x*m_charHeight, str);
    }
}
```

The listing also shows the functions that you need to change to accommodate the `OnPrint()` function. For example, `OnPrepareDC()` no longer sets the viewport origin for each page. `OnDraw()`, on the other hand, contains only the code needed to draw the document in the application's window.

This version of `OnPrint()` works by determining exactly which lines of the document need to be drawn on the current page, and drawing only those lines. MFC passes the current page to `OnPrint()` in the `CPrintInfo` object member `m_nCurPage`. Here's a quick rundown of what the `OnPrint()` function does:

- Calculates the number of the first line to print
- Calculates the number of the last line to print
- Uses the first and last line numbers as the control values in a `for` loop
- Prints a line of text in each iteration of the loop

Figures 8-11 and 8-12 show how the application's pagination now works. In Figure 8-11, you can see that the program no longer prints partial lines on the first page. In Figure 8-12, you can see that the document's second page starts with the next full line of text.

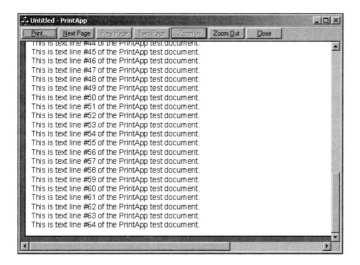

Figure 8-11: Print preview now shows the first page ending with a complete line.

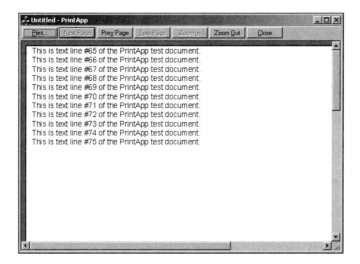

Figure 8-12: The second page shows the rest of the document, starting with the next full line.

The OnEndPrinting() function

The last function to explore is OnEndPrinting() — the counterpart for the OnBeginPrinting() function. MFC calls OnEndPrinting() when the print job completes, giving your application a chance to release resources allocated in `OnBeginPrinting()`. AppWizard overrides `OnEndPrinting()` in your application, as shown here:

```
void CCircleAppView::OnEndPrinting(CDC* /*pDC*/,
    CPrintInfo* /*pInfo*/)
{
    // TODO: add cleanup after printing
}
```

Notice that the `CDC` and `CPrintInfo` objects passed to the function are commented out. You need to remove the comments if you want to access these objects in the body of the function.

Now that you know how to print text documents, it's time to move on to graphics printing. In most cases, graphical screens don't need to deal with text sizes and line spacing. Instead, scaling is accomplished using a physical measurement such as inches or millimeters. In the following sections, you learn how this scaling works.

Printing Graphics in an MFC Application

When you print a text document, you need to be aware of text sizes in order to space the lines of the document correctly. When you print a document that contains graphics, you need to scale all the elements that comprise the document so that the output looks reasonably similar to that on the screen. How you want to perform this scaling depends on the application's needs; this is a choice you need to make as you design your application's user interface. For example, do you want to print the output so that it's the same size as that on the screen, or do you want to enable the user to scale the screen image and printer images separately?

The PrintCircleApp Sample Application

Location: `WinPrgS\Chap08\PrintCircleApp`

On this book's CD-ROM, you can find the PrintCircleApp application that demonstrates the concepts you learn in this section. When you run the application, you can draw circles in the window by clicking in the window. Also, you can change the size or color of the circles by clicking buttons on the toolbar. The program features a ruler at the top of the screen, which indicates the size of the screen's logical inches (as shown in Figure 8-13). Figure 8-14 shows how the circle document appears in print preview. As you can see, the printer output is scaled properly.

Chapter 8: Printing **317**

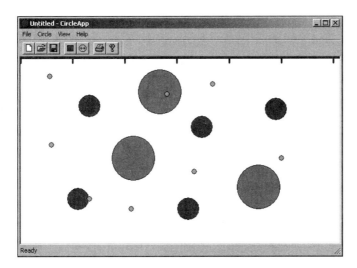

Figure 8-13: The PrintCircleApp screen displaying a set of circles

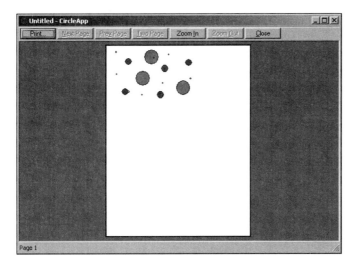

Figure 8-14: PrintCircleApp's print preview showing the document just created

Scaling Between the Screen and Printer

As you now know, the screen's display and the printer usually have different resolutions. That is, the horizontal and vertical dots per inch on the screen may be 96, while the printer's horizontal and vertical dots per inch may be 300 or more. (The horizontal and vertical values aren't necessarily the same.)

The screen has larger dots, so when you print an image on both the screen and the printer, the printer's image looks small.

If you have a hard time understanding how the dots-per-inch measurement of a device affects the size of printed output, imagine that you have a box of BBs and a box of marbles. Lay 100 BBs in a row, and then lay 100 marbles in a row. Which line is longer? Obviously, because marbles are larger than BBs, the 100-marble line is longer than the 100-BB line. A device's dots-per-inch measurements are no more mysterious than BBs and marbles. If you tell Windows to draw a line 100 units long on a 96 DPI device and on a 300 DPI device, the 300 DPI device's line is shorter because the device's dots are smaller.

You can solve this problem in a number of ways. You can use a different mapping mode (instead of the default MM_TEXT) for drawing and printing your graphics. (You learn about mapping modes in Chapter 10.) You can have the user choose a final size for the printed output and scale the output based on that choice. Or, if it suits your application, you simply can draw the images so that a logical inch on the screen comes out as an inch on the printer.

To do this, you call upon the services of your old friend GetDeviceCaps() (see Chapter 2). When you call GetDeviceCaps() with the constant LOGPIXELSX as its single argument, the function returns the number of dots per logical horizontal inch on the screen. Similarly, when you call GetDeviceCaps() with the argument LOGPIXELSY, you get the number of dots per logical vertical inch on the screen. The keyword here is "logical." Because monitors come in different sizes but display the same resolutions, a logical inch on one screen truly may be an inch. On a larger or smaller screen, a logical inch is larger or smaller than an inch.

To perform printer output scaling, the first step is to get the logical dots per inch for the screen. Following is an example of how you can do this:

```
CClientDC clientDC(this);
screenHDotsPerInch =
    clientDC.GetDeviceCaps(LOGPIXELSX);
screenVDotsPerInch =
    clientDC.GetDeviceCaps(LOGPIXELSY);
```

Here, the program first gets a DC for the application's client window. It then calls the DC's GetDeviceCaps() member function to get the screen's logical inch. You can place the previous lines anywhere in the program after the system creates the application's window. In an MFC program, a good place is in the OnCreate() function that responds to the Windows WM_CREATE message.

After getting the screen's logical inch, you need to get the printer's logical inch. To do that, you use code similar to the following snippet:

```
int printerHDotsPerInch =
    pDC->GetDeviceCaps(LOGPIXELSX);
```

```
int printerVDotsPerInch =
    pDC->GetDeviceCaps(LOGPIXELSY);
```

Notice that the `GetDeviceCaps()` function is called through a pointer called pDC. The pDC pointer is the address of a printer DC; so in order to call `GetDeviceCaps()` for the printer, you must have a printer DC already. If you use `OnDraw()` to send data to the printer, you can place the previous lines there. But check the DC's `IsPrinting()` flag to ensure that the DC is a printer DC and not the screen DC, as shown here:

```
float hScale = 1.0;
float vScale = 1.0;

if (pDC->IsPrinting())
{
    int printerHDotsPerInch =
        pDC->GetDeviceCaps(LOGPIXELSX);
    int printerVDotsPerInch =
        pDC->GetDeviceCaps(LOGPIXELSY);
    hScale = (float)printerHDotsPerInch /
        (float)screenHDotsPerInch;
    vScale = (float)printerVDotsPerInch /
        (float)screenVDotsPerInch;
}
```

In this code example, the program not only gets the printer's logical inch, but it also creates horizontal and vertical scaling values by dividing the printer's logical inch by the screen's logical inch. You can use these scaling factors with output coordinates in order to create an appropriate display for both the screen and the printer. For example, suppose the variables x1, y1, x2, and y2 contain the screen coordinates for a shape. You might scale the coordinates as follows:

```
x1 = (int)(x1 * hScale);
y1 = (int)(y1 * vScale);
x2 = (int)(x2 * hScale);
y2 = (int)(y2 * vScale);
```

If the DC passed to `OnDraw()` is a screen DC, hScale and vScale end up set to 1.0. The coordinates, when multiplied by hScale and vScale, stay the same, and the actual values replace the scaling values:

```
x1 = (int)(x1 * 1.0);
y1 = (int)(y1 * 1.0);
x2 = (int)(x2 * 1.0);
y2 = (int)(y2 * 1.0);
```

If the DC is a printer DC, however, hScale and vScale get set to the results of dividing printer logical inches by screen logical inches. Suppose that the screen logical inch is 96 pixels, both horizontally and vertically, and the printer's logical inch is 300, both horizontally and vertically. Substituting actual values for the `printerHDotsPerInch` and `screenHDotsPerInch` variables, you get the following calculation:

```
hScale = 300 / 96;
vScale = 300 / 96;
```

This calculation yields the following results:

```
hScale = 3.125;
vScale = 3.125;
```

These scaling values indicate that the screen's logical inch contains a little over three times as many dots as the printer's logical inch. When printing, all screen coordinates must be multiplied by the scaling values so that a logical inch on the screen equals an inch on the printer:

```
x1 = (int)(x1 * 3.125);
y1 = (int)(y1 * 3.125);
x2 = (int)(x2 * 3.125);
y2 = (int)(y2 * 3.125);
```

The OnCreate() Function

Now that you've experimented with the program a bit, let's see how it performs its printing magic. In order to perform the scaling, the program gets the screen's logical inch in the `OnCreate()` function; ClassWizard adds this function to the application (see Figure 8-15). Here is the program's `OnCreate()` function:

```
int CCircleAppView::OnCreate(LPCREATESTRUCT
    lpCreateStruct)
{
    if (CView::OnCreate(lpCreateStruct) == -1)
        return -1;

    // TODO: Add your specialized creation code here

    CClientDC clientDC(this);
    m_winHDotsPerInch =
        clientDC.GetDeviceCaps(LOGPIXELSX);
    m_winVDotsPerInch =
        clientDC.GetDeviceCaps(LOGPIXELSY);

    return 0;
}
```

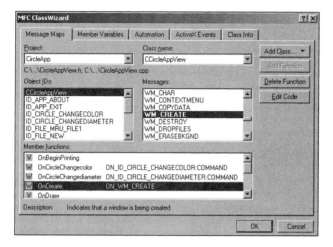

Figure 8-15: Use ClassWizard to add OnCreate() to the view window class.

The OnDraw() Function

PrintCircleApp uses `OnDraw()` for drawing on both the screen and the printer. The following code shows the `OnDraw()` function, which performs the following tasks:

- Initializes the horizontal and vertical scaling variables to 1.0
- If the DC is for the printer, gets the printer's logical inch and divides it by the window's logical inch, resetting the horizontal and vertical scaling variables
- Processes the application's circle document, scaling the output as appropriate
- If the DC is not for the printer, draws a ruler on the screen

```
void CCircleAppView::OnDraw(CDC* pDC)
{
    CCircleAppDoc* pDoc = GetDocument();
    ASSERT_VALID(pDoc);

    // TODO: add draw code for native data here
    float hScale = 1.0;
    float vScale = 1.0;

    if (pDC->IsPrinting())
```

```cpp
    {
        int printHDotsPerInch =
            pDC->GetDeviceCaps(LOGPIXELSX);
        int printVDotsPerInch =
            pDC->GetDeviceCaps(LOGPIXELSY);
        hScale = (float)printHDotsPerInch /
            (float)m_winHDotsPerInch;
        vScale = (float)printVDotsPerInch /
            (float)m_winVDotsPerInch;
    }

    int size = pDoc->m_circleArray.GetSize();

    for (int x=0; x<size; ++x)
    {
        CircleStruct* circle =
            (CircleStruct*)pDoc->m_circleArray.GetAt(x);
        int radius = circle->diameter/2;
        int x1 = circle->point.x-radius;
        int y1 = circle->point.y-radius;
        int x2 = circle->point.x+radius;
        int y2 = circle->point.y+radius;
        COLORREF color = circle->color;
        CBrush brush(color);
        CBrush* oldBrush = pDC->SelectObject(&brush);

        x1 = (int)(x1 * hScale);
        y1 = (int)(y1 * vScale);
        x2 = (int)(x2 * hScale);
        y2 = (int)(y2 * vScale);

        pDC->Ellipse(x1, y1, x2, y2);
        pDC->SelectObject(oldBrush);
    }

    if (!pDC->IsPrinting())
    {
        CPen newPen(PS_SOLID, 3, RGB(0,0,0));
        CPen* pOldPen = pDC->SelectObject(&newPen);
        pDC->MoveTo(0, 1);
        pDC->LineTo(800, 1);

        for (int i=0; i<10; ++i)
        {
            pDC->MoveTo(i*m_winHDotsPerInch, 1);
            pDC->LineTo(i*m_winHDotsPerInch, 10);
        }
        pDC->SelectObject(pOldPen);
    }
}
```

The OnPreparePrinting() Function

Unlike the text-printing application that appears earlier in this chapter, PrintCircleApp doesn't take advantage of the `OnPreparePrinting()`, `OnBeginPrinting()`, and `OnEndPrinting()` functions except to set the maximum page count to 1:

```
BOOL CCircleAppView::OnPreparePrinting(CPrintInfo* pInfo)
{
    // default preparation

    pInfo->SetMaxPage(1);

    return DoPreparePrinting(pInfo);
}
```

Problems & Solutions

Using Physical Measurements as Scaling Factors

PROBLEM: *In the program I'm writing, I don't want to use proportional values as scaling factors; I just want to use inches. That is, when I draw a scaled line, I want to use inches as line coordinates instead of pixel or dot coordinates. Is this possible?*

SOLUTION: Sort of. Although you can't directly tell Windows to draw a line six inches long, you can set up your scaling so that you use inch values as scaling factors (as the numbers you multiply coordinate values by). The trick is to avoid hard-coded screen coordinates completely. Instead, express all coordinates in terms of the scale you want to use. For example, if you want to draw a rectangle 6 inches long and 3.5 inches high, use 6 and 3.5 in the `Rectangle()` function's arguments — but multiply those inch values by the device's logical inch.

To accomplish this, call `GetDeviceCaps()` in your `OnCreate()` function (as shown in the following code) in order to obtain the screen device's logical inch:

```
int CInchAppView::OnCreate(LPCREATESTRUCT lpCreateStruct)
{
    if (CView::OnCreate(lpCreateStruct) == -1)
        return -1;

    // TODO: Add your specialized creation code here

    CClientDC clientDC(this);
    m_screenHInch =
        clientDC.GetDeviceCaps(LOGPIXELSX);
```

Continued

```
    m_screenVInch =
        clientDC.GetDeviceCaps(LOGPIXELSY);

    return 0;
}
```

Then override the view window class's `OnBeginPrinting()` function. In that function, call `GetDeviceCaps()` to get the printer's logical inch:

```
void CInchAppView::OnBeginPrinting(CDC* pDC,
    CPrintInfo* /*pInfo*/)
{
    // TODO: add extra initialization before printing

    m_printerHInch = pDC->GetDeviceCaps(LOGPIXELSX);
    m_printerVInch = pDC->GetDeviceCaps(LOGPIXELSY);
}
```

Now that you have the size of a logical inch for each of the devices, you can use inches as coordinates as long as you multiply those inch coordinates by the appropriate device logical inch. For example, the following code shows how to draw a 6x3.5-inch rectangle on the screen at one inch from the left and top of the window:

```
void CInchAppView::OnDraw(CDC* pDC)
{
    CInchAppDoc* pDoc = GetDocument();
    ASSERT_VALID(pDoc);

    // TODO: add draw code for native data here
    int x1 = (int)(1.0 * m_screenHInch);
    int y1 = (int)(1.0 * m_screenVInch);
    int x2 = (int)(7.0 * m_screenHInch);
    int y2 = (int)(4.5 * m_screenVInch);

    pDC->Rectangle(x1, y1, x2, y2);
}
```

Here's the code for the `OnPrint()` function, which handles sending the rectangle to the printer:

```
void CInchAppView::OnPrint(CDC* pDC, CPrintInfo* pInfo)
{
    // TODO: Add your specialized code here
    //       and/or call the base class

    int x1 = (int)(1.0 * m_printerHInch);
    int y1 = (int)(1.0 * m_printerVInch);
```

Continued

```
        int x2 = (int)(7.0 * m_printerHInch);
        int y2 = (int)(4.5 * m_printerVInch);

        pDC->Rectangle(x1, y1, x2, y2);
}
```

Location: **WinPrgS\Chap08\InchApp**

To see how all this inch-scaling stuff works, you now use MFC AppWizard and ClassWizard to put together an application called InchApp. This application displays and prints a 6-inch rectangle on the screen and on whatever printer is connected to your system, demonstrating the concepts covered in this section. For those of you who are not comfortable with building Visual C++ applications yet, the following steps make clear what you need to do to add simple printing capabilities to your own applications.

1. Select the File menu's New command and create an MFC AppWizard (exe) project called InchApp, as shown in Figure 8-16.

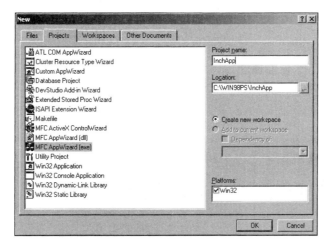

Figure 8-16: The new application is called InchApp.

2. Select Single document in the Step 1 dialog box, as shown in Figure 8-17.

3. Click the Next button three times, accepting the default settings in the Step 2 of 6 and Step 3 of 6 dialog boxes.

4. Turn off the Docking toolbar and Initial status bar options in the Step 4 of 6 dialog box, as shown in Figure 8-18.

Continued

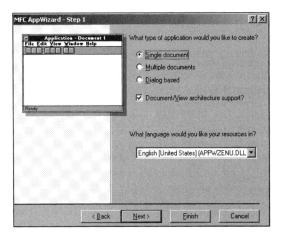

Figure 8-17: The new application uses the single document interface.

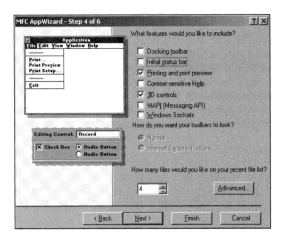

Figure 8-18: The new application has no toolbar or status bar.

5. Click the Next button and select the As a statically linked library option in the Step 5 of 6 dialog box (see Figure 8-19).

Continued

Chapter 8: Printing **327**

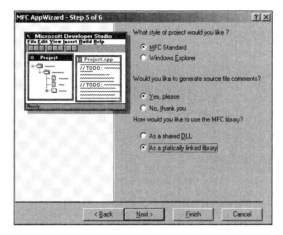

Figure 8-19: The new application links statically to the MFC libraries.

6. Click the Finish button. Your New Project Information dialog box appears and should look like the one shown in Figure 8-20. Click OK to close the box.

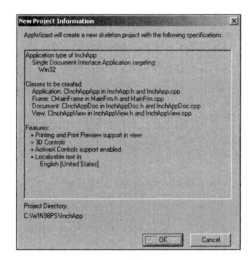

Figure 8-20: The New Project Information dialog box shows the final options for the InchApp application.

Continued

7. Use ClassWizard to add the `OnCreate()` function to the application's `CInchAppView` class (see Figure 8-21).

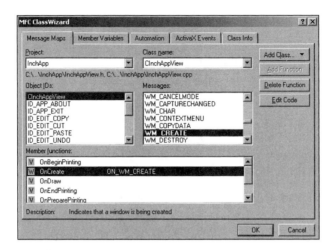

Figure 8-21: You use ClassWizard to add the OnCreate() function.

8. Click the Edit Code button and add the following lines to `OnCreate()`, right after the `TODO: Add your specialized creation code here` comment:

```
CClientDC clientDC(this);
m_screenHInch =
    clientDC.GetDeviceCaps(LOGPIXELSX);
m_screenVInch =
    clientDC.GetDeviceCaps(LOGPIXELSY);
```

9. Use ClassWizard to override the view class's `OnPrint()` function, as shown in Figure 8-22.

10. Click the Edit Code button and add the following lines to `OnPrint()`, right after the `TODO: Add your specialized code here and/or call the base class` comment:

```
int x1 = (int)(1.0 * m_printerHInch);
int y1 = (int)(1.0 * m_printerVInch);
int x2 = (int)(7.0 * m_printerHInch);
int y2 = (int)(4.5 * m_printerVInch);

pDC->Rectangle(x1, y1, x2, y2);
```

Continued

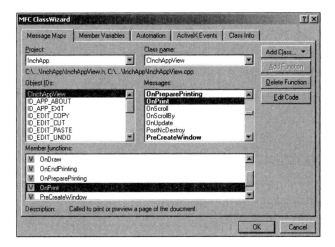

Figure 8-22: You use ClassWizard to override the OnPrint() function.

11. At the end of the `OnPrint()` function, comment out or remove the call to the base class's `OnPrint()` function.

12. Add the following lines to the `CInchAppView` class's `OnDraw()` function, right after the `TODO: add draw code for native data here` comment:

    ```
    int x1 = (int)(1.0 * m_screenHInch);
    int y1 = (int)(1.0 * m_screenVInch);
    int x2 = (int)(7.0 * m_screenHInch);
    int y2 = (int)(4.5 * m_screenVInch);

    pDC->Rectangle(x1, y1, x2, y2);
    ```

13. Add the following line to the `CInchAppView` class's `OnPreparePrinting()` function, right after the default preparation comment:

    ```
    pInfo->SetMaxPage(1);
    ```

14. Add the following lines to the `CInchAppView` class's `OnBeginPrinting()` function, right after the `TODO: add extra initialization before printing` comment:

    ```
    m_printerHInch = pDC->GetDeviceCaps(LOGPIXELSX);
    m_printerVInch = pDC->GetDeviceCaps(LOGPIXELSY);
    ```

15. Also in `OnBeginPrinting()`, remove the comments from the `pDC` DC object's name in the function's parameter list.

Continued

16. Load the `CInchAppView` class's header file and add the following lines to the class's Implementation section, right after the `protected` keyword:

    ```
    int m_printerVInch;
    int m_printerHInch;
    int m_screenVInch;
    int m_screenHInch;
    ```

Now you have completed the InchApp application. Press Ctrl+F5 on your keyboard to compile and run the application. When you do, you see the window shown in Figure 8-23. The window displays a rectangle 6 inches long and 3.5 inches high. Moreover, it displays the rectangle one inch from the left and top of the window. Remember, however, that the window uses logical inches. The actual size of the rectangle depends on the size of your monitor.

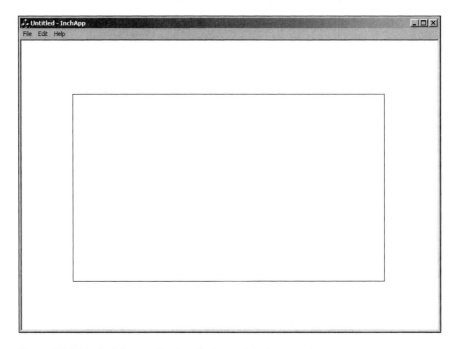

Figure 8-23: The InchApp application displays a 6-inch rectangle.

To see that the scaling works as advertised, select the File menu's Print command. Your printer should print the rectangle. Go ahead and measure it with a ruler. If you don't want to print the page, you can see the printed result in the print preview window shown in Figure 8-24. Because the print preview display is scaled for the screen, you have to estimate the size of the rectangle compared with the rest of the page.

Continued

Chapter 8: Printing

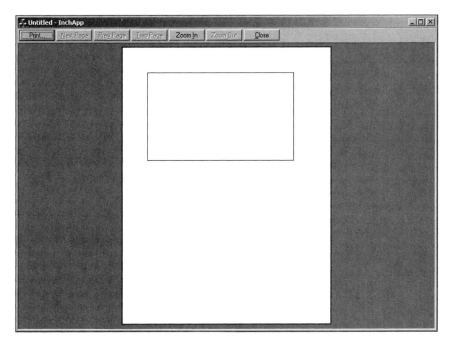

Figure 8-24: InchApp's print preview shows the scaled rectangle.

Summary

Many of the applications you write for Windows 2000 require the capability to print documents. Although printing under Windows can become a complex task, MFC takes over some of the burden. It does this not only by providing a printer context for the print job, but also by handling the Print dialog box and providing functions that enable you to access the printing process at various points.

Also discussed in this chapter:

▶ Printing in a traditional Windows program requires six main steps: getting the printer DC, starting the document, starting pages, rendering the document, ending pages, and ending the document.

▶ The easiest way to add printing capabilities to an MFC program is to select the Printing and print preview option when creating the application with AppWizard.

▶ In an MFC program, the view window's OnDraw() function can render simple documents on both the screen and the printer.

- MFC calls the `OnPreparePrinting()` function when a print or print preview job begins.
- The `OnBeginPrinting()` function is the first place the class has access to the printer DC.
- The `OnPrepareDC()` function is the last chance an MFC application has to manipulate the printer DC before the document is sent to the printer.
- You can override the `OnPrint()` function when you want to output the document's data differently for the printer than for the screen.
- MFC calls `OnEndPrinting()` when the print job is complete.
- When printing graphics, you generally are more concerned with scaling than you are with text sizes, line spacing, pagination, and displaying headers and footers.
- Because screen pixels usually are much larger than a printer's dots, an application must scale text and images when printing.

Part II
Advanced Windows 2000 Programming

Chapter 9: Bitmaps

Chapter 10: Advanced GDI

Chapter 11: Programming the Windows User Interface

Chapter 12: The Registry

Chapter 13: Installing User Applications

Chapter 9

Bitmaps

In This Chapter
- Introducing device-dependent and device-independent bitmaps
- Programming device-dependent bitmaps
- Programming device-independent bitmaps

Windows applications can create attractive displays using only the GDI drawing functions. However, sometimes you want to display detailed images — maybe even photographs — in an application's window. That's when you call upon the power of a *bitmap*. Bitmaps are the most common type of image file used in Windows; they can be as simple as a button icon or as complex as a photographic-quality image. But no matter how you use them, bitmaps make your application look more professional. You had a brief introduction to bitmaps in Chapter 2 when you created a bitmapped brush. In this chapter, you learn even more ways to use bitmaps.

Introducing DDBs and DIBs

A bitmap is nothing fancier than an image that can be displayed on the screen. You might, for example, use a bitmap to display a photo on the screen or to provide an icon for a button. The only way a bitmap differs from other types of images, such as GIF or JPEG pictures, is in the file format. That is, bitmaps are stored differently than other types of image files. There are two varieties of bitmaps: *device-dependent bitmaps (DDBs)* and *device-independent bitmaps (DIBs)*.

DDBs are stored rarely, if ever, on a disk. Instead, applications create and manipulate DDBs in memory. A DDB is device-dependent because it doesn't contain a color palette; its colors depend on the device on which it's displayed (usually the screen). A DDB does not contain other informational structures that a device-independent bitmap contains to indicate how the bitmap should be displayed. Usually, applications use DDBs to transfer image information between memory and the screen. For example, a common use for a DDB is to store a copy of a window's contents so that the window can be redrawn quickly from memory.

A DIB, on the other hand, is stored on disk. Any application that can read bitmap files—which usually have the .BMP file name extension—can read and display the image. Even applications running on different platforms (such as Macintosh) can read and display bitmap files. Unlike DDBs, DIBs include color information. This color information may be in the form of a palette (as in a 256-color image) or stored in the data for each pixel (as in a 24-bit image). In any case, all the information an application needs to display the bitmap is in a DIB's file, including the bitmap's size and other attributes. One example of a DIB is a scanned image saved in the .BMP format. The rest of this chapter explores how you can use both DDBs and DIBs in your Windows applications.

Programming with Device-Dependent Bitmaps

As stated previously, applications usually use DDBs to transfer image information between memory and the screen. Sometimes, different applications running concurrently in Windows 2000 can share image data by passing the information as a DDB in the clipboard, from which the DDB can be pasted into another application's window. No matter how an application uses a DDB, however, there are several steps that the application must perform to create a bitmap object, associate it with the device, and display it. These steps, as performed by an MFC application, are as follows:

1. Create a `CBitmap` object
2. Initialize the `CBitmap` object with a bitmap that is compatible with the current device context
3. Create a memory device context that is compatible with the current device context
4. Select the bitmap into the memory DC
5. Draw on the bitmap through the memory DC
6. Copy the bitmap to the display device

What the application does with the bitmap after creating it depends on the application. In many cases, the application copies the bitmap from memory to the screen. An application also can copy image data from the screen to the bitmap in order to store a copy of the screen in memory or to transfer all or part of the screen image to another application (such as a screen-capture program might do). The following sections describe each of the preceding steps.

Creating and Initializing a Bitmap Object

The MFC libraries feature a class for creating and manipulating DDBs, also called GDI bitmaps. This class, named `CBitmap`, features several ways to create and initialize bitmaps, as well as member functions for changing or obtaining bitmap information. Table 9-1 lists the most common of these functions:

Table 9-1 Functions for Manipulating Bitmaps

Function	Description
`FromHandle()`	Gets a pointer to a `CBitmap` object
`GetBitmap()`	Obtains information about a bitmap and places it into a `BITMAP` structure
`GetBitmapBits()`	Copies a bitmap's data into a buffer
`GetBitmapDimension()`	Gets a bitmap's width and height
`SetBitmapBits()`	Changes the bitmap's data to the given values
`SetBitmapDimension()`	Changes a bitmap's width and height

Creating a `CBitmap` object in your program is easy:

```
CBitmap bitmap;
```

The tricky part is associating the `CBitmap` object with the actual bitmap that the object manipulates. You must do this by calling one of the seven initialization functions listed in Table 9-2.

Table 9-2 Bitmap Initialization Functions

Function	Description
`LoadBitmap()`	Associates a bitmap from the application's resources with the `CBitmap` object. In this case, you have created the bitmap image already (using Visual C++'s bitmap editor) and have added the bitmap to the project's resources.
`LoadOEMBitmap()`	Associates a standard Windows bitmap with the `CBitmap` object. The standard bitmaps represent images such as checks and arrows that are part of the Windows system.
`LoadMappedBitmap()`	Associates a bitmap from the application's resources with the `CBitmap` object, mapping the bitmap's colors to the system colors. As with the `LoadBitmap()` function, you have created the bitmap image already (using Visual C++'s bitmap editor). This bitmap may represent something, like a button, which you want to appear on the screen using system colors the user sets.

Continued

Table 9-2 *(continued)*	
Function	**Description**
`CreateBitmapIndirect()`	Creates a new bitmap from a `BITMAP` structure and associates it with the `CBitmap` object. This function is similar to `CreateBitmap()`, except you store the bitmap information into a `BITMAP` structure rather than pass the information as individual arguments.
`CreateCompatibleBitmap()`	Creates a bitmap that's compatible with the given DC and associates it with the `CBitmap` object. This function easily creates a bitmap to transfer information between the screen and memory. Rather than having to specify all the bitmap's attributes, as you do with `CreateBitmap()`, you simply specify a DC, and the function extracts the attributes it needs from the DC.
`CreateDiscardableBitmap()`	Creates a discardable bitmap that's compatible with the given DC and associates it with the `CBitmap` object. Similar to `CreateCompatibleBitmap()`, except that Windows can discard the resultant bitmap whenever the bitmap is not selected into a DC.

An example of using one of the preceding functions is if you want to create a new bitmap that you can display on the screen. You call `CreateCompatibleBitmap()` to create the bitmap. However, because `CreateCompatibleBitmap()` requires a pointer to a DC as one of its arguments, you first create the DC object. The entire process looks like this:

```
CBitmap bitmap;
CClientDC windowDC(this);
bitmap.CreateCompatibleBitmap(&windowDC, 200, 100);
```

These lines create and initialize a 200x100 bitmap that's compatible with (can be displayed in) the current client window.

Creating the Memory DC

Now that you have the bitmap created, you probably want to draw something on it. After all, a blank bitmap doesn't do you much good. In order to draw on the bitmap, you must select it into a memory DC. This process is similar to selecting a new pen or brush into a window DC. You can think of the bitmap as just another GDI object like a pen or brush. But what the heck is a memory DC? A *memory DC* closely resembles a window DC; the big difference is that a memory DC sits invisibly in memory and is never displayed directly on the screen. In a way, you could say that a memory DC is a buffer that has GDI objects such as pens, brushes, and fonts (not to mention bitmaps) associated with it.

You create a memory DC by creating an object of MFC's `CDC` class, which is the class from which MFC derives the other DC classes:

```
CDC memoryDC;
```

Notice that (unlike when you create a window DC) when you create a memory DC, you don't pass the window's `this` pointer as an argument. That's because `CDC` is a general class for any kind of DC, and not every DC has to be compatible with a client window.

Once you create the `CDC` object to use as a memory DC, you must associate the `CDC` object with an actual DC. The `CDC` class provides a couple of ways to do this, but the most useful for this example is to call the DC object's `CreateCompatibleDC()` function:

```
memoryDC.CreateCompatibleDC(&windowDC);
```

This function takes as its single parameter a pointer to the DC object with which the memory DC should be compatible. Because you want to display the bitmap on the screen, and because the bitmap is compatible with the window's DC, `CreateCompatibleDC()`'s argument is the address of the window DC.

Selecting the Bitmap into the Memory DC

So far, you have a client window with a DC, a bitmap compatible with the window DC, and a memory DC compatible with the window DC. Although these three distinct objects are fully compatible, you have to get them to work together. The first step toward accomplishing that goal is to select the bitmap into the memory DC:

```
CBitmap* pOldBitmap =
    memoryDC.SelectObject(&bitmap);
```

As you can see, you select the bitmap into the DC exactly as you do any other GDI object — by calling the DC's `SelectObject()` function. `SelectObject()`'s single argument is the address of the `CBitmap` object. The call to `SelectObject()` returns a pointer to the DC's previous bitmap. Hold onto this pointer in order to reselect the original bitmap back into the DC. However, don't get any ideas about making use of this default bitmap; it's a single, monochrome pixel.

Note: You can select a bitmap into only a memory DC. Don't try to select a bitmap into a window or printer DC.

Drawing on the Bitmap

When you select a bitmap into a memory DC, you give that DC a useful drawing surface. In the case of a memory DC, this drawing surface is not unlike the drawing surface of a window. You just can't see it. You can, however, direct the same sorts of drawing commands to the memory DC that you direct to a window or printer DC.

To prepare your bitmap, first fill it with a background color. You do this because the bitmap contains whatever random values were in memory at the location that the bitmap was created. Figure 9-1 shows what happens if you forget to clear the bitmap with a background color — a cool effect, but probably not what you want!

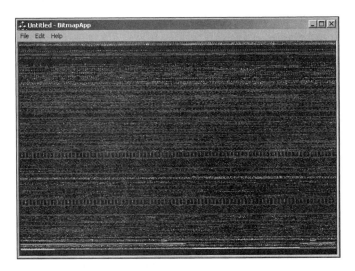

Figure 9-1: A window displaying a bitmap that wasn't cleared

To clear the bitmap, call the DC object's `FillRect()` function:

```
CBrush* pWhiteBrush = new CBrush(RGB(255,255,255));
CRect rect(0, 0, 199, 99);
memoryDC.FillRect(rect, pWhiteBrush);
```

These lines create a white brush and a `CRect` object representing the bitmap's coordinates. Next, call `FillRect()` with the newly created objects. The result is a bitmap filled with white. You can, of course, clear the bitmap to any color you like. Black is another common choice.

With the bitmap cleared, you can draw whatever you like on it by calling the memory DC's drawing functions. For example, the following code draws a line of text and a rectangle on the bitmap:

```
CBrush* pRedBrush = new CBrush(RGB(255,0,0));
CPen* pThickPen =
    new CPen(PS_SOLID, 3, RGB(0,0,0));
CBrush* pOldBrush =
    memoryDC.SelectObject(pRedBrush);
CPen* pOldPen =
    memoryDC.SelectObject(pThickPen);
memoryDC.TextOut(10, 10,
    "This text is going to the bitmap");
memoryDC.Rectangle(50, 50, 150, 75);
memoryDC.SelectObject(pOldBrush);
memoryDC.SelectObject(pOldPen);
memoryDC.SelectObject(pOldBitmap);
delete pRedBrush;
delete pThickPen;
```

Here, the program draws the rectangle using a thick pen and red brush that are created and selected into the memory DC. Figure 9-2 shows the resulting bitmap displayed in a window. Notice how the program selects objects in and out of the DC just as it does for a normal window DC.

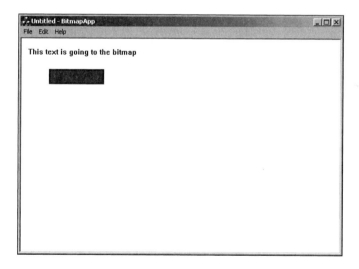

Figure 9-2: A window displaying the bitmap

Copying the Bitmap to the Display

Now your bitmap is drawn and ready to go. The only problem is that you can't see it. To display the bitmap, you must copy it from the memory DC to the window's DC. You can do this a couple of ways, depending on whether you want the bitmap displayed at exactly the same size or you need it displayed larger or smaller. The most common functions to use for copying bitmaps are `BitBlt()` and `StretchBlt()`.

Copying a Bitmap Without Changing its Size

To copy a bitmap to a window without changing the bitmap's size, use the `CDC` class's `BitBlt()`; it is prototyped as follows. Table 9-3 lists the function's argument descriptions.

```
BOOL BitBlt(
    int x,
    int y,
    int nWidth,
    int nHeight,
    CDC* pSrcDC,
    int xSrc,
    int ySrc,
    DWORD dwRop);
```

Table 9-3   The BitBlt() Function's Arguments

Argument	Description
x	The X coordinate of the destination rectangle's upper-left corner.
y	The Y coordinate of the destination rectangle's upper-left corner.
nWidth	The destination rectangle's and bitmap's width.
nHeight	The destination rectangle's and bitmap's height.
pSrcDC	A pointer to the DC that contains the bitmap.
xSrc	The X coordinate of the bitmap's upper-left corner.
ySrc	The Y coordinate of the bitmap's upper-left corner.
dwRop	The specification for the raster operation. For copying a bitmap, use `SRCCOPY`.

Whew! Got all that? The `BitBlt()` function is not as difficult to use as it looks—although it may take you a few tries to get the coordinates just right in some cases. With `BitBlt()`'s arguments, all you do is simply tell Windows where to copy the bitmap and from where the bitmap should be copied. Just think of each DC as a piece of paper with a drawing on it. Now imagine that you're telling someone what part of the first paper should display what part of the second paper.

To copy an entire bitmap, you use a `BitBlt()` call that looks something like this:

```
windowDC.BitBlt(0, 0, 200, 100,
    &memoryDC, 0, 0, SRCCOPY);
```

The DC through which you call `BitBlt()` (in this case, `windowDC`) is the destination DC. The first two `BitBlt()` arguments tell Windows that the bitmap should be copied to the point 0,0 in `windowDC`. The coordinates 0,0 represent the extreme upper-left corner of the window's display area. The second two arguments tell Windows that the bitmap being copied is 200x100 pixels. The third argument tells Windows that `memoryDC` holds the bitmap to be copied, whereas the next two arguments tell Windows the upper-left coordinates of the bitmap at which to start copying. These coordinates don't have to be 0,0. You also can copy only a portion of the bitmap if you like. Finally, the last argument tells Windows how to combine the source and destination pixels — an advanced topic you learn more about in Chapter 10. For now, stick with `SRCCOPY` for this argument.

Copying a Bitmap and Changing its Size

The other function you can use to copy the bitmap is the `CDC` class's `StretchBlt()`, which enables you to stretch or compress the bitmap on the destination DC. Using `StretchBlt()`, you can make any bitmap fit into any size rectangle — although the image may suffer a little from the scaling operation. `StretchBlt()`'s signature follows. Table 9-4 lists the function's argument descriptions.

```
BOOL StretchBlt(
    int x,
    int y,
    int nWidth,
    int nHeight,
    CDC* pSrcDC,
    int xSrc,
    int ySrc,
    int nSrcWidth,
    int nSrcHeight,
    DWORD dwRop);
```

Table 9-4   The StretchBlt() Function's Arguments

Argument	Description
x	The X coordinate of the destination rectangle's upper-left corner.
y	The Y coordinate of the destination rectangle's upper-left corner.
nWidth	The destination rectangle's width.

Continued

Table 9-4 *(continued)*

Argument	Description
nHeight	The destination rectangle's height.
pSrcDC	A pointer to the DC that contains the bitmap.
xSrc	The X coordinate of the bitmap's upper-left corner.
ySrc	The Y coordinate of the bitmap's upper-left corner.
nSrcWidth	The source rectangle's width.
nSrcHeight	The source rectangle's height.
dwRop	The specification for the raster operation. For copying a bitmap, use SRCCOPY.

As you can see from the argument list, StretchBlt() differs from BitBlt() in that StretchBlt() specifies the size of both the destination and source rectangles. StretchBlt() stretches or reduces the source bitmap so that it fits inside the destination rectangle. For example, if you have a 200x100 pixel bitmap that you want to display four times its normal size, you can use a StretchBlt() call like the following:

```
windowDC.StretchBlt(0, 0, 800, 400,
    &memoryDC, 0, 0, 200, 100, SRCCOPY);
```

Notice that the specified destination rectangle is four times larger than the specified source rectangle. These values cause Windows to display the bitmap at four times its normal size (as shown in Figure 9-3), which quadruples the size of the bitmap in Figure 9-2.

Figure 9-3: A window displaying a bitmap at four times its normal size

Creating the BitmapApp Application

Location: `WinPrgS\Chap09\BitmapApp`

Now that you know something about creating and displaying device-dependent bitmaps, you can put this knowledge to practical use. To demonstrate topics already discussed in this chapter, this section builds the BitmapApp application, which enables applications to reproduce their displays more quickly. You can find a complete copy of this application and its source code on this book's CD-ROM.

Sometimes, an application you're writing takes a noticeable amount of time to reproduce its display when the window must be repainted. This problem often arises when the window must repaint many objects in its display. In a case like this, you can supercharge that sluggish display by holding a duplicate of the window's client area in a bitmap in memory. When the application draws to the screen, it also should draw to the bitmap, keeping the bitmap up-to-date. Then, when the window needs to repaint, the application just copies the bitmap to the screen rather than reproducing the display by replaying all the drawing commands.

To get some practice in building bitmap applications, as well as to see bitmap programming techniques in action, start up Visual C++ and perform the following steps to build your own version of the BitmapApp application.

1. Select the File menu's New command and start a new MFC AppWizard (exe) project called BitmapApp in the Projects window, as shown in Figure 9-4.

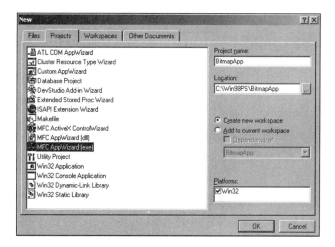

Figure 9-4: The new MFC AppWizard project is called BitmapApp.

2. In the MFC AppWizard - Step 1 dialog box, select the Single document option (as shown in Figure 9-5).

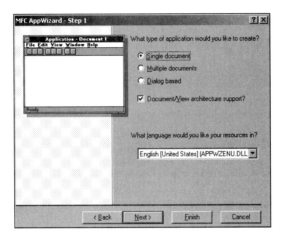

Figure 9-5: The new application uses the single document interface.

3. Click the Next button three times, accepting the default settings in the Step 2 and Step 3 dialog boxes.

4. In the Step 4 dialog box, turn off the Docking toolbar, Initial status bar, and Printing and print preview options (see Figure 9-6).

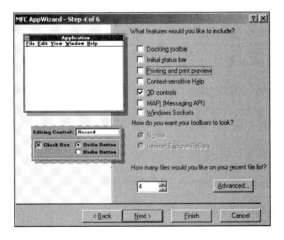

Figure 9-6: The new application has no toolbar, status bar, or print commands.

5. Click the Next button. Accept the Yes, please default option to generate source file comments and then select the As a statically linked library option in the Step 5 dialog box (as shown in Figure 9-7).

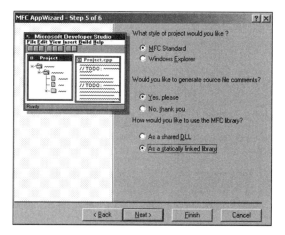

Figure 9-7: The new application links to MFC's static library.

6. Click the Finish button. The New Project Information dialog box appears.
7. Click the OK button, and AppWizard generates the new project.
8. Press Ctrl+W to display ClassWizard, and add the `OnCreate()` function to the `CBitmapAppView` class, as shown in Figure 9-8. Make sure you have `CBitmapAppView` selected in the Class name box.

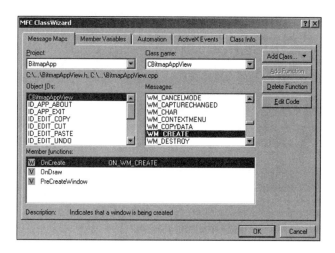

Figure 9-8: ClassWizard adds the OnCreate() function to the program.

9. Click the Edit Code button and add the following lines to `OnCreate()`, right after the `TODO: Add your specialized creation code here` comment:

```
CClientDC windowDC(this);
m_bitmap.CreateCompatibleBitmap(&windowDC, 800, 600);
CDC memoryDC;
memoryDC.CreateCompatibleDC(&windowDC);
CBitmap* pOldBitmap =
    memoryDC.SelectObject(&m_bitmap);
CBrush* pWhiteBrush = new CBrush(RGB(255,255,255));
CRect rect(0, 0, 799, 599);
memoryDC.FillRect(rect, pWhiteBrush);
memoryDC.TextOut(10, 10, "BITMAP");
memoryDC.SelectObject(pOldBitmap);
delete pWhiteBrush;
```

10. In the project workspace window, right-click the `CBitmapAppView` class and select Add Member Variable from the menu that appears (see Figure 9-9).

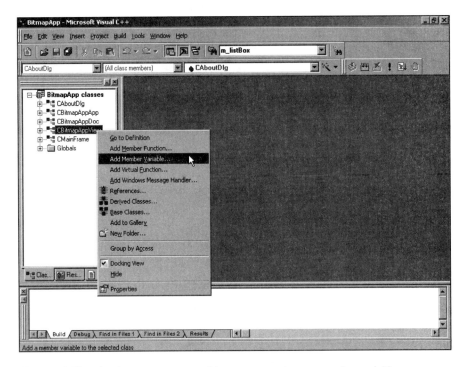

Figure 9-9: The class's pop-up menu enables you to create new member variables.

11. In the Add Member Variable dialog box, create a member variable with the variable type CBitmap and the variable name m_bitmap. Select Protected access, as shown in Figure 9-10. Click OK to dismiss the dialog box.

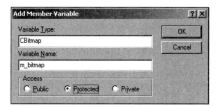

Figure 9-10: The m_bitmap member variable has protected access.

12. Press Ctrl+W to display ClassWizard, and add the OnLButtonDown() function to the CBitmapAppView class.

13. Click the Edit Code button and add the following lines to OnLButtonDown(), right after the TODO: Add your message handler code here and/or call default comment:

```
CClientDC windowDC(this);

CDC memoryDC;
memoryDC.CreateCompatibleDC(&windowDC);
CBitmap* pOldBitmap =
    memoryDC.SelectObject(&m_bitmap);

CBrush* pRedBrush = new CBrush(RGB(255,0,0));
CPen* pThickPen =
    new CPen(PS_SOLID, 3, RGB(0,0,0));

CBrush* pOldMemoryDCBrush =
    memoryDC.SelectObject(pRedBrush);
CBrush* pOldWindowDCBrush =
    windowDC.SelectObject(pRedBrush);
CPen* pOldMemoryDCPen =
    memoryDC.SelectObject(pThickPen);
CPen* pOldWindowDCPen =
    windowDC.SelectObject(pThickPen);

for (int x=0; x<100; ++x)
{
    int x1, y1;

    do
    {
        x1 = rand() % 769;
        y1 = rand() % 569;
    }
```

```
            while (y1 < 30);

            CPoint* pNewPoint = new CPoint(x1, y1);
            m_pointArray.Add(pNewPoint);

            memoryDC.Rectangle(x1, y1, x1+30, y1+30);
            windowDC.Rectangle(x1, y1, x1+30, y1+30);
        }

        memoryDC.SelectObject(pOldMemoryDCBrush);
        memoryDC.SelectObject(pOldMemoryDCPen);
        memoryDC.SelectObject(pOldBitmap);
        windowDC.SelectObject(pOldWindowDCBrush);
        windowDC.SelectObject(pOldWindowDCPen);

        delete pRedBrush;
        delete pThickPen;
```

14. Create a member variable with the variable type `CPtrArray` and the variable declaration `m_pointArray`. Select Protected access. Click OK to dismiss the dialog box.

15. Press Ctrl+W to display ClassWizard, and add the `OnRButtonDown()` function to the `CBitmapAppView` class.

16. Click the Edit Code button and add the following lines to `OnRButtonDown()`, right after the `TODO: Add your message handler code here and/or call default` comment:

    ```
    m_draw = !m_draw;
    Invalidate();
    ```

17. Create a member variable with the variable type `BOOL` and the variable declaration `m_draw`. Select Protected access. Click OK to dismiss the dialog box.

18. Add the following lines to the `CBitmapAppView` class's constructor, after the `TODO: add construction code here` comment:

    ```
    m_draw = FALSE;
    srand((unsigned)time(NULL));
    ```

19. Add the following lines to the `CBitmapAppView` class's destructor:

    ```
            int size = m_pointArray.GetSize();

            for (int x=0; x<size; ++x)
            {
                CPoint* point =
                    (CPoint*)m_pointArray.GetAt(x);
                delete point;
            }

            m_pointArray.RemoveAll();
    ```

Chapter 9: Bitmaps

20. Add the following lines to the `CBitmapAppView` class's `OnDraw()` function, after the `TODO: add draw code for native data here` comment:

```
if (m_draw)
{
    CBrush* pRedBrush = new CBrush(RGB(255,0,0));
    CPen* pThickPen =
        new CPen(PS_SOLID, 3, RGB(0,0,0));
    CBrush* pOldBrush =
        pDC->SelectObject(pRedBrush);
    CPen* pOldPen = pDC->SelectObject(pThickPen);

    int size = m_pointArray.GetSize();

    for (int x=0; x<size; ++x)
    {
        CPoint* point =
            (CPoint*)m_pointArray.GetAt(x);
        int x1 = point->x;
        int y1 = point->y;
        pDC->Rectangle(x1, y1, x1+30, y1+30);
    }

    pDC->TextOut(10, 10, "NO BITMAP");

    pDC->SelectObject(pOldBrush);
    pDC->SelectObject(pOldPen);
    delete pRedBrush;
    delete pThickPen;
}
else
{
    CDC memoryDC;
    memoryDC.CreateCompatibleDC(pDC);
    CBitmap* pOldBitmap =
        memoryDC.SelectObject(&m_bitmap);
    pDC->BitBlt(0, 0, 800, 600,
        &memoryDC, 0, 0, SRCCOPY);
    memoryDC.SelectObject(pOldBitmap);
}
```

You've completed BitmapApp. Press Ctrl+F5 to compile and run the application.

Running the BitmapApp Application

When you run BitmapApp, the main window appears and displays the word BITMAP in the upper-left corner. The word BITMAP means that the window currently displays a bitmap that the application created in memory. Right-click the mouse to switch the display from the bitmap to the display that the application draws from scratch. When you do, the words NO BITMAP appear in the window to show that the application is not displaying the bitmap but is redrawing the window from scratch. You soon discover that switching between the BITMAP and NO BITMAP displays enables you to see the difference a bitmap can make when it comes time to repaint a window.

Don't see much of a difference yet? That's because the window only displays a line of text. To give the application something challenging to display, left-click the window; this causes 100 randomly placed rectangles to appear on the screen. Keep clicking to fill the window with rectangles, as shown in Figure 9-11. Now when you switch between the BITMAP and NO BITMAP displays, you should see a difference in the redraw rate. Keep adding rectangles. The more you add, the longer it takes the NO BITMAP display to refresh. Conversely, the BITMAP display always pops up instantly.

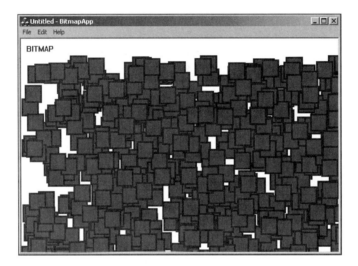

Figure 9-11: BitmapApp holds a duplicate of the window's client area in a bitmap in memory, enabling the application to draw to the screen from the bitmap. This speeds up the recovery process.

Programming with Device-Independent Bitmaps

From a user point of view, you probably are most familiar with the DIB type of bitmap. DIBs are all those files you see with the .BMP file name extension in your Windows folder. You probably even use DIBs as wallpaper on your Windows desktop. They are image files not unlike other types of image files such as GIF, PCX, TIFF, and JPEG. Unlike many of the other image file types, however, DIBs rarely are compressed; this means that their files tend to be much larger than the files of other types of images.

Because DIBs live in disk files, you need to know their file format before you can load them into your application. A DIB file contains four major parts, each of which contains a structure defined by Windows:

File header	BITMAPFILEHEADER
Bitmap header	BITMAPINFOHEADER
Bitmap color table	RGBQUAD
Bitmap image data	No formal structure exists for this element because data represents the actual image.

The BITMAPINFOHEADER and an array of RGBQUAD structures are contained in a BITMAPINFO structure. Figure 9-12 illustrates the structure of a DIB file.

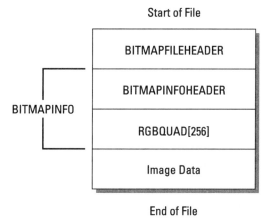

Figure 9-12: A DIB file comprises several types of data structures.

Not all DIBs contain a color table. A 24-bit color DIB, for example, has no color table because the color of each pixel in the image is contained in the data for the pixel.

Loading a DIB File

Loading a bitmap file requires not only reading the file from disk, but also using the various structures to calculate important information about the bitmap. Before you can even load the file, however, you must open the DIB's file. There are several ways to do this, but using MFC's CFile class is among the easiest methods of handling file I/O. (You learn more about the CFile class in Chapter 16.) Following is one method of opening the DIB file:

```
CFile dibFile(fileName, CFile::modeRead);
```

Here, `fileName` is the DIB's file name (including the path), and `modeRead` is the mode in which you should open the file—in this case, read-only mode.

Loading the file header

At the start of the DIB file is the `BITMAPFILEHEADER` structure, which Windows defines as follows. The structure member descriptions, in order, follow the declaration.

```
typedef struct tagBITMAPFILEHEADER {
    WORD bfType;
    DWORD bfSize;
    WORD bfReserved1;
    WORD bfReserved2;
    DWORD bfOffBits;
} BITMAPFILEHEADER, *PBITMAPFILEHEADER;
```

bfType	The ASCII values of the letters BM
bfSize	The bitmap file's size
bfReserved1	Always 0
bfReserved2	Always 0
bfOffBits	The number of bytes from the start of the file to the bitmap's data

After opening the DIB file, load the file's `BITMAPFILEHEADER` structure because this structure contains the information you need to load the bitmap. You can handle that task like this:

```
BITMAPFILEHEADER bitmapFileHeader;
dibFile.Read((void*)&bitmapFileHeader,
    sizeof(BITMAPFILEHEADER));
```

Here, you first declare a `BITMAPFILEHEADER` structure into which you can read the structure's data. Then you call the `CFile` object's `Read()` method to read the data from the file into the structure. `Read()`'s two arguments are the address of where to store the data and the number of bytes to read.

Before you process the remainder of the file, you need to make sure that the file is indeed a DIB. You can do this by checking the `bfType` structure member for the ASCII values of BM, which stands for bitmap. You can check for the bitmap ID in an `if` statement like this:

```
if (bitmapFileHeader.bfType == 0x4d42)
{
    // Process bitmap here
}
```

If the file checks out as a bitmap, you're ready to read the rest of the bitmap file. To do this, you must know the size of the rest of the file. You can calculate this value by getting the size of the entire file and subtracting the size of the BITMAPFILEHEADER structure, which you've read into memory already. The calculation looks something like this:

```
DWORD fileLength = dibFile.GetLength();
DWORD size = fileLength -
    sizeof(BITMAPFILEHEADER);
```

Of course, before you can read in the rest of the bitmap file, you must have a place to put it. You can solve this problem by allocating a chunk of memory:

```
BYTE* pDib = (BYTE*)GlobalAllocPtr(GMEM_MOVEABLE, size);
```

For now, just know that a call to GlobalAllocPtr() returns a pointer to a block of memory. The function's second argument specifies the size of this block. So, after the preceding function call, pDib contains the address of a memory block that's just the right size for the remainder of the DIB's file. You can read the remainder of the file like this:

```
dibFile.Read((void*)pDib, size);
dibFile.Close();
```

Loading the bitmap header and color table

You now have the complete DIB in memory. You may recall that the BITMAPINFO structure (which contains the BITMAPINFOHEADER and RGBQUAD structures) follows the BITMAPFILEHEADER structure in the DIB file. Windows defines the BITMAPINFO structure like this:

```
typedef struct tagBITMAPINFO {
    BITMAPINFOHEADER bmiHeader;
    RGBQUAD bmiColors[1];
} BITMAPINFO, *PBITMAPINFO;
```

Because the buffer to which pDib points contains all the data following the BITMAPFILEHEADER structure, pDib also points to the BITMAPINFO structure. You should save that address like this:

```
BITMAPINFO* pBitmapInfo = (BITMAPINFO*) pDib;
```

Moreover, because the BITMAPINFOHEADER structure is the first member of the BITMAPINFO structure, pDib also contains its address. You can save the address like this:

```
BITMAPINFOHEADER* pBitmapInfoHeader =
    (BITMAPINFOHEADER*) pDib;
```

Windows defines the BITMAPINFOHEADER structure in the following structure declaration. Table 9-5 lists the structure's members.

```
typedef struct tagBITMAPINFOHEADER{
    DWORD   biSize;
```

```
    LONG    biWidth;
    LONG    biHeight;
    WORD    biPlanes;
    WORD    biBitCount;
    DWORD   biCompression;
    DWORD   biSizeImage;
    LONG    biXPelsPerMeter;
    LONG    biYPelsPerMeter;
    DWORD   biClrUsed;
    DWORD   biClrImportant;
} BITMAPINFOHEADER, *PBITMAPINFOHEADER;
```

Table 9-5   BITMAPINFOHEADER's Members

Member	Description
biSize	The size of the structure.
biWidth	The bitmap's width. For Windows 98 and Windows 2000, if biCompression is set to BI_JPEG or BI_PNG, this member is the decompressed JPEG or PNG image file's width.
biHeight	The bitmap's height. A negative value indicates a top-down bitmap. For Windows 98 and Windows 2000, if biCompression is set to BI_JPEG or BI_PNG, this member is the decompressed JPEG or PNG image file's height.
biplanes	Number of bit planes; always 1.
biBitCount	The number of bits per pixel. Must be one of the values 0, 1, 4, 8, 16, 24, or 32. For more information on these values, please consult your Visual C++ documentation.
biCompression	The image's compression type; usually set at 0 for none, but can be BI_RGB, BI_RLE8, BI_RLE4, BI_BITFIELDS, BI_JPEG, or BI_PNG. If you need more information on these values, please consult your Visual C++ documentation.
biSizeImage	The size of the image in bytes. For Windows 98 or Windows 2000, if biCompression is BI_JPEG or BI_PNG, this member is the JPEG or PNG image buffer's size.
biXPelsPerMeter	The target device's horizontal resolution in pixels per meter.
biYPelsPerMeter	The target device's vertical resolution in pixels.
biClrUsed	The number of colors actually used by the bitmap; 0 = all colors used.
biClrImportant	The number of important colors; 0 = all colors important.

Because the DIB's color table follows the `BITMAPINFOHEADER` structure, you can calculate its address by adding the size of the `BITMAPINFOHEADER` to the address stored in `pDib`:

```
RGBQUAD* pRGB = (RGBQUAD*)(pDib +
    pBitmapInfoHeader->biSize);
```

Windows then defines the `RGBQUAD` structure as follows:

```
typedef struct tagRGBQUAD {
    BYTE    rgbBlue;
    BYTE    rgbGreen;
    BYTE    rgbRed;
    BYTE    rgbReserved;
} RGBQUAD;
```

The first three members of this structure hold the red, green, and blue color values (respectively) for the color being defined. The fourth member is always 0. The DIB's color table contains one `RGBQUAD` structure for every color in the bitmap — a color table for a 256-color bitmap is a 256-element array of `RGBQUAD` structures.

At this point, you have pointers to the `BITMAPFILEHEADER`, `BITMAPINFO`, and `BITMAPINFOHEADER` structures, as well as a pointer to the bitmap's color table. You now need the address of the bitmap's image data. To get this address, you need to know the size of the DIB's color table — a value that's not included directly in any of the DIB structures. You do know, however, that each color is represented by an `RGBQUAD` structure. If you can get the number of colors, you can get the size of the color table by multiplying the number of colors by the size of the `RGBQUAD` structure. You learn more about the `RGBQUAD` structure later in this chapter when you study color palettes.

Although the `biClrUsed` structure specifies the number of colors in the DIB, a value of 0 means all the colors are used. So, `biClrUsed` may or may not be useful in determining the number of colors. If `biClrUsed` contains a value other than 0, you're home free. However, if `biClrUsed` is 0, you have to use the `biBitCount` member to determine the number of colors.

The `biBitCount` member tells you the number of bits used to represent each pixel of the image. In images of 256 colors or fewer, these pixel values represent an index into the color table. (If a DIB contains more than 256 colors, it doesn't have a color table.) That is, if a pixel's value is 25, Windows finds the pixel's color in the 25th entry in the DIB's color table. If a pixel uses eight bits, the pixel can be one of 256 colors. (An 8-bit value must be in the range of 0 to 255).

You can see how you can get the number of colors from the bit count. If the bit count is 1, the image uses only two colors; if the bit count is 4, the image uses 16 colors; and if the bit count is 8, the image uses 256 colors. Anything over 256 colors is not relevant to loading the bitmap because you don't have to deal with a color table at all. So, to determine the number of colors in a DIB, you might use code like this:

```
int numberOfColors;

if ((pBitmapInfoHeader->biClrUsed == 0) &&
    (pBitmapInfoHeader->biBitCount < 9))
{
    switch (pBitmapInfoHeader->biBitCount)
    {
        case 1: numberOfColors = 2; break;
        case 4: numberOfColors = 16; break;
        case 8: numberOfColors = 256;
    }
}
else
    numberOfColors =
        (int) pBitmapInfoHeader->biClrUsed;

if (pBitmapInfoHeader->biClrUsed == 0)
    pBitmapInfoHeader->biClrUsed = numberOfColors;
```

Now you're getting somewhere! With the number of colors in hand, you can figure out the size of the color table and then calculate where the bitmap image data starts. You do this by adding the size of the color table to the pDib pointer:

```
DWORD clrTableSize = numberOfColors * sizeof(RGBQUAD);
BYTE* pData = pDib + pBitmapInfoHeader->biSize
    + clrTableSize;
```

Often, folks who create bitmap files leave the BITMAPINFOHEADER structure's biSizeImage member set to 0. Fill in that value by calculating the image size in your program, which you do by multiplying the image's width and height. For example:

```
if (pBitmapInfoHeader->biSizeImage == 0)
{
    DWORD height = pBitmapInfoHeader->biHeight;
    DWORD width = pBitmapInfoHeader->biHeight;
    pBitmapInfoHeader->biSizeImage = height * width;
}
```

And that's all there is to it. Now that you know all the details of loading a bitmap into memory, you can use that knowledge to design a class that manages this sticky task for you.

The Custom CDib Class

Sure, the process of loading a bitmap is complicated. The good news is that you can write the code for managing a bitmap and then use it again and again as needed for any bitmap. In fact, you can place the code into a class and load a bitmap simply by creating an instance of the class. The really good news is that your humble author has written just such a class already, which you can see in Listings 9-1 and 9-2. Listing 9-1 is the class's header file, whereas Listing 9-2 is the class's implementation file.

Name: `cdib.h`
Location: `WinPrgS\Chap09\BitmapApp2`

Listing 9-1: The CDib class's header file

```
#ifndef __CDIB_H
#define __CDIB_H

class CDib : public CObject
{
protected:
    char m_fileName[256];
    RGBQUAD* m_pRGB;
    BYTE* m_pData;
    UINT m_numberOfColors;
    BOOL m_valid;
    BITMAPFILEHEADER* m_pBitmapFileHeader;
    BITMAPINFOHEADER* m_pBitmapInfoHeader;
    BITMAPINFO* m_pBitmapInfo;

public:
    CDib(const char* dibFileName);
    ~CDib();

    char* GetFileName();
    BOOL IsValid();
    DWORD GetSize();
    UINT GetWidth();
    UINT GetHeight();
    UINT GetNumberOfColors();
    RGBQUAD* GetRGB();
    BYTE* GetData();
    BITMAPINFO* GetInfo();

protected:
    void LoadFile();

};

#endif
```

Name: `cdib.cpp`
Location: `WinPrgS\Chap09\BitmapApp2`

Listing 9-2: The CDib class's implementation file

```
#include "stdafx.h"
#include "cdib.h"
#include "windowsx.h"
```

```cpp
CDib::CDib(const char* dibFileName)
{
    strcpy(m_fileName, dibFileName);
    LoadFile();
}

CDib::~CDib()
{
    GlobalFreePtr(m_pBitmapInfo);
}

void CDib::LoadFile()
{
    CFile dibFile(m_fileName, CFile::modeRead);

    BITMAPFILEHEADER bitmapFileHeader;
    dibFile.Read((void*)&bitmapFileHeader,
        sizeof(BITMAPFILEHEADER));

    if (bitmapFileHeader.bfType == 0x4d42)
    {
        DWORD fileLength = dibFile.GetLength();
        DWORD size = fileLength -
            sizeof(BITMAPFILEHEADER);
        BYTE* pDib =
            (BYTE*)GlobalAllocPtr(GMEM_MOVEABLE, size);
        dibFile.Read((void*)pDib, size);
        dibFile.Close();

        m_pBitmapInfo = (BITMAPINFO*) pDib;
        m_pBitmapInfoHeader = (BITMAPINFOHEADER*) pDib;
        m_pRGB = (RGBQUAD*)(pDib +
            m_pBitmapInfoHeader->biSize);
        int m_numberOfColors = GetNumberOfColors();
        if (m_pBitmapInfoHeader->biClrUsed == 0)
            m_pBitmapInfoHeader->biClrUsed =
                m_numberOfColors;
        DWORD colorTableSize = m_numberOfColors *
            sizeof(RGBQUAD);
        m_pData = pDib + m_pBitmapInfoHeader->biSize
            + colorTableSize;
        m_pBitmapInfoHeader->biSizeImage = GetSize();
        m_valid = TRUE;
    }
    else
    {
        m_valid = FALSE;
        AfxMessageBox("This isn't a bitmap file!");
    }
}

BOOL CDib::IsValid()
{
```

```cpp
    return m_valid;
}

char* CDib::GetFileName()
{
    return m_fileName;
}

UINT CDib::GetWidth()
{
    return (UINT) m_pBitmapInfoHeader->biWidth;
}

UINT CDib::GetHeight()
{
    return (UINT) m_pBitmapInfoHeader->biHeight;
}

DWORD CDib::GetSize()
{
    if (m_pBitmapInfoHeader->biSizeImage != 0)
        return m_pBitmapInfoHeader->biSizeImage;
    else
    {
        DWORD height = (DWORD) GetHeight();
        DWORD width = (DWORD) GetWidth();
        return height * width;
    }
}

UINT CDib::GetNumberOfColors()
{
    int numberOfColors;

    if ((m_pBitmapInfoHeader->biClrUsed == 0) &&
        (m_pBitmapInfoHeader->biBitCount < 9))
    {
        switch (m_pBitmapInfoHeader->biBitCount)
        {
            case 1: numberOfColors = 2; break;
            case 4: numberOfColors = 16; break;
            case 8: numberOfColors = 256;
        }
    }
    else
        numberOfColors =
            (int) m_pBitmapInfoHeader->biClrUsed;

    return numberOfColors;
}

BYTE* CDib::GetData()
{
```

```
        return m_pData;
}

RGBQUAD* CDib::GetRGB()
{
    return m_pRGB;
}

BITMAPINFO* CDib::GetInfo()
{
    return m_pBitmapInfo;
}
```

Using the `CDib` class couldn't be easier. First, you create an object of the class:

```
CDib* pBitmap = new CDib("c:\Images\MyBitmap.bmp");
```

The constructor's single argument is a string containing the bitmap's path and file name. That single line is all you need to create the `CDib` object as well as load the DIB file and set all the appropriate pointers. And you thought loading a bitmap was hard.

To ensure that the bitmap file is valid, call the class's `IsValid()` member function:

```
BOOL dibOkay = pBitmap->IsValid();
```

The remaining `CDib` member functions give you access to the information you need to display a DIB. Table 9-6 describes each of the functions.

Table 9-6   The Remaining CDib Member Functions

Function	Description
`GetData()`	Gets a pointer to the DIB's image data
`GetFileName()`	Gets the bitmap's file name
`GetHeight()`	Gets the image's height
`GetInfo()`	Gets a pointer to the DIB's `BITMAPINFO` structure
`GetNumberOfColors()`	Gets the number of colors used in the image
`GetRGB()`	Gets a pointer to the DIB's color table; returns `NULL` if there is no color table
`GetSize()`	Gets the image's size in bytes
`GetWidth()`	Gets the image's width
`IsValid()`	Returns `TRUE` if the `CDib` object is valid

Displaying a DIB

Once you have your bitmap initialized and loaded, you should copy it to the screen. Copying a DIB to the screen is different from copying a DDB to the screen. One big difference is that you don't need to select the DIB into a memory device context. You can copy the image's data directly to the screen. The function you use to copy a DIB reflects another big difference. Rather than use `BitBlt()`, as you do with a DDB, you use `StretchDIBits()` to display a DIB. I provide that function's signature here, followed by its arguments in Table 9-7:

```
int StretchDIBits(
    HDC hdc,
    int XDest,
    int YDest,
    int nDestWidth,
    int nDestHeight,
    int XSrc,
    int YSrc,
    int nSrcWidth,
    int nSrcHeight,
    CONST VOID *lpBits,
    CONST BITMAPINFO *lpBitsInfo,
    UINT iUsage,
    DWORD dwRop
);
```

Table 9-7 StretchDIBits()'s Arguments

Argument	Description
hdc	Handle of the destination DC
XDest	X coordinate of the destination rectangle's upper-left corner
Ydest	Y coordinate of the destination rectangle's upper-left corner
nDestWidth	Width of the destination rectangle
nDestHeight	Height of the destination rectangle
XSrc	X coordinate of the source rectangle's upper-left corner
YSrc	Y coordinate of the source rectangle's upper-left corner
nSrcWidth	Width of the source rectangle
nSrcHeight	Height of the source rectangle
lpBits	Pointer to the bitmap's image data
lpBitsInfo	Pointer to the bitmap's `BITMAPINFO` structure
iUsage	Color table usage; usually `DIB_RGB_COLORS`
dwRop	Raster operation; determines how source and destination pixels are combined

As you can see, `StretchDIBits()` is similar to `BitBlt()`, but the source bitmap doesn't need to supply a memory context handle. Instead, the source bitmap supplies the address of its image data, as well as the address of its `BITMAPINFO` structure. To load and display a bitmap as a `CDib` object, you can use code like this:

```
CDib* pBitmap = new CDib("mybitmap.bmp");

if (!pBitmap->IsValid())
    MessageBox("Couldn't find mybitmap.bmp.",
        "Error", MB_OK | MB_ICONEXCLAMATION);
else
{
    BYTE* pBitmapData = pBitmap->GetData();
    LPBITMAPINFO pBitmapInfo = pBitmap->GetInfo();

    CClientDC windowDC(this);
    StretchDIBits(windowDC.m_hDC, 0, 0, 500, 300,
        0, 0, 500, 300, pBitmapData, pBitmapInfo,
        DIB_RGB_COLORS, SRCCOPY);
}
```

Here, the program first creates a `CDib` object from the `mybitmap.bmp` file. The program then calls the bitmap object's `IsValid()` member function to make sure that the bitmap object is OK to use, displaying an error message box if `IsValid()` returns `FALSE`. If the bitmap object is created successfully, a call to the object's `GetData()` function gets a pointer to the bitmap's image data, and a call to `GetInfo()` gets a pointer to the bitmap's `BITMAPINFO` structure. Both of these pointers function as arguments in the call to `StretchDIBits()`, which displays the bitmap.

Managing Palettes

Although the previous section discusses a general procedure for loading and displaying a bitmap, one important detail was left out: palettes. Any DIB with 256 or fewer colors carries with it a color palette. In order to display the DIB correctly, you must give the DIB's color palette to Windows. Because Windows can run many applications concurrently, dealing with palettes is trickier than you may expect. This is because any of the running applications may need to display images using a color palette at the same time. No two color palettes are likely to be exactly alike (unless they are created alike by design), so how can Windows show two or more applications using two or more different palettes? In this section, you get the answer to that question.

Logical palettes

Windows can display only so many colors at a time. For example, if you run your system in 256-color mode, Windows can display only 256 colors. These 256 colors can be any 256 colors you like (except for the 20 colors Windows reserves for its own use), but 256 colors is the limit that the screen can display in this mode. Windows has a system palette, which holds the 256 colors that the system displays. In most cases, applications need only 20 of these colors to display their windows and data in color. However, when you start displaying more complex graphics such as bitmaps, 20 colors doesn't cut it.

Any application that displays complex images must create a *logical palette,* which is similar to the system palette except that it belongs only to one application. Every running application can create and store its own logical palette. When the application is the topmost window, it gives its logical palette to Windows; in turn, Windows loads the application's colors into the system palette. Then, the application can display its graphics correctly. When the user switches windows, the new topmost application gives Windows its logical palette; Windows loads this logical palette into the system palette.

There is one minor complication. When an application with a palette loses its focus (called the *background application*) and a new application (called the *foreground application*) gives Windows its logical palette, Windows still needs to display the image in the background application as best it can. Windows does this by matching the background application's colors as closely as possible to the foreground application's colors. Then, although the background application's display may not be perfect, it usually is close. However, if the foreground application's logical palette significantly differs from the background application's logical palette, the background application's display suffers a great deal.

An application creates a logical palette by loading color values into a `LOGPALETTE` structure and calling the `CreatePalette()` function. A program might define its `LOGPALETTE` structure like this:

```
struct
{
    WORD Version;
    WORD NumberOfEntries;
    PALETTEENTRY aEntries[256];
} palette = { 0x300, 256 };
```

The structure's three members are a version number (usually 0x300), the number of colors in the palette, and an array of `PALETTEENTRY` structures. There is one element for each color. Windows defines the `PALETTEENTRY` structure like this:

```
typedef struct tagPALETTEENTRY {
    BYTE peRed;
    BYTE peGreen;
    BYTE peBlue;
    BYTE peFlags;
} PALETTEENTRY
```

The structure's first three members are the values for the color's red, green, and blue components. The last member contains a flag that specifies how Windows should handle the color being defined. Usually, you just put a 0 in this member and leave the color management to Windows.

To initialize a palette from a `CDib` object that loads a DIB file, you can use code like this:

```
LPRGBQUAD pRGBTable = pBitmap->GetRGB();
UINT numberOfColors = pBitmap->GetNumberOfColors();

for(UINT x=0; x<numberOfColors; ++x)
{
    palette.aEntries[x].peRed =
        pRGBTable[x].rgbRed;
    palette.aEntries[x].peGreen =
        pRGBTable[x].rgbGreen;
    palette.aEntries[x].peBlue =
        pRGBTable[x].rgbBlue;
    palette.aEntries[x].peFlags = 0;
}
```

In the preceding listing, `pBitmap` is a pointer to a valid `CDib` object. The program copies the color values from the DIB's color table (pointed to by `pRGBTable`) to the members of each `PALETTEENTRY` structure.

After initializing the `LOGPALETTE` structure, you create the palette by calling the aptly named `CreatePalette()` Windows API function. This function returns a handle to the newly created palette (or `NULL` if the function call fails):

```
HPALETTE hPalette =
    ::CreatePalette((LPLOGPALETTE)&palette);
```

Finally, you can give the new palette to Windows. Windows programmers call this process *realizing the palette*. To realize the bitmap's palette, you first select the new palette into the DC and then you call the `RealizePalette()` function. The entire process looks like this:

```
HPALETTE hOldPalette =
    SelectPalette(pDC->m_hDC, hPalette, FALSE);
RealizePalette(pDC->m_hDC);

// Display bitmap here.

SelectPalette(pDC->m_hDC, hOldPalette, FALSE);
DeleteObject(hPalette);
```

Notice that when the program is through with the palette, it selects the old palette back into the DC and calls `DeleteObject()` to get rid of the now unneeded palette.

Managing palette changes

When an application realizes its palette, Windows sends messages to other currently running applications to give them a chance to realize their own palettes as well. When a background application realizes its palette, Windows maps the application's palette to the new system palette. Your application must handle two messages — `WM_PALETTECHANGED` and `WM_QUERYNEWPALETTE` — if it is to work properly under Windows 2000.

Windows sends the WM_PALETTECHANGED message whenever an application changes the system palette. This message signals all applications to realize their palettes and get remapped to the new palette. If an application fails to respond to the WM_PALETTECHANGED message, the palette change may corrupt the application's display beyond reason.

Windows sends the WM_QUERYNEWPALETTE message to an application when the application becomes the topmost window. This message signals the application that it should realize its palette in order to take over the system palette. The application that receives and responds to WM_QUERYNEWPALETTE has the best display because all of its colors are available in the system palette.

In an MFC program, you respond to these important palette messages in the main window's class — usually called CMainFrame. Use ClassWizard to add the OnPaletteChanged() and OnQueryNewPalette() functions to the class. In each function, you must realize the application's current logical palette. How you do this depends on how your application is set up. If you normally realize the palette in the application's OnDraw() function, you can call the view window's Invalidate() function; this causes MFC to call OnDraw().

However, in the case of OnPaletteChanged(), you must make sure your application can differentiate between itself and another application changing the palette because you don't want it to respond to its own message. If it does, the application ends up in an infinite loop as it changes its palette and generates another WM_PALETTECHANGED message. To determine whether it is the application's own view window that changed the palette, have your application check the pFocusWnd pointer passed to the function against a pointer to the view window. If they are the same, write your program so it doesn't realize the application's palette. The following code shows the source code for typical OnPaletteChanged() and OnQueryNewPalette() functions:

```
void CMainFrame::OnPaletteChanged(CWnd* pFocusWnd)
{
    CFrameWnd::OnPaletteChanged(pFocusWnd);

    // TODO: Add your message handler code here

    CView* pView = GetActiveView();
    if (pFocusWnd != pView)
        pView->Invalidate();
}

BOOL CMainFrame::OnQueryNewPalette()
{
    // TODO: Add your message handler code here
    //       and/or call default

    CView* pView = GetActiveView();
```

```
            pView->Invalidate();

            return CFrameWnd::OnQueryNewPalette();
}
```

In the `OnPaletteChanged()` function, the program first gets a pointer to the application's view window. It then compares this pointer to the pointer that represents the window generating the palette change. Only if they aren't the same window does the program invalidate the window, which causes it to realize its palette. In the `OnQueryNewPalette()` function, the program simply gets a pointer to the view window and calls the window's `Invalidate()` function to force the window to redraw its display and realize its palette.

Creating the BitmapApp2 Application

Location: `WinPrgS\Chap09\BitmapApp2`

Now that you've learned a little about device-independent bitmap programming, you can apply that knowledge to building a simple bitmap viewer. Perform the following steps to create your copy of the BitmapApp2 application. These steps not only give you additional experience with Visual C++'s tools, but they also show you step by step how to manage DIBs in a full-fledged application. If you don't want to build the application, you can find a complete copy on this book's CD-ROM.

1. Select the File menu's New command and start a new MFC AppWizard (exe) project called BitmapApp2 in the Projects window.

2. In the MFC AppWizard - Step 1 dialog box, select the Single document option.

3. Click the Next button three times, accepting the default settings in the Step 2 and Step 3 dialog boxes.

4. In the Step 4 dialog box, turn off the Docking toolbar, Initial status bar, and Printing and print preview options.

5. Click the Next button and then select the As a statically linked library option in the Step 5 dialog box.

6. Click the Finish button. The New Project Information dialog box appears.

7. Click the OK button and AppWizard generates the new project.

8. Copy the `CDib.h` and `CDib.cpp` files from the `Chapter09\BitmapApp2` folder of this book's CD-ROM to your BitmapApp2 project's folder.

9. Select the Project menu's Add To Project command and then select Files from the submenu that appears (as shown in Figure 9-13). You use the File command to add new files to your project.

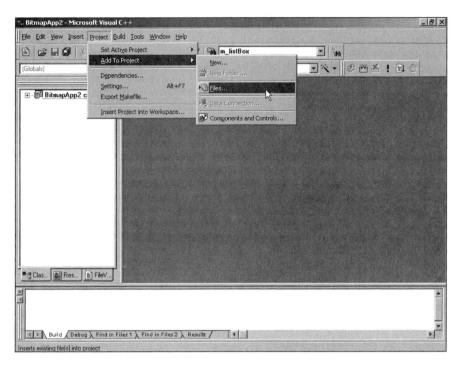

Figure 9-13: The Add To Project command enables you to add non-AppWizard-generated files to your project.

10. Select the cdib.cpp file in the Insert Files into Project dialog box (see Figure 9-14) and click the OK button. Visual C++ adds the file to the project.

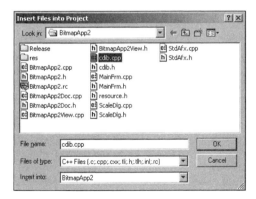

Figure 9-14: Adding the cdib.cpp file to the project gives the program access to the CDib class.

You've completed the basic BitmapApp2 project. You can, if you like, compile and run the project by pressing Ctrl+F5 on your keyboard. However, the program doesn't do much at this point. You still have to modify the default resources and add the source code needed to give the application bitmap-loading capabilities.

Customizing the Application's Resources

Now that you have the basic project set up, you can work on the application's resources. In this section, you add menu commands and a dialog box as well as modify a few of the default resources. Just perform the following steps to complete this portion of the BitmapApp2 application.

1. Select the ResourceView tab in the project workspace window and then bring up the application's accelerators in the resource editor, as shown in Figure 9-15.

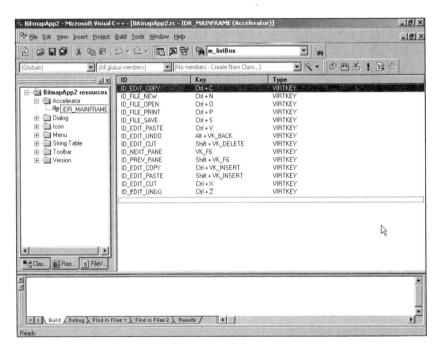

Figure 9-15: The resource editor enables you to add and delete accelerators.

2. Delete all the accelerators except `ID_FILE_OPEN` (see Figure 9-16).

3. Load the application's About dialog box into the editor and change the copyright string to read **Copyright (C) 2000 by IDG Books Worldwide,** as shown in Figure 9-17.

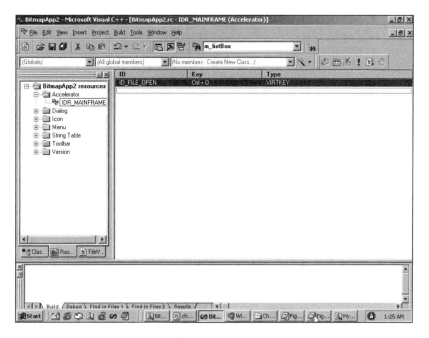

Figure 9-16: The resource editor after deleting the unneeded accelerators

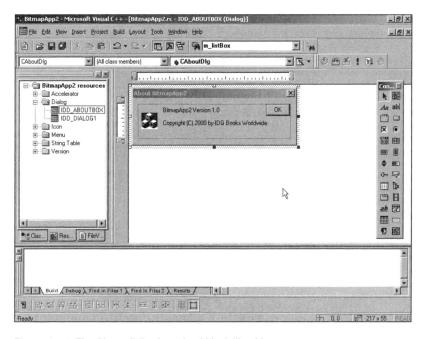

Figure 9-17: The About dialog box should look like this.

Part II: Advanced Windows 2000 Programming

4. Load the application's menu bar into the editor and delete the Edit menu. Also, delete all commands from the File menu except Open and Exit (as shown in Figure 9-18).

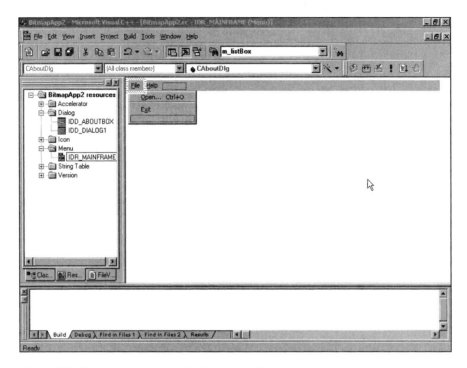

Figure 9-18: The menu bar displayed after deleting the unneeded commands

5. Create a Scale menu in the Menu Item Properties dialog box and give it one item called Set Scaling... with an ID of `ID_SCALE_SETSCALING` (as shown in Figure 9-19).

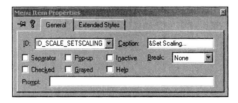

Figure 9-19: The new Scale menu displayed with its Set Scaling... command

6. Select the Insert menu's Resource command and add a new dialog box to the resources.

7. Modify the Set Scaling dialog box so that it looks like the one shown in Figure 9-20. Keep the default ID of `IDC_EDIT1` for the edit control.

Figure 9-20: The new Set Scaling dialog box

8. Double-click the new dialog box. Select the Create a new class option in the Adding a Class dialog box (see Figure 9-21) and click OK.

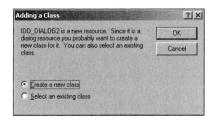

Figure 9-21: This dialog box is the first step to creating a new dialog class.

9. In the New Class dialog box, type `CScaleDlg` into the Name box (see Figure 9-22) and click OK.

Figure 9-22: This dialog box enables you to specify information about the new class including its class name, file name, and base class.

10. In the MFC ClassWizard property sheet, select the Member Variables tab. Double-click the IDC_EDIT1 control ID and associate the m_scale variable with the control. The m_scale variable should have the data type float, as shown in Figure 9-23.

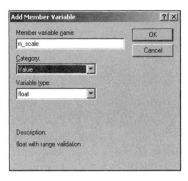

Figure 9-23: The Add Member Variable dialog box enables you to associate variables with the dialog box's controls.

11. Click OK and then enter **1** into the Minimum Value box and **5** into the Maximum Value box (see Figure 9-24). Click OK to dismiss ClassWizard.

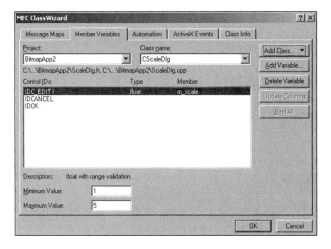

Figure 9-24: The user must enter a value between 1 and 5 into the edit boxes.

The application's resources are complete. You should save your work at this point by selecting the File menu's Save All command. If you like, you can compile and run the program by pressing Ctrl+F5. If you run the program, you see the new menu bar; you also can select the Help menu's

About BitmapApp2 command to call up the application's modified About dialog box.

Adding Source Code

The last thing you must do to finish the BitmapApp2 application is add the functions and source code required to give the application bitmap-loading and bitmap-displaying capabilities. Follow the next set of steps to accomplish this task.

1. Click the ClassView tab of the project workspace window and then right-click the CBitmapApp2Doc class. (You may have to click the + to open the ClassView tree.) A menu appears.

2. Select Add Member Variable from the menu and then define the variable m_pBitmap in the Add Member Variable dialog box (as shown in Figure 9-25). The variable's type should be CDib*, and the access should be Public. Click OK to dismiss the dialog box, and Visual C++ adds the new member variable to the class.

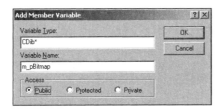

Figure 9-25: BitmapApp2's document class has a single member variable that holds a pointer to the CDib object.

3. Load the BitmapApp2Doc.h header file and add the following line near the top of the file, right after the existing line #endif // _MSC_VER >= 1000. This line enables the document class to access the CDib class.

   #include "CDib.h"

4. Load the BitmapApp2Doc.cpp file and add the following line to the CBitmapApp2Doc class's constructor, right after the TODO: add one-time construction code here comment. This line ensures that the bitmap object's pointer starts off NULL.

   m_pBitmap = NULL;

5. Press Ctrl+W to display ClassWizard, and add the OnFileOpen() function to the class, as shown in Figure 9-26. (Make sure you have CBitmapApp2Doc selected in the Class name box.) When the user selects the Open command on the File menu, the program receives an ID_FILE_OPEN message that causes MFC to call the OnFileOpen() function.

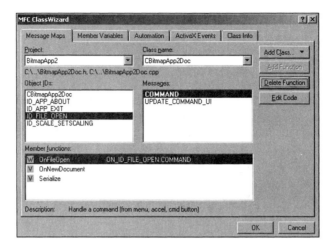

Figure 9-26: ClassWizard associates the OnFileOpen() function with the ID_FILE_OPEN menu command.

6. Click the Edit Code button and add the following lines to the new `OnFileOpen()` function, right after the `TODO: Add your command handler code here` comment:

```
CFileDialog dlg(TRUE, "bmp", "*.bmp");
int result = dlg.DoModal();

if (result == IDOK)
{
    CString path = dlg.GetPathName();
    m_pBitmap = new CDib(path);
    if (m_pBitmap->IsValid())
        SetTitle(path);
    else
        DeleteContents();
}

UpdateAllViews(0);
```

7. Use ClassWizard to override the `DeleteContents()` function in the `CBitmapApp2Doc` class, as shown in Figure 9-27.

8. Click the Edit Code button and add the following lines to the `DeleteContents()` function, right after the `TODO: Add your specialized code here and/or call the base class` comment:

```
if (m_pBitmap)
{
    delete m_pBitmap;
    m_pBitmap = NULL;
}
```

Chapter 9: Bitmaps 377

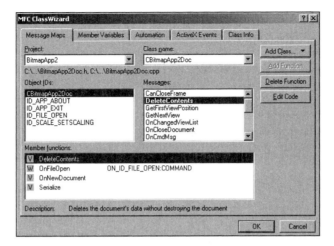

Figure 9-27: ClassWizard overrides the `CDocument` class's `DeleteContents()` function in the `CBitmapApp2Doc` class.

9. Load the `BitmapApp2View` file and add the following line near the top, after the existing line `#include "BitmapApp2View.h"`:

    `#include "ScaleDlg.h"`

10. Right-click the `CBitmapApp2View` class in the project workspace window, select Add Member Variable from the menu that appears, and then define the variable `m_scale` in the Add Member Variable dialog box. The variable's type should be `float`, and the access should be Protected. Click OK to dismiss the dialog box.

11. Add the following line to the `CBitmapApp2View` class's constructor, right after the `TODO: add construction code here` comment:

    `m_scale = 1.0;`

12. Add the following lines to the `CBitmapApp2View` class's `OnDraw()` function, right after the `TODO: add draw code for native data here` comment:

```
CDib* pBitmap = pDoc->m_pBitmap;

if (pBitmap)
{
    BYTE* pBitmapData = pBitmap->GetData();
    LPBITMAPINFO pBitmapInfo = pBitmap->GetInfo();
    int bitmapHeight = pBitmap->GetHeight();
    int bitmapWidth = pBitmap->GetWidth();
    int scaledWidth = (int)(bitmapWidth * m_scale);
    int scaledHeight = (int)(bitmapHeight * m_scale);

    if (pBitmap->GetRGB()) // Has a color table
```

```
            {
                HPALETTE hPalette =
                    CreateBitmapPalette(pBitmap);
                HPALETTE hOldPalette =
                    ::SelectPalette(pDC->m_hDC, hPalette, FALSE);
                ::RealizePalette(pDC->m_hDC);

                StretchDIBits(pDC->m_hDC,
                    10, 10, scaledWidth, scaledHeight,
                    0, 0, bitmapWidth, bitmapHeight,
                    pBitmapData, pBitmapInfo,
                    DIB_RGB_COLORS, SRCCOPY);

                ::SelectPalette(pDC->m_hDC, hOldPalette, FALSE);
                ::DeleteObject(hPalette);
            }
            else
                StretchDIBits(pDC->m_hDC,
                    10, 10, scaledWidth, scaledHeight,
                    0, 0, bitmapWidth, bitmapHeight,
                    pBitmapData, pBitmapInfo,
                    DIB_RGB_COLORS, SRCCOPY);

    }
```

13. Right-click the `CBitmapApp2View` class in the project workspace window, select Add Member Function from the menu that appears, and then define the `CreateBitmapPalette()` function in the Add Member Function dialog box (as shown in Figure 9-28). The function's type should be `HPALETTE`, its signature should be `CreateBitmapPalette(CDib* pBitmap)`, and the access should be Protected. Click OK to dismiss the dialog box.

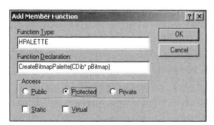

Figure 9-28: BitmapApp2's view class gets a new function called CreateBitmapPalette().

14. Add the following lines to the `CreateBitmapPalette()` function:

```
struct
{
    WORD Version;
    WORD NumberOfEntries;
    PALETTEENTRY aEntries[256];
```

```
    } palette = { 0x300, 256 };

    LPRGBQUAD pRGBTable = pBitmap->GetRGB();
    UINT numberOfColors = pBitmap->GetNumberOfColors();

    for(UINT x=0; x<numberOfColors; ++x)
    {
        palette.aEntries[x].peRed =
            pRGBTable[x].rgbRed;
        palette.aEntries[x].peGreen =
            pRGBTable[x].rgbGreen;
        palette.aEntries[x].peBlue =
            pRGBTable[x].rgbBlue;
        palette.aEntries[x].peFlags = 0;
    }

    HPALETTE hPalette =
        ::CreatePalette((LPLOGPALETTE)&palette);

    return hPalette;
```

15. Use ClassWizard to add the `OnScaleSetscaling()` function to the `CBitmapApp2View` class.

16. Click the Edit Code button and add the following lines to the `OnScaleSetscaling()` function, right after the `TODO: Add your command handler code here` comment:

    ```
    CScaleDlg dlg(this);
    dlg.m_scale = m_scale;

    int result = dlg.DoModal();

    if (result == IDOK)
    {
        m_scale = dlg.m_scale;
        Invalidate();
    }
    ```

17. Use ClassWizard to add the `OnPaletteChanged()` function—which responds to the `WM_PALETTECHANGED` Windows message—to the `CMainFrame` class. Make sure that you select `CMainFrame` in ClassWizard's Class name box.

18. Click the Edit Code button and add the following lines to the `OnPaletteChanged()` function, right after the `TODO: Add your command handler code here` comment:

    ```
    CView* pView = GetActiveView();
    if (pFocusWnd != pView)
        pView->Invalidate();
    ```

380 Part II: Advanced Windows 2000 Programming

19. Use ClassWizard to add the `OnQueryNewPalette()` function—which responds to the `WM_QUERYNEWPALETTE` Windows message—to the `CMainFrame` class.

20. Click the Edit Code button and add the following lines to the `OnQueryNewPalette()` function, right after the `TODO: Add your command handler code here and/or call default` comment:

    ```
    CView* pView = GetActiveView();
    pView->Invalidate();
    ```

You've completed BitmapApp2. To compile and run the application, press Ctrl+F5 on your keyboard.

Running the BitmapApp2 Application

When you run BitmapApp2, the application's window appears. Select the File menu's Open command and use the Open dialog box to select and load a bitmap file. There are four bitmaps included with the program: `1-bit.bmp`, `4-bit.bmp`, `8-bit.bmp`, and `24-bit.bmp`. These files contain 2-color, 16-color, 256-color, and True-Color images, respectively. You also can use the application to load and display any valid bitmap file. Figure 9-29 shows the application displaying the `24-bit.bmp` file.

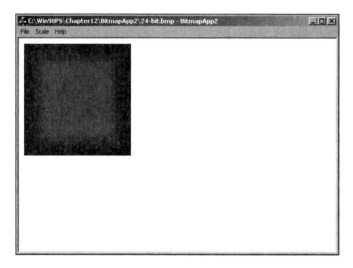

Figure 9-29: BitmapApp2 displaying a 24-bit bitmap

You can use the Scale menu to enlarge the image of a loaded bitmap. First select the Scale menu's Set Scaling command. Then type a value between 1 and 5 into the dialog box that appears. When you click the dialog box's OK button, the displayed bitmap—and any other bitmap you load—gets scaled to the value you choose (see Figure 9-30). You don't have to choose whole numbers for the scaling; you can enter something like 2.75 if you like.

Figure 9-30: The bitmap scaled by a factor of five

When the user selects the File menu's Open command, the `CBitmapApp2Doc` document class's `OnFileOpen()` function takes over:

```
void CBitmapApp2Doc::OnFileOpen()
{
    // TODO: Add your command handler code here

    CFileDialog dlg(TRUE, "bmp", "*.bmp");
    int result = dlg.DoModal();

    if (result == IDOK)
    {
        CString path = dlg.GetPathName();
        m_pBitmap = new CDib(path);
        if (m_pBitmap->IsValid())
            SetTitle(path);
        else
            DeleteContents();
    }

    UpdateAllViews(0);
}
```

In `OnFileOpen()`, the program creates and displays a File dialog box that lists files with a .BMP extension. If the user exits the dialog box via the OK button, the program gets the selected file's path name and calls the `CDib` class's constructor to create and load the bitmap. If the bitmap loads successfully, `OnFileOpen()` calls `SetTitle()` to set the document's title to the file's path name. This title appears in the application's title bar. If the bitmap ends up not valid, the program calls `DeleteContents()` to delete the `CDib` object.

MFC calls the document class's `DeleteContents()` function when the application first runs and whenever you load a new bitmap:

```
void CBitmapApp2Doc::DeleteContents()
{
    // TODO: Add your specialized code here
    //    and/or call the base class

    if (m_pBitmap)
    {
        delete m_pBitmap;
        m_pBitmap = NULL;
    }

    CDocument::DeleteContents();
}
```

`DeleteContents()` makes sure that the application's document (which consists of only the currently selected bitmap) starts fresh each time the user loads a bitmap.

The `OnDraw()` function is where most of the bitmap handling occurs. First, `OnDraw()` gets a pointer to the bitmap from the application's document class:

```
CDib* pBitmap = pDoc->m_pBitmap;
```

Then the program calls various `CDib` member functions to get pointers to the DIB's image data and `BITMAPINFO` structure, as well as the bitmap's dimensions:

```
BYTE* pBitmapData = pBitmap->GetData();
LPBITMAPINFO pBitmapInfo = pBitmap->GetInfo();
int bitmapHeight = pBitmap->GetHeight();
int bitmapWidth = pBitmap->GetWidth();
```

The program then scales the bitmap's dimensions, with the scaling value set by the user:

```
int scaledWidth = (int)(bitmapWidth * m_scale);
int scaledHeight = (int)(bitmapHeight * m_scale);
```

If the bitmap has 256 or fewer colors, it has a color table. In this case, `OnDraw()` creates and realizes a logical palette for the DIB:

```
HPALETTE hPalette =
    CreateBitmapPalette(pBitmap);
```

```
HPALETTE hOldPalette =
    ::SelectPalette(pDC->m_hDC, hPalette, FALSE);
::RealizePalette(pDC->m_hDC);
```

CreateBitmapPalette() is a function you add to the view class. This function creates a logical palette exactly as described in the previous section on palette handling.

With the palette created and realized, the program displays the currently loaded bitmap:

```
StretchDIBits(pDC->m_hDC,
    10, 10, scaledWidth, scaledHeight,
    0, 0, bitmapWidth, bitmapHeight,
    pBitmapData, pBitmapInfo,
    DIB_RGB_COLORS, SRCCOPY);
```

Finally, the program restores the old palette to the DC and deletes the now unneeded DIB palette:

```
::SelectPalette(pDC->m_hDC, hOldPalette, FALSE);
::DeleteObject(hPalette);
```

DIBs without color tables don't require the entire palette processing. A simple call to StretchDIBits() is all it takes to display the bitmap's image in the window.

The double colons (::) in front of function calls indicate Windows API functions and not member functions of an MFC class.

Problems & Solutions

Managing Multi-Image, Device-Independent Bitmaps

PROBLEM: *I want to put all of my application's images into a single bitmap file and then extract the individual images as I need them. Is there some way to do this with Visual C++ under Windows 98?*

SOLUTION: Placing multiple images into a single bitmap file is a time-honored technique for reducing the number of files that must accompany an application. This technique also enables an application to run faster because all its images get loaded into memory at one time — rather than the application having to constantly access the user's disk. In fact, Visual C++ uses the multi-image bitmap technique to organize the images it uses for the toolbar's buttons. Figure 9-31 shows a toolbar bitmap loaded into Microsoft Paint.

Continued

Part II: Advanced Windows 2000 Programming

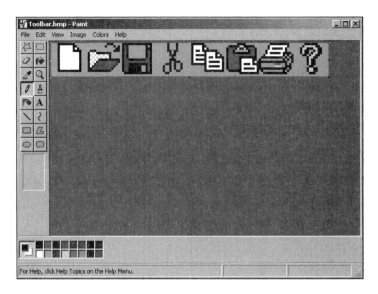

Figure 9-31: Visual C++ places all the toolbar's button images into a single bitmap file.

The first step, of course, is to create your bitmap. You can organize images in your bitmap in a number of ways. The only rule is that you must know the coordinates and size of each image in the bitmap. If the images you use are all the same size, you can end up with a grid of images like that shown in Figure 9-32. However, nothing can stop you from putting images of many different sizes in the same bitmap as long as you know their coordinates.

Figure 9-32: This bitmap contains six images, all the same size.

Notice that the bottom row of images in Figure 9-33 is labeled 1 through 3, whereas the top row is labeled 4 through 6. The images are created this way because Windows bitmaps (except in special cases) are stored as *bottom-up images*. Bottom-up images are stored upside down in memory, which places the images labeled 1 through 3 at the top of the bitmap. Figure 9-33 shows the same grid as Figure 9-32, but this time as it appears in memory.

Continued

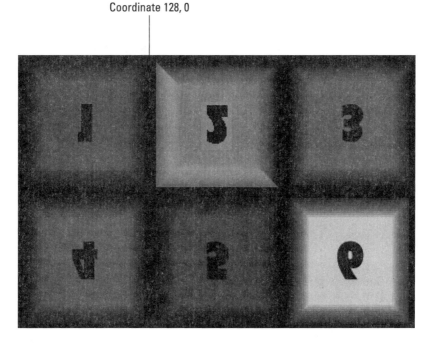

Figure 9-33: DIBs usually are stored upside down in memory. The source coordinates for this DIB's chosen image is the upper-left corner at coordinates 128,0.

The StretchDIBits() function knows how to reverse a bottom-up image so that it appears right side up on the screen. If it didn't, the images would appear upside down. This is still a problem if you have to write your own library of video and image functions (not an easy task). Give a silent thank-you to the Windows programmers for making StretchDIBits() as smart as it is.

When you're ready to display one of the images in the bitmap, you call StretchDIBits() and provide the source coordinates for the image. For example, if you want to display block 2 in Figure 9-33's bitmap, call StretchDIBits() like this:

```
BYTE* pBitmapData = pBitmap->GetData();
LPBITMAPINFO pBitmapInfo = pBitmap->GetInfo();

StretchDIBits(pDC->m_hDC, 20, 20, 128, 128,
    128, 0, 128, 128, pBitmapData,
    pBitmapInfo, DIB_RGB_COLORS, SRCCOPY);
```

Continued

The result of the preceding call to StretchDIBits() looks something like Figure 9-30. The destination coordinates (20, 20) can be just about anything that fits in the window, as long as the width and height values (128, 128) are correct. The source coordinates (128, 0) are where you have to be careful. They specify where in the bitmap the specific image you want is located (see Figure 9-34).

StretchDIBits() then gets that portion of the bitmap (see Figure 9-34), flips it right side up (see Figure 9-35), and displays it on the screen at the destination coordinates (see Figure 9-36).

Figure 9-34: The selected portion of the bitmap

Figure 9-35: The StretchDIBits() function flips the image before displaying it.

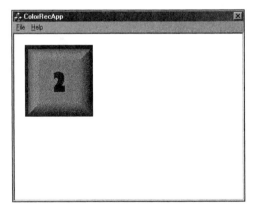

Figure 9-36: This application displays the single chosen image from the multi-image bitmap.

Continued

Chapter 9: Bitmaps

Location: `WinPrgS\Chap09\ColorRecApp`

On this book's CD-ROM, you can find the ColorRecApp application from which the previous code examples and figures are taken. When you run the application, you see the window shown in Figure 9-37. Click any box, and the boxes reorder themselves with the selected box first.

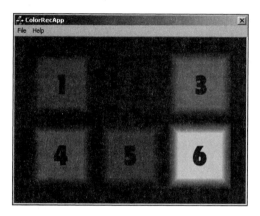

Figure 9-37: This application displays the multi-image bitmap as a single image.

How does the application work? First, the application loads the main bitmap in the `OnCreate()` function, which MFC calls in response to Windows' `WM_CREATE` message:

```
int CColorRecAppView::OnCreate
    (LPCREATESTRUCT lpCreateStruct)
{
    if (CView::OnCreate(lpCreateStruct) == -1)
        return -1;

    // TODO: Add your specialized creation code here

    pBitmap = new CDib("colorrec.bmp");
    if (!pBitmap->IsValid())
        MessageBox("Couldn't find colorrec.bmp.",
            "ColorRecApp Error",
            MB_OK | MB_ICONEXCLAMATION);

    return 0;
}
```

Because the application creates a bitmap object on the heap (that is, by using the `new` operator), the program should delete the bitmap at the end. ColorRecApp performs this task in its `OnDestroy()` function, which MFC calls in response to Windows' `WM_DESTROY` message. `OnDestroy()`, shown in the following code, is `OnCreate()`'s counterpart. Usually, anything you allocate in `OnCreate()` can be deleted in `OnDestroy()`.

Continued

```
void CColorRecAppView::OnDestroy()
{
    CView::OnDestroy();

    // TODO: Add your message handler code here

    if (pBitmap)
        delete pBitmap;
}
```

The program incorporates a simple, six-element array to keep track of the order in which each numbered block should be displayed. Each number in the array, from 0 through 5, represents a block. At the start of the program, the blocks should be displayed in order; so the program initializes the array in the view class's constructor, as shown here:

```
CColorRecAppView::CColorRecAppView()
{
    // TODO: add construction code here

    for (int x=0; x<6; ++x)
        m_colors[x] = x;
}
```

The OnDraw() function has the task of displaying the blocks. The OnDraw() function first fills the window's background with black, and then it gets pointers to the bitmap's image data and BITMAPINFO structure. Next, OnDraw() sets up a for loop that iterates six times — once for each block image. In the for loop, OnDraw() calculates the destination and source coordinates for the current block. A call to StretchDIBits() then displays the block on the screen in its correct location. The OnDraw() function looks like this:

```
void CColorRecAppView::OnDraw(CDC* pDC)
{
    CColorRecAppDoc* pDoc = GetDocument();
    ASSERT_VALID(pDoc);

    // TODO: add draw code for native data here

    if (!pBitmap)
        return;

    CBrush blackBrush(RGB(0,0,0));
    pDC->FillRect(CRect(0,0,435,345), &blackBrush);

    BYTE* pBitmapData = pBitmap->GetData();
    LPBITMAPINFO pBitmapInfo = pBitmap->GetInfo();

    for (int x=0; x<6; ++x)
    {
```

Continued

```
            int destX = x * 128 + 20;
            if (x > 2)
                destX = (x-3) * 128 + 20;

            int destY = 20;
            if (x > 2)
                destY = 148;

            int srcX = m_colors[x] * 128;
            if (m_colors[x] > 2)
                srcX = (m_colors[x] - 3) * 128;

            int srcY = 0;
            if (m_colors[x] > 2)
                srcY = 128;

            StretchDIBits(pDC->m_hDC, destX, destY, 128, 128,
                srcX, srcY, 128, 128, pBitmapData,
                pBitmapInfo, DIB_RGB_COLORS, SRCCOPY);
    }
}
```

When the user clicks the window, the program must determine whether the user clicked a block; if so, the program rearranges the block array as appropriate to the user's selection. All this happens in the OnLButtonDown() function, which MFC calls in response to the WM_LBUTTONDOWN Windows message. In OnLButtonDown(), the program first checks the coordinates at which the user clicked to see whether the coordinates are on the area of the window that contains blocks. If so, the program uses the coordinates to calculate the block on which the user clicked. A for loop then reorders the block array into a temporary array, which is copied back into the original array. The call to Invalidate() forces a call to OnDraw(), which draws the blocks using the new order in the block array. Here's the OnLButtonDown() function:

```
void CColorRecAppView::OnLButtonDown
    (UINT nFlags, CPoint point)
{
    // TODO: Add your message handler code here
    //    and/or call default

    if ((point.x > 20) && (point.x < 404) &&
        (point.y > 20) && (point.y < 276))
    {
        UINT col = ((point.x-20)/128)*128+20;
        UINT row = ((point.y-20)/128)*128+20;
        UINT index = (col/128) + (row/128) * 3;

        UINT temp[6];
        int x;
```

Continued

```
            for (x=0; x<6; ++x)
            {
                temp[x] = m_colors[index];
                ++index;
                if (index > 5)
                    index = 0;
            }
            for (x=0; x<6; ++x)
                m_colors[x] = temp[x];

            Invalidate(FALSE);
        }

        CView::OnLButtonDown(nFlags, point);
    }
```

PROBLEMS & SOLUTIONS

Displaying Nonrectangular Bitmaps

PROBLEM: *The program I'm working on must display images of various shapes, not just rectangles. Unfortunately,* `StretchDIBits()` *only displays rectangular images. How can I get around this limitation?*

SOLUTION: First, the bad news: Windows can display only rectangular images. The good news is that you can trick Windows into displaying a rectangular image so that it looks nonrectangular. The trick involves knowing a little about image masks and raster operations.

A *mask* is an image that prepares a window's client area to receive a "nonrectangular" image. In a way, the mask — when displayed properly — cuts a hole in the window's background image. This hole is the exact shape and size of the nonrectangular image you want to display. To get the mask and image to display properly, you have to use a couple of special raster operations.

What's a raster operation? A *raster operation* determines the way in which a source pixel (such as from a bitmap) combines with a destination pixel (such as in a window). These operations calculate the final value for the pixel by ANDing, ORing, or XORing the values in various ways. Windows defines 15 standard raster operations: BLACKNESS, DSTINVERT, MERGECOPY, MERGEPAINT, NOTSRCCOPY, NOTSRCERASE, PATCOPY, PATINVERT, PATPAINT, SRCAND, SRCCOPY, SRCERASE, SRCINVERT, SRCPAINT, and WHITENESS.

Continued

You learn more about raster operations in Chapter 10. For now, keep the SRCCOPY, SRCAND, and SRCPAINT raster operations in mind. You specify one of these operations when you call StretchDIBits() to display a bitmap. For example, already you're used to seeing SRCCOPY as StretchDIBits()'s last argument:

```
StretchDIBits(pDC->m_hDC, 0, 0, 500, 300,
    0, 0, 500, 300, pBitmapData, pBitmapInfo,
    DIB_RGB_COLORS, SRCCOPY);
```

All the DIBs displayed so far are displayed with the SRCCOPY raster operation, which tells Windows to replace the destination pixels with the source pixels. You use the SRCAND raster operation to display a mask, and the SRCPAINT raster operation to display the final image.

To prepare your nonrectangular image for display, you first create a mask. Suppose that you want to display the cone-like image shown in Figure 9-38. Notice that the cone image is surrounded with black. The black area is the part of the bitmap that you don't want to appear on the screen. You need to create a second bitmap, exactly the same size as the first, which has the black area filled with white and the rest of the image area filled with black (as shown in Figure 9-39). This second image is the mask.

Figure 9-38: Although the bitmap is rectangular, the application needs to display only the cone image.

Figure 9-39: This is the image's mask.

After creating your two images, you're ready to display them in your application. First, you display the mask using the SRCAND raster operation. This gives you the result shown in Figure 9-40. Notice how the mask cuts a hole in the window's background that's just right for the final image. The StretchDIBits() call that displays the mask looks like this:

```
StretchDIBits(windowDC.m_hDC, 20, 20, 128, 128,
    0, 0, 128, 128, pBitmapData, pBitmapInfo,
    DIB_RGB_COLORS, SRCAND);
```

Continued

Now, to display the nonrectangular image, you copy the image to the exact same coordinates to which you copy the mask. This time you use the SRCPAINT raster operation, which combines the source and destination pixels in such a way that only the portion of the image that fits into the mask "cutout" appears on the screen (see Figure 9-41).

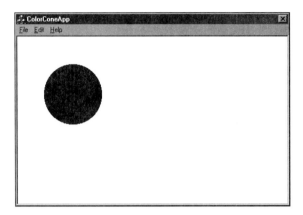

Figure 9-40: The image mask displayed with the SRCAND raster operation

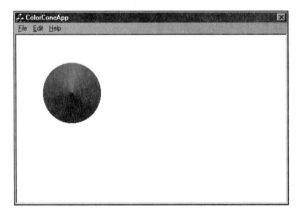

Figure 9-41: The image displayed on top of the mask using the SRCPAINT raster operation

Location: WinPrgS\Chap09\ColorConeApp

On this book's CD-ROM, you can find the ColorConeApp application that demonstrates the techniques discussed here. When you run the application, click anywhere in the window to display the nonrectangular bitmap over the window's background colors. Figure 9-42 shows the application after the user clicks several places in the window.

Continued

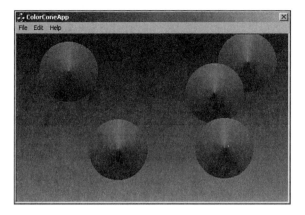

Figure 9-42: The ColorConeApp application demonstrates a display of nonrectangular images.

The program creates and loads its bitmaps in the view window class's `OnCreate()` function:

```
int CColorConeAppView::OnCreate
    (LPCREATESTRUCT lpCreateStruct)
{
    if (CView::OnCreate(lpCreateStruct) == -1)
        return -1;

    // TODO: Add your specialized creation code here

    m_pBackBitmap = new CDib("backgrnd.bmp");
    if (!m_pBackBitmap->IsValid())
        MessageBox("Couldn't find backgrnd.bmp.",
            "ColorConeApp Error",
            MB_OK | MB_ICONEXCLAMATION);

    m_pConeBitmap = new CDib("cone.bmp");
    if (!m_pConeBitmap->IsValid())
        MessageBox("Couldn't find cone.bmp.",
            "ColorConeApp Error",
            MB_OK | MB_ICONEXCLAMATION);

    m_pMaskBitmap = new CDib("conemask.bmp");
    if (!m_pMaskBitmap->IsValid())
        MessageBox("Couldn't find conemask.bmp.",
            "ColorConeApp Error",
            MB_OK | MB_ICONEXCLAMATION);

    return 0;
}
```

Continued

As you can see in the function, there are three bitmaps: the background image, the image mask, and the cone image.

Because the program creates the bitmaps on the heap, using the new operator, the bitmap objects should be deleted when the program ends. The program handles this task in the OnDestroy() function:

```
void CColorConeAppView::OnDestroy()
{
    CView::OnDestroy();

    // TODO: Add your message handler code here

    if (m_pBackBitmap)
        delete m_pBackBitmap;
    if (m_pConeBitmap)
        delete m_pConeBitmap;
    if (m_pMaskBitmap)
        delete m_pMaskBitmap;
}
```

The ColorConeApp application doesn't store the coordinates of the images that display on the screen, so OnDraw() cannot reproduce the entire display when the window needs repainting. However, OnDraw() does display the background image as shown here:

```
void CColorConeAppView::OnDraw(CDC* pDC)
{
    CColorConeAppDoc* pDoc = GetDocument();
    ASSERT_VALID(pDoc);

    // TODO: add draw code for native data here

    if (!m_pBackBitmap)
        return;

    BYTE* pBitmapData = m_pBackBitmap->GetData();
    LPBITMAPINFO pBitmapInfo = m_pBackBitmap->GetInfo();

    StretchDIBits(pDC->m_hDC, 0, 0, 500, 300,
        0, 0, 500, 300, pBitmapData, pBitmapInfo,
        DIB_RGB_COLORS, SRCCOPY);
}
```

The last function of interest in ColorConeApp is OnLButtonDown(), which displays a cone image wherever the user clicks in the application's window. It's here that the program uses the SRCAND and SRCPAINT raster operations to display the image mask and the image, as shown here:

```
void CColorConeAppView::OnLButtonDown
    (UINT nFlags, CPoint point)
{
```

Continued

```
        // TODO: Add your message handler code here
        //      and/or call default

        CClientDC windowDC(this);

        int destX = point.x - 64;
        int destY = point.y - 64;

        BYTE* pBitmapData = m_pMaskBitmap->GetData();
        LPBITMAPINFO pBitmapInfo = m_pMaskBitmap->GetInfo();

        StretchDIBits(windowDC.m_hDC, destX, destY, 128, 128,
            0, 0, 128, 128, pBitmapData, pBitmapInfo,
            DIB_RGB_COLORS, SRCAND);

        pBitmapData = m_pConeBitmap->GetData();
        pBitmapInfo = m_pConeBitmap->GetInfo();

        StretchDIBits(windowDC.m_hDC, destX, destY, 128, 128,
            0, 0, 128, 128, pBitmapData, pBitmapInfo,
            DIB_RGB_COLORS, SRCPAINT);

        CView::OnLButtonDown(nFlags, point);
    }
```

Summary

Bitmaps are versatile images used in virtually every Windows application. However, if you want to do more with bitmaps than just using them as button icons, you have to know how to load and display them. This process can be as simple as accessing a bitmap in the application's resources or as complex as loading a device-independent bitmap from a file, creating a palette, and drawing the image on the screen.

Also discussed in this chapter:

▶ Device-dependent bitmaps (DDBs) mostly transfer image data between the screen and memory.

▶ Device-independent bitmaps (DIBs) hold images that include color tables and other display information.

▶ To draw on a DDB, you must select it into a memory DC.

▶ To display a DDB, you copy the image from the memory DC to a window DC.

▶ To display a DIB, you copy the image data buffer to a window DC.

▶ DIBs contain several types of data structures that an application must be capable of reading and interpreting.

- DIBs reside in their own memory buffers; you don't need to select them into a memory device context.
- An application must create a palette for any DIB containing 256 or fewer colors.
- DIBs with more than 256 colors don't use color tables.
- Applications with palettes must respond to Windows' palette messages.
- You can trick Windows into displaying a rectangular image so that it looks nonrectangular.
- Placing multiple images into a single bitmap enables you to reduce the number of files that must accompany an application.

Chapter 10
Advanced GDI

In This Chapter

- ▶ Understanding physical and logical coordinates
- ▶ Using mapping modes
- ▶ Performing screen magic with drawing modes
- ▶ Creating and displaying regions
- ▶ Creating and displaying paths

Whenever you display data in a window — even something as simple as text — Windows has to go through a complex mapping process to convert logical coordinates into physical coordinates. This mapping process depends on a number of device context attributes including the mapping mode, the window, and the viewport. If all this sounds complicated to you, don't despair. In this chapter, you get the skinny on mapping modes and everything that goes with them. You also learn about drawing modes, specifically raster operations, which help determine what you see on the screen. In addition, you learn about regions, paths, and two ways to specify areas and lines on the screen. Windows' Graphical Device Interface (GDI) manages all this coordinate, mode, raster operation, region, and path stuff. (The GDI, discussed in Chapter 2, comprises Windows' graphics system.)

Physical and Logical Coordinates

As you already know, your monitor's screen displays data by lighting dots in various combinations and colors. These dots, called *pixels*, are the smallest things the monitor can display. To keep everything orderly, pixels are arranged in horizontal rows. How many dots there are in each row, as well as how many rows make up the entire screen, depends on your system's current resolution setting. For example, if you have your monitor set to 640×480, the screen has 480 rows of 640 dots each; if you have your monitor set to 800×600, the screen has 600 rows of 800 pixels each.

Windows manages these rows of dots in several ways using the following coordinates (see Figure 10-1):

Screen coordinates   Origin (the position 0,0) in the screen's upper-left corner

Window coordinates   Origin in the upper-left corner of the full window

Client coordinates   Origin in the upper-left corner of the client window

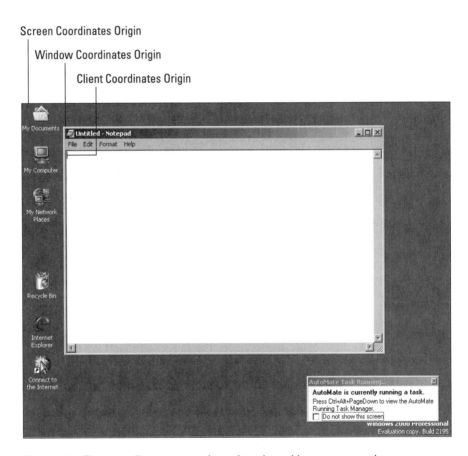

Figure 10-1: Three coordinate systems determine where objects appear on the screen.

No matter which coordinate system you work with, these are the physical coordinates of the display device. Simply stated, *physical coordinates* are actual coordinates on the screen. They're called physical coordinates because they have an actual physical presence in the pixels on the screen.

Logical coordinates are the coordinates you give to GDI functions that display data on the screen. They have no meaning except in relationship to the physical coordinates. For example, when a call to TextOut() tells Windows to display a line of text at the coordinates 20,50, Windows must determine where the coordinates 20,50 are on the physical device. Depending on the mapping mode, which determines how Windows interprets the coordinates, the text can end up anywhere on the screen. You can't, in fact, even calculate where the text will appear unless you know the mapping mode as well as the window and viewport settings. Any set of logical coordinates may or may not end up equal to the physical coordinates. This all becomes clearer as you learn more about mapping modes.

You probably don't have a lot of use for screen or window coordinates in your applications. For that reason, as well as to simplify the following discussions, this chapter uses the client-window system for all physical coordinates.

Mapping Modes

All this talk of physical and logical coordinates may confuse you. After all, up until now when you told Windows to display a line of text at coordinates 20,50 in a window, that line of text showed up at coordinates 20,50, right? You didn't need to monkey around with physical and logical coordinates. This bit of good fortune, however, was due only to the fact that Windows' default mapping mode, MM_TEXT, defines a one-to-one relationship between physical and logical coordinates. That is, the logical coordinates you specified mapped exactly to the same physical coordinates.

For the most part, the default MM_TEXT mapping mode is all you need for most programs. Using the MM_TEXT mapping mode and a little arithmetic, you even can perform scaling and other graphics techniques. However, the title of this chapter contains the word "Advanced;" this means you're not going to get off the hook so easily. The truth is that Windows defines eight mapping modes that determine the way Windows maps logical coordinates to physical coordinates. Table 10-1 lists and describes those modes.

Table 10-1   Windows Mapping Modes

Mode	Description
MM_ANISOTROPIC	The GDI converts logical units to arbitrary units with arbitrarily scaled axes.
MM_HIENGLISH	The GDI converts a logical unit to 0.001 inches, with values of X increasing to the right and values of Y increasing upwards.

Continued

Table 10-1 (continued)

Mode	Description
MM_HIMETRIC	The GDI converts a logical unit to 0.01 millimeters, with values of X increasing to the right and values of Y increasing upwards.
MM_ISOTROPIC	The GDI converts logical units to arbitrary units with equally scaled axes.
MM_LOENGLISH	The GDI converts a logical unit to 0.01 inches, with values of X increasing to the right and values of Y increasing upwards.
MM_LOMETRIC	The GDI converts a logical unit to 0.1 millimeters, with values of X increasing to the right and values of Y increasing upwards.
MM_TEXT	The GDI converts a logical unit to one pixel, with values of X increasing to the right and values of Y increasing down.
MM_TWIPS	The GDI converts a logical unit to one *twip* (1/1440 inches), with values of X increasing to the right and values of Y increasing upwards.

Experimenting with Window and Viewport Origins

CD

Location: WinPrgS\Chap10\MapModeApp

Before you examine each mode, it's helpful for you to first experiment with window and viewport origins. Take a look on this book's CD-ROM for the MapModeApp application. When you run the application, you see the window shown in Figure 10-2. As you can see, the window displays a set of lines drawn at the window's origin, as well as text that shows the current viewport and window origins.

Select the Origins menu's Set Viewport Origin or Set Window Origin commands to change an origin. When you do, a dialog box appears into which you can type the new origin values. Figure 10-3, for example, shows the results when you change the viewport origin to 150,75. Try setting the viewport and window origins to the same value. You discover that they cancel each other out.

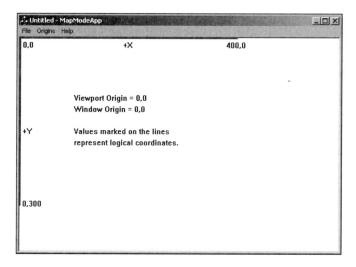

Figure 10-2: The MapModeApp application when it first appears

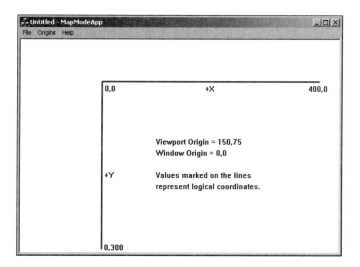

Figure 10-3: The application with its viewport origin changed

The MapModeApp application draws its display in the view class's OnDraw() function, which looks like this:

```
void CMapModeAppView::OnDraw(CDC* pDC)
{
    CMapModeAppDoc* pDoc = GetDocument();
    ASSERT_VALID(pDoc);
```

```
    // TODO: add draw code for native data here

    CPen newPen(PS_SOLID, 3, RGB(255,0,0));
    CPen* oldPen = pDC->SelectObject(&newPen);

    pDC->SetViewportOrg(m_vprtOrgX, m_vprtOrgY);
    pDC->SetWindowOrg(m_winOrgX, m_winOrgY);

    pDC->MoveTo(0, 0);
    pDC->LineTo(400, 0);
    pDC->MoveTo(0, 0);
    pDC->LineTo(0, 300);

    pDC->TextOut(5, 5, "0,0");
    pDC->TextOut(190, 5, "+X");
    pDC->TextOut(5, 160, "+Y");
    pDC->TextOut(380, 5, "400,0");
    pDC->TextOut(5, 290, "0,300");

    char s[81];
    wsprintf(s, "Viewport Origin = %d,%d",
        m_vprtOrgX, m_vprtOrgY);
    pDC->TextOut(100, 100, s);
    wsprintf(s, "Window Origin = %d,%d",
        m_winOrgX, m_winOrgY);
    pDC->TextOut(100, 120, s);
    pDC->TextOut(100, 160, "Values marked on the lines");
    pDC->TextOut(100,180,"represent logical coordinates.");

    pDC->SelectObject(oldPen);
}
```

The application starts the viewport and window origins—represented by the m_vprtOrgX, m_vprtOrgY, m_winOrgX, and m_winOrgY member variables—at all zeroes. When the user changes an origin, the application redraws the window with the new origins.

When the user selects the Set Viewport Origin or Set Window Origin command, the application displays a dialog box. This occurs in the view class's OnOrigins Setviewportorigin() or OnOriginsSetwindoworigin() function, as appropriate for the selected command. The program creates and displays the dialog box; if the user clicks the OK button, the program resets the appropriate member variables with the values extracted from the dialog box. Following are the OnOriginsSetviewportorigin() and OnOriginsSetwindoworigin() functions:

```
void CMapModeAppView::OnOriginsSetviewportorigin()
{
    // TODO: Add your command handler code here

    CVprtDialog dlg;
    dlg.m_x = m_vprtOrgX;
```

```
        dlg.m_y = m_vprtOrgY;

        int result = dlg.DoModal();
        if (result == IDOK)
        {
            m_vprtOrgX = dlg.m_x;
            m_vprtOrgY = dlg.m_y;
            Invalidate();
        }
    }

    void CMapModeAppView::OnOriginsSetwindoworigin()
    {
        // TODO: Add your command handler code here

        CWinDialog dlg;
        dlg.m_x = m_winOrgX;
        dlg.m_y = m_winOrgY;

        int result = dlg.DoModal();
        if (result == IDOK)
        {
            m_winOrgX = dlg.m_x;
            m_winOrgY = dlg.m_y;
            Invalidate();
        }
    }
```

The MM_TEXT Mode

You're ready to examine the mapping modes in more detail. The first one you examine is MM_TEXT, Windows' default mapping mode. If you don't set the mapping mode explicitly in your program, MM_TEXT is what you get. If you've programmed other computers, MM_TEXT is the closest mapping mode to what you probably are accustomed to using. In this mode, the coordinate system's origin is in the upper-left corner of the client window — with X values increasing to the right and Y values increasing as you go down. Figure 10-4 shows the MM_TEXT mapping mode illustrated in a window. Here are the C++ lines that create the display:

```
pDC->MoveTo(0, 0);
pDC->LineTo(400, 0);
pDC->MoveTo(0, 0);
pDC->LineTo(0, 300);

pDC->TextOut(5, 5, "0,0");
pDC->TextOut(190, 5, "+X");
pDC->TextOut(5, 160, "+Y");
pDC->TextOut(380, 5, "400,0");
pDC->TextOut(5, 290, "0,300");
```

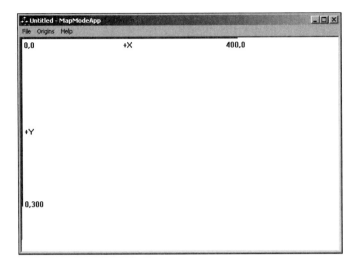

Figure 10-4: This window shows MM_TEXT's X and Y coordinates.

One thing you should notice about Figure 10-4 and the preceding code is that the logical coordinates in the calls to the GDI functions MoveTo( ), LineTo( ), and TextOut( ) map to exactly equivalent physical coordinates. That is, the call to MoveTo(0,0) moves the drawing cursor to the physical coordinates 0,0. When you leave the MM_TEXT mode in its default state, this always occurs. In the figure, the text labeling the onscreen coordinates represents both logical and physical coordinates.

However, to illustrate how physical and logical coordinates can differ, mess with the device context's window and viewport origins. The *window origin* represents the origin related to the logical coordinates, whereas the *viewport origin* represents the origin related to the physical, client-window coordinates. In this use of the word, you can think of the "window" as the entire data view — all or part of which appears on the screen. The viewport represents that portion of the window that actually appears onscreen.

Note

When used in the context of windows and viewports, the word "window" should not be confused with the window object you see on the screen. They have nothing to do with each other, except that the window coordinates (logical coordinates) get mapped to the onscreen window object's client area.

To change the viewport origin, call the DC object's SetViewportOrg( ) function; its signature looks like this:

```
BOOL SetViewportOrg(int X, int Y);
```

This function takes two arguments. The first, X, is the device X coordinate of the new origin; and the second, Y, is the device Y coordinate of the new origin.

When you move the viewport origin, you tell Windows to display the logical 0,0 origin at the new viewport origin. As an example, suppose the program that creates the display in Figure 10-4 calls SetViewportOrg() as follows before drawing the display:

clientDC.SetViewportOrg(50, 50);

This line tells Windows to display the logical coordinate 0,0 at the physical coordinate 50,50. The display then ends up looking like Figure 10-5. Notice how the entire display shifts 50 pixels to the right and 50 pixels down. Now, the coordinates marked on the lines in the figure represent only the logical coordinates.

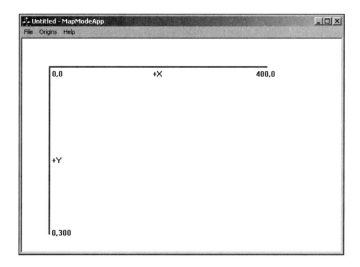

Figure 10-5: This window demonstrates the MM_TEXT mapping mode with a viewport origin of 50,50.

You also can change the window origin; as you may guess, this has the opposite effect of setting the viewport origin. To set the window origin, call the DC object's SetWindowOrg() function, whose signature is as follows:

BOOL SetWindowOrg(int X, int Y);

When you move the window origin, you tell Windows to display the new logical origin at the viewport's 0,0 physical coordinate. As an example, suppose the program that creates the display in Figure 10-4 calls SetWindowOrg() as follows before drawing the display:

clientDC.SetWindowOrg(-50, -50);

This line tells Windows to display the logical coordinate -50,-50 at the physical coordinate 0,0. The display again ends up looking like Figure 10-5. If the call to `SetWindowOrg()` does not specify negative coordinates, the display shifts up and to the left, taking it out of view.

Mapping with a Physical Unit of Measurement

The `MM_TEXT` mode is great for most general-purpose programs. Best of all, using the `MM_TEXT` mode is easy thanks to the one-to-one relationship between the coordinates you provide for functions and the pixels of the display device. Sooner or later, though, you're going to write a program for which it makes sense to scale graphical output using real-world measurements such as inches or millimeters. A drafting program, for example, requires that you use these types of measurements. For these situations, Windows offers the mapping modes you study in this section.

The MM_LOENGLISH and MM_HIENGLISH modes

Although the `MM_TEXT` mapping mode is the one used the most, you have many other options; two include the `MM_LOENGLISH` and `MM_HIENGLISH` modes, which are similar in that they both work with measurements in inches. In the `MM_LOENGLISH` mapping mode, the logical unit is 0.01 inches rather than one pixel as it is in `MM_TEXT`. In `MM_HIENGLISH`, the logical unit is 0.001 inches — giving you an even higher degree of precision.

But the logical units are just one way these mapping modes differ from `MM_TEXT`. In the `MM_LOENGLISH` and `MM_HIENGLISH` modes, the Y coordinates decrease as you move down the display rather than increase as they do with the `MM_TEXT` mapping mode. (The X coordinates still increase from left to right.) This means that, with the default window and viewport origins of 0,0, you have to use negative values for Y in order to see anything on the screen. Figure 10-6 illustrates how the `MM_LOENGLISH` mode looks. These C++ lines create the display:

```
pDC->SetMapMode(MM_LOENGLISH);
pDC->SetViewportOrg(50, 50);

pDC->MoveTo(0, 0);
pDC->LineTo(400, 0);
pDC->MoveTo(0, 0);
pDC->LineTo(0, -300);

pDC->TextOut(5, -5, "0,0");
pDC->TextOut(190, -5, "+X");
pDC->TextOut(5, -160, "-Y");
pDC->TextOut(380, -5, "400,0");
pDC->TextOut(5, -290, "0,-300");
```

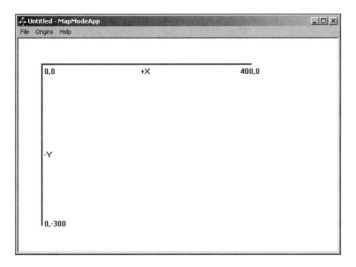

Figure 10-6: This application shows a display drawn in MM_LOENGLISH mapping mode. Notice that the X and Y coordinates use numbers in the hundreds.

You should notice a few things about the preceding code. First, the program sets the mapping mode by calling the device context object's SetMapMode() member function and supplying the new mode as the function's single argument. Second, the program sets the viewport origin (in physical coordinates) to 50,50 so that you more easily can see the lines that are drawn starting with the logical origin (the point marked 0,0 in Figure 10-6). Third, you should notice that all Y coordinates in the MoveTo(), LineTo(), and TextOut() functions are negative. Remember: Y coordinates in these mapping modes increase upwards. To move down the screen, you must use negative Y values—assuming your origin is in the upper-left corner of the screen. Finally, because the logical unit in MM_LOENGLISH mapping mode is 0.01 inches, the horizontal line in the display represents four logical inches (400 x 0.01), and the vertical line represents three logical inches (300 x 0.01).

The MM_HIENGLISH mapping mode uses units 10 times as small as those used with MM_LOENGLISH. This means that, to create the same display shown in Figure 10-6, you have to multiply all the MM_LOENGLISH coordinates by 10. Following are the code that results and Figure 10-7 with the resultant display.

```
pDC->SetMapMode(MM_LOENGLISH);
::SetViewportOrgEx(pDC->m_hDC, 50, 50, NULL);

pDC->MoveTo(0, 0);
pDC->LineTo(400, 0);
pDC->MoveTo(0, 0);
pDC->LineTo(0, -300);
```

```
pDC->TextOut(5, -5, "0,0");
pDC->TextOut(190, -5, "+X");
pDC->TextOut(5, -160, "-Y");
pDC->TextOut(380, -5, "400,0");
pDC->TextOut(5, -290, "0,-300");
```

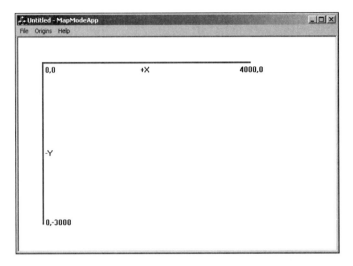

Figure 10-7: This application shows a display drawn in MM_HIENGLISH mapping mode. Notice that the X and Y coordinates use numbers in the thousands.

The MM_LOMETRIC and MM_HIMETRIC modes

The MM_LOMETRIC and MM_HIMETRIC mapping modes are very similar to MM_LOENGLISH and MM_HIENGLISH in that they enable you to scale output to a real-world measurement. The difference is that they use millimeters as logical units, rather than inches. More specifically, in the MM_LOMETRIC mode, the logical unit is 0.1 millimeters; in MM_HIMETRIC, the logical unit is 0.01 millimeters. So, when you want to scale to millimeters, these modes are just the ticket. In both modes, the X coordinates still increase from left to right, and the Y coordinates still decrease from top to bottom. For example, the following code draws two lines 100 millimeters long with one line running left to right and the other running top to bottom:

```
pDC->SetMapMode(MM_LOMETRIC);
pDC->MoveTo(0, 0);
pDC->LineTo(1000, 0);
pDC->LineTo(1000, -1000);
```

The MM_TWIPS Mode

The MM_TWIPS mode uses a form of measurement called *twips* to calculate X and Y coordinates. If you've programmed with Visual Basic, you know the word "twip." If not, a twip is a tiny unit of measurement; there are 1,440 twips in an inch. Outside of the different logical unit, the MM_TWIPS mapping mode works exactly like the MM_LOENGLISH, MM_HIENGLISH, MM_LOMETRIC, and MM_HIMETRIC modes, with X values increasing to the right and Y values decreasing down. Because a twip is equal to 1/20th of a point, this mapping mode can be useful for working with some types of text displays—although I never recall seeing it used. For example, the following code draws two lines four inches (5,760 twips) long with one line running left to right and the other running top to bottom:

```
pDC->SetMapMode(MM_TWIPS);
pDC->MoveTo(0, 0);
pDC->LineTo(5760, 0);
pDC->LineTo(5760, -5760);
```

Scaling Logical Units to Arbitrary Coordinates

When none of the other mapping modes are appropriate, you have to roll your own, so to speak. Two of the mapping modes—MM_ISOTROPIC and MM_ANISOTROPIC—enable you to decide how your coordinates map to physical units. These mapping modes are handy for when you scale to a display that changes size (such as a resizable window), as well as for other special uses. In this section, you see how these mapping modes work.

The MM_ISOTROPIC and MM_ANISOTROPIC modes

Now the fun really starts. All the previous mapping modes represent some specific unit of measure—whether in inches, millimeters, or twips. What if you don't want to use any of these logical units? What if you have something else in mind? Then you can resort to the MM_ISOTROPIC and MM_ANISOTROPIC mapping modes, which enable you to decide how logical units should be scaled to physical coordinates. The only difference between MM_ISOTROPIC and MM_ANISOTROPIC is that the former forces X units of measure to equal exactly Y units of measure and the latter enables you to change even that small restriction. But before you can experiment with the MM_ISOTROPIC and MM_ANISOTROPIC mapping modes, you have to know about window and viewport extents and their close relationship with the mapping modes.

When you decide to use the MM_ISOTROPIC or MM_ANISOTROPIC mapping mode, you must deal with something called *window* and *viewport extents*. The window extents are like the logical coordinates, and the viewport extents are like the physical coordinates to which Windows must map the logical coordinates. The extents really have no meaning by themselves; they are meaningful only when taken as a pair. That is, the ratio between the window and viewport extents is crucial, not the extents' specific values.

Because Windows needs the window extents to set up its mapping properly, you should set the window extents before the viewport extents. You do this by calling the DC object's `SetWindowExt()` function, whose signature looks like this:

```
BOOL SetWindowExt(int nXExtent, int nYExtent);
```

The function's two arguments are the horizontal window extent and the vertical window extent.

After setting the window extents, you can set the viewport extents. Windows then can determine how logical coordinates are mapped to physical coordinates. To set the viewport extents, you call the `SetViewportExt()` function; its signature looks like this:

```
BOOL SetViewportExt(int nXExtent, int nYExtent);
```

The function's two arguments are the horizontal viewport extent and the vertical viewport extent.

If you're confused about how the window and viewport extents work together, consider this example: Suppose that you want to use logical coordinates from 0 to 1000, and you want those logical coordinates mapped to a viewport 100 units square. First, you set the mapping mode to `MM_ISOTROPIC`:

```
CClientDC clientDC(this);
clientDC.SetMapMode(MM_ISOTROPIC);
```

Next, you set the window extents:

```
clientDC.SetWindowExt(1000, 1000);
```

Finally, you set the viewport extents:

```
clientDC.SetViewportExt(100, 100);
```

With the extents set up this way, Windows maps a logical X or Y coordinate of 0 to a viewport coordinate of 0 and maps a logical X or Y coordinate of 1000 to a viewport coordinate of 100. (All other logical coordinates fall somewhere in between.) Answer this one-question pop quiz: Given the extents set in this example, where does Windows map a logical X or Y coordinate of 500? If you say, "to a viewport coordinate of 50," you get an A for the day.

In the previous example, the window extents are set to 1000,1000. The two extents are the same because the mapping mode is `MM_ISOTROPIC`, which requires equal horizontal and vertical extents. If you try to set the extents to unequal values, Windows resets them to be equal.

You can get the current mapping mode and extents by calling the `GetMapMode()`, `GetWindowExtEx()`, and `GetViewportExtEx()` functions.

Chapter 10: Advanced GDI

PROBLEMS & SOLUTIONS

Mapping Modes and the Cartesian System

PROBLEM: *I'm writing a graphing program that needs to plot values into a Cartesian coordinate system. How can I do this with mapping modes?*

SOLUTION: It's important to note that, in most mapping modes, you can use negative or positive logical coordinates just as you can when plotting values in a Cartesian coordinate system. For example, although positive Y values and negative X values don't appear on the screen when the window and viewport origins are set to their default 0,0 values, you still can use positive Y values and negative X values. If you want these coordinates to appear on the screen, just change the window or viewport origin.

Location: `WinPrgS\Chap10\CartesianApp`

CD

Figure 10-8 shows an example **application** called CartesianApp that displays a Cartesian coordinate system in the `MM_LOMETRIC` mapping mode. You can find this application on this book's CD-ROM. When you run the application, select the Graph menu's Graph Line command. A dialog box appears into which you can type the end points for a line. When you exit the dialog box, the program graphs the line on the display.

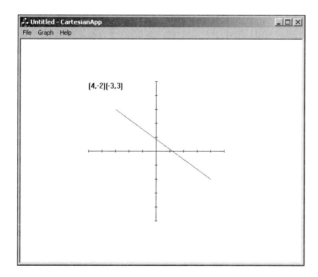

Figure 10-8: The CartesianApp application graphs lines.

Continued

CartesianApp holds the coordinates for the current line in four member variables of the view class. These member variables — called m_x1, m_y1, m_x2, and m_y2 — start off at all zeroes so all you see on the screen is a dot at the graph's origin. When you enter new values for the line's coordinates, the view class's OnDraw() function redraws the display, as shown here:

```
void CCartesianAppView::OnDraw(CDC* pDC)
{
    CCartesianAppDoc* pDoc = GetDocument();
    ASSERT_VALID(pDoc);

    // TODO: add draw code for native data here

    pDC->SetMapMode(MM_LOMETRIC);
    pDC->SetViewportOrg(250, 200);

    // Draw the X and Y axes.
    pDC->MoveTo(-500, 0);
    pDC->LineTo(500, 0);
    pDC->MoveTo(0, 500);
    pDC->LineTo(0, -500);

    // Draw the X axis tick marks.
    for (int x=0; x<11; ++x)
    {
        pDC->MoveTo(-500+(x*100), 10);
        pDC->LineTo(-500+(x*100), -10);
    }

    // Draw the Y axis tick marks.
    for (int y=0; y<11; ++y)
    {
        pDC->MoveTo(-10, 500-(y*100));
        pDC->LineTo(10, 500-(y*100));
    }

    // Graph the line.
    CPen newPen(PS_SOLID, 5, RGB(255,0,0));
    CPen* oldPen = pDC->SelectObject(&newPen);

    pDC->MoveTo(m_x1*100, m_y1*100);
    pDC->LineTo(m_x2*100, m_y2*100);
    char s[81];
    wsprintf(s, "(%d,%d)(%d,%d)",
        m_x1, m_y1, m_x2, m_y2);
    pDC->TextOut(-500, 500, s);

    pDC->SelectObject(oldPen);
}
```

When it comes to graphing programs, CartesianApp is pretty limited. However, if you're a math whiz, you can try adding other types of graphing to the program. How about graphing various types of equations? Good luck!

Chapter 10: Advanced GDI

PROBLEMS & SOLUTIONS

Mapping Modes and Aspect Ratio

PROBLEM: *In the application I'm working on, I want to be sure that square images always look square and round images always look round. Also, I want the current image to always display at its largest possible size. Is there a way to solve this problem with mapping modes?*

SOLUTION: Sure is. Enter *retaining aspect ratio* — the perfect task for the MM_ISOTROPIC mapping mode, which always has equal horizontal and vertical extents. For example, when drawing in MM_ISOTROPIC mode, a 100-unit horizontal line always is the same length as a 100-unit vertical line. By setting the window extents to whatever values are appropriate for your application, you're assured of retaining the aspect ratio of shapes.

To solve your second problem, you need only set the viewport extents to the current width and height of the client window. The only complication here is that whenever the user resizes the window, you have to reset the viewport extents. You can do this by using ClassWizard to add the OnSize() function to your application, as shown in Figure 10-9. OnSize() responds to the WM_SIZE Windows message that Windows sends to the application whenever the user resizes the window.

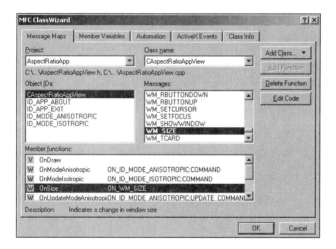

Figure 10-9: Adding the OnSize() message-response function to your application enables you to reset the viewport extents.

Continued

414 Part II: Advanced Windows 2000 Programming

Location: `WinPrgS\Chap10\AspectRatioApp`

On this book's CD-ROM, you can find the AspectRatioApp application. When you run the application, you see the window shown in Figure 10-10. The program is set to the `MM_ISOTROPIC` mapping mode so that the square always looks square.

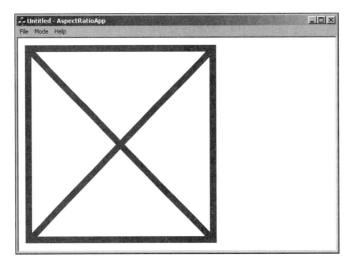

Figure 10-10: AspectRatioApp displays a square in MM_ISOTROPIC mode.

Thanks to the viewport extents, the shape always displays as large as possible no matter how you resize the window (see Figure 10-11).

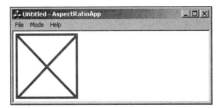

Figure 10-11: The shape stays square regardless of window size.

In the Mode menu, you can change the mapping mode from `MM_ISOTROPIC` to `MM_ANISOTROPIC`. Consequently, the shape's aspect ratio changes to fit the window (see Figure 10-12).

Continued

Chapter 10: Advanced GDI

Figure 10-12: In MM_ANISOTROPIC mode, the shape stretches both horizontally and vertically to fit the window.

AspectRatioApp holds the currently selected mapping mode in the m_mapMode member variable of the view window class and holds the client window's width and height in the m_clientWidth and m_clientHeight variables. The OnDraw() function sets the mapping mode with the m_mapMode variable, and sets the viewport extents with the m_clientWidth and m_clientHeight variables, before drawing its display. Following is the OnDraw() function:

```
void CAspectRatioAppView::OnDraw(CDC* pDC)
{
    CAspectRatioAppDoc* pDoc = GetDocument();
    ASSERT_VALID(pDoc);

    // TODO: add draw code for native data here

    CPen newPen(PS_SOLID, 30, RGB(255,0,0));
    CPen* oldPen = pDC->SelectObject(&newPen);

    pDC->SetMapMode(m_mapMode);
    pDC->SetWindowExt(1000, 1000);
    pDC->SetViewportExt(m_clientWidth,
        m_clientHeight);

    pDC->Rectangle(50, 50, 950, 950);
    pDC->MoveTo(55, 55);
    pDC->LineTo(945, 945);
    pDC->MoveTo(945, 55);
    pDC->LineTo(55, 945);

    pDC->SelectObject(oldPen);
}
```

Continued

Whenever the window gets resized — including when the window first appears — the program must set the values of the `m_clientWidth` and `m_clientHeight` variables. This happens in the view class's `OnSize()` function, as shown here:

```
void CAspectRatioAppView::OnSize
    (UINT nType, int cx, int cy)
{
    CView::OnSize(nType, cx, cy);

    // TODO: Add your message handler code here

    m_clientWidth = cx;
    m_clientHeight = cy;
}
```

`OnSize()`'s two parameters are the new width and height of the client window. The program copies these values into the `m_clientWidth` and `m_clientHeight` variables.

Raster Operations

You may recall from Chapter 9 how you use the raster operations `SRCAND` and `SRCPAINT` to draw nonrectangular images on the screen. These raster operations exemplify the many ways in which you can display any type of data on the screen. The raster operations determine the way that Windows combines a source and destination pixel using logical operators such as `AND`, `OR`, and `XOR`. Many of these raster operations have only esoteric uses that you probably will never need. However, a few have special uses that can make the difference between an amateur application and a professional one. You examine two sets of raster operations in this chapter:

Bitmap raster operations	Used to draw images on the screen
Line raster operations	Used to draw lines on the screen

Bitmap Raster Operations

Bitmap raster operations are the operations you use with functions such as `StretchDIBits()` or `BitBlt()`. As Chapter 9 discusses, these operations can display bitmaps and bitmap masks in various ways. They actually do more than combine source and destination rectangles; some also combine the current brush with the final image. Table 10-2 lists and describes the 15 operation codes.

Table 10-2 Raster Operations for Bitmaps

Operation	Description
BLACKNESS	Fills the destination rectangle with black
DSTINVERT	Inverts the colors of the destination rectangle
MERGECOPY	ANDs the source rectangle's colors with the brush
MERGEPAINT	Inverts the source rectangle and ORs the result with the destination rectangle
NOTSRCCOPY	Inverts the source rectangle and copies it to the destination rectangle
NOTSRCERASE	ORs the source and destination rectangles and then inverts the result
PATCOPY	Replaces the destination rectangle with the brush
PATINVERT	XORs the destination rectangle with the brush
PATPAINT	Inverts the source rectangle and ORs the brush with the result, which is ORed with the destination rectangle
SRCAND	ANDs the source and destination rectangles
SRCCOPY	Replaces the destination rectangle with the source rectangle
SRCERASE	Inverts the destination rectangle and ANDs the result with the source rectangle
SRCINVERT	XORs the source and destination rectangles
SRCPAINT	ORs the source and destination rectangles
WHITENESS	Fills the destination rectangle with white

To display any type of bitmap with one of these raster operations, use the operation code as the last argument in the `StretchDIBits()` or `BitBlt()` functions. For example, the following lines transfer a bitmap from a memory DC to the screen using the `SRCAND` raster operation:

```
pDC->BitBlt(370, 100, 80, 80,
    &memoryDC, 0, 0, SRCAND);
```

Location: `WinPrgS\Chap10\RasterOpApp`

The best way to explore these different raster operations is to see them in action. On this book's CD-ROM, find the RasterOpApp application. When you run the application, you see the window shown in Figure 10-13. In the window, the program displays a bitmap 15 times — using each of the raster operations in the order in which they appear in Table 10-2.

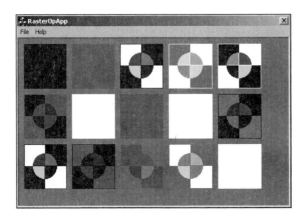

Figure 10-13: RasterOpApp demonstrates the 15 bitmap raster operations.

If you look over the list of raster operations, you may notice that several of them not only combine the source and destination rectangles, but also throw in the current brush as well. A DC's default brush is solid white and has no effect on the appearance of any of the raster operations. However, if you select a different brush into the DC, you can see the effect immediately. To see this happen, click the application's window. The application selects a patterned, black brush into the DC so you can see how the raster operations combine the brush with the source and destination rectangles (see Figure 10-14).

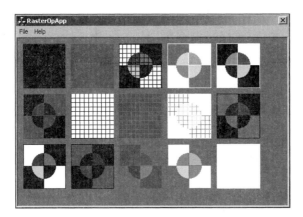

Figure 10-14: RasterOpApp adds a patterned brush to the mix.

Although the solid background color does affect the raster operations, the results aren't very obvious. To get a better look at how the window background affects the process, right-click the window. The application then draws lines on the background so you can see more clearly how the raster operations combine the source and destination rectangles (see Figure 10-15).

Chapter 10: Advanced GDI

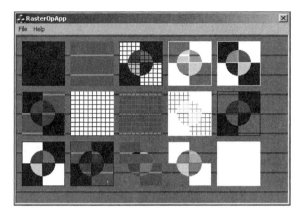

Figure 10-15: RasterOpApp adds lines to the background.

You can find virtually all of the interesting source code for this program in the view class's `OnDraw()` function, which looks like this:

```
void CRasterOpAppView::OnDraw(CDC* pDC)
{
    CRasterOpAppDoc* pDoc = GetDocument();
    ASSERT_VALID(pDoc);

    // TODO: add draw code for native data here

    pDC->FillRect(CRect(0,0, 500, 350),
        new CBrush(RGB(176,150,33)));

    if (m_drawLines)
    {
        CPen* pNewPen =
            new CPen(PS_SOLID, 3, RGB(255,0,0));
        CPen* pOldPen = pDC->SelectObject(pNewPen);

        for (int x=0; x<10; ++x)
        {
            pDC->MoveTo(0, x*35);
            pDC->LineTo(500, x*35);
        }

        pDC->SelectObject(pOldPen);
        delete pNewPen;
    }

    CDC memoryDC;
    memoryDC.CreateCompatibleDC(pDC);
    CBitmap bitmap;
    bitmap.LoadBitmap(IDB_BITMAP1);
    CBitmap* pOldBitmap =
```

```
            memoryDC.SelectObject(&bitmap);

    CBrush* pNewBrush = new CBrush(HS_CROSS, RGB(0,0,0));
    CBrush* pOldBrush;

    if (m_showBrush)
        pOldBrush = pDC->SelectObject(pNewBrush);

    pDC->BitBlt(10, 10, 80, 80,
        &memoryDC, 0, 0, BLACKNESS);
    pDC->BitBlt(100, 10, 80, 80,
        &memoryDC, 0, 0, DSTINVERT);
    pDC->BitBlt(190, 10, 80, 80,
        &memoryDC, 0, 0, MERGECOPY);
    pDC->BitBlt(280, 10, 80, 80,
        &memoryDC, 0, 0, MERGEPAINT);
    pDC->BitBlt(370, 10, 80, 80,
        &memoryDC, 0, 0, NOTSRCCOPY);

    pDC->BitBlt(10, 100, 80, 80,
            &memoryDC, 0, 0, NOTSRCERASE);
    pDC->BitBlt(100, 100, 80, 80,
        &memoryDC, 0, 0, PATCOPY);
    pDC->BitBlt(190, 100, 80, 80,
        &memoryDC, 0, 0, PATINVERT);
    pDC->BitBlt(280, 100, 80, 80,
        &memoryDC, 0, 0, PATPAINT);
    pDC->BitBlt(370, 100, 80, 80,
        &memoryDC, 0, 0, SRCAND);

    pDC->BitBlt(10, 190, 80, 80,
        &memoryDC, 0, 0, SRCCOPY);
    pDC->BitBlt(100, 190, 80, 80,
        &memoryDC, 0, 0, SRCERASE);
    pDC->BitBlt(190, 190, 80, 80,
        &memoryDC, 0, 0, SRCINVERT);
    pDC->BitBlt(280, 190, 80, 80,
        &memoryDC, 0, 0, SRCPAINT);
    pDC->BitBlt(370, 190, 80, 80,
        &memoryDC, 0, 0, WHITENESS);

    if (m_showBrush)
    {
        pDC->SelectObject(pOldBrush);
        delete pNewBrush;
    }

    memoryDC.SelectObject(pOldBitmap);
}
```

OnDraw() draws the window's background and then draws the 15 bitmaps over the background. Notice especially how the different calls to BitBlt()

display exactly the same bitmap, but they do so using a different raster operation.

The OnDraw() function performs the following tasks:

- Fills the window with the background color
- Draws background lines on the display if the user selects this option
- Creates and loads a bitmap
- Creates a patterned brush and selects the brush if the user selects the patterned brush option
- Copies the bitmap to the screen once for each of the defined raster operations
- Restores the DC

Line Drawing Modes

Displaying bitmaps represents only one way that Windows uses raster operations. Windows also uses raster operations when it draws lines on the screen. When you draw lines on a display — whether you draw a rectangle, an ellipse, a straight line, or some other shape — Windows replaces the source pixels with the color of the current pen. This is similar to using the SRCCOPY operation with bitmaps. However, you're not stuck with this one type of raster operation. Windows defines 16 raster operations that you can use when drawing lines. Table 10-3 lists and describes these raster operations.

Table 10-3   Raster Operations for Drawing Lines

Operation	Description
R2_BLACK	Draws a black line
R2_WHITE	Draws a white line
R2_NOP	Draws no line
R2_NOT	Draws a line that's the inverse of the screen color
R2_COPYPEN	Draws a line in the pen color
R2_NOTCOPYPEN	Draws a line that's the inverse of the pen color
R2_MERGEPENNOT	Draws a line that ORs the pen color and the inverse of the screen color
R2_MASKPENNOT	Draws a line that ANDs the pen and the inverse of the screen

Continued

Table 10-3 (continued)

Operation	Description
R2_MERGENOTPEN	Draws a line that ORs the screen color and the inverse of the pen color
R2_MASKNOTPEN	Draws a line that ANDs the screen color and the inverse of the pen
R2_MERGEPEN	Draws a line that ORs the pen color and the screen color
R2_NOTMERGEPEN	Draws a line that is the inverse of the pen ORed with the screen color
R2_MASKPEN	Draws a line that ANDs the pen and the screen color
R2_NOTMASKPEN	Draws a line that's the inverse of the pen ANDed with the screen color
R2_XORPEN	Draws a line that XORs the pen with the screen color
R2_NOTXORPEN	Draws a line that is the inverse of the pen XORed with the screen color

For normal drawing, you don't need to concern yourself with the drawing mode at all. But when you need them, the different raster operations are one function call away. To set the drawing mode for the current DC, call the DC object's SetROP2() member function:

```
pDC->SetROP2(R2_NOT);
```

The function's single argument is one of the previously listed raster operation codes.

Location: WinPrgS\Chap10\LineModeApp

As with the bitmap raster operations, the best way to understand line-drawing modes is to see them in action. On this book's CD-ROM, you can find the LineModeApp application. When you run the application, you see the window shown in Figure 10-16. In the window, the program draws 16 lines using each of the raster operations in the order in which they are listed in Table 10-3.

Although the solid background color does affect the raster operations, the results aren't obvious. To get a better look at how the window background affects the process, click the window. The application then draws lines on the background so you can see more clearly how the raster operations combine the pen and screen colors (see Figure 10-17).

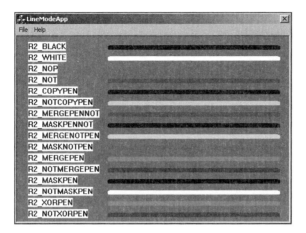

Figure 10-16: LineModeApp draws lines using all 16 raster operations.

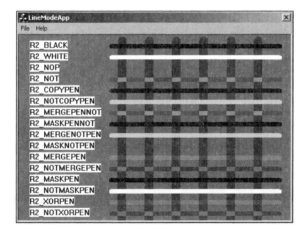

Figure 10-17: LineModeApp adds lines to the background.

The view class's `OnDraw()` function — which draws the window's background and then draws the 16 lines and their labels over the background — contains all of the pertinent source code for LineModeApp, as shown in Listing 10-1:

Listing 10-1: The OnDraw() Function

```
void CLineModeAppView::OnDraw(CDC* pDC)
{
    CLineModeAppDoc* pDoc = GetDocument();
    ASSERT_VALID(pDoc);

    // TODO: add draw code for native data here
```

```cpp
    pDC->FillRect(CRect(0,0, 500, 380),
        new CBrush(RGB(176,150,33)));

    CPen* pOldPen;

    if (m_drawLines)
    {
        CPen redPen(PS_SOLID, 16, RGB(255,0,0));
        pOldPen = pDC->SelectObject(&redPen);

        for (int x=0; x<6; ++x)
        {
            pDC->MoveTo(190+x*50, 10);
            pDC->LineTo(190+x*50, 380);
        }

        pDC->SelectObject(pOldPen);
    }

    CPen newPen(PS_SOLID, 8, RGB(0,0,255));
    pOldPen = pDC->SelectObject(&newPen);

    pDC->TextOut(20, 10, "R2_BLACK");
    pDC->SetROP2(R2_BLACK);
    pDC->MoveTo(170, 20);
    pDC->LineTo(480, 20);
    pDC->TextOut(20, 30, "R2_WHITE");
    pDC->SetROP2(R2_WHITE);
    pDC->MoveTo(170, 40);
    pDC->LineTo(480, 40);
    pDC->TextOut(20, 50, "R2_NOP");
    pDC->SetROP2(R2_NOP);
    pDC->MoveTo(170, 60);
    pDC >LineTo(480, 60);
    pDC->TextOut(20, 70, "R2_NOT");
    pDC->SetROP2(R2_NOT);
    pDC->MoveTo(170, 80);
    pDC->LineTo(480, 80);
    pDC->TextOut(20, 90, "R2_COPYPEN");
    pDC->SetROP2(R2_COPYPEN);
    pDC->MoveTo(170, 100);
    pDC->LineTo(480, 100);
    pDC->TextOut(20, 110, "R2_NOTCOPYPEN");
    pDC->SetROP2(R2_NOTCOPYPEN);
    pDC->MoveTo(170, 120);
    pDC->LineTo(480, 120);
    pDC->TextOut(20, 130, "R2_MERGEPENNOT");
    pDC->SetROP2(R2_MERGEPENNOT);
    pDC->MoveTo(170, 140);
    pDC->LineTo(480, 140);
    pDC->TextOut(20, 150, "R2_MASKPENNOT");
    pDC->SetROP2(R2_MASKPENNOT);
    pDC->MoveTo(170, 160);
```

```
    pDC->LineTo(480, 160);
    pDC->TextOut(20, 170, "R2_MERGENOTPEN");
    pDC->SetROP2(R2_MERGENOTPEN);
    pDC->MoveTo(170, 180);
    pDC->LineTo(480, 180);
    pDC->TextOut(20, 190, "R2_MASKNOTPEN");
    pDC->SetROP2(R2_MASKNOTPEN);
    pDC->MoveTo(170, 200);
    pDC->LineTo(480, 200);
    pDC->TextOut(20, 210, "R2_MERGEPEN");
    pDC->SetROP2(R2_MERGEPEN);
    pDC->MoveTo(170, 220);
    pDC->LineTo(480, 220);
    pDC->TextOut(20, 230, "R2_NOTMERGEPEN");
    pDC->SetROP2(R2_NOTMERGEPEN);
    pDC->MoveTo(170, 240);
    pDC->LineTo(480, 240);
    pDC->TextOut(20, 250, "R2_MASKPEN");
    pDC->SetROP2(R2_MASKPEN);
    pDC->MoveTo(170, 260);
    pDC->LineTo(480, 260);
    pDC->TextOut(20, 270, "R2_NOTMASKPEN");
    pDC->SetROP2(R2_NOTMASKPEN);
    pDC->MoveTo(170, 280);
    pDC->LineTo(480, 280);
    pDC->TextOut(20, 290, "R2_XORPEN");
    pDC->SetROP2(R2_XORPEN);
    pDC->MoveTo(170, 300);
    pDC->LineTo(480, 300);
    pDC->TextOut(20, 310, "R2_NOTXORPEN");
    pDC->SetROP2(R2_NOTXORPEN);
    pDC->MoveTo(170, 320);
    pDC->LineTo(480, 320);

    pDC->SelectObject(pOldPen);
}
```

At this point, you should be able to read through the listing and understand what's happening. Notice especially how the different calls to BitBlt() display exactly the same line, but they do so using a different raster operation. And, yes, you can shorten the OnDraw() function by drawing the lines in a loop, but that also makes the program a little more difficult to follow.

The OnDraw() function performs the following tasks:

- Fills the window with the background color
- Draws background lines on the display if the user selects this option
- Creates and selects a blue pen
- Draws one line in each of the defined line-drawing raster operations
- Restores the DC

426 Part II: Advanced Windows 2000 Programming

PROBLEMS & SOLUTIONS

The Magic of R2_XORPEN

PROBLEM: *I heard somewhere about a drawing mode that can draw and erase lines without changing the background image. Is there really a way to do this seemingly magical feat?*

SOLUTION: Yep. What you heard about is the R2_XORPEN drawing mode. Using this drawing mode, you can draw a line over any background image and then restore the image by redrawing the same line a second time (still using the R2_XORPEN drawing mode). Many Windows applications use this drawing technique to implement things such as rubber-band lines, boxes, and ellipses.

Location: `WinPrgS\Chap10\MagicRectApp`

On this book's CD-ROM, you can find the MagicRectApp application that demonstrates the R2_XORPEN drawing technique. When you run the application, you see the window shown in Figure 10-18. Click the window to draw a series of rectangles in R2_XORPEN mode (see Figure 10-19). When you click a second time, the rectangles vanish without disturbing the background image.

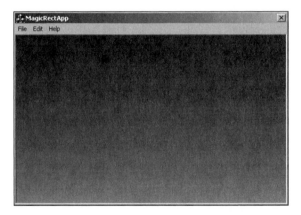

Figure 10-18: MagicRectApp displays a bitmapped background.

Continued

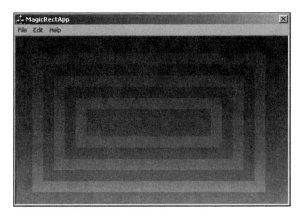

Figure 10-19: The program draws rectangles in R2_XORPEN mode.

The program displays its bitmap in the OnDraw() function. This ensures that the window's background always is drawn properly when the window needs repainting. Following is the OnDraw() function. (If you don't understand how the bitmap gets displayed, you can review bitmaps in Chapter 9.)

```
void CMagicRectAppView ::OnDraw(CDC* pDC)
{
    CMagicRectAppDoc* pDoc = GetDocument();
    ASSERT_VALID(pDoc);

    // TODO: add draw code for native data here

    if (!m_pBackBitmap)
        return;

    BYTE* pBitmapData = m_pBackBitmap->GetData();
    LPBITMAPINFO pBitmapInfo = m_pBackBitmap->GetInfo();

    StretchDIBits(pDC->m_hDC, 0, 0, 500, 300,
        0, 0, 500, 300, pBitmapData, pBitmapInfo,
        DIB_RGB_COLORS, SRCCOPY);
}
```

When the user clicks the application's window, Windows sends the application a WM_LBUTTONDOWN message. This message causes MFC to call the CMagicRectAppView class's OnLButtonDown() message-response function:

```
void CMagicRectAppView::OnLButtonDown
    (UINT nFlags, CPoint point)
{
    // TODO: Add your message handler code here
    //    and/or call default
```

```
    CClientDC windowDC(this);

    CPen bluePen(PS_SOLID, 20, RGB(0,0,255));
    CPen* pOldPen = windowDC.SelectObject(&bluePen);
    windowDC.SelectStockObject(NULL_BRUSH);

    windowDC.SetROP2(R2_XORPEN);
    windowDC.Rectangle(40, 40, 450, 270);
    windowDC.Rectangle(80, 80, 410, 230);
    windowDC.Rectangle(120, 120, 370, 190);

    windowDC.SelectObject(pOldPen);

    CView::OnLButtonDown(nFlags, point);
}
```

In OnLButtonDown( ), the program creates a window DC, selects a wide blue pen, selects the stock NULL_BRUSH, sets the drawing mode to R2_XORPEN, and then draws several nested rectangles. The next time the user clicks the window, OnLButtonDown( ) again draws the rectangles in R2_XORPEN mode — but this time the rectangles are drawn on top of the previous rectangles, which restores the background image.

The SelectStockObject( ) function enables you to select GDI objects that Windows already has created. Selecting the NULL_BRUSH object effectively tells Windows not to fill shapes, such as rectangles, with a color. Other stock objects include BLACK_BRUSH, DKGRAY_BRUSH, GRAY_BRUSH, HOLLOW_BRUSH, LTGRAY_BRUSH, WHITE_BRUSH, BLACK_PEN, NULL_PEN, and WHITE_PEN.

Now, the next time you drag a rubber-band line in a drawing program or drag a rectangle around a group of icons, you'll remember raster operations and be pleased with yourself because you know how this little bit of graphics magic works.

Using Regions

In many programs shown so far in this book, you use rectangles not only as shapes on the screen but also to determine what portion of the screen or bitmap with which you want to work. Rectangles are everywhere in Windows programming — so much so that MFC even has a class, CRect, for managing them. However, rectangles aren't the only way you can specify a portion of the screen; you also can use a *region*. A region is as simple as a rectangle or as complex as a set of rectangles, ellipses, and polygons. In a nutshell, a region is an area of the screen that isn't restricted to a rectangular shape.

Creating and Drawing a Region

In MFC, the `CRgn` class represents Windows regions. Thanks to the class's member functions, you can use a `CRgn` object to manage a nonrectangular area more easily. But before you can call upon those member functions, you must create a `CRgn` object; you do so like this:

```
CRgn region;
```

After creating the region, you must tell MFC what the region looks like. There are several types of regions from which to choose, each with its own creation function. Table 10-4 lists and describes those functions, all of which are members of the `CRgn` class.

Table 10-4   CRgn Functions

Function	Description
`CreateEllipticRgn()`	Creates an elliptical region
`CreateEllipticRgnIndirect()`	Creates an elliptical region from a `RECT` structure
`CreatePolygonRgn()`	Creates a polygonal region
`CreatePolyPolygonRgn()`	Creates a region containing multiple polygons
`CreateRectRgn()`	Creates a rectangular region
`CreateRectRgnIndirect()`	Creates a rectangular region from a `RECT` structure
`CreateRoundRectRgn()`	Creates a rectangular region with rounded corners

You can paint a region in several ways, using the `FillRgn()`, `FrameRgn()`, `InvertRgn()`, and `PaintRgn()` member functions of the DC object. For example, the following code paints regions with the `FillRgn()` function (as seen in Figure 10-20):

```
CClientDC* pDC = new CClientDC(this);

CRgn region1;
CRgn region2;
CRgn region3;

region1.CreateRectRgn(40, 40, 300, 300);
region2.CreateEllipticRgn(160, 160, 550, 300);
POINT points[5] = {
```

```
    120, 20, 420, 150, 420, 180, 130, 230, 20, 20};
region3.CreatePolygonRgn(points, 5, WINDING);

pDC->FillRgn(&region1, new CBrush(RGB(255,0,0)));
pDC->FillRgn(&region2, new CBrush(RGB(0,255,0)));
pDC->FillRgn(&region3, new CBrush(RGB(0,0,255)));

delete pDC;
```

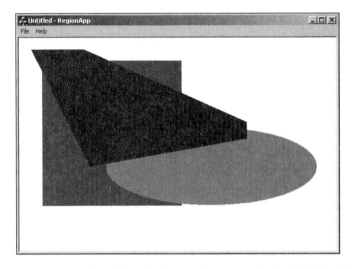

Figure 10-20: This window displays regions created with the FillRgn() function.

As you can see in the preceding code, CreateRectRgn() and CreateElliptic Rgn() both take the coordinates of a rectangle as their arguments. The Create PolygonRgn() function, however, takes as arguments an array of POINT structures, the number of points in the array, and a filling mode (which can be ALTERNATE or WINDING).

Combining Regions

Location: WinPrgS\Chap10\RegionApp

One thing that makes regions so powerful is that you can combine several regions into one. You do this by calling a region object's CombineRgn() member function. This function takes three arguments: the address of the first region to combine, the address of the second region to combine, and the combine mode (RGN_AND, RGN_COPY, RGN_DIFF, RGN_OR, or RGN_XOR). The RegionApp sample application on this book's CD-ROM shows how to combine regions using different modes. When you run the application, you see the window shown in Figure 10-21. This figure displays the three combined regions using the RGN_XOR mode—the result you get from this code:

```
CClientDC* pDC = new CClientDC(this);

CRgn region1;
CRgn region2;
CRgn region3;

region1.CreateRectRgn(40, 40, 300, 300);
region2.CreateEllipticRgn(160, 160, 550, 300);
POINT points[5] = {
    120, 20, 420, 150, 420, 180, 130, 230, 20, 20};
region3.CreatePolygonRgn(points, 5, WINDING);

region1.CombineRgn(&region1, &region2, RGN_XOR);
region1.CombineRgn(&region1, &region3, RGN_XOR);
pDC->FillRgn(&region1, new CBrush(RGB(255,0,0)));

delete pDC;
```

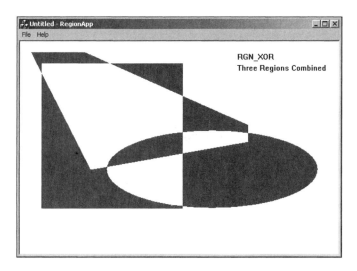

Figure 10-21: RegionApp displaying three regions in RGN_XOR mode

When the RGN_XOR mode combines two regions, only areas that are unique to one area or the other appear in the combined region. That is, no overlapping areas are included.

Figure 10-21 may appear to show overlapping areas because the display is the result of two calls to CombineRgn() rather than just one. Essentially, three regions are combining. If you want to get a clearer picture of the combination process, right-click the window. The application then removes the third region from the combined region to show that the RGN_XOR mode really does remove overlapped areas (see Figure 10-22). Right-click the window again to put the third region back, and you see that what appeared to be an overlapped area really fell over an area that the first combination removed.

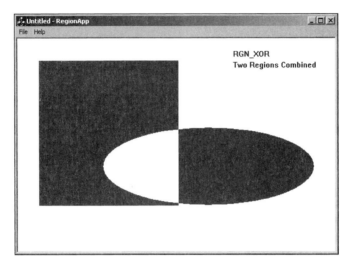

Figure 10-22: RegionApp displaying two regions in RGN_XOR mode

Figure 10-23 shows the three regions combined in RGN_AND mode. In this mode, only areas the regions have in common appear in the combination. Whereas RGN_XOR showed only non-overlapped areas, RGN_AND shows only overlapped areas. If you want to simplify the display, then right-click the display to remove the third region from the combined regions.

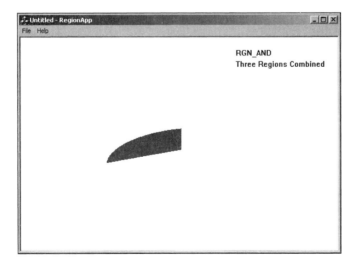

Figure 10-23: RegionApp displaying three regions in RGN_AND mode

Figure 10-24 shows the three regions combined in `RGN_COPY` mode. In this mode, the region given in `CombineRgn()`'s first argument is copied to the new region. In this case, the display looks the same whether you view two or three regions combined into one. The first region is the only one that makes it through the process.

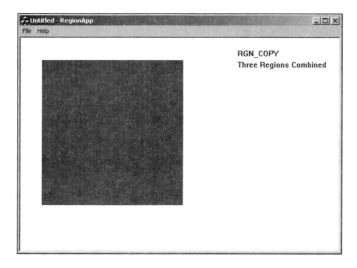

Figure 10-24: RegionApp displaying three regions in RGN_COPY mode

Figure 10-25 shows the three regions combined in `RGN_DIFF` mode. Now the areas of the second and third regions are removed from the first region, leaving only a portion of the original rectangle.

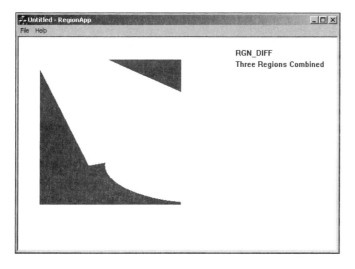

Figure 10-25: RegionApp displaying three regions in RGN_DIFF mode

Finally, Figure 10-26 shows the three regions combined in RGN_OR mode. This is probably the easiest mode to understand. All the areas of all the regions become part of the combined region, including overlapped and non-overlapped areas. When you want to combine regions, this is probably the result that first springs to mind because the combined region includes all of the source regions.

As is typical for this chapter's programs, all the fun shows up in the view class's OnDraw( ) function of RegionApp, shown here:

```
void CRegionAppView::OnDraw(CDC* pDC)
{
    CRegionAppDoc* pDoc = GetDocument();
    ASSERT_VALID(pDoc);

    // TODO: add draw code for native data here
    switch (m_combineMode)
    {
    case RGN_AND:
        pDC->TextOut(400,20, "RGN_AND"); break;
    case RGN_COPY:
        pDC->TextOut(400,20, "RGN_COPY"); break;
    case RGN_DIFF:
        pDC->TextOut(400,20, "RGN_DIFF"); break;
    case RGN_OR:
        pDC->TextOut(400,20, "RGN_OR"); break;
    case RGN_XOR:
        pDC->TextOut(400,20, "RGN_XOR"); break;
    }

    if (m_showOnlyTwo)
        pDC->TextOut(400, 40, "Two Regions Combined");
    else
        pDC->TextOut(400, 40, "Three Regions Combined");

    CRgn region1;
    CRgn region2;
    CRgn region3;

    region1.CreateRectRgn(40, 40, 300, 300);
    region2.CreateEllipticRgn(160, 160, 550, 300);
    POINT points[5] = {
        120, 20, 420, 150, 420, 180, 130, 230, 20, 20};
    region3.CreatePolygonRgn(points, 5, WINDING);

    region1.CombineRgn(&region1, &region2,
        m_combineMode);
    if (!m_showOnlyTwo)
        region1.CombineRgn(&region1, &region3,
            m_combineMode);

    pDC->FillRgn(&region1, new CBrush(RGB(255,0,0)));
}
```

There's nothing too tricky going on in OnDraw(). The previous discussion should prepare you to understand the code.

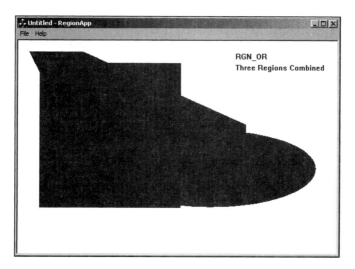

Figure 10-26: RegionApp displaying three regions in RGN_OR mode

The preceding OnDraw() function performs the following tasks:

- Prints a text label for the selected region mode
- Prints a text label specifying whether the display combines two or three shapes
- Creates and initializes three region objects
- Combines the regions according to the currently selected options
- Draws the combined region in the window

The CRgn class has several other member functions you might find useful. Take some time to look the class up in your online Visual C++ documentation and see what the class has to offer.

Using Paths

Paths are similar to regions, except paths contain lines and curves rather than shapes such as rectangles and ellipses. As with regions, however, you must create paths before you can display them. Once the path is created, the program can render it on the screen in various ways. In this section, you learn how to create and display paths.

Creating a Path

You start a path by calling the DC object's `BeginPath()` member function. The system then stores any lines you draw, rather than displaying the lines on the screen. When you're finished creating the path, you call the DC object's `EndPath()` member function. The following example creates a path that represents a four-sided polygon:

```
pDC->BeginPath();

pDC->MoveTo(20, 20);
pDC->LineTo(400, 100);
pDC->LineTo(500, 300);
pDC->LineTo(100, 200);
pDC->LineTo(20, 20);

pDC->EndPath();
```

Here, the program starts a path and then draws four lines. These lines are stored in the path, rather than rendered on the screen. The call to `EndPath()` ends the path.

Rendering a Path

Now that you have all those lines stored, you may wonder what to do with them. As you may guess, Windows 2000 supplies functions for displaying paths. Those functions, which are encapsulated in MFC's DC classes, are as follows:

StrokePath()	Draws the path using the current pen
FillPath()	Fills the path with the current brush
StrokeAndFillPath()	Draws and fills the path

So to draw the path used in the previous example, you can use the following line:

```
pDC->StrokePath();
```

Because you can define only one path at a time, you don't need to supply any kind of path ID, handle, or object to `StrokePath()`, `FillPath()`, or `StrokeAndFillPath()`. However, rendering the path also destroys it.

Defining Subpaths

A path can contain any number of *subpaths*, which are nothing more than paths within a path. When you call a function in a path that changes the drawing position, such as MoveTo(), you start a new subpath at the new position. When you render the path, by calling StrokePath() for instance, the system renders all subpaths of the path. In this way, a path can define a set of shapes on the screen. For example, the following lines create three distinct figures when rendered. Notice the call to the CloseFigure() function:

```
pDC->BeginPath();

pDC->MoveTo(20, 20);
pDC->LineTo(400, 100);
pDC->LineTo(500, 300);
pDC->LineTo(100, 200);
pDC->CloseFigure();

pDC->MoveTo(450, 50);
pDC->LineTo(550, 50);
pDC->LineTo(550, 150);
pDC->LineTo(450, 150);
pDC->CloseFigure();

pDC->MoveTo(50, 250);
pDC->LineTo(100, 250);
pDC->LineTo(100, 300);
pDC->LineTo(50, 300);
pDC->CloseFigure();

pDC->EndPath();
```

Here, the call to BeginPath() starts the path. The first call to MoveTo() then starts the first subpath, which comprises three lines. The call to CloseFigure() causes the system to finish the first figure by drawing a line between the starting and ending points. After creating the first subpath, the second call to MoveTo() starts another subpath (also consisting of three lines). Finally, the program creates a third subpath before calling EndPath() to end the path.

The PathApp Sample Program

Location: WinPrgS\Chap10\PathApp

On this book's CD-ROM, you can find the PathApp application that demonstrates rendering paths. When you run the application, you see the window shown in Figure 10-27; this figure displays a path rendered with the

StrokePath() function. To see the other types of path rendering, click the window. With the first click, the program renders the path with FillPath() (see Figure 10-28); with the second click, the program renders the path with StrokeAndFillPath() (see Figure 10-29).

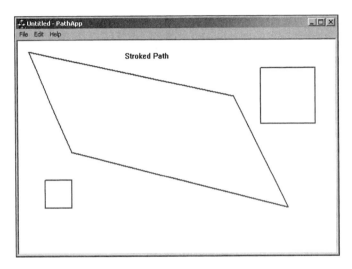

Figure 10-27: PathApp rendering with StrokePath()

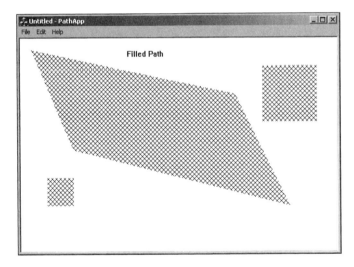

Figure 10-28: PathApp rendering with FillPath()

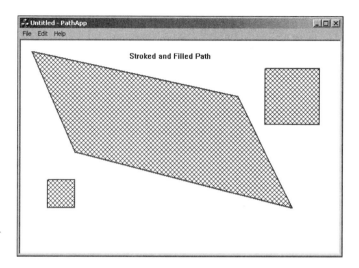

Figure 10-29: PathApp rendering with StrokeAndFillPath()

Here is the PathApp application's `OnDraw()` function, in which the program creates and renders the path according to the currently selected rendering style:

```
void CPathAppView::OnDraw(CDC* pDC)
{
    CPathAppDoc* pDoc = GetDocument();
    ASSERT_VALID(pDoc);

    // TODO: add draw code for native data here

    pDC->BeginPath();

    pDC->MoveTo(20, 20);
    pDC->LineTo(400, 100);
    pDC->LineTo(500, 300);
    pDC->LineTo(100, 200);
    pDC->CloseFigure();

    pDC->MoveTo(450, 50);
    pDC->LineTo(550, 50);
    pDC->LineTo(550, 150);
    pDC->LineTo(450, 150);
    pDC->CloseFigure();

    pDC->MoveTo(50, 250);
    pDC->LineTo(100, 250);
    pDC->LineTo(100, 300);
    pDC->LineTo(50, 300);
    pDC->CloseFigure();
```

```
    pDC->EndPath();

    CPen redPen(PS_SOLID, 2, RGB(255,0,0));
    CPen* pOldPen = pDC->SelectObject(&redPen);
    CBrush patBrush(HS_DIAGCROSS, RGB(0,0,255));
    CBrush* pOldBrush = pDC->SelectObject(&patBrush);

    if (m_renderStyle == 0)
    {
        pDC->StrokePath();
        pDC->TextOut(200, 20, "Stroked Path");
    }
    else if (m_renderStyle == 1)
    {
        pDC->FillPath();
        pDC->TextOut(200, 20, "Filled Path");
    }
    else
    {
        pDC->StrokeAndFillPath();
        pDC->TextOut(200, 20, "Stroked and Filled Path");
    }

    pDC->SelectObject(pOldPen);
    pDC->SelectObject(pOldBrush);
}
```

The function first creates a path containing three subpaths, after which it creates a thick, red pen and a patterned brush. It then selects these new GDI objects into the DC. The m_renderStyle member variable determines whether the program renders the path with StrokePath(), FillPath(), or StrokeAndFillPath(). The value of this variable changes each time the user clicks the window.

Note

Paths are a powerful tool for creating complex regions because you can convert any path to a region by calling the region object's CreateFromPath() member function. CreateFromPath() takes as a single argument the address of the DC containing the path.

Summary

By manipulating window and viewport origins and extents, you can control how Windows maps logical coordinates to the screen. This gives you the power to create displays that represent any type of coordinate system you need. Drawing modes enable you to pull off some seemingly magical stunts when displaying bitmaps or drawing lines. You even can make graphics appear and disappear without damaging a background image, regardless of the complexity of the background. Finally, regions and paths provide techniques for specifying nonrectangular areas of the screen.

Also discussed in this chapter:

- Physical coordinates represent the pixels on the screen, whereas logical coordinates are the coordinates you supply to GDI drawing functions.
- Windows automatically maps logical coordinates to physical coordinates.
- By changing the window or viewport origin, an application can control where on the display it draws data without changing the logical coordinates supplied to drawing functions.
- Mapping modes determine how Windows orients the X and Y axes and how Windows specifies the unit of measure applied to logical coordinates.
- When using the `MM_ISOTROPIC` and `MM_ANISOTROPIC` mapping modes, you can specify the window and viewport extents that control how Windows maps logical coordinates to physical coordinates.
- Bitmap drawing modes, such as `SRCAND` and `SRCPAINT`, enable you to combine source pixels, screen pixels, and the current brush in various ways.
- Line-drawing modes, such as `R2_COPYPEN` and `R2_XORPEN`, determine how the current pen combines with the screen color.
- Regions are areas of the screen defined by rectangles, polygons, and ellipses.
- Paths comprise a set of lines or subpaths that you can render on the screen in various ways or that you can convert to a complex region.

Chapter 11

Programming the Windows User Interface

In This Chapter

▶ Programming drag-and-drop applications

▶ Creating and manipulating shortcuts

▶ Adding icons to the system tray

▶ Working with the shell namespace

▶ Exploring DNA, Active Directory, and MTS

Windows 2000 features a whole host of advanced user-interface features that you may or may not need as you program your Windows applications. Such features include the shell namespace, shortcuts, taskbar, drag-and-drop, user-interface extensions, and Active Directory. Some of these Windows 2000 features are too advanced to cover in detail in this chapter. I introduce such topics, including Active Directory, in this chapter. For more thorough coverage, read *Windows 2000 Programming Bible* by John Paul Mueller (IDG Books Worldwide). This book concentrates solely on the advanced features of Windows 2000.

Using Drag-and-Drop

Windows' *user-interface shell* is a library of functions that implements many of the advanced features you can use in your Windows applications. Drag-and-drop functionality has been around for some time and is built into the user-interface shell. Enabling a program to respond to drag-and-drop is easy, and it provides your applications with a powerful mechanism by which the user can indicate which files the application should load and process.

Location: `WinPrgS\Chap11\DragDrop2`

CD

On this book's CD-ROM, you can find the DragDrop2 example program that demonstrates adding basic drag-and-drop functionality to a Windows application. When you run the DragDrop2 application, a narrow window appears. Drag one or more files from Windows Explorer into the DragDrop2 window, and the file names of the dropped files appear in the DragDrop2 window, as shown in Figure 11-1.

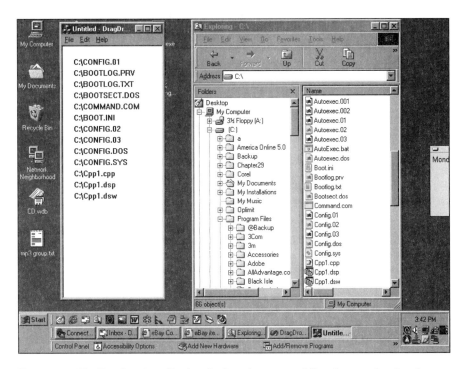

Figure 11-1: The DragDrop2 application displays the names of files that you drop into its window.

Registering as a Drag-and-Drop Application

To respond to drag-and-drop operations, your application first must register with Windows as a drag-and-drop application. You do this by calling the DragAcceptFiles() function, which DragDrop2 does in the view class's OnCreate() function. The OnCreate() function looks like this:

```
int CDragDrop2View::OnCreate(LPCREATESTRUCT lpCreateStruct)
{
    if (CView::OnCreate(lpCreateStruct) == -1)
    return -1;
    // TODO: Add your specialized creation code here
    DragAcceptFiles(TRUE);
    return 0;
}
```

As you can see, DragAcceptFiles() requires a single argument, which is a Boolean value specifying whether the application can (TRUE) or cannot (FALSE) accept drag-and-drop files.

Handling the WM_DROPFILES Message

Once you have your application registered for drag-and-drop, the application must respond to the WM_DROPFILES Windows message. This message indicates that the user has dropped something on your application's window. If you write a conventional Windows program—that is, a program that doesn't use MFC or some other framework—the wParam parameter for the WM_DROPFILES message is a handle to a data structure that contains information about the item or items dropped on the application's window. In the case statement for the message, you cast wParam to a handle. The case statement might look something like this:

```
case WM_DROPFILES:
{
    HDROP hDropInfo = (HANDLE)wParam;
    /* Handle the message here. */
}
```

Getting the Dropped File Names

To retrieve the number of files dropped, the program should call the DragQueryFile() function like this:

```
int numFiles = DragQueryFile(hDropInfo, -1, NULL, 0);
```

Here, hDropInfo is the handle to the HDROP structure that is passed in the wParam parameter.

The program then can get the actual file names of the dropped files by calling DragQueryFile() in a loop something like this:

```
char lpszFile[MAX_PATH];
for (int x=0; x<numFiles; ++x)
{
    DragQueryFile(hDropInfo, x, lpszFile, sizeof(lpszFile));
    // Do something with the file name here.
}
```

In this call to DragQueryFile(), the function's four arguments are described as follows:

hDropInfor	A handle to an HDROP structure
x	The index of the file name to retrieve
lpszFile	A pointer to the buffer that should receive the file name
sizeof(lpszFile)	The size of the buffer

Ending a Drag-and-Drop Operation

When the program is finished handling the `WM_DROPFILES` message, it should call the `DragFinish()` function like this:

```
DragFinish(hDropInfo);
```

This function's single argument is a handle to the `HDROP` structure.

The DragDrop2 Application

In the DragDrop2 example program, which uses MFC, the `OnDropFiles()` function handles the `WM_DROPFILES` Windows message. That function looks like this:

```
void CDragDrop2View::OnDropFiles(HDROP hDropInfo)
{
    // TODO: Add your message handler code here and/or call default
    char lpszFile[MAX_PATH];
    // Get the number of files.
    m_numFiles = DragQueryFile(hDropInfo, -1, NULL, 0);
    if (m_numFiles > 20)
        m_numFiles = 20;
    for (int x=0; x<m_numFiles; ++x)
    {
        DragQueryFile(hDropInfo, x, lpszFile, sizeof(lpszFile));
        fileNames[x] = lpszFile;
    }

    Invalidate();
    // Signal that the drag and drop operation is over.
    DragFinish(hDropInfo);
    CView::OnDropFiles(hDropInfo);
}
```

In this function, `fileNames[]` is an array of `CString` objects. This array is defined as a member of the view class like this:

```
CString m_fileNames[20];
```

Once your program has the names of the dropped files, it can perform the required processing. For example, the application can open the file and display its contents in an editor. The DragDrop2 example program does not perform file processing. It settles for only displaying the file names, which the program does in the view class's `OnDraw()` function:

```
void CDragDrop2View::OnDraw(CDC* pDC)
{
    CDragDrop2Doc* pDoc = GetDocument();
    ASSERT_VALID(pDoc);
    // TODO: add draw code for native data here
    for (int x=0; x<m_numFiles; ++x)
        pDC->TextOut(20, 20+x*20, m_fileNames[x]);
}
```

Manipulating Shortcuts

No one who uses Windows can fail to notice the user interface's reliance on *shortcuts,* which are like pointers to files and objects installed on the system. Shortcuts can reference just about any type of Windows object including files, drives, printers, programs, Internet addresses, and more. The user instantly can recognize a shortcut, which appears as an icon with a boxed arrow in the lower-left corner. Although users can create their own shortcuts easily using Windows Explorer, Windows applications also create shortcuts. Installation programs, for example, often place shortcuts to installed applications on the user's desktop.

To create a shortcut in an application, you need to learn about two COM interfaces: IShellLink and IPersistFile. If you don't understand COM, don't panic. Using these COM interfaces is actually quite easy, requiring only that you understand a few simple steps. For example, to install a shortcut on the user's desktop, your program must perform the following actions:

1. Initialize COM
2. Create an IShellLink object
3. Use the IShellLink interface to obtain a pointer to the IPersistFile interface
4. Initialize the new shortcut through the IShellLink interface
5. Use the IPersistFile interface to save the new shortcut
6. Release all COM pointers
7. Uninitialize COM

The following sections describe each of these steps in detail. You'll soon see how easy it is to use COM objects to manipulate the Windows user interface.

Initializing COM

Before you can create COM objects and obtain pointers to their interfaces, you must initialize COM. Your program completes this task with one function call, as shown here:

```
HRESULT hResult = CoInitializeEx(NULL, COINIT_MULTITHREADED);
```

As you can see, the CoInitializeEx() function returns an HRESULT value. You should check this return value to ensure that COM initialized successfully. You do this by comparing the result to S_OK, which indicates that the function call succeeded:

```
if (hResult == S_OK)
{
    // Continue here.
}
```

```
else
{
    // Handle COM failure here.
}
```

The `CoInitializeEx()` function requires two arguments. The first is always NULL. The second determines the type of threading to use. For most cases, use the `COINIT_MULTITHREADED` flag. If you're interested in other settings for this flag, look up the `CoInitializeEx()` function and the `COINIT` enumeration in your Visual C++ online help.

Creating an IShellLink Object

Once you have COM initialized, the next step is to create an `IShellLink` COM object. You create the object like this:

```
IShellLink *pShellLink;
hResult = CoCreateInstance(CLSID_ShellLink, NULL,
    CLSCTX_INPROC_SERVER, IID_IShellLink,
    (void **)&pShellLink);
```

The `CoCreateInstance()` function requires five arguments, which are described as follows:

CLSID_ShellLink	The class ID of the object to create. In this case, `CLSID_ShellLink` identifies the `IShellLink` object.
NULL	A pointer to the outer object, which is used only with object aggregation (a topic beyond the scope of this book). In most cases, use NULL for this argument.
CLSCTX_INPROC_SERVER	A flag that specifies the context in which the system runs executable code. The `CLSCTX_INPROC_SERVER` flag specifies that the object runs in the same process as the application that calls `CoCreateInstance()`. For more information on this flag, look up the `CLSCTX` enumeration in your Visual C++ online help.
IID_IShellLink	The class ID of the COM interface for which the program needs a pointer. In this case, `IDD_IShellLink` is the class ID for the `IShellLink` interface.
&pShellLink	The address of the variable in which to store the acquired pointer.

Getting an IPersistFile Interface Pointer

Now that you have the `IShellLink` object and have a pointer to its `IShellLink` interface, you can get a pointer to the object's `IPersistFile` interface. If you have experience with COM, you already know that you acquire an interface pointer through an object by calling that object's `QueryInterface()` function. If you have no COM experience, you just learned something new! Here's the function call that acquires a pointer to the `IShellLink` object's `IPersistFile` interface:

```
IPersistFile *pPersistFile;
hResult = pShellLink->QueryInterface(IID_IPersistFile,
    (void **)&pPersistFile);
```

The `QueryInterface()` function requires two arguments. The first argument is the ID of the interface for which you want a pointer, and the second is the address of the variable that holds the pointer. As you can see, the `IPersistFile` interface's ID is `IID_IPersistFile`.

Initializing the New Shortcut

You now have pointers to the `IShellLink` and `IPersistFile` interfaces, which means you finally can start creating your new shortcut. To do this, you must call a couple of functions in the `IShellLink` interface. Table 11-1 lists and describes the functions provided in the `IShellLink` interface.

Table 11-1   Functions of the IShellLink Interface

Function	Description
GetArguments()	Gets the `IShellLink` object's command-line arguments
GetDescription()	Gets the `IShellLink` object's description string
GetHotkey()	Gets the `IShellLink` object's hot key
GetIconLocation()	Gets the path and index of the `IShellLink` object's icon
GetIDList()	Gets the `IShellLink` object's list of item identifiers
GetPath()	Gets the `IShellLink` object's path and file name
GetShowCmd()	Gets the `IShellLink` object's show command
GetWorkingDirectory()	Gets the `IShellLink` object's working directory
Resolve()	Updates the `IShellLink` object's path and list of identifiers

Continued

Table 11-1 *(continued)*

Function	Description
SetArguments()	Sets the IShellLink object's command-line arguments
SetDescription()	Sets the IShellLink object's description string
SetHotkey()	Sets the IShellLink object's hot key
SetIconLocation()	Sets the path and index of the IShellLink object's icon
SetIDList()	Sets the IShellLink object's list of item identifiers
SetPath()	Sets the IShellLink object's path and file name
SetRelativePath()	Sets the IShellLink object's relative path
SetShowCmd()	Sets the IShellLink object's Show command
SetWorkingDirectory()	Sets the IShellLink object's working directory

The two functions of special interest in this case are SetPath() and SetDescription(). The SetPath() function specifies the path of the object with which the shortcut is associated. For example, if you want to create a shortcut to your computer's config.sys file, the call to SetPath() looks like this:

```
pShellLink->SetPath("c:\\config.sys");
```

The SetDescription() function sets the string that appears as the shortcut's label. In the case of the shortcut to the config.sys file, the call to SetDescription() might look like this:

```
pShellLink->SetDescription("Shortcut to config.sys");
```

Saving a Shortcut

With your new shortcut created, you now need to store it someplace. The IPersistFile interface provides the function needed to accomplish this task: Save(). Because the Save() function requires the path to which you want to save the shortcut, the program first constructs the path. A logical place to store the shortcut is on the user's desktop. To do that, you can use code like the following:

```
char savePath[MAX_PATH];
GetWindowsDirectory(savePath, MAX_PATH);
int len = strlen(savePath);
strcpy(&savePath[len], "\\desktop\\config.lnk");
```

Then you convert the path to Unicode format for the `Save()` function:

```
OLECHAR widePath[MAX_PATH];
MultiByteToWideChar(CP_ACP, 0,
    savePath, -1, widePath, MAX_PATH);
```

Finally, the program can call `Save()` to store the shortcut in the user's desktop directory, which causes the shortcut's icon to appear on the user's desktop:

```
pPersistFile->Save(widePath, TRUE);
```

Releasing Pointers and Uninitializing COM

The last step is to release the pointers to the `IShellLink` and `IPersistFile` interfaces. *You never use the* `delete` *operator on a pointer to a COM interface.* This is because COM objects keep a count of the number of processes using the object, and the object stays in memory until its reference count goes to 0. When you acquire a pointer to an interface, the object that implements the interface increments its counter. When you release the pointer, the object decrements its counter. To release an interface pointer, you call the interface's `Release()` function like this:

```
pInterface->Release();
```

Here, `pInterface` is a pointer to the interface to be released. In the case of the `IShellLink` and `IPersistFile` interfaces, the calls to release look something like this:

```
pPersistFile->Release();
pShellLink->Release();
```

Finally, to uninitialize COM, your application need only call the `CoUninitialize()` function like this:

```
CoUninitialize();
```

The Shortcut Example Application

Location: `WinPrg5\Chap11\Shortcut`

Everything you just learned about shortcuts comes together in the example program Shortcut, which you can find on this book's CD-ROM. When you run the program, the application's main window appears. Click the window to create a shortcut for your `config.sys` file. The shortcut's icon should appear on your desktop.

The only function in Shortcut that pertains to the creation of shortcuts is the view class's `OnLButtonDown()` function, which appears here:

```
void CShortcutView::OnLButtonDown(UINT nFlags, CPoint point)
{
```

```
// TODO: Add your message handler code here and/or call default
IShellLink *pShellLink;
IPersistFile *pPersistFile;

HRESULT hResult = CoInitialize(NULL);
if (hResult == S_OK)
{
    hResult = CoCreateInstance(CLSID_ShellLink, NULL,
        CLSCTX_INPROC_SERVER, IID_IShellLink,
        (void **)&pShellLink);
    if (hResult == S_OK)
    {
        hResult = pShellLink->QueryInterface(IID_IPersistFile,
            (void **)&pPersistFile);
        if (hResult == S_OK)
        {
            hResult = pShellLink->SetPath("c:\\config.sys");
            pShellLink->SetDescription
                ("Shortcut to config.sys");
            char savePath[MAX_PATH];
            GetWindowsDirectory(savePath, MAX_PATH);
            int len = strlen(savePath);
            strcpy(&savePath[len], "\\desktop\\config.lnk");
            OLECHAR widePath[MAX_PATH];
            MultiByteToWideChar(CP_ACP, 0,
                savePath, -1, widePath, MAX_PATH);
            pPersistFile->Save(widePath, TRUE);
            pPersistFile->Release();
        }
        pShellLink->Release();
    }
}
else
    MessageBox("COM Initialization failed");
CoUninitialize();
CView::OnLButtonDown(nFlags, point);
}
```

Manipulating Icons in the System Tray

Every Windows machine from Windows 95 up has an area—usually at the bottom of the screen—called the *taskbar*. The taskbar holds the Start menu, an area for icons that the user wants immediate access to, an area for showing the icons of running processes, and the system tray. The *system tray* contains icons that display system status information (such as the time and battery power) and enable the user to access various utilities and accessories easily. Every machine has different icons in the system tray, depending upon the programs that are installed on the machine.

Adding an Icon to the Tray

Any application can display its icon in the system tray. It's just a matter of initializing a NOTIFYICONDATA structure and calling the Shell_NotifyIcon() function. Windows declares the NOTIFYICONDATA structure as follows. Note that version 5 of this structure includes additional members not shown here:

```
typedef struct _NOTIFYICONDATA {
    DWORD cbSize;
    HWND hWnd;
    UINT uID;
    UINT uFlags;
    UINT uCallbackMessage;
    HICON hIcon;
    TCHAR szTip[64];
} NOTIFYICONDATA, *PNOTIFYICONDATA;
} NOTIFYICONDATA, *PNOTIFYICONDATA;
```

Table 11-2 lists the structure's members and their descriptions.

Table 11-2 Members of the NOTIFYICONDATA Structure

Member	Description
cbSize	The size of the NOTIFYICONDATA structure
hIcon	The icon's handle
hWnd	The handle of the window to be notified when the user manipulates the icon
szTip	A pointer to the string to be used as a standard tooltip, which can be a maximum of 64 characters
uCallbackMessage	A message ID that the system should use when sending tray-icon notifications to the window
uFlags	Flags that specify the valid members of the NOTIFYICONDATA structure; can be a combination of NIF_ICON, NIF_MESSAGE, and NIF_TIP
uID	The icon's ID

Note

Version 5.0 of the NOTIFYICONDATA structure provides additional members that support expanded tray icon functionality. If you're interested in the 5.0 version, look up NOTIFYICONDATA in your Visual C++ online help.

The following code snippet demonstrates how a program initializes the `NOTIFYICONDATA` structure in preparation for placing an icon in the system tray:

```
NOTIFYICONDATA notifyIconData;
notifyIconData.cbSize = sizeof(NOTIFYICONDATA);
notifyIconData.uFlags = NIF_MESSAGE|NIF_ICON|NIF_TIP;
notifyIconData.hIcon =
    LoadIcon(NULL, MAKEINTRESOURCE(ID_MYLOGO));
notifyIconData.uID = (UINT)ID_MYLOGO;
notifyIconData.hWnd = hWnd;
notifyIconData.uCallbackMessage = TRAY_MESSAGE;
strcpy(notifyIconData.szTip, "MyApp QuickStart");
```

Once the `NOTIFYICONDATA` structure is ready to go, the application calls the `Shell_NotifyIcon()` function like this:

```
Shell_NotifyIcon(NIM_ADD, &notifyIconData);
```

The `Shell_NotifyIcon()` function's first argument is a flag that specifies what task the function call is to perform. This argument can be one of the values in Table 11-3. The second argument is the address of the initialized `NOTIFYICONDATA` structure.

Table 11-3 Shell_NotifyIcon Task Identifiers

Value	Description
NIM_ADD	Adds an icon to the system tray
NIM_DELETE	Deletes an icon in the system tray
NIM_MODIFY	Modifies an icon in the system tray

Responding to Icon Events

Now that you have the icon in the system tray, you want it to do more than sit there looking pretty. Thanks to the information you supplied in the `NOTIFYICONDATA` structure, the system can inform your program of actions the user performs on the icon. Specifically, your program can receive notifications of mouse events such as `WM_MOUSEMOVE`, `WM_LBUTTONDOWN`, `WM_RBUTTONDOWN`, `WM_LBUTTONDBLCLK`, and `WM_RBUTTONDBLCLK`.

Your application receives these notifications by responding to the user-defined message ID placed in the `NOTIFYICONDATA` structure's `uCallback Message` member. When your application receives the notification message, the specific event's ID is in the `lParam` parameter. A function, which is called from your application's message loop and that responds to the notification, might look like this:

```
void OnTrayMessage(WPARAM wParam, LPARAM lParam)
{
    UINT msgID = (UINT)lParam;
    switch (msgID)
    {
    case WM_LBUTTONDOWN:
        // Handle left click here.
        break;

    case WM_LBUTTONDBLCLK:
        // Handle left double click here.
        break;
    case WM_RBUTTONDOWN:
        // Handle right click here.
        break;

    case WM_RBUTTONDBLCLK:
        // Handle right double click here.
        break;
    case WM_MOUSEMOVE:
        // Handle mouse move messages here.
    }
}
```

Removing an Icon from the Tray

When the application no longer needs the icon in the system tray, it can remove the icon in much the same way that it places the icon there. Simply initialize the NOTIFYICONDATA structure and call Shell_NotifyIcon(). The following code lines show how you can accomplish this task:

```
NOTIFYICONDATA notifyIconData;
notifyIconData.cbSize = sizeof(NOTIFYICONDATA);
notifyIconData.uID = (UINT)ID_MYLOGO;
notifyIconData.hWnd = m_hWnd;

Shell_NotifyIcon(NIM_DELETE, &notifyIconData);
```

As you can see, the NOTIFYICONDATA structure's uID and hWnd members identify the icon you want removed and the window on whose behalf the operation is to be performed.

The TrayApp Example Application

Location: WinPrgS\Chap11\TrayApp

On this book's CD-ROM, you can find the TrayApp example application that demonstrates all the techniques discussed in this section. When you run the program, the application's main window appears (as shown in Figure 11-2).

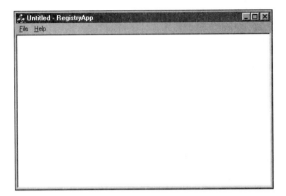

Figure 11-2: TrayApp main window

Click the window to place an icon on the system tray. Right-click the window to remove the icon. Before removing the icon, however, move the mouse over the icon and click with both the left and right mouse buttons. Every mouse action results in either a response in the window's display or in a message box.

When you left-click the window, the application must place an icon in the system tray. The application's view class handles this task in the OnLButtonDown() function, as shown here:

```
void CTrayAppView::OnLButtonDown(UINT nFlags, CPoint point)
{
    // TODO: Add your message handler code here and/or call default
    NOTIFYICONDATA notifyIconData;
    notifyIconData.cbSize = sizeof(NOTIFYICONDATA);
    notifyIconData.uFlags = NIF_MESSAGE|NIF_ICON|NIF_TIP;
    notifyIconData.hIcon =
        LoadIcon(NULL, MAKEINTRESOURCE(IDI_WINLOGO));
    notifyIconData.uID = (UINT)IDI_WINLOGO;
    notifyIconData.hWnd = m_hWnd;
    notifyIconData.uCallbackMessage = TRAY_MESSAGE;
    strcpy(notifyIconData.szTip, "A Tray Tip!");
    Shell_NotifyIcon(NIM_ADD, &notifyIconData);
    CView::OnLButtonDown(nFlags, point);
}
```

A right-click tells the application to remove the icon, which is handled in the view class's OnRButtonDown() function:

```
void CTrayAppView::OnRButtonDown(UINT nFlags, CPoint point)
{
    // TODO: Add your message handler code here and/or call default
    NOTIFYICONDATA notifyIconData;
    notifyIconData.cbSize = sizeof(NOTIFYICONDATA);
    notifyIconData.uID = (UINT)IDI_WINLOGO;
    notifyIconData.hWnd = m_hWnd;
```

```
        Shell_NotifyIcon(NIM_DELETE, &notifyIconData);
        CView::OnRButtonDown(nFlags, point);
}
```

Finally, mouse actions on the icon in the system tray generate the user-defined TRAY_MESSAGE Windows message. TrayApp defines that message like this:

```
const TRAY_MESSAGE = WM_USER + 1;
```

The program uses the view class's message map to associate the TRAY_MESSAGE message with the message-response function OnTrayMessage(). The view class's message map looks as follows:

```
BEGIN_MESSAGE_MAP(CTrayAppView, CView)
    //{{AFX_MSG_MAP(CTrayAppView)
    ON_WM_LBUTTONDOWN()
    ON_WM_RBUTTONDOWN()
    //}}AFX_MSG_MAP
    ON_MESSAGE(TRAY_MESSAGE, OnTrayMessage)
END_MESSAGE_MAP()
```

The ON_MESSAGE entry in the message map specifies that the OnTrayMessage() function should handle TRAY_MESSAGE messages. That function looks like this:

```
void CTrayAppView::OnTrayMessage(WPARAM wParam, LPARAM lParam)
{
    static int test = 0;
    UINT msgID = (UINT)lParam;
    switch (msgID)
    {
    case WM_LBUTTONDOWN:
        MessageBox("Tray Icon Left Clicked.");
        break;
    case WM_LBUTTONDBLCLK:
        MessageBox("Tray Icon Left Double-Clicked.");
        break;
    case WM_RBUTTONDOWN:
        MessageBox("Tray Icon Right Clicked.");
        break;
    case WM_RBUTTONDBLCLK:
        MessageBox("Tray Icon Right Double-Clicked.");
        break;
    case WM_MOUSEMOVE:
        CString msg;
        msg.Format("Mouse Move: %d", test++);
        CClientDC clientDC(this);
        clientDC.TextOut(20, 60, msg);
    }
}
```

The Shell Namespace

You can think of the *shell namespace* as an extended directory structure. Whereas your hard disk directory represents all the files and folders on your hard disk, the shell namespace is a directory for all of the objects installed on your system. These objects include not only the usual disk drives, but also printers, network resources, the Recycle Bin, and so on.

At the very top of the shell namespace hierarchy is the desktop—named, appropriately enough, Desktop. Whatever objects are currently associated with the desktop appear below Desktop in the hierarchy. These objects usually include My Computer, Recycle Bin, My Documents, My Briefcase, and Network Neighborhood, as well as any folders that the user places on the desktop. Beneath My Computer, you find system resources that include all your disk drives, Printers, Control Panel, Dial-Up Networking, Scheduled Tasks, and so on.

The following terms apply when discussing the shell namespace:

Folder	A set of objects in the shell namespace. Folders can contain other folders and/or file objects. Each folder is a COM object that implements the `IShellFolder` interface.
File object	A non-folder item inside a folder.
Virtual folder	A folder not associated with actual storage devices and the file system. For example, the Printers folder contains file objects that represent the printers installed on the system, rather than data files stored on the hard disk.
Item identifier	An ID that identifies a specific object in the shell namespace. This ID takes the form of a binary data structure.
PIDL	A pointer to a list of item IDs.

Enumerating the Contents of a Folder

Although it's a somewhat complex process, your application can discover the contents of any folder in the shell namespace. In fact, with a little work, an application can acquire the entire hierarchy of items in the shell namespace—much as Windows Explorer does when it displays the objects of the shell namespace in its left-hand pane. The steps required to enumerate a folder in the shell namespace are as follows:

1. Get a pointer to the `IShellFolder` interface.
2. Get a pointer to the `IMalloc` interface.
3. Get a pointer to the `IEnumIDList` interface.

Chapter 11: Programming the Windows User Interface

4. Retrieve a PIDL for the next item in the enumeration.
5. Determine what type of identifier the PIDL represents.
6. Process the item.
7. Free the memory allocated for the PIDL.
8. Repeat steps 4 through 7 until all items are enumerated.
9. Release the `IShellFolder, IEnumIDList,` and `IMalloc` interfaces.

The NamespaceApp Application

Location: `WinPrgS\Chap11\Namespace`

CD

On this book's CD-ROM, you can find the NamespaceApp example application that demonstrates all the techniques discussed in this section. When you run the program, the application's main window appears and displays the names of all folders in the first level (the Desktop level) of the shell namespace. The following sections explain how the program works.

The OnCreate() function

The application enumerates the contents of the Desktop folder with no intervention from you. It does this because the application performs the enumeration in the view class's `OnCreate()` function, which MFC calls when the view window is created. The `OnCreate()` function looks like this:

```
int CNamespaceAppView::OnCreate(LPCREATESTRUCT lpCreateStruct)
{
    if (CView::OnCreate(lpCreateStruct) == -1)
        return -1;
    // TODO: Add your specialized creation code here
    LPSHELLFOLDER lpShellFolder;
    LPMALLOC lpMalloc;
    LPENUMIDLIST lpEnumIDList;

    m_nameCount = 0;
    HRESULT hResult = SHGetDesktopFolder(&lpShellFolder);
    if (hResult == NOERROR)
    {
        hResult = ::SHGetMalloc(&lpMalloc);
        if (hResult == NOERROR)
        {
            hResult = lpShellFolder->EnumObjects(NULL,
                SHCONTF_FOLDERS | SHCONTF_NONFOLDERS,
                &lpEnumIDList);
            if (hResult == NOERROR)
                ProcessFolder(lpShellFolder, lpMalloc,
                    lpEnumIDList);
            lpMalloc->Release();
            lpEnumIDList->Release();
```

```
            Invalidate();
        }
        lpShellFolder->Release ();
    }
    return 0;
}
```

You need to explore this function line by line in order to understand what's going on in this program. The `OnCreate()` function first declares pointers to the `IShellFolder`, `IMalloc`, and `IEnumIDList` interfaces:

```
LPSHELLFOLDER lpShellFolder;
LPMALLOC lpMalloc;
LPENUMIDLIST lpEnumIDList;
```

Next, the function sets the member variable `m_nameCount` to 0:

```
m_nameCount = 0;
```

This variable holds the number of folder names that the application stores in the array `m_names[]`, which the `OnDraw()` function uses to display the folder names in the view window.

The function now calls `SHGetDesktopFolder()` to get a pointer to the Desktop folder's `IShellFolder` interface:

```
HRESULT hResult = SHGetDesktopFolder(&lpShellFolder);
```

As you can see, this function returns an `HRESULT` value. Before continuing, the program checks that the return value equals `NOERROR`. If it does, then the `SHGetDesktopFolder()` function successfully returned an `IShellFolder` interface pointer:

```
if (hResult == NOERROR)
{
    ...
}
```

The next step is to call `SHGetMalloc()` to get a pointer to the `IMalloc` interface, which the program must use to allocate and free any memory needed by the COM interfaces:

```
hResult = ::SHGetMalloc(&lpMalloc);
```

This function also returns an `HRESULT` value that must be checked against `NOERROR`.

Now, the program calls `EnumObjects()` through the `IShellFolder` interface pointer to acquire a pointer to the `IEnumIDList` interface:

```
hResult = lpShellFolder->EnumObjects(NULL,
    SHCONTF_FOLDERS | SHCONTF_NONFOLDERS, &lpEnumIDList);
```

Chapter 11: Programming the Windows User Interface   **461**

This function requires three arguments, which are described as follows:

NULL	The handle of the parent window that provides the enumeration with user input. If no user input is required, this argument is NULL.
SHCONTF_FOLDERS | SHCONTF_NONFOLDERS	A set of flags that specifies the types of items to enumerate. Table 11-4 lists the possible values for this argument.
&lpEnumIDList	The address where the function should store the IEnumIDList pointer.

Table 11-4   EnumObjects() Flags

Value	Description
SHCONTF_FOLDERS	Includes folder items in the enumeration
SHCONTF_NONFOLDERS	Includes non-folder items in the enumeration
SHCONTF_INCLUDEHIDDEN	Includes hidden items in the enumeration
SHCONTF_INIT_ON_FIRST_NEXT	Delays validation of the enumeration object until the first call to Next()
SHCONTF_NETPRINTERSRCH	Includes printer objects in the enumeration

If the program gets the IEnumIDList pointer successfully, it calls the user-defined function ProcessFolder(). This function retrieves the names of the Desktop folders:

```
if (hResult == NOERROR)
    ProcessFolder(lpShellFolder, lpMalloc, lpEnumIDList);
```

Finally, the program releases the IMalloc, IEnumIDList, and IShellFolder interface pointers and invalidates the view window to force a call to the OnDraw() function:

```
lpMalloc->Release();
lpEnumIDList->Release();
Invalidate();
lpShellFolder->Release();
```

The ProcessFolder() function

The `ProcessFolder()` function is where the NamespaceApp program retrieves the names of the folders that the program displays in the window. That function looks like this:

```
void CNamespaceAppView::ProcessFolder(LPSHELLFOLDER lpShellFolder,
    LPMALLOC lpMalloc, LPENUMIDLIST lpEnumIDList)
{
    STRRET strRet;
    ULONG numFetched;
    LPITEMIDLIST lpItemIDList;

    HRESULT hResult = lpEnumIDList->Next(1,
        &lpItemIDList, &numFetched);
    while (hResult == NOERROR)
    {
        ULONG attributes = SFGAO_FOLDER;
        lpShellFolder->GetAttributesOf(1,
            (const struct _ITEMIDLIST **)&lpItemIDList, &attributes);
        if (attributes & SFGAO_FOLDER)
        {
            hResult = lpShellFolder->
                GetDisplayNameOf(lpItemIDList, SHGDN_NORMAL, &strRet);
            if (m_nameCount < 20)
                m_names[m_nameCount++] = strRet.cStr;
        }
        lpMalloc->Free(lpItemIDList);
        hResult = lpEnumIDList->Next(1, &lpItemIDList,
                &numFetched);
    }
}
```

Note that `ProcessFolder()` **receives as arguments the** `IShellFolder`, `IMalloc`, **and** `IEnumIDList` **pointers that the program creates in** `OnCreate()`.

The function first declares the local variables it needs, which includes a PIDL (a pointer to an `ITEMIDLIST`):

```
STRRET strRet;
ULONG numFetched;
LPITEMIDLIST lpItemIDList;
```

The function then calls `lpEnumIDList->Next()` to get the first folder PIDL:

```
HRESULT hResult = lpEnumIDList->Next(1,
    &lpItemIDList, &numFetched);
```

Chapter 11: Programming the Windows User Interface **463**

The Next() function requires three arguments, which are described as follows:

1	The number of item ID lists to be placed at the address given in the second argument
&lpItemIDList	The address of an array of ITEMIDLIST pointers
&numFetched	The address of a variable that will receive the number of item ID lists retrieved

The Next() function returns NOERROR until there are no items left to retrieve. Then the function returns S_FALSE.

If the Next() function retrieves a valid item ID list, the program calls lpShellFolder->GetAttributesOf() to get the item's attributes:

```
ULONG attributes = SFGAO_FOLDER;
lpShellFolder->GetAttributesOf(1,
    (const struct _ITEMIDLIST **)&lpItemIDList, &attributes);
```

This function requires three arguments, which are described as follows:

1	The number of items for which to get attributes.
&lpItemIDList	The address of the PIDL that points to the item ID lists.
&attributes	The address of a ULONG variable that contains the attributes for which to search. GetAttributesOf() also returns flags in this variable. Because there are more than 25 different flags that can combine to form this value, I don't list them here. Please refer to your Visual C++ online documentation for more information.

The ProcessFolder() function now checks the returned attribute flags for the type of item the program wants. If the attributes check out, the program calls lpShellFolder->GetDisplayNameOf() to get the item's display name and then adds the name to the m_names[] array:

```
if (attributes & SFGAO_FOLDER)
{
    hResult = lpShellFolder->
        GetDisplayNameOf(lpItemIDList, SHGDN_NORMAL, &strRet);
    if (m_nameCount < 20)
        m_names[m_nameCount++] = strRet.cStr;
}
```

The `GetDisplayNameOf()` function requires three arguments, which are described as follows:

`lpItemIDList`	The address of the item's PIDL.
`SHGDN_NORMAL`	A flag that specifies how the name should be returned. `SHGDN_NORMAL` specifies the item's full name, whereas `SHGDN_INFOLDER` requests a name relative to the containing folder.
`&strRet`	The address of a `STRRET` structure, which is where the function returns the requested name. As you can see in the preceding code, the `cStr` member of the `STRRET` structure holds the name's string.

Although the system allocates the memory required to store the item ID lists, your application must free this memory. You do this through the `IMalloc` interface like this:

`lpMalloc->Free(lpItemIDList);`

The `ProcessFolder()` function continues the enumeration until the last folder is processed.

Advanced Windows 2000 Features

In this section, you get a quick look at some advanced Windows 2000 features. However, I do not cover these features in any detail in this book. If these technologies sound like something you need or want to know more about, you can find detailed information in *Windows 2000 Programming Bible* by John Paul Mueller (IDG Books Worldwide).

DNA

DNA is the acronym for Microsoft's *Distributed interNet Application* architecture, which encompasses the myriad technologies developed by Microsoft for application development. In Microsoft's own words, "Windows DNA defines a framework for delivering solutions that meet the demanding requirements of corporate computing, the Internet, intranets, and global electronic commerce, while reducing overall development and deployment costs." As such, DNA divides client-server application development into three tiers:

- Navigation and user interface
- Business logic
- Data storage

In addition, DNA provides a host of services that help developers meet development goals. Those services include the following:

- Active Server Pages (ASP)
- COM components
- Component services
- Dynamic HTML (DHTML)
- Microsoft data access components
- Microsoft message queuing
- Windows security services

Active Directory

Active Directory is a distributed directory service that simplifies many of the tasks associated with accessing and maintaining networked resources and data. Using Active Directory, an administrator can manage an entire network from his or her desk rather than having to go from one workstation to another in order to gather the information. Active Directory, of course, does this while maintaining complete data security. In addition, both users and programmers can take advantage of Active Directory. Users get easy access to better online support, while programmers gain new tools to make their distributed applications more network-friendly.

MTS

MTS stands for *Microsoft Transaction Server*. According to Microsoft, MTS is "a new category of product that makes it easier to develop and deploy high-performance, scaleable, and reliable distributed applications. This is achieved by combining the technology of component-based development and deployment environments with the reliability and scalability of transaction processing monitors."

In MTS, transactions are units of execution that must be successful or unsuccessful fully. For example, if a user attempts to purchase a product over the Internet, the transaction must be completed fully or ignored. That is, users don't want their credit card information accepted if the connection goes down before the completion of the sale. To fulfill this promise, MTS transactions have the following attributes:

Atomicity	Every update in the entire transaction must be performed successfully or the entire transaction fails and no updates are recorded.
Consistency	When the transaction is complete, the results are always exactly as expected.

Isolation   One transaction cannot affect another.

Durability   The transaction should be capable of surviving reasonable levels of failure.

Summary

The Windows 2000 system provides many ways to manipulate the user interface using various API functions as well as COM interfaces such as `IShellLink`, `IPersistFile`, `IShellFolder`, `IMalloc`, and `IEnumIDList`.

Also discussed in this chapter:

- An application registers itself for drag-and-drop operations by calling the `DragAcceptFiles()` API function.
- An application handles drag-and-drop operations by responding to the `WM_DROPFILES` Windows message.
- The `DragQueryFile()` function returns the number of files dropped on an application's windows, as well as the names of the dropped files.
- An application calls the `DragFinish()` API function to finish a drag-and-drop operation.
- To initialize and uninitialize COM, an application calls the `CoInitializeEx()` and `CoUninitialize()` functions respectively.
- To create a COM object, an application can call the `CoCreateInstance()` API function.
- Using the `IShellLink` and `IPersistFile` COM interfaces, an application can create and store a shortcut.
- To display or remove an icon in the system tray, an application calls the `Shell_NotifyIcon()` function.
- Using the `IShellFolder`, `IMalloc`, and `IEnumIDList` COM interfaces, a program can manipulate the shell namespace.

Chapter 12

The Registry

In This Chapter

- Introducing the Registry
- Exploring the structure of the Registry
- Using the Registry Editor and Registry files
- Examining the Win32 Registry API
- Manipulating the Registry with the Registry API

One of the most mysterious parts of the Windows 2000 system is the Registry. The truth is that managing the Registry from your application is not as difficult as you may think. (It's certainly not any harder than handling files.) Although it's true that the Registry contains a seemingly endless amount of esoteric data, you don't need to pay attention to most of it. The average software developer needs to know only the basic structure of the Registry and a handful of Registry management functions. In this chapter, you see how to use the Registry in your applications.

Overview of the Registry

The *Registry* is much like a database that stores the settings needed to ensure that the Windows system and its hardware and applications can find the information they need to run correctly. In this role, the Registry replaces the `win.ini` file, as well as the application-created `.ini` files, that earlier versions of Windows used to store this important information. For example, where an application called MyApplication once stored its configuration information in a file called `MyApplication.ini`, this application now stores its configuration information in the Registry. There, it is available not only to itself but also to any other process that happens to need that information.

Because the Registry is the central repository for all Windows configuration information, as well as for data about everything from your favorite applications to the ActiveX controls installed on your system, the Registry is one complex beast. For this reason, many programmers are intimidated from managing the Registry in their applications — to the point that some applications still rely on `.ini` files to store configuration information. In the following sections, you discover that there's no reason to feel intimidated by the Registry as long as you know its general structure and the functions needed to manage the information stored there.

How the Registry Is Organized

Because there are many different types of information stored in the Registry, the Registry divides the information into five general areas — the names for which are called *keys*. The easiest way to understand the Registry's general organization is to view it with the *Registry Editor,* a Registry manipulation tool that comes with Windows. To run the Registry Editor, click your Start menu, choose the Run option, and type **regedit** into the dialog box that appears. When you run the Registry Editor, you see a window like that shown in Figure 12-1.

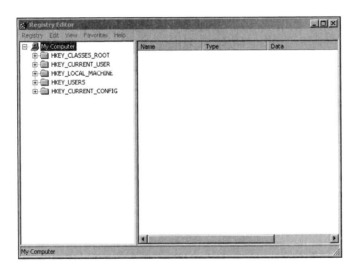

Figure 12-1: The Registry Editor

As you can see, the Registry Editor starts off by displaying the five general areas of the Registry. These areas have the key names HKEY_CLASSES_ROOT, HKEY_CURRENT_USER, HKEY_LOCAL_MACHINE, HKEY_USERS, HKEY_CURRENT_CONFIG, and HKEY_DYN_DATA. Each of these Registry areas contains a specific type of information, as shown in Table 12-1.

Table 12-1   The Main Registry Keys

Key Name	Description
HKEY_CLASSES_ROOT	Defines document, file-viewer, and interface-extension classes and properties. Also, provides the information that ensures DDE and OLE compatibility with the Windows 3.1 registration database.
HKEY_CURRENT_USER	Stores user preferences for the current user, including information about environment variables, program groups, printers, colors, and so on. You can store application preferences here as well.
HKEY_LOCAL_MACHINE	Stores information about the physical state of the computer system. You can find data associated with hardware and software installed on the machine, as well as plug-and-play and network security information.
HKEY_USERS	Stores the default user configuration, as well as the configurations for each user registered with the system. When new users log on, their configuration information is copied to the HKEY_CURRENT_USER section of the Registry.
HKEY_CURRENT_CONFIG	Stores hardware configuration information. This key is mapped to an HKEY_LOCAL_MACHINE subkey.
HKEY_DYN_DATA	Stores dynamic Registry data, which is data that changes frequently. Rather than storing this information on disk with the rest of the Registry data, processes, such as VxDs that support dynamic data, provide it at run time.

If you double-click one of the main keys in Registry Editor's window, the key expands to show its *subkeys* (as shown in Figure 12-2).

Clicking a subkey reveals even more subkeys. You can continue to click the revealed subkeys until you reach the Registry values stored in the most deeply nested subkey, as shown in Figure 12-3.

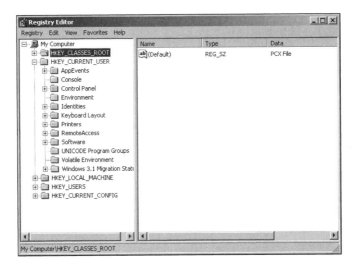

Figure 12-2: Displaying subkeys in Registry Editor

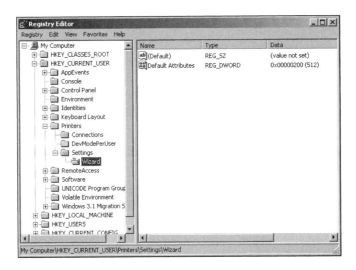

Figure 12-3: Displaying Registry values

The thing to notice about the Registry's organization is that it looks a whole lot like the file-system hierarchy you can display in Windows Explorer. In fact, you can equate *Registry keys* with folders on your hard drive. (The Registry Editor even displays a folder icon for keys.) Just like folders, keys are associated with no actual values except for their names. Similarly, you can think of *Registry values* as the files on your hard drive, in that Registry values are the objects that contain actual data. What kind of data? Table 12-2 lists the types of data that you can store as Registry values.

Table 12-2 Data Types Used in the Registry

Data Type	Description
REG_BINARY	Binary data.
REG_DWORD	32-bit number.
REG_DWORD_BIG_ENDIAN	32-bit number in which the low-order byte is the most significant byte of a word.
REG_DWORD_LITTLE_ENDIAN	32-bit number in the same format as REG_DWORD. Most commonly used in Windows NT and Windows 2000.
REG_EXPAND_SZ	Null-terminated Unicode or ANSI string that holds environment variables in their unexpanded forms.
REG_LINK	Unicode symbolic link.
REG_MULTI_SZ	Array of null-terminated strings. The array itself terminates with two null characters.
REG_NONE	No type.
REG_QWORD	64-bit number.
REG_QWORD_LITTLE_ENDIAN	The same as REG_QWORD.
REG_RESOURCE_LIST	Device-driver resource list.
REG_SZ	Null-terminated Unicode or ANSI string.

Manipulating the Registry

There are three main ways to modify the Registry. You can start the Registry Editor to add, delete, or edit entries; you can create Registry files and merge their contents with the Registry; or you can use the Registry functions provided by the Win32 API. Which method you use depends on the situation and your preferences.

Using the Registry Editor

If you need to make quick changes in your system's Registry, the Registry Editor is the way to go. Using the Registry Editor, you can search for keys, add keys, edit values, and more. You accomplish all this by accessing the commands on Registry Editor's menu bar. For example, Figure 12-4 shows the results of a first search for FrontPage. Note that, almost certainly, another search finds yet another FrontPage entry in the Registry (if FrontPage is installed on the system) because an application can, and usually does, place many different entries in the Registry.

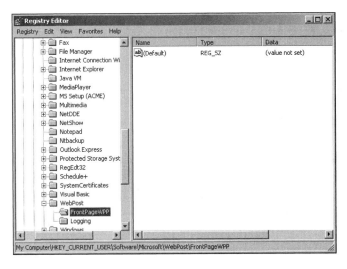

Figure 12-4: Searching for FrontPage in the Registry

Note

You must use care when editing your Registry because a mistake can result in an inability to start Windows.

Using the Registry Files

A *Registry file* is a special text file that you can import into, or export from, the Registry. If you look on the Registry Editor's Registry menu, you find the Import Registry File and Export Registry File commands. Your application's installation program can automate the merging of Registry files into the Registry. Moreover, you can do the merge by double-clicking the Registry file in Windows Explorer. Following is an example of the contents of a Registry file:

```
REGEDIT4

[HKEY_USERS\.DEFAULT\Control Panel\Desktop]
"DragFullWindows"="0"
"FontSmoothing"="0"
"Wallpaper"=""
"TileWallpaper"="0"
"ScreenSaveTimeOut"="840"
"UserPreferencemask"=hex:be,00,00,00
"WallpaperStyle"="0"
"ScreenSaveActive"="0"
"ScreenSaveLowPowerActive"="0"
"ScreenSavePowerOffActive"="0"
"CursorBlinkRate"="500"

[HKEY_USERS\.DEFAULT\Control Panel\Desktop\WindowMetrics]
```

```
"Shell Icon BPP"="16"
"IconSpacingFactor"="100"
"BorderWidth"="-15"
"ScrollWidth"="-240"
"ScrollHeight"="-240"
"CaptionWidth"="-270"
"CaptionHeight"="-270"
"SmCaptionWidth"="-195"
"SmCaptionHeight"="-225"
"MenuWidth"="-270"
"MenuHeight"="-270"
"IconSpacing"="-1125"
"IconVerticalSpacing"="-1125"
"MinAnimate"="0"

[HKEY_USERS\.DEFAULT\Control Panel\Desktop\ResourceLocale]
@="00000409"
```

You can see here that each Registry value is specified by the value's name in quotes followed by an equals sign and the actual value, also in quotes. Notice how the keys that lead to the values are expressed in a path not unlike the path you might see that leads to files on your disk drive.

Registry files are a good way to create default settings for an application when you first install the application. However, to record Registry settings that may change each time the application runs (for example, saving user preferences), you need to use Win32's Registry API. (I cover this topic in the next section.) Because you can use the Win32 Registry API to perform virtually any operation on the Registry, this chapter does not go into further detail on Registry files. For more information on this topic, please refer to the Windows documentation included with Visual C++.

Using the Registry API

The Win32 API provides a set of functions for managing the contents of the Registry. These operations include the usual adding and deleting of keys, searching for and acquiring values in the Registry, and much more. Table 12-3 lists and describes the most often used functions of the Win32 Registry API.

Table 12-3   The Win32 Registry API Functions

Function	Description
RegCloseKey()	Closes an open key
RegCreateKeyEx()	Creates a key
RegDeleteKey()	Deletes a key

Continued

Table 12-3 *(continued)*

Function	Description
RegDeleteValue()	Deletes a Registry value
RegEnumKeyEx()	Enumerates a key's subkeys
RegEnumValue()	Enumerates a key's values
RegFlushKey()	Flushes all Registry write operations
RegOpenKeyEx()	Opens a key
RegQueryInfoKey()	Returns information about a key
RegQueryValueEx()	Returns a Registry value
RegSetValueEx()	Sets a Registry value

You use the functions listed in Table 12-3 when writing Win32 (32-bit) applications, which (at this point) is all you should do. This is because, except for backwards compatibility, Win16 is obsolete. However, Windows still supports the Win16 Registry APIs to ensure that older applications run properly. Because you may encounter these functions in older source code, Table 12-4 lists and describes the Win16 Registry API functions. You should not use them in new projects.

Table 12-4 The Win16 Registry API Functions

Function	Description
RegCloseKey()	Closes an open key
RegCreateKey()	Creates a key
RegDeleteKey()	Deletes a key
RegEnumKey()	Enumerates a key's subkeys
RegOpenKey()	Opens a key
RegQueryValue()	Returns a Registry value
RegSetValue()	Sets a Registry value

The RegistryApp Sample Program

Location: `WinPrg5\Chap12\RegistryApp`

On this book's CD-ROM, you can find the RegistryApp application that demonstrates how to use the Win32 Registry API to record and read user preferences with the Registry. Specifically, when the user closes the application, RegistryApp remembers the size and position of its window. It then restores that size and position when the user restarts the application. To see RegistryApp in action, run `RegistryApp.exe`. When you do, you see a window like that shown in Figure 12-5.

Figure 12-5: The running RegistryApp application

Change the size and position of the window and then close the application. Finally, rerun the application, and it automatically restores its size and position. In the following sections, you explore the code that makes RegistryApp tick.

Writing User Preferences to the Registry

As you now know, when the user closes a Windows application, Windows generates a `WM_DESTROY` message. In the case of RegistryApp, the `WM_DESTROY` message causes a call to the `CMainFrame` class's `OnDestroy()` message-response function. This is where RegistryApp saves, into the Registry, the current size and position of its window. The `OnDestroy()` function looks like this:

```
void CMainFrame::OnDestroy()
{
    CFrameWnd::OnDestroy();

    // TODO: Add your message handler code here

    HKEY keyHandle1, keyHandle2, keyHandle3;
    CString str;
```

```
        DWORD disp;
        RECT rect;

        // Get the window's current size and position.
        GetWindowRect(&rect);
        DWORD xpos = rect.left;
        DWORD ypos = rect.top;
        DWORD width = rect.right - rect.left;
        DWORD height = rect.bottom - rect.top;

        // Open the Software key under HKEY_CURRENT_USER.
        RegOpenKeyEx(HKEY_CURRENT_USER, "Software",
            0, KEY_ALL_ACCESS, &keyHandle1);

        // Create the MyCompany key under Software.
        RegCreateKeyEx(keyHandle1, "MyCompany", 0, "",
            REG_OPTION_NON_VOLATILE, KEY_ALL_ACCESS, NULL,
            &keyHandle2, &disp);

        // Create the MyApplication key under MyCompany.
        RegCreateKeyEx(keyHandle2, "MyApplication", 0, "",
            REG_OPTION_NON_VOLATILE, KEY_ALL_ACCESS, NULL,
            &keyHandle3, &disp);

        // Add the XPosition value to MyApplication.
        RegSetValueEx(keyHandle3, "XPosition",
            0, REG_DWORD, (BYTE*)&xpos, sizeof(DWORD));

        // Add the YPosition value to MyApplication.
        RegSetValueEx(keyHandle3, "YPosition",
            0, REG_DWORD, (BYTE*)&ypos, sizeof(DWORD));

        // Add the Width value to MyApplication.
        RegSetValueEx(keyHandle3, "Width",
            0, REG_DWORD, (BYTE*)&width, sizeof(DWORD));

        // Add the Height value to MyApplication.
        LONG result = RegSetValueEx(keyHandle3, "Height",
            0, REG_DWORD, (BYTE*)&height, sizeof(DWORD));

        if (result != ERROR_SUCCESS)
            MessageBox("Registry error");

        // Close all the open keys.
        RegCloseKey(keyHandle1);
        RegCloseKey(keyHandle2);
        RegCloseKey(keyHandle3);
}
```

Now, examine the function line by line. `OnDestroy()` **first declares the variables it needs to complete its task:**

```
HKEY keyHandle1, keyHandle2, keyHandle3;
```

The `HKEY` data type, defined by Windows, is the data type you use for the key values that many of the Registry functions return or require as arguments. In this case, the function stores the handles to three Registry keys in the `keyHandle1`, `keyHandle2`, and `keyHandle3` variables.

The function also declares string, double-word, and `RECT` variables:

```
CString str;
DWORD disp;
RECT rect;
```

You see how RegistryApp uses these values as you explore the rest of the function, starting with the `RECT` structure. The function sets the contents of the `RECT` structure by calling `GetWindowRect()` to retrieve the size and position of the window:

```
// Get the window's current size and position.
GetWindowRect(&rect);
DWORD xpos = rect.left;
DWORD ypos = rect.top;
DWORD width = rect.right - rect.left;
DWORD height = rect.bottom - rect.top;
```

Now that the program has the window's size and position, it's time to open some Registry keys. The first step is to call `RegOpenKeyEx()` to open the Software subkey located under the `HKEY_CURRENT_USER` main key:

```
// Open the Software key under HKEY_CURRENT_USER.
RegOpenKeyEx(HKEY_CURRENT_USER, "Software",
    0, KEY_ALL_ACCESS, &keyHandle1);
```

Next, the program must create (or open, if the key already exists) the subkey under which the software distributor's application keys are stored. In this case, assume that the company that developed and distributes RegistryApp is named My Company. A call to `RegCreateKeyEx()` creates a new key for the company or opens an existing one:

```
// Create the MyCompany key under Software.
RegCreateKeyEx(keyHandle1, "MyCompany", 0, "",
    REG_OPTION_NON_VOLATILE, KEY_ALL_ACCESS, NULL,
    &keyHandle2, &disp);
```

As you can see, this function sports nine (yikes!) arguments. These arguments are described, in order, as follows:

keyHandle1	A handle to the key under which the new subkey is created.
"MyCompany"	The name of the key to open or create.
0	A reserved value that must always be 0.

Continued

Continued	
" "	A string that specifies the new object's class. For local-machine (vs. remote) Registry keys, set this value to a null string.
REG_OPTION_NON_VOLATILE	A value that specifies the key's options. Can be REG_OPTION_NON_VOLATILE (the default), REG_OPTION_VOLATILE, or REG_OPTION_BACKUP_RESTORE. For normal usage, specify REG_OPTION_NON_VOLATILE, meaning that the key remains in the Registry even after the system is restarted.
KEY_ALL_ACCESS	A value that specifies the key's access. Can be KEY_CREATE_LINK, KEY_CREATE_SUB_KEY, KEY_ENUMERATE_SUB_KEYS, KEY_EXECUTE, KEY_NOTIFY, KEY_QUERY_VALUE, KEY_SET_VALUE, KEY_ALL_ACCESS, KEY_READ, and KEY_WRITE. For most uses, specify KEY_ALL_ACCESS.
NULL	A pointer to a SECURITY_ATTRIBUTES structure that specifies security attributes for the key. For normal usage, simply supply a NULL value.
&keyHandle2	The address of the HKEY variable that receives the handle of the opened or created key.
&disp	The address of a DWORD value that receives the value REG_CREATED_NEW_KEY or REG_OPENED_EXISTING_KEY after the key is opened or created.

The RegCreateKeyEx() function returns a long integer value that indicates whether the function call succeeded. A return value of ERROR_SUCCESS indicates success; any other return value indicates an error. Except for the last call to the Registry API, the RegistryApp program doesn't check the return value of the function calls. This is because if any function call fails, they all will. Essentially, the result of the final call to retrieve a value from the Registry is enough to know whether the preceding function calls succeeded. If you need to locate a problem, however, you must check the return values of each function call.

The next step is to call RegCreateKeyEx() a second time to create or open the specific application's key. For example, assume that the name of the application that MyCompany is registering is MyApplication. The following function call creates or opens the application's key in the Registry:

```
// Create the MyApplication key under MyCompany.
RegCreateKeyEx(keyHandle2, "MyApplication", 0, "",
    REG_OPTION_NON_VOLATILE, KEY_ALL_ACCESS, NULL,
    &keyHandle3, &disp);
```

Now, the program can set the Registry values that represent the user's application preferences. RegistryApp does this with the `RegSetValueEx()` function:

```
// Add the XPosition value to MyApplication.
RegSetValueEx(keyHandle3, "XPosition",
    0, REG_DWORD, (BYTE*)&xpos, sizeof(DWORD));
```

The `RegSetValueEx()` function requires six arguments. The following list describes these arguments in the order they appear in the function call:

`keyHandle3`	A handle to the open key under which the value is stored or created
`"XPosition"`	A string that specifies the value's name
`0`	A reserved value that must be 0
`REG_DWORD`	The type of value that is stored; can be one of the data types listed in Table 12-2
`&xpos`	A pointer to the value that is associated with the value's name
`sizeof(DWORD)`	The size of the value

This first call to `RegSetValueEx()` stores the window's X position in the Registry. The program also must store the window's Y position, as well as its width and height. RegistryApp accomplishes this task with three additional calls to `RegSetValueEx()`:

```
// Add the YPosition value to MyApplication.
RegSetValueEx(keyHandle3, "YPosition",
    0, REG_DWORD, (BYTE*)&ypos, sizeof(DWORD));

// Add the Width value to MyApplication.
RegSetValueEx(keyHandle3, "Width",
    0, REG_DWORD, (BYTE*)&width, sizeof(DWORD));

// Add the Height value to MyApplication.
LONG result = RegSetValueEx(keyHandle3, "Height",
    0, REG_DWORD, (BYTE*)&height, sizeof(DWORD));
```

Notice that the program stores the result from the final call to `RegSetValueEx()`. The program uses `result` to determine whether the Registry value is stored successfully:

```
if (result != ERROR_SUCCESS)
    MessageBox("Registry error");
```

Finally, the last task is to close the open Registry keys like this:

```
// Close all the open keys.
RegCloseKey(keyHandle1);
RegCloseKey(keyHandle2);
RegCloseKey(keyHandle3);
```

Reading User Preferences from the Registry

When the user runs RegistryApp, MFC calls the main window class's `PreCreateWindow()` function. This is where the application can set the window's size and position before the window is displayed. Logically, then, this is where RegistryApp retrieves the user preferences from the Registry. In RegistryApp, the `PreCreateWindow()` function looks like this:

```
BOOL CMainFrame::PreCreateWindow(CREATESTRUCT& cs)
{
    if( !CFrameWnd::PreCreateWindow(cs) )
        return FALSE;
    // TODO: Modify the Window class or styles here by modifying
    //   the CREATESTRUCT cs

    HKEY keyHandle1, keyHandle2, keyHandle3;
    CString str;
    DWORD valType;
    DWORD xpos, ypos;
    DWORD width, height;
    DWORD valSize = sizeof(DWORD);

    // Open the Software key under HKEY_CURRENT_USER.
    RegOpenKeyEx(HKEY_CURRENT_USER, "Software",
        0, KEY_ALL_ACCESS, &keyHandle1);

    // Open the MyCompany key under Software.
    RegOpenKeyEx(keyHandle1, "MyCompany",
        0, KEY_ALL_ACCESS, &keyHandle2);

    // Open the MyApplication key under MyCompany.
    RegOpenKeyEx(keyHandle2, "MyApplication",
        0, KEY_ALL_ACCESS, &keyHandle3);

    // Get the value of XPosition.
    RegQueryValueEx(keyHandle3, "XPosition",
        0, (LPDWORD) &valType, (LPBYTE) &xpos,
        (LPDWORD) &valSize);
```

```
    // Get the value of YPosition.
    RegQueryValueEx(keyHandle3, "YPosition",
        0, (LPDWORD) &valType, (LPBYTE) &ypos,
        (LPDWORD) &valSize);

    // Get the value of Width.
    RegQueryValueEx(keyHandle3, "Height",
        0, (LPDWORD) &valType, (LPBYTE) &height,
        (LPDWORD) &valSize);

    // Get the value of Height.
    LONG result = RegQueryValueEx(keyHandle3, "Width",
        0, (LPDWORD) &valType, (LPBYTE) &width,
        (LPDWORD) &valSize);

    if (result == ERROR_SUCCESS)
    {
        cs.cx = width;
        cs.cy = height;
        cs.x = xpos;
        cs.y = ypos;
    }

    // Close all the open keys.
    RegCloseKey(keyHandle1);
    RegCloseKey(keyHandle2);
    RegCloseKey(keyHandle3);

    return TRUE;
}
```

Now, examine the function line by line. `PreCreateWindow()` first declares the variables it needs to complete its task:

```
HKEY keyHandle1, keyHandle2, keyHandle3;
CString str;
DWORD valType;
DWORD xpos, ypos;
DWORD width, height;
DWORD valSize = sizeof(DWORD);
```

You see how RegistryApp uses these values as you explore the rest of the function. Now the program starts to manipulate the Registry by opening the `Software` subkey located under the `HKEY_CURRENT_USER` main key:

```
// Open the Software key under HKEY_CURRENT_USER.
RegOpenKeyEx(HKEY_CURRENT_USER, "Software",
    0, KEY_ALL_ACCESS, &keyHandle1);
```

Next, the program must open the subkey under which the software distributor's application keys are stored:

```
// Open the MyCompany key under Software.
RegOpenKeyEx(keyHandle1, "MyCompany",
    0, KEY_ALL_ACCESS, &keyHandle2);
```

The next step is to call RegOpenKeyEx() a second time to open the specific application's key:

```
// Open the MyApplication key under MyCompany.
RegOpenKeyEx(keyHandle2, "MyApplication",
    0, KEY_ALL_ACCESS, &keyHandle3);
```

Now, the program can start to retrieve the user-preference values from the Registry by calling the RegQueryValueEx() function:

```
// Get the value of XPosition.
RegQueryValueEx(keyHandle3, "XPosition",
    0, (LPDWORD) &valType, (LPBYTE) &xpos,
    (LPDWORD) &valSize);
```

The RegQueryValueEx() function requires six arguments, which are described in order as follows:

keyHandle3	A handle to the key under which the value is stored
"XPosition"	The name of the value to retrieve
0	A reserved value that must be 0
&valType	The address of a DWORD that receives the type of data stored in the Registry value
&xpos	A pointer to the variable that receives the value
&valSize	The size of the value

To get the remaining user-preference values, the program calls RegQueryValueEx() an additional three times:

```
// Get the value of YPosition.
RegQueryValueEx(keyHandle3, "YPosition",
    0, (LPDWORD) &valType, (LPBYTE) &ypos,
    (LPDWORD) &valSize);

// Get the value of Width.
RegQueryValueEx(keyHandle3, "Height",
    0, (LPDWORD) &valType, (LPBYTE) &height,
    (LPDWORD) &valSize);

// Get the value of Height.
LONG result = RegQueryValueEx(keyHandle3, "Width",
    0, (LPDWORD) &valType, (LPBYTE) &width,
    (LPDWORD) &valSize);
```

If the Registry function calls succeed, the program sets the members of the cs structure. This structure controls the window's size and position:

```
if (result == ERROR_SUCCESS)
{
    cs.cx = width;
    cs.cy = height;
    cs.x = xpos;
    cs.y = ypos;
}
```

Finally, RegistryApp closes all open keys:

```
// Close all the open keys.
RegCloseKey(keyHandle1);
RegCloseKey(keyHandle2);
RegCloseKey(keyHandle3);
```

Summary

Managing the Registry can be as simple or as complex as you need. For most applications, however, a few function calls to the Registry API are all it takes to move information to and from the Registry. In this chapter, you learned the techniques needed to accomplish these tasks. In the next chapter, you learn to create installation programs for your applications.

Also discussed in this chapter:

- The Registry is much like a database that stores the settings needed to ensure that the Windows system and its hardware and applications can find the information they need to run correctly.
- If you need to make quick changes in your system's Registry, use the Registry Editor.
- A Registry file is a special text file that you can import into, or export from, the Registry.
- An application calls the RegOpenKeyEx() API function to open a registry key.
- To create a registry key, an application calls the RegCreateKeyEx() function.
- To set a registry value, an application calls the RegSetValueEx() API function.
- Using the RegQueryValueEx() API function, an application can retrieve a registry value.

Chapter 13

Installing User Applications

In This Chapter

- Exploring different packaging models
- Installing and running InstallShield
- Creating a basic installation package

Every Windows product needs a way for the user to install the application on his or her machine. Unfortunately, creating an installation program by hand can be a grueling process. Thank the gods of the binary realm that Visual C++ includes a sophisticated tool called InstallShield that makes creating an installation program, if not exactly a snap, then at least hugely easier than doing it the old-fashioned way. In this chapter, you get a hands-on look at InstallShield and the process of creating installation packages for your applications.

Product Packaging

How you package your application depends a great deal on how the application is distributed and where it is used. For example, if you put together a product for commercial distribution in a shrink-wrapped box, you package the product differently than if you package a shareware product for distribution over the Internet. (In this use of the term, *packaging* means the way the files that comprise the product are distributed to the user — not the packaging materials, such as a box and manual.)

With the shrink-wrap packaging model, you prepare your product's files to distribute commercially — usually placing the installation files on a CD-ROM or, less commonly these days, on floppy disks. This type of packaging requires an appealing, high-quality installation interface that the user can use to install the product with as few headaches as possible. If you skimp on the installation user interface, you can plan on a lot of technical support phone calls, as well as a lot of bad will generated toward your company.

When packaging a product for use within a company, however, the installation interface needs to be more flexible than fancy in order to accommodate the many different options and features that you can install on a LAN. The size of the installation is usually less important — unlike the shareware packaging model in which you need to create the smallest distribution file you can because your main distribution channel probably is the Internet (and other online resources).

The same is true if you plan to distribute the application on floppy disks (which are considerably cheaper to produce than CD-ROMs). Creating a small shareware distribution package can be a challenge, requiring that you fine-tune and strip the application's resources (graphics, help files, and so on) to their minimum. Often, a shareware developer creates a trial version of the product that leaves out the extras in order to accommodate the downloading requirements of the potential user.

Whatever type of installation program you need, InstallShield can help you create it. In the following sections, you get hands-on experience with InstallShield as you create a set of installation files for a simple application.

Using InstallShield

Regardless of your chosen packaging model, Visual C++ comes with an excellent tool called *InstallShield* that generates high-quality installation packages. If you install InstallShield at the same time you install Visual C++, you can find it in Visual C++'s Tools menu. You also can run InstallShield from its command on the Start menu, which is located in the Microsoft Visual Studio 6.0 Tools submenu. If you haven't installed InstallShield yet, you can find its `setup.exe` file in the `Ishield` directory on one of your Visual Studio or Visual C++ CD-ROMs.

In this section, you use InstallShield to create a CD-ROM distribution package — the most common of the installation media types. Because InstallShield is such a complex program (although much easier to use than trying to create your installation program by hand), this chapter doesn't have the space to go into detail on many of InstallShield's options. However, by creating a basic installation program, you learn enough about InstallShield to get started. For more information on InstallShield, you can consult the included Help files or log onto InstallShield's Web site at `http://support.installshield.com/docs/default.asp`.

Determining the Files to Package

No matter what packaging model you need to use, the first step is to figure out exactly what files must be part of the installation package. Obviously, there is more than one solution to this problem because every application uses different types of files. Your application might be as simple as a single executable file or it might require library files, help files, data files, and any number of other types of files. As a programmer, you need to know what these files are, where to find them, and how to package them.

Not all files your application uses are necessarily obvious. For example, if you link to the dynamic MFC libraries rather than the static libraries, you need to include the appropriate DLLs — mfc42.dll and msvcrt.dll — in your application package. The user's machine may or may not have them installed already. To find such dependencies for your application, use the Depends application that comes packaged with the Windows SDK and usually is installed with Microsoft Visual Studio. Figure 13-1 shows the Depends utility.

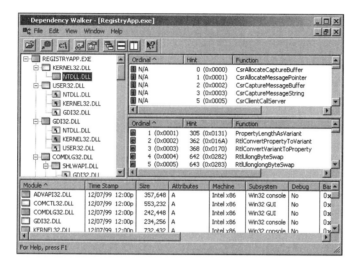

Figure 13-1: The Depends utility can locate application dependencies.

Note You do not need to install all dependencies shown in the Depends utility's window on the user's machine. For example, the kernel32.dll, gdi32.dll, advapi32.dll, and user32.dll libraries shown in Figure 13-1 are all files installed at the time the user installs Windows.

Creating an Application to Install

Once you have all your files gathered, you can get started packing them into a complete installation program for your application. In this section, you use InstallShield to produce such an install program. First, though, you need an application to install. For the purposes of this demonstration, just about any application will do. But to keep things simple, and to keep us all on the same page, load up Visual C++ and create an MFC AppWizard application using all the AppWizard defaults. That is, when the MFC AppWizard - Step 1 dialog box appears (Figure 13-2), simply click the Finish button.

Note If you haven't installed InstallShield yet, now's the time to do it. The remainder of this chapter relies on InstallShield for Microsoft Visual C++ 6, which comes with Visual C++.

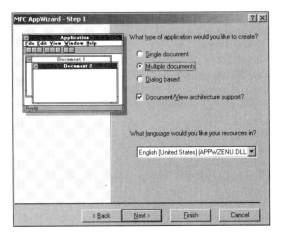

Figure 13-2: Click the Finish button to create the default application.

After creating the project, build and run it. The project's main window should look like Figure 13-3. This is the application for which you'll create an installation program.

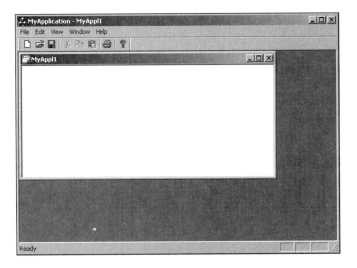

Figure 13-3: The MyApplication project's main window

Starting an InstallShield Project

Perform the following steps to start an InstallShield project. This project serves as the starting point for the complete installation program that you create in this chapter.

1. Run InstallShield from your Start menu. When you do, you see the window shown in Figure 13-4.

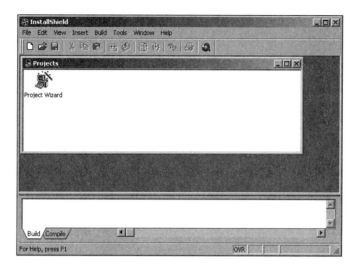

Figure 13-4: InstallShield's main window

2. Double-click the Project Wizard icon in the Projects window. The Project Wizard - Welcome dialog box appears. Type **My Application** into the Application Name box and type **My Company** into the Company Name box, as shown in Figure 13-5.

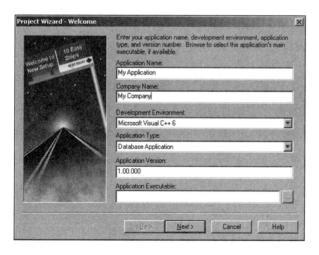

Figure 13-5: The Project Wizard - Welcome dialog box

3. Click the button to the right of the Application Executable box (the button with the ellipsis), and then use the Open dialog box that appears to locate the `MyApplication.exe` file. When you do, the path for the file appears in the Application Executable text box.

4. Click the Next button. The Project Wizard - Choose Dialogs dialog box appears. This is where you choose the dialog boxes that you want to appear during your application's installation. For this demonstration, leave only the Choose Destination Location and Setup Complete checkboxes selected (as shown in Figure 13-6).

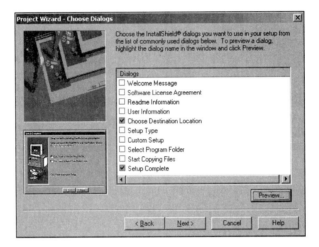

Figure 13-6: Use this dialog box to select the dialog boxes that appear during application installation.

5. Click the Next button. The Project Wizard - Choose Target Platforms dialog box appears. Here you can select the platforms on which you run your application, as shown in Figure 13-7. For this project, leave all platforms selected.

6. Click the Next button to view the language selections, as shown in Figure 13-8. This version of InstallShield supports only English, so leave everything as it is.

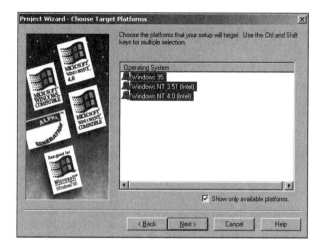

Figure 13-7: You need to tell InstallShield the platforms on which you want to run the application.

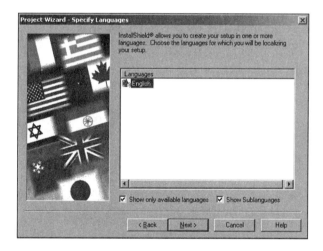

Figure 13-8: In this dialog box, you can select the supported languages.

7. Press the Next button, and the Project Wizard - Specify Setup Types dialog box appears (see Figure 13-9). This is where you can specify different types of installations. By now, you're familiar with the Compact, Custom, and Typical types of installations; I'm sure you have seen them many times as you've installed software on your machine. However, because you don't need different installation types for this example, turn off all the selections in this dialog box.

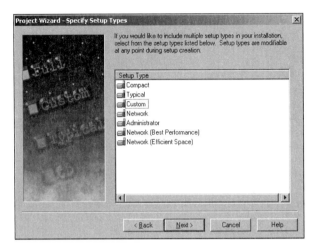

Figure 13-9: Here's where you specify the different installation types your installation program supports.

8. Click the Next button, and the Project Wizard - Specify Components dialog box appears (see Figure 13-10). This is where you tell InstallShield how you divide your installation into components. A *component* is a single, but complete, unit that can include one or more files. For example, when you install Visual Studio, a dialog box displays components such as Visual C++, Visual Basic, and Visual J++. In this case, the only components you need to install are the program files and the shared DLLs, so remove the Example Files and Help Files components from the Components frame. (To remove a component, select it and click the Delete button).

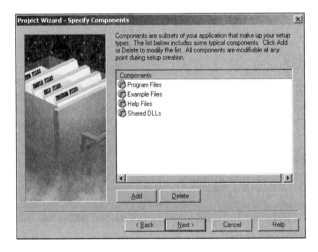

Figure 13-10: Every installation is comprised of components.

9. Click the Next button. The Project Wizard - Specify File Groups dialog box appears. Components are comprised of file groups, which are the files needed to install the component. For this demonstration, you need only the Program Executable Files and Shared DLLs file groups. Delete the others so that the dialog box looks like Figure 13-11.

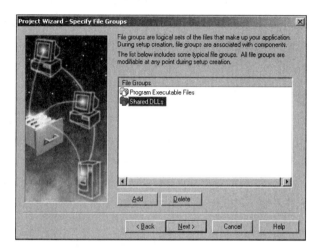

Figure 13-11: Components are comprised of file groups.

10. Click the Next button, and the Project Wizard - Summary dialog box appears, as shown in Figure 13-12. Click the Finish button to create the new project.

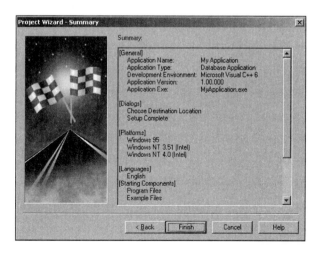

Figure 13-12: The Summary dialog box lists all the choices you made.

At this point, the InstallShield window looks like Figure 13-13. To the left is a tabbed window in which you can select the various elements of the installation. You need to modify much of the information associated with the pages in this pane. To the right is a window that displays your installation's script. You don't need to modify the displayed code by hand—although you can if you want. Instead, use InstallShield's options to specify the details needed to complete the script.

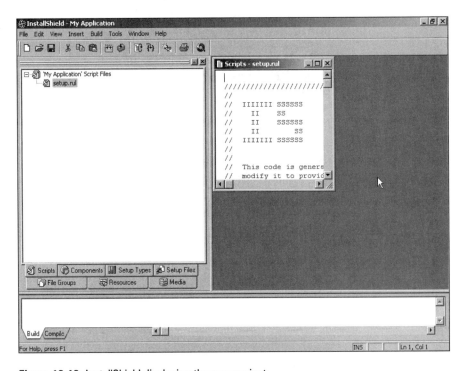

Figure 13-13: InstallShield displaying the new project

Completing Component Setup

All you really have now is an installation shell. InstallShield requires a lot more information to complete the installation program. The first thing you should do is complete the setup of the installation components. Although you told InstallShield about the components you want to include, you haven't told InstallShield any details about the components yet. Perform the following steps to complete this important task.

1. Click the Components tab in InstallShield's left-hand pane. The Component-Program Files window appears (see Figure 13-14). In case you haven't figured it out (wake up!), this is where you supply information about the Program Files component.

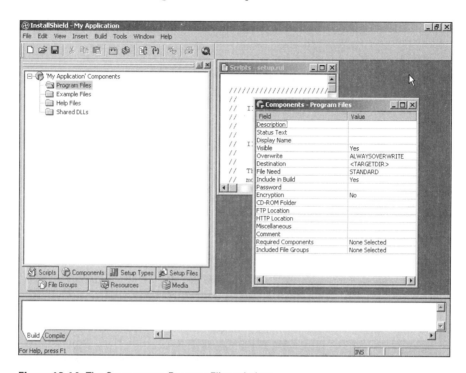

Figure 13-14: The Components-Program Files window

2. Double-click the Description field. The Properties dialog box, where you can enter a description for this component, appears. The installation program displays to the user the description you enter here, so don't use a lot of technical jargon. In this case, enter this text: **This component comprises the files needed to run the MyApplication application.** (Refer to Figure 13-15.) Click the OK button to add the description to the Components - Program Files window.

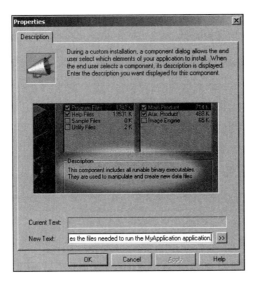

Figure 13-15: Entering a component description

3. Using the same procedure, set the Status Text field by typing the following: **Copying program files....** The install program displays this message to the user as it copies the Program Files component to the user's machine.

4. Double-click the Required Components field. The Required Components page of the Properties dialog box appears. Here, you tell InstallShield whether any components require the installation of other components. In this case, the Shared DLLs component must be installed with the Program Files component because the application does not run without it. Click the Shared DLLs entry, followed by the Add button. The dialog box then looks like Figure 13-16. Click OK to finalize your selection.

5. Double-click the Included File Groups field. The Included File Groups page of the Properties dialog box appears (see Figure 13-17). Here, you tell InstallShield the file groups needed to install the Program Files component.

Chapter 13: Installing User Applications **497**

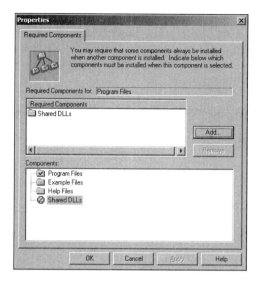

Figure 13-16: The Shared DLLs is a required component.

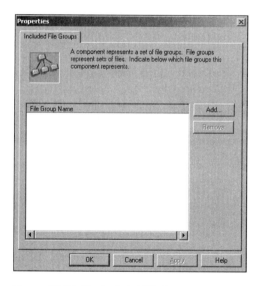

Figure 13-17: The Included File Groups page of the Properties dialog box

6. Click the Add button to display the file groups defined for this project. The Add File Group dialog box appears, as shown in Figure 13-18. This application has only one file group in the Program Files component. Click Program Executable Files and then OK to associate this file group with the Program Files component.

Figure 13-18: The Add File Group dialog box

7. Click OK in the Properties dialog box. Your Components - Program Files window now should look like Figure 13-19.

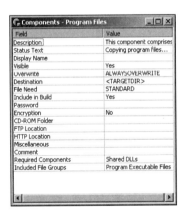

Figure 13-19: The finished entries in the Component - Program Files window

Set up the Shared DLLs component using the same process you use for the Program Files component:

- In the Description field, enter **Libraries required by the application.**
- In the Status Text field, enter **Copying library files....**
- On the Included File Groups page, select the Shared DLLs file group.

The finished Components - Shared DLLs window should look like Figure 13-20.

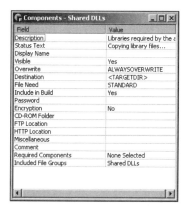

Figure 13-20: The finished entries in the Component - Shared DLLs window

You're finished setting up your installation project's components. The next step is to set up the file groups, which you do in the following section.

Completing File Group Setup

Your installation program is much closer to completion, but InstallShield still requires a bit more information. Now, you must complete setting up the installation's file groups. In the previous section, you told InstallShield all about the components you want to include — even telling InstallShield which file groups go with which components — but you haven't told InstallShield any details about the file groups yet. You remedy that problem by performing the following steps to complete the installation's file groups.

1. Click the File Groups tab in InstallShield's left-hand pane. The File Groups - Program Executable Files window appears (see Figure 13-21). However, you don't need this window to set up your file groups for this basic installation project.

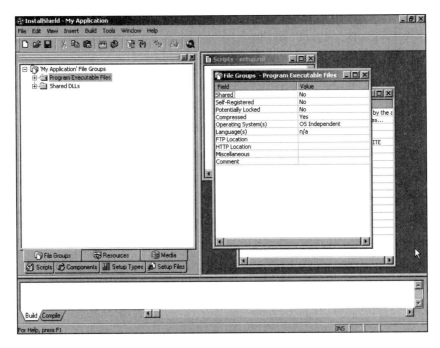

Figure 13-21: The File Groups - Program Executable Files window

2. Click the plus sign to the left of the Program Executable Files file group in the InstallShield's left-hand pane. Then, click the Links entry that appears. When you do, the File Groups - Program Executable Files\Links window appears (as shown in Figure 13-22).

3. Right-click inside the File Groups - Program Executable Files\Links window and select the Insert File Link(s) command from the pop-up menu that appears. The Insert file link(s) into File Group dialog box appears. Select the MyApplication.exe file, as shown in Figure 13-23, and click Open. The file appears in the window.

4. Follow the same procedure for the Shared DLLs file group. In this group, add the mfc42.dll and msvcrt.dll files; you can find these files in several places on your hard disk. Just do a search to locate them.

You're finished setting up your installation project's file groups. The next step is to tell InstallShield where to place your application's shortcut on the Start menu.

Chapter 13: Installing User Applications 501

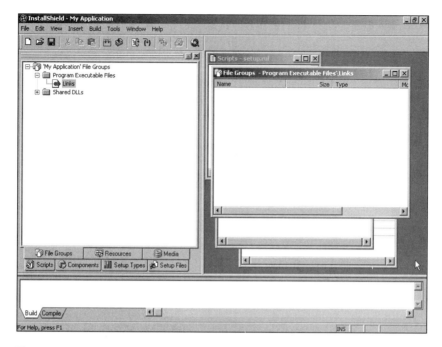

Figure 13-22: The File Groups - Program Executable Files\Links window

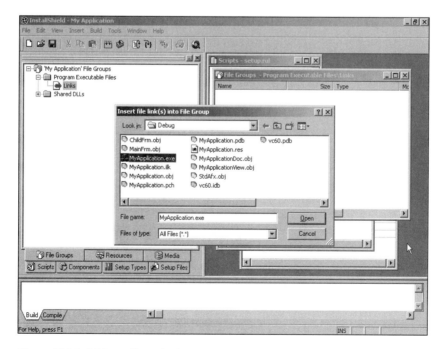

Figure 13-23: Adding a file to the file group

Creating the Media

Your final task is to select the type of media you want for the installation, which you can do with InstallShield's Media Build Wizard. To complete this task and build the final installation files, perform the following steps.

1. Select the Media Build Wizard command from InstallShield's Build menu. The Media Build Wizard window appears, as shown in Figure 13-24.

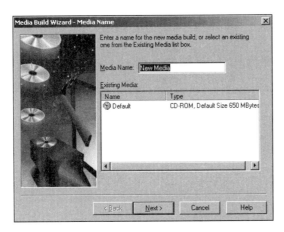

Figure 13-24: The Media Build Wizard window

2. Click the Default entry in the Existing Media list. This selects a CD-ROM installation. Click the Next button, and the Disk Type page of the wizard appears, as shown in Figure 13-25. The CD-ROM entry should be selected already in this window. Notice, however, the other media types you can choose.

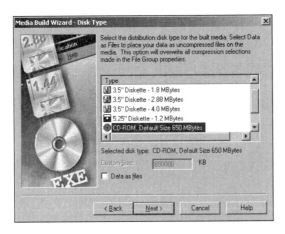

Figure 13-25: The Disk Type page of the Media Build Wizard

3. Click the Next button (leaving the CD-ROM media selected). The Build Type page appears. Select the Full Build option, as shown in Figure 13-26.

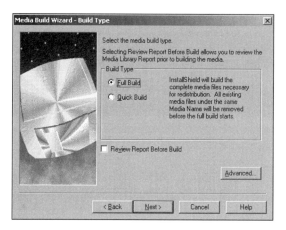

Figure 13-26: You want to perform a full build.

4. Click the Next button three more times, making note of the different wizard pages that appear. (You shouldn't need to change any of the information on these pages.) On the Summary page (see Figure 13-27), click the Finish button to generate your installation files.

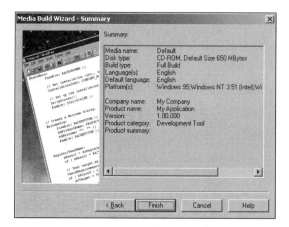

Figure 13-27: The Summary page displays all your selections.

After building your installation project, you can find the final files on your hard disk (as shown in Figure 13-28). These are the files that you burn onto the installation CD-ROM. You can, however, test the installation without actually making a CD-ROM. Just run your installation's `setup.exe` program.

InstallShield not only installs the application, but it also sets things up so that the user easily can uninstall the application from the application list in Control Panel's Add/Remove Programs properties window (shown in Figure 13-29).

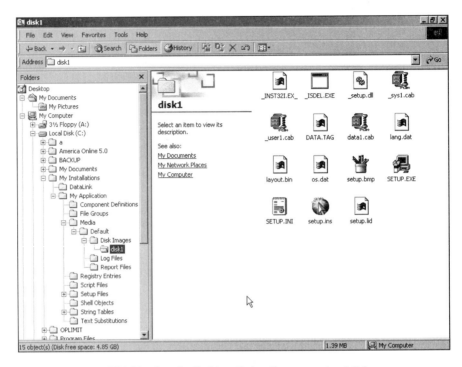

Figure 13-28: InstallShield writes the final installation files to your hard disk.

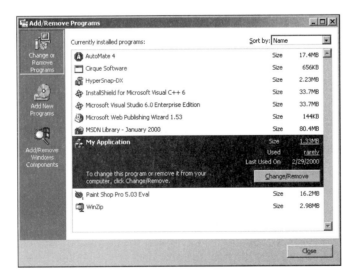

Figure 13-29: InstallShield also sets up the application so that you can uninstall it easily.

Chapter 13: Installing User Applications

PROBLEMS & SOLUTIONS

Adding the Application to the Start Menu

PROBLEM: *When I install my application, I want a shortcut added to the user's Start menu. How can I accomplish this with InstallShield?*

SOLUTION: Instructing InstallShield to add an application shortcut to the user's Start menu is fairly easy. Using the installation you develop in this chapter as an example, simply perform the following steps.

1. Click the Resources tab in InstallShield's left-hand pane. The Resources pane appears, in which you can see the String Table, Registry Entries, and Shell Objects selections (as shown in Figure 13-30). You may have to click the plus sign to the left of the "My Application Resources" entry to display the selections.

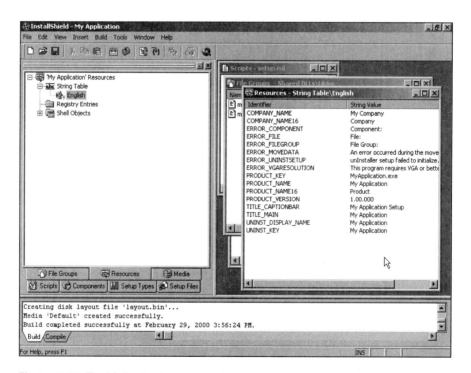

Figure 13-30: The MyApplication project's Resources pane

Continued

2. Click the plus sign to the left of the Shell Objects item to display the Explorer Shell entry. Continue opening the subfolders until you open the Programs folder, as shown in Figure 13-31.

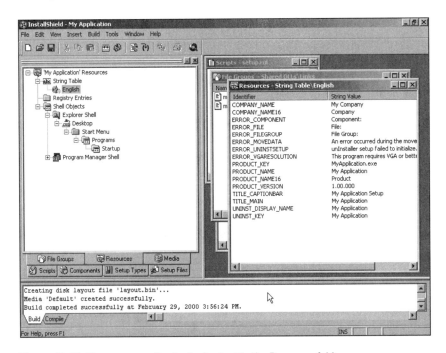

Figure 13-31: Place your application's shortcut in the Programs folder.

3. Right-click the Programs folder. Click the New command on the menu that appears and then select the Shortcut command from the submenu. Change the shortcut's name to My Application, as shown in Figure 13-32.

4. In the Shell Objects - Shortcuts window, double-click the Shortcut Text field. The Shortcut Properties dialog box appears. Enter **My Application** into the Shortcut Text text box. This text appears in the user's Start menu.

5. In the Target text box, type <TARGETDIR>\MyApplication.exe. This entry tells InstallShield where to find the file that must be associated with the shortcut. The <TARGETDIR> string is a variable that holds the path where the application is installed. You can't enter this path explicitly because the user may decide to install the application in a different location than the one the installation program suggests.

6. Enter 0 into the Icon Index box. This tells InstallShield that the icon to display in the Start menu is the first icon defined in the application's executable file. If the icon is defined in a different file, you enter the path to the file in the Icon File text box. When you're finished, the Shortcut Properties dialog box should look like Figure 13-33.

Continued

Chapter 13: Installing User Applications   **507**

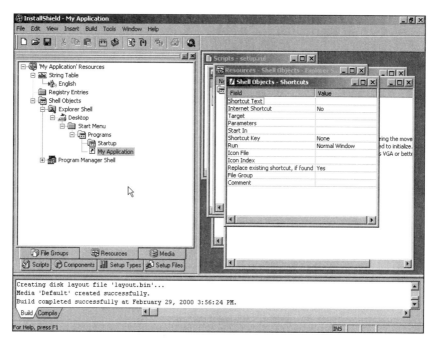

Figure 13-32: The new shortcut's name is My Application.

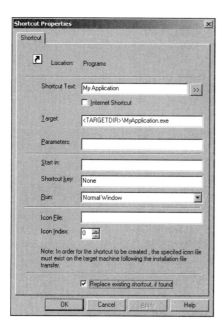

Figure 13-33: Defining the application's Start menu shortcut

Continued

7. Click OK to close the dialog box and finalize your entries, which appear in the Shell Objects - Shortcuts window (see Figure 13-34).

Figure 13-34: The Shell Objects - Shortcuts window

8. Double-click File Group in the Shell Objects - Shortcuts window. The Shortcut Properties dialog box appears containing the File Group page, as shown in Figure 13-35. Select Program Executable Files and click OK.

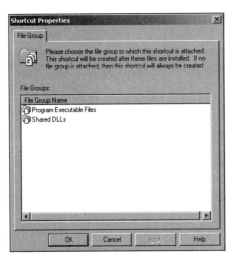

Figure 13-35: The File Group page

After completing these steps, you must rebuild the installation to ensure that your changes become part of your application installation package.

Summary

Although there are a lot of details to deal with, creating an installation program using InstallShield is much easier than trying to write one by hand. In fact, you can create your application's installation files without writing a single line of code — which is hard to beat. In the next part of this book, you learn about system programming techniques such as handling memory, processes, and input devices.

Also discussed in this chapter:

- Installation methods depend upon how the program will be distributed.
- You can use the Depends tool to discover the files on which your application depends.
- An installation comprises one or more components, which are a set of related file groups.
- Components comprise one or more file groups, which are sets of related files.
- After providing InstallShield with all your installation's details, you must specify a media type, which is the type of media that'll be used to distribute the application.

Part III
OS Core Programming

Chapter 14: Process Control

Chapter 15: Input Devices: The Mouse and the Keyboard

Chapter 16: File Handling

Chapter 17: The Clipboard

Chapter 14

Process Control

In This Chapter

- Understanding processes, threads, and priorities
- Exploring user interface threads and worker threads
- Using thread synchronization

Windows 2000 is a complex operating system that does an impressive job juggling multiple processes so that they seem to execute concurrently. From the user's point of view, Windows 2000's multitasking enables Windows to run multiple applications at the same time. Windows 2000 programmers, however, know that there's a lot more going on under the hood, where each application may contain several threads. Each of these threads, in turn, acts as a kind of mini-process.

Programming multiple threads can be a tricky process. You can't just throw a bunch of code into a thread and expect everything to run smoothly. You must be concerned with how the threads work together, and especially how the threads use shared resources. In this chapter, you learn a few thread programming tricks that might keep you out of trouble.

Processes, Threads, and Priorities

Under Windows 2000, a *process* is more or less equivalent to a running application. For example, when you run your Web browser, you're creating a Windows process. But a process doesn't necessarily have to have a window or even appear on the screen at all. A *thread,* on the other hand, is a distinct path of execution within a process. All processes have at least one initial thread, which is called the *primary thread.* A process may also start any number of *secondary threads,* which can perform concurrent tasks on behalf of the process.

Priority Settings for Processes and Threads

Each process and thread has a *priority* setting that determines when it runs and how much CPU time it gets. Specifically, Windows 2000's scheduler assigns CPU time to each process and thread based on the priority of the process and its thread. These priorities change constantly as Windows attempts to keep every thread running smoothly.

Processes are assigned to one of six priority classes, defined by Windows 2000:

ABOVE_NORMAL_PRIORITY_CLASS	Process is scheduled between NORMAL_PRIORITY_CLASS and HIGH_PRIORITY_CLASS processes.
BELOW_NORMAL_PRIORITY_CLASS	Process is scheduled under NORMAL_PRIORITY_CLASS processes.
HIGH_PRIORITY_CLASS	Process is scheduled over IDLE_PRIORITY_CLASS and NORMAL_PRIORITY_CLASS processes.
IDLE_PRIORITY_CLASS	Process is scheduled only when all other processes are blocked (i.e., have no messages to process).
NORMAL_PRIORITY_CLASS	Process is scheduled as normal.
REALTIME_PRIORITY_CLASS	Process is scheduled over all other priority classes.

Normally, a process should be assigned the NORMAL_PRIORITY_CLASS priority level. The other priority classes are for special circumstances. The HIGH_PRIORITY_CLASS and REALTIME_ PRIORITY_CLASS, in particular, should be used with caution, as they are capable of slowing other processes to a crawl.

Always remember that the CPU is a shared resource and that other applications running on the user's system are vying for their fair share of CPU time. Never set a process's or thread's priority level higher than it needs to be. In most cases, the NORMAL_PRIORITY_CLASS or THREAD_PRIORITY_NORMAL setting works just fine.

Threads also get a *relative* priority setting that's calculated from both the priority that the programmer requests for the thread and the priority of the thread's containing process. This final thread priority, which can be a value from 0 to 31, is called the *base priority level.* Windows 2000 defines thread priority classes to enable you to set the appropriate priority level for a thread's task. For example, a thread that receives data from a modem requires a higher priority than a thread that reads data from a disk file because the modem thread cannot afford to miss even a single byte of incoming data, whereas the file thread's data is available whenever the thread needs it. Table 14-1 lists the thread priority classes and their descriptions.

Table 14-1   Thread Priority Classes

Thread Priority Classes	Descriptions
THREAD_PRIORITY_IDLE	Thread's base priority level is 1 when the thread is contained in a HIGH_ PRIORITY_CLASS or lower process. Thread's base priority level is 16 when the thread is contained in a REALTIME_ PRIORITY_ CLASS process.
THREAD_PRIORITY_LOWEST	Thread's base priority level is two less than the containing process's priority level.
THREAD_PRIORITY_BELOW_NORMAL	Thread's base priority level is one less than the containing process's priority level.
THREAD_PRIORITY_NORMAL	Thread's base priority level is the same as the containing process's priority level.
THREAD_PRIORITY_ABOVE_NORMAL	Thread's base priority level is one higher than the containing process's priority level.
THREAD_PRIORITY_HIGHEST	Thread's base priority level is two higher than the containing process's priority level.
THREAD_PRIORITY_CRITICAL	Thread's base priority level is 15 when the thread is contained in a HIGH_ PRIORITY_CLASS or lower process. Thread's base priority level is 31 when the thread is contained in a REALTIME_ PRIORITY_ CLASS process.

Normally, a high-priority thread gets the first crack at CPU time. The high-priority thread then runs until it no longer has messages to process, at which point Windows schedules another thread.

Because most threads — including high-priority threads — spend a lot of time waiting for messages, low-priority threads usually get all the CPU time they need. However, Windows raises the priority level of threads that haven't run for a while in order to ensure that every thread gets its fair share of CPU time. Windows may also raise a thread's priority if that thread is holding a resource needed by a higher-priority thread. This is because the higher-priority thread is effectively blocked until the lower-priority thread releases the shared resource. Finally, Windows slightly raises the priority of threads whose containing processes are in the foreground application. Conversely, Windows slightly lowers the priority of threads whose containing processes are in the background.

You can temporarily set a thread's priority to a higher level in order to ensure better performance for the user. (This is what Windows does when a process moves from the background to the foreground.) However, when the thread's need for a higher priority expires, remember to return the priority to its previous lower setting.

MFC provides a special class for threads, called `CWinThread`. You can derive your own thread classes from `CWinThread` and then use the class's member functions to manipulate the thread. You can do this in two ways, depending upon whether you're creating a worker thread or a user interface thread.

Worker Threads and User Interface Threads

Windows applications programmed with MFC feature two types of threads: *worker threads* and *user interface (UI) threads*. A *UI thread* processes Windows messages and so can create and manage user-interface elements such as windows and controls. A *worker thread* does not process Windows messages and is used to perform background tasks, such as controlling an animation sequence or calculating the contents of a spreadsheet.

Creating a Worker Thread

Obviously, because a worker thread handles no Windows messages, it's often much easier to program than a UI thread. In fact, in your MFC programs, you can get a worker thread going with a single function call:

```
CWinThread* thread = AfxBeginThread(ThreadProc, pParam);
```

This function call creates and runs a thread with normal priority. `ThreadProc` is the address of the function that represents the thread, and `pParam` is a 32-bit value that is passed to the thread function. In other words, when the preceding call executes, MFC calls `ThreadProc()`, running the function as a secondary thread. `ThreadProc()` receives the `pParam` value as its single parameter, as you can see in the following `ThreadProc()` signature:

```
UINT ThreadProc(LPVOID pParam);
```

Of course, you can call your thread's function anything you like; you don't have to stick with `ThreadProc()`. For example, the following is a thread function that displays a message box on the screen and then exits, ending the thread:

```
UINT MessageThread(LPVOID pParam)
{
    char* pMessage = (char*) pParam;
    CWnd* pMainWnd = AfxGetMainWnd();
    ::MessageBox(pMainWnd->m_hWnd,
        pMessage, "Thread Message", MB_OK);
    return 0;
}
```

This `MessageThread()` function performs the following tasks:

- Casts the pParam parameter to a char pointer
- Gets a pointer to the application's main window
- Displays a message box, using the main window's handle and the message passed to the function

For more information on window handles, please refer to Chapter 3.

The line that starts the thread might look like this:

```
AfxBeginThread (MessageThread,
    "Greetings from your thread!");
```

Notice the way that `MessageThread()` uses the `pParam` parameter in order to pass the address of the string to display in the message box. You can use this parameter to pass any 32-bit value, including something simple like a window handle or something snazzier like a pointer to a structure containing information needed by the thread.

Location: **WinPrgS\Chap14\ThreadApp1**

On this book's CD-ROM, you'll find a simple program that implements the `MessageThread()` function in the application's view class. Although `MessageThread()` is defined in the view class's implementation file, it is not a member function of the class. Defining `MessageThread()` in the view class's implementation file is just a convenience, because the view class's `OnLButtonDown()` function starts the thread. Figure 14-1 shows ThreadApp1 in action, sending you a message from a running thread. When you run the application, click the window to start the thread.

How does the thread end? When the `MessageThread()` function ends, so does the thread it represents. As ThreadApp1's user, to end the thread in ThreadApp1, you dismiss the message box. `MessageThread()` then executes its return statement and ends, taking the thread with it.

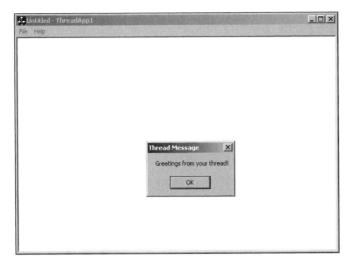

Figure 14-1: The ThreadApp1 application's thread displays its message box, informing you that the thread is running.

The call to `AfxBeginThread()` isn't quite as simple as it looks. There are actually many more parameters than those shown in the previous sample code segment. However, most of the parameters have default values. The complete `AfxBeginThread()` signature looks like this:

```
CWinThread* AfxBeginThread(
    AFX_THREADPROC pfnThreadProc,
    LPVOID pParam,
    int nPriority = THREAD_PRIORITY_NORMAL,
    UINT nStackSize = 0,
    DWORD dwCreateFlags = 0,
    LPSECURITY_ATTRIBUTES lpSecurityAttrs = NULL);
```

As you can see, the full `AfxBeginThread()` takes six parameters, shown here in the order they appear in the signature:

`pfnThreadProc`	The address of the function that implements the thread.
`pParam`	A 32-bit value that is passed to the thread function.
`nPriority`	The thread's initial priority level.
`nStackSize`	The maximum stack size.
`dwCreateFlags`	A flag specifying how the thread should be started. A value of 0 executes the thread immediately upon creation; a value of `CREATE_SUSPENDED` suspends the thread after it's created.
`LpSecurityAttrs`	A pointer to a `SECURITY_ATTRIBUTES` structure.

In most cases, the default values for AfxBeginThread()'s parameters work fine. If you want to dig further into the innards of threads, you can find more information about these parameters in your Visual C++ online documentation.

Creating a UI Thread

Because UI threads must contain a message loop, they are more complicated to deal with than worker threads. Instead of just writing a thread function and calling AfxBeginThread() to start it, you must derive a custom thread class from MFC's CWinThread class. This thread class must override the class's InitInstance() function, where the thread can perform any initialization tasks. MFC calls InitInstance() when it first creates the thread. It's also a good idea to override ExitInstance(), which is the counterpart of InitInstance(). MFC calls ExitInstance() before MFC destroys the thread object so that the thread can clean up after itself.

When you create your main application with AppWizard, you can use ClassWizard to create your thread class as follows:

1. Press Ctrl+W to display ClassWizard.

2. Click the Add Class button and select New from its drop-down menu, as shown in Figure 14-2.

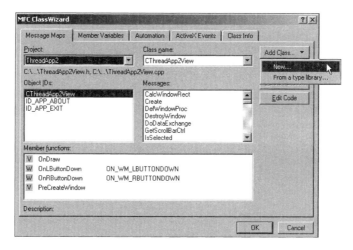

Figure 14-2: The MFC ClassWizard dialog box displayed while creating a new class.

3. After the New Class dialog box appears, type the name of the new class in the Name box. Then select CWinThread in the Base class box, as shown in Figure 14-3.

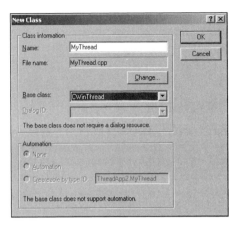

Figure 14-3: The New Class dialog box, showing the name and base class of the new class

4. Click OK to create the thread class. ClassWizard reappears with the thread class selected, as shown in Figure 14-4. Notice how ClassWizard has already overridden the `InitInstance()` and `ExitInstance()` member functions for you, listing their names in the Member functions box.

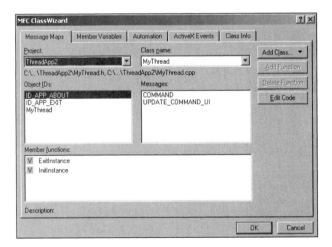

Figure 14-4: ClassWizard displaying the new thread class

Following are the header and implementation files of the thread class that ClassWizard creates for you. (I've edited some of the ClassWizard stuff from the files.) Whether or not you take advantage of ClassWizard to create your thread class, you can use the source code in the listings as the skeleton for other UI thread classes you might want to create:

```
class MyThread : public CWinThread
{
    DECLARE_DYNCREATE(MyThread)
protected:
    MyThread();

// Attributes
public:

// Operations
public:

// Overrides
    // ClassWizard generated virtual function overrides
    //{{AFX_VIRTUAL(MyThread)
    public:
    virtual BOOL InitInstance();
    virtual int ExitInstance();
    //}}AFX_VIRTUAL

// Implementation
protected:
    virtual ~MyThread();

    // Generated message map functions
    //{{AFX_MSG(MyThread)
        // NOTE - the ClassWizard will add and remove member functions
here.
    //}}AFX_MSG

    DECLARE_MESSAGE_MAP()
};
#include "stdafx.h"
#include "ThreadApp2.h"
#include "MyThread.h"

#ifdef _DEBUG
#define new DEBUG_NEW
#undef THIS_FILE
static char THIS_FILE[] = __FILE__;
#endif


//////////////////////////////////////////////////////
// MyThread

IMPLEMENT_DYNCREATE(MyThread, CWinThread)

MyThread::MyThread()
{
}
```

```
MyThread::~MyThread()
{
}

BOOL MyThread::InitInstance()
{
    // TODO:  perform and per-thread initialization here
    return TRUE;
}

int MyThread::ExitInstance()
{
    // TODO:  perform any per-thread cleanup here
    return CWinThread::ExitInstance();
}

BEGIN_MESSAGE_MAP(MyThread, CWinThread)
    //{{AFX_MSG_MAP(MyThread)
        // NOTE - the ClassWizard will add and\
remove mapping macros here.
    //}}AFX_MSG_MAP
END_MESSAGE_MAP()
```

In order to give this thread something to do, you might have it create a window in its InitInstance() function. That source code might look something like this:

```
BOOL MyThread::InitInstance()
{
    CFrameWnd* pFrameWnd = new CFrameWnd();
    pFrameWnd->Create(NULL, "Thread Window");
    pFrameWnd->ShowWindow(SW_SHOW);
    pFrameWnd->UpdateWindow();
    return TRUE;
}
```

Finally, the main program needs to start the UI thread. This is done much like starting a worker thread, by calling a version of AfxBeginThread():

```
AfxBeginThread(RUNTIME_CLASS(MyThread));
```

Here, the function's single parameter is a pointer to the CRuntimeClass structure representing the thread class. The RUNTIME_CLASS MFC macro very nicely generates the structure for you. All you have to do is give the macro the class's name. Although it doesn't require the 32-bit pParam parameter, this version of AfxBeginThread() has exactly the same default parameters as the version you used to create a worker thread.

You probably won't have much call for creating UI threads in your programs. Most secondary threads, after all, are worker threads. For that reason, the remainder of this chapter concentrates on worker threads.

PROBLEMS & SOLUTIONS

Process-to-Thread Communication

PROBLEM: *How can my program communicate with a thread?*

SOLUTION: Often when you program threads, you need a way for the thread and its containing process to communicate. There are actually several ways to do this. The easiest method is to define a global variable that both the thread and the process can access. You could, for example, set up an integer variable as a flag to signal when a thread should end.

To implement this technique, first define a global variable that the program and thread can use as a communication channel:

```
int threadFlag;
```

Then set the global variable to an appropriate starting value and start the thread:

```
    threadFlag = 1;
    HWND hWnd = GetSafeHwnd();
    AfxBeginThread(FlagThread, hWnd);
```

The thread function then gets to work, doing whatever processing is necessary, while constantly checking the value of the global variable:

```
UINT FlagThread(LPVOID pParam)
{
    while(threadFlag == 1)
    {
        // The thread does its work here.
    }
    return 0;
}
```

To stop the thread, the program only needs to change the value of the global variable:

```
threadFlag = 0;
```

When the thread's `while` loop checks `threadFlag`, the loop ends, which, in this case, also ends the thread.

Using global variables to communicate between a process and a thread is a simple method, but not always the best. A more elegant way to perform similar communication is with an *event object*. To learn more about event objects, read "Using Event Objects," later in this chapter.

Thread Synchronization

You might think at this point that using threads is downright easy. This is a perfect example of how a little knowledge can be dangerous. When you start programming threads, you can quickly run into serious trouble if you don't consider something called *thread synchronization*. Using thread synchronization techniques ensures that multiple threads don't simultaneously access critical shared resources.

Suppose your program defines a data structure that holds information the application requires to generate its display. This data might be, for example, the contents of a spreadsheet. The application has a thread that reads the spreadsheet data in order to display values in each cell on the screen. Meanwhile, another thread enables the user to edit the contents of the spreadsheet.

Without thread synchronization, this situation is a disaster waiting to happen. Why? You can't allow the calculation thread to access the data at the same time as the edit thread. If the threads access the data simultaneously, the calculation thread may read a data element that is in the process of being edited — getting, for example, a value of 30 instead of 3,000. Obviously, such bad data reads would make the spreadsheet useless.

In order to avoid such problems, Visual C++ defines four MFC synchronization objects you can use in your multithreaded programs:

Events	Used as flags to pass signals between threads
Critical Sections	Used within a process as keys to gain access to shared resources
Mutexes	Work like critical sections, except they can synchronize threads in multiple processes, rather than in just a single process
Semaphores	Enable multiple threads, up to a given limit, to access shared resources

Using Event Objects

Event objects are little more than sophisticated flags — that is, an event object can be on or off. When an event object is on, it is said to be in its signaled state. Conversely, when the event object is off, it is in its nonsignaled state. Threads can watch for changes in an event object's signal state in order to determine whether it's safe to run. With MFC, you can create automatic or manual event objects.

Automatic event objects

In Visual C++, the MFC class `CEvent` represents event objects. To create an event object, you usually create a global `CEvent` object:

```
CEvent eventObj;
```

Although they're not shown in this line, `CEvent`'s constructor actually has four parameters. All of these have default values, as you can see in the following function signature:

```
CEvent(
    BOOL bInitiallyOwn = FALSE,
    BOOL bManualReset = FALSE,
    LPCTSTR lpszName = NULL,
    LPSECURITY_ATTRIBUTES lpsaAttribute = NULL );
```

The four parameters, in order, are as follows:

bInitiallyOwn	Determines the starting signal state (TRUE = signaled; FALSE = nonsignaled).
bManualReset	Determines whether this is a manual (TRUE) or automatic (FALSE) event. An automatic event automatically sets itself back to the nonsignaled state.
lpszName	Assigns a name to the event object.
lpsaAttribute	Acts as a pointer to a SECURITY_ATTRIBUTES structure.

In order to use the `CEvent` class (and other thread synchronization classes) in your program, you must add the line `#include "afxmt.h"` to the file that references the `CEvent` class.

After creating the event object, you start the secondary thread that you'll synchronize using the event object. For example, you might start the thread like this:

```
AfxBeginThread(EventThread, hWnd);
```

Here, `EventThread` is the thread that must wait for the event object to be signaled; however, when you call `AfxBeginThread()`, the thread starts to execute immediately. Inside the thread function, therefore, you need to add code that forces the thread to wait for the signaled event. You do this by calling the event object's `Lock()` member function.

For example, here is an event function that displays a message box when it first starts:

```
UINT EventThread(LPVOID pParam)
{
```

```
    HWND hWnd = (HWND) pParam;
    ::MessageBox(hWnd, "Thread started",
        "Thread Message", MB_ICONEXCLAMATION | MB_OK);

    eventObj.Lock();

    ::MessageBox(hWnd, "Thread unblocked",
        "Thread Message", MB_ICONEXCLAMATION | MB_OK);

    return 0;
}
```

The function performs the following tasks:

- Displays a message box telling the user that the thread has started
- Calls the event object's `Lock()` member function, which blocks the thread from continuing until the event object is placed in its signaled state
- Displays a second message box when the event object is signaled

How, you might ask, does a program set an event object to its signaled state? You signal an event object by calling its `SetEvent()` member function:

```
eventObj.SetEvent();
```

Location: **WinPrgS\Chap14\ThreadApp2**

To see all this event object stuff in action, check out the ThreadApp2 application on this book's CD-ROM. There you'll find a sample application that demonstrates the use of `CEvent` objects to control a thread. When you run the application, its frame window appears, after which you can click in the window's client area to start a secondary thread. When the thread starts, it displays the message box shown in Figure 14-5.

Here is the thread function from ThreadApp2:

```
UINT EventThread(LPVOID pParam)
{
    HWND hWnd = (HWND) pParam;
    ::MessageBox(hWnd, "Thread started",
        "Thread Message", MB_ICONEXCLAMATION | MB_OK);

    eventObj.Lock();

    ::MessageBox(hWnd, "Thread unblocked",
        "Thread Message", MB_ICONEXCLAMATION | MB_OK);

    return 0;
}
```

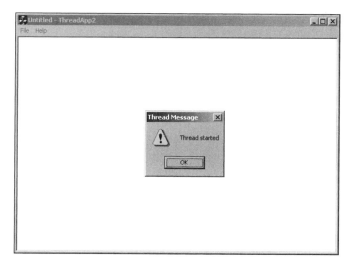

Figure 14-5: The Thread Message message box displays when the secondary thread begins.

You can see that, after displaying the message box, the thread blocks itself by locking the event object. At this point, the thread is suspended, waiting for the event object to become signaled. In a full application, the program's primary thread might be preparing a data structure that the second thread must process. In that case, the second thread mustn't start processing the data structure until the first thread has finished with it.

To unblock ThreadApp2's secondary thread, right-click the window's client area. You then see the message box shown in Figure 14-6. At this point in a full application, the thread would begin whatever task it was designed to do, after which the thread would end or go back into a blocked state, waiting for more data to process. In ThreadApp2, you can stop the thread by dismissing the second message box.

To see automatic events in action, start more than one instance of the thread by clicking several times in the window. (You have to close a thread's message box before you can click again, of course.) Each time you click, an instance of the `EventThread()` thread begins and then suspends in order to wait for the event object to be signaled.

The next step is to signal the event object, which you do by right-clicking the window. When you right-click the window the first time, the program sets the event object to its signaled state, and the first thread wakes up. Because the event object is automatic, it immediately goes back to its nonsignaled state, which means other threads you have started stay suspended. Right-clicking again signals the event object and wakes up the next running thread, and so on for all threads you started.

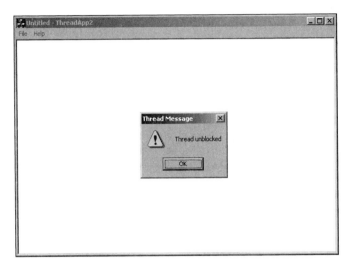

Figure 14-6: After right-clicking your window's client area, this message box appears, enabling you to unblock the secondary thread.

Thread Communication with Event Objects

PROBLEM: *How can I use event objects to communicate between a program and a secondary thread?*

SOLUTION: In the previous Problems and Solutions section, "Process-to-Thread Communication," you learned the secret of using a global variable to communicate between a program and a thread. You can also establish this type of communication using event objects in place of global variables. This technique is more elegant and a bit safer.

Location: `WinPrgS\Chap14\EventThread`

On this book's CD-ROM, you can find the EventThread application, which demonstrates using event objects to communicate between the program and the thread. To implement the event object communication technique, the program first includes the `afxmt.h` header file in the view class's implementation file:

```
#include "afxmt.h".
```

Continued

Then the program defines global event objects that the program and thread can use as communication channels. In this example, the event objects control the starting and stopping of the thread:

```
CEvent comEventStart;
CEvent comEventEnd;
```

The program starts the thread in response to the WM_CREATE message, which occurs when the program is first started. In an MFC program, you can respond to WM_CREATE by using ClassWizard to create the OnCreate() message-response function, as shown here:

```
int CEventThreadView::OnCreate
    (LPCREATESTRUCT lpCreateStruct)
{
    if (CView::OnCreate(lpCreateStruct) == -1)
        return -1;

    // TODO: Add your specialized creation code here

    HWND hWnd = GetSafeHwnd();
    AfxBeginThread(EventThread, hWnd);

    return 0;
}
```

As you can see, OnCreate() starts the thread. However, because the thread is designed so that it doesn't start processing until the comEventStart event object becomes signaled, the thread immediately suspends. Here is the thread function:

```
UINT EventThread(LPVOID pParam)
{
    BOOL runThread = TRUE;

    HWND hWnd = (HWND) pParam;
    ::MessageBox(hWnd, "Thread started.",
        "Thread Message",
        MB_ICONEXCLAMATION | MB_OK);

    comEventStart.Lock();

    ::MessageBox(hWnd, "Thread processing.",
        "Thread Message",
        MB_ICONEXCLAMATION | MB_OK);

    while(runThread)
    {
        // Perform the thread's task here.
        int retCode = ::WaitForSingleObject(
            comEventEnd.m_hObject, 0);
        if (retCode == WAIT_OBJECT_0)
```

Continued

```
                runThread = FALSE;
        }

        ::MessageBox(hWnd, "Thread ending.",
            "Thread Message",
            MB_ICONEXCLAMATION | MB_OK);

        return 0;
}
```

When you click in the application's window, MFC calls the `OnLButtonDown()` function. This then calls the `comEventStart` event object's `SetEvent()` member function to set the event to its signaled state:

```
void CEventThreadView::OnLButtonDown(UINT nFlags,
    CPoint point)
{
    // TODO: Add your message handler code here
    // and/or call default

    comEventStart.SetEvent();

    CView::OnLButtonDown(nFlags, point);
}
```

The thread unblocks and enters its `while` loop, where it begins whatever processing it was designed to do. Inside the `while` loop, the thread constantly calls the Windows API function `WaitForSingleObject()` in order to monitor the state of the `comEventEnd` event object. The advantage of calling `WaitForSingleObject()`, rather than the usual `Lock()` member function, is that `WaitForSingleObject()` returns a value. This means that the thread can poll the event object without actually blocking.

`WaitForSingleObject()` takes two arguments: the handle of the event object and the length of time (in milliseconds) to wait. A value of 0 for the wait time causes `WaitForSingleObject()` to return a value immediately. When `WaitForSingleObject()` returns `WAIT_OBJECT_0`, the event object has entered its signaled state, meaning, in this case, that the thread should end.

To end the thread, right-click the application's window. MFC calls the program's `OnRButtonDown()` function, which calls the `comEventEnd` event object's `SetEvent()` function, and the thread ends:

```
void CEventThreadView::OnRButtonDown(UINT nFlags,
    CPoint point)
{
    // TODO: Add your message handler code here
    // and/or call default

    comEventEnd.SetEvent();

    CView::OnRButtonDown(nFlags, point);
}
```

You may have noticed the double colon (::) in front of the call to `WaitForSingleObject()`. Use this symbol to indicate that a function call is a Windows API function, rather than an MFC function. The double colon makes it possible to call Windows API functions that are also defined in MFC with the same name. For example, if you call `MessageBox()` within an MFC class, MFC assumes you want to call the MFC version of `MessageBox()`. If, for some reason, you actually wanted to call the Windows API version, you'd preface the function call with the double colon:

```
::MessageBox();
```

However, you can use the double colon any time you call a Windows API function, even if the function doesn't have an MFC counterpart. By doing this, you make it easy to see when you're calling MFC functions and when you're calling Windows API functions.

Manual Event Objects

In the previous section, you saw how automatic event objects wake a single thread instance and then go back into their nonsignaled state. If you want to wake up all instances of a thread simultaneously, you need to create a manual event object, which you might do like this:

```
CEvent eventObj(FALSE, TRUE);
```

If you remember the arguments for the `CEvent` constructor, you know that the first `FALSE` parameter specifies that the event object will start in its nonsignaled state; the second argument of `TRUE` specifies that the event object is manual, rather than automatic.

Location: **WinPrgS\Chap14\ThreadApp3**

When the manual event object becomes signaled, it stays signaled until the program explicitly calls the object's `ResetEvent()` member function. This means that all threads waiting for the event object can unblock, as you can discover with the ThreadApp3 program, found on this book's CD-ROM.

When you run ThreadApp3, you see a window much like ThreadApp2's window. Now, however, the program assigns numbers to the threads you start. You can start as many instances of the program's secondary thread as you like, with each getting a unique number. Figure 14-7 shows the program creating a third thread.

After creating the number of threads you want, each thread is blocked, waiting for the event object to become signaled. To signal the event object, right-click the window. When you do, all threads become unblocked, as shown in Figure 14-8.

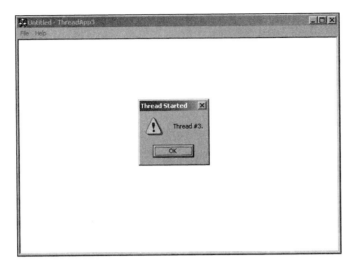

Figure 14-7: ThreadApp3 creating a third thread instance

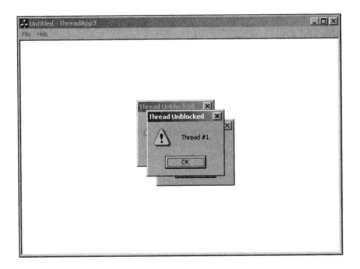

Figure 14-8: ThreadApp3's secondary threads unblock simultaneously.

ThreadApp3's `OnLButtonDown()` and `OnRButtonDown()` functions look exactly like ThreadApp2's. The thread function, `EventThread()`, however, has some new wrinkles, as shown here:

```
UINT EventThread(LPVOID pParam)
{
    static int threadNum = 0;
    char str[81];
```

```
        ++threadNum;
        wsprintf(str, "Thread #%d.", threadNum);
        HWND hWnd = (HWND) pParam;
        ::MessageBox(hWnd, str, "Thread Started",
            MB_ICONEXCLAMATION | MB_OK);

        eventObj.Lock();

        ::MessageBox(hWnd, str, "Thread Unblocked",
            MB_ICONEXCLAMATION | MB_OK);

        return 0;
}
```

Now `EventThread()` uses a static variable, `threadNum`, to hold the thread number. Each time the user starts a thread, the program increments `thread Num` and uses its new value to construct a text string for the message box.

When you use a thread function to create multiple instances of a thread, you must be sure that the function causes no re-entrance problems. That is, the function must be very careful in dealing with data objects, because each thread instance may access the same objects. This isn't a problem for local variables because each thread instance gets its own stack. However, global and static variables are potential land mines. For instance, the `threadNum` variable in the preceding `EventThread()` function could cause trouble if two thread instances tried to access it at the same time, although that shouldn't happen in ThreadApp3.

Using Critical Sections

You can think of a *critical section object* as a kind of key that unlocks access to a shared resource. When one thread owns the critical section object, other threads that want to access the locked resource must suspend their execution until the first thread hands over the key.

Visual C++ supports critical sections through its MFC `CCriticalSection` class. Creating a critical section object is even easier than creating an event object. This is because the class's constructor takes no arguments:

```
CCriticalSection criticalSection;
```

When a thread wants to access a shared resource, the thread calls the critical section object's `Lock()` member function, which effectively hands the resource key to the calling thread (assuming no other thread already owns the critical object):

```
criticalSection.Lock();
```

If some other thread has already locked the critical section, the thread calling Lock() is blocked until the critical section is again freed. Otherwise, the thread becomes the critical section's owner and can access the shared resource. When the thread has completed whatever task it must perform on the shared resource, it releases the critical section object by calling the Unlock() member function:

criticalSection.Unlock();

Location: **WinPrg5\Chap14\ThreadApp4**

On this book's CD-ROM, you can find an application that demonstrates critical sections. When you run the program, click the window's client area. When you do, the program starts two separate threads. The first thread grabs the critical section object and displays a message box, telling you that the thread has started. The second thread also starts and attempts to gain ownership of the critical section object. Because the first thread already owns the critical section, however, the second thread blocks.

When you dismiss the message box, the first thread unlocks the critical section and displays a message box informing you of that fact. This action wakes up the second thread, which grabs the critical section object and displays its own message box. At this point, you have two message boxes on the screen, as shown in Figure 14-9. Finally, when you dismiss the second thread's start-up message box, the thread releases the critical section object and displays its final message box.

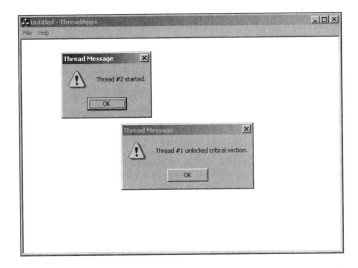

Figure 14-9: ThreadApp4's first thread releases the critical section object.

If you found all that hard to follow, take a look at the following code, which shows the `OnLButtonDown()` function defined in ThreadApp4's view class:

```
void CThreadApp4View::OnLButtonDown(UINT nFlags, CPoint point)
{
    // TODO: Add your message handler code here and/or call default

    HWND hWnd = GetSafeHwnd();
    AfxBeginThread(CriticalThread1, hWnd);
    AfxBeginThread(CriticalThread2, hWnd);

    CView::OnLButtonDown(nFlags, point);
}
```

When the user clicks the application's window, MFC calls `OnLButtonDown()`, where `CriticalThread1` and `CriticalThread2` are started together. This results in the `CriticalThread1()` and `CriticalThread2()` functions executing one after the other.

Now look at this code, which is the source code for the first thread function, `CriticalThread1()`:

```
UINT CriticalThread1(LPVOID pParam)
{
    criticalSection.Lock();

    HWND hWnd = (HWND) pParam;
    ::MessageBox(hWnd, "Thread #1 started.",
        "Thread Message", MB_ICONEXCLAMATION | MB_OK);

    criticalSection.Unlock();

    ::MessageBox(hWnd,
        "Thread #1 unlocked critical section.",
        "Thread Message", MB_ICONEXCLAMATION | MB_OK);

    return 0;
}
```

As you can see, this thread function immediately locks the critical section, which prevents the second thread from doing so. After locking the critical section, the function displays the message box, which halts the thread until you dismiss the message box from the screen. The instant you do, the function unlocks the critical section, giving the second thread a chance to lock it and commence executing. The source code for `CriticalThread2()` looks almost exactly like that for `CriticalThread1()`. The only difference is the name of the thread and the strings that identify the thread.

PROBLEMS & SOLUTIONS

Suspended and Sleeping Threads

PROBLEM: *How can I suspend a thread for a set period of time?*

SOLUTION: There may be situations in which your thread must have a built-in timer. For example, you may want to use a thread to control an animation sequence. To do this, the thread must time the interval between one frame of the animation and the next. Although you can call `SuspendThread()` to suspend a thread, you can't specify a time limit. Moreover, the thread cannot re-awaken itself. To awaken the suspended thread, some other process or thread must call `ResumeThread()`.

Luckily, there is a thread function that works well for timing purposes, `Sleep()`, which you call like this:

```
Sleep(1000);
```

The function's single parameter is the number of milliseconds the thread should sleep. Therefore, the previous line puts the thread to sleep for approximately 1,000 ms, or one second.

Using Mutexes

You use a *mutex* (which is short for "mutually exclusive") synchronization object almost exactly as you use a critical section object. The big difference is that whereas critical sections can only communicate from within a single process, mutexes can communicate across process boundaries. This means that you can use a mutex to synchronize resources between different running applications, something that's way beyond a critical section's capabilities.

Visual C++ supports mutexes with the MFC `CMutex` class. You create a mutex in the application as a global object:

```
CMutex mutex(FALSE, "mutex1");
```

Here, the `CMutex` constructor takes two arguments. However, the `CMutex` constructor actually has three parameters, all of which have default values. The full signature looks like this:

```
CMutex(
    BOOL bInitiallyOwn = FALSE,
    LPCTSTR lpszName = NULL,
    LPSECURITY_ATTRIBUTES lpsaAttribute = NULL );
```

The parameters, which are very similar to those used for automatic event objects, are described in order as follows:

bInitiallyOwn	Specifies whether the mutex starts off locked (TRUE) or unlocked (FALSE).
lpszName	Assigns a name to the mutex. The name is used by different processes to identify the mutex in the system.
lpsaAttribute	Acts as a pointer to a SECURITY_ATTRIBUTES structure.

Once you have the mutex created, you use it exactly like a critical section object, calling the object's Lock() member function when the program is about to access a shared resource:

`mutex.Lock();`

When the program is finished with the resource, it calls the mutex's Unlock() member function:

`mutex.Unlock();`

Location: **WinPrgS\Chap14\ThreadApp5**

If you'd like to experiment with mutexes, take a look at the ThreadApp5 program on this book's CD-ROM. Following is the application's thread function:

```
UINT MutexThread(LPVOID pParam)
{
    HWND hWnd = (HWND) pParam;
    ::MessageBox(hWnd, "Thread started.",
        "Thread Message", MB_ICONEXCLAMATION | MB_OK);

    mutex.Lock();

    ::MessageBox(hWnd, "Mutex locked.",
        "Thread Message", MB_ICONEXCLAMATION | MB_OK);

    mutex.Unlock();

    ::MessageBox(hWnd, "Mutex unlocked.",
        "Thread Message", MB_ICONEXCLAMATION | MB_OK);

    return 0;
}
```

This function performs the following tasks:

- Displays a message box telling the user that the thread has started
- Locks the mutex
- Displays a message box telling the user that the mutex is locked
- Unlocks the mutex
- Displays a message box telling the user that the mutex is unlocked

To see the mutex in action, follow these steps:

1. Run two instances of the application and resize the windows so that they fit next to each other on the screen.
2. Click each of the windows to start the secondary threads. When you do, a message box appears for each application, telling you that the threads have started, as shown in Figure 14-10.

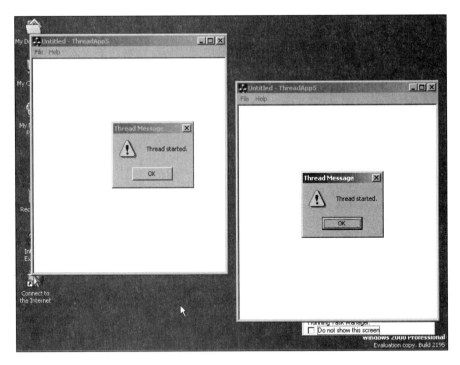

Figure 14-10: After you click each window, these message boxes appear to tell you the secondary threads have started.

Chapter 14: Process Control **539**

3. Dismiss one of the message boxes. The associated application instance locks the mutex and displays a message box telling you that the mutex is locked, as shown in Figure 14-11.

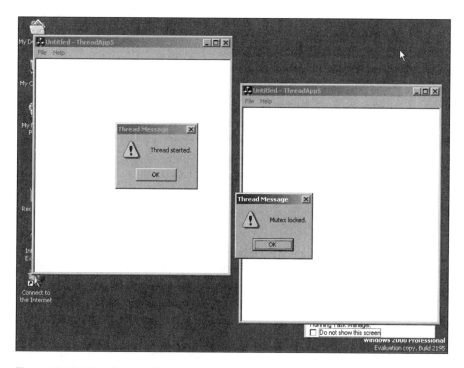

Figure 14-11: After the associated application instance locks the mutex, it displays this message box.

4. Without dismissing the "Mutex locked" message box (which will cause the application to unlock the mutex), dismiss the second instance's "Thread started" message box. Nothing happens. You don't see a "Mutex locked" message box for the second instance because the first instance still has the mutex locked (see Figure 14-12).

5. Click the first application instance's "Mutex locked" message box in order to unlock the mutex. Immediately, the first thread releases the mutex and the second one grabs it, as shown by the message boxes that appear in Figure 14-13. As you can see, mutexes really do work across process boundaries.

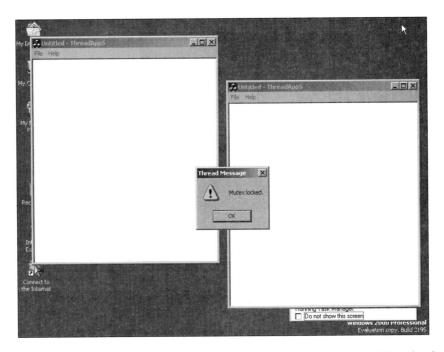

Figure 14-12: The "Mutex locked" message box is displayed while the second thread waits for the mutex to be unlocked.

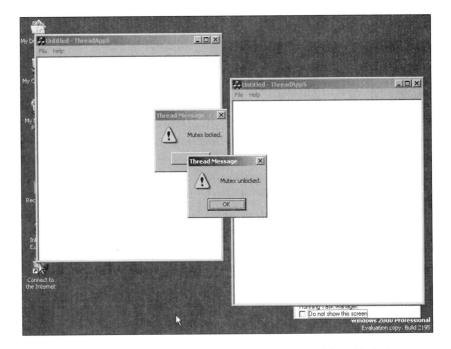

Figure 14-13: The first thread unlocks the mutex, and the second thread locks it.

Using Semaphores

Semaphores enable an application to limit the number of threads that access a resource. This is very different from critical sections or mutexes, which always limit accessibility to a single thread at a time. A semaphore starts with an initial resource count, which represents the current status of the semaphore, and a maximum resource count, which represents the greatest number of threads that can access the resource simultaneously. Like a mutex, a semaphore can be used to synchronize threads within a single process, as well as to synchronize threads between multiple processes.

When a thread locks a semaphore, the semaphore reduces its resource count by one. When the resource count reaches zero, any other thread that tries to lock the resource is blocked; it can't resume until another thread releases the semaphore, which increments the resource count.

Visual C++ supports semaphores through the MFC CSemaphore class. When you create a semaphore object, you specify the initial resource count and the maximum resource count. If you're going to use the semaphore across process boundaries, you also need to specify a semaphore name. You might create a semaphore object like this:

```
CSemaphore semaphore(3, 3, "semaphore1");
```

Although they're not shown in this line, CSemaphore's constructor actually has four parameters, all of which have default values, as you can see in the following function signature:

```
CSemaphore(
    LONG lInitialCount = 1,
    LONG lMaxCount = 1,
    LPCTSTR pstrName = NULL,
    LPSECURITY_ATTRIBUTES lpsaAttributes = NULL);
```

The four parameters, in order, are as follows:

lInitialCount	Specifies the semaphore's initial resource count
lMaxCount	Specifies the semaphore's maximum resource count
pstrName	Assigns a name to the semaphore object
lpsaAttributes	Acts as a pointer to a SECURITY_ATTRIBUTES structure

Just as with other synchronization objects, such as critical sections and mutexes, when a thread is about to access the shared resource, it calls the semaphore's Lock() member function. This causes the semaphore to decrement its resource count. When the thread is finished with the shared resource, it calls the semaphore object's Unlock() member function, which increments the semaphore's resource count.

Location: **WinPrgS\Chap14\ThreadApp6**

On this book's CD-ROM, you can find the ThreadApp6 application, which demonstrates using semaphores to control a resource between several running applications. In the application's view class, the program creates a semaphore as described previously:

```
CSemaphore semaphore(3, 3, "semaphore1");
```

To start a thread, the user clicks ThreadApp6's window. This causes MFC to call the view class's `OnLButtonDown()` member function, as shown here:

```
void CThreadApp6View::OnLButtonDown(UINT nFlags,
    CPoint point)
{
    // TODO: Add your message handler code here
    // and/or call default

    HWND hWnd = GetSafeHwnd();
    AfxBeginThread(SemaphoreThread, hWnd);

    CView::OnLButtonDown(nFlags, point);
}
```

As you can see, `OnLButtonDown()` calls `AfxBeginThread()` to start the `SemaphoreThread` secondary thread, represented by the `Semaphore Thread()` function. Following is the `SemaphoreThread()` function:

```
UINT SemaphoreThread(LPVOID pParam)
{
    HWND hWnd = (HWND) pParam;
    ::MessageBox(hWnd, "Thread started.",
        "Thread Message", MB_ICONEXCLAMATION | MB_OK);

    semaphore.Lock();

    ::MessageBox(hWnd, "Semaphore locked.",
        "Thread Message", MB_ICONEXCLAMATION | MB_OK);

    semaphore.Unlock();

    ::MessageBox(hWnd, "Semaphore unlocked.",
        "Thread Message", MB_ICONEXCLAMATION | MB_OK);

    return 0;
}
```

Notice how much this function looks like `MutexThread()` from the ThreadApp5 application. The only real difference is that `SemaphoreThread()` locks and unlocks a semaphore rather than a mutex.

The `SemaphoreThread()` function performs the following tasks:

- Displays a message box telling the user that the thread has started

- Locks the semaphore, which decrements the semaphore's resource count

- Displays a message box telling the user that the semaphore is locked

- Unlocks the semaphore, which increments the semaphore's resource count

- Displays a message box telling the user that the semaphore is unlocked

When you run a single instance of ThreadApp6, nothing interesting happens. The application simply displays message boxes that show what the program is up to, when threads start, and when semaphores lock and unlock. Things get interesting when you run more instances of the application than the semaphore's maximum resource count allows. To see what I mean, perform the following steps:

1. Run four instances of ThreadApp6.

2. Resize and position the windows so that they all fit on the screen.

3. Click each of the windows in order to start each application's secondary thread. Four message boxes appear, informing you that the threads have started (see Figure 14-14).

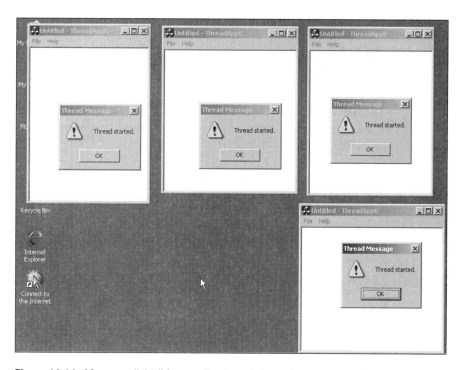

Figure 14-14: After you click all four application windows, these message boxes appear to inform you that the secondary threads have started.

4. Click the OK button on three of the message boxes. Three new message boxes appear, informing you that the three associated threads have locked the semaphore, as shown in Figure 14-15. (You may have to move the message boxes around in order to see them all.)

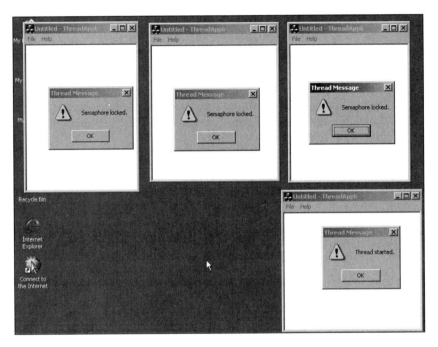

Figure 14-15: To inform you that you've exceeded the semaphore's maximum resource count, message boxes appear, showing that their threads have locked the semaphore.

5. Click the OK button on the remaining "Thread started" message box. The message box goes away, but no new message box tells you that the thread has locked the semaphore (see Figure 14-16). This is because the semaphore has a maximum resource count of three, and three threads have already locked the semaphore.

6. Dismiss one of the "Semaphore locked" message boxes. The associated thread displays its "Semaphore unlocked" message box. At the same time, the fourth, waiting thread immediately grabs the semaphore and locks it, as indicated by its "Semaphore locked" message box (see Figure 14-17).

7. Close all message boxes. Each thread unlocks the semaphore and ends.

Chapter 14: Process Control 545

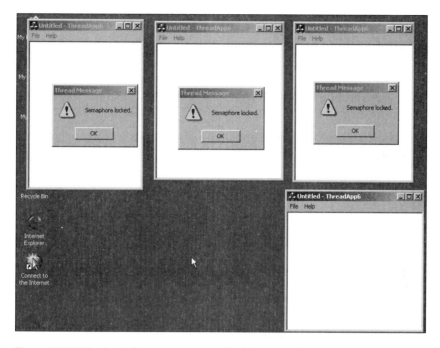

Figure 14-16: The fourth instance cannot yet lock the semaphore, as it has a maximum resource count of three.

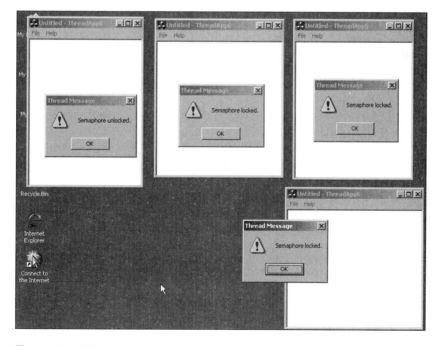

Figure 14-17: While one thread unlocks the semaphore, another locks it.

Summary

Using threads, you can assign time-consuming tasks to functions that run concurrently with the main program. In this way, you take better advantage of the Windows operating system to provide your application's user with a more responsive interface. However, multithreaded applications can become very complex and lead to unexpected and sometimes disastrous problems. You should use multithreading only when there is a clear advantage to doing so and not just because you want your application to incorporate the latest technology.

Also discussed in this chapter:

- Processes are more or less equivalent to running applications.
- Threads are distinct paths of execution within a process.
- Processes and threads both have priority settings that determine how much CPU time they get.
- A worker thread does not process Windows messages and therefore has no user interface.
- A UI thread does process Windows messages and therefore can display windows and other UI elements.
- Thread synchronization enables you to protect shared resources from concurrent access by multiple threads.
- Event objects pass signals between threads.
- Critical section objects act as keys that enable access to protected resources.
- Mutexes are like critical sections that work across process boundaries.
- Semaphores enable a maximum number of threads to access shared resources.

Chapter 15

Input Devices: The Mouse and the Keyboard

In This Chapter
- Understanding input events
- Responding to mouse messages
- Responding to keyboard messages

A computer can have any number of input devices, but the mouse and the keyboard are the most common ones. Because the mouse and keyboard are everywhere, this chapter describes how Windows 2000 handles their input. Once you know the basics, it's simple to add input routines to your MFC programs. In fact, basic mouse and keyboard handling is as easy to implement as adding a message-response function or two to your MFC program, something that Visual C++'s ClassWizard can help you do.

Input Events and Messages

As you already know, virtually everything that happens in a Windows application occurs in response to events. Input devices like the mouse and the keyboard are no different. Whenever the user moves the mouse or types on the keyboard, the system captures the input events and sends a flood of messages to the application. The application then must decide which messages to handle and which to pass back to Windows for default processing.

Because many of the user interface objects used in a Windows program, such as menus and dialog boxes, handle mouse and keyboard input automatically, a Windows application responds to input messages only for special, application-specific purposes. For example, a paint program may respond to mouse events so that the user can draw a line in the application's window, whereas a word-processing application may respond to keyboard events so that the user can type a document.

Both the mouse and the keyboard generate their own types of messages. For example, the mouse generates Windows messages such as `WM_MOUSEMOVE`, `WM_LBUTTONDOWN`, and `WM_RBUTTONDBLCLK`. The keyboard, on the other hand, generates messages such as `WM_KEYDOWN` and `WM_KEYUP`. When you want your application to respond to a specific mouse or keyboard event, you simply create a message-response function for the message. MFC then automatically routes the message to the message-response function, where you can handle it as you see fit.

Handling the Mouse

Now that you have a general idea of how the mouse and the keyboard communicate with a Windows application, you can explore the details and learn exactly how to add mouse and keyboard support to your Windows applications. In this section, you will concentrate on the mouse, which most users rely upon at least as much as a keyboard — if not more.

Client-Area Mouse Messages

The *client area* is the part of the window in which an application can draw. Windows sends client-area mouse messages to your application whenever the mouse pointer is over the client area of a window owned by your application. You may recall that the mouse communicates with an application using mouse event messages such as `WM_MOUSEMOVE`. For example, when the user moves the mouse over the application window's client area, the application receives a stream of `WM_MOUSEMOVE` messages, which tell the application not only that the mouse is moving, but also the location of the mouse at the time Windows generated the message.

When the mouse moves outside of the application window's client area, the application stops receiving client-area mouse messages. Instead, Windows sends the mouse messages to whatever window (including the desktop) the mouse happens to be over. When the mouse moves back over the window's client area, Windows redirects the mouse messages to the application. (An exception to this rule is when the application has captured the mouse, which means that Windows directs all mouse messages to the application even when the mouse is outside of the application's window. You learn about capturing the mouse a little later in this chapter, in the section "Capturing Mouse Messages.")

Table 15-1 describes the 18 client-area mouse messages that your application can receive.

Table 15-1 Client-Area Mouse Messages

Message	Description
WM_CAPTURECHANGED	The window is losing the mouse capture.
WM_LBUTTONDBLCLK	Left mouse button was double-clicked.
WM_LBUTTONDOWN	Left mouse button was pressed.
WM_LBUTTONUP	Left mouse button was released.
WM_MBUTTONDBLCLK	Middle mouse button was double-clicked.
WM_MBUTTONDOWN	Middle mouse button was pressed.
WM_MBUTTONUP	Middle mouse button was released.
WM_MOUSEACTIVATE	The mouse cursor was in an inactive window when the user pressed a mouse button.
WM_MOUSEHOVER	The mouse cursor hovered over the window's client area for the hover time set by a call to TrackMouseEvent().
WM_MOUSELEAVE	The mouse cursor has left the client area of the window specified by call to TrackMouseEvent().
WM_MOUSEMOVE	Mouse has moved over the client area.
WM_MOUSEWHEEL	The mouse wheel was rotated.
WM_RBUTTONDBLCLK	Right mouse button was double-clicked.
WM_RBUTTONDOWN	Right mouse button was pressed.
WM_RBUTTONUP	Right mouse button was released.
WM_XBUTTONDBLCLK	Mouse X button was double-clicked.
WM_XBUTTONDOWN	Mouse X button was pressed down.
WM_XBUTTONUP	Mouse X button was released.

Nonclient-Area Mouse Messages

Windows also sends *nonclient-area* mouse messages to your application. These types of mouse messages occur when the mouse is over any area of the application's window except the client area. For example, the application receives nonclient-area mouse messages when the mouse is over the window's title bar or control buttons. Most applications ignore nonclient-area mouse messages, because they are best handled by Windows itself. When the user double-clicks a window's title bar, for example, Windows restores the window's size to its previous setting.

You don't usually want to interfere with Windows' default handling of nonclient-area mouse messages because, if you do, the application's window may stop responding to the user as the user expects it to. However, there are times when responding to nonclient-area mouse messages enables an application to implement extra features. An application might, for example, intercept nonclient messages in order to enhance the way a window's title bar responds to the mouse.

Normally, an application ignores nonclient-area mouse messages. However, there are 15 nonclient-area mouse messages that your application may receive. These are similar to their client-area counterparts, as you can see in Table 15-2, which lists the nonclient-area mouse messages and their descriptions.

Table 15-2 Nonclient-Area Mouse Messages

Message	Description
WM_NCLBUTTONDBLCLK	Left mouse button was double-clicked.
WM_NCLBUTTONDOWN	Left mouse button was pressed.
WM_NCLBUTTONUP	Left mouse button was released.
WM_NCMBUTTONDBLCLK	Middle mouse button was double-clicked.
WM_NCMBUTTONDOWN	Middle mouse button was pressed.
WM_NCMBUTTONUP	Middle mouse button was released.
WM_NCMOUSEHOVER	The mouse cursor hovered over the window's non-client area for the hover time set by a call to `TrackMouseEvent()`.
WM_NCMOUSELEAVE	The mouse cursor has left the non-client area of the window specified by call to `TrackMouseEvent()`.
WM_NCMOUSEMOVE	Mouse has moved over the non-client area.
WM_NCRBUTTONDBLCLK	Right mouse button was double-clicked.
WM_NCRBUTTONDOWN	Right mouse button was pressed.
WM_NCRBUTTONUP	Right mouse button was released.
WM_NCXBUTTONDBLCLK	Mouse X button was double-clicked.
WM_NCXBUTTONDOWN	Mouse X button was pressed down.
WM_NCXBUTTONUP	Mouse X button was released.

PROBLEMS & SOLUTIONS

Responding to Nonclient-Area Mouse Messages

PROBLEM: *How can I respond to nonclient-area mouse messages in an MFC program? ClassWizard doesn't allow me to add nonclient messages to a class's message map.*

SOLUTION: Although ClassWizard tries to dissuade you from capturing nonclient-area messages (with good reason), MFC does define message-map macros and message-response functions for all the nonclient-area messages. To handle these messages in an application, you must add the macros and functions to your program by hand, without the help of ClassWizard. For example, the following message map associates the WM_NCMOUSEMOVE message with the OnNcMouseMove( ) message-response function:

```
BEGIN_MESSAGE_MAP(CMainFrame, CFrameWnd)
    //{{AFX_MSG_MAP(CMainFrame)
        // NOTE - the ClassWizard will add and remove mapping macros here.
        //    DO NOT EDIT what you see in these blocks of generated code !
    //}}AFX_MSG_MAP
    ON_WM_NCMOUSEMOVE()
END_MESSAGE_MAP()
```

Notice that the message map is from the CMainFrame class, which represents the main frame window in an MFC application. It is the frame window that owns the nonclient areas, so it is the frame window that gets the nonclient-area messages.

You must also provide the OnNcMouseMove( ) function, because ClassWizard won't do it for you. In your frame window's declaration, you declare the message-response function like this:

```
afx_msg void OnNcMouseMove(UINT nHitTest, CPoint point);
```

The OnNcMouseMove( ) function itself looks something like this:

```
void CMainFrame::OnNcMouseMove(UINT nHitTest, CPoint point)
{
    // Do stuff here...

    CFrameWnd::OnNcMouseMove(nHitTest, point);
}
```

Continued

Location: **WinPrgS\Chap15\NCMouse**

Don't forget to pass the message on to the base class's OnNcMouseMove() function. You want to be sure that nonclient-area messages get their normal, default processing. You can find a sample program called NCMouse on this book's CD-ROM. NCMouse tracks WM_NCMOUSEMOVE messages, displaying the mouse coordinates in the application's window. To generate the messages, move the mouse pointer over the nonclient areas of the window, as shown in Figure 15-1.

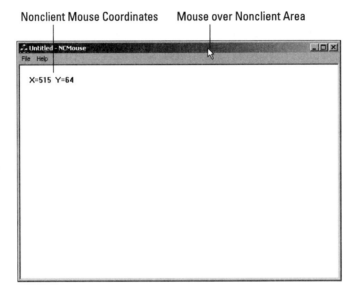

Figure 15-1: The NCMouse application displays mouse coordinates when the mouse is over the window's nonclient area.

The Mouse Sample Application

Now that you have mouse-handling concepts tucked under your belt, you can put those concepts to work. In this section, you'll examine, and experiment with, an application that demonstrates the mouse programming techniques discussed in this chapter. You'll see how to respond to mouse messages, as well as how to capture the mouse in an application.

Responding to mouse messages

Location: `WinPrgS\Chap15\Mouse`

The Mouse sample program on this book's CD-ROM illustrates how to intercept and respond to mouse messages. When you run the program, its main window appears. At first this window is blank, but the instant you move the mouse over the window, `WM_MOUSEMOVE` messages appear in the window, showing the mouse's coordinates at the time of the message. Click the left mouse button when the mouse is over the window, and not only do the `WM_LBUTTONDOWN` and `WM_LBUTTONUP` messages appear in the window, but the coordinates where the event took place also appear. Ditto for right mouse button clicks. Figure 15-2 shows the Mouse application in action, with the various events it handles displayed in the window.

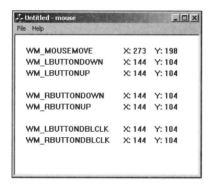

Figure 15-2: The Mouse application displayed with the events it's currently handling.

The Mouse application also demonstrates mouse capture techniques. There may be times when your application needs to receive mouse messages even when the mouse isn't over the application's client area. For example, in a paint program, users may hold down the left mouse button as they draw a line in the window. If a user accidentally drags the mouse pointer outside of the paint application's window, the application must continue to receive mouse messages. Otherwise, if the user releases the mouse button outside of the window, the application will have no way of knowing that the user isn't still drawing.

Capturing mouse messages

To see mouse capture working, place the mouse pointer over the Mouse application's client area. Then hold down the right mouse button as you move the mouse around the screen. Even when the mouse leaves the application's window, the window continues to receive mouse messages.

When you move the mouse without holding down the right mouse button, the application stops receiving mouse messages the instant the mouse pointer leaves the application's client area.

For a more detailed look at message flow with and without mouse capture, run a second instance of the Mouse application. When the mouse pointer is over the first instance, Windows sends all mouse messages to that instance. Figure 15-3 shows two instances of the Mouse application. Notice that the mouse pointer is over the first instance, so Windows directs mouse messages to that window.

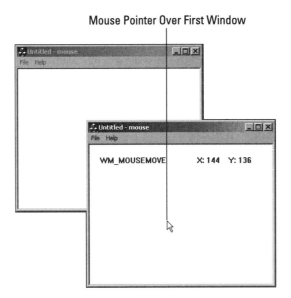

Figure 15-3: The first instance of the Mouse application displayed while receiving mouse messages

In Figure 15-4, the user has moved the mouse pointer over the second instance of the Mouse application. Now, Windows sends all mouse messages to the second instance's window, as you can tell by the appearance of the WM_MOUSEMOVE message in the window's client area.

Finally, Figure 15-5 shows the results of the user holding down the right mouse button when moving the mouse from the first instance of Mouse to the second instance. The first instance captures the mouse, so Windows sends all mouse messages to the first instance even when the mouse pointer is over the second (or over any other window). Notice that the WM_MOUSEMOVE coordinates are now negative. This is because WM_MOUSEMOVE coordinates are always relative to the upper-left corner of the window that has captured the mouse.

Chapter 15: Input Devices: The Mouse and the Keyboard

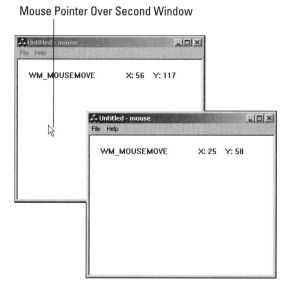

Figure 15-4: The second instance of the Mouse application displays output while receiving mouse messages.

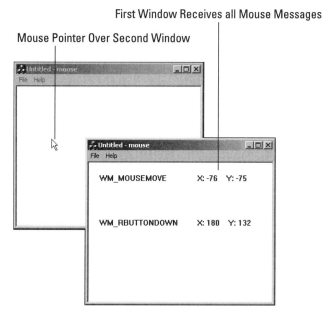

Figure 15-5: After the first instance of the Mouse application captures the mouse, mouse coordinates appear in the first instance's window.

Examining the Mouse application

Location: WinPrgS\Chap15\Mouse

As you've surely guessed, the Mouse application responds to mouse messages thanks to the message-response functions defined in the view window's class, CMouseView. This class is contained in the mouseView.cpp file on this book's CD-ROM. As is the rule in an MFC program, CMouseView uses a message map to associate messages with the appropriate message-response functions. The following code shows how the CMouseView class defines its message map:

```
BEGIN_MESSAGE_MAP(CMouseView, CView)
    //{{AFX_MSG_MAP(CMouseView)
    ON_WM_MOUSEMOVE()
    ON_WM_LBUTTONDOWN()
    ON_WM_LBUTTONUP()
    ON_WM_RBUTTONDOWN()
    ON_WM_RBUTTONUP()
    ON_WM_LBUTTONDBLCLK()
    ON_WM_RBUTTONDBLCLK()
    //}}AFX_MSG_MAP
END_MESSAGE_MAP()
```

Each of the macros that comprise the body of the message map associates a mouse message with its appropriate message handler. For example, the ON_WM_MOUSEMOVE macro tells MFC to call the OnMouseMove() function when the window receives a WM_MOUSEMOVE message. Similarly, the message map tells MFC to call OnLButtonDown() when the window receives a WM_LBUTTONDOWN message.

The text that appears in the Mouse application's window is displayed from the view class's message-response functions. For example, the following code shows the OnMouseMove() function:

```
void CMouseView::OnMouseMove(UINT nFlags, CPoint point)
{
    // TODO: Add your message handler code here and/or call default
    char str[50];
    CClientDC dc(this);
    dc.TextOut(20, 20, "WM_MOUSEMOVE");
    wsprintf(str, "X: %d    Y: %d    ", point.x, point.y);
    dc.TextOut(200, 20, str);

    CView::OnMouseMove(nFlags, point);
}
```

The Mouse application receives a stream of these messages as the mouse pointer moves over the application's window. The CPoint object that's passed as the function's second parameter contains the location of the mouse pointer at the time of the event. `OnMouseMove()` creates a display string from the `CPoint` object and displays the string in the application's window.

The `OnLButtonDown()`, `OnLButtonUp()`, `OnLButtonDblClk()`, and `OnRButtonDblClk()` functions all work similarly, translating the `CPoint` object into a display string that's drawn in the application's window. The `OnRButtonDown()` and `OnRButtonUp()` functions, however, have a little extra work to do, because it's in those functions that the application captures and releases the mouse.

Problems & Solutions

Handling Mouse and Keyboard Events

PROBLEM: *How can I tell if the user has clicked a mouse button with either the Shift or Ctrl key pressed?*

SOLUTION: You may have noticed that the MFC message-response functions for mouse messages receive two parameters: `nFlags` and `point`. You already know that `point` is a `CPoint` object containing the mouse's coordinates at the time of the message. The secret to discovering whether the user has performed a Shift-click or a Ctrl-click is to examine the `nFlags` parameter. In fact, you can determine the state of both the Ctrl and Shift keys, as well as all the mouse buttons, from the bits contained in `nFlags`. You can even tell whether the user has pressed more than one mouse button simultaneously.

Visual C++ defines a number of constants that you can use as bit masks to discover the contents of the bit flags in `nFlags`. The constants are `MK_CONTROL` (the Ctrl key flag), `MK_LBUTTON` (the left mouse button flag), `MK_MBUTTON` (the middle mouse button flag), `MK_RBUTTON` (the right mouse button flag), and `MK_SHIFT` (the Shift key flag). To determine the state of a key or mouse button, perform a bitwise AND against `nFlags`. For example, to determine whether the Shift key was pressed at the time of a mouse click, perform the following calculation:

```
BOOL shift = nFlags & MK_SHIFT;
```

The following code shows the `OnRButtonDown()` function, which not only displays information about the mouse message, but also calls `SetCapture()` to capture the mouse. After the call to `SetCapture()`, Windows directs all mouse messages to the Mouse application, regardless of where the mouse pointer happens to be:

```
void CMouseView::OnRButtonDown(UINT nFlags, CPoint point)
{
    // TODO: Add your message handler code here and/or call default

    SetCapture();

    char str[50];
    CClientDC dc(this);
    dc.TextOut(20, 100, "WM_RBUTTONDOWN");
    wsprintf(str, "X: %d    Y: %d    ", point.x, point.y);
    dc.TextOut(200, 100, str);

    CView::OnRButtonDown(nFlags, point);
}
```

When the user releases the right mouse button, the Mouse application releases the mouse capture. This event happens in the `OnRButtonUp()` function, as shown here:

```
void CMouseView::OnRButtonUp(UINT nFlags, CPoint point)
{
    // TODO: Add your message handler code here and/or call default
    ReleaseCapture();

    char str[50];
    CClientDC dc(this);
    dc.TextOut(20, 120, "WM_RBUTTONUP");
    wsprintf(str, "X: %d    Y: %d    ", point.x, point.y);
    dc.TextOut(200, 120, str);

    CView::OnRButtonUp(nFlags, point);
}
```

Here, `OnRButtonUp()` calls the `ReleaseCapture()` function, which is the counterpart to `SetCapture()`. After the call to `ReleaseCapture()`, Windows goes back to sending mouse messages to the window over which the mouse is positioned. That is, the Mouse application goes back to receiving mouse messages only when the mouse pointer is over the application's client area.

Note

Windows 3.x allowed an application to capture the mouse for an indefinite amount of time. If the application that captured the mouse failed to release the mouse, no other application could ever receive mouse messages. Windows 2000 solves this problem by allowing the mouse capture to continue for only as long as a mouse button remains pressed. That is, the Mouse application would run fine under Windows 2000 if the call to `ReleaseCapture()` were left out of the `OnRButtonUp()` function. However, in the spirit of good programming, you should always release the mouse after capturing it.

Handling the Keyboard

Just as Windows sends messages to an application when the user moves or clicks the mouse, so too does Windows send messages to an application when the user types on the keyboard. The big difference between mouse messages and keyboard messages is that mouse messages get sent to the window where the mouse is positioned, and keyboard messages always get sent to the window with the input focus, which is usually the topmost window on the screen.

There are several ways your application can capture and respond to keyboard events. Which keyboard message you respond to depends on how you plan to use the keystrokes in your program. For example, one type of keyboard message sends only printable characters to your application, while others enable you to respond to the many special keys on the keyboard, such as the F keys, the arrow keys, the Delete key, and so on.

Keyboard Messages

Your application can respond to three main keyboard messages: WM_CHAR, WM_KEYDOWN, and WM_KEYUP. (Other, less-used, messages include WM_DEADCHAR and WM_SYSCHAR.) There are also two special messages — WM_SYSKEYDOWN and WM_SYSKEYUP — for system keys Alt and F10, for which Windows reserves special functions. Just as with nonclient-area mouse messages, you must be careful how you handle system keys. If you cripple their default behaviors, Windows will stop working the way the user expects it to work.

When the user presses and releases a key, Windows actually sends all three main keyboard messages. When the key goes down, Windows sends the WM_KEYDOWN and WM_CHAR messages. When the user releases the key, Windows sends the WM_KEYUP message. By responding to the appropriate message, you can create just about any kind of keyboard handler you need.

One exception to the preceding series of events is if the user presses a system key. For example, if the user presses the Alt key, Windows sends the application a WM_SYSKEYDOWN message. If the user presses another key along with the Alt key, Windows still sends WM_SYSKEYDOWN, instead of WM_KEYDOWN. Of course, when the user releases the Alt key, Windows sends the WM_SYSKEYUP message.

Another exception is when the user presses a key that doesn't represent a printable character. Such keys are the F1 through F12 function keys, the Delete key, the arrow keys, and so on. Pressing and releasing one of these keys results in WM_KEYDOWN and WM_KEYUP messages, but no WM_CHAR messages. This is because WM_CHAR messages are sent only for keys that represent printable characters.

Each of the keyboard messages includes additional information about the keystroke. This additional information is packaged in the wParam and lParam parameters that the application receives as part of the message. If you're programming with MFC, the appropriate message-response functions "crack" these parameters into their individual components. For example, the signature for MFC's OnChar() function, which responds to the WM_CHAR message, looks like this:

```
void OnChar(UINT nChar, UINT nRepCnt, UINT nFlags)
```

Here, the cracked parameters are nChar, nRepCnt, and nFlags. The nChar parameter holds the keystroke's character; nRepCnt holds the number of times the key repeated; and nFlags holds more detailed information stored in its bits, as described in Table 15-3. The MFC OnKeyDown() and OnKeyUp() message-response functions, which respond to the WM_KEYDOWN and WM_KEYUP messages, receive the same parameters as OnChar().

Table 15-3 nFlag Data Fields

Bits	Description
0-15	The key's repeat count
16-23	The key's scan code
24	Extended key flag (0=not extended key; 1=extended key, such as a function key or a numeric keypad key)
25-28	Used internally by Windows
29	Alt key flag (0=Alt not pressed; 1=Alt pressed)
30	Previous key state flag (0=single stroke; 1=repeating stroke)
31	Press or release flag (0=key pressed; 1=key released)

The Keys Sample Application

Location: WinPrgS\Chap15\Keys

The Keys sample program on this book's CD-ROM illustrates how to intercept and respond to WM_CHAR messages. When you run the program, its main window appears. At first this window is blank, but when you press a key on your keyboard, the key's character appears in the window. As long as you press a key that represents a printable character, the appropriate character appears in the window. However, because the Keys application responds only to WM_CHAR messages, special keys such as F2, Ctrl, Insert, and End have no effect on the application's display. Figure 15-6 shows the Keys application in action, with a keystroke displayed in its window.

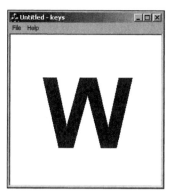

Figure 15-6: The Keys application with the "W" keystroke displayed in its window

Examining the Keys Application

Thanks to MFC's powerful message mapping, there's not a heck of a lot to know about the Keys application. As with any MFC window that responds to Windows messages, Keys' view window, represented by the `CKeysView` class, defines a message map that associates the `WM_CHAR` message with the `OnChar()` function, as shown here:

```
BEGIN_MESSAGE_MAP(CKeysView, CView)
    //{{AFX_MSG_MAP(CKeysView)
    ON_WM_CHAR()
    //}}AFX_MSG_MAP
END_MESSAGE_MAP()
```

The character that appears in the Keys application's window is stored in a `CString` member variable called `m_displayString`. The string is initialized with a new character every time a `WM_CHAR` message is processed by the `OnChar()` function, as shown here:

```
void CKeysView::OnChar(UINT nChar, UINT nRepCnt, UINT nFlags)
{
    // TODO: Add your message handler code here and/or call default

    m_displayString = nChar;
    Invalidate();

    CView::OnChar(nChar, nRepCnt, nFlags);
}
```

After assigning the new character to `m_displayString`, `OnChar()` calls `Invalidate()`, which forces the window to redraw itself. The view class's `OnDraw()` function displays the character, after creating a suitably large font. The following code sample shows the Keys application's `OnDraw()` function. If you don't understand how to create fonts, you can find the gory details in Chapter 4.

```
void CKeysView::OnDraw(CDC* pDC)
{
    CKeysDoc* pDoc = GetDocument();
    ASSERT_VALID(pDoc);

    // TODO: add draw code for native data here

    CFont font;
    font.CreateFont(200, 0, 0, 0, FW_BOLD, 0, 0, 0, DEFAULT_CHARSET,
        OUT_CHARACTER_PRECIS, CLIP_CHARACTER_PRECIS, DEFAULT_QUALITY,
        DEFAULT_PITCH | FF_DONTCARE, NULL);
    pDC->SelectObject(&font);
    pDC->TextOut(60, 40, m_displayString);
}
```

The KeyDown Sample Application

When programming Windows and MFC, there's always more than one way to skin the proverbial cat. Although responding to the WM_CHAR message may be all you need for some applications, the other mouse messages pass more keystrokes to your application, giving you better control over the keyboard.

CD

Location: WinPrgS\Chap15\KeyDown

The KeyDown sample program on this book's CD-ROM illustrates how to intercept and respond to WM_KEYDOWN and WM_KEYUP messages. When you run the program, you see a blank window. Start typing, and WM_KEYDOWN and WM_KEYUP messages appear in the window. Each WM_KEYDOWN message displayed in the window also provides useful information about the keystroke. Moreover, the KeyDown application responds to almost every key on the keyboard, rather than just the keys associated with printable characters.

Figure 15-7 shows KeyDown's display after the user has held down the F2 key for a second or two. Notice how the key repeated 10 times, but the Repeat value was always 1. This indicates that the system was able to keep up with the incoming keystrokes. Had the system been bogged down, it might have lumped several WM_KEYDOWN messages into a single one and then set nRepCnt to the number of keystrokes represented by the single message.

Another thing to notice about Figure 15-7 is how the character associated with the F2 keystroke is reported as "Q." This anomaly is caused by the fact that the nChar value for the F2 key, as well as for other special keys, represents a virtual key code, which you learn about in the following "Problems and Solutions" section.

Also, notice how the first WM_KEYDOWN message has a Previous value of 0. This is how you can tell that this WM_KEYDOWN message represents the first keystroke for the key. The remaining F2 keystrokes all have Previous values of 1, indicating that they resulted from the user holding down the key rather than pressing the key repeatedly.

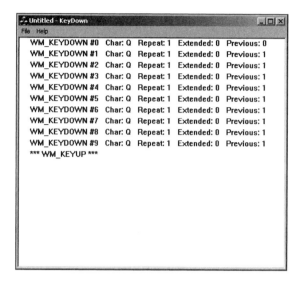

Figure 15-7: KeyDown displayed after the F2 key is held down for one to two seconds

Finally, the Extended value for all of the F2 keystrokes is 0, indicating that F2 is not an extended key. The extended keys include Insert, Home, PgUp, PgDn, Delete, and End. The arrow keys and the keypad's Enter and forward-slash keys are also extended keys. For example, Figure 15-8 shows the KeyDown application after the user has pressed several of the arrow keys. As you can see, the Extended value indicates that the keystrokes were made on extended keys.

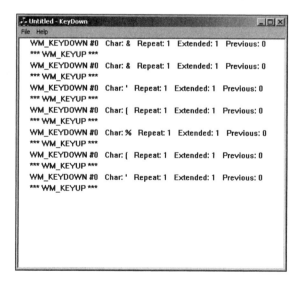

Figure 15-8: The KeyDown application showing extended keys

PROBLEMS & SOLUTIONS

Using Virtual Key Codes

PROBLEM: *How can I respond to special keys like F2 or the arrow keys when receiving keyboard messages?*

SOLUTION: Previously, I mentioned that the nChar parameter that MFC keyboard message-response functions receive can contain the actual character pressed or, in this case of special keys, a virtual key code. Visual C++ defines constants that represent all the virtual key codes you'll ever need, as you can see in Table 15-4, which lists the most commonly used. Just compare the nChar value with the appropriate constant in order to determine the key that was pressed. For example, to determine whether the user pressed the F2 key, you might write something like this:

```
if (nChar == VK_F2)
{
    // Handle F2 key here
}
```

Remember that if you want to respond to special keys, your application must watch for the WM_KEYDOWN and WM_KEYUP messages. The WM_CHAR message reports only keystrokes that result in printable characters.

Table 15-4 Virtual Key Codes

Code	Key
VK_ADD	+ on keypad
VK_BACK	Backspace
VK_CANCEL	Ctrl-Break
VK_CAPITAL	Caps Lock
VK_CLEAR	5 on keypad, Num Lock off
VK_CONTROL	Ctrl
VK_DECIMAL	. on keypad
VK_DELETE	Delete
VK_DIVIDE	/ on keypad
VK_DOWN	Down arrow
VK_END	End
VK_ESCAPE	Esc

Continued

Code	Key
VK_F1	F1
VK_F10	F10
VK_F11	F11
VK_F12	F12
VK_F2	F2
VK_F3	F3
VK_F4	F4
VK_F5	F5
VK_F6	F6
VK_F7	F7
VK_F8	F8
VK_F9	F9
VK_HOME	Home
VK_INSERT	Insert
VK_LEFT	Left arrow
VK_MENU	Alt
VK_MULTIPLY	* on keypad
VK_NEXT	PgDn
VK_NUMLOCK	Num Lock
VK_NUMPAD0	0 on keypad
VK_NUMPAD1	1 on keypad
VK_NUMPAD2	2 on keypad
VK_NUMPAD3	3 on keypad
VK_NUMPAD4	4 on keypad
VK_NUMPAD5	5 on keypad
VK_NUMPAD6	6 on keypad
VK_NUMPAD7	7 on keypad
VK_NUMPAD8	8 on keypad
VK_NUMPAD9	9 on keypad
VK_PAUSE	Pause
VK_PRIOR	PgUp
VK_RETURN	Enter

Continued

Table 15-4 *(continued)*

Code	Key
VK_RIGHT	Right arrow
VK_SCROLL	Scroll Lock
VK_SHIFT	Shift
VK_SNAPSHOT	Print Screen
VK_SPACE	Spacebar
VK_SUBTRACT	- on keypad
VK_TAB	Tab
VK_UP	Up arrow

Examining the KeyDown Application

As you've come to expect, KeyDown sets up a message map in its view class, CKeyDownView, which associates the messages it wants to handle with the message-response functions that handle them. In this case, the application must respond to WM_KEYDOWN and WM_KEYUP messages, so the message map looks like this:

```
BEGIN_MESSAGE_MAP(CKeyDownView, CView)
    //{{AFX_MSG_MAP(CKeyDownView)
    ON_WM_KEYDOWN()
    ON_WM_KEYUP()
    //}}AFX_MSG_MAP
END_MESSAGE_MAP()
```

The application stores the incoming messages in a CStringArray object. The view class's OnDraw() function is then charged with the task of displaying the contents of the array, as shown here:

```
void CKeyDownView::OnDraw(CDC* pDC)
{
    CKeyDownDoc* pDoc = GetDocument();
    ASSERT_VALID(pDoc);

    // TODO: add draw code for native data here

    for (int x=0; x<20; ++x)
    {
        CString s = m_stringArray.GetAt(x);
        pDC->TextOut(20, x*20, s);
    }
}
```

Chapter 15: Input Devices: The Mouse and the Keyboard

Using the string array enables the program to create a pseudo-scrolling display without being stuck with all the code required to set up a real scrolling window. The array is updated in the OnKeyDown() and OnKeyUp() functions. These functions manipulate the contents of the array such that it appears in the window as a scrolling list. The following code shows OnKeyDown(), which has the more complicated task of not only reporting the message, but also of deciphering the extra information that the KeyDown application displays with the WM_KEYDOWN message:

```
void CKeyDownView::OnKeyDown(UINT nChar, UINT nRepCnt,
    UINT nFlags)
{
    // TODO: Add your message handler code here
    //    and/or call default

    char c[80];
    wsprintf(c, "WM_KEYDOWN #%d    Char: %c   \
Repeat: %d    Extended: %d    Previous: %d",
        m_keyDownCount++, nChar, nRepCnt,
        (nFlags > 8) & 0x01, (nFlags > 14) & 0x01);

    CString str(c);

    if (m_stringCount < 20)
        m_stringArray.SetAt(m_stringCount++, str);
    else
    {
        for (int x=0; x<19; ++x)
        {
            CString s = m_stringArray.GetAt(x+1);
            m_stringArray.SetAt(x, s);
        }
        m_stringArray.SetAt(19, str);
    }

    Invalidate();

    CView::OnKeyDown(nChar, nRepCnt, nFlags);
}
```

Here, also, is the OnKeyUp() function:

```
void CKeyDownView::OnKeyUp(UINT nChar, UINT nRepCnt,
    UINT nFlags)
{
    // TODO: Add your message handler code here
    //    and/or call default

    m_keyDownCount = 0;

    if (m_stringCount < 20)
        m_stringArray.SetAt(m_stringCount++,
            "*** WM_KEYUP ***");
```

```
    else
    {
        for (int x=0; x<19; ++x)
        {
            CString s = m_stringArray.GetAt(x+1);
            m_stringArray.SetAt(x, s);
        }
        m_stringArray.SetAt(19, "*** WM_KEYUP ***");
    }

    Invalidate();

    CView::OnKeyUp(nChar, nRepCnt, nFlags);
}
```

PROBLEMS & SOLUTIONS

Tracking the Shift, Ctrl, and Alt Keys

PROBLEM: *How can I determine whether the user has pressed the Shift, Ctrl, or Alt key along with a keystroke?*

SOLUTION: The keyboard messages don't include information on the Shift and Ctrl keys, but they do give you the state of the Alt key in bit 13 of the nFlags parameter. To discover the state of the Alt key, you might write a code line like this:

```
BOOL altDown = (nFlags > 13) & 0x01;
```

Normally, though, you don't need to check explicitly for the Alt key, because if the Alt key is pressed, you get WM_SYSKEYDOWN and WM_SYSKEYUP messages instead of WM_KEYDOWN and WM_KEYUP.

What about Shift and Ctrl? Although information about these keys is not included with the keyboard messages' other baggage, you can still get this state information easily enough by calling the Windows API function GetKeyState(). This handy function takes a single argument, which is a value representing the key you want to check. Visual C++ defines constants—VK_SHIFT, VK_CONTROL, and VK_MENU—for these values (refer to Table 15-4). For example, to check the state of the Shift key, you'd write something like this:

```
int shiftDown = ::GetKeyState(VK_SHIFT);
```

GetKeyState() returns a negative value if the key is pressed and a nonnegative value if the key is not pressed.

Summary

Virtually every program you write will require some sort of mouse and keyboard handling. These two devices are, after all, the main way that users enter information into a computer. This chapter has shown you the basic techniques for responding to the mouse and the keyboard in an MFC application. Along the way, you learned a few extra tricks, such as capturing the mouse and determining when the user is holding down the Shift, Ctrl, or Alt keys.

Also discussed in this chapter:

- Windows sends messages to an application when the user manipulates the mouse or types on the keyboard.
- When the mouse pointer is over a window's client area, the window receives client-area mouse messages.
- When the mouse pointer is over the window's nonclient area (title bar, border, or controls), the window receives nonclient-area mouse messages.
- A window can capture the mouse in order to force Windows to send all mouse messages to the window, even when the mouse pointer is outside the window's boundaries.
- Windows sends various types of character codes with the WM_CHAR message, including ASCII values and key codes for extended keys.
- A Windows application can capture key-down and key-up messages, or just receive character messages.
- Windows defines a set of virtual key-code constants that represent the keys of the keyboard.

Chapter 16

File Handling

In This Chapter

▶ Implementing document/view architecture
▶ Understanding persistent objects
▶ Handling files with the `CFile` class

When you're programming with Visual C++, you have several methods of file handling available. These include taking advantage of MFC's document/view architecture, using archive objects to create persistent classes, and using MFC's `CFile` class to manipulate files more directly. If you create your application using MFC's document/view architecture, file handling comes almost for free, with the document class's `Serialize()` member function doing most of the work for you. When you use the `CFile` class, you can manipulate files more like you used to in DOS programs — by opening a file, writing data to the file, and then closing the file. In this chapter, you learn the various ways you can save and load data to and from a disk file.

The Document/View Architecture

MFC's document/view architecture enables your application to separate the way data is stored from the way it's viewed. Specifically, the application's document class is responsible for holding the data for the currently open document, as well as for serializing the data to and from a disk file. The view class, on the other hand, displays the data and enables the user to edit the data in whatever way is appropriate for the application.

Although many things about the document/view architecture relate only indirectly to file I/O, the document and view classes work together so tightly that it's difficult to separate one element of the architecture from the other. Therefore, in this section, you learn not only how to save and load documents using the document and view classes, but also how to construct an application that employs the document/view architecture.

The easiest way to implement the document/view architecture in an application is to create the application with AppWizard. The source code that AppWizard generates contains all the nuts and bolts required to implement functioning document and view classes. You only need to add the source code to handle the specific type of data for your application. To implement the document/view architecture, you must complete the following steps:

1. Use AppWizard to create a skeleton application.
2. Declare the data objects needed to hold the document's data in the document class.
3. Complete the document class's `OnNewDocument()` function in order to initialize a new document.
4. Override the `DeleteContents()` function in the document class in order to delete data from the previous document.
5. Complete the document class's `Serialize()` function in order to save and load document data.
6. Complete the view class's `OnDraw()` function in order to display the contents of the current document.
7. In the view class, add the code needed to enable the user to edit the document's data.

Location: `WinPrg5\Chap16\String`

On this book's CD-ROM, you can find the source code and executable file for the String application, a program that uses the document/view architecture to enable the user to save, load, and edit an array of strings. In the following sections, you examine each of the seven previous steps as they apply to the building of the String application.

Step 1: Create a Skeleton Application

You should already know how to create a new application with AppWizard. If you need a refresher course, please refer to your Visual C++ documentation. To create the String application, start a new project workspace called `string`. Then, use the following settings in AppWizard's six wizard pages to finish the skeleton application:

  Step 1 of 6 page — Select the single document interface.

  Step 2 of 6 page — Accept all default settings.

  Step 3 of 6 page — Accept all default settings.

  Step 4 of 6 page — Shut off all features except 3D controls.

  Step 5 of 6 page — Select the statically linked library.

  Step 6 of 6 page — Accept all default settings.

When you click the Finish button on the Step 6 of 6 wizard page, you should see the New Project Information dialog box shown in Figure 16-1.

Chapter 16: File Handling

Figure 16-1: After choosing settings in the six wizard pages for the String application, AppWizard displays the New Project Information dialog box.

Step 2: Declare the Document's Data Objects

The next step is to declare member variables where the application can store its data. Because the String application's data consists of an array of strings, the MFC CStringArray class is the perfect data type. Add a data member called m_strArray to the CStringDoc document class. This data member should be an object of the CStringArray class and have public access, as shown in Figure 16-2.

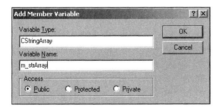

Figure 16-2: Here's the document class's new data member after adding m_strArray to the CStringDoc document class.

Step 3: Complete the OnNewDocument() Function

Whenever the user creates a new document, MFC calls the document class's OnNewDocument() function, which gives the application a chance to initialize the new document. In the case of the String application, `OnNewDocument()` adds a header string to the string array. Every String document has this editable header string, which the application displays at the top of the window. Following is the completed `OnNewDocument()` function:

```
BOOL CStringDoc::OnNewDocument()
{
    if (!CDocument::OnNewDocument())
        return FALSE;

    // TODO: add reinitialization code here
    // (SDI documents will reuse this document)

    m_strArray.Add("DEFAULT HEADER STRING");

    return TRUE;
}
```

Step 4: Override the DeleteContents() Function

When the user creates a new application document (either explicitly or just by starting the application), MFC calls `DeleteContents()` so the application can delete any data objects that remain from the previous document. This gives the new document a fresh start. Because MFC calls `DeleteContents()` when the application first runs, you must be sure to check for empty documents in order to avoid crashing the program when there is no previous document. You don't want to try to access objects before they've been created. You can override `DeleteContents()` using ClassWizard, as shown in Figure 16-3. Following is String's completed `DeleteContents()` function. (The call to `m_strArray.RemoveAll()` is safe even if the array is empty.)

```
void CStringDoc::DeleteContents()
{
    // TODO: Add your specialized code here and/or call the base class

    m_strArray.RemoveAll();

    CDocument::DeleteContents();
}
```

Step 5: Complete the Serialize() Function

The document class's `Serialize()` function is where the document's data is loaded from or saved to disk. `Serialize()`'s single parameter is a `CArchive` object that can serialize many types of data, including classes like `CString`. To serialize data to the archive, use the << operator. To serialize data from the archive, use the >> operator. MFC defines both of these operators in the `CArchive` class so that you can easily save and load many types of data.

Chapter 16: File Handling

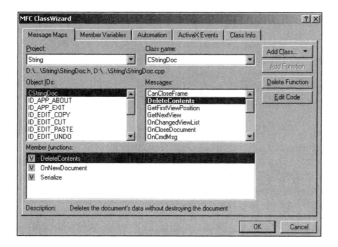

Figure 16-3: Override `DeleteContents()` with ClassWizard.

Unfortunately, a `CStringArray` object is not one of the data types supported by the `CArchive` class. Therefore, in order to save or load the strings contained in the `m_strArray` data member, the program extracts the strings from the array before serializing them. The completed `Serialize()` function looks like this:

```
void CStringDoc::Serialize(CArchive& ar)
{
    int size;

    if (ar.IsStoring())
    {
        // TODO: add storing code here

        size = m_strArray.GetSize();
        ar << size;
        for (int x=0; x<size; ++x)
        {
            CString str = m_strArray.GetAt(x);
            ar << str;
        }
    }
    else
    {
        // TODO: add loading code here

        ar > size;
        for (int x=0; x<size; ++x)
        {
            CString str;
            ar > str;
            m_strArray.Add(str);
```

```
        }
        UpdateAllViews(NULL);
    }
}
```

In the `Serialize()` function, notice the call to `UpdateAllViews()` after loading a document. This call ensures that the document's view is updated with the newly loaded data.

One great thing about many MFC classes is that they are *persistent,* which means that they are fully capable of serializing their contents without your having to extract the data manually. You learn more about persistent classes later in this chapter. For now, take a look at the following code, which shows an alternative way to write the `Serialize()` function, taking advantage of the `CStringArray` class's persistence:

```
void CStringDoc::Serialize(CArchive& ar)
{
    m_strArray.Serialize(ar);

    if (ar.IsStoring())
    {
        // TODO: add storing code here

    }
    else
    {
        // TODO: add loading code here

        UpdateAllViews(NULL);
    }
}
```

In this version of the function, the program merely calls the `m_strArray`'s `Serialize()` function to handle the saving and loading tasks. The only other thing the document class's `Serialize()` function must do is call `UpdateAllViews()` to update the application's view window.

Step 6: Complete the OnDraw() Function

In your application's view class, the `OnDraw()` function is charged with displaying the current document in the application's window. How you display this data in your own applications is, of course, completely dependent upon the data and how you think it's best displayed. In the case of the String application, the display is just a list of the string array's contents, as shown in Figure 16-4. Following is the `CStringView` class's completed `OnDraw()` function:

```
void CStringView::OnDraw(CDC* pDC)
{
    CStringDoc* pDoc = GetDocument();
```

```
ASSERT_VALID(pDoc);

// TODO: add draw code for native data here

int row = 20;
int size = pDoc->m_strArray.GetSize();
for (int x=0; x<size; ++x)
{
    CString str = pDoc->m_strArray.GetAt(x);
    pDC->TextOut(20, row, str);
    if (x=0)
        row += 40;
    else
        row += 20;
}
}
```

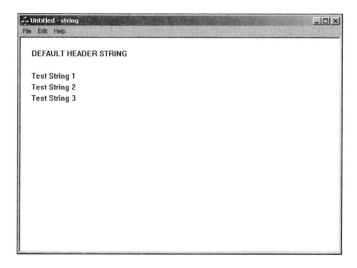

Figure 16-4: The String application displaying its document

Step 7: Add Editing Code

The final task in implementing an application with the document/view architecture is enabling the user to edit the document. In the String application, the user can add strings to the array, as well as change the header string, by selecting the Add String or Change Header commands, respectively. These commands display a dialog box in which the user types the new information. Here are the functions that display the dialog boxes and add the new data to the document:

```
void CStringView::OnEditAddstring()
{
    // TODO: Add your command handler code here
```

```
    CStringDoc* pDoc = GetDocument();
    CAddStringDlg dialog;
    int result = dialog.DoModal();

    if (result == IDOK)
    {
        CString str = dialog.m_string;
        pDoc->m_strArray.Add(str);
        Invalidate();
    }
}

void CStringView::OnEditChangeheader()
{
    // TODO: Add your command handler code here

    CStringDoc* pDoc = GetDocument();
    CChangeHeaderDlg dialog;
    int result = dialog.DoModal();

    if (result == IDOK)
    {
        CString str = dialog.m_header;
        pDoc->m_strArray.SetAt(0, str);
        Invalidate();
    }
}
```

Figure 16-5 shows the dialog box that adds a string to the document. The dialog box that changes the header looks about the same.

Figure 16-5: The String application provides a dialog box for adding a string.

Persistent Objects

A persistent object can serialize its state and contents. A good example of a persistent object is the CStringArray object you used in the previous section to store document data. To save or load the object's contents to and from a file, you only needed to call the object's Serialize() function with a reference to a CArchive object. MFC classes, however, aren't the only classes that can be serialized. Any class that you create can be made persistent, simply by following a few easy steps:

1. Derive your new class from MFC's CObject class.
2. Include the DECLARE_SERIAL macro in the class's declaration.

3. Provide a default constructor for the class.
4. Provide a Serialize() function in the class.
5. Include the IMPLEMENT_SERIAL macro in the class's definition.

Location: **WinPrgS\Chap16\PersistCircleApp**

On this book's CD-ROM is a new version of PrintCircleApp. You originally developed the program in Chapter 8. The new version, called PersistCircle App, uses a persistent class to store the document's circles. From the user's point of view, this new version works just like the old one; the differences are all internal. For example, the following code shows the header file for the class that the program uses to store its document data:

```
/////////////////////////////////////////////////
// CCircles.h
/////////////////////////////////////////////////

struct CircleStruct
{
    CPoint point;
    COLORREF color;
    int diameter;
};

class CCircles : public CObject
{
    DECLARE_SERIAL(CCircles)

    CCircles();

protected:
    CPtrArray m_circleArray;

public:
    void AddCircle(CPoint point, COLORREF color,
        int diameter);
    int GetCircleCount();
    void GetCircle(int circleNum, CircleStruct* circle);
    void DeleteAllCircles();
    void Serialize(CArchive& ar);
};
```

As you can see, CCircles is derived from CObject. The class declaration also includes the DECLARE_SERIAL macro. (The macro's single argument is the name of the class you're declaring as serializable.) The new class also provides a default constructor. The constructor is defined in the class's implementation file.

The CCircles class has a single data member, which is an object of the CPtrArray class. The original program used the CPtrArray class to store the circles that make up a document. The CCircles class uses the CPtrArray object, m_circleArray, in exactly the same way. Now, however, the details of handling m_circleArray are hidden from the main program, which accesses the array only through the public member functions provided by CCircles. The public member functions, along with their descriptions, are listed here:

AddCircle()	Adds a circle to the circle array
DeleteAllCircles()	Deletes all circles from the circle array
GetCircle()	Gets the data for a given circle
GetCircleCount()	Returns the current number of circles in the circle array
Serialize()	Performs object serialization for the class

The header file declares the class's Serialize() function. The class also has to define the Serialize() function, which it does in its implementation file, as shown here:

```
/////////////////////////////////////////////////
// CCircles.cpp
/////////////////////////////////////////////////

#include "stdafx.h"
#include "CCircles.h"

IMPLEMENT_SERIAL(CCircles, CObject, 1)

CCircles::CCircles()
{
}

void CCircles::AddCircle(CPoint point,
    COLORREF color, int diameter)
{
    CircleStruct* circle = new CircleStruct;
    circle->point = point;
    circle->color = color;
    circle->diameter = diameter;
    m_circleArray.Add(circle);
}

int CCircles::GetCircleCount()
{
    return m_circleArray.GetSize();
}

void CCircles::GetCircle(int circleNum,
    CircleStruct* circle)
{
    CircleStruct* circleStruct =
        (CircleStruct*)m_circleArray.GetAt(circleNum);
```

```
        circle->point = circleStruct->point;
        circle->color = circleStruct->color;
        circle->diameter = circleStruct->diameter;
    }

    void CCircles::DeleteAllCircles()
    {
        int size = GetCircleCount();
        for (int x=0; x<size; ++x)
        {
            CircleStruct* circle =
                (CircleStruct*)m_circleArray.GetAt(x);
            delete circle;
        }
        m_circleArray.RemoveAll();
    }

    void CCircles::Serialize(CArchive& ar)
    {
        CObject::Serialize(ar);

        if (ar.IsStoring())
        {
            CircleStruct circle;
            int size = GetCircleCount();
            ar << size;

            for (int x=0; x<size; ++x)
            {
                GetCircle(x, &circle);
                ar << circle.point;
                ar << circle.color;
                ar << circle.diameter;
            }
        }
        else
        {
            int size;
            ar > size;

            for (int x=0; x<size; ++x)
            {
                CPoint point;
                COLORREF color;
                int diameter;
                ar > point;
                ar > color;
                ar > diameter;
                AddCircle(point, color, diameter);
            }

        }
    }
```

The first thing to notice here is the `IMPLEMENT_SERIAL` macro. The macro's three arguments are the name of the class you're declaring as serializable, the name of the immediate base class, and a schema, or version, number.

The most important part of this class (at least from the point of view of file handling) is the `Serialize()` function, which is what makes `CCircles` persistent. The `Serialize()` function, which transfers the object's data (or state) to and from a file, looks quite a bit like the `Serialize()` function you wrote for the document class in the original version of the program. Here is the original document class's `Serialize()` function:

```
void CCircleAppDoc::Serialize(CArchive& ar)
{
    if (ar.IsStoring())
    {
        // TODO: add storing code here
        int size = m_circleArray.GetSize();
        ar << size;

        for (int x=0; x<size; ++x)
        {
            CircleStruct* circle =
                (CircleStruct*)m_circleArray.GetAt(x);
            ar << circle->point;
            ar << circle->color;
            ar << circle->diameter;
        }
    }
    else
    {
        // TODO: add loading code here
        int size;
        ar > size;
        m_circleArray.SetSize(size);

        for (int x=0; x<size; ++x)
        {
            CPoint point;
            COLORREF color;
            int diameter;
            ar > point;
            ar > color;
            ar > diameter;
            CircleStruct* circle = new CircleStruct;
            circle->point = point;
            circle->color = color;
            circle->diameter = diameter;
            m_circleArray.SetAt(x, circle);
        }

        UpdateAllViews(NULL);
    }
}
```

Compare this older version with the new `Serialize()` function. The main difference is that `CCircles`'s `Serialize()` function calls the class's own member functions where appropriate, rather than always calling `CPtrArray` member functions.

Now that `CCircles` handles most of the serialization, how does the document class save a document? The following code shows the document class's new `Serialize()` function:

```
void CCircleAppDoc::Serialize(CArchive& ar)
{
    m_circles.Serialize(ar);

    if (ar.IsStoring())
    {
        // TODO: add storing code here
    }
    else
    {
        // TODO: add loading code here

        UpdateAllViews(NULL);
    }
}
```

As you can see, all it does is call `m_circles.Serialize()`. Note that `m_circles` is a `CCircles` object that then handles the serialization, whether the application is loading or saving the object. In the case of loading a document, `CCircleAppDoc::Serialize()` must also call `UpdateAllViews()` to ensure that the view window is updated with the newly loaded document.

Other functions in the original application have also changed in this new version. For example, the following code shows how the new view class's `OnLButtonDown()` member function adds a circle to the document, by calling a `CCircles` member function rather than a `CPtrArray` member function:

```
void CCircleAppView::OnLButtonDown(UINT nFlags,
    CPoint point)
{
    // TODO: Add your message handler code here
    //    and/or call default

    // Draw the new circle.
    CClientDC clientDC(this);
    CBrush brush(m_currentColor);
    CBrush* oldBrush = clientDC.SelectObject(&brush);
    int radius = m_currentDiameter / 2;
    clientDC.Ellipse(point.x-radius, point.y-radius,
        point.x+radius, point.y+radius);
    clientDC.SelectObject(oldBrush);

    // Store the new circle in the document.
```

```
    CCircleAppDoc* pDoc = GetDocument();
    pDoc->m_circles.AddCircle(point,
        m_currentColor, m_currentDiameter);

    CView::OnLButtonDown(nFlags, point);
}
```

Ditto for OnDraw(), which displays the circles in the view window. The following code shows the new OnDraw() function:

```
void CCircleAppView::OnDraw(CDC* pDC)
{
    CCircleAppDoc* pDoc = GetDocument();
    ASSERT_VALID(pDoc);

    // TODO: add draw code for native data here
    int size = pDoc->m_circles.GetCircleCount();

    for (int x=0; x<size; ++x)
    {
        CircleStruct circle;
        pDoc->m_circles.GetCircle(x, &circle);
        int radius = circle.diameter/2;
        int x1 = circle.point.x-radius;
        int y1 = circle.point.y-radius;
        int x2 = circle.point.x+radius;
        int y2 = circle.point.y+radius;
        COLORREF color = circle.color;
        CBrush brush(color);
        CBrush* oldBrush = pDC->SelectObject(&brush);
        pDC->Ellipse(x1, y1, x2, y2);
        pDC->SelectObject(oldBrush);
    }
}
```

A few other changes have been made to the document and view classes in order to accommodate the change from the CPtrArray data storage to the persistent CCircles object. If you want to examine those changes, you can find the complete source code on this book's CD-ROM.

PROBLEMS & SOLUTIONS

Saving Persistent and Nonpersistent Objects with Document/View Architecture

PROBLEM: *How do I save and load both persistent objects and nonpersistent objects in a program using the document/view architecture?*

Continued

Chapter 16: File Handling

SOLUTION: In order to avoid a lot of confusing source code, the program examples in this book tend to be overly simplified compared to real-world applications. For example, a real paint application would have much more complex data to serialize than does the trivial circle sample program. Some of this complex data may be stored in persistent classes, whereas other document data may be stored in nonpersistent data objects.

The good news is that a document's Serialize() function doesn't force you into an either/or situation. If you need to save both persistent objects and nonpersistent objects, write a Serialize() function like the one shown here:

```
void CCircleAppDoc::Serialize(CArchive& ar)
{
    m_circles.Serialize(ar);

    if (ar.IsStoring())
    {
        // TODO: add storing code here

        ar << msg;
    }
    else
    {
        // TODO: add loading code here

        ar > msg;

        UpdateAllViews(NULL);
    }
}
```

Here, the function first serializes persistent objects and then, in the if statement, saves or loads nonpersistent objects.

If you try this combined approach to serialization, be sure that you save the data objects in the same order that you load them. This is true, of course, for any type of file handling. There's nothing magical about serialization.

Location: `WinPrgS\Chap16\PersistCircleApp2`

On this book's CD-ROM, you'll find yet another version of the circle program. This version displays a message string in the window along with the circles, as shown in Figure 16-6. You can edit the message string by selecting the Circle menu's Change Message command. The program's document class serializes the circle data and the message string as previously described.

Continued

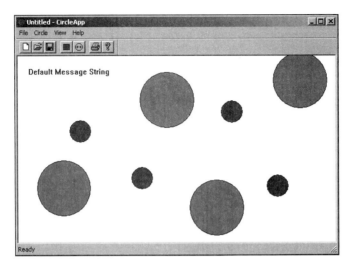

Figure 16-6: This version of the circle program serializes both persistent and nonpersistent data objects.

Reminding Users to Save Modified Files

PROBLEM: *How can I remind a user to save a modified file before closing it?*

SOLUTION: This handy feature is actually built into the MFC document classes. To take advantage of the feature, call the `SetModifiedFlag()` member function whenever the user changes the document. Then, when the user goes to close the document, MFC warns that the file needs saving. When the user saves the file, the document class clears the modified flag.

The following code shows the `OnCircleChangemessage()` function from the PersistCircleApp2 version of the circle application:

```
void CCircleAppView::OnCircleChangemessage()
{
    // TODO: Add your command handler code here
```

Continued

```
        CCircleAppDoc* pDoc = GetDocument();
        CMessageDlg dialog;
        dialog.m_message = pDoc->msg;
        int result = dialog.DoModal();
        if (result == IDOK)
        {
            pDoc->msg = dialog.m_message;
            pDoc->SetModifiedFlag();
            Invalidate();
        }
    }
```

This is the function that enables the user to change the message string displayed in the window. Notice the call to pDoc->SetModifiedFlag() in the if statement. That call is all it takes to tell the document class that the document needs to be saved. There's another call to SetModifiedFlag() in the view class's OnLButtonDown() function, where the view class adds circles to the display in response to the user's button clicks. Figure 16-7 shows the circle application when the user tries to exit the application before saving a modified file.

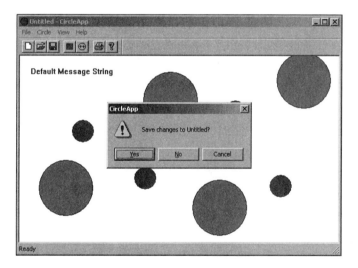

Figure 16-7: The circle application displayed with a dialog box asking whether the user wants to save the file; this dialog box appears when the user attempts to exit before saving a modified file.

File Handling with the CFile Class

Taking advantage of the document/view architecture and creating persistent objects are both great ways to manipulate files in your Visual C++ programs. However, sometimes you just want to handle the file yourself—opening, closing, reading, and writing a file directly. If this is the case, you might want to look into MFC's CFile class, which enables you to manipulate files more directly. Table 16-1 lists the member functions of the CFile class.

Table 16-1   CFile Member Functions

Function	Description
Abort()	Closes a file regardless of errors
Close()	Closes a file
Duplicate()	Creates a duplicate file object
Flush()	Flushes data not yet written
GetFileName()	Retrieves the file's name
GetFilePath()	Retrieves the file's complete path
GetFileTitle()	Retrieves the file's title
GetLength()	Returns the file's length
GetPosition()	Returns the file pointer
GetStatus()	Retrieves the file's status
LockRange()	Locks a portion of the file
Open()	Opens a file
Read()	Reads data from a file
ReadHuge()	Reads data from a file, using a DWORD read count
Remove()	Deletes a file
Rename()	Renames a file
Seek()	Positions the file pointer
SeekToBegin()	Positions the file pointer at the beginning of the file
SeekToEnd()	Positions the file pointer at the end of the file
SetFilePath()	Sets the file's path
SetLength()	Changes the file's length
SetStatus()	Sets the file's status
UnlockRange()	Unlocks a portion of the file
Write()	Writes data to a file
WriteHuge()	Writes data to a file, using a DWORD write count

To create a file, you simply create a `CFile` object by calling the `CFile` class's constructor with a file name and the appropriate access flags:

```
CFile file("testfile.txt",
    CFile::modeCreate | CFile::modeWrite);
```

Writing to the file is as easy as calling the file object's `Write()` member function:

```
file.Write("This is a test", 14);
```

`Write()`'s two arguments are the address of the data to write and the length of the data.

Finally, you close the file by calling . . . you guessed it . . . the `Close()` member function:

```
file.Close();
```

The `CFile` class defines a number of mode flags that you can use when you open or create a file. Table 16-2 lists these flags along with their descriptions.

Table 16-2 CFile File Mode Flags

Flag	Description
`CFile::modeCreate`	Creates a new file. If the file exists, its length is truncated to 0 length.
`CFile::modeNoInherit`	Disallows file inheritance by child processes.
`CFile::modeNoTruncate`	Disallows the file to be truncated if the file exists.
`CFile::modeRead`	Opens the file as read-only.
`CFile::modeReadWrite`	Opens the file for read and write access.
`CFile::modeWrite`	Opens the file as write-only.
`CFile::shareCompat`	Maps to `CFile::ShareExclusive`.
`CFile::shareDenyNone`	Opens the file, but doesn't deny read or write access to other processes.
`CFile::shareDenyRead`	Opens the file and denies read access to other processes.
`CFile::shareDenyWrite`	Opens the file and denies write access to other processes.
`CFile::shareExclusive`	Opens the file and denies read and write access to other processes.
`CFile::typeBinary`	Sets the binary mode in derived classes.
`CFile::typeText`	Sets the text mode in derived classes.

Reading from a file is just as easy as writing to one, as the following source code lines show:

```
CFile file("testfile.txt", CFile::modeRead);
char s[81];
int numBytes = file.Read(s, 80);
s[numBytes] = 0;
file.Close();
```

These lines perform the following actions:

- Open the file for reading
- Read up to 80 bytes into a character array
- Append a zero to the character array in order to form a C string
- Close the file

As you can see, the `Read()` function returns the number of bytes read from the file. The other `CFile` member functions are just as easy to use, especially if you're already familiar with C file handling.

PROBLEMS & SOLUTIONS

Detecting Errors When Handling Files with the CFile Class

PROBLEM: *When I'm handling files with the `CFile` class, how do I know whether the operations went OK or whether an error occurred?*

SOLUTION: Many of the `CFile` member functions throw `CFileException` exceptions when file operations fail. To handle errors, you should enclose your file-handling code in `try/catch` program blocks and then watch for the specific errors your program may generate. The following code shows how you might add error handling to your `CFile` file operations. You place the code that may generate errors in the `try` program block, and then place the error-handling code in the `catch` block:

```
try
{
    CFile file("testfile.txt", CFile::modeRead);
    char s[81];
    int numBytes = file.Read(s, 80);
    s[numBytes] = 0;
    file.Close();
}
catch (CFileException* fe)
{
```

Continued

```cpp
switch (fe->m_cause)
{
    case CFileException::fileNotFound:
        MessageBox("File not found",
            fe->m_strFileName);
        break;
    case CFileException::generic:
        MessageBox("Generic file error",
            fe->m_strFileName);
        break;
    case CFileException::badPath:
        MessageBox("Bad path",
            fe->m_strFileName);
        break;
    case CFileException::tooManyOpenFiles:
        MessageBox("Too many open files",
            fe->m_strFileName);
        break;
    case CFileException::accessDenied:
        MessageBox("Access denied",
            fe->m_strFileName);
        break;
    case CFileException::invalidFile:
        MessageBox("Invalid file",
            fe->m_strFileName);
        break;
    case CFileException::removeCurrentDir:
        MessageBox("Can't remove directory",
            fe->m_strFileName);
        break;
    case CFileException::directoryFull:
        MessageBox("Directory full",
            fe->m_strFileName);
        break;
    case CFileException::badSeek:
        MessageBox("Bad seek",
            fe->m_strFileName);
        break;
    case CFileException::hardIO:
        MessageBox("Hardware error",
            fe->m_strFileName);
        break;
    case CFileException::sharingViolation:
        MessageBox("Sharing violation",
            fe->m_strFileName);
        break;
    case CFileException::lockViolation:
        MessageBox("Lock violation",
            fe->m_strFileName);
        break;
```

Continued

```
              case CFileException::diskFull:
                  MessageBox("Disk full",
                      fe->m_strFileName);
                  break;
              case CFileException::endOfFile:
                  MessageBox("End of file",
                      fe->m_strFileName);
                  break;
        }
    }
```

A `CFileException` object contains the error that occurred in its `m_cause` member variable and the name of the file that caused the error in its `m_strFileName` member variable. As you can see in the preceding code, `CFile` objects can generate many different errors. Of course, in the sample listing, not all the errors could be generated by the calls to the `CFile` constructor and the `Read()` and `Close()` functions. The other error types are included in the listing for the sake of completeness.

Summary

No matter what type of application you're programming, Visual C++ features a file-handling method perfect for the task. Whether you want to deal with files directly or incorporate persistent objects into your project, MFC's document/view architecture provides a framework that makes it easy to provide professional-level document saving and loading features.

Also discussed in this chapter:

- MFC's document/view architecture separates the data that makes up a document from the way the user views and edits the document.
- Using AppWizard, you can create a skeleton program that supports the document/view architecture with a few mouse clicks.
- The document class's `Serialize()` member function is where data loading and saving occurs.
- You can create your own *persistent objects* (objects that can serialize their contents and states) easily by using the `DECLARE_SERIAL` and `IMPLEMENT_SERIAL` macros and by writing a `Serialize()` function for the class.
- MFC's `CFile` class provides object-oriented advantages, while at the same time enabling you to manage files directly.

Chapter 17

The Clipboard

In This Chapter

▶ Understanding the clipboard's standard data formats
▶ Using registered and private clipboard formats
▶ Providing multiple types of clipboard data

One of the big advantages of an operating system like Windows 2000 is its ability to share data between applications. Under Windows, you can share data in several ways, including using ActiveX to link or embed data objects. You learn about ActiveX in Part 4 of this book. For now, the easiest way to get data from one application to another is through the clipboard.

When using the clipboard, you can specify your application's document data type in various ways. Other applications that understand the data type can use their cut and paste functions to transfer the data to and from the clipboard, as well as render the data in their windows. It's up to you, as the programmer, to decide how your application's data should be represented in the clipboard. Windows gives you several options:

Standard formats	Windows defines a number of standard formats, such as text and bitmap, that applications can use to transfer data to and from the clipboard.
Private "display" formats	Windows also defines formats that the Windows clipboard viewer can display in a standard format but that are interpreted differently by an application that knows how to extract additional information from the data.
Registered formats	Applications can create their own clipboard formats and register the formats with Windows. Then, any application that understands the custom format can copy and paste data to and from the clipboard, as well as render the data in its window.

In the following sections, you learn how to use these methods of managing data with the clipboard.

Standard Formats

When you think about the clipboard, you often think in terms of copying text from one application and pasting it into another. Although this is the clipboard's most common use, it can handle other types of data as well. In fact, Windows defines a set of constants that programs use to identify the current contents of the clipboard. These constants and their purposes are listed in Table 17-1.

Table 17-1 Constants Used to Identify Clipboard Contents

Constant	Description
CF_BITMAP	A device-dependent bitmap.
CF_DIB	A device-independent bitmap (DIB).
CF_DIBV5	A device-independent bitmap with a BITMAPV5HEADER structure.
CF_DIF	Data Interchange Format (DIF) data.
CF_DSPBITMAP	Bitmap associated with a private format.
CF_DSPENHMETAFILE	Enhanced metafile associated with a private format.
CF_DSPMETAFILEPICT	Metafile-picture associated with a private format.
CF_DSPTEXT	Text associated with a private format.
CF_ENHMETAFILE	An enhanced metafile handle.
CF_GDIOBJFIRST through CF_GDIOBJLAST	Values for application-defined GDI object clipboard formats.
CF_HDROP	An HDROP handle for a list of files.
CF_LOCALE	A handle to the locale identifier for Clipboard text.
CF_METAFILEPICT	A special type of metafile that includes data stored in a METAFILEPICT structure.
CF_OEMTEXT	Text that uses the OEM character set.
CF_OWNERDISPLAY	Owner-display Clipboard format.
CF_PALETTE	A palette handle.
CF_PENDATA	Windows for Pen Computing pen extensions.
CF_PRIVATEFIRST through CF_PRIVATELAST	Values for private Clipboard formats.

Chapter 17: The Clipboard

Constant	Description
CF_RIFF	Nonstandard audio data.
CF_SYLK	Microsoft Symbolic Link (SYLK) data.
CF_TEXT	Plain text that's terminated with a NULL character. The text has carriage return and linefeed characters at the end of each line.
CF_TIFF	Tagged Image File Format (TIFF) picture data.
CF_WAVE	Standard audio data.
CF_UNICODETEXT	Unicode text Clipboard format.

As you can see, many of these clipboard formats have specific uses that you don't run into too often. The most commonly used formats are CF_TEXT and CF_BITMAP, for transferring text and image data between applications.

A Clipboard Example Application

As an example of transferring data in a standard format to the clipboard, you will examine a new version of the circle application that you created in Chapter 8. This new version has been modified to include a Copy command that creates a bitmap from the current document data and transfers the bitmap to the clipboard. Any application that can display bitmaps — such as Microsoft Paint — can then display a circle document.

The type of data created by an application's Copy command is completely dependent on the application; Windows really has nothing to do with it. However, when working with images, a Copy command usually creates bitmaps because there is no standard clipboard format. If the application wanted to copy data in another format to the clipboard, such as PCX, the application would have to register a custom clipboard format.

Location: WinPrgS\Chap17\CBCircleApp

You can find the new version of the circle application on this book's CD-ROM. When you run the program, you will immediately see that this version of the program has an Edit menu containing Copy and Paste commands. The Copy command copies the entire current document as a bitmap to the clipboard. You can then display the bitmap in an application such as Microsoft Paint, Microsoft Word, or any other application that can display bitmaps, by selecting the appropriate command, usually Paste.

To see the Copy command in action, follow these steps:

1. Run CBCircleApp.
2. When the application's main window appears, paint a few circles.

3. Select CBCircleApp's Copy command, as shown in Figure 17-1.

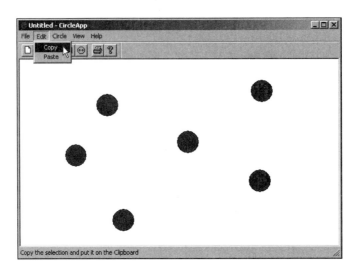

Figure 17-1: The Copy command copies the CircleApp document to the clipboard as a bitmap.

4. Run Microsoft Paint.
5. Select Microsoft Paint's Paste command from the Edit menu. The CBCircleApp document appears in Paint's window.

Copying a Bitmap to the Clipboard

Now that you've seen the clipboard in action, it's time to look behind the scenes and see how an application copies an image to the clipboard. Copying a bitmap to the clipboard is an easy process if you already have the bitmap created and ready to go. First, you call OpenClipboard() to open the clipboard:

```
BOOL open = OpenClipboard();
```

This function, which is a member function of the MFC CWnd class, returns TRUE if the clipboard opens successfully, and FALSE otherwise.

If the clipboard opens, you call EmptyClipboard():

```
::EmptyClipboard();
```

This Windows function call not only removes all previous data from the clipboard, but also makes your application the clipboard owner. As long as your application owns the clipboard, other applications cannot access it.

Chapter 17: The Clipboard

With the clipboard open and empty, you can then call Windows' SetClipboardData() function to copy the bitmap to the clipboard:

```
::SetClipboardData(CF_BITMAP, hBitmap);
```

SetClipboardData()'s two arguments are the data format (in this case, CF_BITMAP) and a handle to the data object. At this point, the clipboard owns the data, and your application should no longer access the data directly.

Most applications pass a copy of the data object to the clipboard so that the application can continue to access the original data.

The final step is to close the clipboard:

```
::CloseClipboard();
```

When you close the clipboard, you release your application's hold on it so that other applications can access the clipboard if they need to.

Because the clipboard is a shared system resource, an application should retain control of the clipboard only for a short period of time. The application should close the clipboard the instant it's finished with it.

The CBCircleApp application does its clipboard copying in the view class's OnEditCopy() function, which is the function that responds to the Edit menu's Copy command, as shown here:

```
void CCircleAppView::OnEditCopy()
{
    // TODO: Add your command handler code here

    BOOL open = OpenClipboard();
    if (open)
    {
        ::EmptyClipboard();

        CClientDC clientDC(this);
        CBitmap* pBitmap = new CBitmap();
        pBitmap->CreateCompatibleBitmap(&clientDC,
            800, 600);

        CDC memoryDC;
        memoryDC.CreateCompatibleDC(&clientDC);
        memoryDC.SelectObject(pBitmap);

        CBrush whiteBrush(RGB(255,255,255));
        memoryDC.FillRect(CRect(0,0,799,599),
            &whiteBrush);

        RenderDisplay(&memoryDC);

        HBITMAP hBitmap = (HBITMAP) *pBitmap;
        ::SetClipboardData(CF_BITMAP, hBitmap);
```

```
        ::CloseClipboard();
    }
}
```

If you're not familiar with bitmap handling, `OnEditCopy()` is probably befuddling. To learn more about bitmaps, go back to Chapter 9, read up on the subject, and meet the rest of us back here. The following overview of the function provides a general idea of what's going on. The `OnEditCopy()` function performs the following tasks:

- Opens and empties the clipboard:

  ```
  BOOL open = OpenClipboard();
  if (open)
  {
      ::EmptyClipboard();
  ```

- Creates an 800×600 bitmap that's compatible with the current display:

  ```
  CClientDC clientDC(this);
  CBitmap* pBitmap = new CBitmap();
  pBitmap->CreateCompatibleBitmap(&clientDC,
      800, 600);
  ```

- Creates a memory device context and selects the bitmap into it:

  ```
  CDC memoryDC;
  memoryDC.CreateCompatibleDC(&clientDC);
  memoryDC.SelectObject(pBitmap);
  ```

- Fills the bitmap with white:

  ```
  CBrush whiteBrush(RGB(255,255,255));
  memoryDC.FillRect(CRect(0,0,799,599),
      &whiteBrush);
  ```

- Calls the member function that draws the circle document onto the bitmap:

  ```
  RenderDisplay(&memoryDC);
  ```

- Transfers the bitmap to the clipboard:

  ```
  HBITMAP hBitmap = (HBITMAP) *pBitmap;
  ::SetClipboardData(CF_BITMAP, hBitmap);
  ```

- Closes the clipboard:

  ```
  ::CloseClipboard();
  ```

`RenderDisplay()` is a member function of the view class and does almost exactly what the original circle application's `OnDraw()` function did. In fact, in this version of the program, the `OnDraw()` function calls `RenderDisplay()`, too. The following code shows `RenderDisplay()` and `OnDraw()` for your comparison:

```
void CCircleAppView::RenderDisplay(CDC* pDC)
{
```

```cpp
    CCircleAppDoc* pDoc = GetDocument();

    int size = pDoc->m_circleArray.GetSize();

    for (int x=0; x<size; ++x)
    {
        CircleStruct* circle =
            (CircleStruct*)pDoc->m_circleArray.GetAt(x);
        int radius = circle->diameter/2;
        int x1 = circle->point.x-radius;
        int y1 = circle->point.y-radius;
        int x2 = circle->point.x+radius;
        int y2 = circle->point.y+radius;
        COLORREF color = circle->color;
        CBrush brush(color);
        CBrush* oldBrush = pDC->SelectObject(&brush);
        pDC->Ellipse(x1, y1, x2, y2);
        pDC->SelectObject(oldBrush);
    }
}

void CCircleAppView::OnDraw(CDC* pDC)
{
    CCircleAppDoc* pDoc = GetDocument();
    ASSERT_VALID(pDoc);

    // TODO: add draw code for native data here
    int size = pDoc->m_circleArray.GetSize();

    for (int x=0; x<size; ++x)
    {
        CircleStruct* circle =
            (CircleStruct*)pDoc->m_circleArray.GetAt(x);
        int radius = circle->diameter/2;
        int x1 = circle->point.x-radius;
        int y1 = circle->point.y-radius;
        int x2 = circle->point.x+radius;
        int y2 = circle->point.y+radius;
        COLORREF color = circle->color;
        CBrush brush(color);
        CBrush* oldBrush = pDC->SelectObject(&brush);
        pDC->Ellipse(x1, y1, x2, y2);
        pDC->SelectObject(oldBrush);
    }
}
```

As mentioned before, when you pass the bitmap (or any other data) to the clipboard, you should no longer access the bitmap in your application. The data belongs to the clipboard. If you need to access the data, you can extract it from the clipboard just as any other application would have to, or you can make a private copy of the data before passing it to the clipboard.

Once the clipboard is closed, it owns the data it contains. You should not attempt to access the data except through the clipboard. For this reason, if your application needs continuous access to the data, it must make a copy of that data.

For example, if the circle application needed to keep the bitmap's image on its display, it would have to redraw the bitmap when the window is redrawn. This requires having continual access to the bitmap retrieved from the clipboard, which requires that the application copy the bitmap before closing the clipboard. You might copy the bitmap in the OnEditPaste() function as follows:

1. Create a new MFC bitmap object from the data returned into the BITMAP structure:

   ```
   CBitmap myBitmap;
   myBitmap.CreateBitmapIndirect(&bitmapStruct);
   ```

2. Create a second memory DC into which the application can copy the bitmap:

   ```
   CDC dstMemDC;
   dstMemDC.CreateCompatibleDC(&clientDC);
   ```

3. Select the new bitmap object into the new memory DC:

   ```
   dstMemDC.SelectObject(myBitmap);
   ```

4. Copy the clipboard's bitmap (which is selected into the srcMemDC memory DC) into the new memory DC:

   ```
   dstMemDC.BitBlt(0, 0, bitmapStruct.bmWidth,
       bitmapStruct.bmHeight, &srcMemDC,
       0, 0, SRCCOPY);
   ```

Pasting a Bitmap from the Clipboard

Once you have copied a bitmap to the clipboard, you'll probably want to do something with it. Luckily, the new version of the circle application not only can copy bitmaps to the clipboard, it also can paste a bitmap from the clipboard into its display. However, because the program doesn't retain a copy of the bitmap, the bitmap display is only temporary. That is, when the window redraws itself, it draws only the current document, without any pasted bitmaps. Nor can the application print the pasted bitmap image.

To see the Paste command in action, follow these steps:

1. Run CBCircleApp.
2. Run Microsoft Paint.
3. Draw something in Paint's display.
4. Use Paint's selection tool to select and copy a piece of the display area (see Figure 17-2).

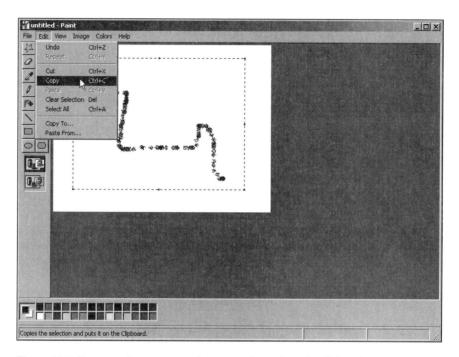

Figure 17-2: You can select a rectangular area and copy it to the clipboard as a bitmap.

5. Switch to CBCircleApp and select the Paste command. The Paint bitmap appears in the application's window.

Accessing and displaying data stored in the clipboard is a fairly simple process. First, you call `IsClipboardFormatAvailable()` to see whether the clipboard holds the type of data the application's looking for:

```
BOOL bitmapAvailable =
    IsClipboardFormatAvailable(CF_BITMAP);
```

The function's single argument is the format of the data for which you're checking. `IsClipboardFormatAvailable()` returns `TRUE` if the requested format is available, and `FALSE` otherwise.

If the format the application needs is available in the clipboard, you open the clipboard and call `GetClipboardData()` to obtain a handle to the data in the clipboard:

```
OpenClipboard();
HBITMAP hBitmap =
    (HBITMAP)::GetClipboardData(CF_BITMAP);
```

The `GetClipboardData()` function's single argument is the format of the data. If the call is successful, the function returns a handle to the data object. Otherwise, the return value is `NULL`.

As always, when you're through with the clipboard, you close it:

```
CloseClipboard();
```

The CBCircleApp application does its clipboard pasting in the view class's OnEditPaste() function, which responds to the Edit menu's Paste command:

```
void CCircleAppView::OnEditPaste()
{
    // TODO: Add your command handler code here

    BOOL bitmapAvailable =
        IsClipboardFormatAvailable(CF_BITMAP);
    if (bitmapAvailable)
    {
        OpenClipboard();
        HBITMAP hBitmap =
            (HBITMAP)::GetClipboardData(CF_BITMAP);

        CBitmap* bitmap = CBitmap::FromHandle(hBitmap);
        BITMAP bitmapStruct;
        bitmap->GetBitmap(&bitmapStruct);

        CClientDC clientDC(this);

        CDC srcMemDC;
        srcMemDC.CreateCompatibleDC(&clientDC);
        srcMemDC.SelectObject(bitmap);

        clientDC.BitBlt(0, 0, bitmapStruct.bmWidth,
            bitmapStruct.bmHeight, &srcMemDC,
            0, 0, SRCCOPY);

        CloseClipboard();
    }
}
```

Here, the function retrieves the bitmap from the clipboard exactly as previously described. However, before closing the clipboard, the function displays the bitmap in the window's client area. To do this, the program first creates an MFC bitmap object from the bitmap handle returned from the clipboard:

```
CBitmap* bitmap = CBitmap::FromHandle(hBitmap);
```

It then gets information about the bitmap, storing the information in a BITMAP structure:

```
BITMAP bitmapStruct;
bitmap->GetBitmap(&bitmapStruct);
```

Next, the program creates a device context for the window's client area:

```
CClientDC clientDC(this);
```

With a client DC in hand, the program can create a memory DC that's compatible with the client DC:

```
CDC srcMemDC;
srcMemDC.CreateCompatibleDC(&clientDC);
```

The memory DC will hold the bitmap just retrieved from the clipboard. To get the bitmap into the DC, the program calls `SelectObject()`:

```
srcMemDC.SelectObject(bitmap);
```

Finally, the program displays the bitmap by copying it from the memory DC to the client DC, which represents the window's client area:

```
clientDC.BitBlt(0, 0, bitmapStruct.bmWidth,
    bitmapStruct.bmHeight, &srcMemDC,
    0, 0, SRCCOPY);
```

Again, for a more detailed description of bitmaps and MFC's `CBitmap` class, please consult Chapter 9. You may also want to look over Chapter 2 for information about using device contexts and GDI objects.

Registered and Private Clipboard Formats

Although the standard clipboard formats defined by Windows include many common types of data, you may create an application containing data that doesn't fall into one of these types. For example, think about the circle application you created in Chapter 8. If that application supported clipboard copy and paste functions, what data format would you use to copy the file? You could transfer data as a bitmap, but using the bitmap format would cause the document to lose the data that defines the size, location, and color of each circle. This would leave you with nothing more than a picture of the document at the time it was copied into the clipboard, instead of a complete circle application document.

To overcome this type of problem, applications can define their own types of clipboard data. One way to do this is to transfer data using the standard clipboard types, but interpret the data differently in the application. For example, the circle application could use the plain text format to transfer the size, location, and color of each circle in a document as a series of text lines:

```
APP=CIRCLEAPP
COUNT=3
DIAMETER=40
X=116
Y=59
RED=255
GREEN=0
BLUE=0
DIAMETER=40
X=140
Y=206
```

```
RED=255
GREEN=0
BLUE=0
DIAMETER=100
X=266
Y=145
RED=128
GREEN=128
BLUE=255
```

The previous lines fully describe three circles in a circle application document. However, whereas a text application would paste these text lines as they are into the document window, the circle application (or an application that understands the circle application's data format) would know that it needs to parse the individual values from the text in order to re-create the `CircleStruct` structures that these lines represent.

When this data is pasted into the clipboard, it might not use the `CF_TEXT` format. Instead, it might use the `CF_DSPTEXT` format, which tells an application that the data is in text form but should be interpreted in some other way. An application that knows how to render data from the circle application watches for data in the `CF_DSPTEXT` format.

When the clipboard contains `CF_DSPTEXT` data, the application checks the first line of the text to see whether the circle application created the data (after all, any application can use `CF_DSPTEXT` in its own way for its own document data). If the text checks out as a circle application document, the application then parses the text lines, re-creating the original circle document.

Following are the constants you can use when copying or pasting clipboard data in special formats:

CF_DSPTEXT	Data of the `CF_TEXT` type not necessarily interpreted as text
CF_DSPBITMAP	Data of the `CF_BITMAP` type not necessarily interpreted as image data
CF_DSPMETAFILEPICT	Data of the `CF_METAFILEPICT` type not necessarily interpreted as a metafile picture
CF_DSPENHMETAFILE	Data of the `CF_ENHMETAFILE` type not necessarily interpreted as a metafile handle

The "DSP" in the previous constant names stands for "display," meaning that Windows' clipboard viewer can display these data types in their normal format (i.e., as text, bitmaps, and so on), but applications that understand the special data format can display the data as it was designed to be displayed.

Registering a Private Format

Another way to manage custom data types with the clipboard is to register a private clipboard data format. To do this, you devise your own format name, such as CF_CIRCLES, and register it with Windows. Your application, and other applications that understand the private data type, can then transfer data to and from the clipboard using the private format.

To register the private format in your program, call RegisterClipboardFormat():

```
int formatID = ::RegisterClipboardFormat("CF_CIRCLES");
```

The function returns an ID that identifies the format, and the function's single argument is the string that identifies the format.

PROBLEMS & SOLUTIONS

Delayed Rendering

PROBLEM: *If my application needs to copy a large data object, such as a full-screen bitmap, to the clipboard, doesn't the object continue to consume a lot of memory as long as it's in the clipboard? Is there some way to make better use of memory in this case?*

SOLUTION: It's true that any data object in the clipboard continues to take up memory until the object is removed. If that data object happens to be very large, a lot of memory can be wasted. If you're concerned about the wasted memory, there's a more memory-efficient way of handling the clipboard. This method involves something called *delayed rendering*.

When you use delayed rendering, you give the clipboard the data type (for example, CF_BITMAP) of a data object, but you don't provide the data object itself until an application tries to paste the data into a document. At that point, you create the data object and pass it to the clipboard.

Setting up the clipboard for delayed rendering is easy — just pass NULL as SetClipboardData()'s second argument, rather than passing the handle to the data object. For example, if you wanted to use delayed rendering with a bitmap, you might write the following lines:

```
BOOL open = OpenClipboard();
if (open)
{
    ::EmptyClipboard();
    ::SetClipboardData(CF_BITMAP, NULL);
    ::CloseClipboard();
}
```

Continued

That's all there is to it. However, you still need to supply the bitmap (or whatever data format you're using) when an application tries to paste from the clipboard. Windows uses three messages to manage delayed rendering:

WM_RENDERFORMAT	Windows sends this message when an application calls GetClipboardData( ) in order to obtain the contents of the clipboard. This is your application's signal to supply the data object.
WM_RENDERALLFORMATS	Windows sends this message if your application tries to terminate while it is still the owner of a clipboard containing NULL data objects. In response, you must supply handles for all data objects originally given to the clipboard as NULL.
WM_DESTROYCLIPBOARD	Windows sends this message when another application becomes the clipboard owner. In this case, the NULL data objects no longer exist, so your application is no longer responsible for providing handles to them.

When your application receives WM_RENDERFORMAT, you must pass the data object to the clipboard. You do this by calling SetClipboardData( ), this time supplying a handle to the object, rather than supplying NULL. Note that you should not call OpenClipboard( ) or CloseClipboard( ) in response to the WM_RENDERFORMAT message.

When your application receives WM_RENDERALLFORMATS, you must open and empty the clipboard, after which you must supply data objects to the clipboard for every NULL data object the application placed on the clipboard. The difference between WM_RENDERFORMAT and WM_RENDERALLFORMATS is that, with the latter, you supply all data formats the application passed to the clipboard, rather than just a requested format. Also, you must call OpenClipboard( ), EmptyClipboard( ), and CloseClipboard( ) when handing WM_RENDERALLFORMATS.

When your application receives WM_DESTROYCLIPBOARD, you don't have to do anything except release any resources you were holding in order to be able to handle WM_RENDERFORMAT or WM_RENDERALLFORMATS messages.

Location: **WinPrgS\Chap17\DelayedRender**

On this book's CD-ROM, you can find an application that demonstrates delayed rendering under MFC. To see delayed rendering work, run both the DelayedRender application and Notepad, sizing and positioning the windows so that they are both fully visible. Select DelayedRender's Copy command, and a message box tells you that the application is setting up delayed rendering (see Figure 17-3).

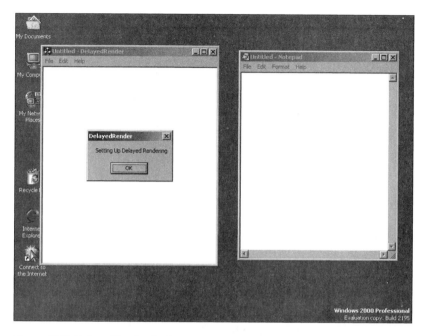

Figure 17-3: DelayedRender displays a message box when it's setting up the clipboard for delayed rendering.

Now, dismiss the message box, switch to Notepad, and select its Paste command. The text "A Test of Delayed Rendering" appears in the window. This text line wasn't passed to the clipboard until Notepad asked for it — an example of delayed rendering.

Next, highlight some text in Notepad's window and select Notepad's Copy command. Notepad takes over ownership of the clipboard, so Windows sends a WM_DESTROYCLIPBOARD message to DelayedRender, which you can verify by the message box that appears over DelayedRender's window (see Figure 17-4).

As a last experiment, switch back to DelayedRender, dismiss the message box, and select the Copy command. A message box tells you that the application is again setting up for delayed rendering. Dismiss the message box and close DelayedRender. A message box appears, telling you that the application is rendering all formats (in this case, there's only one format).

The source code that accomplishes this clipboard magic is fairly simple. When the user selects the Copy command, the view class's OnEditCopy() function creates a global memory block containing a line of text:

```
m_hText = ::GlobalAlloc(GHND, 29);
m_pText = (char*) ::GlobalLock(m_hText);
strcpy(m_pText, "A Test of Delayed Rendering.");
::GlobalUnlock(m_hText);
```

Continued

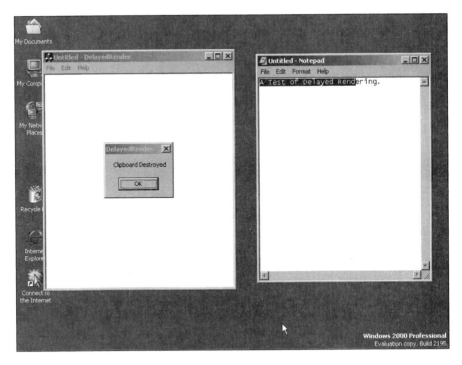

Figure 17-4: DelayedRender notifies you when it loses ownership of the clipboard.

This line of text represents the object that will utilize delayed rendering, simulating the user selecting and copying a large block of text from a document.

After storing the text in its memory block, `OnEditCopy()` passes the data type to the clipboard, but it passes `NULL` as the data object handle:

```
BOOL open = OpenClipboard();
if (open)
{
    ::EmptyClipboard();
    ::SetClipboardData(CF_TEXT, NULL);
    ::CloseClipboard();
}
```

When the user tries to paste from the clipboard, MFC calls the view class's `OnRenderFormat()` function:

```
void CDelayedRenderView::OnRenderFormat(UINT nFormat)
{
    if (nFormat == CF_TEXT)
        ::SetClipboardData(CF_TEXT, m_hText);
}
```

Continued

As you can see, `OnRenderFormat()` checks for the clipboard data type and, if the type is `CF_TEXT`, calls `SetClipboardData()` to give the text to the clipboard.

When DelayedRender terminates while owning the clipboard, MFC calls `OnRenderAllFormats()`. The `OnRenderAllFormats()` function, which handles the WM_RENDERALLFORMATS message, is similar to `OnRenderFormat()`, except it must open and close the clipboard, as well as render the text object:

```
void CDelayedRenderView::OnRenderAllFormats()
{
    MessageBox("Rendering All Formats");

    OpenClipboard();
    ::EmptyClipboard();
    ::SetClipboardData(CF_TEXT, m_hText);
    ::CloseClipboard();
}
```

Finally, `OnDestroyClipboard()`, which handles the WM_DESTROYCLIPBOARD message, simply deletes the text block, because the clipboard no longer needs it:

```
void CDelayedRenderView::OnDestroyClipboard()
{
    MessageBox("Clipboard Destroyed");

    if (m_pText != NULL)
        delete m_pText;
}
```

Multiple Clipboard Data Formats

In the spirit of sharing, applications that copy data to the clipboard should enable as many target applications as possible to display the data. This often means supplying data to the clipboard in more than one format. For example, the circle application could supply both a private clipboard data format and a normal bitmap image of the current display. Then, although bitmap-compatible applications wouldn't be able to edit a circle document, they could at least display an image of the document that was created by the circle application.

Supplying multiple data formats to the clipboard is as easy as creating the various types of data and passing them to the clipboard one after the other. Other applications can then check for a specific type (for example, `CF_BITMAP`) and, if the data exists in that format, extract it from the clipboard and display it. The more formats your application can provide to the clipboard, the better the chance that other applications can display the document.

Multiple Formats in Action

Location: `WinPrgS\Chap17\CBCircleApp2`

On this book's CD-ROM, you can find a version of CBCircleApp that copies its document to the clipboard in two forms: as a bitmap and as a text file. The text file is a list of each circle's attributes as described in the previous section. The data this version of CBCircleApp copies to the clipboard makes it possible for three types of applications to display data from CBCircleApp:

Any CBCircleApp-compatible application	Currently, only CBCircleApp itself fits this bill, but you could design your own applications that understand the text data format that CBCircleApp copies to the clipboard. These types of applications can re-create the actual CBCircleApp document and even enable the user to edit the document.
Most paint programs	Any program that can display a bitmap can display the bitmap that CBCircleApp copies to the clipboard. Such an application can display the CBCircleApp document exactly as it originally appeared. However, the display is only an image and not a real CBCircleApp document. (Many full-fledged word processors and other types of applications can also display bitmaps.)
Any text application	Most text-editing applications can display the text form of a CBCircleApp document. Unfortunately, such an application cannot re-create the actual document or even necessarily display the graphical image of the original document.

As you can see, although several types of applications can read CBCircleApp data from the clipboard, applications other than CBCircleApp-compatible applications lose something in the translation. A bitmap-compatible application loses all the data that describes the individual circles in the document, whereas a plain-text application loses all visual aspects of a CBCircleApp document, although it retains a complete description of each circle.

To see how CBCircleApp's multiple clipboard formats work, perform the following steps:

1. Start Microsoft Paint, Notepad, and CBCircleApp2.
2. Draw a few circles in CBCircleApp2's display.
3. Select the Copy command on CBCircleApp2's Edit menu. CBCircleApp2 copies the current document to the clipboard, both as a bitmap and as a text description.

4. Switch to Microsoft Paint and select its Paste command. The CBCircleApp2 bitmap appears in Paint's display.

5. Switch to Notepad and select its Paste command. The text version of the CBCircleApp2 document appears in Notepad's window, as shown in Figure 17-5.

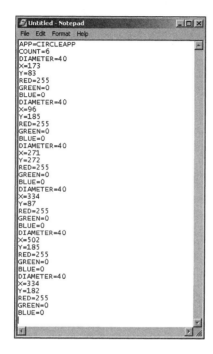

Figure 17-5: Notepad can display the CBCircleApp2 text from the clipboard.

6. Switch back to CBCircleApp2 and select the New command, either from the File menu or from the toolbar. CBCircleApp2 clears its window.

7. Create a few new circles in CBCircleApp2's window.

8. Select CBCircleApp2's Paste command. CBCircleApp2 reads the text version of the old CBCircleApp2 document from the clipboard and re-creates the original document from the information, pasting the old circle document in with the new one, as shown in Figure 17-6.

The document you create by merging the clipboard data with the current document is a full CBCircleApp2 document. You can save it, add circles to it, and reload it. You can even copy it to the clipboard.

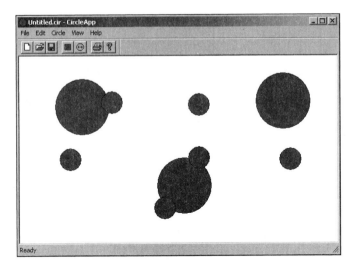

Figure 17-6: Here, CBCircleApp2 has pasted the circles from the clipboard in with the new circles.

Copying CircleApp Data in Multiple Formats

The following code shows the OnEditCopy() function, which MFC calls when the user selects the Edit menu's Copy command:

```
void CCircleAppView::OnEditCopy()
{
    // TODO: Add your command handler code here

    BOOL open = OpenClipboard();
    if (open)
    {
        ::EmptyClipboard();
        CBitmap* pBitmap = RenderAsBitmap();
        HBITMAP hBitmap = (HBITMAP) *pBitmap;
        ::SetClipboardData(CF_BITMAP, hBitmap);
        HGLOBAL hText = RenderAsText();
        ::SetClipboardData(CF_TEXT, hText);
        ::CloseClipboard();
    }
}
```

This function creates two versions of the circle document and makes both versions available to the clipboard. This enables several types of applications to display the document in one form or another. The function performs the following tasks:

- Opens and empties the clipboard
- Creates a bitmap version of the document

- Gives the bitmap to the clipboard
- Creates a text version of the document
- Gives the text version to the clipboard
- Closes the clipboard

As you can see in the listing, all of the details of rendering the document in its different formats are contained in the RenderAsBitmap() and RenderAsText() functions. The RenderAsBitmap() function is not unlike the OnEditCopy() function in the previous version of the circle application, as seen here:

```
CBitmap* CCircleAppView::RenderAsBitmap()
{
    CClientDC clientDC(this);
    CBitmap* pBitmap = new CBitmap();
    pBitmap->CreateCompatibleBitmap(&clientDC,
        800, 600);

    CDC memoryDC;
    memoryDC.CreateCompatibleDC(&clientDC);
    memoryDC.SelectObject(pBitmap);

    CBrush whiteBrush(RGB(255,255,255));
    memoryDC.FillRect(CRect(0,0,799,599),
        &whiteBrush);

    RenderDisplay(&memoryDC);

    return pBitmap;
}
```

This function performs the following tasks:

- Creates a bitmap that's compatible with the current display
- Creates a memory device context
- Selects the bitmap into the memory DC
- Clears the bitmap with white
- Draws the current circle document onto the bitmap
- Returns from the function a pointer to the bitmap

The RenderDisplay() function called from RenderAsBitmap() is exactly the same as the RenderDisplay() function in the previous CBCircleApp version. Moreover, as in that previous version, RenderDisplay() not only draws the document when a bitmap is needed for the clipboard, but also draws the document in CBCircleApp2's window.

The `RenderAsText()` function is fairly complicated because it must take the data that represents each circle in the document and convert it into an ASCII representation. The following code shows the function:

```
HGLOBAL CCircleAppView::RenderAsText()
{
    CCircleAppDoc* pDoc = GetDocument();

    HGLOBAL hMemBlock = ::GlobalAlloc(GHND, 64000);
    char* pMemBlock = (char*) ::GlobalLock(hMemBlock);

    strcpy(pMemBlock, "APP=CIRCLEAPP");
    int index = 13;
    pMemBlock[index++]='\r';
    pMemBlock[index++]='\n';
    int size = pDoc->m_circleArray.GetSize();
    ValueToText("COUNT", size, index, pMemBlock);

    for (int x=0; x<size; ++x)
    {
        CircleStruct* circle =
            (CircleStruct*)pDoc->m_circleArray.GetAt(x);
        int diameter = circle->diameter;
        int x1 = circle->point.x;
        int y1 = circle->point.y;
        COLORREF color = circle->color;

        ValueToText("DIAMETER", diameter,
            index, pMemBlock);
        ValueToText("X", x1, index, pMemBlock);
        ValueToText("Y", y1, index, pMemBlock);
        int red = GetRValue(color);
        ValueToText("RED", red, index, pMemBlock);
        int green = GetGValue(color);
        ValueToText("GREEN", green, index, pMemBlock);
        int blue = GetBValue(color);
        ValueToText("BLUE", blue, index, pMemBlock);
    }

    pMemBlock[index] = 0;
    ::GlobalUnlock(hMemBlock);

    return hMemBlock;
}
```

This function performs the following tasks:

- Gets a pointer to the document object, which holds the document's data
- Allocates a block of memory for the text
- Creates the text header elements that identify the text and specify the number of circles defined in the text

- Iterates through the circle array, converting each data member to a text description
- Returns from the function a handle to the memory block containing the text

As you can see in `RenderAsText()`, the `ValueToText()` function actually creates a line of text and copies it into the text buffer. Here is the `ValueToText()` function:

```
void CCircleAppView::ValueToText(char* label,
    int value, int& index, char* pMemBlock)
{
    char s[80];
    wsprintf(s, "%s=%d\r\n", label, value);
    int len = strlen(s);
    for (int i=0; i<len; ++i)
        pMemBlock[index++] = s[i];
}
```

As you can see, `ValueToText()` takes four parameters: the text label for the line, the integer associated with the label, the current index into the text buffer, and a pointer to the text buffer. The function turns these values into a text line that looks something like this:

`DIAMETER=40`

Of course, the function also creates lines for the X, Y, RED, GREEN, and BLUE labels associated with a circle's data.

Pasting CircleApp Data in Multiple Formats

When the user selects the Paste command from CBCircleApp2's Edit menu, the program must determine whether the clipboard contains CBCircleApp2 data. If it does, the program can copy the data from the clipboard and then extract the information needed to re-create the document. `OnEditPaste()`, shown here, is the function that handles the Paste command:

```
void CCircleAppView::OnEditPaste()
{
    // TODO: Add your command handler code here

    BOOL textAvailable =
        ::IsClipboardFormatAvailable(CF_TEXT);
    if (!textAvailable)
        return;

    OpenClipboard();
    HANDLE hCircleText = ::GetClipboardData(CF_TEXT);
    char* pClipboardText =
        (char*)GlobalLock(hCircleText);
    int textSize = ::GlobalSize(hCircleText);
```

```
            char* pCircleText = (char*)malloc(textSize);
            strcpy(pCircleText, pClipboardText);
            ::CloseClipboard();

            char s[80];
            int index = 0;
            do
                s[index] = pCircleText[index];
            while (pCircleText[index++] != '\n');

            int result = strcmp(s, "APP=CIRCLEAPP\r\n");

            if (result != 0)
                return;

            int count = ParseCircleText(index, pCircleText);
            for (int x=0; x<count; ++x)
            {
                CircleStruct* circle = new CircleStruct;
                circle->diameter =
                    ParseCircleText(index, pCircleText);
                circle->point.x =
                    ParseCircleText(index, pCircleText);
                circle->point.y =
                    ParseCircleText(index, pCircleText);
                int red = ParseCircleText(index, pCircleText);
                int green = ParseCircleText(index, pCircleText);
                int blue = ParseCircleText(index, pCircleText);
                COLORREF color = RGB(red,green,blue);
                circle->color = color;

                CCircleAppDoc* pDoc = GetDocument();
                pDoc->m_circleArray.Add(circle);
            }

            Invalidate();
}
```

Because the OnEditPaste() function is so important to understanding the way CBCircleApp2 handles the Paste command, the following paragraphs describe the function one piece at a time.

OnEditPaste() first checks whether the clipboard holds data in the CF_TEXT format:

```
BOOL textAvailable =
    ::IsClipboardFormatAvailable(CF_TEXT);
if (!textAvailable)
    return;
```

If the clipboard contains no data in the CF_TEXT format, the function immediately returns because this version of the circle application cannot process any clipboard data except its own private type of text data.

If `CF_TEXT` data is available, the program opens the clipboard and gets a handle to the text contained in the clipboard:

```
OpenClipboard();
HANDLE hCircleText = ::GetClipboardData(CF_TEXT);
```

Next, `OnEditPaste()` gets a pointer to the clipboard text, gets the size of the text, and creates a memory block where it can copy the text:

```
char* pClipboardText =
    (char*)GlobalLock(hCircleText);
int textSize = ::GlobalSize(hCircleText);
char* pCircleText = (char*)malloc(textSize);
```

With the new text buffer in hand, the program copies the clipboard text to the new buffer and then closes the clipboard:

```
strcpy(pCircleText, pClipboardText);
::CloseClipboard();
```

The next task is to determine whether CBCircleApp2 created the text in the clipboard. To do this, the program checks the first text line:

```
    char s[80];
    int index = 0;
    do
        s[index] = pCircleText[index];
    while (pCircleText[index++] != '\n');
```

In CBCircleApp2 text data, the first line should be APP=CIRCLEAPP, followed by a carriage return and linefeed. The program checks for this signature and returns if it doesn't find it:

```
int result = strcmp(s, "APP=CIRCLEAPP\r\n");
if (result != 0)
    return;
```

At this point in `OnEditPaste()`, the program has confirmed that the text in the clipboard is CBCircleApp2 data. The next step is to extract from the text the values that define each circle in the document. The local member function `ParseCircleText()` handles this task, with `OnEditPaste()` first getting the circle count:

```
int count = ParseCircleText(index, pCircleText);
```

The `ParseCircleText()` function returns the next integer in the text data. The function's two arguments are the current index into the data and a pointer to the data. Because the index is passed by reference, `ParseCircleText()` changes the index value to point to the next line of text in the data.

The program uses the circle count in a `for` statement that extracts the data needed to re-create each circle in the document. In the loop, the program first creates a new `CircleStruct` object for the current circle:

```
CircleStruct* circle = new CircleStruct;
```

The program then calls `ParseCircleText()` several times in order to extract the diameter and location values for the circle:

```
circle->diameter =
    ParseCircleText(index, pCircleText);
circle->point.x =
    ParseCircleText(index, pCircleText);
circle->point.y =
    ParseCircleText(index, pCircleText);
```

The program also extracts the red, green, and blue color components and uses them to create a `COLORREF` value for the circle:

```
int red = ParseCircleText(index, pCircleText);
int green = ParseCircleText(index, pCircleText);
int blue = ParseCircleText(index, pCircleText);
COLORREF color = RGB(red,green,blue);
circle->color = color;
```

Finally, the loop gets a pointer to the document and adds the newly re-created circle object to the document class's circle array:

```
CCircleAppDoc* pDoc = GetDocument();
pDoc->m_circleArray.Add(circle);
```

The loop repeats this process until it has re-created each of the circle objects represented in the text data. The loop then ends, and `OnEditPaste()` calls `Invalidate()` to force the application to redisplay the current document, which now has new circle objects pasted from the clipboard.

The following code shows the `ParseCircleText()` function, which is responsible for extracting the integer values that represent the circles in the text data. The function is straight C++, with no Windows code complicating things, so you should have no difficulty understanding how it works:

```
int CCircleAppView::ParseCircleText(int& index,
    char * pCircleText)
{
    while (pCircleText[index++] != '=');

    char s[80];
    int i = 0;
    while (pCircleText[index] != '\r')
        s[i++] = pCircleText[index++];

    s[i] = 0;
    index += 3;
    int value = atoi(s);

    return value;
}
```

Summary

Applications can share data in several ways, but the clipboard is the easiest method to implement for this purpose. Using the clipboard, you can transfer many types of data — including text and bitmaps — from one application to another.

Also discussed in this chapter:

▶ You can transfer clipboard data using standard formats, standard private formats, or registered private formats.

▶ Opening and emptying the clipboard transfers clipboard ownership to the program that opened and emptied the clipboard.

▶ Closing the clipboard releases the application's ownership of the clipboard.

▶ When trying to paste data from the clipboard, you must determine what type of data is stored in the clipboard.

▶ Because the clipboard owns data it contains, you must make a copy of the data before manipulating it.

▶ When copying large data objects to the clipboard, a program can implement delayed rendering, and so use memory more efficiently.

▶ By copying data in multiple formats to the clipboard, many different applications can better share the data.

Part IV
ActiveX Programming

Chapter 18: Introduction to ActiveX

Chapter 19: Containers

Chapter 20: Servers

Chapter 21: Automation

Chapter 22: ActiveX Controls

Chapter 18

Introduction to ActiveX

In This Chapter

- Looking back at OLE 1.0
- Advancing the technology with OLE 2.0
- Introducing COM and ActiveX
- Understanding ActiveX applications and components

If you've ever cracked open an ActiveX programming manual and started to read, you most likely had a humbling experience. ActiveX, and the COM system upon which it's built, is a complex beast — downright mind-boggling. Expert programmers take a year or more to wade through all the documentation and figure out how to put the concepts to work. Although your chances of mastering this new technology without a year of full-time work on ActiveX are slim, you shouldn't give up hope.

MFC encapsulates much of ActiveX into the classes that make up the MFC application frameworks. Moreover, AppWizard can create skeleton applications that support ActiveX, leaving you to only fine-tune the result. This makes ActiveX manageable even for the weekend programmer. In this chapter, you get an introduction to ActiveX. The remaining chapters in Part 4 provide hands-on projects to get you started with ActiveX.

OLE 1.0

Microsoft has long been pursuing the idea that documents, rather than applications, should be the focus of an operating system. In other words, users should never be concerned with what application does what job. They should need to know only the type of document they want to create, letting the operating system find and load the appropriate application. Moreover, when users want to create a document containing different types of data elements — for example, both text and graphics — they shouldn't have to leave the editing environment in order to create the new data. Instead, the appropriate editing tools should merge with the current application, providing a seamless document creation and editing experience. This whole idea of a "document-centric" operating system started with a technology Microsoft dubbed OLE (object linking and embedding). Figure 18-1 illustrates this concept.

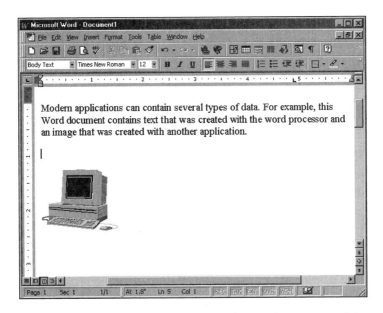

Figure 18-1: With OLE, applications can contain more than one type of data.

OLE is a system that enables applications to more easily share data in two ways: data linking and data embedding. The application that holds the linked or embedded data is called a *container application,* whereas the application that supplies editing services for the linked or embedded data is called the *server application.* (And there's nothing to stop an application from being both a container and a server.) When a data set is *linked* into a document (see Figure 18-2), the document maintains a connection to the data set as part of the document. However, the linked data stays in its own file as a discrete object. Because the document maintains only a link to the data set, the document stays up-to-date as the data set changes.

When a data set is *embedded* into a document, the document no longer maintains a connection with the data set's file. Instead, the data set is actually copied into the document. Because there is no longer a connection between the containing document and the original data set, when the data set changes, the document doesn't reflect the changes, as shown in Figure 18-3. To update the embedded data, the user has to load the document and change the data manually.

Chapter 18: Introduction to ActiveX

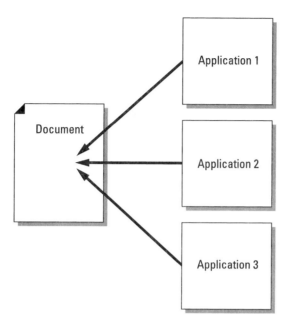

Figure 18-2: Linked data remains in its own file.

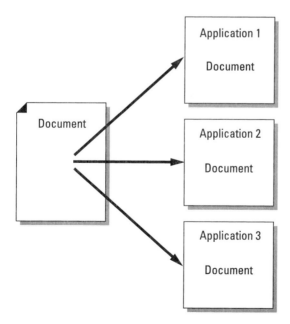

Figure 18-3: Embedded data is copied into the containing document.

Whether a document links or embeds a data set, the application that created the data can edit the data easily. Usually, the user double-clicks the linked or embedded item, which causes the editing application to appear in its own window; or, if it supports in-place editing, the editor can actually merge its toolbars and menus with the application that contains the linked or embedded data.

OLE 2.0

OLE was a step in the right direction, but it lacked many features that would enable applications to take a second seat to documents. OLE 2.0 extends OLE's abilities to include not only data sharing between applications, but also functionality sharing between applications. By creating an application as a set of programmable objects (also called *OLE components*), applications can call upon one another for the capabilities they need, further generalizing the concept of an application.

For example, if a text-editing application needs to spell-check a document, it doesn't necessarily need to have its own spell-checker. Instead, it can call upon a spell-checker object that some other application has already registered with the system. Figure 18-4 illustrates this idea. Notice how the word processor in the figure supplies three programmable objects that can be accessed by other applications. The text editor is currently calling upon the services of the spell-checking component.

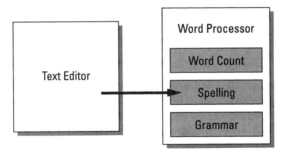

Figure 18-4: Applications can supply programmable objects that can be accessed by other applications.

In Figure 18-4, the word processor is the *OLE server* (because it's providing a service), and the text editor is an *OLE client* (because it's using a service). The process of controlling another application's programmable objects is called *OLE automation*. Therefore, you could also call the word processor an automation server and call the text editor an automation client. Whatever terminology you want to use, programmable objects blur the boundaries between one application and another, making all the applications in the system seem to work together.

As you can see, OLE automation provides advantages to both application users and developers. Users can take full advantage of the capabilities represented by all applications installed in the system, without having to know where those capabilities originate. The user can concentrate on the document and let the applications take care of themselves.

Developers, on the other hand, face a double-edged sword. Although they no longer need to reinvent software that's been developed and installed on the user's system, they must now support OLE, which adds another layer of complexity to the development process — one that's perceived as insurmountable by many programmers. Luckily, as you'll see in the following chapters, Visual C++ developers can let MFC handle most of the intricacies of developing OLE applications.

OLE 2.0 also introduced the concept of *OLE controls,* programmable objects that can be embedded into an application and so become an integral part of the application in much the same way an embedded document becomes a part of a containing document. Originally, OLE controls were conceived as a way to create buttons, sliders, progress indicators, and other types of custom controls. (They are called OLE *controls,* after all.) However, the idea soon grew to include mini-applications that offer complex services to host applications. For example, Figure 18-5 shows an application containing a Microsoft calendar control. As you can see, this control goes way beyond a custom button or slider, being more akin to a complete application than a lowly button.

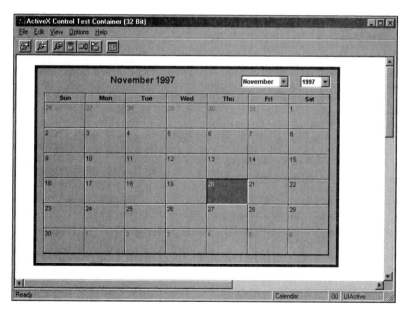

Figure 18-5: Microsoft's calendar control demonstrates how OLE controls can be complex, mini-applications.

Component Object Model (COM)

COM is the technology that provides the underpinnings of OLE. Put simply, COM is a specification for creating binary objects. These binary objects can communicate with one another, controlling functions and setting properties. In short, a binary object is like a program that loads into the system, but is not necessarily visible on the screen. Dynamic link libraries (DLLs) are a similar type of object, in that they contain functions that other modules in the system can call.

The COM specification is a set of rules that dictates how binary objects are created. These rules define a method through which applications can query a binary object to discover the types of interfaces the object supports. Some of these interfaces are standard, whereas others are proprietary. In any case, by adhering to the specifications, objects can be accessed and manipulated by any OLE-capable application.

Luckily, if you're programming with Visual C++ and MFC, you don't have to know much about COM, although it's always a good idea to have a little background on the technology you're using. As you'll soon discover, Visual C++'s amazing AppWizard can provide your application with most of the basic OLE functionality your program needs. All you have to do is refine the generated source code for your specific purposes.

Distributed Component Object Model (DCOM)

DCOM is an extension of COM that enables component services to function over different types of networks, including local-area networks (LANs), wide-area networks (WANs), and even the Internet.

ActiveX

A couple of years ago, COM and OLE were the big programming buzzwords. Now, programmers throw the word "ActiveX" around like celebrity names at a Hollywood party. When Microsoft recently turned its attention to the Internet, it occurred to the powers that be that there was no reason why the Internet should not be treated as just another peripheral, such as a disk drive or CD-ROM drive. Why not make the Internet so accessible from the user's computer that it seems to become part of the operating system? With this idea came the necessity of extending OLE 2.0 so that it encompassed not just the user's local system, but also any network to which the local system was connected. ActiveX was born.

ActiveX could have been called OLE 3.0, but the capabilities of OLE had gone so far beyond object linking and embedding that the original moniker was more confusing than descriptive. Therefore, Microsoft named this newly expanded technology ActiveX. Now, virtually everywhere the word OLE would have been used, the word ActiveX is substituted. For example, OLE components are now ActiveX components, OLE controls are now ActiveX controls, and OLE documents are now ActiveX documents.

All of these objects that share the word ActiveX in their names are more powerful than their old OLE counterparts, however. They are now objects that expand the original OLE concepts to the Web. ActiveX controls, for example, can be placed in Web pages and transmitted automatically to the browser that's viewing the Web page. ActiveX documents, too, are much more powerful than OLE documents. Not only can these objects be transmitted over the Web, ActiveX documents also tell the receiving browser how the document should be displayed. You can think of an ActiveX document as being a storage object for information that can be interpreted, displayed, and manipulated by a receiving application.

COM+

COM+ is a massively enhanced version of COM that provides not only the services originally supplied by COM, but also a host of new services that enable the creation of component-based distributed applications (applications built from components that are designed to function over a network). The added services include those of Microsoft Transaction Server 2.0, which is a system for building and managing intranet and Internet applications.

COM+ also features improvements in the way threading is handled, as well as improved security services. The new features have such high-tech names as neutral threading, role-based security, object pooling, queued components, automatic transactions, and other stuff in which only advanced programmers are interested. Suffice it to say that COM+ is COM on steroids.

ActiveX Applications and Components

In the following chapters, you'll learn to program several types of ActiveX projects using AppWizard and MFC. As you work through these chapters, keep in mind that ActiveX is an immense technology worthy of a complete book (or books) of its own. In fact, Microsoft's own ActiveX manuals run to thousands of pages. Although Part IV of this book provides only an introduction to ActiveX, the following chapters cover the major types of ActiveX projects: containers, servers, automation, and ActiveX controls. The remaining sections in this chapter introduce you to these concepts.

ActiveX Container Applications

An ActiveX *container* is an application that holds linked or embedded data. Such an application must not only be able to display the linked or embedded data, but it must also be able to enable the user to select, move, delete, and edit the data. Figure 18-6, for example, shows Microsoft Word displaying a document that contains an embedded graphic.

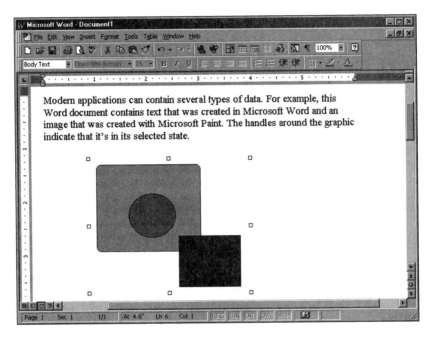

Figure 18-6: Microsoft Word can act as a container application.

In the figure, you can see that the graphic object displays sizing handles that the user can use to resize the image. The user can also move the image to any position in the document, as well as delete the image by selecting the Edit menu's Clear command or by pressing the Delete key on the keyboard.

When Microsoft Word contains linked or embedded data, it's acting as an ActiveX container. Many Windows applications support ActiveX in this way. In Chapter 19, you'll discover how to program your own ActiveX container applications.

ActiveX Server Applications

In the previous section, you saw Microsoft Word acting as a container application. The graphic (a real masterpiece, no?) embedded in the Word document was created with Microsoft Paint, which makes Paint the server application. If the user wants to edit the embedded graphic, he or she can double-click the item. The server then should respond in one of two ways: by opening the graphic in a separate editing window or by merging its user interface with Word's.

Which way the server responds depends on how the client and server were programmed. If the applications support in-place editing (recommended), ActiveX merges the server's toolbars and menus with the container application's. This enables the user to edit the item without ever switching windows or applications. Figure 18-7 shows Microsoft Word after the user has double-clicked the Paint graphic. In the figure, Paint has merged its toolbars and menus with Word's.

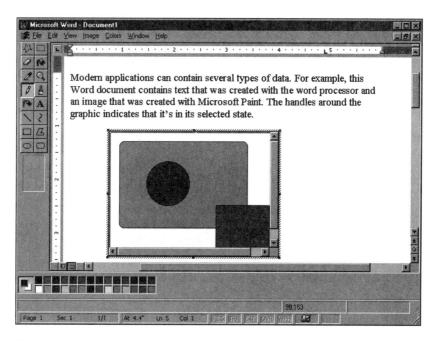

Figure 18-7: Paint's toolbars and menu bars are now merged with Word's.

The user can now edit the graphic just as if the graphic were loaded into Paint. In Figure 18-8, for example, the user has used Paint's ellipse tool to add two filled ellipses to the image. Because ActiveX makes all of Paint's tools available in the toolbar, adding the ellipses takes only seconds.

When users are finished editing, they click somewhere outside of the graphic, and Word's window returns to normal, restoring its own toolbars and menus. The newly edited graphic appears in the document. In Chapter 19, you'll learn to create server applications that support in-place editing.

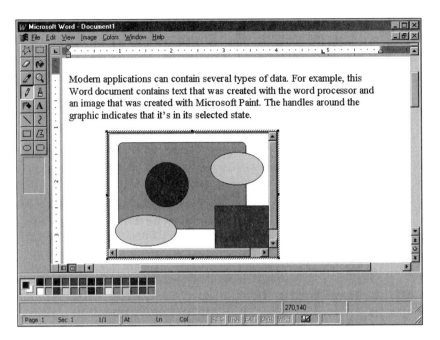

Figure 18-8: Here the user has edited the image using Paint's tools.

ActiveX Automation Applications

Just as you have containers and servers with object linking and embedding, so you have automation clients and automation servers with ActiveX automation. An automation-client application reaches out into the system to control a component of another application, called the *automation server*. Of course, the process isn't quite that simple. Both applications must be specially programmed to take advantage of ActiveX automation.

For example, an application that hasn't been programmed to be an automation client cannot access programmable objects made available by an automation server. Conversely, an application that hasn't been programmed as an automation server cannot share its functionality with other applications in the system, even if the other applications support ActiveX automation.

Creating automation servers means defining interfaces that provide access to properties and methods of the programmable objects supplied by the server. On the client side, when an application wants to access a programmable object, it must know how to obtain a reference to the object's interface, as well as how to manage the object's properties and call the object's methods. Re-using the spell-checker example, an application that wants to take advantage of another application's spell-checker (assuming that the spell-checker is a programmable object) would acquire a reference to the spell-checker's interface, and then it would call the spell-checker's functions through that interface. You learn to create automation applications, both clients and servers, in Chapter 21.

ActiveX Controls

The last type of ActiveX project you'll learn about in Part IV is ActiveX controls. As mentioned previously in this chapter, ActiveX controls are like mini-applications that you can embed into other applications. They take the concept of programmable components and separate those components from the server. That is, ActiveX components are complete entities unto themselves and do not need to be managed by a server application.

One of the biggest advantages of ActiveX controls is their capability to provide computing power to Web pages on the Internet. In this way, ActiveX controls can act much like Java applets. Virtually any type of program you can conceive of can be programmed as an ActiveX control and included in a Web page. When the user logs onto the Web page, the system checks whether the ActiveX control is available locally. If it isn't, the system automatically downloads the control and displays it in the Web page. You learn to program ActiveX controls in Chapter 22.

ActiveX Documents

Once the Web took over nearly everyone's computers, Microsoft decided it needed to expand its new document-oriented philosophy to the Internet. ActiveX documents are Microsoft's answer to enabling Web browsers and other ActiveX client applications to interpret and display documents in much the same way OLE documents enabled data sharing on a local computer system. ActiveX documents are, to put it simply, super-powered OLE documents.

One way ActiveX documents are super-powered compared with OLE documents is their capability to be transmitted over the Internet to a remote ActiveX client application, usually a Web browser. In much the same way your local computer system can link or embed a Microsoft Paint document into a Microsoft Word document, so too can a Web browser embed an ActiveX document in its window. However, this ActiveX document may or may not be located on the local computer. It may have been received from the other side of the world.

ActiveX documents are also super-powered in the way they take the concept of a document to a whole new level. In fact, many ActiveX documents don't look like documents at all, but rather like complete applications running inside a client application's window. For example, an ActiveX document that represents a 3-D scene would contain not only the data that defines the scene (the traditional idea of a document), but also all the information needed for a client application to display and manipulate the 3-D scene.

An ActiveX document is a complete document package that includes not only the document's data, but also the tools needed to manage the document. You could say that an ActiveX document knows how to manage itself, making it easy for a client application to display the document.

Summary

Now that you have a general idea of what ActiveX is and what it does, you're ready to get your hands dirty with some actual ActiveX programming. In the following chapter, you create your first ActiveX container application. In the remaining ActiveX chapters, you discover even more about this complex but exciting technology.

Also discussed in this chapter:

- OLE 1.0 enables applications to link and embed data.
- Linked data maintains a connection to its data set and therefore changes automatically when the original data is updated.
- Embedded data is copied into a document and so doesn't update itself when the original data changes.
- OLE 2.0 extended OLE to include OLE controls.
- ActiveX is the most recent version of OLE, which has been extended to support a networked environment.
- ActiveX controls, which are like mini-applications, can be embedded in other applications and in Web pages.
- An ActiveX document is a complete document package that includes not only the document's data, but also the tools needed to manage the document.
- An ActiveX container application can link or embed data created by another application.
- An ActiveX client application uses services supplied by an ActiveX **server** application.
- Automation enables an application to manipulate another application's programmable components.

Chapter 19

Containers

In This Chapter

▶ Creating a skeleton container application
▶ Modifying an ActiveX item's class
▶ Using the mouse to select items
▶ Deleting embedded items

To be a fully compliant Windows 2000 application, a program must support ActiveX. One way a program can support ActiveX is to be an *ActiveX container*, which is an application that can link or embed files created by other applications. You got an introduction to container applications in Chapter 18. In this chapter, you build your own ActiveX container application using AppWizard and other Visual C++ tools. This application, called ContainerApp, shows you how to link or embed objects in an application's document, as well as how to enable users to edit, move, and delete objects.

Note

Programming container applications is a complex task that cannot be fully explained in a single chapter. This chapter is only an introduction to the programming techniques required to create a basic container application. After you master the topics in this chapter, if you want to learn more about ActiveX, you should pick up a book that concentrates on ActiveX programming.

Creating a Skeleton Container Application

CD

Location: `WinPrgS\Chap19\ContainerApp`

Just as with all AppWizard applications, your container application begins as an AppWizard project for which Visual C++ generates the basic source code for the program's classes. In a container application, these classes include not only the usual application, frame window, document (now derived from the `COleDocument` class instead of `CDocument`), and view window classes, but also an additional class derived from MFC's `COleClientItem` class. In this application, AppWizard will call the derived class `CContainerAppCntrItem`. This class represents any linked or embedded item in the application's window. To create the skeleton for ContainerApp, perform the following steps:

1. Start a new AppWizard project called ContainerApp, as shown in Figure 19-1.

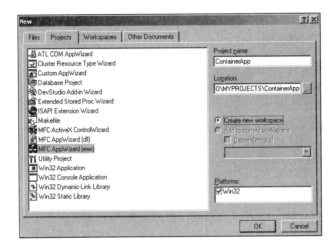

Figure 19-1: The new container application project is called ContainerApp.

2. In the MFC AppWizard - Step 1 dialog box, select the Single Document option.

3. Click the Next button twice, accepting the default options in the Step 2 dialog box.

4. In the Step 3 of 6 dialog box, select the Container option and click the Next button.

   Selecting the Container feature tells AppWizard to generate the ActiveX source code needed to create a skeleton container application. The skeleton application will be able to link and embed data created by other applications.

5. In the Step 4 of 6 dialog box, turn off all features except 3D Controls, and then click the Next button.

6. In the Step 5 of 6 dialog box, select the As a Statically Linked Library option. Accept the default "Yes, please" to generate source file comments.

7. Click the Finish button.

8. Click the OK button, and AppWizard generates the source code files for the skeleton application.

You've now completed the ContainerApp skeleton application. Save your work by selecting the Save All command on Visual C++'s File menu.

If you compile and run the application, you can test it by linking or embedding an item into the application's current document. To do this, select the Edit menu's Insert New Object command. The Insert Object dialog box appears, as shown in Figure 19-2. You can choose to create a new item of the type selected in the Object Type box, or you can choose a file to link or embed into the document.

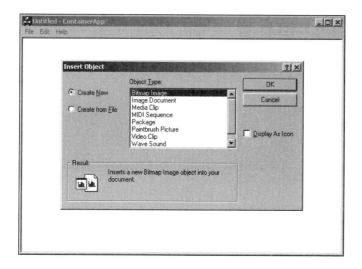

Figure 19-2: The skeleton application already supports linking and embedding.

Double-click the Bitmap Image object type. The application creates a new bitmap image and embeds it into the document. At the same time, Microsoft Paint's toolbars and menus merge with ContainerApp's (assuming that, on your system, Paint is still the application registered as the editor for bitmaps), as shown in Figure 19-3. You haven't added even one line of code on your own, yet the application already has ActiveX functionality, thanks to AppWizard's Container option.

Use Paint's tools to draw a few shapes on the bitmap. Because the container application now sports all of Paint's tools and menus, you can do almost anything with the bitmap that you could do if you were actually running Paint.

Unfortunately, the skeleton application supports no item-selection functions, so you can't deselect the bitmap and get back to the regular application. You can, however, save the current document (including its embedded item) and then reload it, which has the same effect of deselecting the embedded item. To do this, select the File menu's Save command. After saving the file, select the File menu's New command to clear the window and start a new document. Now, use the Open command to reopen the saved document. You can also select the document from the File menu's document list.

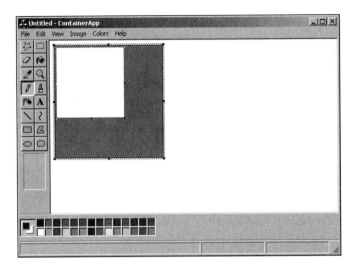

Figure 19-3: Here, an empty bitmap object is embedded into the application's document.

When you reload the document, you see a window something like the one shown in Figure 19-4. (What you see depends on the figure you drew, of course.) If you want to bring back Paint's tools in order to edit the bitmap, you can find the bitmap item represented on the Edit menu. If you select Edit from the Bitmap Image Object's submenu, ActiveX again merges Paint's tools and menus into ContainerApp. If you select the Open command from the submenu, Paint itself runs as a stand-alone application.

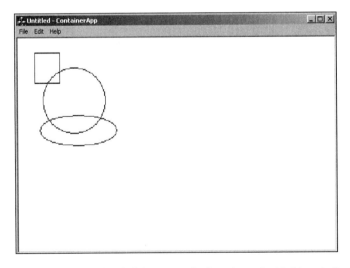

Figure 19-4: The reloaded document displays the embedded item in its deselected state.

Managing Embedded Object Size and Position

The first step toward completing ContainerApp is to add code to the CContainerAppCntrItem class so that embedded items can manage their own sizes and positions. When AppWizard generated the CContainerApp CntrItem class, it created hard-coded coordinates for objects of the class. You don't want to use hard-coded sizes and coordinates because users will want to size and position embedded items as is appropriate for their current document. Perform the following steps to complete the CContainerAppCntrItem class:

1. In the Project Workspace window, select the ClassView tab, and then right-click CContainerAppCntrItem (you may have to click the + sign to open the class tree) and select the Add Member Variable command from the menu that appears.

2. In the Add Member Variable dialog box, type CRect in the Variable Type box, type m_objectRect in the Variable Name box, and select Public access, as shown in Figure 19-5.

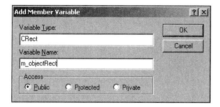

Figure 19-5: The m_objectRect member variable will hold the object's size and position.

Here, you're adding the m_objectRect member variable to the class that represents items embedded in the application's document. This member variable will hold the object's size and position.

3. In the Project Workspace window, double-click the CContainerApp CntrItem class's OnChangeItemPosition() function (see Figure 19-6). (You may have to click the + sign to open the class tree.) The function appears in Visual C++'s edit window.

Figure 19-6: Double-clicking the function brings the source code up in the edit window.

4. Add the following lines to the function, right after the TODO comment:

   ```
   m_objectRect = rectPos;
   CContainerAppDoc* pDoc = GetDocument();
   pDoc->SetModifiedFlag();
   pDoc->UpdateAllViews(NULL);
   ```

   When the user changes the position of an embedded item, MFC calls the OnChangeItemPosition() function. The lines you added to the function save the item's new position and update all views of the document to reflect the new position.

5. Add the following line to the OnGetItemPosition() function, after deleting the call to SetRect() that's already there:

   ```
   rPosition = m_objectRect;
   ```

   When the framework needs the location of an embedded item, it calls the OnGetItemPosition() function. The line you added sets the position to the coordinates saved in the m_objectRect object.

6. Add the following line to the CContainerAppCntrItem class's constructor:

   ```
   m_objectRect.SetRect(20, 20, 150, 150);
   ```

This line initializes the item's starting position. That is, when the user creates a new item, the item will first appear in the size and position contained in m_objectRect.

7. Add the following line to the CContainerAppCntrItem class's Serialize() function, right after the TODO: add storing code here comment:

        ar << m_objectRect;

   This line saves the item's size and position when the rest of the document is saved.

8. Add the following line to the CContainerAppCntrItem class's Serialize() function, right after the TODO: add loading code here comment:

        ar >> m_objectRect;

   This line loads the item's size and position when the rest of the document is loaded.

You now have completed the CContainerAppCntrItem class. You should save your work before continuing. You can also compile and run the application, although at this point the application won't run any differently than the previous version, except that new objects start off smaller when first added to the document.

Using the Mouse to Select Items

The next step toward completing ContainerApp is to enable the user to select and deselect embedded items. This includes not only clicking the object for selection, but also starting the editing process by double-clicking the object. The following steps show how to add item selection to ContainerApp:

1. In the CContainerAppView class's OnDraw() function, remove or comment out all the lines following the TODO: remove this code when final draw code is complete comment.

   The lines you removed displayed an embedded object in the default location in the container application's window. You've removed these lines so that the application can display multiple items at the locations contained in their m_objectRect member variables.

2. Add the following lines to the OnDraw() function, in place of the lines you removed in Step 1:

        POSITION pos = pDoc->GetStartPosition();

        while(pos != NULL)
        {
            CContainerAppCntrItem* pObject =
                (CContainerAppCntrItem*) pDoc->GetNextItem(pos);
            pObject->Draw(pDC, pObject->m_objectRect);
            CRectTracker tracker;

```
        SetupTracker(&tracker, pObject);
        tracker.Draw(pDC);
    }
```

These lines step through all the items embedded in the current document, drawing the items in their proper positions. The `CRectTracker` object draws the appropriate outline around the object, depending on the item's state. (`CRectTracker` objects also display the appropriate mouse cursor for an object.) `SetupTracker()`, which initializes a tracker object, is a function you'll add to the program yourself later in these steps.

3. Press Ctrl+W on your keyboard to display ClassWizard. Then add the `OnSetCursor()` function (which MFC calls in response to a `WM_SETCURSOR` Windows message) to the `CContainerAppView` class, as shown in Figure 19-7. Make sure you have `CContainerAppView` selected in ClassWizard's Class name box.

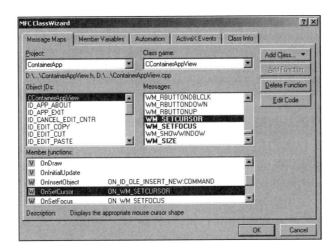

Figure 19-7: ClassWizard adding the OnSetCursor() function to the program

4. Add the following lines to the `OnSetCursor()` function, right after the `TODO` comment:

```
if ((m_pSelection != NULL) && (pWnd == this))
{
    CRectTracker tracker;
    SetupTracker(&tracker, m_pSelection);
    BOOL cursorSetByTracker =
        tracker.SetCursor(this, nHitTest);
    if (cursorSetByTracker)
        return TRUE;
}
```

These lines check whether the cursor is over a selected embedded item. If it is, the program creates a `CRectTracker` object to set the cursor to the appropriate shape for the selected item. The `pWnd` variable is a pointer to the window that received the `WM_SETCURSOR` message, and `m_pSelection`, which is a member variable of the view class, is a pointer to any selected item.

5. Press Ctrl+W on your keyboard to display ClassWizard. Then add the `OnLButtonDown()` function to the `CContainerAppView` class.

6. Add the following lines to the `OnLButtonDown()` function, right after the `TODO` comment:

    ```
    CContainerAppCntrItem* pHitItem = GetHitItem(point);
    SetObjectAsSelected(pHitItem);

    if (pHitItem == NULL)
        return;

    CRectTracker tracker;
    SetupTracker(&tracker, pHitItem);
    UpdateWindow();

    if (!tracker.Track(this, point))
        return;

    Invalidate();

    pHitItem->m_objectRect = tracker.m_rect;
    CContainerAppDoc* pDoc = GetDocument();
    pDoc->SetModifiedFlag();
    ```

    These lines first determine whether the button click is to select or deselect an item. If the click is to select the item, a `CRectTracker` object draws the appropriate border around the item. Calling the tracker's `Track()` member function enables the user to manipulate the item, after which the window is updated and the document marked as dirty (needing to be saved). The `GetHitItem()` function determines whether the mouse was clicked over an embedded item. You'll add `GetHitItem()` to the program later in these steps.

7. Press Ctrl+W on your keyboard to display ClassWizard. Then add the `OnLButtonDblClk()` function to the `CContainerAppView` class.

8. Add the following lines to the `OnLButtonDblClk()` function, right after the `TODO` comment:

    ```
    OnLButtonDown(nFlags, point);

    if (m_pSelection == NULL)
        return;

    SHORT keyState = GetKeyState(VK_CONTROL);
    LONG oleVerb;

    if (keyState < 0)
        oleVerb = OLEIVERB_OPEN;
    ```

```
    else
        oleVerb = OLEIVERB_PRIMARY;

m_pSelection->DoVerb(oleVerb, this);
```

These lines first call `OnLButtonDown()` to tackle the item-selection task. Then, if the user has selected an item (rather than deselected an item), the program gets the state of the keyboard's Ctrl key. Holding down the Ctrl key when double-clicking an item signals that the item should be opened. If the Ctrl key isn't pressed, the double-click should trigger the item's primary verb, which is often edit. As you can see, Visual C++ defines constants for these standard OLE verbs. (An OLE verb is an action that can be performed on an ActiveX object.)

9. Right-click the `CContainerAppView` class in the Project Workspace window, select Add Member Function from the menu, and add the `SetupTracker()` function to the class. To do this, the Function Type should be `void`, the Function Declaration should be `SetupTracker(CRectTracker* pTracker, CContainerAppCntrItem* pObject)`, and the Access should be Protected, as shown in Figure 19-8.

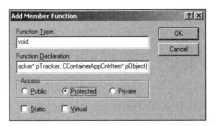

Figure 19-8: Adding the SetupTracker() function to the program

10. Add the following lines to the `SetupTracker()` function:

```
pTracker->m_rect = pObject->m_objectRect;

if (pObject == m_pSelection)
    pTracker->m_nStyle |= CRectTracker::resizeInside;

OLE_OBJTYPE objType = pObject->GetType();

if (objType == OT_EMBEDDED)
    pTracker->m_nStyle |= CRectTracker::solidLine;
else if (objType == OT_LINK)
    pTracker->m_nStyle |= CRectTracker::dottedLine;

UINT objectState = pObject->GetItemState();

if ((objectState == COleClientItem::activeUIState) ||
    (objectState == COleClientItem::openState))
    pTracker->m_nStyle |= CRectTracker::hatchInside;
```

The SetupTracker() function is where you can really see the tracker object at work. In the function, the program gets the size of the selected item and then, through the tracker object, draws resize handles on the item. Then the program determines whether the item is linked or embedded, and draws the appropriate outline for the item's OLE state. Finally, if the item is being edited, the program draws a crosshatch pattern on the item in the document, indicating that it's not currently available.

11. Right-click the CContainerAppView class in the Project Workspace window, select Add Member Function from the menu, and add the GetHitItem() function to the class. To do this, the Function Type should be CContainerAppCntrItem*, the Function Declaration should be GetHitItem(CPoint point), and the Access should be Protected.

12. Add the following lines to the GetHitItem() function:

    ```
    CContainerAppCntrItem* pObjectHit = NULL;
    CContainerAppDoc* pDoc = GetDocument();
    BOOL objectHit;

    POSITION pos = pDoc->GetStartPosition();

    while (pos != NULL)
    {
        CContainerAppCntrItem* pObject =
            (CContainerAppCntrItem*)pDoc->GetNextItem(pos);
        objectHit = pObject->m_objectRect.PtInRect(point);

        if (objectHit)
            pObjectHit = pObject;
    }

    return pObjectHit;
    ```

    In the GetHitItem() function, the program loops through all the items, comparing their positions with the point passed into the function as its single parameter. If the given point falls inside an item, that item is considered "hit" and is passed back from the function.

13. Right-click the CContainerAppView class in the Project Workspace window, select Add Member Function from the menu, and add the SetObjectAsSelected() function to the class. To do this, the Function Type should be void, the Function Declaration should be SetObjectAsSelected(CContainerAppCntrItem* pObject), and the Access should be Protected.

14. Add the following lines to the SetObjectAsSelected() function:

    ```
    CContainerAppDoc* pDoc = GetDocument();

    if ((m_pSelection != pObject) || (pObject == NULL))
    {
        COleClientItem* pActiveObject =
    ```

```
                    pDoc->GetInPlaceActiveItem(this);

    if ((pActiveObject != pObject) &&
            (pActiveObject != NULL))
        pActiveObject->Close();
}

m_pSelection = pObject;
Invalidate();
```

In the `SetObjectAsSelected()` function, the program determines whether the user clicked an empty portion of the window or an item. If an item is being selected, and there's already another item selected, the function closes the previously selected item. The `m_pSelection` member variable gets the pointer to the selected item, and the call to `Invalidate()` updates the window.

You now have completed the ContainerApp application. You should save your work and then compile and run the application. When you do, the main window appears. You can embed an object in the current document just as you did with earlier versions of the program. Now, however, when you click in the window outside of the embedded object, the program reverts to its own menus.

If you click the object to select it, sizing handles appear on the object's border and the mouse pointer changes into a cross cursor, indicating that the object can be dragged to a new location (see Figure 19-9). By dragging the object's sizing handles with the mouse pointer, you can make the object any size you like (see Figure 19-10). The image in the object automatically resizes as well.

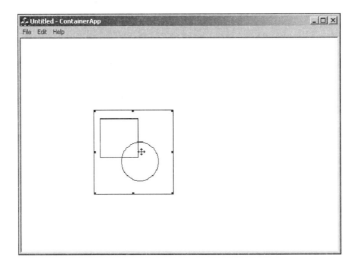

Figure 19-9: The user can now move embedded objects in ContainerApp.

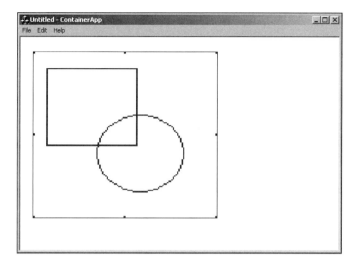

Figure 19-10: The user can now resize embedded objects in ContainerApp.

One problem with the earlier versions of ContainerApp was that its documents could hold only a single embedded object. This new version can hold multiple embedded and linked items. Figure 19-11, for example, shows the application with both a bitmap and a WordPad object embedded in the window.

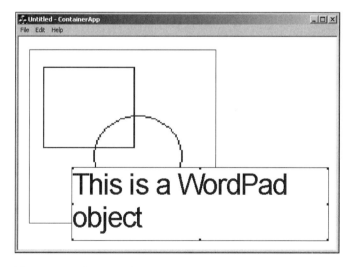

Figure 19-11: ContainerApp can manage multiple embedded objects.

PROBLEMS & SOLUTIONS

Deleting Embedded Items

PROBLEM: *OK, the ContainerApp application works. But once I embed an item in the application's window, although I can move it around and resize it, I can't get rid of it. There must be some way of deleting linked or embedded objects, right?*

SOLUTION: Enabling users to delete an embedded item isn't difficult. You just have to call the selected item's Delete() member function. However, you do need to add the Delete command to the application's user interface. Commonly, you'll add some sort of Delete command to the application's Edit menu, as well as respond to the keyboard's Delete key. You should already be familiar with creating and responding to menu commands. Here, you'll see how to respond to the Delete key in order to delete an embedded item.

To add a Delete command to the ContainerApp application, load the project and then press Ctrl+W to display ClassWizard. Add the OnKeyDown() function to the program, as shown in Figure 19-12. In OnKeyDown(), you need to check whether the user pressed the Delete key and whether an item is selected. If both of these conditions are true, you call the selected item's Delete() function and then call UpdateAllViews() to redraw all the view windows that may be displaying the document. Following is the final OnKeyDown() function:

```
void CContainerAppView::OnKeyDown
    (UINT nChar, UINT nRepCnt, UINT nFlags)
{
    // TODO: Add your message handler code here
    //    and/or call default
    if ((m_pSelection == NULL) || (nChar != VK_DELETE))
        return;

    m_pSelection->Delete();
    m_pSelection = NULL;
    CContainerAppDoc* pDoc = GetDocument();
    pDoc->UpdateAllViews(NULL);

    CView::OnKeyDown(nChar, nRepCnt, nFlags);
}
```

Continued

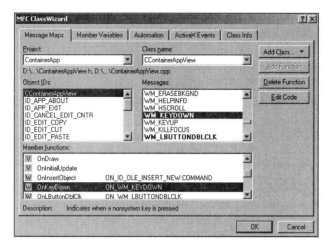

Figure 19-12: ClassWizard adds the OnKeyDown() function to the program.

Summary

AppWizard does an amazing job of generating the code an application needs to be an ActiveX container. Still, the basic functionality supplied by AppWizard is rarely adequate for a complete application. AppWizard leaves many details of implementing a container to the programmer. In this chapter, you learned how to give the skeleton container application extra capabilities, such as enabling the user to select, move, and delete embedded items.

Also discussed in this chapter:

▶ AppWizard provides options for generating several types of ActiveX applications.

▶ In an MFC program, an object of the COleClientItem class represents embedded items.

▶ MFC calls a COleClientItem-derived object's OnChangeItemPosition() member function when the user moves an embedded item.

▶ MFC calls a COleClientItem-derived object's OnGetItemPosition() member function when the program needs the item's current position.

▶ Embedded objects can store their sizes and positions in data members of the class, as well as save and load their sizes and positions in their Serialize() functions.

▶ CRectTracker objects draw the appropriate borders around embedded items, as well as set mouse cursors.

- By overloading the view class's `OnSetCursor()` function, a container application can change the mouse cursor when the cursor passes over embedded items.
- When the user double-clicks an embedded item, the program should perform the appropriate OLE verb on the item.
- To delete an embedded item, call the item's `Delete()` member function.

Chapter 20

Servers

In This Chapter

▶ Creating a skeleton server application
▶ Modifying the application's resources
▶ Completing the document class
▶ Completing the server item class
▶ Customizing the view class
▶ Running a server application

As you learned in the previous chapter, to be fully compliant with Windows 2000 application guidelines, a program must support ActiveX. You previously learned that a program can support ActiveX by being an ActiveX *container,* which is an application that can link or embed files created by other applications. Another way an application can support ActiveX is by being an ActiveX *server,* which is an application that can link or embed its documents into a container application's window, although it can also run as a stand-alone application if needed. As you'll learn, creating a basic server application with Visual C++ is even easier (compared to writing one from scratch, that is) than creating a container application.

In this chapter, you put together the ServerApp application, which supports ActiveX server features such as OLE menus, ActiveX document classes, ActiveX frame-window classes, and server item classes. You'll also learn how to program a server to draw its items when those items are embedded in another application's window.

Programming server applications is a complex task that cannot be fully explained in a single chapter. This chapter is only an introduction to the programming techniques required to create a basic server application. After you master the topics in this chapter, if you want to learn more about ActiveX, you should pick up a book that concentrates on ActiveX programming.

Creating a Skeleton Server Application

Location: `WinPrgS\Chap20\ServerApp`

Just as with all AppWizard applications, your server application begins as an AppWizard project for which Visual C++ generates the basic source code for the program's classes. In a server application, these classes include not only the usual application, frame window, document (now derived from the `COleServerDoc` class instead of `CDocument`), and view window classes, but also an additional class derived from MFC's `COleServerItem` class. In ServerApp, AppWizard names the derived class `CServerAppSrvrItem`. This class represents the server side of any of the application's items, linked or embedded, in a container application's window. To create the skeleton server application, perform the following steps:

You should read through all the application-building steps in this chapter, whether or not you actually build the server application yourself, because the steps include explanations of the programming techniques needed to build a server application.

1. Start a new AppWizard project called ServerApp, as shown in Figure 20-1.

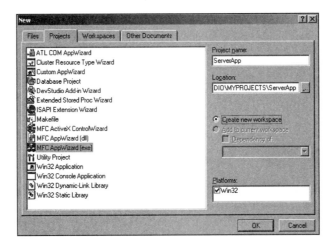

Figure 20-1: The new server application project is called ServerApp.

2. In the MFC AppWizard - Step 1 dialog box, select the Single Document option.

3. Click the Next button twice, accepting the default options in the Step 2 dialog box.

4. In the Step 3 of 6 dialog box, select the Full-server option, as shown in Figure 20-2, and click the Next button.

   Selecting the Full-server feature tells AppWizard to generate the source code needed to create a skeleton ActiveX server application. The skeleton application will be able to link and embed its documents into applications that act as ActiveX containers. (A mini-server application, another option you can select, cannot run as a stand-alone application and supports only embedded objects.)

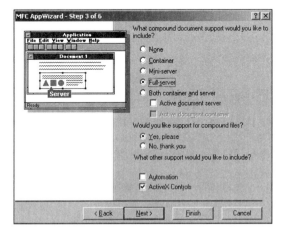

Figure 20-2: AppWizard can generate the code needed to create a server application.

5. In the Step 4 of 6 dialog box, turn off all features except 3-D Controls, and then click the Next button.

6. In the Step 5 of 6 dialog box, select the As a Statically Linked Library option. Accept the "Yes, please" default option to generate source file comments.

7. Click the Finish button.

8. Click the OK button, and AppWizard generates the source code files for the skeleton application.

You've now completed the ServerApp skeleton application. Save your work by selecting the Save All command on Visual C++'s File menu.

If you compile and run the application, you can test it by linking or embedding its document into the ContainerApp application you created in Chapter 18. To do this, start ContainerApp and select the Edit menu's Insert New Object command. The Insert Object dialog box appears. In the Object Type box, find Server Document, as shown in Figure 20-3.

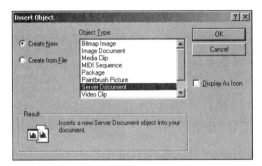

Figure 20-3: The ServerApp application has already registered its document type with the Windows system Registry.

 Make sure you have compiled and run ServerApp before running Container App. If you fail to run ServerApp, Visual C++ won't register the application's document type in your system Registry, and you won't find the Server Document document type in the Insert Object dialog box.

Server Document is the default document type provided by ServerApp. If you select this document type from the Insert New Object dialog box, Windows embeds a document from ServerApp into the currently open ContainerApp document, as shown in Figure 20-4. Something interesting has happened as well. As long as the Server Document object is selected for editing, ServerApp's menus take the place of ContainerApp's.

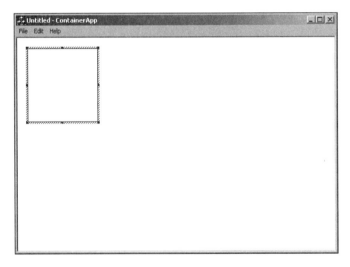

Figure 20-4: ContainerApp shows off its new Server Document object along with ServerApp's menu bar.

To see that this ActiveX feature is working, click the ContainerApp window to deselect the Server Document object. Then, look at the Help menu. You'll see the command About ContainerApp. Now double-click the Server Document object to select it for editing. Again, look at the Help menu. The About ContainerApp command has been replaced with About ServerApp, proving that ServerApp's menus appear in ContainerApp's window. If you had created a toolbar for the ServerApp application, it would have appeared in ContainerApp's window as well.

Customizing the Application's Resources

Now that you have the basic application built, you can customize the resources in order to add a dialog box and complete the application's menus. Perform the following steps to complete the ServerApp application's resources:

1. Select the Resource command from Visual C++'s Insert menu. When the Insert Resource dialog box appears, select the Dialog resource and click the New button.

2. Use the dialog-box editor to create the dialog box shown in Figure 20-5, using the default IDs for all controls.

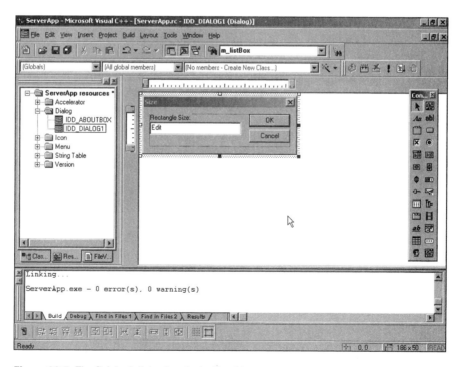

Figure 20-5: The finished dialog box looks like this.

The server application will display a single rectangle as the contents of its document. The dialog box will enable the user to specify the size of the rectangle.

3. Double-click the dialog box you just created to bring up the Adding a Class dialog box. Select the Create a New Class option and click OK.

4. Name the new class `CSizeDlg` in the New Class dialog box (see Figure 20-6) and click the OK button.

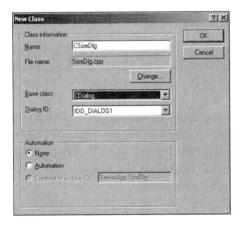

Figure 20-6: The new dialog class will be called CSizeDlg.

5. In the MFC Class Wizard property sheet, click the Member Variables tab to display the Member Variables page. Double-click `IDC_EDIT1` and create a variable for the control, as shown in Figure 20-7.

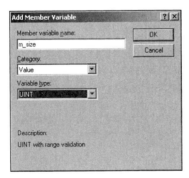

Figure 20-7: The m_size member variable will hold the value the user enters into the edit box.

6. Back in ClassWizard, enter **10** and **100** as `m_size`'s minimum and maximum allowable values (see Figure 20-8). Then click OK to close the ClassWizard property sheet.

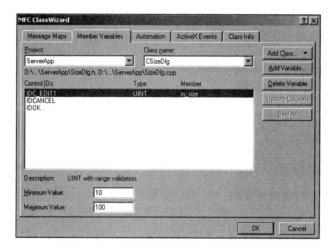

Figure 20-8: The minimum and maximum acceptable values for m_size are 10 and 100, respectively.

7. In the ResourceView page of the Project Workspace window, double-click the `IDR_MAINFRAME` menu ID to display the menu in the menu editor.

8. Add the Rectangle menu shown in Figure 20-9 with the Size submenu, giving the Size command the ID `ID_RECTANGLE_SIZE`.

9. Add the Rectangle menu to the `IDR_SRVR_EMBEDDED` (see Figure 20-10) and `IDR_SRVR_INPLACE` (see Figure 20-11) menus. Use the `ID_RECTANGLE_SIZE` ID for the Size command on each menu.

   As you can tell from the menu IDs, Windows will use these additional menus to display menu bars in a container application that's editing a ServerApp document. The double bars in the `IDR_SRVR_INPLACE` menu specify where additional menus can be merged into the menu bar.

You've now completed the application's resources. To save your work, select the Save All command from Visual C++'s File menu.

Part IV: ActiveX Programming

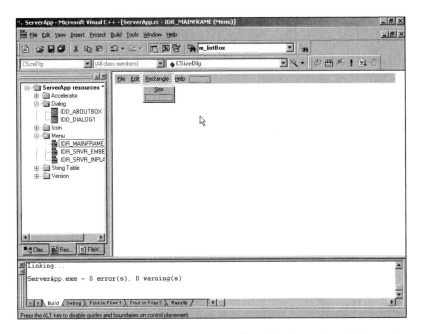

Figure 20-9: The user will be able to call up the Size dialog box using the Rectangle menu's Size command.

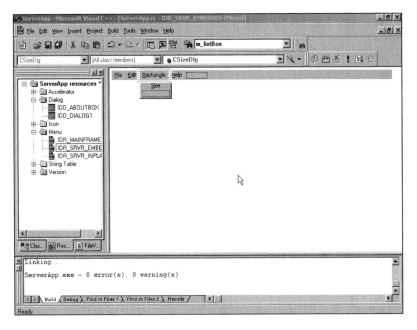

Figure 20-10: You should duplicate server editing commands in the IDR_SRVR_ EMBEDDED menu.

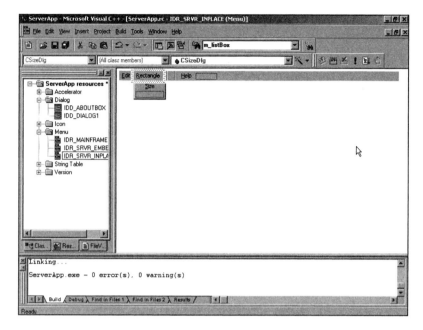

Figure 20-11: You should also duplicate server editing commands in the IDR_SRVR_INPLACE menu.

Completing the Application's Document Class

As in any MFC program, ServerApp's document class holds the data that represents the application's currently open document. An ActiveX server application's document class is much like any other application's document class, providing not only member variables to hold the document's data, but also providing the code needed to initialize a new document, as well as to save and load a document. Perform the following steps to complete ServerApp's document class, CServerAppDoc:

1. Right-click CServerAppDoc in the ClassView page of the Project Workspace window, and select Add Member Variable from the menu that appears.

2. When the Add Member Variable dialog box appears, type UINT in the Variable Type box, type m_size in the Variable Declaration box, and select the Public access option, as shown in Figure 20-12.

    The m_size variable will hold the size of the rectangle that appears in the ServerApp document. This variable is the only value that determines how a ServerApp document looks on the screen.

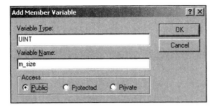

Figure 20-12: A ServerApp document consists of only the value of a single variable.

3. Add the following line to the document class's Serialize() function. Place the line after the add storing code here comment.

    ar << m_size;

4. Add the following line to the document class's Serialize() function. Place the line after the add loading code here comment.

    ar >> m_size;

5. Press Ctrl+W to display ClassWizard, and add the OnEditCopy() function to the document class, as shown in Figure 20-13.

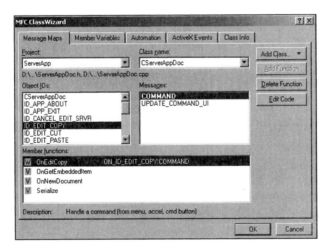

Figure 20-13: You use ClassWizard to add the OnEditCopy() function to the document class.

6. Click the Edit Code button and then add the following lines to the new OnEditCopy() function:

    ```
    CServerAppSrvrItem* pItem = GetEmbeddedItem();
    pItem->CopyToClipboard(TRUE);
    ```

Now, when the user selects a Paste Link command, the `OnEditCopy()` function copies the Server Document item to the clipboard.

7. Add the following line to the `CServerAppDoc` class's `OnNewDocument()` member function, right after the `TODO` comment:

   ```
   m_size = 50;
   ```

   This line initializes the rectangle size to its default value.

You have now completed the ServerApp application's document class. Select the File menu's Save All command to save your work.

Completing the Server Item's Class

In the previous chapter, you learned that AppWizard creates a class derived from `COleClientItem` that represents the ActiveX object currently embedded in the container's document. The server, too, has a similar class, but the server version of the class represents an ActiveX item for which the server is supplying editing functions. You could say that this server item class, derived from `COleServerItem`, is the other side of the ActiveX item coin.

On the container side, the ActiveX object (represented by an object of the `COleClientItem` class) has to know its own size and where it's positioned. On the server side of things, the same object (now represented by the `COleServerItem` class) has to know how to draw itself. That is, although the container application positions the ActiveX item in the window, it is the server application that displays the item.

To complete ServerApp's server item class, you need to provide the code that draws the item. Similar to an application's view class, a server item class contains an `OnDraw()` function, which determines how the item looks when drawn in a container application's window. To complete ServerApp's `CServerAppSrvrItem` class, add the following lines to the class's `OnDraw()` function:

```
pDC->SetMapMode(MM_TEXT);
int x = pDoc->m_size + 10;
int y = pDoc->m_size + 10;
pDC->Rectangle(10, 10, x, y);
```

The `OnDraw()` function displays the inactive embedded object in a container application's window. The mapping mode should be set to the same mode used in the view class's `OnDraw()` function, which draws the document in the server's window when the server is being run as a stand-alone application.

Completing the View Class

In an ActiveX server application, the *view class* is responsible for displaying a document when the application is running as a stand-alone application. The view class also supplies editing functions for the application. These editing functions are usually callable from a container application through the server menus that Windows merges with the container's menus (when the user selects an embedded item for editing). In the following steps, you complete the view class's `OnDraw()` function, as well as enable the user to display the Size dialog box. Using the Size dialog box, the user can edit a ServerApp document, by changing the size of the rectangle that represents the document.

1. Add the following lines to the `CServerAppView` class's `OnDraw()` function:

   ```
   pDC->SetMapMode(MM_TEXT);
   int x = pDoc->m_size + 10;
   int y = pDoc->m_size + 10;
   pDC->Rectangle(10, 10, x, y);
   ```

   These lines draw the document when it's being displayed in the server application's own window. Notice that these lines are identical to the lines you added to the item's `OnDraw()` function.

2. Press Ctrl+W to display ClassWizard, and then add the `OnRectangleSize()` message-response function, as shown in Figure 20-14.

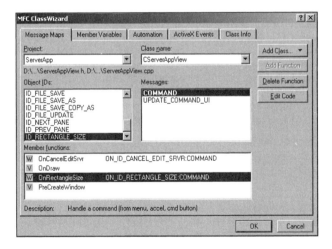

Figure 20-14: Use ClassWizard to add the OnRectangleSize() function to the document class.

3. Add the following lines to the `OnRectangleSize()` function:

   ```
   CSizeDlg dlg;
   ```

```
CServerAppDoc* pDoc = GetDocument();
dlg.m_size = pDoc->m_size;

int result = dlg.DoModal();
if (result == IDOK)
{
    pDoc->m_size = dlg.m_size;
    pDoc->SetModifiedFlag();
    pDoc->NotifyChanged();
    Invalidate();
}
```

The `OnRectangleSize()` function sets up the Size dialog box and displays it to the user. If the user dismisses the dialog box with the OK button, `OnRectangleSize()` sets the document's `m_size` member variable to the new value entered by the user and then updates both the locally displayed document and the embedded item (if any). Calling the document class's `NotifyChanged()` function is all it takes to notify any items embedded in containers that their displays need to be repainted.

4. Add the following line to the top of the view class's implementation file (`ServerAppView.cpp`), after the line `#include "ServerAppView.h"` that's already there:

   `#include "SizeDlg.h"`

You've now completed the ServerApp sample ActiveX server application. Select the Build ServerApp.exe command from Visual C++'s Build menu to compile and link your changes.

Running the Server Application

There are actually several ways to run a server application. First, you can run the server just like any other application, as a stand-alone program that enables the user to create and edit documents. Second, you can run a server application as an in-place editing tool in a container application by selecting for editing an embedded item in a container application's window. Finally, you can run the server application by selecting for editing a linked item in a container application. In this case, the server runs in its own window, editing the file to which the linked item is associated.

Running ServerApp as a Stand-Alone Application

To run ServerApp on its own, double-click the program's executable file or run the application from Visual C++ by selecting the Execute command. When you do, you see the window shown in Figure 20-15. The rectangle in the window's upper-left corner represents the application's default document, which consists of a rectangle with a size of 50.

664   Part IV: ActiveX Programming

The only way you can edit the document in this simple example is to change the size of the rectangle. You do this by selecting the Rectangle menu's Size command, which displays the Size dialog box. In this dialog box, you can specify a size from 10 to 100 for the rectangle. Figure 20-16 shows the application after the user has given the rectangle a new size of 100.

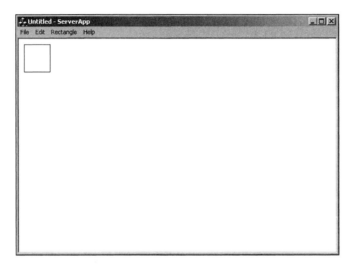

Figure 20-15: This is ServerApp running as a stand-alone application.

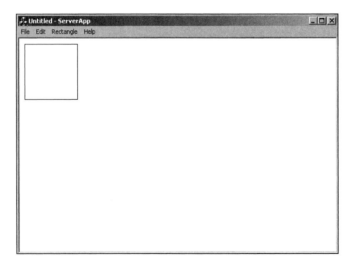

Figure 20-16: Here, the rectangle has been reset to size 100.

Before closing the ServerApp application, save the document under the name `test.srv`. Later in this chapter, you'll use this file to link an item into a container application's window.

Running ServerApp as an In-Place Editor

To run ServerApp in-place, you must first start a container application. Luckily, you just created such an application in the previous chapter. Therefore, run ContainerApp and select its Insert New Object command from the Edit menu. Select Server Document in the Object Type box of the Insert Object dialog box (refer back to Figure 20-3 for a refresher of what this looks like). Click OK to embed the item into the container application's window (see Figure 20-17).

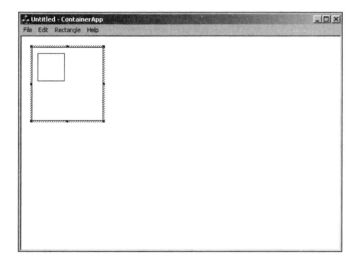

Figure 20-17: Here's ContainerApp with its embedded Server Document item.

Notice in Figure 20-17 that not only did the application embed a ServerApp document object, but it also ran ServerApp in-place, so that you can edit the embedded object. You can see that ServerApp is running in-place because its menus have replaced ContainerApp's menus. Go ahead and select the Size command from the Rectangle menu. The Size dialog box appears just as if you were running ServerApp rather than Container App (which, in a way, you are). Change the rectangle size to 10 and then click outside of the object to deselect it. Windows restores ContainerApp's menus, as shown in Figure 20-18. The solid line around the ServerApp item means that the item is embedded in the container window.

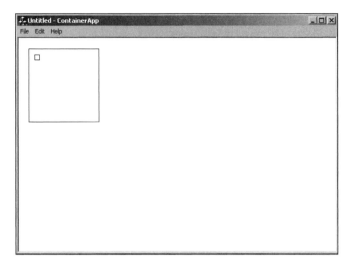

Figure 20-18: The rectangle has been reset to size 10.

Running ServerApp as an Editor for a Linked Item

In the previous section, you embedded a ServerApp item into ContainerApp's window. Because the item is embedded, the item's data (the rectangle) exists only as a part of the container application's document. That is, the item used in ContainerApp doesn't have a file of its own. When you link a ServerApp item, on the other hand, you select a ServerApp file. In this case, when the file is edited, the linked item in the container window changes automatically to the new version of the document.

To try this out, again select the Insert New Object command from ContainerApp's Edit menu. When the Insert Object dialog box appears, select the Create from File option. The Object Type box changes to a File text box with a Browse button, as shown in Figure 20-19. Use the Browse button to locate and select the `test.srv` file you saved when running ServerApp as a stand-alone application. Then, select the Link option in the Insert Object dialog box. Click OK to link the file into ContainerApp's window.

When the newly linked ServerApp item first appears, it covers the previously embedded item. Use your mouse to drag the linked item to a new location in the window, as shown in Figure 20-20. Notice that the new item sports a dashed border, which indicates that the item is linked.

Chapter 20: Servers **667**

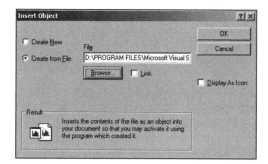

Figure 20-19: You can use the Insert Object dialog box to link, as well as embed, items.

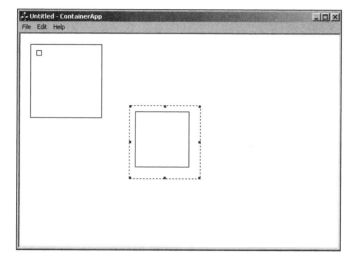

Figure 20-20: Now there are embedded and linked ServerApp items in ContainerApp's window.

To edit the linked item, double-click it. Windows starts ServerApp in a separate window and loads the linked file into the window (see Figure 20-21).

You can now edit the item by bringing up the Size dialog box (select the Rectangle menu's Size command) and changing the rectangle's size. When you close the ServerApp application and save the changed file, the linked item in ContainerApp changes too, as shown in Figure 20-22.

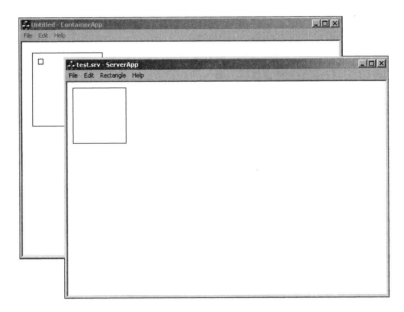

Figure 20-21: When editing a linked item, both ContainerApp and ServerApp are on the screen.

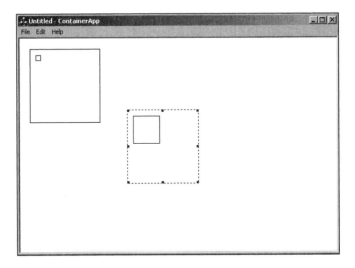

Figure 20-22: Once a linked item has been edited, it changes in the container application to reflect the changes made to the source file.

That's all there is to building and running a basic server application. Of course, your own server applications will feature more complex document types and will require more sophisticated programming. Still, this chapter's sample program ought to get you started with creating your own ActiveX server applications.

Summary

A basic server application is easier to build than a container application. Still, there's a lot to learn in order to master the programming of ActiveX server applications. This chapter presented an introduction to server programming. If you want to know more, you should pick up an ActiveX programming book that covers writing container and server applications with Visual C++ and MFC.

Also discussed in this chapter:

- When you select AppWizard's Full-server option, AppWizard can generate a complete server skeleton application.
- In an MFC program, an object of the COleServerItem class represents server items.
- AppWizard-generated server applications have three menu resources that enable the application's menus to appear in the stand-alone application, as well as in in-place and linked-item versions of the application.
- A server application's document class holds the document's data, as well as supplies the programming needed to save and load the document.
- MFC calls a COleClientItem-derived object's OnDraw() member function to render the item in a container application's window.
- A server application creates an object derived from the COleServerItem class for each item linked or embedded in a container application's window.
- A server application's view class contains the OnDraw() function, which displays the application's data when the application runs in its own window (rather than in-place).

Chapter 21

Automation

In This Chapter

- Building an automation server application
- Building an automation client application
- Controlling an automation server from the client application

Automation enables you to create applications that can control one another. Using automation, you can design features in one program and then be able to use those features in any other program you write—reusability at its best. You might, for example, have an application that can, among other things, count the number of words in a document. If you make this application into an automation server, other applications can call the function that counts words and not need to implement that function themselves. In this chapter, you'll learn how to create both automation server and automation client applications.

In this chapter, you'll put together the AutoServerApp application, which supports automation features such as properties and methods that can be accessed by a client application. Along the way, you'll learn to define an interface through which client applications can control an automation server. Because a server application is only half the picture, you'll also create a client application called AutoClientApp.

Note

Programming automation applications is a complex task that cannot be fully explained in a single chapter. This chapter is only an introduction to the programming techniques required to create basic automation server and client applications. After you master the topics in this chapter, if you want to learn more about ActiveX, you should pick up a book that concentrates on ActiveX programming.

The Automation Server Application

CD

Location: WinPrgS\Chap21\AutoServerApp

In the first part of this chapter, you'll learn to program a simple automation server. As you already know, an automation server provides some sort of service that can be accessed and controlled by a client application. For example, an automation server might provide a spell-checker that other applications can use to spell-check their documents. In this chapter, you won't create a server that sophisticated, but you will get a quick look at how this handy technology works. You can find this section's sample application, AutoServerApp, on this book's CD-ROM.

Creating a Skeleton Automation Server

AppWizard can get your automation server started, leaving you to fill in the details appropriate for your specific application. Creating an automation server using AppWizard is not unlike creating any other type of application. You just specify slightly different AppWizard options. Perform the following steps to create the AutoServerApp skeleton application:

Note

You should read through all the application-building steps in this chapter, whether or not you actually build the automation server application yourself, because the steps include explanations of the programming techniques needed to build an automation server application.

1. Start a new AppWizard project called AutoServerApp, as shown in Figure 21-1.

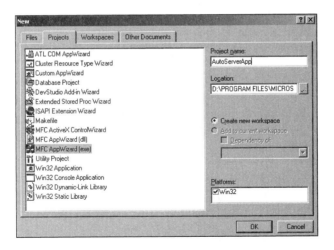

Figure 21-1: The new automation server application is called AutoServerApp.

2. In the MFC AppWizard - Step 1 dialog box, select the Single Document option.

3. Click the Next button twice, accepting the default options in the Step 2 dialog box.

4. In the Step 3 of 6 dialog box, select the Automation and ActiveX Controls option. Click the Next button.

   Selecting the Automation feature tells AppWizard to generate the source code needed to create a skeleton automation server application. The skeleton application will be able to define properties and methods that can be accessed by other applications.

5. In the Step 4 of 6 dialog box, turn off all features except 3-D Controls and then click the Next button.

6. In the Step 5 of 6 dialog box, select the As a Statically Linked Library option.

7. Click the Finish button.

8. Click the OK button, and AppWizard generates the source code files for the skeleton application.

You've now completed the AutoServerApp skeleton application. Save your work by selecting the Save All command on Visual C++'s File menu. At this point, the application does nothing useful, so you don't need to compile the source files. Instead, continue on to the next set of steps, where you complete the automation server's resources.

Customizing the Automation Server's Resources

Now that you have the basic application built, you can customize the resources in order to add a dialog box and complete the application's menus. Perform the following steps to complete the AutoServerApp application's resources:

1. Select the Resource command from Visual C++'s Insert menu. When the Insert Resource dialog box appears, select the Dialog resource and click the New button.

2. Create the dialog box shown in Figure 21-2, using the IDs IDC_XPOS, IDC_YPOS, and IDC_DIAMETER for the edit controls.

   The automation server will display a single circle as the contents of its document. The dialog box will enable the user to specify the position and size of the circle.

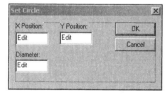

Figure 21-2: The finished dialog box looks like this.

3. Double-click the dialog box you just created to bring up the Adding a Class dialog box, as shown in Figure 21-3. Select the Create a new class option and click OK.

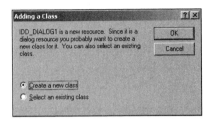

Figure 21-3: You must create a new class for the dialog box.

4. Name the new class CCircleDlg in the New Class dialog box (see Figure 21-4) and click the OK button.

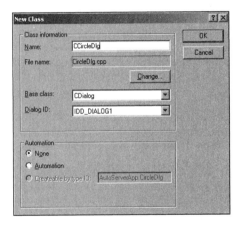

Figure 21-4: The new dialog class will be called CCircleDlg.

5. In the MFC ClassWizard property sheet, click the Member Variables tab to display the Member Variables page. Double-click IDC_DIAMETER to display the Add Member Variable dialog box, and create a UINT variable called m_diameter for the control, as shown in Figure 21-5. This member variable will hold the document's circle-diameter value.

6. Create UINT member variables called m_xpos and m_ypos for the IDC_XPOS and IDC_YPOS edit controls. Click ClassWizard's OK button to finalize the dialog box's class.

7. In the ResourceView page of the Project Workspace window, double-click the IDR_MAINFRAME menu ID to display the menu in the menu editor.

Figure 21-5: The m_diameter member variable will hold the value the user enters into the Diameter edit box.

8. Add the Circle menu shown in Figure 21-6, giving the submenu's Set Circle command the ID `ID_CIRCLE_SETCIRCLE`.

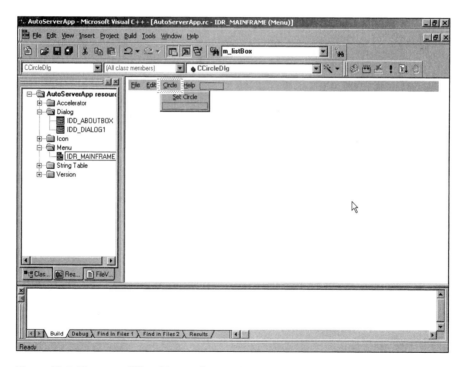

Figure 21-6: The user will be able to call up the Set Circle dialog box using the Circle menu's Set Circle command.

You've now completed the application's resources. To save your work, select the Save All command from Visual C++'s File menu.

Completing the Automation Server's Document Class

As in any MFC program, AutoServerApp's document class holds the data that represents the application's currently open document. An automation server application's document class is much like any other application's document class, providing not only member variables to hold the document's data, but also providing the code needed to initialize a new document, as well as to save and load a document. Perform the following steps to complete AutoServerApp's document class, CAutoServerAppDoc:

1. Right-click CAutoServerAppDoc in the ClassView page of the Project Workspace window and select Add Member Variable from the menu that appears.

2. When the Add Member Variable dialog box appears, type UINT in the Variable Type box, type m_diameter in the Variable Name box, and select the Public access option, as shown in Figure 21-7.

    The m_diameter variable will hold the diameter of the circle that appears in the AutoServerApp document.

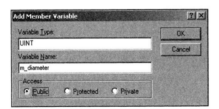

Figure 21-7: An AutoServerApp document consists of values that determine the position and size of a circle.

3. Create two more public UINT member variables called m_xpos and m_ypos.

    These variables will hold the position of the circle that appears in the AutoServerApp document.

4. Add the following lines to the document class's Serialize() function. Place the lines after the add storing code here comment:

    ```
    ar << m_diameter;
    ar << m_xpos;
    ar << m_ypos;
    ```

5. Add the following line to the document class's Serialize() function. Place the line after the add loading code here comment:

    ```
    ar >> m_diameter;
    ar >> m_xpos;
    ar >> m_ypos;
    ```

6. Add the following lines to the `CAutoServerAppDoc` class's `OnNewDocument()` member function, right after the `TODO` comment:

   ```
   m_diameter = 100;
   m_xpos = 30;
   m_ypos = 30;
   ```

   These lines initialize the circle's size and position to the default values.

   You have now completed the AutoServerApp application's document class. Select the File menu's Save All command to save your work.

Completing the Automation Server's View Class

In the following steps, you complete the view class's `OnDraw()` function, as well as enable the user to display the Set Circle dialog box. Using the Set Circle dialog box, the user can edit an AutoServerApp document by changing the size and position of the circle that represents the document.

1. Add the following lines to the `CAutoServerAppView` class's `OnDraw()` function:

   ```
   pDC->Ellipse(pDoc->m_xpos, pDoc->m_ypos,
       pDoc->m_diameter + pDoc->m_xpos,
       pDoc->m_diameter + pDoc->m_ypos);
   ```

   These lines draw the circle that's displayed as the application's document.

2. Press Ctrl+W to display ClassWizard, and then add the `OnCircleSetcircle()` message-response function, as shown in Figure 21-8.

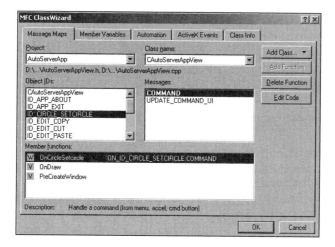

Figure 21-8: Use ClassWizard to add the OnCircleSetcircle() function to the view class.

3. Add the following lines to the `OnCircleSetcircle()` function:

```
CCircleDlg dlg;
CAutoServerAppDoc* pDoc = GetDocument();
dlg.m_diameter = pDoc->m_diameter;
dlg.m_xpos = pDoc->m_xpos;
dlg.m_ypos = pDoc->m_ypos;

int result = dlg.DoModal();

if (result == IDOK)
{
    pDoc->m_diameter = dlg.m_diameter;
    pDoc->m_xpos = dlg.m_xpos;
    pDoc->m_ypos = dlg.m_ypos;
    pDoc->SetModifiedFlag();
    Invalidate();
}
```

The `OnCircleSetcircle()` function sets up the Set Circle dialog box and displays it to the user. If the user dismisses the dialog box with the OK button, `OnCircleSetcircle()` sets the document's member variables to the new values entered by the user and then updates the displayed document.

4. Add the following line to the top of the view class's implementation file (`AutoServerAppView.cpp`), after the line `#include "AutoServerAppView.h"` that's already there:

```
#include "CircleDlg.h"
```

You've now completed AutoServerApp's view class. Select the File menu's Save All command to save your work. At this point, you can compile and run the application. If you do, you'll discover that it runs just like any other AppWizard application, with no obvious automation features. You can select the Circle menu's Set Circle command to change the circle's size and location (see Figure 21-9), but that's about it. To create the automation server, you must define properties and methods, which you do in the next section.

Defining the Server's Properties and Methods

To enable an automation client application to control the automation server, the server must define an interface consisting of properties and methods. Properties are similar to member variables, and methods are similar to member functions, but properties and methods are part of the automation server's interface, rather than part of a class. To add properties and methods to AutoServerApp, perform the following steps:

1. Press Ctrl+W to display ClassWizard, and then select the Automation page, as shown in Figure 21-10.

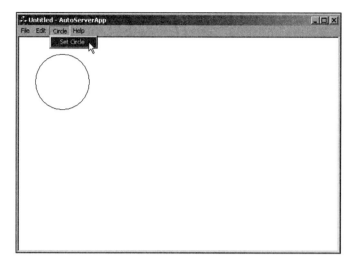

Figure 21-9: At this point, AutoServerApp runs with no obvious automation features.

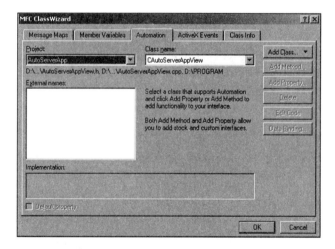

Figure 21-10: You use ClassWizard's Automation page to add properties and methods.

2. Select `CAutoServerAppDoc` in the Class name box and click the Add Property button.

3. In the Add Property dialog box, enter `Diameter` in the External name box, select `short` in the Type box, and select the Get/Set methods option (see Figure 21-11).

`Diameter` will be the name of the property that client applications use to control the size of the circle object. To retrieve this value from the automation server, a client application calls the `GetDiameter()` method. Similarly, to change the Diameter property, a client application calls the `SetDiameter()` method.

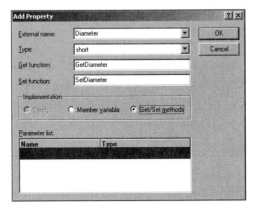

Figure 21-11: The Diameter property controls the circle's size.

4. Add two more properties, called `xPosition` and `yPosition`, to the interface, following the same procedure given in Step 3. ClassWizard's Automation page should look like the one shown in Figure 21-12 when you're finished.

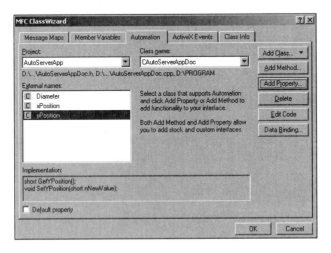

Figure 21-12: ClassWizard displays the three new properties.

5. In ClassWizard, click the Add Method button. In the Add Method dialog box, type `DisplayServerWindow` in the External name box (the Internal name box will mirror your typing) and select `void` in the Return type box, as shown in Figure 21-13. Click OK to dismiss the Add Method dialog box.

   The `DisplayServerWindow()` method enables client applications to display the server application's window.

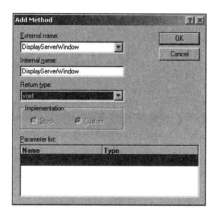

Figure 21-13: ClassWizard can also define methods for the automation interface.

6. With `DisplayServerWindow` highlighted in ClassWizard's External name box, click the Edit Code button. Add the following lines to the `DisplayServerWindow()` method:

   ```
   CFrameWnd* pWnd = (CFrameWnd*)AfxGetMainWnd();
   pWnd->ActivateFrame(SW_SHOW);
   ```

   Now, when a client application calls `DisplayServerWindow()`, the server gets a pointer to the main window and displays the window by calling its `ActivateFrame()` function.

7. In the `GetDiameter()` method, replace the `return` statement with the following line:

   ```
   return (short)m_diameter;
   ```

   When a client application calls `GetDiameter()`, the method returns the value of `m_diameter`, which is the circle's current size.

8. Add the following lines to the `SetDiameter()` method:

   ```
   m_diameter = nNewValue;
   UpdateAllViews(NULL);
   SetModifiedFlag();
   ```

When a client application calls `SetDiameter()`, the method receives the new value in the `nNewValue` parameter. The method saves the new value in `m_diameter` and then redraws all views so that the new diameter has an immediate effect on the display.

9. In the `GetXPosition()` method, replace the return statement with the following line:

    ```
    return (short)m_xpos;
    ```

    When a client application calls `GetXPosition()`, the method returns the value of `m_xpos`, which is the circle's horizontal position.

10. Add the following lines to the `SetXPosition()` method:

    ```
    m_xpos = nNewValue;
    UpdateAllViews(NULL);
    SetModifiedFlag();
    ```

    When a client application calls `SetXPosition()`, the method receives the new value in the `nNewValue` parameter. The method saves the new value in `m_xpos` and then redraws all views so that the new horizontal position has an immediate effect on the display.

11. In the `GetYPosition()` method, replace the `return` statement with the following line:

    ```
    return (short)m_ypos;
    ```

    When a client application calls `GetYPosition()`, the method returns the value of `m_ypos`, which is the circle's vertical position.

12. Add the following lines to the `SetYPosition()` method:

    ```
    m_ypos = nNewValue;
    UpdateAllViews(NULL);
    SetModifiedFlag();
    ```

    When a client application calls `SetYPosition()`, the method receives the new value in the `nNewValue` parameter. The method saves the new value in `m_ypos` and then redraws all views so that the new vertical position has an immediate effect on the display.

You've now completed the AutoServerApp sample application. Select the Build AutoServerApp.exe command from Visual C++'s Build menu to compile and link your changes. Although AutoServerApp now supports ActiveX automation through its new interface, you still need a client application that knows how to control the server. You'll build the client application in the next section.

The Automation Client Application

Location: `WinPrgS\Chap21\AutoClientApp`

Automation is a two-sided process. Once you have a server application that supplies automation services, you need a client application to take advantage of those services. In this section, you'll construct a client application that knows how to access AutoServerApp's automation interface. After completing the client application, you'll discover how the server and client work together. You can find this section's sample application, AutoClientApp, on this book's CD-ROM.

Creating the Automation Client Skeleton

AppWizard can get your client server started just as easily as it got your server application started. Then you can fill in the details that are appropriate for your specific client application. As you'll soon see, creating an automation client application using AppWizard is not unlike creating any other type of application. Perform the following steps to create the AutoClientApp skeleton application:

1. Start a new AppWizard project called AutoClientApp, as shown in Figure 21-14.

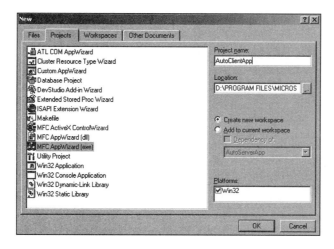

Figure 21-14: The new automation client application project is called AutoClientApp.

2. In the MFC AppWizard - Step 1 dialog box, select the Single Document option.

3. Click the Next button three times, accepting the default options in the Step 2 and Step 3 dialog boxes.

4. In the Step 4 of 6 dialog box, turn off all features except 3-D Controls and then click the Next button.

5. In the Step 5 of 6 dialog box, select the As a Statically Linked Library option. Accept the "Yes, please" default option to generate source file comments.

6. Click the Finish button.

7. Click the OK button, and AppWizard generates the source code files for the skeleton application.

Customizing the Client Application's Resources

Now that you have the basic client application built, you can customize the resources in order to complete the application's menus. In the ResourceView page of the Project Workspace window, double-click the IDR_MAINFRAME menu ID to display the menu in the menu editor. Then, add the Automation menu shown in Figure 21-15, assigning commands and IDs as listed in Table 21-1.

Table 21-1 Automation Menu Commands and IDs

Command	ID
Set Diameter	ID_AUTOMATION_SETDIAMETER
Set X Position	ID_AUTOMATION_SETXPOSITION
Set Y Position	ID_AUTOMATION_SETYPOSITION
Display Window	ID_AUTOMATION_DISPLAYWINDOW

You've now completed the application's resources. To save your work, select the Save All command from Visual C++'s File menu.

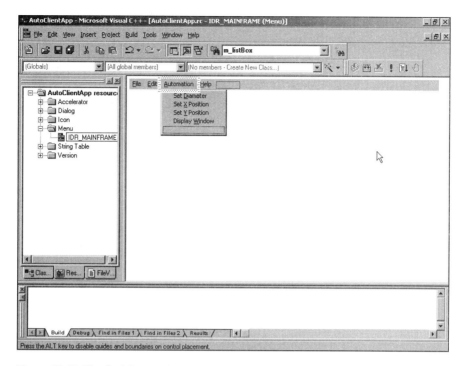

Figure 21-15: The final Automation menu should look like this.

Completing the Client Application's View Class

The client application's view class is charged with responding to menu messages. Because some of those menu messages must manipulate the server application, the view class must have access to the server application's properties and methods. This access is provided by an interface that you can create from the server application's type library. To create that interface and the menu commands' message-response functions, follow these steps:

1. Press Ctrl+W to display ClassWizard, and then select the Message Maps page. Click the Add Class button and select the From a type library option, as shown in Figure 21-16. The Import from Type Library dialog box appears.

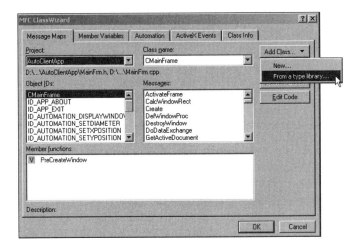

Figure 21-16: ClassWizard can create classes from type libraries.

2. In the Import from Type Library dialog box, navigate to the AutoServer App.tlb file in your server application's Release or Debug directory, as shown in Figure 21-17. Double-click the AutoServerApp.tlb file to select it.

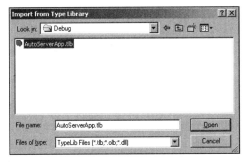

Figure 21-17: The required type library is part of your AutoServerApp project.

3. In the Confirm Classes dialog box (see Figure 21-18), click OK to accept the suggested names for the new class and the class's source code files. Click OK to dismiss ClassWizard.

The type library contains information about the server's properties and methods. ClassWizard can read the type library and create a class that represents the interface represented by the class library. This new class makes it easy for your application to access the server's properties and call the server's methods.

Figure 21-18: ClassWizard converts the server's interface into a class.

4. In the ClassView page of the Project Workspace window, right-click the `CAutoClientAppView` class and select Add Member Variable from the menu that appears.

5. In the Add Member Variable dialog box, type `IAutoServerApp` into the Variable Type box, type `m_server` into the Variable Name box, and select the Protected access option. Click OK to add the member variable to the view class.

    `IAutoServerApp` is the class you created from the server application's type library. The `m_server` object, which the program creates from `IAutoServerApp`, will represent the server's interface in the client application. That is, the client application will be able to access the server through the `m_server` object.

6. If it's not already there, add the following line to the top of the `AutoClientAppView.h` file, right after the `#endif` directive that's already there:

    ```
    #include "AutoServerApp.h"
    ```

7. Press Ctrl+W to display ClassWizard, and add the `OnAutomation Setdiameter()` message-response function. (Make sure you select `CAutoClientAppView` in the Class Name box.)

8. Add the following lines to the new `OnAutomationSetdiameter()` function:

    ```
    int diameter = m_server.GetDiameter();
    diameter += 25;
    if (diameter > 300)
        diameter = 100;
    m_server.SetDiameter(diameter);
    ```

    These lines get the current circle diameter from the server, calculate a new diameter, and call the server to set the new diameter.

9. Press Ctrl+W to display ClassWizard, and add the `OnAutomation Setxposition()` message-response function.

10. Add the following lines to the new `OnAutomationSetxposition()` function:

    ```
    int xpos = m_server.GetXPosition();
    xpos += 50;
    if (xpos > 320)
        xpos = 30;
    m_server.SetXPosition(xpos);
    ```

    These lines get the current circle's horizontal position from the server, calculate a new position, and call the server to set the new position.

11. Press Ctrl+W to display ClassWizard, and add the `OnAutomationSety position()` message-response function.

12. Add the following lines to the new `OnAutomationSetyposition()` function:

    ```
    int ypos = m_server.GetYPosition();
    ypos += 50;
    if (ypos > 320)
        ypos = 30;
    m_server.SetYPosition(ypos);
    ```

    These lines get the current circle's vertical position from the server, calculate a new position, and call the server to set the new position.

13. Press Ctrl+W to display ClassWizard, and add the `OnAutomation Displaywindow()` message-response function.

14. Add the following line to the new `OnAutomationDisplaywindow()` function:

    ```
    m_server.DisplayServerWindow();
    ```

    This line calls the server's `DisplayServerWindow()` method to display the server's main window, which remains hidden unless the client calls this method.

15. Press Ctrl+W to display ClassWizard, and add the `OnCreate()` message-response function, as shown in Figure 21-19.

16. Add the following lines to the new `OnCreate()` function, right after the `TODO: Add your specialized creation code here` comment:

    ```
    BOOL loaded =
        m_server.CreateDispatch("AutoServerApp.Document");

    if (!loaded)
        return -1;
    ```

    These lines load the automation server. If the server fails to load, the return value of -1 tells MFC that the window cannot be created properly and the application should terminate.

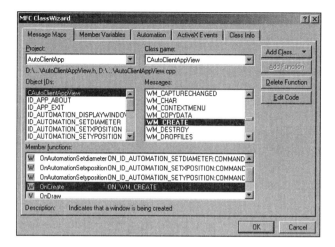

Figure 21-19: Use ClassWizard to add the OnCreate() function.

You've now completed the client application's view class. Next, you'll add the code needed to initialize ActiveX, after which you'll experiment with the server and client applications to get a firsthand look at how they work together.

Initializing ActiveX in the Client Application

You'll be pleased to know that the AutoClientApp application is almost complete. The final step is to enable ActiveX by calling the MFC AfxOleInit() function. If you fail to do this, your client application will be unable to access the server. The best place to call AfxOleInit() is in the application class's InitInstance() function. Load the CAutoClientAppApp class's implementation file and add the following lines to the very beginning of the Init Instance() function, right after the function's opening brace:

```
BOOL OleEnabled = AfxOleInit();
    if (!OleEnabled)
        return FALSE;
```

You've now completed the automation client application. In the following section, you'll finally get to run both the server and the client and see the power of automation.

Controlling the Server from the Client

Now that you've created both an automation server application and a client application, you're ready to see ActiveX automation in action. First, be sure that you've run the server application at least once. When you run the server the first time, it registers itself with Windows as an automation server. Until the server has been registered with Windows, the client application cannot control it.

If the server application is still running, close it. You don't need to have the server running in order to control it from the client; the client application loads the server automatically. Run the AutoClientApp application, and you'll see the window shown in Figure 21-20.

Figure 21-20: This is AutoClientApp when you first run it.

When you start AutoClientApp, although you can't see the server application, it's already loaded into memory. To prove this, select the Set Diameter command from the AutoClientApp's Automation menu. Nothing happened? Select the Set Diameter command a few more times. Still nothing? Actually, a lot is going on behind the scenes. Every time you select the Set Diameter command, AutoClientApp calls the automation server and changes the circle's diameter. The problem is that the server's window isn't visible, so you can't see the changes.

To remedy this problem, select the Display Window command from AutoClientApp's Automation menu. Up pops the server's window, and there you can see that your Set Diameter selections really did have an effect, because the circle is much larger than its default size, as shown in Figure 21-21. Arrange both windows (you can make the client application window smaller to save room) so that you can see them both.

Now, select the Set Diameter, Set X Position, and Set Y Position commands from the client application's Automation menu. As you select these commands, you can watch the server application responding just as if you were selecting the commands from its own menu. Changing the X and Y positions results in moving the circle, as shown in Figure 21-22.

Chapter 21: Automation **691**

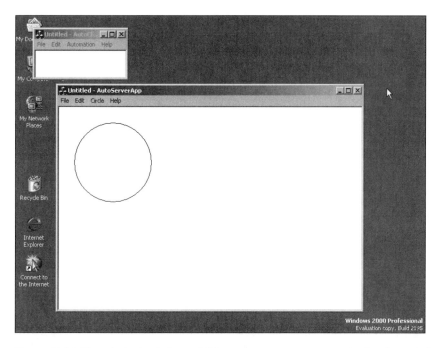

Figure 21-21: To make both windows visible on the screen, you can make the client window fairly small.

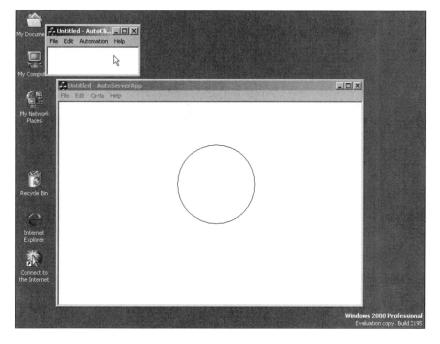

Figure 21-22: You can use the client application to move around the circle shown in the server application's window.

PROBLEMS & SOLUTIONS

Accessing Properties Directly

PROBLEM: *I want to be able to provide access to an automation server's properties without bothering with Get and Set methods. Is there some way I can give the properties public access but still keep the application aware of when a property changes?*

SOLUTION: For most automation servers, indirect access to property values (using Get and Set methods) is the best way to go, in the same way that you usually give a class's member variables protected or private access attributes. However, rules are made to be broken, and there may be times when it makes sense to enable direct access of properties. In these cases, you can create a notification method for each property, which will be called whenever the property changes. Other applications, however, will be able to access the property's storage variable directly.

When you use ClassWizard to create your automation server's interface, select the Member variable option in the Add Property dialog box instead of Get/Set methods. For example, in Figure 21-23, the programmer is creating AutoServerApp's `Diameter` property using the Member variable option. Notice in the figure how ClassWizard defines a notification method for the property. In the figure, the notification method is called `OnDiameterChanged()`. This is the function that is called whenever an application changes the associated property directly.

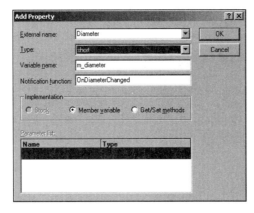

Figure 21-23: ClassWizard can also create notification functions for properties.

Summary

Using automation servers, you can provide program functionality to any application that can access the server. In this way, you can develop features once and reuse those features in future projects. In fact, any application that can create an interface class from the server's type library can access an object's properties and methods. A server can even provide multiple interfaces and so offer a set of features to other programs.

Also discussed in this chapter:

- AppWizard provides options for generating ActiveX automation applications.
- An automation server provides programmable objects comprised of properties and methods to other applications.
- An automation client uses the features of an automation server.
- Automation servers expose their programmable objects to clients through an interface that ClassWizard can convert to a class.
- Normally, a client application indirectly accesses an object's properties through Get and Set methods.
- An interface can also include public properties that are associated with notification methods.

Chapter 22
ActiveX Controls

In This Chapter

- ▶ Creating a skeleton ActiveX control
- ▶ Creating an ActiveX control's user interface
- ▶ Creating a control's properties and methods
- ▶ Responding to a control's button
- ▶ Testing an ActiveX control

ActiveX controls are like mini-applications that you can embed in other applications' windows. ActiveX controls are popping up all over the Word Wide Web, used in much the same way that some people use Java applets. Because ActiveX controls can do just about anything a small application can do, they enable Web developers to create Web pages that actually do something inside the user's browser rather than just present information. On Web sites, you can find ActiveX controls that do everything from play tic-tac-toe to calculate the payment schedule on a loan. In this chapter, you get an introduction to creating ActiveX controls. Along the way, you'll create a working ActiveX control called Scramble.

Note

Programming ActiveX controls is a complex task that cannot be fully explained in a single chapter. This chapter is only an introduction to the programming techniques required to create a basic ActiveX control. After you master the topics in this chapter, if you want to learn more about ActiveX controls, you should pick up a book that concentrates on ActiveX control programming.

Creating a Skeleton ActiveX Control

CD

Location: `WinPrgS\Chap22\Scramble`

Just as you used AppWizard in previous projects to create skeleton programs, so too can you use Visual C++'s ActiveX ControlWizard to create a skeleton control. The resultant skeleton control is fully functional without your having to enter even one line of code. Of course, if you want to create a useful control, you'll have to do a little programming. In this section, you use ActiveX ControlWizard to create the basic control. In later sections, you'll change this skeleton control into a simple word-scramble game. Perform the following steps to create the skeleton control:

Note

You should read through all the application-building steps in this chapter, whether or not you actually build the ActiveX control yourself, because the steps include explanations of the programming techniques needed to build an ActiveX control.

1. Start a new MFC ActiveX ControlWizard project called Scramble, as shown in Figure 22-1.

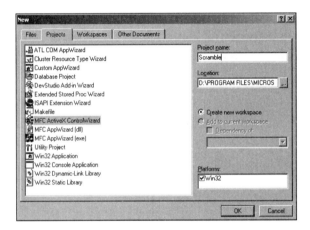

Figure 22-1: The new control project is called Scramble.

2. In the MFC ActiveX ControlWizard - Step 1 of 2 dialog box, accept all default options and click the Finish button (see Figure 22-2).

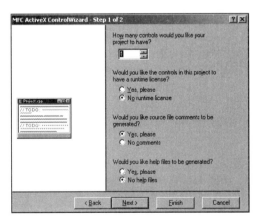

Figure 22-2: The default options will work fine for the sample ActiveX control.

3. Your New Project Information dialog box should look like the one in Figure 22-3, except your install directory may be different depending on

the directory you chose when you created the project in Step 1.

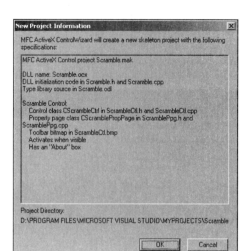

Figure 22-3: The New Project Information dialog box displays the ActiveX control's final options.

4. Click the OK button, and ControlWizard generates the source code files for the skeleton application.

You've now completed the Scramble skeleton ActiveX control. Save your work by selecting the Save All command on Visual C++'s File menu. At this point, the application does nothing useful, so you don't need to compile the source files. Instead, continue on to the next set of steps, where you complete the control's user interface.

Creating the ActiveX Control's User Interface

Not all ActiveX controls are interactive in nature. For example, an ActiveX control might do nothing more than display a line of scrolling text. However, Scramble, being a simple game, requires a user interface through which the user can communicate with the control. In this section, you create that interface by completing the following steps:

1. Right-click CScrambleCtrl in the ClassView page of the Project Workspace window and select the Add Member Variable command in the menu that appears.

2. In the Add Member Variable dialog box, type CEdit in the Variable Type box, type m_edit in the Variable Name box, and select the Protected access option, as shown in Figure 22-4. The edit box you're adding to the class allows the user to enter information into the control.

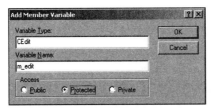

Figure 22-4: The edit control enables the user to enter information into the control.

3. Bring up the Add Member Variable dialog box again and type CButton in the Variable Type box, type m_button in the Variable Name box, and select the Protected access option (see Figure 22-5). This button will be another interactive element of the ActiveX control, enabling the user to tell the control to process text entered into the edit box.

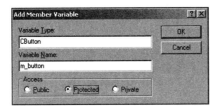

Figure 22-5: The button control will enable the user to finalize entries in the edit control.

4. Press Ctrl+W to display ClassWizard, and add the OnCreate() function, as shown in Figure 22-6.

5. Add the following lines to the OnCreate() function:

```
m_edit.Create(WS_CHILD | WS_BORDER | WS_VISIBLE |
    ES_AUTOHSCROLL, CRect(20, 70, 120, 100),
    this, IDC_EDIT);
m_button.Create("Submit", WS_CHILD | WS_BORDER |
    WS_VISIBLE | BS_PUSHBUTTON,
    CRect(130, 70, 230, 100), this, IDC_BUTTON);
```

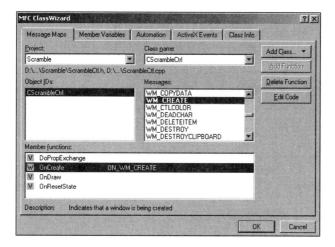

Figure 22-6: ClassWizard adding the OnCreate() function

6. Replace the `pdc->Ellipse(rcBounds)` line in the OnDraw() function with the following lines:

```
pdc->TextOut(20, 50, "Enter Answer:");

LOGFONT logFont;
logFont.lfHeight = 32;
logFont.lfWidth = 0;
logFont.lfEscapement = 0;
logFont.lfOrientation = 0;
logFont.lfWeight = FW_BOLD;
logFont.lfItalic = 0;
logFont.lfUnderline = 0;
logFont.lfStrikeOut = 0;
logFont.lfCharSet = ANSI_CHARSET;
logFont.lfOutPrecision = OUT_DEFAULT_PRECIS;
logFont.lfClipPrecision = CLIP_DEFAULT_PRECIS;
logFont.lfQuality = PROOF_QUALITY;
logFont.lfPitchAndFamily = VARIABLE_PITCH | FF_ROMAN;
strcpy(logFont.lfFaceName, "Times New Roman");

CFont font;
font.CreateFontIndirect(&logFont);
CFont* pOldFont = pdc->SelectObject(&font);
pdc->TextOut(20, 10, "ERSBCMLA");
pdc->SelectObject(pOldFont);
```

The OnDraw() function draws the control in the same way the OnDraw() function in a regular MFC application draws an application's window. In this case, OnDraw() displays two strings in the control, one of them with a large font.

7. Select the Resource Symbols command from Visual C++'s View menu. The Resource Symbols dialog box appears, displaying the resource IDs defined in the program (see Figure 22-7).

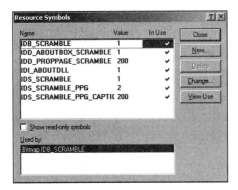

Figure 22-7: The Resource Symbols dialog box enables you to see defined IDs and how the IDs are used.

8. Click the New button and type IDC_EDIT in the New Symbol dialog box's Name box, as shown in Figure 22-8. (Visual C++ automatically provides a value.) Click OK to add the new resource symbol to the project. You'll use this ID to identify the ActiveX control's edit box.

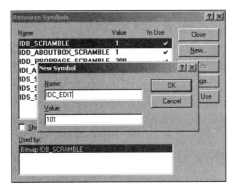

Figure 22-8: You can add resource symbols for the controls you added.

9. Click the New button again and type IDC_BUTTON in the New Symbol dialog box's Name box. Click OK to add the new symbol to the project. You'll use this ID to identify the ActiveX control's button.

You've now completed the control's basic user interface. At this point, you can see what the control looks like when it's embedded in a program. First, select the Build Scramble.ocx command from Visual C++'s Build menu. Visual

C++ compiles and links the control. Just as important, Visual C++ registers the new control with the system so that you can include it in other applications or in Web pages.

To get a look at the new control, select the ActiveX Control Test Container command from Visual C++'s Tools menu. The test container application appears. In the text container's Edit menu, Select the Insert New Control command (see Figure 22-9). In the Insert Control dialog box, find the Scramble Control (see Figure 22-10) and double-click it. The control appears in the test container's window.

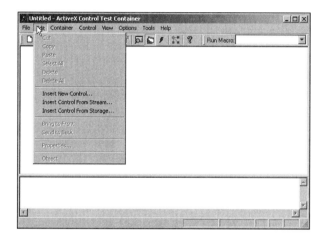

Figure 22-9: Selecting the Insert New Control command enables you to display your new control.

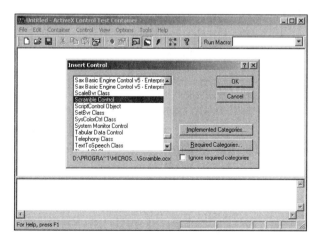

Figure 22-10: The Insert Control dialog box lists the controls that are registered on your machine.

When the control first appears, use your mouse to resize and move it. Figure 22-11 shows the control after it's been resized and moved. That strange word at the top of the control is a scrambled version of "Scramble," the control's default puzzle. When the control is fully functioning, the user will be able to enter the answer to the puzzle in the edit box and click the Submit button to submit the answer to the control.

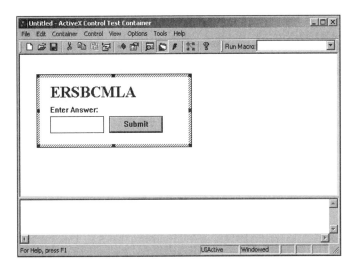

Figure 22-11: Here's the Scramble control displayed in a container window.

Creating Properties and Methods

As you know, an ActiveX *control* is a mini-application that can be placed in other applications' windows or in Web pages. By creating properties and methods for the control, you enable the control's user (*user* in this case means the person adding the control to a window) to customize the way the control looks and acts. For example, currently the Scramble control presents only a single word to unscramble. Once a player has solved that puzzle, there needs to be a way to replace the old puzzle with a new one. You can do this by making the scrambled word a property.

Methods are another feature of a control that determines how the control looks and acts. They are functions in a control that can be called from the control's container. The Scramble control already has one method generated by AppWizard, the function that displays its About dialog box. This method is called `AboutBox()` and looks like the following:

```
void CScrambleCtrl::AboutBox()
{
    CDialog dlgAbout(IDD_ABOUTBOX_SCRAMBLE);
```

```
    dlgAbout.DoModal();
}
```

You can add other methods to your controls as well. The scramble control, for example, will have methods for setting and getting properties. You create control properties in much the same way you create properties for automation applications. Perform the following steps to add properties and methods to the Scramble control:

1. Press Ctrl+W to display ClassWizard, and then click the Automation tab to display the Automation page.

2. Click the Add Property button. When the Add Property dialog box appears, select the Get/Set methods option, type `ScrambleString` in the External name box (ClassWizard automatically fills in the Get and Set function names as you type), and select BSTR in the Type box, as shown in Figure 22-12. Click OK to create the property.

   The `ScrambleString` property of the Scramble control will hold the scrambled string. The BSTR is a data type used with strings in automation functions.

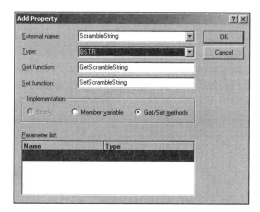

Figure 22-12: You use the Add Property dialog box to create your control's properties.

3. Click the Add Property button again. When the Add Property dialog box appears, select the Get/Set methods option, type `AnswerString` in the External name box, and select BSTR in the Type box. Click OK to create the property.

   The `AnswerString` property of the Scramble control will hold the unscrambled string.

4. Right-click `CScrambleCtrl` in the ClassView page of the Project Workspace window and select Add Member Variable from the menu that appears.

5. In the Add Member Variable dialog box, type CString in the Variable Type box, type m_scrambleStr in the Variable Name box, and select the Protected access option, as shown in Figure 22-13.

   The m_scrambleStr member variable will hold the string assigned to the ScrambleString property.

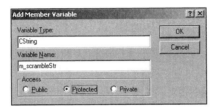

Figure 22-13: Controls, like other classes, can define member variables.

6. Display the Add Member Variable dialog box again; type CString in the Variable Type box, type m_answerStr in the Variable Name box, and select the Protected access option.

   The m_answerStr member variable will hold the string assigned to the AnswerString property.

7. Add the following line to the GetScrambleString() method, after the TODO comment:

   ```
   strResult = m_scrambleStr;
   ```

   This line sets the string to be returned by the function to the string stored in the m_scrambleStr member variable.

8. Add the following lines to the SetScrambleString() method, after the TODO comment:

   ```
   m_scrambleStr = lpszNewValue;
   InvalidateControl();
   ```

   These lines set the m_scrambleStr member variable to the new string value and then redraw the control.

9. Add the following line to the GetAnswerString() method, after the TODO comment:

   ```
   strResult = m_answerStr;
   ```

   This line sets the string to be returned by the function to the string stored in the m_answerStr member variable.

10. Add the following lines to the `SetAnswerString()` method, after the `TODO` comment:

    ```
    m_answerStr = lpszNewValue;
    InvalidateControl();
    ```

    These lines set the `m_answerStr` member variable to the new string value and then redraw the control.

11. In the `OnDraw()` function, change the `"ERSBCMLA"` in the call to `TextOut()` to `m_scrambleStr`.

    The `OnDraw()` function will now display the current value of the `ScrambleString` property instead of a hard-coded value.

12. Add the following lines to the end of the `CScrambleCtrl()` constructor:

    ```
    m_scrambleStr = "ERSBCMLA";
    m_answerStr = "SCRAMBLE";
    ```

    These lines give the `ScrambleString` and `AnswerString` properties their default values.

You've now created your ActiveX control's properties and methods. In the next section, you'll write the code that makes the control's button behave as it should.

Responding to the Control's Button

You're almost there now. All you have to do is make the control's button respond to the user's clicks. You can do this using Windows messages, as you'll see when you complete the following steps:

1. Right-click `CScrambleCtrl` in the ClassView page of the Project Workspace window and select Add Member Function from the menu that appears.

2. In the Add Member Function dialog box, type `afx_msg void` in the Function Type box, type `OnButtonClicked()` in the Function Declaration box, and select the Protected access option, as shown in Figure 22-14.

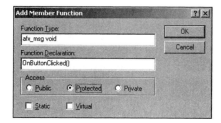

Figure 22-14: Controls can also define member functions.

3. Add the following line to the `CScrambleCtrl` class's message map (found near the top of the `ScrambleCtrl.cpp` file), right after the `ON_OLEVERB()` macro that's already there:

   ```
   ON_BN_CLICKED(IDC_BUTTON, OnButtonClicked)
   ```

4. Add the following lines to the `OnButtonClicked()` function:

   ```
   CString str;
   m_edit.GetWindowText(str);
   str.MakeUpper();

   if (str == m_answerStr)
       m_edit.SetWindowText("Correct!");
   else
       m_edit.SetWindowText("Incorrect");
   ```

Now, when the user clicks the Submit button, the control's `OnButtonClicked()` function gets called, which extracts the contents of the edit box and compares the contents with the string that holds the scramble puzzle's answer. The function changes the edit box's contents to "Correct!" or "Incorrect," depending on the result of the comparison. You'll see this in action in just a moment.

You've now completed the Scramble control. Select the Build menu's Build Scramble.ocx command to compile, link, and register the control.

Testing the ActiveX Control

Now that you're done building the control, you can see Scramble do its stuff. Run ActiveX Control Text Container from Visual C++'s Tools menu. When the application appears, select the Insert New Control command from the container's Edit menu. Double-click Scramble Control in the Insert Control dialog box, and then resize and position the control, as shown in Figure 22-15.

Type the word "**Scramble**" into the edit box and click the Submit button. The word "Correct!" should appear in the edit box, because you've typed the answer to the default scramble, as shown in Figure 22-16.

The control wouldn't be much good if it were only capable of supplying one scramble puzzle. Fortunately, Scramble enables you to change its properties and create your own scramble puzzles. To try this, select the Ambient Properties command from the container application's Container menu. The Properties dialog box appears. Select `AnswerString` in the Property list box, type **CONTROL** (all uppercase) into the Value box, and click the Apply button.

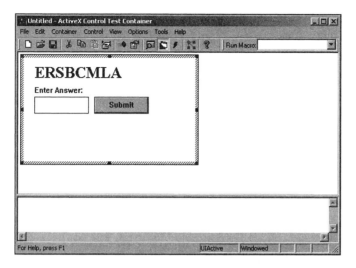

Figure 22-15: Here's the container application with the Scramble control.

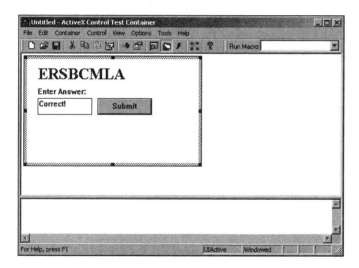

Figure 22-16: Here's the Scramble control after the user solves the puzzle.

Now, using the same procedure you used to set the AnswerString property, set the ScrambleString property to LORTNOC. When you click the Apply button, the control's displayed scramble string changes to the new one. If you type **CONTROL** into the text box and click the Submit button, the control tells you that you've entered the correct answer.

PROBLEMS & SOLUTIONS

Placing an ActiveX Control on a Web Page

PROBLEM: *I've got an ActiveX control that was created for my Web site, but I can't figure out how to include it in an HTML document. Help!*

SOLUTION: Including an ActiveX control in your Web page isn't much harder than including a Java applet. The biggest difference is that ActiveX controls are identified by a GUID (globally unique ID), and before you can add a control to a Web page, you have to know what that GUID is. An easy way to find the GUID is to look up the control in your Registry.

First, click your Windows 2000 Start menu and select the Run command. When the Run dialog box appears, type `regedit` into the Open box and click the OK button. The Registry Editor appears on your screen and displays the main folders in your system's Registry.

Select the Edit menu's Find command. In the Find dialog box, type **Scramble Control** and click the Find Next button. The Registry Editor searches for the Scramble control in the registry. Press F3 to search again, until you find the SCRAMBLE.ScrambleCtrl.1 entry in the left-hand pane. You'll see that this entry has a subfolder called CLSID pane. Click CLSID to display the control's GUID (also known as a class ID, or CLSID).

Double-click the word "default" in the right-hand pane to bring up the ID in the Value Data box of the Edit String dialog box. Then, press Ctrl+C to copy the ID to the clipboard. You'll need the ID to add the control to your HTML document, and it's a heck of a lot easier to copy it this way than to try to type it manually. Close the Registry Editor.

The next step is to add the control to your HTML file, which you do with the `<OBJECT>` tag. The following is an example HTML document for the Scramble control:

```
<HTML>

<HEAD>
  <TITLE>ActiveX Control Example</TITLE>
</HEAD>

<BODY>
<CENTER>

<OBJECT classid="clsid:3206DCA8-6CA1-11D1-AB9F-50C153C10000"
  id=Scramble height=150 width=300>
</OBJECT>
Continued
</CENTER>
</BODY>
</HTML>
```

Continued

The <OBJECT> tag is similar to many other HTML tags, containing attributes that enable you to control the element's ID and size. The most important thing to notice about the <OBJECT> tag is the way it specifies the control's `classid` attribute. The value for this attribute is the GUID you found with the Registry Editor.

Summary

ActiveX controls take the idea of automation one step further, by enabling you to embed a programmable object into an application's window or a Web page. Creating an ActiveX control with Visual C++ and MFC is much easier than programming one from scratch, thanks to the MFC ActiveX Control Wizard. Using this handy wizard, you can concentrate on writing the code that makes your control do what it needs to do, rather than having to write the general code common to all ActiveX controls.

Also discussed in this chapter:

- Visual C++ provides the ActiveX ControlWizard, which is similar to AppWizard, for creating ActiveX controls.
- An MFC ActiveX control paints its display in the `OnDraw()` function, the same as any other MFC program.
- ActiveX controls feature properties that can be changed by applications or by scripts in a Web page.
- Container applications can call an ActiveX control's methods.
- The ActiveX Control Test Container application enables you to test ActiveX controls without having to write your own container applications or create an HTML document.
- You use the <OBJECT> tag to place ActiveX controls in an HTML document.

Part V
Multimedia Programming

Chapter 23: DirectDraw

Chapter 24: DirectSound

Chapter 25: DirectInput

Chapter 26: Direct3D

Chapter 23

DirectDraw

In This Chapter

- Creating a DirectDraw program
- Preparing Visual C++ for DirectDraw
- Creating a DirectDraw object
- Setting the screen access level
- Setting the display mode
- Creating DirectDraw surfaces
- Creating offscreen surfaces
- Creating DirectDraw palettes
- Examining a sample DirectDraw application

This is the first chapter in an exploration of Microsoft's DirectX technologies. DirectX enables programmers to create multimedia programs for Windows unlike typical Windows programs. The most substantial feature in new DirectX applications is their capability to attain the graphical speeds needed to create even sophisticated games, something that Windows on its own has historically been poor at doing. In fact, DirectX is almost solely responsible for the explosion of new game titles for the Windows operating system. Previously, most games were written for DOS.

DirectX comprises several libraries, the most important of which are Direct Draw, DirectSound, DirectInput, and Direct3D. This chapter focuses on DirectDraw; subsequent chapters cover the other libraries.

DirectDraw is sophisticated enough to warrant a thousand-page book of its own. Of course, this chapter doesn't have a thousand pages to dedicate to DirectDraw, but there is enough space to give you a taste of DirectDraw programming. You can then decide whether it's a topic that you want to pursue further. After you master the topics in this chapter, if you want to learn more about DirectDraw, you should pick up a book that concentrates on DirectDraw programming.

In order to run DirectDraw programs, you must have DirectX installed on your system. Windows 2000 comes with DirectX 7.0 built in. However, if you need to, you can get a copy of the DirectX 7.0 SDK from Microsoft by pointing your Web browser to http://www.microsoft.com/directx.

Creating a DirectDraw Program

In this chapter, you'll examine the basic steps you must complete to create most DirectDraw applications and build a sample DirectDraw program. To create a DirectDraw program, you must complete the following main steps:

1. Create a DirectDraw object. The DirectDraw object is the object through which you can access other DirectDraw capabilities.

2. Set the screen access level. Normally, a DirectDraw program requests exclusive control of the screen and palette, which prevents other programs from changing settings behind DirectDraw's back.

3. Set the display mode. The display mode determines the size of the screen and the number of colors that can be displayed.

4. Create a DirectDraw primary surface. A DirectDraw primary surface represents the display you see on the screen. The primary surface is often associated with one or more back buffers, which are used to animate the display.

5. Create offscreen surfaces for bitmaps. Most DirectDraw programs must display bitmaps, probably a lot of bitmaps. Offscreen surfaces are areas of memory where bitmaps reside.

6. Create DirectDraw palettes for surfaces. Just as with a conventional Windows program, the screen colors in a DirectDraw program are determined by a palette. Usually, the program constructs the DirectDraw palette from a bitmap's color table.

After completing these basic steps, your program can use DirectDraw to perform whatever graphics functions are required by your specific application. In many cases, your programs will use back buffers and bitmaps to animate the display. These techniques require additional programming steps. You'll learn how to add back buffers to your program in the "Creating the Primary DirectDraw Surface" section of this chapter, and you'll take a closer look at bitmaps in the "Creating Offscreen Surfaces" section later in this chapter.

Often, DirectDraw programs are written without the use of application frameworks such as MFC. This is because MFC can bring with it a lot of extra baggage that slows down an application—especially a game—that needs to run at its fastest speed. Compared with adding DirectDraw to an MFC program, though, creating a non-MFC DirectDraw program is straightforward. Getting DirectDraw to run properly in an MFC program is the tricky part. The main part of this chapter focuses on writing an MFC DirectDraw program, and the "Problems and Solutions" section illustrates how to write such a program without MFC.

Adding DirectDraw Files to Your Visual C++ Project

The DirectDrawApp sample program that you'll examine later in this chapter was created by AppWizard as an SDI (single document) application with no extras such as a toolbar or status bar. By now, you should be comfortable with creating this type of skeleton application. There are a couple of extra steps, however, that you need to complete before you can compile and run an MFC DirectDraw program.

Adding the ddraw.h Header File to Your Program

First, you must include in your program the ddraw.h header file, which contains declarations for the various DirectDraw functions, structures, and data types. Because the ddraw.h header file is included with Visual C++'s other header files, you only need to add the following line to modules that access the DirectDraw libraries:

```
#include <ddraw.h>
```

The angle brackets around the file name indicate that the header file is located in one of the default header-file directories, rather than in the project's directory. To see the default directories, select the Options command on Visual C++'s Tools menu. When the Options property sheet appears, select the Directories page and select Include Files in the Show directories for list box (see Figure 23-1). DirectDrawApp includes the ddraw.h file in its view class's header file, called DirectDrawAppView.h.

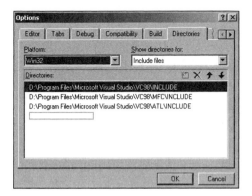

Figure 23-1: You can view and change the default directories in the Options property sheet.

Adding the ddraw.lib File to Your Program

Now that you've included the ddraw.h header file, you shouldn't have any problems compiling your DirectDraw program. Unfortunately, you'll quickly discover that the program won't link because it can't find the DirectDraw libraries. To correct this problem, you must add the ddraw.lib file to your project, as illustrated in the following steps:

1. Select the Add to Project command on Visual C++'s Project menu.
2. Select the Files command from the submenu that appears, as shown in Figure 23-2.

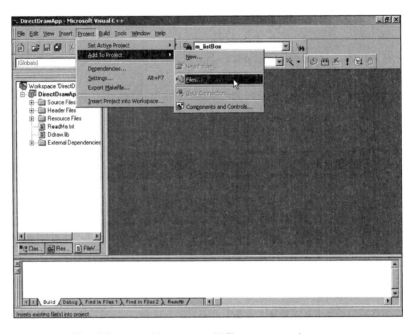

Figure 23-2: Visual C++ enables you to add files to your project.

3. Navigate to your c:\ProgramFiles\Microsoft Visual Studio\Vc98\lib directory in the Insert Files into Project dialog box.
4. Select the ddraw.lib file, as shown in Figure 23-3.

Now Visual C++ is set up to compile and link a DirectDraw program.

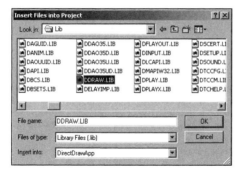

Figure 23-3: DirectDraw programs must link to the ddraw.lib file.

Creating a DirectDraw Object

To use DirectDraw in a program, you need to first create a DirectDraw object, through which you'll acquire access to the DirectDraw functions and objects. To create a DirectDraw object, you call `DirectDrawCreate()`, as follows:

```
LPDIRECTDRAW pDDraw;
HRESULT result = DirectDrawCreate(NULL,
    &pDDraw, NULL);
if (result != DD_OK)
{
    // Handle DirectDraw failure.
}
```

`LPDIRECTDRAW` represents a pointer to a DirectDraw object. In this case, the pointer is called `pDDraw`. You pass the address of the pointer as `DirectDrawCreate()`'s second argument (you'll usually use `NULL` for the other two arguments). If the function call succeeds, `DirectDrawCreate()` places the address of the DirectDraw object into the `pDDraw` pointer. To ensure that this pointer is valid, you must check `DirectDrawCreate()`'s return value, which should be `DD_OK` if the call succeeded. If the call fails, you can't use DirectDraw in the program.

Setting the Screen Access Level

With a pointer to a DirectDraw object in hand, your application can take over control of the computer's display. You do this by calling the DirectDraw object's `SetCooperativeLevel()` function:

```
result = pDDraw->SetCooperativeLevel(hFrameWnd,
    DDSCL_EXCLUSIVE | DDSCL_FULLSCREEN);
if (result != DD_OK)
{
    // Handle screen access failure.
}
```

SetCooperativeLevel() takes two arguments: the handle of the application's main window and the screen access flags. Usually, you'll use DDSCL_EXCLUSIVE | DDSCL_FULLSCREEN for the flags, giving your application exclusive access to the entire screen. Such access causes the application to run as a full-screen application, rather than a windowed application. SetCooperativeLevel(), like DirectDrawCreate(), returns DD_OK if the function call succeeds. If the call fails, you probably can't use DirectDraw in the program.

Setting the Display Mode

Your DirectDraw application's next task is to set the screen mode, which determines the size of the screen and the number of colors that can be displayed. You do this by calling the DirectDraw object's SetDisplayMode() function:

```
result = pDDraw->SetDisplayMode(640, 480, 8);
if (result != DD_OK)
{
    // Handle display mode failure.
}
```

SetDisplayMode()'s three arguments are the screen's horizontal resolution, the screen's vertical resolution, and the color depth expressed in color bits. The previous call to SetDisplayMode() creates a 640×480 screen with 256 colors (8-bit color). If the function succeeds, SetDisplayMode() returns DD_OK. If the call fails, you'll probably want to terminate the program, because the display won't be set up properly.

Creating the Primary DirectDraw Surface

Every DirectDraw program must have a primary *surface,* which is the object that represents the screen display. Often, a DirectDraw program will also have one or more back buffers associated with the primary surface. As mentioned at the beginning of this chapter, a back buffer enables you to add animation functionality to your DirectDraw program. More specifically, when a program creates back buffers, the program can perform *page-flipping,* a programming technique that makes smooth animation possible. (You'll learn about page-flipping when you examine the DirectDrawApp application later in this chapter.)

To create a primary surface with a back buffer, you call the DirectDraw object's CreateSurface() function, which involves initializing DDSURFACEDESC and DDSCAPS structures, as shown here:

```
LPDIRECTDRAWSURFACE pSurface;
DDSURFACEDESC ddsd;

memset(&ddsd, 0, sizeof(ddsd));
```

```
ddsd.dwSize = sizeof(ddsd);
ddsd.ddsCaps.dwCaps = DDSCAPS_PRIMARYSURFACE |
    DDSCAPS_FLIP | DDSCAPS_COMPLEX;
ddsd.dwBackBufferCount = 1;
ddsd.dwFlags = DDSD_CAPS | DDSD_BACKBUFFERCOUNT;
HRESULT result = pDDraw->CreateSurface(&ddsd,
    &pSurface, NULL);
if (result != DD_OK)
{
    // Handle surface-creation failure.
}
```

The DDSURFACEDESC structure, which is defined by DirectDraw, holds the data that describes a DirectDraw surface. There's not enough room in this chapter to fully describe this structure. However, the preceding example creates a primary surface with one back buffer. You can use this code verbatim to accomplish the same task. In the example code, the program first calls memset() to zero out the entire structure. The remaining lines then set the structure to create a flippable (you'll learn about page-flipping soon) primary surface with one back buffer.

The CreateSurface() function takes three arguments: the address of the DDSURFACEDESC structure, the address of a LPDIRECTDRAWSURFACE pointer, and NULL.

An LPDIRECTDRAWSURFACE pointer is the address of a DirectDraw surface. In the example, the LPDIRECTDRAWSURFACE pointer is called pSurface. If the call to CreateSurface() succeeds, CreateSurface() places the address of the new primary surface in pSurface and returns DD_OK. If the call fails, the pointer will be invalid, and you won't be able to manipulate the DirectDraw surface.

Once you have the primary surface pointer, you need to get a pointer to the associated back buffer (if you requested a back buffer). You do this by calling the DirectDraw surface object's GetAttachedSurface() function. Assuming that the previous example came first in the program, you would call the DirectDraw surface object's GetAttachedSurface() function:

```
DDSCAPS ddsCaps;
LPDIRECTDRAWSURFACE pBackBuf;
ddsCaps.dwCaps = DDSCAPS_BACKBUFFER;
result = pSurface->
    GetAttachedSurface(&ddsCaps, &pBackBuf);
if (result != DD_OK)
{
    // Handle function failure.
}
```

The DDSCAPS_BACKBUFFER flag in the DDSCAPS structure specifies that GetAttachedSurface() should get the back-buffer pointer. GetAttachedSurface() returns DD_OK if it succeeds. If the function call fails, the back-buffer pointer will be invalid, and your program will have no way to access the back buffer.

Creating Offscreen Surfaces

Once you have your main DirectDraw surfaces, you'll need additional surfaces for storing images. Most DirectDraw applications create their screens using many bitmaps to animate their displays. These bitmaps (which are usually DIBs) have to be stored in memory, where they'll be easily accessible in the program. DirectDraw uses offscreen surfaces for these bitmap storage areas. Creating an offscreen surface is similar to creating primary and back-buffer surfaces. The difference is the way you initialize the DDSURFACEDESC structure, as shown here:

```
LPDIRECTDRAWSURFACE pOffScrnSurf;
DDSURFACEDESC ddsd;
memset(&ddsd, 0, sizeof(ddsd));
ddsd.dwSize = sizeof(ddsd);
ddsd.dwHeight = 200;
ddsd.dwWidth = 200;
ddsd.dwFlags = DDSD_CAPS |
    DDSD_HEIGHT | DDSD_WIDTH;
ddsd.ddsCaps.dwCaps = DDSCAPS_OFFSCREENPLAIN;
HRESULT result = pDDraw->
    CreateSurface(&ddsd, &pOffScrnSurf, NULL);

if (result != DD_OK)
{
    // Handle failure.
}
```

The code here creates a 200×200 offscreen surface. As you can see, to create the surface, the program first initializes the DDSURFACEDESC structure and then calls the DirectDraw object's CreateSurface() function. As usual with DirectDraw functions, CreateSurface() returns DD_OK if it succeeds.

Creating DirectDraw Palettes

After creating the offscreen surfaces for your bitmaps, you copy the bitmaps onto the surfaces. You'll see how to tackle that task later in this chapter, when you examine the sample program. Before you can display those bitmaps, however, you have to create another type of DirectDraw object, a DirectDraw palette, which determines the colors you see on the screen. You create a DirectDraw palette by calling the DirectDraw object's CreatePalette() function:

```
PALETTEENTRY paletteEntries[256];
LPDIRECTDRAWPALETTE pDDrawPal;
HRESULT result = pDDraw->CreatePalette(DDPCAPS_8BIT,
    paletteEntries, &pDDrawPal, NULL);

if (result != DD_OK)
{
```

```
            // Handle palette failure.
    }
```

`CreatePalette()` requires four arguments, shown here in order:

- A flag indicating the type of palette to create (`DDPCAPS_8BIT` for 256 colors)
- The address of a `PALETTEENTRY` structure containing the colors
- The address of a `LPDIRECTDRAWPALETTE` pointer
- `NULL`

If the function call succeeds, `CreatePalette()` returns `DD_OK`. (You already learned about `PALETTEENTRY` structures in Chapter 9. Please refer to that chapter if you need a quick refresher.)

Exploring the DirectDrawApp Sample Application

Location: `WinPrgS\Chap23\DirectDrawApp`

On this book's CD-ROM, you'll find the DirectDrawApp sample application, which is an MFC program that incorporates DirectDraw in order to display a simple animation sequence. When you run the program, your screen turns black, with a pulsing rectangle in the middle, as shown in Figure 23-4. (Before running the program, you may need to change your computer's display settings to any 256-color mode.) To exit the program, press Esc on your keyboard.

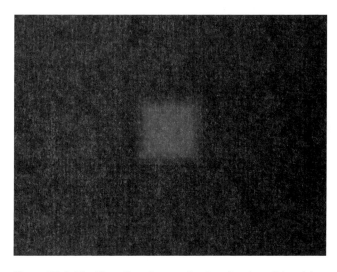

Figure 23-4: The DirectDrawApp application showing off its tricks.

DirectDrawApp's OnInitialUpdate() Function

Now that you've seen the program in action, take a look at the source code to see how the application initializes and manipulates DirectDraw. In an MFC program, a good place to initialize DirectDraw is in the view class's OnInitialUpdate() function, which you add to the class with ClassWizard, as shown in Figure 23-5. MFC calls OnInitialUpdate() once when the view class is first updated. At that point, the application's main window, represented by the CMainFrame class, has its window handle, which you need to create DirectDraw surfaces. Here is DirectDrawApp's OnInitialUpdate() function:

```
void CDirectDrawAppView::OnInitialUpdate()
{
    CView::OnInitialUpdate();

    // TODO: Add your specialized code here
    //    and/or call the base class

    InitMemberVariables();

    BOOL okay = InitDirectDraw();
    if (!okay)
        return;

    okay = CreateDDrawSurfaces();
    if (!okay)
        return;

    okay = ClearDDrawSurface(m_pBackBuf);
    if (!okay)
        return;

    okay = CreateOffScreenSurface();
    if (!okay)
        return;

    InitImages();

    if (m_DDrawOK)
    {
        DibToSurface(m_pDib, &CRect(0,0,488,499),
            m_pImages, &CPoint(0,0));
        SetTimer(1, 100, 0);
    }
}
```

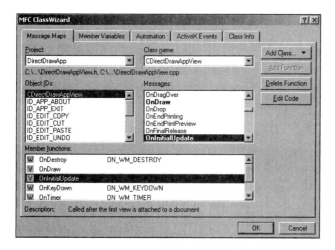

Figure 23-5: ClassWizard overriding the view class's OnInitialUpdate() function.

As you can see, the function calls other member functions — `InitMemberVariables()`, `InitDirectDraw()`, `CreateDDrawSurfaces()`, `ClearDDrawSurface()`, `CreateOffScreenSurface()`, `InitImages()`, and `DibToSurface()` — to get the program set up for its animated display. If any of these functions fail, `OnInitialUpdate()` immediately returns, discontinuing any further DirectDraw initialization. This action leaves `m_DDrawOK` (a member variable of the view class) set to `FALSE`, which indicates to other functions that they should not call any DirectDraw functions.

DirectDrawApp's InitMemberVariables() Function

The `InitMemberVariables()` function initializes the view class's member variables to their default values. The member variables are declared in the view class's header file like this:

```
UINT m_frame;
CDib* m_pDib;
BOOL m_DDrawOK;
LPDIRECTDRAW m_pDDraw;
LPDIRECTDRAWSURFACE m_pSurface;
LPDIRECTDRAWSURFACE m_pBackBuf;
LPDIRECTDRAWSURFACE m_pImages;
LPDIRECTDRAWPALETTE m_pDDrawPal;
```

Here is the `InitMemberVariables()` function:

```
void CDirectDrawAppView::InitMemberVariables()
{
```

```
    m_frame = 0;
    m_pDib = NULL;
    m_DDrawOK = FALSE;
    m_pDDraw = NULL;
    m_pSurface = NULL;
    m_pBackBuf = NULL;
    m_pImages = NULL;
    m_pDDrawPal = NULL;
}
```

The program uses the following variables:

m_frame	An animation frame counter
m_pDib	A pointer to the program's bitmap object
m_DDrawOK	A flag indicating whether DirectDraw initialized successfully
m_pDDraw	A pointer to the application's DirectDraw object
m_pSurface	A pointer to the primary DirectDraw surface
m_pBackBuf	A pointer to the DirectDraw back-buffer surface
m_pImages	A pointer to the DirectDraw offscreen surface
m_pDDrawPal	A pointer to the DirectDraw palette object

DirectDrawApp's InitDirectDraw() Function

In DirectDrawApp, it's the `InitDirectDraw()` function that creates the DirectDraw object, sets the screen access level, and sets the display mode. The following code shows the `InitDirectDraw()` function:

```
BOOL CDirectDrawAppView::InitDirectDraw()
{
    HRESULT result = DirectDrawCreate(NULL,
        &m_pDDraw, NULL);
    if (result != DD_OK)
        return FALSE;

    CWnd* pFrameWnd = AfxGetMainWnd();
    HWND hFrameWnd = pFrameWnd->m_hWnd;
    result =
        m_pDDraw->SetCooperativeLevel(hFrameWnd,
            DDSCL_EXCLUSIVE | DDSCL_FULLSCREEN);
    if (result != DD_OK)
        return FALSE;

    result = m_pDDraw->SetDisplayMode(640, 480, 8);
    if (result != DD_OK)
        return FALSE;
```

```
    return TRUE;
}
```

Notice how the function calls `AfxGetMainWnd()` to get a pointer to the frame window and, through the pointer, to get access to the window's handle. If you had tried to place this code in the view class's `OnCreate()` function, you would have discovered that the main window had not yet been created and so doesn't have a handle. As with other DirectDrawApp initialization functions, if any initialization step fails, the function immediately returns, without trying to perform any further initialization.

DirectDrawApp's CreateDDrawSurfaces() Function

DirectDrawApp's `CreateDDrawSurfaces()` function creates the DirectDraw primary and back-buffer surfaces. The following code shows the `CreateDDrawSurfaces()` function. As with other DirectDrawApp initialization functions, if any step fails, the function immediately returns, without trying to perform further initialization:

```
BOOL CDirectDrawAppView::CreateDDrawSurfaces()
{
    DDSURFACEDESC ddsd;
    DDSCAPS ddsCaps;

    memset(&ddsd, 0, sizeof(ddsd));
    ddsd.dwSize = sizeof(ddsd);
    ddsd.ddsCaps.dwCaps = DDSCAPS_PRIMARYSURFACE |
        DDSCAPS_FLIP | DDSCAPS_COMPLEX;
    ddsd.dwBackBufferCount = 1;
    ddsd.dwFlags = DDSD_CAPS | DDSD_BACKBUFFERCOUNT;
    HRESULT result = m_pDDraw->
        CreateSurface(&ddsd, &m_pSurface, NULL);
    if (result != DD_OK)
        return FALSE;

    ddsCaps.dwCaps = DDSCAPS_BACKBUFFER;
    result = m_pSurface->
        GetAttachedSurface(&ddsCaps, &m_pBackBuf);
    if (result != DD_OK)
        return FALSE;

    return TRUE;
}
```

If you need a refresher on how this function works, please refer back to the section "Creating the Primary DirectDraw Surface."

DirectDrawApp's ClearDDrawSurface() Function

DirectDrawApp's `ClearDDrawSurface()` function initializes a surface's memory area to all black (always color index 0 in Windows 2000). Basically, the function gets a pointer to the memory area and fills the area with zeroes. Little in DirectDraw is that simple, however, including, as you'll soon see, this function. Following is the `ClearDDrawSurface()` function:

```
BOOL CDirectDrawAppView::ClearDDrawSurface
    (LPDIRECTDRAWSURFACE pSurface)
{
    BOOL okay = FALSE;
    HRESULT result;
    DDSURFACEDESC ddsd;

    memset(&ddsd, 0, sizeof(ddsd));
    ddsd.dwSize = sizeof(ddsd);

    BOOL endLoop = FALSE;
    do
    {
        result = pSurface->Lock(NULL, &ddsd,
            DDLOCK_SURFACEMEMORYPTR, NULL);

        if (result == DDERR_SURFACELOST)
        {
            m_pSurface->Restore();
            m_pImages->Restore();
        }
        else if (result != DDERR_WASSTILLDRAWING)
            endLoop = TRUE;
    }
    while (!endLoop);

    if (result == DD_OK)
    {
        UINT height = ddsd.dwHeight;
        UINT width = ddsd.lPitch;
        char* buffer = (char*)ddsd.lpSurface;
        memset(buffer, 0, height * width);
        pSurface->Unlock(ddsd.lpSurface);
        okay = TRUE;
    }

    return okay;
}
```

Before manipulating surface memory, the surface must be locked by calling the surface object's `Lock()` function. When the program tries to lock the surface, it may encounter a couple of problems. First, if the user switches to another program or performs some other similar event, the program may lose its DirectDraw surfaces. In this case, the program must call every surface's `Restore()` function. (In a full-featured DirectDraw program, the images in the surfaces may also need to be restored. That is, after restoring the surface objects, your program may have to copy the bitmaps back onto the surfaces.) The `Lock()` function returns `DDERR_SURFACELOST` if the surfaces need to be restored. `ClearDDrawSurface()` handles this error by restoring the surfaces.

`Lock()`'s function signature is shown next. The function's four arguments are described, in order, following the signature.

```
HRESULT Lock(
  LPRECT lpDestRect,
  LPDDSURFACEDESC lpDDSurfaceDesc,
  DWORD dwFlags,
  HANDLE hEvent
```

lpDestRect	A pointer to a `RECT` structure containing the destination rectangle to lock.
lpDDSurfaceDesc	A pointer to the DirectDraw surface.
dwFlags	Flags indicating the type of lock to perform.
hEvent	A handle to an event. It's currently not used, so it should be `NULL`.

Another problem the program may encounter is trying to lock a surface while DirectDraw is still drawing the screen. In this case, `Lock()` returns `DDERR_WASSTILLDRAWING`, and your program must loop back and try `Lock()` again. Eventually, `Lock()` should return `DD_OK`, and your program can proceed. `Lock()`'s second argument is the address of a `DDSURFACEDESC` structure, which, when the function succeeds, will contain the address of the surface memory in its `lpSurface` member. You'll need this pointer to access the surface memory.

When the function has finished with the surface memory, it unlocks the surface with a call to the surface object's `Unlock()` function, whose single argument is the address of the surface memory to unlock.

DirectDrawApp's CreateOffScreenSurface() Function

DirectDrawApp's `CreateOffScreenSurface()` function creates the offscreen surface in which the program stores its single bitmap. The surface is created exactly as described earlier in this chapter. However, besides creating the offscreen surface, the function also specifies a transparent color for the surface. A *transparent color* is a color in a bitmap that you don't want to appear on the screen when the bitmap is copied. By defining a transparent color, you can display nonrectangular images on the screen, in much the same way you did in Chapter 9 when you displayed bitmaps using masks. The `CreateOffScreenSurface()` function looks like this:

```
BOOL CDirectDrawAppView::CreateOffScreenSurface()
{
    DDSURFACEDESC ddsd;

    memset(&ddsd, 0, sizeof(ddsd));
    ddsd.dwSize = sizeof(ddsd);
    ddsd.dwHeight = 499;
    ddsd.dwWidth = 488;
    ddsd.dwFlags = DDSD_CAPS |
        DDSD_HEIGHT | DDSD_WIDTH;
    ddsd.ddsCaps.dwCaps = DDSCAPS_OFFSCREENPLAIN;
    HRESULT result = m_pDDraw->
        CreateSurface(&ddsd, &m_pImages, NULL);

    if (result != DD_OK)
        return FALSE;

    DDCOLORKEY ddck;
    ddck.dwColorSpaceLowValue = 35;
    ddck.dwColorSpaceHighValue = 35;
    m_pImages->SetColorKey(DDCKEY_SRCBLT, &ddck);

    return TRUE;
}
```

As you can see here, to specify a transparent color for a DirectDraw surface, you first initialize a `DDCOLORKEY` structure with the low and high indexes of the transparent colors. In the case of a single transparent color, the low and high indexes are the same. After setting the index values, you call the surface object's `SetColorKey()` function to set the transparent color. In the `CreateOffScreenSurface()` function, the program selects color index 35 as a transparent color. This selection means that any pixel in the bitmap that has a color index of 35 will not appear when the image is copied.

DirectDrawApp's InitImages() Function

DirectDrawApp's `InitImages()` function loads the bitmap from disk and calls `CreateDDrawPal()`, which creates a DirectDraw palette from the bitmap's color table:

```
void CDirectDrawAppView::InitImages()
{
    m_pDib = new CDib("frames.bmp");
    m_pDDrawPal =
        CreateDDrawPal(m_pDDraw, m_pDib);
```

```
        if (m_pDDrawPal != NULL)
        {
            HRESULT result =
                m_pSurface->SetPalette(m_pDDrawPal);
            if (result == DD_OK)
                m_DDrawOK = TRUE;
        }
    }
```

If the program creates the DirectDraw palette object successfully, `InitImages()` calls the surface object's `SetPalette()` function to assign the palette to the surface. `SetPalette()` takes a `LPDIRECTDRAWPALETTE` value (which is a pointer to a DirectDraw palette object) as its single argument and returns `DD_OK` if the function successfully sets the palette. If you don't remember the `CDib` class, you should review Chapter 9.

DirectDrawApp's CreateDDrawPal() Function

DirectDrawApp's `CreateDDrawPal()` function creates a DirectDraw palette object from a DIB's color table, as shown in the following code. If you remember creating palettes in Chapter 9, you'll see some familiar material here:

```
LPDIRECTDRAWPALETTE CDirectDrawAppView::CreateDDrawPal
    (LPDIRECTDRAW pDDraw, CDib * pDib)
{
    PALETTEENTRY paletteEntries[256];
    LPDIRECTDRAWPALETTE pDDrawPal;
    LPRGBQUAD pRGB = pDib->GetRGB();

    for (int x=0; x<256; ++x)
    {
        paletteEntries[x].peRed = pRGB[x].rgbRed;
        paletteEntries[x].peGreen = pRGB[x].rgbGreen;
        paletteEntries[x].peBlue = pRGB[x].rgbBlue;
    }

    HRESULT result = pDDraw->CreatePalette(DDPCAPS_8BIT,
        paletteEntries, &pDDrawPal, NULL);

    if (result != DD_OK)
        pDDrawPal = NULL;

    return pDDrawPal;
}
```

Basically, the function copies the colors from the DIB's color table into a `PALETTEENTRY` structure and then calls the DirectDraw object's `CreatePalette()` function to create the palette object.

CreatePalette() takes four arguments:

- A flag specifying the palette type (DDPCAPS_8BIT creates a 256-color palette)
- The address of the PALETTEENTRY structure
- The address of a pointer to a DirectDraw palette object
- NULL

If CreatePalette() returns DD_OK, the function returns a pointer to the palette object. If the call to CreatePalette() succeeds, the function returns DD_OK.

DirectDrawApp's DibToSurface() Function

You can use GDI functions to draw on a DirectDraw surface. However, GDI functions are often slow, one of the reasons you're using DirectDraw in the first place. More important, there are no GDI functions for displaying DIBs, which are the most common image type used with DirectDraw programs. For these reasons, DirectDraw programmers often write their own graphics display routines. One such routine you've already seen is ClearDDrawSurface(), which fills a DirectDraw surface with black pixels. Now you can take a look at DibToSurface(), a function that copies all or part of a DIB to a DirectDraw surface:

```
void CDirectDrawAppView::DibToSurface(CDib * pDib,
    CRect * srcRect, LPDIRECTDRAWSURFACE pSurface,
    CPoint * destPt)
{
    DDSURFACEDESC ddsd;

    memset(&ddsd, 0, sizeof(ddsd));
    ddsd.dwSize = sizeof(ddsd);

    HRESULT result;
    BOOL endLoop = FALSE;
    do
    {
        result = pSurface->Lock(NULL, &ddsd,
            DDLOCK_SURFACEMEMORYPTR, NULL);

        if (result == DDERR_SURFACELOST)
        {
            m_pImages->Restore();
            m_pSurface->Restore();
        }
        else if (result != DDERR_WASSTILLDRAWING)
            endLoop = TRUE;
    }
    while (!endLoop);
```

```
        if (result == DD_OK)
        {
            char* pSurfData = (char*)ddsd.lpSurface +
                (destPt->y * ddsd.lPitch) + destPt->x;

            UINT dibH = pDib->GetHeight();
            UINT dibW = pDib->GetWidth();
            UINT srcH = (UINT)srcRect->Height();
            UINT srcW = (UINT)srcRect->Width();

            char* pDibData = (((char*)pDib->GetData()) +
                (dibH-1) * dibW) - srcRect->top *
                dibW + srcRect->left;

            for (UINT x=0; x<srcH; ++x)
            {
                memcpy(pSurfData, pDibData, srcW);

                pSurfData += ddsd.lPitch;
                pDibData -= dibW;
            }

            pSurface->Unlock(NULL);
        }
}
```

`DibToSurface()` gets called in `OnInitialUpdate()`. There, `DibToSurface()` copies the entire frames.bmp image into the `m_pImages` offscreen surface. Once `DibToSurface()` copies the image to the surface, DirectDraw can do its part to create the program's display. `DibToSurface()` requires four arguments:

`pDib`	A pointer to the `CDib` object that represents the bitmap to copy
`srcRect`	A pointer to a `CRect` object holding the source rectangle
`pSurface`	A pointer to the destination DirectDraw surface
`dstPoint`	A pointer to a `CPoint` object holding the destination coordinates of the surface

Like `ClearDDrawSurface()`, `DibToSurface()` must lock the DirectDraw surface before it can access the surface memory. It must also unlock the surface when it's finished with it. The part of the function that copies bitmap data to the surface is straight C++ that calculates the destination address for the data, calculates the address of a row of bitmap data, and copies that bitmap data to the surface. There has been no effort to optimize the function. You C++ experts out there should be able to streamline the function quite a bit, if you feel compelled to do so.

DirectDrawApp's OnTimer() Function

DirectDrawApp's `OnTimer()` function is where the animation actually occurs. The `OnInitialUpdate()` function gets a Windows timer started, which causes Windows to send `WM_TIMER` events to the application ten times a second. In an MFC program, an application can handle these messages in the view class's `OnTimer()` message-response function, which you add to the class using ClassWizard. The `OnTimer()` function looks like this:

```
void CDirectDrawAppView::OnTimer(UINT nIDEvent)
{
    // TODO: Add your message handler code here
    //    and/or call default

    int x, y;

    m_frame += 1;
    if (m_frame > 7)
        m_frame = 0;

    switch (m_frame)
    {
        case 0: x = 1;   y = 1;   break;
        case 1: x = 163; y = 1;   break;
        case 2: x = 325; y = 1;   break;
        case 3: x = 1;   y = 163; break;
        case 4: x = 163; y = 163; break;
        case 5: x = 325; y = 163; break;
        case 6: x = 1;   y = 325; break;
        case 7: x = 163; y = 325;
    }

    ClearDDrawSurface(m_pBackBuf);

    m_pBackBuf->BltFast(250, 170, m_pImages,
        CRect(x, y, x+160, y+160),
        DDBLTFAST_SRCCOLORKEY | DDBLTFAST_WAIT);

    m_pSurface->Flip(NULL, DDFLIP_WAIT);

    CView::OnTimer(nIDEvent);
}
```

In DirectDrawApp, the `OnTimer()` function first increments the animation frame counter in order to determine which image to display next. The function then gets the coordinates in the bitmap for the appropriate image. (The frames.bmp bitmap contains all eight images used in the animation, as seen in Figure 23-6.)

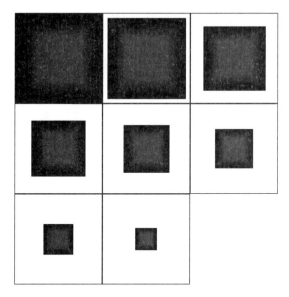

Figure 23-6: The frames that make up the program's animation sequence

The function then clears the back-buffer surface and calls the back-buffer surface's BltFast() function, which copies the appropriate portion of the bitmap to the back buffer. BltFast() takes five arguments:

- A destination X coordinate
- A destination Y coordinate
- A pointer to the offscreen surface containing the image to copy
- A pointer to a CRect object holding the source rectangle
- Flags specifying the type of operation

In the OnTimer() function, the flags used with BltFast() are DDBLTFAST_SRCCOLORKEY and DDBLTFAST_WAIT, with the former specifying that the copy should use the transparent color keys, and the latter specifying that the function should automatically deal with the DDERR_WASSTILLDRAWING error.

Finally, OnTimer() calls the primary surface object's Flip() function, which brings the back buffer into view on the screen and makes the original primary surface memory into the new back buffer. This flipping between the primary and back-buffer surfaces is what produces the animation, similar to those flip books you get in boxes of Cracker Jacks.

DirectDrawApp's OnKeyDown() Function

DirectDrawApp's `OnKeyDown()` function enables the user to terminate the program. MFC calls `OnKeyDown()` whenever the user presses a key on the keyboard, which generates a `WM_KEYDOWN` message. You add the `OnKeyDown()` function to your MFC program using ClassWizard. In DirectDrawApp, `OnKeyDown()` looks like this:

```
void CDirectDrawAppView::OnKeyDown(UINT nChar,
    UINT nRepCnt, UINT nFlags)
{
    // TODO: Add your message handler code here
    //    and/or call default

    if (nChar == VK_ESCAPE)
    {
        CWnd* pParentWnd = GetParentFrame();
        pParentWnd->PostMessage(WM_CLOSE);
    }

    CView::OnKeyDown(nChar, nRepCnt, nFlags);
}
```

DirectDrawApp's version of `OnKeyDown()` watches for the Esc key. When that keystroke arrives, the function sends a `WM_CLOSE` message to the application's frame window, which closes the application.

DirectDrawApp's OnDestroy() Function

MFC calls the `OnDestroy()` function just before the window is destroyed, so it's also a good place to release resources that the program may have allocated for the window. In the case of DirectDrawApp, those resources are the various DirectDraw objects and the bitmap object. To release DirectDraw objects, you don't call delete on their pointers. Instead, you call their `Release()` functions, but you must be sure to release the objects in the right order, as shown in the following code:

```
void CDirectDrawAppView::OnDestroy()
{
    CView::OnDestroy();

    // TODO: Add your message handler code here

    KillTimer(1);

    if (m_pDDrawPal != NULL)
        m_pDDrawPal->Release();

    if (m_pSurface != NULL)
        m_pSurface->Release();
```

```
        if (m_pDDraw != NULL)
            m_pDDraw->Release();

        if (m_pDib != NULL)
            delete m_pDib;
}
```

As you can see, you first need to release the palettes, followed by the surfaces, and last of all, the DirectDraw object. You can add the `OnDestroy()` function to your program using ClassWizard.

DirectDraw creates its objects following the specifications for COM objects. This is why you must call the DirectDraw object's `Release()` functions, rather than destroy them via the `delete` operator. Because COM objects can be used by more than one process, the objects keep internal counters. These counters are incremented when a program creates the object, and decremented when the program calls the object's `Release()` function. When the object's count is decremented to zero, the system removes the object from memory.

PROBLEMS & SOLUTIONS

Writing a Conventional DirectDraw Windows Application

PROBLEM: *OK, now I know how to write an MFC DirectDraw program. What if I prefer to do without the extra baggage and write my program without MFC? What's the trick?*

SOLUTION: Truth be told, many programmers create their DirectDraw programs without help from MFC. The easiest way to accomplish this task is to write a traditional Windows program, but write it as a C++ program rather than a C program. The reason for this is because the syntax for calling DirectDraw functions in a C program is fairly clumsy, whereas the C++ syntax is what you're already used to using.

If you've forgotten how to write a traditional Windows application, you might want to take the time now to review Chapter 1.

To create a DirectDraw application as a conventional Windows program, first write the basic application as you normally would, providing a `WinMain()` function that defines and registers your window class, as well as contains the application's message loop. You'll also need to provide a Windows procedure that responds to the many messages for which Windows will target your application. In your basic Windows procedure, you'll want to respond at least to the `WM_DESTROY` message.

Continued

Part V: Multimedia Programming

Location: `WinPrgS\Chap23\DirectDrawApp2`

Once you have the basic application built, you can add the DirectDraw program code. In your Windows procedure, respond to the `WM_CREATE` message by initializing your program and setting up DirectDraw. You then might start a Windows timer to control an animation sequence, calling DirectDraw's `Flip()` method to display the back buffer. As you can see in the following code, the entire process is actually less complicated than trying to wedge DirectDraw into an MFC program. You can find the program on this book's CD-ROM. When you run the program, the screen switches between the back buffer and the window. Press Escape to quit the program.

```
#include <windows.h>
#include <ddraw.h>

/* Function prototypes */
LRESULT CALLBACK WndProc(HWND hWnd, UINT message,
    WPARAM wParam, LPARAM lParam);
void InitVariables();
BOOL InitDirectDraw(HWND hWnd);
BOOL CreateDDrawSurfaces();
BOOL ClearDDrawSurface(LPDIRECTDRAWSURFACE pSurface);

/* Global variables */
LPDIRECTDRAW pDDraw;
LPDIRECTDRAWSURFACE pSurface;
LPDIRECTDRAWSURFACE pBackBuf;

int WINAPI WinMain(HINSTANCE hCurrentInst,
    HINSTANCE hPrevInstance, PSTR lpszCmdLine,
    int nCmdShow)
{
    WNDCLASS wndClass;
    HWND hWnd;
    MSG msg;
    UINT width;
    UINT height;

    wndClass.style = CS_HREDRAW | CS_VREDRAW;
    wndClass.lpfnWndProc = WndProc;
    wndClass.cbClsExtra = 0;
    wndClass.cbWndExtra = 0;
    wndClass.hInstance = hCurrentInst;
    wndClass.hIcon = LoadIcon(NULL, IDI_APPLICATION);
    wndClass.hCursor = LoadCursor(NULL, IDC_ARROW);

    wndClass.hbrBackground = GetStockObject(WHITE_BRUSH);
    wndClass.lpszMenuName = NULL;
    wndClass.lpszClassName = "DDrawApp";

    RegisterClass(&wndClass);
```

Continued

```
        width = GetSystemMetrics(SM_CXSCREEN) / 2;
        height = GetSystemMetrics(SM_CYSCREEN) / 2;

        hWnd = CreateWindow(
          "DDrawApp",            /* Window class's name.    */
          "DirectDraw App",      /* Title bar text.         */
          WS_OVERLAPPEDWINDOW,   /* The window's style.     */
          10,                    /* X position.             */
          10,                    /* Y position.             */
          width,                 /* Width.                  */
          height,                /* Height.                 */
          NULL,                  /* Parent window's handle. */
          NULL,                  /* Menu handle.            */
          hCurrentInst,          /* Instance handle.        */
          NULL);                 /* No additional data.     */

        ShowWindow(hWnd, nCmdShow);
        UpdateWindow(hWnd);

        while (GetMessage(&msg, NULL, 0, 0))
        {
            TranslateMessage(&msg);
            DispatchMessage(&msg);
        }

        return msg.wParam;
}

LRESULT CALLBACK WndProc(HWND hWnd, UINT message,
    WPARAM wParam, LPARAM lParam)
{
    switch(message)
    {
        case WM_CREATE:
            InitVariables();
            InitDirectDraw(hWnd);
            CreateDDrawSurfaces();
            ClearDDrawSurface(pBackBuf);
            SetTimer(hWnd, 1, 1000, 0);
            return 0;

        case WM_TIMER:
            pSurface->Flip(NULL, DDFLIP_WAIT);
            return 0;

        case WM_KEYDOWN:
            if (wParam == VK_ESCAPE)
                PostQuitMessage(0);
            return 0;

        case WM_DESTROY:
```

Continued

```
                KillTimer(hWnd, 1);
                if (pSurface != NULL)
                    pSurface->Release();

                if (pDDraw != NULL)
                    pDDraw->Release();

                PostQuitMessage(0);
                return 0;
        }

    return DefWindowProc(hWnd, message, wParam, lParam);
}

void InitVariables()
{
    pDDraw = NULL;
    pSurface = NULL;
    pBackBuf = NULL;
}

BOOL InitDirectDraw(HWND hWnd)
{
    HRESULT result = DirectDrawCreate(NULL,
        &pDDraw, NULL);
    if (result != DD_OK)
        return FALSE;

    result = pDDraw->SetCooperativeLevel(hWnd,
        DDSCL_EXCLUSIVE | DDSCL_FULLSCREEN);
    if (result != DD_OK)
        return FALSE;

    result = pDDraw->SetDisplayMode(640, 480, 8);
    if (result != DD_OK)
        return FALSE;

    return TRUE;
}

BOOL CreateDDrawSurfaces()
{
    DDSURFACEDESC ddsd;
    DDSCAPS ddsCaps;

    memset(&ddsd, 0, sizeof(ddsd));
    ddsd.dwSize = sizeof(ddsd);
    ddsd.ddsCaps.dwCaps = DDSCAPS_PRIMARYSURFACE |
        DDSCAPS_FLIP | DDSCAPS_COMPLEX;
    ddsd.dwBackBufferCount = 1;
    ddsd.dwFlags = DDSD_CAPS | DDSD_BACKBUFFERCOUNT;
```

Continued

```
        HRESULT result = pDDraw->
            CreateSurface(&ddsd, &pSurface, NULL);
        if (result != DD_OK)
            return FALSE;

        ddsCaps.dwCaps = DDSCAPS_BACKBUFFER;
        result = pSurface->
            GetAttachedSurface(&ddsCaps, &pBackBuf);
        if (result != DD_OK)
            return FALSE;

        return TRUE;
    }

    BOOL ClearDDrawSurface(LPDIRECTDRAWSURFACE pSurface)
    {
        BOOL okay = FALSE;
        HRESULT result;
        DDSURFACEDESC ddsd;

        memset(&ddsd, 0, sizeof(ddsd));
        ddsd.dwSize = sizeof(ddsd);

        BOOL endLoop = FALSE;
        do
        {
            result = pSurface->Lock(NULL, &ddsd,
                DDLOCK_SURFACEMEMORYPTR, NULL);

            if (result == DDERR_SURFACELOST)
                pSurface->Restore();
            else if (result != DDERR_WASSTILLDRAWING)
                endLoop = TRUE;
        }
        while (!endLoop);

        if (result == DD_OK)
        {
            UINT height = ddsd.dwHeight;
            UINT width = ddsd.lPitch;
            char* buffer = (char*)ddsd.lpSurface;
            memset(buffer, 0, height * width);
            pSurface->Unlock(ddsd.lpSurface);
            okay = TRUE;
        }

        return okay;
    }
```

Continued

Although this program initializes DirectDraw in much the same way as this chapter's previous program, DirectDrawApp, it doesn't manipulate bitmaps. The bitmap manipulations were left out so that you could better see what it takes to get DirectDraw up and running in a traditional Windows program. The program does, however, perform simple animation. When you run the program, it continually flips between the primary and back buffers. To terminate the program, simply press your keyboard's Esc key. All of the DirectDraw code in the program should be familiar to you by now. If you don't understand the program, you need to reread this chapter from the beginning.

Summary

Getting DirectDraw set up and ready to run is actually not as complex a process as you might think. You just create a DirectDraw main object, create a few DirectDraw surfaces (primary, back-buffer, and offscreen), create palettes for your bitmaps, and load the bitmaps into their offscreen surfaces. Of course, what you do with DirectDraw after you get it up and running is the real art of DirectDraw programming. This chapter gave you a quick introduction to the technology; it would take hundreds of pages to describe all of DirectDraw's capabilities.

Now that you've had a little experience with DirectDraw, you might want to spend some time on your own investigating the DirectX libraries. The DirectX SDK includes hundreds of pages of documentation that'll let you pick up where you left off here.

Also discussed in this chapter:

- A DirectDraw application must first create a DirectDraw object.
- The application can set up the display by calling `SetCooperativeLevel()` and `SetDisplayMode()` through the DirectDraw object.
- The primary DirectDraw surface represents the screen display.
- Primary DirectDraw surfaces are often associated with back-buffer surfaces that can be used for page-flipping.
- Offscreen DirectDraw surfaces provide storage for the images a program needs to create its display.
- DirectDraw palettes provide the colors for a display.

Chapter 24

DirectSound

In This Chapter

▶ Creating a DirectSound program
▶ Preparing Visual C++ for DirectSound
▶ Creating a DirectSound object
▶ Setting the sound-hardware access level
▶ Creating DirectSound buffers
▶ Examining a sample DirectSound application

DirectSound is probably the second most important component of the DirectX libraries. What, after all, would a modern game or multimedia application be without sound? Using DirectSound, you can let Windows' drivers worry about the system's sound card. You just create your sound effects, load them into the program, and play them. In this chapter, you'll learn how to get started with DirectSound.

Programming DirectSound is a complex task that cannot be fully explained in a single chapter. This chapter is only an introduction to the programming techniques required to create a basic DirectSound application. After you master the topics in this chapter, if you want to learn more about DirectSound, you should pick up a book that concentrates on DirectX programming.

In order to run DirectSound programs, you must have DirectX installed on your system. Windows 2000 already has DirectX 7.0 built in. However, if you need it, you can get a copy of the DirectX 5.0 SDK from Microsoft by pointing your Web browser to http://www.microsoft.com/directx.

Creating a DirectSound Program

Because DirectDraw and DirectSound were developed together, you'll see a lot of similarities in the ways you use them in your programs. As with the previous chapter, in this chapter you will build a sample DirectSound application while examining the basic steps you must complete to create most DirectSound applications.

To create a DirectSound program, you must complete the following main steps:

1. Create a DirectSound object. The DirectSound object is the object through which you can access other DirectSound capabilities.

2. Set the sound-hardware access level. Normally, a DirectSound program requests normal control of the system's sound hardware, which gives the application non-exclusive access to the sound card.

3. Create DirectSound secondary buffers. A DirectSound secondary buffer represents a sound in your program. You'll usually create a secondary sound buffer for each sound you want to play.

After completing these basic steps, your program can use DirectSound to play the sound effects loaded into your application.

Note

Often, DirectSound programs are written without the use of an application framework such as MFC. This is because MFC can bring with it a lot of extra baggage that slows down an application — especially a game — that needs to run at its fastest speed. Compared with adding DirectSound to an MFC program, though, creating a non-MFC DirectSound program is straightforward. Getting DirectSound to run properly in an MFC program is the tricky part. The main part of this chapter, therefore, focuses on writing an MFC DirectSound program, and the "Problems and Solutions" section illustrates how to write such a program without MFC.

Adding DirectSound Files to Your Visual C++ Project

The DirectSoundApp sample program that you'll examine later in this chapter was created by AppWizard as an SDI (single document) application with no extras such as a toolbar or status bar. By now, you should be comfortable with creating this type of skeleton application. There are a couple of extra steps, however, that you need to complete before you can compile and run an MFC DirectSound program.

Adding the dsound.h Header File

First, you must include in your program the dsound.h header file, which contains declarations for the various DirectSound functions, structures, and data types. Because the dsound.h header file is included with Visual C++'s other header files, you only need to add the following line to modules that access the DirectSound libraries:

```
#include <dsound.h>
```

The angle brackets around the file name indicate that the header file is located in one of the default header-file directories, rather than in the project's directory.

Now that you've included the dsound.h header file, you should have no trouble compiling your DirectSound program.

Adding the dsound.lib File

As with DirectDraw, you'll quickly discover that the program won't link because it can't find the DirectSound libraries. To correct this problem, you must add the dsound.lib file to your project. To do this, follow these steps:

1. Select the Add to Project command on Visual C++'s Project menu (see Figure 24-1).

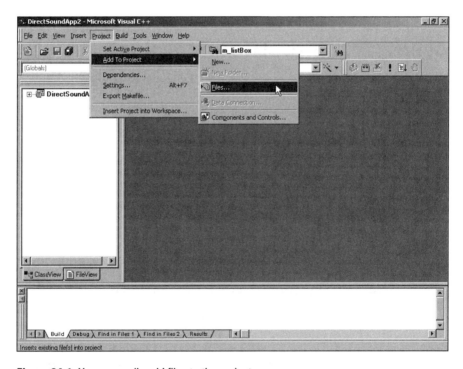

Figure 24-1: You can easily add files to the project.

2. Select the Files command from the submenu that appears.
3. Navigate to your c:\ProgramFiles\Microsoft Visual Studio\Vc98\lib directory in the Insert Files Into Project dialog box.
4. Select the dsound.lib file, as shown in Figure 24-2.

Part V: Multimedia Programming

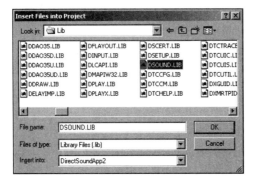

Figure 24-2: DirectSound programs must link to the dsound.lib file.

Now, Visual C++ is set up to compile and link a DirectSound program.

Creating a DirectSound Object

To use DirectSound in a program, you must create a DirectSound object, through which you'll acquire access to the DirectSound functions. To create a DirectSound object, call `DirectSoundCreate()`:

```
LPDIRECTSOUND pDS;
HRESULT result =
    DirectSoundCreate(NULL, &pDS, NULL);
if (result != DS_OK)
{
    // Handle DirectSound failure.
}
```

`LPDIRECTSOUND` represents a pointer to a DirectSound object. In this case, the pointer is called pDS. You pass the address of the pointer as `DirectSoundCreate()`'s second argument (you'll usually use NULL for the other two arguments). If the function call succeeds, `DirectSoundCreate()` places the address of the DirectSound object into the pDS pointer. To ensure that this pointer is valid, you must check `DirectSoundCreate()`'s return value, which should be DS_OK if the call succeeds.

Setting the Sound-Hardware Access Level

With a pointer to a DirectSound object in hand, your application can access the computer's sound card. You do this by calling the DirectSound object's `SetCooperativeLevel()` function:

```
result = pDS->
    SetCooperativeLevel(hMainWnd, DSSCL_NORMAL);
if (result != DS_OK)
```

```
{
    // Handle sound access failure.
}
```

`SetCooperativeLevel()` takes two arguments: the handle of the application's main window and the sound-hardware access flags. Usually, you'll use `DSSCL_NORMAL` for the flags, giving your application access to sound hardware but still allowing multitasking to function properly. `SetCooperativeLevel()`, like `DirectSoundCreate()`, returns `DS_OK` if the function call succeeds.

Creating the Secondary DirectSound Buffer

Every DirectSound object is associated with a primary sound buffer. You don't have to create the primary buffer; DirectSound does it for you. You do, however, have to create secondary buffers for your sound effects. To create a secondary buffer, you call the DirectSound object's `CreateSoundBuffer()` function, which involves initializing a `DSBUFFERDESC` structure, as shown in the following code example:

```
DSBUFFERDESC dsbd;
memset(&dsbd, 0, sizeof(DSBUFFERDESC));
dsbd.dwSize = sizeof(DSBUFFERDESC);
dsbd.dwBufferBytes = bufferSize;
dsbd.lpwfxFormat =
    (LPWAVEFORMATEX) pwfe;
dsbd.dwFlags = DSBCAPS_CTRLDEFAULT;

HRESULT result = pDS->CreateSoundBuffer(&dsbd,
    &pBuffer, NULL);
if (result != DS_OK)
{
    // Handle buffer failure.
}
```

The `DSBUFFERDESC` structure, which is defined by DirectSound, holds the data that describes a DirectSound surface. The preceding example creates a secondary buffer for a wave file described in the `pwfe` `WAVEFORMATEX` structure. (You'll see this structure later in the chapter, when you examine the DirectSoundApp sample program.) The `bufferSize` variable is the size of the buffer needed to hold the wave file's data.

The `CreateSoundBuffer()` function takes three arguments: the address of the `DSBUFFERDESC` structure, the address of a `DIRECTSOUNDBUFFER` pointer, and `NULL`.

An `LPDIRECTSOUNDBUFFER` pointer is the address of a DirectSound secondary buffer. In the example, the `LPDIRECTSOUNDBUFFER` pointer is called `pBuffer`. If the call to `CreateSoundBuffer()` succeeds, `CreateSoundBuffer()` places the address of the new secondary buffer in `pBuffer` and returns `DD_OK`.

Exploring the DirectSoundApp Application

Location: `WinPrgS\Chap24\DirectSoundApp`

On this book's CD-ROM, you'll find the DirectSoundApp sample application, which is an MFC program that incorporates DirectSound in order to play a simple sound effect. When you run the program, you see the window shown in Figure 24-3. Click the window to hear the sound effect played by DirectSound.

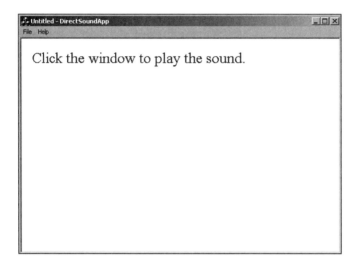

Figure 24-3: The DirectSoundApp application prompts the user to play a DirectSound sound effect.

In the following sections, you'll examine DirectSoundApp more closely and see how it implements DirectSound using the techniques described in this chapter.

DirectSoundApp's View-Class Constructor

Now that you've seen the program in action, take a look at the source code to see how the application initializes and manipulates DirectSound. The view class's constructor initializes the class's member variables to their default values:

```
CDirectSoundAppView::CDirectSoundAppView()
{
    // TODO: add construction code here

    m_pBuffer = NULL;
    m_pWave = NULL;
    m_DSOK = FALSE;
```

```
    m_bufSize = 0;
    m_pDS = NULL;
}
```

The member variables are declared in the view class's header file:

```
DWORD m_bufSize;
LPDIRECTSOUND m_pDS;
BOOL m_DSOK;
CWave* m_pWave;
LPDIRECTSOUNDBUFFER m_pBuffer;
```

The program uses the following variables:

m_bufSize	Size of the wave file's data
m_pDS	Pointer to the application's DirectSound object
m_DSOK	Flag indicating whether DirectSound initialized successfully
m_pWave	Pointer to the CWave object that contains the sound data
m_pBuffer	Pointer to the secondary DirectSound buffer

DirectSoundApp's OnInitialUpdate() Function

In an MFC program, a good place to initialize DirectSound is in the view class's OnInitialUpdate() function, which you add to the class with ClassWizard, as shown in Figure 24-4. MFC calls OnInitialUpdate() once when the view class is first updated. At that point, the application's main window, represented by the CMainFrame class, has its window handle, which you need to call SetCooperativeLevel(). The following code shows DirectSoundApp's OnInitialUpdate() function:

```
void CDirectSoundAppView::OnInitialUpdate()
{
    CView::OnInitialUpdate();

    // TODO: Add your specialized code here
    //    and/or call the base class

    BOOL okay = InitDirectSound();
    if (!okay)
        return;

    okay = CreateSoundBuffer();
    if (!okay)
        return;

    m_DSOK = LoadWaveData();
}
```

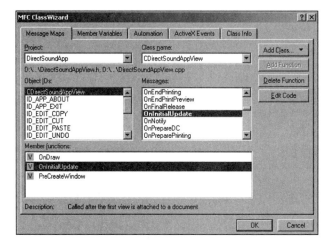

Figure 24-4: ClassWizard overriding the view class's OnInitialUpdate() function.

As you can see, the function calls other member functions — InitDirectSound(), CreateSoundBuffer(), and LoadWaveData() — to get the program set up for playing sound effects. If any of these functions fail, OnInitialUpdate() immediately returns, discontinuing any further DirectSound initialization. This action leaves m_DSOK (a member variable of the view class) set to FALSE, which indicates to other functions that they should not call DirectSound functions.

DirectSoundApp's InitDirectSound() Function

In DirectSoundApp, it's the InitDirectSound() function that creates the DirectSound object and sets the sound-hardware access level. The following code shows the InitDirectSound() function:

```
BOOL CDirectSoundAppView::InitDirectSound()
{
    HRESULT result =
        DirectSoundCreate(NULL, &m_pDS, NULL);
    if (result != DS_OK)
        return FALSE;

    CWnd* pMainWnd = AfxGetMainWnd();
    HWND hMainWnd = pMainWnd->m_hWnd;
    result = m_pDS->SetCooperativeLevel(hMainWnd,
        DSSCL_NORMAL);
    if (result != DS_OK)
        return FALSE;

    return TRUE;
}
```

Notice how the function calls `AfxGetMainWnd()` to get a pointer to the frame window and, through the pointer, get access to the window's handle. If you had tried to place this code in the view class's `OnCreate()` function, you would have discovered that the main window had not yet been created and so doesn't have a handle. As with other DirectSoundApp initialization functions, if any step fails, the function immediately returns, without trying to perform any further initialization.

DirectSoundApp's CreateSoundBuffer() Function

DirectSoundApp's `CreateSoundBuffer()` function creates the DirectSound secondary buffer, using the techniques described previously in this chapter. The following code shows the `CreateSoundBuffer()` function:

```
BOOL CDirectSoundAppView::CreateSoundBuffer()
{
    LPWAVEFORMATEX pwfe;
    DSBUFFERDESC dsbd;

    m_pWave = new CWave("metal.wav");
    if (!m_pWave->IsValid())
        return FALSE;
    pwfe = m_pWave->GetFormat();
    m_bufSize = m_pWave->GetSize();

    memset(&dsbd, 0, sizeof(DSBUFFERDESC));
    dsbd.dwSize = sizeof(DSBUFFERDESC);
    dsbd.dwBufferBytes = m_bufSize;
    dsbd.lpwfxFormat =
        (LPWAVEFORMATEX) pwfe;
    dsbd.dwFlags = DSBCAPS_CTRLDEFAULT;

    HRESULT result = m_pDS->CreateSoundBuffer(&dsbd,
        &m_pBuffer, NULL);
    if (result != DS_OK)
        return FALSE;

    return TRUE;
}
```

Notice that the function defines a pointer to a `WAVEFORMATEX` structure, which holds information about a wave file that's needed in order to create a DirectSound buffer. As with other DirectSoundApp initialization functions, if any step fails, the function immediately returns, without trying to perform further initialization.

The CWave Class

CWave is a custom class, much like the CBitmap class you developed in Chapter 9, that loads a wave sound file and provides the information about the file needed by DirectSound. A CWave object was created near the beginning of the CreateSoundBuffer() function. Completely describing the programming techniques for loading a wave file is beyond the scope of this chapter. However, if you know something about Windows' multimedia library, you can explore the CWave class to see how it works. Following is the class's header file and implementation file:

```
#ifndef __CWAVE_H
#define __CWAVE_H

#include <mmsystem.h>

class CWave : public CObject
{
protected:
    LPCSTR m_filename;
    WAVEFORMATEX m_wfe;
    BYTE* m_pData;
    DWORD m_size;
    BOOL m_valid;

public:
    CWave(LPCSTR filename);
    ~CWave();

    BOOL IsValid();
    DWORD GetSize();
    BYTE* GetData();
    LPCSTR GetFilename();
    LPWAVEFORMATEX GetFormat();

protected:
    BOOL LoadFile(LPCSTR filename);
};

#endif

#include <stdafx.h>
#include <afxwin.h>
#include "windowsx.h"
#include "cwave.h"

CWave::CWave(LPCSTR filename)
{
    m_filename = filename;
    m_pData = NULL;
    m_size = 0;
    m_valid = LoadFile(filename);
}
```

```
CWave::~CWave()
{
    GlobalFreePtr(m_pData);
}

BOOL CWave::IsValid()
{
    return m_valid;
}

DWORD CWave::GetSize()
{
    return m_size;
}

LPWAVEFORMATEX CWave::GetFormat()
{
    return &m_wfe;
}

BYTE* CWave::GetData()
{
    return m_pData;
}

LPCSTR CWave::GetFilename()
{
    return m_filename;
}

BOOL CWave::LoadFile(LPCSTR filename)
{
    MMCKINFO mmCkiRiff;
    MMCKINFO mmCkiChunk;

    HMMIO hMMIO = mmioOpen((char*)filename, NULL,
        MMIO_READ | MMIO_ALLOCBUF);
    if (hMMIO == NULL)
        return FALSE;

    mmCkiRiff.fccType = mmioFOURCC('W', 'A', 'V', 'E');
    MMRESULT mmResult = mmioDescend(hMMIO, &mmCkiRiff,
        NULL, MMIO_FINDRIFF);
    if (mmResult != MMSYSERR_NOERROR)
        return FALSE;

    mmCkiChunk.ckid = mmioFOURCC('f', 'm', 't', ' ');
    mmResult = mmioDescend(hMMIO, &mmCkiChunk,
        &mmCkiRiff, MMIO_FINDCHUNK);
    if (mmResult != MMSYSERR_NOERROR)
        return FALSE;

    LONG numBytes = mmioRead(hMMIO, (char*)&m_wfe,
```

```
            sizeof(WAVEFORMATEX));
    if (numBytes == -1)
        return FALSE;

    mmResult = mmioAscend(hMMIO, &mmCkiChunk, 0);
    if (mmResult != MMSYSERR_NOERROR)
        return FALSE;

    mmCkiChunk.ckid = mmioFOURCC('d', 'a', 't', 'a');
    mmResult = mmioDescend(hMMIO, &mmCkiChunk,
        &mmCkiRiff, MMIO_FINDCHUNK);
    if (mmResult != MMSYSERR_NOERROR)
        return FALSE;

    m_size = mmCkiChunk.cksize;
    m_pData = (BYTE*)GlobalAllocPtr(GMEM_MOVEABLE, m_size);
    if (m_pData == NULL)
        return FALSE;

    numBytes = mmioRead(hMMIO, (char*)m_pData, m_size);
    if (numBytes == -1)
        return FALSE;
    mmioClose(hMMIO, 0);

    return TRUE;
}
```

If you're not interested in how to load a wave file, you can just add the class to your programs and call its member functions as needed. To create an object of the class, you call the class's constructor with the file name of the wave file you want to load. The constructor not only creates the CWave object, but also loads the file and stores information you'll need as you create your DirectSound object and buffers. The CWave class's methods are listed here, along with their descriptions:

CWave()	Constructs a CWave object from the given wave file
IsValid()	Returns TRUE if the CWave object is valid
GetSize()	Returns the size of the sound data as a DWORD
GetData()	Returns a pointer to the sound data
GetFilename()	Returns the wave file's file name
GetFormat()	Returns a pointer to the wave file's WAVEFORMATEX structure

You'll learn more about using the CWave class as you explore the rest of the DirectSoundApp application in the following sections.

DirectSoundApp's LoadWaveData() Function

In the `LoadWaveData()` function, DirectSoundApp transfers the sound data from the `CWave` object to the secondary DirectSound buffer, as shown here:

```
BOOL CDirectSoundAppView::LoadWaveData()
{
    LPVOID pBlock1;
    DWORD bytesBlock1;
    LPVOID pBlock2;
    DWORD bytesBlock2;

    HRESULT result = m_pBuffer->Lock(0, m_bufSize,
        &pBlock1, &bytesBlock1, &pBlock2,
        &bytesBlock2, 0);
    if (result != DS_OK)
        return FALSE;

    DWORD waveSize = m_pWave->GetSize();
    BYTE* pWaveData = m_pWave->GetData();
    memcpy((void*)pBlock1, pWaveData, waveSize);

    m_pBuffer->Unlock(pBlock1, bytesBlock1,
        pBlock2, bytesBlock2);

    delete m_pWave;

    return TRUE;
}
```

Before transferring data to a buffer, the program must lock the buffer by calling the `DIRECTSOUNDBUFFER` object's `Lock()` function. The `Lock()` function takes seven arguments:

- The buffer position at which to start locking data (0 = beginning)
- The number of bytes to lock
- The address of a pointer that will get the address of the first sound block
- The address of a `DWORD` that will hold the number of bytes in the first sound block
- The address of a pointer that will get the address to the second sound block
- The address of a `DWORD` that will hold the number of bytes in the second sound block
- A locking flag; usually 0

After `LoadWaveData()` locks the sound buffer, the `pBlock1`, `bytesBlock1`, `pBlock2`, and `bytesBlock2` variables will contain the values described above. `LoadWaveData()` uses the `pBlock1` pointer as the destination for the `memcpy()` command that copies the wave data to the DirectSound buffer.

After copying the data, `LoadWaveData()` calls the buffer object's `Unlock()` function and deletes the `CWave` object. `Unlock()` takes the `pBlock1`, `bytesBlock1`, `pBlock2`, and `bytesBlock2` variables as its arguments.

DirectSoundApp's OnLButtonDown() Function

Now that the wave file's data has been loaded into the DirectSound secondary buffer, the sound effect is ready to play. When the user clicks in the application's window, DirectSoundApp plays the sound by calling the buffer object's `Play()` function. This happens in the view class's `OnLButtonDown()` function, which responds to the WM_LBUTTONDOWN Windows message:

```
void CDirectSoundAppView::OnLButtonDown(UINT nFlags, CPoint point)
{
    // TODO: Add your message handler code here and/or call default

    if (m_DSOK)
    {
        m_pBuffer->SetCurrentPosition(0);
        m_pBuffer->Play(0, 0, 0);
    }

    CView::OnLButtonDown(nFlags, point);
}
```

As you can see in this listing, the program calls the sound buffer object's `SetCurrentPosition()` function to set the starting point to the first byte in the buffer, and then it calls `Play()` to play the sound effect.

DirectSoundApp's OnDestroy() Function

Finally, when the user closes the application, DirectSoundApp must release the DirectSound objects it created. As with DirectDraw, you don't call the `delete` operator on a DirectSound pointer. Instead, you call the DirectSound object's `Release()` function. DirectSoundApp takes care of these final details in the `OnDestroy()` function, which MFC calls just before the view window is destroyed. `OnDestroy()` releases the secondary buffer and then releases the main DirectSound object. You can add `OnDestroy()` to your AppWizard-generated programs using ClassWizard. The final function looks like this:

```
void CDirectSoundAppView::OnDestroy()
{
    CView::OnDestroy();

    // TODO: Add your message handler code here

    if (m_pBuffer != NULL)
        m_pBuffer->Release();
```

```
        if (m_pDS != NULL)
            m_pDS->Release();
}
```

DirectSound creates its objects following the specifications for COM objects. This is why you must call DirectSound objects' Release() functions, rather than destroy them via the delete operator. Because COM objects can be used by more than one process, the objects keep internal counters. These counters are incremented when a program creates the object, and decremented when the program calls the object's Release() function. When the object's count is decremented to zero, the system removes the object from memory.

PROBLEMS & SOLUTIONS

Writing a Conventional DirectSound Windows Application

PROBLEM: *Now I know how to write an MFC DirectSound program. What if I prefer to write my program without MFC?*

SOLUTION: Just as with DirectDraw, the easiest way to accomplish this task is to write a traditional Windows program, but write it as a C++ program rather than a C program. Then you can avoid the clumsy syntax required to call DirectSound functions from a C program.

If you've forgotten how to write a traditional Windows application, you might want to take the time now to review Chapter 1.

To create a DirectSound application as a conventional Windows program, first write the basic application as you normally would, providing a WinMain() function that defines and registers your window class, as well as contains the application's message loop. You'll also need to provide a Windows procedure that responds to the many messages for which Windows will target your application. In your basic Windows procedure, you'll want to respond at least to the WM_DESTROY message.

Location: WinPrgS\Chap24\DirectSoundApp2

Once you have the basic application built, you can add the DirectSound program code. In your Windows procedure, respond to the WM_CREATE message by initializing your program and setting up DirectSound. As you can see in the following program, the entire process is actually less complicated than trying to wedge DirectSound into an MFC program. You can find the complete program on this book's CD-ROM:

```
#include <windows.h>
#include <windowsx.h>
#include <dsound.h>
```

Continued

```c
/* Function prototypes */
LRESULT CALLBACK WndProc(HWND hWnd, UINT message,
    WPARAM wParam, LPARAM lParam);
void InitVariables();
BOOL InitDirectSound(HWND hWnd);
BOOL LoadWaveFile(char* filename);
BOOL CreateSoundBuffer();

/* Global variables */
LPDIRECTSOUND pDS;
LPDIRECTSOUNDBUFFER pDSBuffer;
WAVEFORMATEX wfe;
BYTE* pSoundData;
DWORD soundSize;

int WINAPI WinMain(HINSTANCE hCurrentInst,
    HINSTANCE hPrevInstance, PSTR lpszCmdLine,
    int nCmdShow)
{
    WNDCLASS wndClass;
    HWND hWnd;
    MSG msg;
    UINT width;
    UINT height;

    wndClass.style = CS_HREDRAW | CS_VREDRAW;
    wndClass.lpfnWndProc = WndProc;
    wndClass.cbClsExtra = 0;
    wndClass.cbWndExtra = 0;
    wndClass.hInstance = hCurrentInst;
    wndClass.hIcon = LoadIcon(NULL, IDI_APPLICATION);
    wndClass.hCursor = LoadCursor(NULL, IDC_ARROW);
    wndClass.hbrBackground = GetStockObject(WHITE_BRUSH);
    wndClass.lpszMenuName = NULL;
    wndClass.lpszClassName = "DSoundApp";

    RegisterClass(&wndClass);

    width = GetSystemMetrics(SM_CXSCREEN) / 2;
    height = GetSystemMetrics(SM_CYSCREEN) / 2;

    hWnd = CreateWindow(
            "DSoundApp",         /* Window class's name.     */
            "DirectSound App",   /* Title bar text.          */
            WS_OVERLAPPEDWINDOW, /* The window's style.      */
            10,                  /* X position.              */
            10,                  /* Y position.              */
            width,               /* Width.                   */
            height,              /* Height.                  */
            NULL,                /* Parent window's handle.  */
            NULL,                /* Menu handle.             */
            hCurrentInst,        /* Instance handle.         */
```

Continued

```
                    NULL);              /* No additional data.    */

    ShowWindow(hWnd, nCmdShow);
    UpdateWindow(hWnd);

    while (GetMessage(&msg, NULL, 0, 0))
    {
        TranslateMessage(&msg);
        DispatchMessage(&msg);
    }

    return msg.wParam;
}

LRESULT CALLBACK WndProc(HWND hWnd, UINT message,
    WPARAM wParam, LPARAM lParam)
{
    HDC hDC;
    PAINTSTRUCT paintStruct;

    switch(message)
    {
        case WM_CREATE:
            InitVariables();
            InitDirectSound(hWnd);
            LoadWaveFile("metal.wav");
            CreateSoundBuffer();
            return 0;

        case WM_PAINT:
            hDC = BeginPaint(hWnd, &paintStruct);
            TextOut(hDC, 10, 10,
                "Click the window to play the sound.", 35);
            EndPaint(hWnd, &paintStruct);
            return 0;

        case WM_LBUTTONDOWN:
            pDSBuffer->SetCurrentPosition(0);
            pDSBuffer->Play(0, 0, 0);
            return 0;

        case WM_DESTROY:
            if (pDSBuffer != NULL)
                pDSBuffer->Release();
            if (pDS != NULL)
                pDS->Release();
            GlobalFreePtr(pSoundData);
            PostQuitMessage(0);
            return 0;
    }
```

Continued

```
        return DefWindowProc(hWnd, message, wParam, lParam);
}

void InitVariables()
{
    pDSBuffer = NULL;
    pDS = NULL;
}

BOOL InitDirectSound(HWND hWnd)
{
    HRESULT result =
        DirectSoundCreate(NULL, &pDS, NULL);
    if (result != DS_OK)
        return FALSE;

    result = pDS->SetCooperativeLevel(hWnd,
        DSSCL_NORMAL);
    if (result != DS_OK)
        return FALSE;

    return TRUE;
}

BOOL LoadWaveFile(char* filename)
{
    MMCKINFO mmCkiRiff;
    MMCKINFO mmCkiChunk;

    HMMIO hMMIO = mmioOpen((char*)filename, NULL,
        MMIO_READ | MMIO_ALLOCBUF);
    if (hMMIO == NULL)
        return FALSE;

    mmCkiRiff.fccType = mmioFOURCC('W', 'A', 'V', 'E');
    MMRESULT mmResult = mmioDescend(hMMIO, &mmCkiRiff,
        NULL, MMIO_FINDRIFF);
    if (mmResult != MMSYSERR_NOERROR)
        return FALSE;

    mmCkiChunk.ckid = mmioFOURCC('f', 'm', 't', ' ');
    mmResult = mmioDescend(hMMIO, &mmCkiChunk,
        &mmCkiRiff, MMIO_FINDCHUNK);
    if (mmResult != MMSYSERR_NOERROR)
        return FALSE;

    LONG numBytes = mmioRead(hMMIO, (char*)&wfe,
        sizeof(WAVEFORMATEX));
    if (numBytes == -1)
        return FALSE;
```

Continued

```
    mmResult = mmioAscend(hMMIO, &mmCkiChunk, 0);
    if (mmResult != MMSYSERR_NOERROR)
        return FALSE;

    mmCkiChunk.ckid = mmioFOURCC('d', 'a', 't', 'a');
    mmResult = mmioDescend(hMMIO, &mmCkiChunk,
        &mmCkiRiff, MMIO_FINDCHUNK);
    if (mmResult != MMSYSERR_NOERROR)
        return FALSE;

    soundSize = mmCkiChunk.cksize;
    pSoundData =
        (BYTE*)GlobalAllocPtr(GMEM_MOVEABLE, soundSize);
    if (pSoundData == NULL)
        return FALSE;

    numBytes = mmioRead(hMMIO, (char*)pSoundData, soundSize);
    if (numBytes == -1)
        return FALSE;

    mmioClose(hMMIO, 0);
    return TRUE;
}

BOOL CreateSoundBuffer()
{
    DSBUFFERDESC dsbd;
    LPVOID pBlock1;
    DWORD bytesBlock1;
    LPVOID pBlock2;
    DWORD bytesBlock2;

    memset(&dsbd, 0, sizeof(DSBUFFERDESC));
    dsbd.dwSize = sizeof(DSBUFFERDESC);
    dsbd.dwBufferBytes = soundSize;
    dsbd.lpwfxFormat =
        (LPWAVEFORMATEX) &wfe;
    dsbd.dwFlags = DSBCAPS_CTRLDEFAULT;

    HRESULT result = pDS->CreateSoundBuffer(&dsbd,
        &pDSBuffer, NULL);
    if (result != DS_OK)
        return FALSE;

    result = pDSBuffer->Lock(0, soundSize,
        &pBlock1, &bytesBlock1, &pBlock2,
        &bytesBlock2, 0);
    if (result != DS_OK)
        return FALSE;

    memcpy((void*)pBlock1, pSoundData, soundSize);
```

Continued

```
                pDSBuffer->Unlock(pBlock1, bytesBlock1,
                    pBlock2, bytesBlock2);

                return TRUE;
}
```

The preceding program, even though it's a traditional C-style Windows program, initializes DirectSound in much the same way as this chapter's first program, DirectSoundApp. In fact, the program looks and acts very similar. When you run the application, click the window to hear the sound effect. All of the DirectSound code in the program should be familiar to you by now. If you don't understand the program, you need to reread this chapter from the beginning.

Summary

As you've probably noticed, programming DirectSound is a little easier than programming DirectDraw. All you have to do is create a main DirectSound object, create a buffer for your sound data, load the data into the buffer, and play it. Still, if you decide to explore this DirectX library further, there's a lot more to learn. Once you master DirectDraw and DirectSound, however, you'll be well on your way to creating professional-quality Windows multimedia programs that run properly on any Windows 2000 system.

Also discussed in this chapter:

- A DirectSound application must create a DirectSound object.
- The application can set up the sound hardware by calling `SetCooperativeLevel()`.
- The primary DirectSound buffer, which DirectSound creates automatically, represents the sound being played.
- Secondary DirectSound buffers hold the sound data that your program will play.
- A DirectSound buffer object's `Play()` function sends sound data to a sound card.
- You shut down DirectSound by calling the DirectSound object's, and each buffer's, `Release()` function.

Chapter 25
DirectInput

In This Chapter

▶ Creating a DirectInput program
▶ Preparing Visual C++ for DirectInput
▶ Creating a DirectInput object
▶ Creating a DirectInput device
▶ Setting the device data format
▶ Setting the device access level
▶ Acquiring a DirectInput device
▶ Examining a sample DirectInput application

All programs need to deal with input devices, which are the links between humans and the computer. Games and other types of multimedia programs are no different. Most games, in fact, enable players to choose between different types of input devices, most notably the mouse, keyboard, and joystick. For computer games, the mouse and the keyboard are the most important input devices because, while many computer systems may not have a joystick, virtually all of them have a mouse or keyboard. As with the other DirectX features, DirectInput lets programmers handle these devices in a more efficient manner than is possible with Windows API functions. In this chapter, you'll learn how you can add basic DirectInput functionality to your programs.

Note

Programming DirectInput is a complex task that cannot be fully explained in a single chapter. This chapter is only an introduction to the programming techniques required to create a basic DirectInput application. After you master the topics in this chapter, if you want to learn more about DirectInput, you should pick up a book that concentrates on DirectX programming.

In order to run DirectInput programs, you must have DirectX installed on your system. Windows 2000 comes with DirectX 7.0 built in. However, if you should need it, you can get a copy of the DirectX SDK from Microsoft by pointing your Web browser to http://www.microsoft.com/directx.

Creating a DirectInput Program

DirectInput may not be as famous as its DirectDraw and DirectSound cousins, because it works behind the scenes rather than on the screen, but it's still an important part of the DirectX libraries. Using DirectInput, applications programmers can gain control over input devices at an almost hardware level. In this chapter, you'll examine the basic steps you must complete to create most DirectInput applications, along with the source code needed to create them.

To create a DirectInput program, you must complete the following main steps. After completing the main steps, other implementation details depend upon the type of DirectInput device you create. The main steps are as follows:

1. Create a DirectInput object. The DirectInput object is the object through which you can access other DirectInput capabilities.

2. Create a DirectInput device. A DirectInput device is an object that represents a physical input device, such as a mouse, keyboard, joystick, or other type of controller.

3. Set the device data format. Setting a device's data format tells DirectInput how the device is to be used and how its data should be arranged.

4. Set the device access level. The device access level, also called the *cooperative level,* determines how the device can be shared with other processes.

5. Acquire the device. Before an application can receive data from a device, the application must acquire the device. Once the device is acquired, the application begins to receive input data.

After completing these basic steps, your program can use DirectInput to receive input from the DirectInput device.

Often, DirectX programs are written without the use of an application framework such as MFC. This is because MFC can bring with it a lot of extra baggage that slows down an application—especially a game—that needs to run at its fastest speed. Compared with adding DirectInput to an MFC program, though, creating a non-MFC DirectInput program is straightforward. Getting DirectInput to run properly in an MFC program is the tricky part. The main part of this chapter, therefore, focuses on writing an MFC DirectInput program, and the "Problems and Solutions" section illustrates how to write such a program without MFC.

Adding DirectInput Files to Your Visual C++ Project

The DirectInputApp sample program that you'll examine later in this chapter was created by AppWizard as an SDI (single document) application with no extras such as a toolbar or status bar. By now, you should be comfortable with creating this type of skeleton application. There are a couple of extra steps, however, that you need to complete before you can compile and run an MFC DirectInput program.

Adding the dinput.h Header File

First, you must include in your program the dinput.h header file, which contains declarations for the various DirectInput functions, structures, and data types. You do that like this:

```
#include <dinput.h>
```

The angle brackets around the file name indicate that the header file is located in one of the default header-file directories, rather than in the project's directory.

Adding the dinput.lib and dxguid.lib Files

Now that you've included the dinput.h header file, you shouldn't have any difficulty compiling your DirectInput program. Unfortunately, you'll quickly discover that the program won't link because it can't find the DirectInput libraries. To correct this problem, you must add the dinput.lib and dxguid.lib files to your project. To do this, follow these steps:

1. Select the Add to Project command from Visual C++'s Project menu.
2. Select the Files command from the submenu that appears (see Figure 25-1).
3. Navigate to your Visual C++ include directory in the Insert Files into Project dialog box.
4. Select the dinput.lib and dxguid.lib files, as shown in Figure 25-2.

Now Visual C++ is set up to compile and link a DirectInput program.

764   Part V: Multimedia Programming

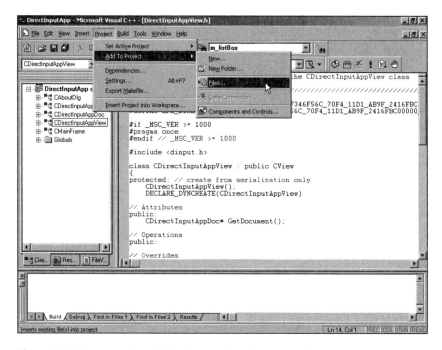

Figure 25-1: You can easily add files to your DirectInput project.

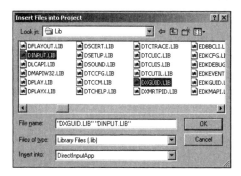

Figure 25-2: DirectInput programs must link to the dinput.lib and dxguid.lib library files.

Creating a DirectInput Object

To use DirectInput in a program, you must create a DirectInput object, through which you'll acquire access to the DirectInput functions. To create a DirectInput object, call `DirectInputCreate()`, as follows:

```
LPDIRECTINPUT pDInput;
HINSTANCE hInstance = AfxGetInstanceHandle();
```

```
HRESULT result = DirectInputCreate(hInstance,
    DIRECTINPUT_VERSION, &pDInput, NULL);
if (FAILED(result))
{
    // Handle DirectInput failure.
}
```

DirectInputCreate( )'s arguments are as follows:

- The application's instance handle
- The predefined DIRECTINPUT_VERSION constant
- The address of a DIRECTINPUT pointer
- NULL

LPDIRECTINPUT represents a pointer to a DirectInput main object. In this case, the pointer is called pDInput. You pass the address of the pointer as DirectInputCreate( )'s second argument. If the function call succeeds, DirectInputCreate( ) places the address of the DirectInput main object into the pDInput pointer. To ensure that this pointer is valid, you must check DirectInputCreate( )'s return value. When you don't need to handle a specific error return value, the FAILED( ) macro is a handy tool for discovering whether the DirectInput function call succeeded. There's also a SUCCEEDED( ) macro.

Creating a DirectInput Device

Once you have your main DirectInput object, you can call the function that creates the DirectInput device object, which represents the physical device the application must control. To create the device, call the DirectInput object's CreateDevice( ) function:

```
LPDIRECTINPUTDEVICE pDIMouse;
HRESULT result = pDInput&CreateDevice(GUID_SysMouse,
    &pDIMouse, NULL);
 if (FAILED(result))
 {
     // Handle device failure.
 }
```

LPDIRECTINPUTDEVICE represents a pointer to a DirectInput device. In this case, the pointer is called pDIMouse. You pass the address of the pointer as CreateDevice( )'s second argument. (The first argument is a predefined ID for the device you want to create.) If the function call succeeds, CreateDevice( ) places the address of the DirectInput device into the pDIMouse pointer. As with many DirectInput functions, to ensure that the returned pointer is valid, you must check CreateDevice( )'s return value.

Setting the Data Format

Before you can receive data from a device, DirectInput has to know how to handle that data. You provide this information by calling the device object's `SetDataFormat()` function:

```
HRESULT result = pDIMouse->SetDataFormat(&c_dfDIMouse);
if (FAILED(result))
{
    // Handle the failure.
}
```

The `SetDataFormat()` function's single argument is a pointer to the structure that describes how the device should return data. DirectInput provides predefined structures for the keyboard, mouse, and joystick. In the preceding case, the function supplies the `c_dfDIMouse` structure to specify default mouse handling.

Setting the Device Access Level

With a pointer to a DirectInput device in hand, your application can set the type of device access the application needs. You do this by calling the device object's `SetCooperativeLevel()` function:

```
CWnd* pMainWnd = AfxGetMainWnd();
HWND hMainWnd = pMainWnd->m_hWnd;
HRESULT result = pDIMouse->SetCooperativeLevel(hMainWnd,
    DISCL_NONEXCLUSIVE | DISCL_FOREGROUND);
if (FAILED(result))
{
    // Handle failure.
}
```

`SetCooperativeLevel()` takes two arguments: the handle of the application's main window and the device access flags. Usually, you'll use `DISCL_NONEXCLUSIVE | DISCL_FOREGROUND` for the flags, giving your application non-exclusive access to the device when the application is the foreground process, but still allowing multitasking to function properly.

Acquiring the Device

The last thing your application must do in order to receive data from the device is acquire the device. Acquiring the device associates the device with your application in much the same way capturing the mouse acquires the mouse device in a regular Windows application. When you've acquired a device, all its input goes to your application until another process gets switched to the foreground and acquires the device on its behalf. To acquire a device, you call the device object's `Acquire()` function:

```
HRESULT result = pDIMouse->Acquire();
if (FAILED(result))
{
    // Handle failure.
}
```

As with most DirectInput functions, `Acquire()` returns a result value that you can check with the `FAILED()` or `SUCCEEDED()` macro. In this example's case, if the `FAILED` macro results in a value of `TRUE`, the body of the `if` statement will execute.

Exploring the DirectInputApp Application

Location: `WinPrgS\Chap25\DirectInputApp`

On this book's CD-ROM, you'll find the DirectInputApp sample application, which is an MFC program that incorporates DirectInput in order to control the mouse. When you run the program, you see the window shown in Figure 25-3. Move the mouse pointer around the screen and watch how the mouse values change in the window. Also, click the mouse buttons. When you do, the data for the button changes from 0 to 1 on the screen.

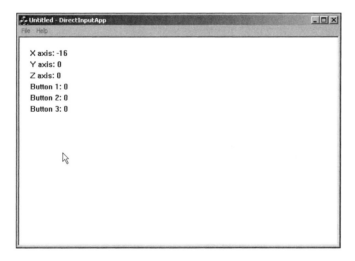

Figure 25-3: The DirectInputApp application tracks relative mouse movement.

When used with DirectInput, a mouse isn't so much a pointing device as it is a replacement for a joystick. That is, the mouse device reports relative mouse movement data, rather than the X and Y coordinates you're used to receiving from a mouse. The relative mouse data indicates the direction the mouse moved and how far the mouse moved since the last time the mouse data was read. Whenever the mouse is at rest, the X, Y, and Z axis data remain at zero. The faster the mouse moves from this virtual origin, the higher the reported mouse values become. (Which values change the most depends on the direction you move the mouse.)

In the following sections, you'll examine DirectInputApp more closely, learning how it implements DirectInput using the techniques described previously in this chapter.

DirectInputApp's View-Class Constructor

Now that you've seen the program in action, take a look at the source code to see how the application initializes and manipulates DirectInput, as shown here:

```
CDirectInputAppView::CDirectInputAppView()
{
    // TODO: add construction code here

    m_DIOK = FALSE;
    m_button3 = 0;
    m_button2 = 0;
    m_button1 = 0;
    m_mouseZ = 0;
    m_mouseY = 0;
    m_mouseX = 0;
    m_pDIMouse = NULL;
    m_pDInput = NULL;
}
```

Here, the view class's constructor initializes the class's member variables to their default values. The member variables are declared in the view class's header file like this:

```
BOOL m_DIOK;
int m_button3;
int m_button2;
int m_button1;
int m_mouseZ;
int m_mouseY;
int m_mouseX;
LPDIRECTINPUTDEVICE m_pDIMouse;
LPDIRECTINPUT m_pDInput;
```

The program uses the following variables:

m_DIOK	Flag indicating whether DirectInput initialized successfully
m_button3	Status of mouse button 3
m_button2	Status of mouse button 2
m_button1	Status of mouse button 1
m_mouseZ	Relative mouse movement on the Z axis
m_mouseY	Relative mouse movement on the Y axis
m_mouseX	Relative mouse movement on the X axis
m_pDIMouse	Pointer to the DirectInput mouse device
m_pDInput	Pointer to the application's DirectInput object

DirectInputApp's OnInitialUpdate() Function

In an MFC program, a good place to initialize DirectInput is in the view class's `OnInitialUpdate()` function, which you add to the class with ClassWizard, as shown in Figure 25-4. MFC calls `OnInitialUpdate()` once when the view class is first updated. At that point, the application's main window, represented by the `CMainFrame` class, has its window handle, which you need in order to call `SetCooperativeLevel()`. Here is DirectInputApp's `OnInitialUpdate()` function:

```
void CDirectInputAppView::OnInitialUpdate()
{
    CView::OnInitialUpdate();

    // TODO: Add your specialized code here
    //    and/or call the base class

    HINSTANCE hInstance = AfxGetInstanceHandle();
    HRESULT result = DirectInputCreate(hInstance,
        DIRECTINPUT_VERSION, &m_pDInput, NULL);
    if (FAILED(result))
        return;

    result = m_pDInput->CreateDevice(GUID_SysMouse,
        &m_pDIMouse, NULL);
    if (FAILED(result))
        return;

    result = m_pDIMouse->SetDataFormat(&c_dfDIMouse);
    if (FAILED(result))
        return;

    CWnd* pMainWnd = AfxGetMainWnd();
    HWND hMainWnd = pMainWnd->m_hWnd;
```

```
        result = m_pDIMouse->SetCooperativeLevel(hMainWnd,
            DISCL_NONEXCLUSIVE | DISCL_FOREGROUND);
        if (FAILED(result))
            return;

        m_DIOK = TRUE;
        SetTimer(1, 100, NULL);
}
```

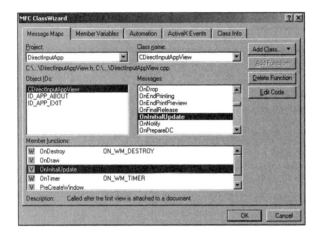

Figure 25-4: ClassWizard overriding the view class's OnInitialUpdate() function

As you can see, the function initializes DirectInput using the techniques you learned earlier in this chapter. If any of these functions fail, OnInitialUpdate() immediately returns, discontinuing any further DirectInput initialization. This action leaves m_DIOK (a member variable of the view class) set to FALSE, which indicates to other functions that they should not call DirectInput functions.

Notice that, near the end of the OnInitialUpdate() function, the program starts a Windows timer. DirectInputApp uses this timer to simulate a game loop, in which a game program continually polls its input devices. In this case, the program's OnTimer() function, where DirectInputApp reads mouse data, gets called ten times a second.

DirectInputApp's OnTimer() Function

DirectInputApp's OnTimer() function responds to the WM_TIMER messages that Windows sends to the application when the OnInitialUpdate() function starts the Windows timer, as shown here:

```
void CDirectInputAppView::OnTimer(UINT nIDEvent)
{
    // TODO: Add your message handler code here
    //    and/or call default
```

```
        if (m_DIOK)
        {
            DIMOUSESTATE dims;

            HRESULT result = m_pDIMouse->Acquire();
            if (FAILED(result))
                return;

            result = m_pDIMouse->
                GetDeviceState(sizeof(DIMOUSESTATE), &dims);
            if (FAILED(result))
                return;

            m_mouseX = dims.lX;
            m_mouseY = dims.lY;
            m_mouseZ = dims.lZ;
            m_button1 = (dims.rgbButtons[0] & 0x80) > 0;
            m_button2 = (dims.rgbButtons[1] & 0x80) > 0;
            m_button3 = (dims.rgbButtons[2] & 0x80) > 0;

            Invalidate();
        }

        CView::OnTimer(nIDEvent);
    }
```

In the preceding function, the program acquires the mouse and then calls the mouse device's `GetDeviceState()` function, which returns the state of the mouse in the members of a `DIMOUSESTATE` structure. After the call to `GetDeviceState()`, the `DIMOUSESTATE` structure (called `dims`) will contain X, Y, and Z axis movement data in its `lX`, `lY`, and `lZ` members, respectively. The structure will also contain mouse button data in its `rgbButtons[]` byte array, with each element of the array representing a specific button (0 represents button 1, 1 represents button 2, and so on). The button data is tucked into the byte's high-order bit, so to extract the information, you must AND the value with 0x80, which masks out the other bits. `OnTimer()` not only uses the bit mask to extract the button information, but it also uses the result in a Boolean expression that sets the appropriate mouse-button variable to either 0 or 1.

You add `OnTimer()` to your AppWizard-generated program using ClassWizard.

DirectInputApp's OnDraw() Function

After `OnTimer()` reads the mouse data, it calls `Invalidate()` to redraw the window with the new information. In an MFC program, this action causes the frameworks to call the view class's `OnDraw()` function, where the application renders its display:

```
void CDirectInputAppView::OnDraw(CDC* pDC)
{
```

```
    CDirectInputAppDoc* pDoc = GetDocument();
    ASSERT_VALID(pDoc);

    // TODO: add draw code for native data here

    char s[81];
    wsprintf(s, "X axis: %d", m_mouseX);
    pDC->TextOut(20, 20, s);
    wsprintf(s, "Y axis: %d", m_mouseY);
    pDC->TextOut(20, 40, s);
    wsprintf(s, "Z axis: %d", m_mouseZ);
    pDC->TextOut(20, 60, s);

    wsprintf(s, "Button 1: %d", m_button1);
    pDC->TextOut(20, 80, s);
    wsprintf(s, "Button 2: %d", m_button2);
    pDC->TextOut(20, 100, s);
    wsprintf(s, "Button 3: %d", m_button3);
    pDC->TextOut(20, 120, s);
}
```

DirectInputApp's `OnDraw()` function displays the most recent mouse data by converting the data to strings and displaying the strings with the `TextOut()` function.

DirectInputApp's OnDestroy() Function

Finally, when the user closes the application, DirectInputApp must release the DirectInput objects it created. Again, as with DirectDraw and DirectSound, you don't call the `delete` operator on a DirectInput pointer. Instead, you call the `Release()` function. DirectInputApp takes care of these final details in the `OnDestroy()` function, which MFC calls just before the view window is destroyed, as shown here:

```
void CDirectInputAppView::OnDestroy()
{
    CView::OnDestroy();

    // TODO: Add your message handler code here

    KillTimer(1);

    if (m_pDIMouse != NULL)
    {
        m_pDIMouse->Unacquire();
        m_pDIMouse->Release();
    }

    if (m_pDInput != NULL)
        m_pDInput->Release();
}
```

In DirectInputApp, `OnDestroy()` destroys the Windows timer, releases the mouse device, and then releases the main DirectInput object. You can add `OnDestroy()` to your AppWizard-generated programs using ClassWizard.

Note

DirectInput creates its objects following the specifications for COM objects. This is why you must call DirectInput objects' `Release()` functions, rather than destroy them via the `delete` operator. Because COM objects can be used by more than one process, the objects keep internal counters. These counters are incremented when a program creates the object, and decremented when the program calls the object's `Release()` function. When the object's count is decremented to zero, the system removes the object from memory.

PROBLEMS & SOLUTIONS

Writing a Conventional DirectInput Windows Application

PROBLEM: *Now I know how to write an MFC DirectInput program. What if I'd prefer to write my program without MFC?*

SOLUTION: Just as with DirectDraw or DirectSound, the easiest way to accomplish this task is to write a traditional Windows program, but write it as a C++ program rather than a C program. Then you can avoid the clumsy syntax required to call DirectInput functions from a C program.

Cross-Reference

If you've forgotten how to write a traditional Windows application, you might want to take the time now to review Chapter 1.

To create a DirectInput application as a conventional Windows program, first write the basic application as you normally would, providing a `WinMain()` function that defines and registers your window class, as well as contains the application's message loop. You'll also need to provide a Windows procedure that responds to the many messages for which Windows will target your application. In your basic Windows procedure, you'll want to respond at least to the `WM_DESTROY` message.

CD

Location: `WinPrgS\Chap25\DirectInputApp2`

Once you have the basic application built, you can add the DirectInput program code. In your Windows procedure, respond to the `WM_CREATE` message by initializing your program and setting up DirectInput. As you can see in the following program, the process is actually less complicated than trying to wedge DirectInput into an MFC program. You can find the program on this book's CD-ROM.

```
#include <windows.h>
#include <windowsx.h>
```

Continued

```c
#include <dinput.h>

/* Function prototypes */
LRESULT CALLBACK WndProc(HWND hWnd, UINT message,
    WPARAM wParam, LPARAM lParam);
void InitVariables();
BOOL InitDirectInput(HWND hWnd);

/* Global variables */
LPDIRECTINPUT pDInput;
LPDIRECTINPUTDEVICE pDIMouse;
int button3;
int button2;
int button1;
int mouseZ;
int mouseY;
int mouseX;
HINSTANCE hInstance;

int WINAPI WinMain(HINSTANCE hCurrentInst,
    HINSTANCE hPrevInstance, PSTR lpszCmdLine,
    int nCmdShow)
{
    WNDCLASS wndClass;
    HWND hWnd;
    MSG msg;
    UINT width;
    UINT height;

    hInstance = hCurrentInst;

    wndClass.style = CS_HREDRAW | CS_VREDRAW;
    wndClass.lpfnWndProc = WndProc;
    wndClass.cbClsExtra = 0;
    wndClass.cbWndExtra = 0;
    wndClass.hInstance = hCurrentInst;
    wndClass.hIcon = LoadIcon(NULL, IDI_APPLICATION);
    wndClass.hCursor = LoadCursor(NULL, IDC_ARROW);
    wndClass.hbrBackground = GetStockObject(WHITE_BRUSH);
    wndClass.lpszMenuName = NULL;
    wndClass.lpszClassName = "DInputApp";

    RegisterClass(&wndClass);

    width = GetSystemMetrics(SM_CXSCREEN) / 2;
    height = GetSystemMetrics(SM_CYSCREEN) / 2;

    hWnd = CreateWindow(
        "DInputApp",           /* Window class's name. */
        "DirectInput App",     /* Title bar text.      */
        WS_OVERLAPPEDWINDOW,   /* The window's style.  */
```

Continued

```
        10,                 /* X position.             */
        10,                 /* Y position.             */
        width,              /* Width.                  */
        height,             /* Height.                 */
        NULL,               /* Parent window's handle. */
        NULL,               /* Menu handle.            */
        hCurrentInst,       /* Instance handle.        */
        NULL);              /* No additional data.     */

    ShowWindow(hWnd, nCmdShow);
    UpdateWindow(hWnd);
    while (GetMessage(&msg, NULL, 0, 0))
    {
        TranslateMessage(&msg);
        DispatchMessage(&msg);
    }

    return msg.wParam;
}

LRESULT CALLBACK WndProc(HWND hWnd, UINT message,
    WPARAM wParam, LPARAM lParam)
{
    HDC hDC;
    PAINTSTRUCT paintStruct;
    HRESULT result;

    switch(message)
    {
        case WM_CREATE:
            InitVariables();
            InitDirectInput(hWnd);
            return 0;

        case WM_PAINT:
            hDC = BeginPaint(hWnd, &paintStruct);
            char s[81];
            wsprintf(s, "X axis: %d", mouseX);
            TextOut(hDC, 20, 20, s, strlen(s));
            wsprintf(s, "Y axis: %d", mouseY);
            TextOut(hDC, 20, 40, s, strlen(s));
            wsprintf(s, "Z axis: %d", mouseZ);
            TextOut(hDC, 20, 60, s, strlen(s));

            wsprintf(s, "Button 1: %d", button1);
            TextOut(hDC, 20, 80, s, strlen(s));
            wsprintf(s, "Button 2: %d", button2);
            TextOut(hDC, 20, 100, s, strlen(s));
            wsprintf(s, "Button 3: %d", button3);
            TextOut(hDC, 20, 120, s, strlen(s));
```

Continued

```
                    EndPaint(hWnd, &paintStruct);
                    return 0;

            case WM_TIMER:
                DIMOUSESTATE dims;

                result = pDIMouse->Acquire();
                if (FAILED(result))
                    return 0;

                result = pDIMouse->
                    GetDeviceState(sizeof(DIMOUSESTATE), &dims);
                if (FAILED(result))
                    return 0;
                mouseX = dims.lX;
                mouseY = dims.lY;
                mouseZ = dims.lZ;
                button1 = (dims.rgbButtons[0] & 0x80) > 0;
                button2 = (dims.rgbButtons[1] & 0x80) > 0;
                button3 = (dims.rgbButtons[2] & 0x80) > 0;

                InvalidateRect(hWnd, NULL, TRUE);
                return 0;

            case WM_DESTROY:
                KillTimer(hWnd, 1);
                if (pDIMouse != NULL)
                {
                    pDIMouse->Unacquire();
                    pDIMouse->Release();
                }

                if (pDInput != NULL)
                    pDInput->Release();

                PostQuitMessage(0);
                return 0;
        }

        return DefWindowProc(hWnd, message, wParam, lParam);
    }

    void InitVariables()
    {
        button3 = 0;
        button2 = 0;
        button1 = 0;
        mouseZ = 0;
        mouseY = 0;
        mouseX = 0;
        pDIMouse = NULL;
```

Continued

```
        pDInput = NULL;
}

BOOL InitDirectInput(HWND hWnd)
{
    HRESULT result = DirectInputCreate(hInstance,
        DIRECTINPUT_VERSION, &pDInput, NULL);
    if (FAILED(result))
        return FALSE;

    result = pDInput->CreateDevice(GUID_SysMouse,
        &pDIMouse, NULL);
    if (FAILED(result))
        return FALSE;
    result = pDIMouse->SetDataFormat(&c_dfDIMouse);
    if (FAILED(result))
        return FALSE;

    result = pDIMouse->SetCooperativeLevel(hWnd,
        DISCL_NONEXCLUSIVE | DISCL_FOREGROUND);
    if (FAILED(result))
        return FALSE;

    SetTimer(hWnd, 1, 100, NULL);

    return TRUE;
}
```

The preceding program, in spite of being a traditional C-style Windows program, initializes DirectInput in much the same way as this chapter's previous program, DirectInputApp. In fact, the program looks and acts very similar. When you run the application, move the mouse around and click the mouse's buttons. The application's display continually reports on the mouse actions. All of the DirectInput code in the program should be familiar to you by now. If you don't understand the program, you should reread this chapter from the beginning.

Summary

Besides the mouse, DirectInput also provides support for a keyboard and a joystick. In fact, the word "joystick" actually refers to many types of controllers, including not only an actual joystick, but also trackballs, controller pads, and any other input device that doesn't fit into the mouse or keyboard category.
As you can see, DirectInput gives your application the tools it needs to support a wide variety of input devices, one or more of which should be perfect for your program.

Also discussed in this chapter:

- A DirectInput application must create a DirectInput main object.
- A DirectInput application must also create a device object.
- The application can set up input-device sharing by calling the device object's `SetCooperativeLevel()` function.
- Setting a device's data format tells DirectInput how to present device data to the application.
- Before an application can receive data from a DirectInput device, it must acquire the device.
- After acquiring a device, the application can obtain data from the device by calling the device object's `GetDeviceState()` function.

Chapter 26
Direct3D

In This Chapter

- Creating a Direct3D program
- Creating a Direct3D main object
- Creating a clipper object
- Creating a Direct3D device
- Creating Direct3D frames and meshes
- Creating a viewport
- Adding lights to a Direct3D scene
- Preparing Visual C++ for Direct3D
- Examining a sample Direct3D application

Now that you've taken a look at most of the DirectX libraries, you should be ready for the real high-tech stuff! Direct3D is without a doubt the most complex of the DirectX libraries (at least from a programmer's point of view). It features a large number of interfaces that you need to learn to program, and it requires quite a bit of knowledge of 3-D programming basics. Using Direct3D, applications programmers can create fabulous 3-D games like Doom or Tomb Raider without having to worry about loading specific drivers for the user's hardware. In this chapter, you'll get a look at how you can add basic Direct3D functionality to your programs.

Note

Programming Direct3D is a complex task that cannot be fully explained in a single chapter. This chapter is only an introduction to the programming techniques required to create a basic Direct3D application. After you master the topics in this chapter, if you want to learn more about Direct3D, you should pick up a book that concentrates on Direct3D programming.

In order to run Direct3D programs, you must have DirectX installed on your system. Windows 2000 has DirectX 7.0 built in. However, if you should need it, you can get a copy of the DirectX SDK from Microsoft by pointing your Web browser to http://www.microsoft.com/directx.

Creating a Direct3D Program

Creating a Direct3D program isn't a process that's easily defined in a list of numbered steps. This is because there are many ways to put together a Direct3D program and many choices you must make along the way. Still, there are certain steps that most Direct3D programs will require. In this section, you'll examine these basic steps and learn how to implement them with source code.

To create a Direct3D program, you usually complete at least the steps outlined in this section. After completing the main steps, other implementation details depend upon the type of Direct3D program you're writing. The main steps are as follows:

1. Create a Direct3D main object. The Direct3D main object is the object through which you can access other Direct3D capabilities.

2. Create a DirectDraw clipper object. Direct3D draws upon DirectDraw for some of its power, the clipper object being a good example. The clipper object enables a Direct3D application's window to update properly without overwriting other windows on the screen.

3. Create a Direct3D device. Once you have a clipper object, you can use it to create a Direct3D device that's appropriate for the application's window. It's the device that draws your 3-D scenes, as well as interfaces with whatever 3-D hardware may be installed on the user's system.

4. Create a root frame (discussed later in this chapter). Direct3D objects are positioned and oriented using frames. Every Direct3D application has a root frame that acts as the parent (or container, if you like) for other frames.

5. Create meshes for objects that will be displayed in the scene. A *mesh* is a group of polygons that are connected in order to create some sort of 3-D shape.

6. Create frames for the meshes. Each object in a 3-D scene must be associated with a frame, which determines the object's position and orientation in a scene.

7. Create a viewport for the scene. Much like a viewfinder in a camera, a viewport determines what part of a 3-D scene appears on the screen.

8. Add lights to the scene. Like lamps in a dark room, Direct3D lights determine not only how bright a scene can be, but also the color of the scene and the way light reflects from objects in the scene.

After completing these basic steps, your program can use Direct3D to render a 3-D scene on the screen. In the following sections, you'll take a closer look at each of these steps, examining the source code required to implement them.

Creating a Direct3D Main Object

To use Direct3D in a program, you must create a Direct3D main object, through which you'll acquire access to the Direct3D interfaces. To create a Direct3D object (in retained mode), call Direct3DRMCreate(), as follows:

```
LPDIRECT3DRM pD3D;
HRESULT result = Direct3DRMCreate(&pD3D);
if (result != D3DRM_OK)
{
    // Handle Direct3D failure.
}
```

LPDIRECT3DRM represents a pointer to a Direct3D retained-mode main object. In this case, the pointer is called pD3D. You pass the address of the pointer as Direct3DRMCreate()'s single argument. If the function call succeeds, Direct3DRMCreate() places the address of the Direct3D main object into the pD3D pointer. To ensure that this pointer is valid, you must check Direct3DRMCreate()'s return value, which will be D3DRM_OK if the function succeeds.

Direct3D programs can be written in *retained* or *immediate* mode. Retained mode Direct3D programs are easier to write and so are more common. The retained mode is a high-level programming interface that's built on top of the immediate mode. The immediate mode provides programmers with a detailed, low-level programming interface.

Creating a Clipper Object

Although 3-D worlds can represent large virtual areas, that image of the world is constrained by the screen, or even the window, through which you must view it. A DirectDraw clipper object that's associated with a window manages the way that the scene can appear on the screen. In a multi-windowed environment, for example, the clipper object ensures that a Direct3D window's display doesn't overwrite other areas of the screen, particularly other applications' windows that may overlap the Direct3D application's window. You create a clipper object by calling DirectDrawCreateClipper():

```
LPDIRECTDRAWCLIPPER pClipper;
HRESULT result =
    DirectDrawCreateClipper(0, &pClipper, 0);
if (result != DD_OK)
{
    // Handle clipper failure.
}
```

Part V: Multimedia Programming

LPDIRECTDRAWCLIPPER represents a pointer to a DIRECTDRAWCLIPPER object. In this case, the pointer is called pClipper. You pass the address of the pointer as DirectDrawCreateClipper()'s second argument. (The first and third arguments can be zero.) If the function call succeeds, DirectDrawCreateClipper() places the address of the clipper object into the pClipper pointer. To ensure that this pointer is valid, you must check DirectDrawCreateClipper()'s return value, which will be DD_OK if the function succeeds.

Once you've created the clipper object, you must associate it with the window it'll manage. You do this by calling the clipper object's SetHWnd() function:

```
result = pClipper->SetHWnd(0, hWnd);
if (result != DD_OK)
{
    // Handle clipper failure.
}
```

SetHWnd() takes zero as its first argument and the window's handle as the second argument. The function returns DD_OK if it succeeds.

Creating a Direct3D Device

While the clipper object may manage how Direct3D draws its scenes, it's the device that does the actual drawing. Therefore, it should come as no surprise that your program must create a Direct3D device. One way an application can perform this task is by calling the main Direct3D object's CreateDeviceFromClipper() function:

```
RECT rect;
::GetClientRect(hWnd, &rect);
LPDIRECT3DRMDEVICE pDevice;
HRESULT result = pD3D->
    CreateDeviceFromClipper(pClipper, NULL,
    rect.right, rect.bottom, &pDevice);
if (result != D3DRM_OK)
{
    // Handle device failure.
}
```

Before calling CreateDeviceFromClipper(), the preceding example calls GetClientRect() to obtain the size of the window's client area, which the program needs to create the device. LPDIRECT3DRMDEVICE represents a pointer to a DIRECT3DRMDEVICE object. In this case, the pointer is called pDevice. You pass the address of the pointer as CreateDeviceFrom

Clipper()'s fifth argument. The CreateDeviceFromClipper() arguments are as follows:

- A pointer to the clipper object
- A GUID for the device (NULL for the ramp color model)
- The width of the window for which the device will be created
- The height of the window for which the device will be created
- The address of the LPDIRECT3DRMDEVICE pointer

If the function call succeeds, CreateDeviceFromClipper() places the address of the device object into the pDevice pointer. To ensure that this pointer is valid, you must check CreateDeviceFromClipper()'s return value, which will be D3DRM_OK if the function succeeds.

After creating the device, you can stick with the default flat shading model, or you can go with the more realistic-looking Gouraud shading. The flat shading model applies lighting effects such that you can see each of the polygons that a shape comprises (see Figure 26-1).

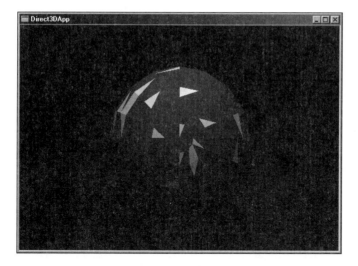

Figure 26-1: With flat shading, you can see the polygons that make up an object.

Gouraud shading, on the other hand, calculates shades using color averages, thus creating more realistic surfaces (see Figure 26-2). To set the shading model, call the device object's SetQuality() function:

```
pDevice->SetQuality(D3DRMRENDER_GOURAUD);
```

Figure 26-2: With Gouraud shading, surfaces look smoother and more realistic.

Creating the Root Frame

As you've already learned, Direct3D scenes comprise many objects, each of which is positioned inside a frame object. It is the frame object that determines an object's orientation and position in the scene. All the object frames in a scene are children of the root frame. Obviously, before you can create child frames, you must create the root frame, which you do by calling the main Direct3D object's CreateFrame() function:

```
LPDIRECT3DRMFRAME pParentFrame;
HRESULT result = pD3D->CreateFrame(0, &pParentFrame);
if (result != D3DRM_OK)
{
    // Handle frame failure.
}
```

LPDIRECT3DRMFRAME represents a pointer to a DIRECT3DRMFRAME object. In this case, the pointer is called pParentFrame. You pass the address of the pointer as CreateFrame()'s second argument. The first argument is the address of the parent frame, or zero if you're creating a parent frame. If the function call succeeds, CreateFrame() places the address of the frame object into the pParentFrame pointer. To ensure that this pointer is valid, you must check CreateFrame()'s return value, which will be D3DRM_OK if the function succeeds.

Creating Meshes for Objects

At this point, you have Direct3D initialized and raring to go. All you have to do now (as if this were an easy task) is create a 3-D scene to display. An object in a Direct3D scene is represented by a *mesh,* which is a collection of polygons linked together such that they create a 3-D object. Direct3D offers several ways to create meshes, but the easiest is to use a mesh builder object, which is represented by the Direct3DRMMeshBuilder interface. You create a mesh builder object by calling the main Direct3D object's CreateMeshBuilder() function:

```
LPDIRECT3DRMMESHBUILDER pMeshBuilder;
HRESULT result = pD3D->CreateMeshBuilder(&pMeshBuilder);
if (result != D3DRM_OK)
{
    // Handle mesh builder failure.
}
```

LPDIRECT3DRMMESHBUILDER represents a pointer to a DIRECT3DRMMESH BUILDER object. In this case, the pointer is called pMeshBuilder. You pass the address of the pointer as CreateMeshBuilder()'s single argument. If the function call succeeds, CreateMeshBuilder() places the address of the mesh builder object into the pMeshBuilder pointer. To ensure that this pointer is valid, you must check CreateMeshBuilder()'s return value, which will be D3DRM_OK if the function succeeds.

With the mesh builder created, you can create the actual mesh, by calling the mesh builder object's Load() function:

```
HRESULT result = pMeshBuilder->Load(fileName,
    NULL, D3DRMLOAD_FROMFILE, NULL, NULL );
if (result != D3DRM_OK)
{
    // Handle mesh load failure.
}
```

In this case, thanks to the D3DRMLOAD_FROMFILE flag, Load() is looking for a file whose name is fileName. This file should use Direct3D's X file format (no, Scully and Mulder had nothing to do with it), a type of file that you can create from 3D Studio objects using Direct3D's CONV3DS utility. If the file loads successfully, Load() returns D3DRM_OK.

Creating Frames for Meshes

You may remember that all objects in a Direct3D scene must be associated with frames, which determine the object's orientation and position. A mesh is no different. Once you've created a mesh, you can't add it to your 3-D world until you've associated it with a frame. Another call to `CreateFrame()` takes care of this task:

```
LPDIRECT3DRMFRAME pFrame;
HRESULT result =
    pD3D->CreateFrame(pParentFrame, &pFrame);
if (result != D3DRM_OK)
{
    // Handle frame failure.
}
```

Notice that, in this case, `CreateFrame()` gets the parent frame pointer as its first argument. This is because the new frame will be a child of the parent frame.

Once the child frame exists, a call to the frame's `AddVisual()` function associates the mesh (represented by the mesh builder object) with the frame:

```
pFrame->AddVisual(pMeshBuilder);
```

The Viewport

Now you've created a 3-D scene that contains an object. Unfortunately, there's no way yet to see the object because you haven't told Direct3D the position from which you want to view the scene. You take care of this little detail by creating a *viewport,* which not only determines your viewing position and angle, but also the clipping planes that determine what portion of the 3-D world is available for viewing. Imagine that you're standing in a room facing a window. As you move toward or away from the window, your view of the outside world changes. In this way, a viewport is similar to a window.

Creating the Viewport Frame

To create a viewport, you first create the frame that'll position and orient the viewport:

```
LPDIRECT3DRMFRAME pEye;
HRESULT result = pD3D->CreateFrame(pParentFrame, &pEye);
if (result != D3DRM_OK)
{
    // Handle frame failure.
}
```

Again, notice that this new frame, whose pointer is called pEye, is created as a child frame of pParentFrame.

After creating the frame object, you call the `SetPosition()` function to position the frame inside the parent frame:

```
pEye->SetPosition(pParentFrame, D3DVALUE(0),
    D3DVALUE(0),D3DVALUE(-40.0));
```

Chapter 26: Direct3D

As you can see, `SetPosition()` takes four arguments:

- A pointer to the parent frame
- The new position on the X axis
- The new position on the Y axis
- The new position on the Z axis

Think of the frame as an eye (which is, of course, where the name `pEye` comes from). Before being positioned, everything added to the 3-D scene ends up centered on the 3-D world's origin, which is position 0,0,0. Therefore, when you first place the eye in the 3-D scene, it'll actually be inside the 3-D object (represented by the mesh builder object) that you just placed in the same position. In order to see the object, then, you have to pull the eye back. That's why, in the call to `SetPosition()`, the Z position is set to -40. Negative numbers pull the eye back from the scene, whereas positive numbers push the eye forward. For example, while the Z value of -40 will enable you to see the object, a positive value in this case will put the eye behind the object, where the object will still be invisible.

The `D3DVALUE` data type is a floating-point value used in Direct3D. You should cast most numerical values you pass to Direct3D functions to the `D3DVALUE` type. (Consult the Direct3D documentation for a function's signature to determine the data types of the arguments.) Also, many Direct3D functions return values of the `D3DVALUE` data type.

Creating the Viewport

Once you have the viewport's frame, you can create the viewport, which you do by calling the main Direct3D object's `CreateViewport()` function:

```
LPDIRECT3DRMVIEWPORT pViewport;
result = pD3D->CreateViewport(pDevice, pEye, 0, 0,
    pDevice->GetWidth(), pDevice->GetHeight(),
    &pViewport);
if (result != D3DRM_OK)
{
    // Handle viewport failure.
}
```

`LPDIRECT3DRMVIEWPORT` represents a pointer to a `DIRECT3DRMVIEWPORT` object. In this case, the pointer is called `pViewport`. You pass the address of the pointer as one of `CreateViewport()`'s seven arguments:

- A pointer to the device object
- A pointer to the frame
- The X position of the viewport
- The Y position of the viewport

- The viewport's width
- The viewport's height
- The address of the viewport pointer

If the function call succeeds, `CreateViewport()` places the address of the viewport object into the `pViewport` pointer. To ensure that this pointer is valid, you must check `CreateViewport()`'s return value, which will be `D3DRM_OK` if the function succeeds.

Adding Lights

You may have placed an eye in the 3-D scene, but it's still darn dark in there. The last thing you must do to prepare your 3-D scene is add lighting. Direct3D supports many types of lighting, including positional, directional, ambient, and spotlights. In this example, you'll see how to use positional lighting. As lighting is a complex topic beyond the scope of this chapter, only positional lighting will be discussed, giving you a taste of what Direct3D is all about. If you want to learn about the other types of lighting, you can look them up in the Direct3D documentation or in a Direct3D programming book.

Creating the Light Object

The first step is to create your light object, by calling the main Direct3D object's `CreateLightRGB()` function:

```
LPDIRECT3DRMLIGHT pLight;
HRESULT result = pD3D->
    CreateLightRGB(D3DRMLIGHT_DIRECTIONAL,
    D3DVALUE(1.0), D3DVALUE(1.0),
    D3DVALUE(1.0), &pLight);
if (result != D3DRM_OK)
{
    // Handle light failure.
}
```

`LPDIRECT3DRMLIGHT` represents a pointer to a `DIRECT3DRMLIGHT` object. In this case, the pointer is called `pLight`. You pass the address of the pointer as one of `CreateLightRGB()`'s five arguments:

- A flag indicating the type of light to create
- The light's red intensity
- The light's green intensity
- The light's blue intensity
- The address of the light's pointer

If the function call succeeds, `CreateLightRGB()` places the address of the light object into the `pLight` pointer. To ensure that this pointer is valid, you must check `CreateLightRGB()`'s return value, which will be `D3DRM_OK` if the function succeeds. If the function fails, you'll have no lighting for your 3-D scene.

Creating the Light's Child Frame

After creating the light, you need to create its child frame, which controls the light's position and orientation in the parent frame:

```
LPDIRECT3DRMFRAME pLightFrame;
result = pD3D->CreateFrame(pParentFrame, &pLightFrame );
if (result != D3DRM_OK)
{
    return FALSE;
}
```

To add the light to the frame, you call the frame's `AddLight()` function, whose single argument is the light object's pointer:

```
pLightFrame->AddLight(pLight);
```

Finally, you position the light by calling the frame's `SetOrientation()` function:

```
pLightFrame->SetOrientation(pParentFrame,
    D3DVALUE(0.0), D3DVALUE(-1.0), D3DVALUE(1.0),
    D3DVALUE(0.0), D3DVALUE(1.0), D3DVALUE(0.0));
```

Following are `SetOrientation()`'s arguments:

- A pointer to the parent frame
- The X coordinate of the forward vector
- The Y coordinate of the forward vector
- The Z coordinate of the forward vector
- The X coordinate of the up vector
- The Y coordinate of the up vector
- The Z coordinate of the up vector

A *vector* is a line that indicates which way an object is pointing. In the `SetOrientation()` function, the forward vector is the direction that the light should face, and the up vector is the light's height.

The Direct3DApp Sample Application

The Direct3DApp sample program that you'll examine in this chapter is an MFC program, but it wasn't created by AppWizard. Instead, the program was written "from scratch." Still, Direct3DApp is an MFC program and takes advantage of the CWinApp and CFrameWnd classes.

Building a New Direct3D Application

Location: WinPrgS\Chap26\Direct3DApp

To run or compile Direct3DApp, you can simply access the project's files on this book's CD-ROM. However, doing so won't help you set up other programs for Direct3D. Therefore, in this section, you'll learn how to build a new project for Direct3DApp, a task that includes getting the project ready for Direct3D.

Assuming that all you have to start with are the application's source code files (Direct3DApp.h, Direct3DApp.cpp, Direct3DWin.h, and Direct3DWin.cpp), you must perform the following steps to get the program compiled and running:

1. Select the New command from Visual C++'s File menu.

2. In the New property sheet, select Win32 Application on the Projects page, type **Direct3DApp** in the Project Name box, and select the project's destination directory in the Location box, as shown in Figure 26-3. Click the OK button to create the project.

   Visual C++ creates an empty project for which you must supply the source code and library files.

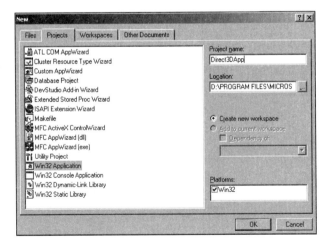

Figure 26-3: Direct3DApp starts off life as a Win32 Application project.

3. Copy the Direct3DApp.h, Direct3DApp.cpp, Direct3DWin.h, and Direct3DWin.cpp files from this book's CD-ROM to your new Direct3DApp project directory.

4. Select the Add to Project command from Visual C++'s Project menu, and then select Files from the submenu that appears (see Figure 26-4).

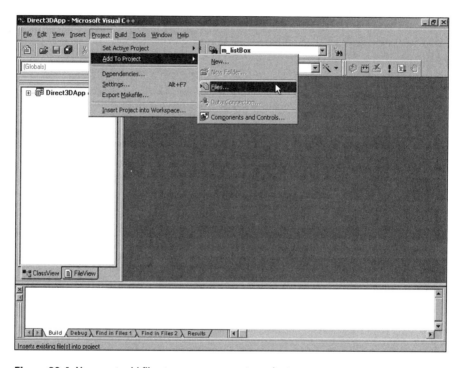

Figure 26-4: You must add files to your new, empty project.

5. In the Insert Files into Project dialog box, select the Direct3DApp.cpp and Direct3DWin.cpp files (see Figure 26-5), and then click OK.

   Visual C++ adds the source code file to the project.

6. Again, select the Add to Project command from Visual C++'s Project menu, and then select Files from the submenu that appears.

Part V: Multimedia Programming

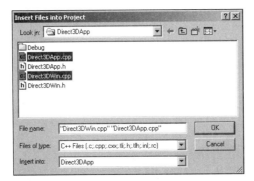

Figure 26-5: Select the project's source code in the dialog box.

7. In the Insert Files into Project dialog box, navigate to your Visual C++ installation's lib folder, select the d3drm.lib and ddraw.lib files (see Figure 26-6), and then click OK.

   Visual C++ adds the DirectDraw and Direct3D library files to the project.

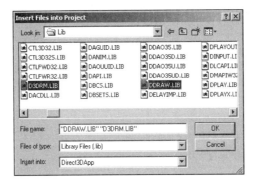

Figure 26-6: Select the library files the project needs.

8. Select the Set Active Configuration command from Visual C++'s Build menu. In the Set Active Project Configuration dialog box, select Direct3DApp - Win32 Release (see Figure 26-7) and click OK.

   Visual C++ is now set to develop the release version of the program, rather than the debugging version.

Chapter 26: Direct3D   793

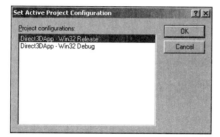

Figure 26-7: The release configuration doesn't include debugging information in your files, so the program's executable is smaller.

9. Select the Settings command from the Project menu. When the Project Settings property page appears, select Use MFC in a Static Library in the Microsoft Foundation Classes drop-down list box, as shown in Figure 26-8.

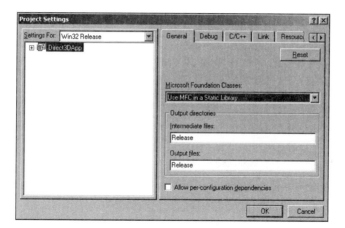

Figure 26-8: When an application uses MFC, it must link to the MFC libraries.

The project is now ready to compile.

Note

Applications that use Direct3D must include the appropriate header files in any modules that access Direct3D interfaces. First, the application must include the #define INITGUID definition. Then, the program must include the d3drm.h header file, and may also require the d3drmwin.h and ddraw.h header files as well.

Running Direct3DApp

Location: `WinPrgS\Chap26\Direct3DApp`

On this book's CD-ROM, you'll find the Direct3DApp program. This program not only shows you how to create a basic Direct3D program, it also shows you how to write MFC programs without the help of AppWizard, which is always handy when you don't want to monkey around with the document and view classes that AppWizard insists on generating.

Before you try to run Direct3DApp, copy it to your hard drive and be sure to copy the Bigship1.x file to the same directory. Rename the file model.x. You can find Bigship1.x in your DirectX installation's Media folder, along with other X files you can display with Direct3DApp.

When you run Direct3DApp, you see the window shown in Figure 26-9. (The quality of the 3-D model may vary depending on your hardware.) Although you can't tell from the figure, the ship model slowly rotates around its Y axis, giving you a view of the model from all sides. When viewing the program, pay particular attention to the lighting, how the scene's single light causes shadows and reflections on the ship's body. That's a lot of 3-D for just a few pages of source code!

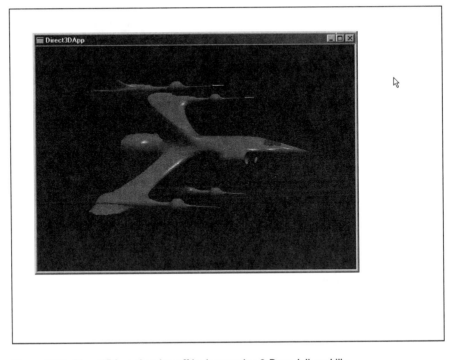

Figure 26-9: Direct3DApp showing off its impressive 3-D modeling skills.

Writing an AppWizardless MFC Application

Before you start digging into Direct3DApp's Direct3D code, you might want to see how to create a non-AppWizard MFC program with only an application and main-window class. The following sections reveal how you can accomplish this handy trick, starting with a program's application class.

Creating the application class's header file

If you look at the following source code, you'll see the header file for Direct3DApp's application class. Two things are important in the listing:

- The application class is derived from `CWinApp`.
- The application class overrides the base class's `InitInstance()` function.

```
#ifndef __DIRECT3DAPP_H
#define __DIRECT3DAPP_H

class Direct3DApp : public CWinApp
{
public:
    Direct3DApp();
    ~Direct3DApp();
    virtual BOOL InitInstance();
};

#endif
```

Remember that the application class represents what goes on behind the scenes in a Windows application. For example, the application class handles the message loop that retrieves and dispatches Windows messages. One thing an application object doesn't have is a window — at least not until you give it one, which you do in `InitInstance()`.

Creating the application class's implementation file

The following source code shows the application class's implementation file:

```
#include <AfxExt.h>
#include <d3drm.h>
#include "Direct3DApp.h"
#include "Direct3DWin.h"

Direct3DApp app;

Direct3DApp::Direct3DApp()
{
}

Direct3DApp::~Direct3DApp()
```

```
{
}

BOOL Direct3DApp::InitInstance()
{
    Direct3DWin* pMainWnd = new Direct3DWin;
    pMainWnd->ShowWindow(SW_SHOWNORMAL);
    pMainWnd->UpdateWindow();

    m_pMainWnd = pMainWnd;

    return TRUE;
}
```

In the `InitInstance()` function, the program creates an object of the `Direct3DWin` class, which is the application's main-window class and where all the Direct3D stuff lives. After creating the window object, `InitInstance()` calls the `ShowWindow()` and `UpdateWindow()` functions to bring up the window on the screen. Finally, the function assigns the window's pointer to the application class's `m_pMainWnd` member variable, which tells the application that it now owns the window and can begin sending it messages.

That's all there is to it. The `Direct3DWin` class handles everything else in the program, including responding to Windows messages, and creating, displaying, and animating its 3-D scene.

Creating the main window class's header file

The following source code shows the `Direct3DWin` class's header file. This class represents the application's main window that you see on the screen. It's also the link between the application and Direct3D:

```
#ifndef __DIRECT3DWIN_H
#define __DIRECT3DWIN_H

class Direct3DWin : public CFrameWnd
{
public:
    Direct3DWin();
    ~Direct3DWin();

protected:
    LPDIRECT3DRM m_pD3D;
    LPDIRECT3DRMDEVICE m_pDevice;
    LPDIRECT3DRMVIEWPORT m_pViewport;
    LPDIRECT3DRMFRAME m_pParentFrame;
    LPDIRECT3DRMFRAME m_pEye;
    LPDIRECT3DRMMESHBUILDER m_pMeshBuilder;
    LPDIRECTDRAWCLIPPER m_pClipper;
    BOOL m_D3DOK;

    BOOL MakeScene();
    BOOL CreateMesh();
```

```
    BOOL CreateViewport();
    BOOL CreateLight();

    afx_msg int OnCreate(LPCREATESTRUCT lpCreateStruct);
    afx_msg void OnPaint();
    afx_msg void OnTimer(UINT nIDEvent);
    afx_msg void OnDestroy();

    DECLARE_MESSAGE_MAP()
};

#endif
```

You should notice a few things about the class declared in the header file:

- The `Direct3DWin` class is derived from MFC's `CFrameWnd` class.
- The class declares member variables for all the main Direct3D pointers the program will need.
- The `MakeScene()`, `CreateMesh()`, `CreateViewport()`, and `CreateLight()` member functions implement the program's Direct3D functionality.
- The class responds to `WM_CREATE`, `WM_PAINT`, `WM_TIMER`, and `WM_DESTROY` windows messages with functions that are associated with the messages in the class's message map.

Creating the window class's implementation file

Here is the window class's implementation file:

```
#include <AfxExt.h>
#define INITGUID
#include <d3drm.h>
#include <d3drmwin.h>
#include "Direct3DWin.h"

BEGIN_MESSAGE_MAP(Direct3DWin, CFrameWnd)
    ON_WM_CREATE()
    ON_WM_PAINT()
    ON_WM_TIMER()
    ON_WM_DESTROY()
END_MESSAGE_MAP()

Direct3DWin::Direct3DWin()
{
    m_D3DOK = FALSE;
    m_pD3D = NULL;
    m_pDevice = NULL;
    m_pViewport = NULL;
    m_pParentFrame = NULL;
    m_pEye = NULL;
    m_pMeshBuilder = NULL;
```

```
    m_pClipper = NULL;
    Create(NULL, "Direct3DApp");
}

Direct3DWin::~Direct3DWin()
{
}

int Direct3DWin::OnCreate(LPCREATESTRUCT)
{
    HRESULT result = Direct3DRMCreate(&m_pD3D);
    if (result != D3DRM_OK)
        return 0;

    result = DirectDrawCreateClipper(0, &m_pClipper, 0);
    if (result != DD_OK)
        return 0;
    result = m_pClipper->SetHWnd(0, m_hWnd);
    if (result != DD_OK)
        return 0;

    RECT rect;
    ::GetClientRect(m_hWnd, &rect);
    result = m_pD3D->CreateDeviceFromClipper(m_pClipper,
        NULL, rect.right, rect.bottom, &m_pDevice);
    if (result != D3DRM_OK)
        return 0;
    m_pDevice->SetQuality(D3DRMRENDER_GOURAUD);

    m_pD3D->CreateFrame(0, &m_pParentFrame);
    if (result != D3DRM_OK)
        return 0;

    BOOL succeeded = MakeScene();
    if (!succeeded)
        return 0;

    m_D3DOK = TRUE;

    SetTimer(1, 100, NULL);

    return 0;
}

BOOL Direct3DWin::MakeScene()
{
    BOOL succeeded = CreateMesh();
    if (!succeeded)
        return FALSE;

    succeeded = CreateViewport();
    if (!succeeded)
        return FALSE;
```

```cpp
        succeeded = CreateLight();
        if (!succeeded)
            return FALSE;

        return TRUE;
    }

    BOOL Direct3DWin::CreateMesh()
    {
        HRESULT result =
            m_pD3D->CreateMeshBuilder(&m_pMeshBuilder);
        if (result != D3DRM_OK)
            return FALSE;

        result = m_pMeshBuilder->Load("model.x",
            NULL, D3DRMLOAD_FROMFILE, NULL, NULL );
        if (result != D3DRM_OK)
        {
            MessageBox("MODEL.X file missing. Please place\n\
 a Direct3D X file with this name\nin the Direct3DApp folder.");
            return FALSE;
        }

        LPDIRECT3DRMFRAME pFrame;
        result =
            m_pD3D->CreateFrame(m_pParentFrame, &pFrame);
        if (result != D3DRM_OK)
            return FALSE;
        pFrame->AddVisual(m_pMeshBuilder);
        pFrame->SetRotation(m_pParentFrame, D3DVALUE(0.0),
            D3DVALUE(1.0), D3DVALUE(0.0), D3DVALUE(0.05));
        pFrame->Release();
        pFrame = NULL;

        return TRUE;
    }

    BOOL Direct3DWin::CreateViewport()
    {
        HRESULT result = m_pD3D->
            CreateFrame(m_pParentFrame, &m_pEye);
        if (result != D3DRM_OK)
            return FALSE;
        m_pEye->SetPosition(m_pParentFrame, D3DVALUE(0),
            D3DVALUE(0), D3DVALUE(-40.0));
        result = m_pD3D->CreateViewport(m_pDevice, m_pEye,
            0, 0, m_pDevice->GetWidth(),
            m_pDevice->GetHeight(), &m_pViewport);
        if (result != D3DRM_OK)
            return FALSE;

        return TRUE;
    }
```

Part V: Multimedia Programming

```cpp
BOOL Direct3DWin::CreateLight()
{
    LPDIRECT3DRMLIGHT pLight;
    HRESULT result = m_pD3D->
        CreateLightRGB(D3DRMLIGHT_DIRECTIONAL,
        D3DVALUE(1.0), D3DVALUE(1.0), D3DVALUE(1.0),
        &pLight);
    if (result != D3DRM_OK)
        return FALSE;

    LPDIRECT3DRMFRAME pLightFrame;
    result = m_pD3D->CreateFrame(m_pParentFrame,
        &pLightFrame );
    if (result != D3DRM_OK)
        return FALSE;

    pLightFrame->AddLight(pLight);
    pLightFrame->SetOrientation(m_pParentFrame,
        D3DVALUE(0.0), D3DVALUE(-1.0), D3DVALUE(1.0),
        D3DVALUE(0.0), D3DVALUE(1.0), D3DVALUE(0.0));
    pLight->Release();
    pLight = NULL;
    pLightFrame->Release();
    pLightFrame = NULL;

    return TRUE;
}

void Direct3DWin::OnPaint()
{
    BOOL repaint = GetUpdateRect(NULL);
    if (!repaint)
        return;

    PAINTSTRUCT pstruct;
    BeginPaint(&pstruct);

    if (m_D3DOK)
    {
        LPDIRECT3DRMWINDEVICE pWndDevice;
        m_pDevice->
            QueryInterface(IID_IDirect3DRMWinDevice,
            (void**)&pWndDevice);
        pWndDevice->HandlePaint(pstruct.hdc);
        pWndDevice->Release();
    }
    else
        ::TextOut(pstruct.hdc, 20, 20,
            "Direct3D failed to start.", 25);

    EndPaint(&pstruct);
}
```

```cpp
void Direct3DWin::OnTimer(UINT nIDEvent)
{
    if (m_D3DOK)
        m_pD3D->Tick(D3DVALUE(1));
}

void Direct3DWin::OnDestroy()
{
    if (m_pMeshBuilder)
        m_pMeshBuilder->Release();

    if (m_pEye)
        m_pEye->Release();

    if (m_pViewport)
        m_pViewport->Release();

    if (m_pParentFrame)
        m_pParentFrame->Release();

    if (m_pDevice)
        m_pDevice->Release();

    if (m_pD3D)
        m_pD3D->Release();

    if (m_pClipper)
        m_pClipper->Release();
}
```

You should take a little time to look over this source code until you understand how it fits in with the application class. You should also understand the general Direct3D programming techniques used in the program. In the sections that follow, you'll examine this application in detail to see how it creates and displays its Direct3D animated scene.

In the listing, you can see that the `OnCreate()` function gets Direct3D up and running. Each step required to build the 3-D scene is implemented in its own function. These functions, which you'll soon examine in greater detail, are `MakeScene()`, `CreateMesh()`, `CreateViewport()`, and `CreateLight()`.

The Direct3DWin class's constructor

The window class's constructor has the usual job of initializing member variables:

```cpp
m_D3DOK = FALSE;
m_pD3D = NULL;
m_pDevice = NULL;
m_pViewport = NULL;
m_pParentFrame = NULL;
m_pEye = NULL;
m_pMeshBuilder = NULL;
m_pClipper = NULL;
```

This initialization is especially important for the Direct3D pointers because if the pointers don't start off NULL, the OnDestroy() function may try to call their Release() functions when the program terminates, even if the objects weren't created successfully. Calling a function through an uninitialized pointer is a good way to give your application's user nasty surprises.

The class's constructor also creates the Window element (the window you see on the screen) that's associated with the class:

```
Create(NULL, "Direct3DApp");
```

Direct3DWin inherits its Create() function from the CFrameWnd base class. Its two arguments provide a pointer to the parent window (NULL means no parent) and the window's title.

The OnDestroy() function

As mentioned in the previous section, the OnDestroy() function releases the Direct3D pointers. For example, here's how OnDestroy() releases the mesh builder and viewport frame objects:

```
if (m_pMeshBuilder)
    m_pMeshBuilder->Release();

if (m_pEye)
    m_pEye->Release();
```

OnDestroy() releases the other Direct3D objects the same way. You can see why it's important that the pointers start off NULL. If Direct3D initialization fails, OnDestroy() is going to get those pointers as they were initialized in the class's constructor.

The OnCreate() function

MFC calls the OnCreate() function in response to the WM_CREATE message, which Windows sends just before the window appears. Direct3DApp uses OnCreate() to set up the basic Direct3D system. First, OnCreate() creates the main Direct3D object:

```
HRESULT result = Direct3DRMCreate(&m_pD3D);
if (result != D3DRM_OK)
    return 0;
```

Notice how if the Direct3D creation process fails, the function returns a zero, which tells the application to go ahead and create the window. In this case, the m_D3DOK flag stays set to FALSE, and the window's OnPaint() function will know to display an error message. Every step of the Direct3D setup uses the same type of error handling, immediately returning from the function if trouble rears its ugly head.

After creating the main Direct3D object, the program creates and initializes its clipper object:

```
result = DirectDrawCreateClipper(0, &m_pClipper, 0);
if (result != DD_OK)
    return 0;
result = m_pClipper->SetHWnd(0, m_hWnd);
if (result != DD_OK)
    return 0;
```

As you learned previously, the SetHWnd() function requires the window's handle. The m_hWnd is a member variable of the Direct3DWin class. The class inherits this member variable from the CWnd class.

The next step is to create the Direct3D device, which OnCreate() does as follows:

```
RECT rect;
::GetClientRect(m_hWnd, &rect);
result = m_pD3D->CreateDeviceFromClipper(m_pClipper,
    NULL, rect.right, rect.bottom, &m_pDevice);
if (result != D3DRM_OK)
    return 0;
m_pDevice->SetQuality(D3DRMRENDER_GOURAUD);
```

For the last step of the basic Direct3D setup, OnCreate() creates the application's parent Direct3D frame:

```
m_pD3D->CreateFrame(0, &m_pParentFrame);
if (result != D3DRM_OK)
    return 0;
```

Near the end of its duties, having successfully initialized Direct3D, OnCreate() calls the locally defined MakeScene() function, which, despite its name, doesn't throw a tantrum, but instead creates the application's 3D scene:

```
BOOL succeeded = MakeScene();
if (!succeeded)
    return 0;
```

If MakeScene() executes successfully, OnCreate() sets the m_D3DOK flag to TRUE so that the rest of the program knows that everything with Direct3D is hunky-dory:

```
m_D3DOK = TRUE;
```

The last thing OnCreate() does is set a Windows timer:

```
SetTimer(1, 100, NULL);
```

This Windows timer, which is the engine that drives the program's 3-D animation, will cause WM_TIMER messages to arrive at the window ten times a second. As you'll soon see, the OnTimer() function handles the WM_TIMER messages "handily."

The MakeScene() function

Direct3DApp's `MakeScene()` function performs the task of putting together a 3-D scene for the application to show off. However, rather than perform its tasks directly, it calls other locally defined functions to complete the deed. The first of these functions is `CreateMesh()`, which `MakeScene()` calls like this:

```
BOOL succeeded = CreateMesh();
if (!succeeded)
    return FALSE;
```

`MakeScene()` gets the viewport and light created the same way, by calling `CreateViewport()` (the local version, not the Direct3D version) and `CreateLight()`:

```
succeeded = CreateViewport();
if (!succeeded)
    return FALSE;

succeeded = CreateLight();
if (!succeeded)
    return FALSE;
```

If any of these function calls fail, `MakeScene()` returns a value of `FALSE`, which causes `OnCreate()` to immediately stop and return, leaving m_D3DOK with a value of `FALSE`.

The CreateMesh() function

`CreateMesh()` is where the real Direct3D scene creation starts. First, the function creates the mesh builder object:

```
HRESULT result =
    m_pD3D->CreateMeshBuilder(&m_pMeshBuilder);
if (result != D3DRM_OK)
    return FALSE;
```

If the mesh builder creation fails, `CreateMesh()` returns `FALSE` to `MakeScene()`, which then returns `FALSE` to `OnCreate()`, which then returns without further Direct3D initialization, which leaves m_D3DOK with a value of `FALSE`. (Whew! The webs we weave.)

The next task for `CreateMesh()` is to load the 3-D object into the mesh builder:

```
result = m_pMeshBuilder->Load("model.x",
    NULL, D3DRMLOAD_FROMFILE, NULL, NULL );
if (result != D3DRM_OK)
{
    MessageBox("MODEL.X file missing. Please place\n\
a Direct3D X file with this name\nin the Direct3DApp folder.");
    return FALSE;
}
```

Chapter 26: Direct3D

Finally, the new mesh needs an orientation and position in the 3-D scene, which means it needs a frame. `CreateMesh()` creates the frame as follows:

```
LPDIRECT3DRMFRAME pFrame;
result =
    m_pD3D->CreateFrame(m_pParentFrame, &pFrame);
if (result != D3DRM_OK)
    return FALSE;
```

Then the program adds the mesh to the frame:

```
pFrame->AddVisual(m_pMeshBuilder);
```

To prepare Direct3D for animation, the program calls the frame object's `SetRotation()` function:

```
pFrame->SetRotation(m_pParentFrame, D3DVALUE(0.0),
    D3DVALUE(1.0), D3DVALUE(0.0), D3DVALUE(0.05));
```

This function call tells Direct3D to rotate the frame around the Y axis. `SetRotation()`'s arguments are described as follows:

- A pointer to the parent frame
- The X coordinate of the vector around which to rotate
- The Y coordinate of the vector around which to rotate
- The Z coordinate of the vector around which to rotate
- The amount of rotation in radians

Finally, because the program doesn't need to access the mesh object's frame, `CreateMesh()` releases the frame object and sets its pointer to `NULL`:

```
    pFrame->Release();
    pFrame = NULL;
```

The CreateViewport() function

Now, with the mesh object created, the program needs to construct a viewport. The first step in completing this task is to create the viewport's frame, which will determine the orientation and position of the view:

```
HRESULT result = m_pD3D->
    CreateFrame(m_pParentFrame, &m_pEye);
if (result != D3DRM_OK)
    return FALSE;
```

Now that the program has its viewport frame, it can position the frame for the required viewing angle and distance:

```
m_pEye->SetPosition(m_pParentFrame, D3DVALUE(0),
    D3DVALUE(0), D3DVALUE(-40.0));
```

The last step is to create the viewport and associate it with its frame:

```
result = m_pD3D->CreateViewport(m_pDevice, m_pEye,
    0, 0, m_pDevice->GetWidth(),
    m_pDevice->GetHeight(), &m_pViewport);
if (result != D3DRM_OK)
    return FALSE;
```

The CreateLight() function

With all the scene objects constructed, and a viewport pointing at the scene, it's time to put some light on the subject. This magic happens in the CreateLight() function, which first creates a single directional light:

```
LPDIRECT3DRMLIGHT pLight;
HRESULT result = m_pD3D->
    CreateLightRGB(D3DRMLIGHT_DIRECTIONAL,
    D3DVALUE(1.0), D3DVALUE(1.0), D3DVALUE(1.0),
    &pLight);
if (result != D3DRM_OK)
    return FALSE;
```

The three color values of 1.0 produce a bright, white light. After its creation, the light needs a frame to orient and position it in the scene:

```
LPDIRECT3DRMFRAME pLightFrame;
result = m_pD3D->CreateFrame(m_pParentFrame,
    &pLightFrame );
if (result != D3DRM_OK)
    return FALSE;
```

With the frame created, the program can add the light to the frame and orient it as needed to light the scene as required by the program:

```
pLightFrame->AddLight(pLight);
pLightFrame->SetOrientation(m_pParentFrame,
    D3DVALUE(0.0), D3DVALUE(-1.0), D3DVALUE(1.0),
    D3DVALUE(0.0), D3DVALUE(1.0), D3DVALUE(0.0));
```

After adding the light to the scene, the program no longer needs to access the light or its frame, so it releases both of these objects and sets their pointers to NULL:

```
pLight->Release();
pLight = NULL;
pLightFrame->Release();
pLightFrame = NULL;
```

The OnPaint() function

In an MFC program that doesn't use a window derived from the CView class, it's the OnPaint() function, rather than OnDraw(), that creates the application's display. In a Direct3D program, creating the display is just a matter of creating a window device and calling its `HandlePaint()` function. This happens in Direct3DApp's `OnPaint()` function, which first calls `GetUpdateRect()` to determine whether any portion of the window actually needs to be redrawn:

```
BOOL repaint = GetUpdateRect(NULL);
if (!repaint)
    return;
```

If `GetUpdateRect()` returns FALSE, there's really nothing that `OnPaint()` needs to do, so the function returns. If `GetUpdateRect()` returns TRUE, however, some portion of the window needs to be redrawn. To handle this eventuality, the program first calls `BeginPaint()`, which, unlike in `OnDraw()`, is required in `OnPaint()`:

```
    PAINTSTRUCT pstruct;
    BeginPaint(&pstruct);
```

Next, `OnPaint()` checks the `m_D3DOK` flag to see whether the program's Direct3D objects are valid. If Direct3D is ready to go, the program creates a window device, calls its `HandlePaint()` function, and finally releases the device:

```
if (m_D3DOK)
{
    LPDIRECT3DRMWINDEVICE pWndDevice;
    m_pDevice->
        QueryInterface(IID_IDirect3DRMWinDevice,
        (void**)&pWndDevice);
    pWndDevice->HandlePaint(pstruct.hdc);
    pWndDevice->Release();
}
```

As you can see, the program gets a pointer to the window device by calling the Direct3D device's `QueryInterface()` function. This function's first argument is the ID for the requested interface, and the second argument is the address of a pointer to the requested interface. If the call to `QueryInterface()` succeeds (which it should, as we already know that the interface exists), the function places the address of the interface into the `pWndDevice` pointer.

If Direct3D didn't initialize properly earlier in the program, `m_D3DOK` will be FALSE, and `OnPaint()` will do nothing more than display an error message:

```
    else
        ::TextOut(pstruct.hdc, 20, 20,
            "Direct3D failed to start.", 25);
```

Finally, `OnPaint()` calls `EndPaint()` to tell Windows that the painting is complete:

```
EndPaint(&pstruct);
```

The OnTimer() function

The last thing of interest in the Direct3DApp program is the way the Direct3D animation works. Believe it or not, all it takes is a single call to the main Direct3D object's `Tick()` function to advance the animation to the next frame. This happens in the program's `OnTimer()` function, which responds to the WM_TIMER messages arriving at the window ten times a second.

`OnTimer()` first checks the m_D3DOK flag to be sure that the Direct3D object is valid. Then the function calls `Tick()` to rotate the 3-D model one step:

```
if (m_D3DOK)
    m_pD3D->Tick(D3DVALUE(1));
```

`Tick()`'s single argument controls the speed of the animation. A value of 1 causes the animation to proceed exactly as was requested when the program called `SetRotation()` in the locally defined `CreateMesh()` function. In Direct3DApp, the `Tick()` argument of 1 causes the model to rotate 0.05 radians. A smaller argument makes the rotation speed proportionately slower, while a larger argument makes the rotation proportionately faster. For example, in Direct3DApp, a `Tick()` argument of 0.5 causes the model to rotate only 0.025 radians, whereas an argument of 2 causes the model to rotate 0.10 radians.

PROBLEMS & SOLUTIONS

Writing a Conventional Direct3D Windows Application

PROBLEM: *Now I know how to write an MFC Direct3D program. What if I'd prefer to write my program without MFC?*

SOLUTION: Just as with DirectDraw or DirectSound, the easiest way to accomplish this task is to write a traditional Windows program, but write it as a C++ program rather than a C program. Then you can avoid the clumsy syntax required to call Direct3D functions from a C program.

Note

If you've forgotten how to write a traditional Windows application, you might want to take the time now to review Chapter 1.

To create a Direct3D application as a conventional Windows program, first write the basic application as you normally would, providing a `WinMain()` function that defines and registers your window class, as well as contains the application's message loop. You'll also need to provide a Windows procedure that responds to the many messages for which Windows will target your application. In your basic Windows procedure, you'll want to respond at least to the WM_DESTROY message.

Continued

Chapter 26: Direct3D

Location: **WinPrgS\Chap26\Direct3DApp2**

Once you have the basic application built, you can add the Direct3D program code. In your Windows procedure, respond to the WM_CREATE message by initializing your program and setting up Direct3D. As you can see in the following source code, the entire process is actually less complicated than trying to wedge Direct3D into an MFC program. You can find the program on this book's CD-ROM.

```
#define INITGUID
#include <windows.h>
#include <windowsx.h>
#include <d3drm.h>
#include <d3drmwin.h>

/* Function prototypes */
LRESULT CALLBACK WndProc(HWND hWnd, UINT message,
    WPARAM wParam, LPARAM lParam);
void InitVariables();
BOOL InitDirect3D(HWND hWnd);
BOOL MakeScene();
BOOL CreateMesh();
BOOL CreateViewport();
BOOL CreateLight();

/* Global variables */
LPDIRECT3DRM pD3D;
LPDIRECT3DRMDEVICE pDevice;
LPDIRECT3DRMVIEWPORT pViewport;
LPDIRECT3DRMFRAME pParentFrame;
LPDIRECT3DRMFRAME pEye;
LPDIRECT3DRMMESHBUILDER pMeshBuilder;
LPDIRECTDRAWCLIPPER pClipper;

int WINAPI WinMain(HINSTANCE hCurrentInst,
    HINSTANCE hPrevInstance, PSTR lpszCmdLine,
    int nCmdShow)
{
    WNDCLASS wndClass;
    HWND hWnd;
    MSG msg;
    UINT width;
    UINT height;

    wndClass.style = CS_HREDRAW | CS_VREDRAW;
    wndClass.lpfnWndProc = WndProc;
    wndClass.cbClsExtra = 0;
    wndClass.cbWndExtra = 0;
    wndClass.hInstance = hCurrentInst;
    wndClass.hIcon = LoadIcon(NULL, IDI_APPLICATION);
    wndClass.hCursor = LoadCursor(NULL, IDC_ARROW);
    wndClass.hbrBackground = GetStockObject(WHITE_BRUSH);
```

Continued

```c
        wndClass.lpszMenuName = NULL;
        wndClass.lpszClassName = "D3DApp";

        RegisterClass(&wndClass);

        width = GetSystemMetrics(SM_CXSCREEN) / 2;
        height = GetSystemMetrics(SM_CYSCREEN) / 2;
        hWnd = CreateWindow(
            "D3DApp",           /* Window class's name.    */
            "Direct3D App",     /* Title bar text.         */
            WS_OVERLAPPEDWINDOW, /* The window's style.    */
            10,                 /* X position.             */
            10,                 /* Y position.             */
            width,              /* Width.                  */
            height,             /* Height.                 */
            NULL,               /* Parent window's handle. */
            NULL,               /* Menu handle.            */
            hCurrentInst,       /* Instance handle.        */
            NULL);              /* No additional data.     */

        ShowWindow(hWnd, nCmdShow);
        UpdateWindow(hWnd);

        while (GetMessage(&msg, NULL, 0, 0))
        {
            TranslateMessage(&msg);
            DispatchMessage(&msg);
        }

        return msg.wParam;
    }
    LRESULT CALLBACK WndProc(HWND hWnd, UINT message,
        WPARAM wParam, LPARAM lParam)
    {
        HDC hDC;
        PAINTSTRUCT paintStruct;
        BOOL repaint;

        switch(message)
        {
            case WM_CREATE:
                InitVariables();
                InitDirect3D(hWnd);
                return 0;

            case WM_PAINT:
                repaint = GetUpdateRect(hWnd, NULL, FALSE);
                if (!repaint)
                    return 0;

                hDC = BeginPaint(hWnd, &paintStruct);
```

Continued

Chapter 26: Direct3D

```
                LPDIRECT3DRMWINDEVICE pWndDevice;
                pDevice->QueryInterface(
                    IID_IDirect3DRMWinDevice,
                    (void**)&pWndDevice);
                pWndDevice->HandlePaint(hDC);
                pWndDevice->Release();

                EndPaint(hWnd, &paintStruct);

                return 0;

            case WM_TIMER:
                pD3D->Tick(D3DVALUE(1));
                return 0;

            case WM_DESTROY:
                if (pMeshBuilder)
                    pMeshBuilder->Release();

                if (pEye)
                    pEye->Release();

                if (pViewport)
                    pViewport->Release();

                if (pParentFrame)
                    pParentFrame->Release();

                if (pDevice)
                    pDevice->Release();

                if (pD3D)
                    pD3D->Release();

                if (pClipper)
                    pClipper->Release();

                PostQuitMessage(0);
                return 0;
        }

        return DefWindowProc(hWnd, message, wParam, lParam);
    }

    void InitVariables()
    {
        pD3D = NULL;
        pDevice = NULL;
        pViewport = NULL;
        pParentFrame = NULL;
        pEye = NULL;
```

Continued

```
    pMeshBuilder = NULL;
    pClipper = NULL;
}

BOOL InitDirect3D(HWND hWnd)
{
    HRESULT result = Direct3DRMCreate(&pD3D);
    if (result != D3DRM_OK)
        return FALSE;
    result = DirectDrawCreateClipper(0, &pClipper, 0);
    if (result != DD_OK)
        return FALSE;
    result = pClipper->SetHWnd(0, hWnd);
    if (result != DD_OK)
        return FALSE;

    RECT rect;
    GetClientRect(hWnd, &rect);
    result = pD3D->CreateDeviceFromClipper(pClipper,
        NULL, rect.right, rect.bottom, &pDevice);
    if (result != D3DRM_OK)
        return FALSE;
    pDevice->SetQuality(D3DRMRENDER_GOURAUD);

    pD3D->CreateFrame(0, &pParentFrame);
    if (result != D3DRM_OK)
        return FALSE;

    BOOL succeeded = MakeScene();
    if (!succeeded)
        return FALSE;

    SetTimer(hWnd, 1, 100, NULL);

    return TRUE;
}

BOOL MakeScene()
{
    BOOL succeeded = CreateMesh();
    if (!succeeded)
        return FALSE;

    succeeded = CreateViewport();
    if (!succeeded)
        return FALSE;

    succeeded = CreateLight();
    if (!succeeded)
        return FALSE;
```

Continued

```
        return TRUE;
}

BOOL CreateMesh()
{
    HRESULT result =
        pD3D->CreateMeshBuilder(&pMeshBuilder);
    if (result != D3DRM_OK)
        return FALSE;
    result = pMeshBuilder->Load("model.x",
        NULL, D3DRMLOAD_FROMFILE, NULL, NULL );
    if (result != D3DRM_OK)
    {
        MessageBox(0, "MODEL.X file missing. Please place\n\
a Direct3D X file with this name\nin the Direct3DApp folder.",
            "File Missing", MB_OK | MB_ICONEXCLAMATION);
        return FALSE;
    }

    LPDIRECT3DRMFRAME pFrame;
    result =
        pD3D->CreateFrame(pParentFrame, &pFrame);
    if (result != D3DRM_OK)
        return FALSE;
    pFrame->AddVisual(pMeshBuilder);
    pFrame->SetRotation(pParentFrame, D3DVALUE(0.0),
        D3DVALUE(1.0), D3DVALUE(0.0), D3DVALUE(0.05));
    pFrame->Release();
    pFrame = NULL;

    return TRUE;
}

BOOL CreateViewport()
{
    HRESULT result = pD3D->
        CreateFrame(pParentFrame, &pEye);
    if (result != D3DRM_OK)
        return FALSE;
    pEye->SetPosition(pParentFrame, D3DVALUE(0),
        D3DVALUE(0), D3DVALUE(-40.0));
    result = pD3D->CreateViewport(pDevice, pEye,
        0, 0, pDevice->GetWidth(),
        pDevice->GetHeight(), &pViewport);
    if (result != D3DRM_OK)
        return FALSE;

    return TRUE;
}
```

Continued

```
BOOL CreateLight()
{
    LPDIRECT3DRMLIGHT pLight;
    HRESULT result = pD3D->
        CreateLightRGB(D3DRMLIGHT_DIRECTIONAL,
        D3DVALUE(1.0), D3DVALUE(1.0), D3DVALUE(1.0),
        &pLight);
    if (result != D3DRM_OK)
        return FALSE;
    LPDIRECT3DRMFRAME pLightFrame;
    result = pD3D->CreateFrame(pParentFrame,
        &pLightFrame );
    if (result != D3DRM_OK)
        return FALSE;

    pLightFrame->AddLight(pLight);
    pLightFrame->SetOrientation(pParentFrame,
        D3DVALUE(0.0), D3DVALUE(-1.0), D3DVALUE(1.0),
        D3DVALUE(0.0), D3DVALUE(1.0), D3DVALUE(0.0));
    pLight->Release();
    pLight = NULL;
    pLightFrame->Release();
    pLightFrame = NULL;

    return TRUE;
}
```

This program, in spite of being a traditional C-style windows program, initializes Direct3D in much the same way as this chapter's first program, Direct3DApp. In fact, the program looks and acts very similar. That is, when you run the application, a rotating 3-D model appears in the window. All of the Direct3D code in the program should be familiar to you by now. If you don't understand the program, you should reread this chapter from the beginning.

Summary

This concludes your all-too-brief introduction to the Direct3D programming libraries. As mentioned before, this introduction is only a starting point. Entire books have been written on Direct3D programming, not to mention on 3-D graphics programming in general. If you're new to 3-D programming, this chapter may seem more confusing than helpful. If so, get yourself a good 3-D graphics programming book and learn the basics. Then, come back to this chapter.

Also discussed in this chapter:

▶ A Direct3D application must create a Direct3D main object.

▶ A DirectDraw clipper object manages a Direct3D window.

- A Direct3D application must create a device object.
- Direct3D objects are oriented and positioned using frames.
- A Direct3D model is created from a mesh, which is a collection of polygons.
- A Direct3D viewport determines how a scene can be viewed.
- Direct3D lights not only enable you to see objects in a 3-D world, but also cause shadows and reflections.

Part VI
Internet Programming

Chapter 27: WinInet

Chapter 28: Internet Explorer

Chapter 27

WinInet

In This Chapter

- Introducing WinInet
- Writing an HTTP application
- Writing an FTP application
- Examining a sample WinInet application

With the Internet slowly but surely dominating our lives, it should come as no surprise that MFC includes classes that enable programmers to create Internet applications more easily than ever before. The WinInet classes make it possible to create HTTP, FTP, and Gopher Internet applications without having to handle (or even know about) all the nitty-gritty details. To introduce you to this topic, this chapter provides an overview of the WinInet classes. Moreover, because HTTP and FTP sessions are the most common type of Internet access, this chapter also features sections about how to use WinInet to create these types of applications. The FTP section, in fact, features an FTP application that enables you to browse FTP servers and download files.

Introducing WinInet

As mentioned previously, WinInet is a collection of MFC classes that simplifies the task of writing Internet applications, including the handling of HTTP, FTP, and Gopher sessions. WinInet includes classes for managing Internet sessions, connections, and files. In fact, using WinInet, you can forget about things like TCP/IP protocol and WinSock, major stumbling blocks for new Internet programmers. Table 27-1 describes the WinInet classes.

Table 27-1 The WinInet Classes

Class	Description
CFileFind	Enables Internet file searches
CFtpConnection	Manages the connection to an FTP server
CFtpFileFind	Enables Internet file searches on an FTP server
CGopherConnection	Manages a connection to a Gopher server
CGopherFile	Manages files on a Gopher server
CGopherFileFind	Enables Internet file searches on a Gopher server
CGopherLocator	Retrieves a Gopher locator from a gopher server
CHttpConnection	Manages the connection to an HTTP server
CHttpFile	Enables an application to read HTTP files
CInternetConnection	Manages a connection to an Internet server
CInternetException	Represents exceptions that occur during Internet sessions
CInternetFile	Enables high-level Internet file access
CInternetSession	Manages one or more Internet sessions

Virtually all Internet access these days is through HTTP or FTP connections. For that reason, this chapter concentrates on these types of applications, as well as on the WinInet classes that support these types of Internet connections. In the rest of this section, you get a closer look at the following classes, which enable you to create both HTTP and FTP applications: CInternetSession, CInternetConnection, CHttpConnection, CFtpConnection, CInternetFile, CHttpFile, CFileFind, CFtpFileFind, and CInternetException.

The CInternetSession Class

No matter what type of Internet program you're writing with WinInet, the first step is to create an Internet session. A CInternetSession object can handle one or more Internet sessions simultaneously and can even handle connections to a proxy server. The CInternetSession object can interpret and connect to URLs that you specify using the object's member functions. Moreover, a CInternetSession object can create HTTP, FTP, and Gopher connections on behalf of your application. Table 27-2 lists the class's member functions, along with their descriptions.

Table 27-2 The CInternetSession Class's Member Functions

Function	Description
Close()	Closes the Internet connection
EnableStatusCallback()	Enables a status callback function for asynchronous operations
GetCookie()	Gets the specified cookie
GetCookieLength()	Gets the specified cookie's length
GetContext()	Gets the session's context value
GetFtpConnection()	Starts an FTP session
GetGopherConnection()	Starts a Gopher session
GetHttpConnection()	Starts an HTTP session
OnStatusCallback()	Updates an asynchronous operation's status
OpenURL()	Opens a given URL
QueryOption()	Provides error handling for operations
ServiceTypeFromHandle()	Gets the type of Internet service
SetCookie()	Sets a cookie for the specified URL
SetOption()	Sets a session's options

The CInternetConnection Class

The `CInternetConnection` class is the base class for the other more specific WinInet connection types, such as `CHttpConnection` and `CFtpConnection`. As such, this class defines the basic functionality for an Internet connection. All WinInet programs must establish an Internet session (through `CInternetSession`) and an Internet connection (through a class derived from `CInternetConnection`) to communicate over the Internet. Following is a list of `CInternetConnection`'s member functions, which are all inherited by classes derived from `CInternetSession`.

GetContext()	Gets the connection's context ID
GetSession()	Gets a pointer to the connection's session object
GetServerName()	Gets the name of the connection's server

The CHttpConnection Class

The `CHttpConnection` class represents a connection to an HTTP server, which is the type of connection that browsers use to display Web pages (see Figure 27-1). Unlike most MFC classes, you don't create a `CHttpConnection` object directly, but rather call the `CInternetSession GetHttpConnection()` member function. Or, you can connect to an HTML document from an HTTP connection by calling the `CInternetSession` object's `OpenURL()` function. Because `CHttpConnection` has `CInternetConnection` as a base class, it inherits that class's member functions. It also defines one of its own, `OpenRequest()`, which opens an HTTP connection.

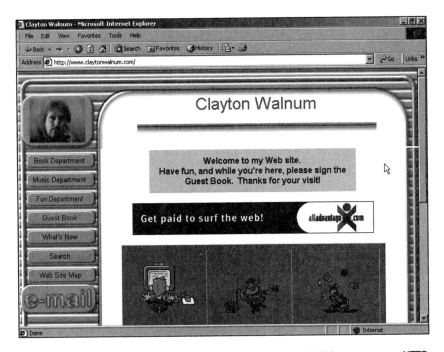

Figure 27-1: Microsoft Internet Explorer displaying the author's Web page over an HTTP connection.

The CFtpConnection Class

The `CFtpConnection` class represents a connection to an FTP server, which is used mainly to upload and download files to and from the server. Like `CHttpConnection`, you don't create a `CFtpConnection` object directly, but rather call the `CInternetSession GetFtpConnection()` member function. Because `CFtpConnection` has `CInternetConnection` as a base class, it inherits that class's member functions. It also defines many of its own, which are listed and described in Table 27-3.

Table 27-3 The CFtpConnection Class's Member Functions

Function	Description
Close()	Closes the connection to an FTP server
CreateDirectory()	Creates a directory on an FTP server
GetCurrentDirectory()	Gets the connection's current directory
GetCurrentDirectoryAsURL()	Gets the connection's current directory as a URL
GetFile()	Downloads a file from an FTP server
OpenFile()	Opens a file on an FTP server
PutFile()	Uploads a file to an FTP server
Remove()	Removes a file from an FTP server
RemoveDirectory()	Removes a directory from an FTP server
Rename()	Renames a file on an FTP server
SetCurrentDirectory()	Changes to the given FTP directory

The CInternetFile Class

The CInternetFile class is the base class for the other more specific WinInet file classes, CHttpFile and CGopherFile. As such, this class defines the basic functionality for an Internet file object, allowing WinInet programs to access files using Internet file transfer protocols. However, you don't create CInternetFile objects in your programs. Instead, you create an object from a class that's derived from CInternetFile. Table 27-4 lists CInternetFile's member functions, which are all inherited by classes derived from CInternetFile.

Table 27-4 The CInternetFile Class's Member Functions

Function	Description
Abort()	Closes the file without regard for errors
Close()	Closes a CInternetFile object
Flush()	Flushes the file
Read()	Reads bytes from the file
ReadString()	Reads characters from the file
Seek()	Positions the file's pointer

Continued

Table 27-4 *(continued)*

Function	Description
SetReadBufferSize()	Sets the size of the file's read buffer
SetWriteBufferSize()	Sets the size of the file's write buffer
Write()	Writes bytes to the file
WriteString()	Writes a string to the file

The CHttpFile Class

The CHttpFile class enables an application to access and read files over an HTTP connection. Because WinInet derives CHttpFile from CInternetFile, the class inherits all of CInternetFile's member functions, as well as defines a set of its own that are specific to handling HTTP files. Table 27-5 lists those functions and their descriptions.

Table 27-5   The CHttpFile Class's Member Functions

Function	Description
AddRequestHeaders()	Adds headers to an HTTP server request
Close()	Closes a file
EndRequest()	Ends a request that was sent by a call to SendRequestEx()
GetFileURL()	Gets a file's URL
GetObject()	Gets a request verb's target object
GetVerb()	Gets a request verb
QueryInfo()	Gets the response or request headers
QueryInfoStatusCode()	Gets an HTTP request's status code
SendRequest()	Sends a request to an HTTP server
SendRequestEx()	Sends a request to an HTTP server (an extended version of SendRequest())

The CFileFind Class

The CFileFind class is the base class for the other, more specific, WinInet file-find classes, CFtpFileFind and CGopherFileFind. As such, this class defines the basic functionality for a file-find object, allowing WinInet programs to do file searches on the local system, as well as over an Internet connection. Besides finding files, `CFileFind` objects can request information about files, including path, file name, creation time, URL, length, directory, and other file attributes. Table 27-6 lists `CFileFind`'s member functions.

Table 27-6 The CFileFind Class's Member Functions

Function	Description
Close()	Terminates a search
FindFile()	Searches for a file
FindNextFile()	Finds the next file in a file search
GetCreationTime()	Gets the file's creation time
GetFileName()	Gets the file's file name
GetFilePath()	Gets the file's path
GetFileTitle()	Gets the file's title, which is the name without the extension
GetFileURL()	Gets the file's URL
GetLastAccessTime()	Gets the file's last access time
GetLastWriteTime()	Gets the files last change time
GetLength()	Gets the file's length
GetRoot()	Gets the file's root directory
IsArchived()	Returns TRUE if the file is archived
IsCompressed()	Returns TRUE if the file is compressed
IsDirectory()	Returns TRUE if the file is a directory
IsDots()	Returns TRUE if the file name is "." or ".."
IsHidden()	Returns TRUE if the file is hidden
IsNormal()	Returns TRUE if the file is normal
IsReadOnly()	Returns TRUE if the file is read-only
IsSystem()	Returns TRUE if the file is a system file
IsTemporary()	Returns TRUE if the file is temporary
MatchesMask()	Specifies attributes of the file for which to search

The CFtpFileFind Class

The `CFtpFileFind` class, which WinInet derives from `CFileFind`, enables FTP applications to search for files, as well as to obtain information about files. `CFtpFileFind` inherits much of its functionality from `CFileFind`, but also defines three functions of its own that refine certain operations for FTP access. The following list describes these additional member functions:

FindFile()	Finds a file on an FTP server
FindNextFile()	Continues a file search from a previous call to FindFile()
GetFileURL()	Gets the URL, including path, of the found file

The CInternetException Class

When an error occurs during a WinInet Internet session, it's an object of the CInternetException class that usually reports it. Many WinInet functions throw CInternetException objects, so your program should supply try and catch program blocks to ensure that the exceptions are handled properly. Because WinInet derives CInternetException from MFC's CException class, you can use the inherited member functions to obtain information about a specific exception.

Writing an HTTP Application

Just about every Internet user on the planet uses an HTTP application to browse the Web, whether they know it or not. It's the HTTP portion of a Web browser that reads HTML code from a Web page and converts it to the page's visual representation. Because HTTP is so important, in this section you'll learn about basic HTTP programming with WinInet.

If you don't consider the task of parsing (reading and interpreting) and rendering an HTTP document (a task that can't be handled with the WinInet classes), creating an HTTP application with WinInet is criminally easy, involving five main steps:

1. Start an Internet session.
2. Open the connection to the HTTP server.
3. Read the HTTP file from the server.
4. Close the HTTP connection.
5. Close the Internet session. In the following sections, you'll examine these steps in detail, as implemented using the WinInet classes.

Starting an Internet Session

No matter what type of Internet program you're writing with WinInet, the first step is to create an Internet session. To set up an Internet session, you create an object of the `CInternetSession` class:

```
CInternetSession session;
```

On a basic level, that's all there is to creating your Internet session. If you're an advanced Internet programmer, `CInternetSession`'s constructor provides additional control over the session through its many arguments, which all have default values. MFC declares the `CInternetSession` constructor like this:

```
CInternetSession(
    LPCTSTR pstrAgent = NULL,
    DWORD dwContext = 1,
    DWORD dwAccessType = INTERNET_OPEN_TYPE_PRECONFIG,
    LPCTSTR pstrProxyName = NULL,
    LPCTSTR pstrProxyBypass = NULL,
    DWORD dwFlags = 0);
```

Each of the constructor's arguments is described, in order, as follows. If you're interested in supplying any of these arguments to the `CInternetSession` constructor, please look for additional details in your Visual C++ online documentation.

`pstrAgent`	A pointer to the name of the application that owns the Internet session
`dwContext`	The context ID with which the session object will be associated
`dwAccessType`	The type of Internet access the session will use
`pstrProxyName`	The CERN proxy name if the access will be through a CERN proxy
`pstrProxyBypass`	A list of addresses that may be ignored during proxy access
`dwFlags`	Flags for selecting additional options

Opening the Connection to an HTTP Server

To establish a connection with an HTTP server, you can call the session object's `OpenURL()` function to read the HTML document from the given URL:

```
CHttpFile* httpFile =
    (CHttpFile*)internetSession.OpenURL(url);
```

The `OpenURL()` function actually has five arguments, all of which except the first have default values. The function's full signature looks like this:

```
CStdioFile* OpenURL(
    LPCTSTR pstrURL,
    DWORD dwContext = 1,
    DWORD dwFlags = INTERNET_FLAG_TRANSFER_ASCII,
    LPCTSTR pstrHeaders = NULL,
    DWORD dwHeadersLength = 0);
```

`OpenURL()`'s arguments are described in order below:

pstrURL	The URL from which to read
dwContext	A context value used with callback functions
dwFlags	File-handling flags
pstrHeaders	Headers to be sent to the server
dwHeadersLength	The length of the headers

How you handle the pointer returned by `OpenURL()` depends on the type of connection. With an FTP connection, the `OpenURL()` function returns a pointer to a `CStdioFile` object, which you must cast to a `CHttpFile` pointer.

After getting the file-object pointer, you can set the file's read-buffer size:

```
httpFile->SetReadBufferSize(4096);
```

Due to a bug in WinInet, before you can use the file object, you must set its buffer size by calling the file object's `SetReadBufferSize()` function.

Reading a File from an HTTP Server

Once you have your connection established, you can read from the file easily by calling the file object's `ReadString()` function:

```
CString string;
httpFile->ReadString(string);
```

The `ReadString()` function takes a reference to a `CString` object into which it places the string read from the file. An overloaded version of the function accepts a pointer to a string, as well as a value indicating the maximum number of characters to read as arguments. Because `ReadString()` may throw a `CInternetException` object, you should call this function from within a `try` program block.

Closing the Connection and Session

When you've finished with your HTTP session, you must close both the connection and the session:

```
httpFile->Close();
session.Close();
```

Creating an HTTP Session

Now that you know all the details, you might like to see those details put together into a block of source code that actually does something. The following source code creates an HTTP session that connects to an HTTP server and reads 100 lines of the default HTML file:

```
CString htmlLines[100];
CString url = "http://www.microsoft.com";

CInternetSession session;

try
{
    CHttpFile* file =
        (CHttpFile*)session.OpenURL(url);
    file->SetReadBufferSize(2046);

    for (int index=0; index<100; ++index)
        file->ReadString(htmlLines[index]);

    file->Close();
}
catch (CInternetException* pException)
{
    pException->ReportError();
}

session.Close();
```

Before you can access WinInet classes in a program, you must include the WinInet header file, afxinet.h. The header file declares the classes, functions, and constants used in WinInet programming.

Of course, the real trick is what you do with those HTML lines once you have them. Rendering an HTML document is an immense task. As an example, if you created an MFC AppWizard program with an OnLButtonDown() function that contained the code shown in the previous listing, when you clicked in the application's window, the program would connect to Microsoft's Web site and read 100 lines of HTML code from the default Web page. Of course, you won't see anything happening unless you do something with the HTML code the function reads.

Writing an FTP Application

Writing an FTP application that just connects to an FTP server and reads the root directory isn't much more complicated than connecting to an HTTP server and reading an HTML file. The basic steps are as follows:

1. Start an Internet session.
2. Open the connection to the FTP server.
3. Get the server's current directory.
4. Read file names from the directory.
5. Close the FTP connection.
6. Close the Internet session.

In the following sections, you'll examine these steps in detail, as implemented using the WinInet classes.

Opening an FTP Connection

Starting a WinInet Internet session for an FTP application is no different than starting one for an HTTP application. Just create an object of the `CInternetSession` class:

```
CInternetSession session;
```

To open an FTP connection to a server, call the session object's `GetFtpConnection()` function:

```
CFtpConnection* pConnection =
    session.GetFtpConnection(m_site);
```

The `GetFtpConnection()` function has five arguments. However, all but the first have default values. In the preceding code, `m_site` is a string containing the FTP server's address—for example, `ftp.microsoft.com`. The function's full signature looks like this:

```
CFtpConnection* GetFtpConnection(
    LPCTSTR pstrServer,
    LPCTSTR pstrUserName = NULL,
    LPCTSTR pstrPassword = NULL,
    INTERNET_PORT nPort = INTERNET_INVALID_PORT_NUMBER,
    BOOL bPassive = FALSE);
```

The five arguments are described in order as follows:

pstrServer	A string containing the server's name
pstrUserName	A string containing the user's login name
pstrPassword	A string containing the user's password
nPort	The server's TCP/IP port number
bPassive	A flag that sets active or passive mode

As an example, suppose you want to access a server named ftp.myserver.com with a user name of Casper and a password of The Ghost. Your call to GetFtpConnection() would look something like this:

```
CFtpConnection* pConnection =
    session.GetFtpConnection("ftp.myserver.com",
    "Casper", "The Ghost");
```

Of course, in a full-featured program, you'd use string variables for the server name, user name, and password, rather than hard-coded values as shown in the example. After all, what good is an FTP program that can connect to only one account on only one server?

Getting the Root Directory

Once you've established a connection with the server, minimally, you'll want to browse the root directory. The first step in accomplishing that task is to get the name of the root directory, which will probably always be "/". However, getting the directory from the server gives you a chance to use the CFtpConnection class's object GetCurrentDirectory() function:

```
CString directory;
succeeded = pConnection->
    GetCurrentDirectory(directory);
```

GetCurrentDirectory() returns the directory's name in the function's single argument, which is a reference to a CString object.

Reading a Directory

Now your application is ready to read the contents of the root directory, which is not unlike reading a directory in a regular non-Internet application. First, you create a CFtpFileFind object:

```
CFtpFileFind fileFind(pFtpConnection);
```

The class's constructor takes as its single argument a pointer to the `CFtpConnection` object.

Next, you call the `CFtpFileFind` object's `FindFile()` function, which returns a Boolean value indicating whether there was a file to find:

```
BOOL gotAFile = fileFind.FindFile();
```

If `FindFile()` returns `TRUE`, you know that the directory is not empty. (If it returns `FALSE`, there are no files in the directory.) You can then call `FindNextFile()` as many times as needed to read all the directory's file names:

```
gotAFile = fileFind.FindNextFile();
```

`FindNextFile()` returns a Boolean value that indicates whether there is another file to find. To read the entire directory, continually call `FindNextFile()` in a loop until the function returns `FALSE`. The entire process of reading file names from a directory on an FTP server looks like the following code:

```
CString fileName;
CFtpFileFind fileFind(pConnection);
BOOL gotAFile = fileFind.FindFile();
while (gotAFile)
{
    gotAFile = fileFind.FindNextFile();
    fileName = fileFind.GetFileName();
    // Do something with the file name.
}
```

Closing the Connection and Session

When you've finished with your FTP session, you must close both the connection and the session:

```
pConnection->Close();
session.Close();
```

Running the FTPAccessApp Application

Location: WinPrgS\Chap27\FTPAccessApp

Before you write a sample FTP application, it would be helpful for you to see what one can do. On this book's CD-ROM, you'll find the FTPAccessApp application, which really puts the WinInet FTP classes to the test. When you run the application, you see the window shown in Figure 27-2. The main window is divided into three columns that display the contents of any FTP directory you log onto.

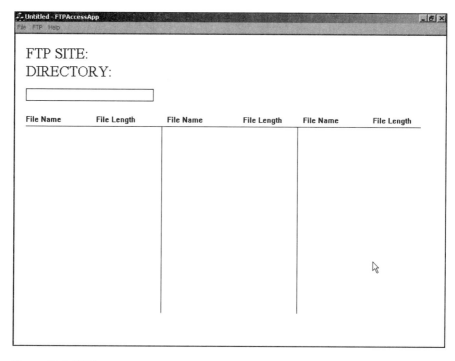

Figure 27-2: FTPAccessApp's main window will be your view into the Internet.

To get started, select the FTP menu's Connect command in the application. When you do, the Connect dialog box appears (see Figure 27-3), into which you can type the information needed to connect to an FTP server. (Microsoft's FTP server comes up as the default the first time you see the dialog box. To connect to Microsoft, just press Enter.) If your connection requires no password, simply enter the name of the FTP server and select OK. You'll then log onto the selected FTP server as an anonymous user.

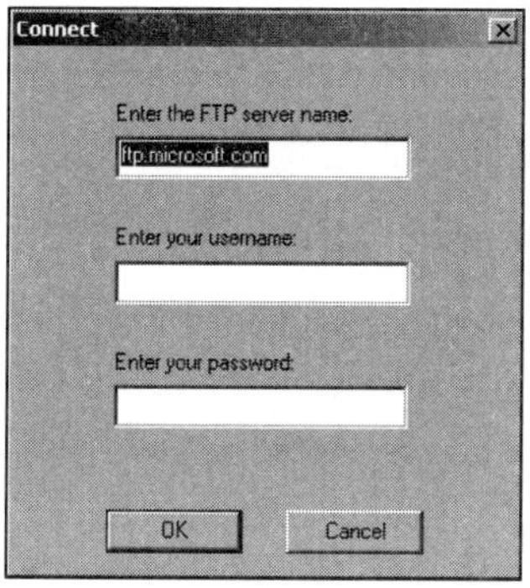

Figure 27-3: You choose an FTP server in the Connect dialog box.

Status messages in the upper-right corner of the window keep you informed as the program makes its connection and reads file names from the server. After the program completes reading the file names on the server, it displays the results in the window. One limitation of this simple example program is that it can display only 45 files. Any more than that and you're out of luck. (Fixing this limitation sounds like a good project for you folks who like to tinker.) Figure 27-4 shows FTPAccessApp after it logs onto Microsoft's server.

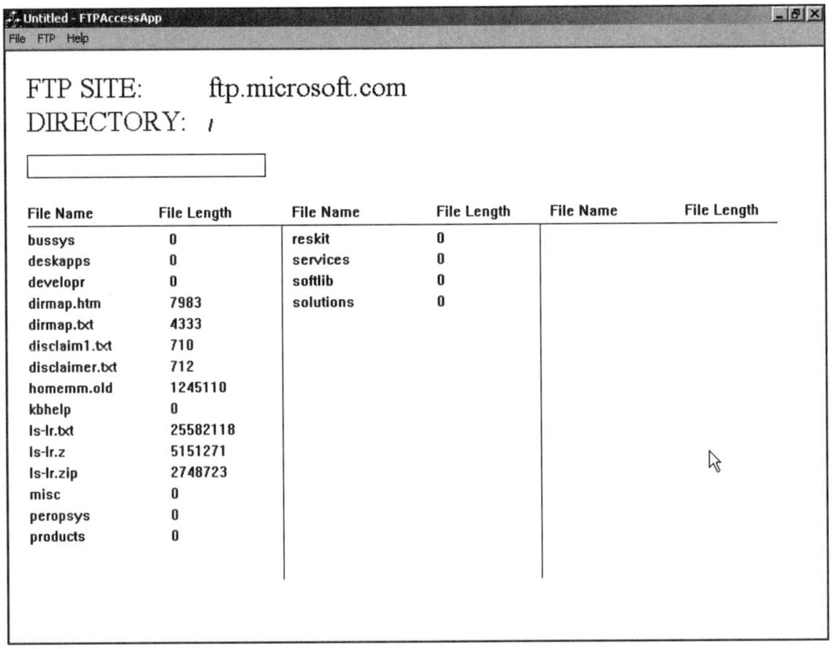

```
 Untitled - FTPAccessApp                                              _ | 8 | X |
File  FTP  Help

FTP SITE:       ftp.microsoft.com
DIRECTORY:   /

┌─────────────────┐
│                 │
└─────────────────┘

File Name      File Length     File Name      File Length     File Name      File Length
bussys           0             reskit           0
deskapps         0             services         0
developr         0             softlib          0
dirmap.htm       7983          solutions        0
dirmap.txt       4333
disclaim1.txt    710
disclaimer.txt   712
homemm.old       1245110
kbhelp           0
ls-lr.txt        25582118
ls-lr.z          5151271
ls-lr.zip        2748723
misc             0
peropsys         0
products         0
```

Figure 27-4: FTPAccessApp explores Microsoft's FTP server.

Now that you're logged onto a server, you can start to browse. To move to another directory, double-click the directory in the window. The entry turns red, the mouse cursor changes into an hourglass, and the program again negotiates with the server. After reading the file names for the new directory, the results appear on the screen. If no file names appear, the directory is empty.

The MOVE TO PREVIOUS DIRECTORY command becomes active when you're no longer on the root directory. You can double-click this command to move back up through the server's directory tree. The directory line near the top of the window keeps you informed of your current location.

As you browse through the server's directory, you may come across a file you want to download. No problem. Just right-click the file's entry. The file's name turns green, and FTPAccessApp asks whether you want to download the file (see Figure 27-5). Click OK to download the file, or click Cancel to terminate the download command. When the download is complete (it could take a while, depending on the size of the file), you'll find the file in FTPAccessApp's directory.

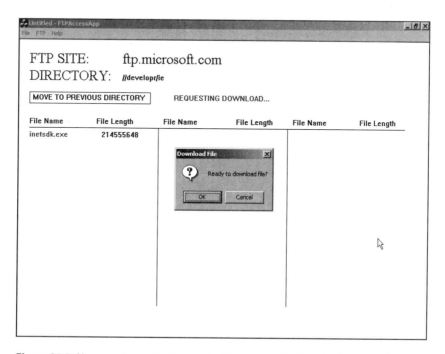

Figure 27-5: You can choose to download a file or abort the download command.

Creating the FTPAccessApp Sample Application

Now that you've seen the application work, in the following sections, you'll examine the source code to see how the application handles the FTP connection.

Examining the Member Variables

FTPAccessApp is an AppWizard-generated program, and virtually everything that happens in FTPAccessApp happens in the view class. Obviously, then, all the important member variables are declared in the view class's header file. Those declarations look like this:

```
CString m_fileNames[45];
DWORD m_fileLengths[45];
```

Part VI: Internet Programming

```
CString m_curDirectory;
CString m_site;
int m_fileCount;
CString m_password;
CString m_username;
```

The following list describes how the program uses each of these variables:

m_fileNames[]	A string array that holds the file names for the current directory
m_fileLengths[]	A DWORD array that holds the lengths of the files in the current directory
m_curDirectory	A string that holds the name of the current directory, complete with path
m_site	A string that holds the name of the currently accessed FTP server
m_fileCount	An integer that holds the number of files in the current directory
m_password	A string that holds the password for the current FTP connection
m_username	A string that holds the user name for the current FTP connection

FTPAccessApp initializes these member variables in the view class's constructor, which looks like this:

```
CFTPAccessAppView::CFTPAccessAppView()
{
    // TODO: add construction code here

    m_fileCount = 0;
    m_site = "";
    m_curDirectory = "";
    m_username = "";
    m_password = "";

    for (int x=0; x<45; ++x)
    {
        m_fileNames[x] = "";
        m_fileLengths[x] = 0;
    }
}
```

Creating the OnDraw() Function

Many of the variables you examined in the previous section contain information to be displayed on the screen. Because FTPAccessApp is an AppWizard-generated program, it draws its display in the view class's OnDraw() function, as shown here:

```
void CFTPAccessAppView::OnDraw(CDC* pDC)
{
    CFTPAccessAppDoc* pDoc = GetDocument();
    ASSERT_VALID(pDoc);

    // TODO: add draw code for native data here

    LOGFONT logFont;
    logFont.lfHeight = 32;
    logFont.lfWidth = 0;
    logFont.lfEscapement = 0;
    logFont.lfOrientation = 0;
    logFont.lfWeight = 400;
    logFont.lfItalic = 0;
    logFont.lfUnderline = 0;
    logFont.lfStrikeOut = 0;
    logFont.lfCharSet = ANSI_CHARSET;
    logFont.lfOutPrecision = OUT_DEFAULT_PRECIS;
    logFont.lfClipPrecision = CLIP_DEFAULT_PRECIS;
    logFont.lfQuality = PROOF_QUALITY;
    logFont.lfPitchAndFamily = VARIABLE_PITCH | FF_ROMAN;
    strcpy(logFont.lfFaceName, "Times New Roman");

    CFont font;
    font.CreateFontIndirect(&logFont);
    CFont* pOldFont = pDC->SelectObject(&font);

    pDC->TextOut(20, 20, "FTP SITE:");
    pDC->TextOut(200, 20, m_site);
    pDC->TextOut(20, 52, "DIRECTORY:");

    pDC->SelectObject(pOldFont);
    pDC->TextOut(200, 62, m_curDirectory);

    pDC->Rectangle(20, 98, 255, 120);
    if (m_curDirectory.GetLength() > 1)
        pDC->TextOut(26, 100,
            "MOVE TO PREVIOUS DIRECTORY");
```

```
            pDC->TextOut(20, 145, "File Name");
            pDC->TextOut(150, 145, "File Length");
            pDC->TextOut(280, 145, "File Name");
            pDC->TextOut(420, 145, "File Length");
            pDC->TextOut(530, 145, "File Name");
            pDC->TextOut(660, 145, "File Length");
            pDC->MoveTo(20, 165);
            pDC->LineTo(750, 165);
            pDC->MoveTo(270, 165);
            pDC->LineTo(270, 500);
            pDC->MoveTo(520, 165);
            pDC->LineTo(520, 500);

            for (int x=0; x<m_fileCount; ++x)
            {
                int col, row;

                if (x < 15)
                {
                    col = 20;
                    row = 170 + x * 20;
                }
                else if (x < 30)
                {
                    col = 280;
                    row = 170 + (x - 15) * 20;
                }
                else
                {
                    col = 540;
                    row = 170 + (x - 30) * 20;
                }

                pDC->TextOut(col, row, m_fileNames[x]);

                if ((m_fileNames[x] != ""))
                {
                    char s[80];
                    wsprintf(s, "%d", m_fileLengths[x]);
                    pDC->TextOut(col+140, row, s);
                }
            }
        }
```

This function creates a large font for the FTP SITE and DIRECTORY labels near the top of the window. After displaying these labels, `OnDraw()` returns to the default font, drawing the remaining labels and any file names that may be stored in the file array. `OnDraw()` draws lines with the `Rectangle()`, `MoveTo()`, and `LineTo()` functions. Near the end of the `OnDraw()` function, you can see that the program has to go through a few gyrations to get the file names to print properly in the different columns.

Creating the OnFtpConnect() Function

Before the application can display data in its `OnDraw()` function, it must read that data from an FTP site. When the user selects the FTP menu's Connect command, the view class's message map sets the `OnFtpConnect()` function into action:

```
void CFTPAccessAppView::OnFtpConnect()
{
    // TODO: Add your command handler code here

    CFTPDialog dialog(this);
    if (m_site == "")
        m_site = "ftp.microsoft.com";
    dialog.m_ftpEdit = m_site;
    dialog.m_nameEdit = m_username;
    dialog.m_passwordEdit = m_password;

    int result = dialog.DoModal();
    if (result != IDOK)
        return;

    m_site = dialog.m_ftpEdit;
    m_username = dialog.m_nameEdit;
    m_password = dialog.m_passwordEdit;
    BeginWaitCursor();
    OpenFTPDirectory("");
    EndWaitCursor();

    Invalidate();
}
```

This function is charged with the task of bringing up the Connect dialog box, retrieving the user's entries from said dialog box, and turning things over to the locally defined `OpenFTPDirectory()` function, which takes the user's dialog box entries and turns them into an actual FTP connection.

Notice how the call to `OpenFTPDirectory()` is sandwiched between calls to `BeginWaitCursor()` and `EndWaitCursor()` function calls. This is the magic that displays and removes the hourglass cursor, signaling the user that the system is tied up trying to accomplish something. In this case, that "something" is logging onto an FTP server.

In the preceding listing, the program creates a `CFTPDialog` dialog box, sets the dialog box's edit controls to the current FTP settings, and displays the dialog box with the `DoModal()` function. If the user exits the dialog box by clicking the OK button, the program reads the user's entries from the dialog box, transferring them to the member variables that store the FTP settings for the class. Calling the locally defined `OpenFTPDirectory()` function (you'll examine this function in the next section) creates the FTP connection and logs onto the server. The call to `Invalidate()` then causes the program to update its display with any data the program reads from the FTP server.

Creating the OpenFTPDirectory() Function

The `OpenFTPDirectory()` function overflows with cool FTP stuff, as shown here:

```
void CFTPAccessAppView::OpenFTPDirectory(CString directory)
{
    DisplayStatusMessage("ESTABLISHING CONNECTION...");

    try
    {
        CInternetSession session;
        CFtpConnection* pConnection =
            session.GetFtpConnection(m_site,
                m_username, m_password);
        BOOL succeeded;
        if (directory == "")
            succeeded = pConnection->
                GetCurrentDirectory(m_curDirectory);
        else
            succeeded =
             pConnection->SetCurrentDirectory(directory);
        if (succeeded)
        {
            ReadFileNames(pConnection);
            session.Close();
            delete pConnection;
            if (directory != "")
                m_curDirectory = directory;
        }
        else
            MessageBox(
                "Cannot access the\nrequested directory",
                "Open Directory",
                MB_OK | MB_ICONINFORMATION);
    }
    catch (CInternetException* pException)
    {
        pException->ReportError();
    }
}
```

First, the function calls the locally defined `DisplayStatusMessage()` function to tell the user that the program's working to establish a connection. Then it creates a `CInternetSession` object and establishes an FTP connection by calling the object's `GetFtpConnection()` member function.

The function then examines the directory variable, the value of which is passed into the function as a parameter. If `OpenFTPDirectory()` is called with directory equal to an empty string, the calling function wants to open the root directory, rather than move to a new directory. This causes a call to `GetCurrentDirectory()` rather than `SetCurrentDirectory()`, which is called if directory contains a directory name.

If everything goes OK, the program calls the locally defined ReadFileNames(), which does the actual file-name reading for the directory. When that function returns, OpenFTPDirectory() closes the session and deletes the connection object. If the program wasn't able to open the directory, it displays a message box notifying the user of the problem. If any CInternetException errors occur, they're handled in the catch program block by calling the exception object's ReportError() function.

Creating the ReadFileNames() Function

Whenever FTPAccessApp needs to read file names from a server's directory, it calls ReadFileNames(), which looks like this:

```
void CFTPAccessAppView::ReadFileNames(CFtpConnection* pFTP)
{
    DisplayStatusMessage("READING DIRECTORY...");

    int fileCount = 0;
    CFtpFileFind fileFind(pFTP);
    BOOL gotAFile = fileFind.FindFile();
    while (gotAFile && (fileCount < 45))
    {
        gotAFile = fileFind.FindNextFile();
        m_fileNames[fileCount] = fileFind.GetFileName();
        m_fileLengths[fileCount] = fileFind.GetLength();
        ++fileCount;
        if (fileCount == 45)
            MessageBox("Can't Display all files");
    }

    m_fileCount = fileCount;
}
```

This function starts off by displaying a status message in the window, after which it creates a CFtpFileFind object with which the function will examine the current server directory. The program calls the CFtpFileFind object's FindFile() and FindNextFile() functions to read in all the file names in the directory. If there are more than 45 files in the directory, the program presents a message box telling the user that the entire directory could not be read. When ReadFileNames() has done its stuff, the m_fileCount member variable will contain the number of files to display, and the m_fileNames[] and m_fileLengths[] arrays will contain the file information that the program received from the GetFileName() and GetLength() functions.

Creating the OnLButtonDblClk() Function

The user can move to a new directory by double-clicking the directory's name in FTPAccessApp's window. That double-click causes MFC to call the OnLButtonDblClk() function, which is associated with the

WM_LBUTTONDBLCLK message through the view class's message map. OnLButtonDblClk() looks like this:

```
void CFTPAccessAppView::OnLButtonDblClk(UINT nFlags, CPoint point)
{
    // TODO: Add your message handler code here
    //    and/or call default

    BeginWaitCursor();

    if ((point.x > 22) && (point.x < 253) &&
        (point.y > 97) && (point.y < 118))
        MoveToPreviousDirectory();

    int index, col, row;
    BOOL selectionOK =
        InitSelection(point, index, col, row);
    if (!selectionOK)
        return;

    CClientDC clientDC(this);
    clientDC.SetTextColor(RGB(255,0,0));
    clientDC.TextOut(col, row, m_fileNames[index]);

    CString targetDir =
        m_curDirectory + '/' + m_fileNames[index];

    OpenFTPDirectory(targetDir);

    EndWaitCursor();
    Invalidate();

    CView::OnLButtonDblClk(nFlags, point);
}
```

This function first displays the hourglass cursor, and then it checks the mouse click's coordinates to see whether the user double-clicked the MOVE TO PREVIOUS DIRECTORY button. If so, the MoveToPreviousDirectory() function takes over.

Otherwise, the program calls InitSelection() to check that the mouse click was on a valid entry in the window and to calculate the values needed by the program to manage the selected entry. Those values are stored in the index, col, and row variables, which hold the index of the selected item (its position in the file array), and the column and row, in pixels, at which the item's name appears on the screen.

The program then displays the selected file name in red, adds the selection to the current path, and calls OpenFTPDirectory() to open that new path, after which it turns off the wait cursor and calls Invalidate() to force an update of the screen.

Creating the OnRButtonDown() Function

When users want to download a file, they right-click its name in the application's window. This causes MFC to call the OnRButtonDown() function, which responds to WM_RBUTTONDOWN Windows messages, as shown here:

```
void CFTPAccessAppView::OnRButtonDown(UINT nFlags, CPoint point)
{
    // TODO: Add your message handler code here
    //    and/or call default

    BeginWaitCursor();

    int index, col, row;
    BOOL selectionOK =
        InitSelection(point, index, col, row);
    if (!selectionOK)
        return;

    CClientDC clientDC(this);
    clientDC.SetTextColor(RGB(0,128,0));
    clientDC.TextOut(col, row, m_fileNames[index]);

    DownloadFile(m_fileNames[index]);
    EndWaitCursor();
    Invalidate();

    CView::OnRButtonDown(nFlags, point);
}
```

In the function, the program first displays the hourglass cursor and then calls InitSelection() to check where the user clicked and to initialize those all-important index, col, and row variables you learned about in the previous section. With the user's click verified, OnRButtonDown() then displays the selected item in green and calls the locally defined DownloadFile() function to do the dirty work, after which the program turns off the wait cursor and updates the screen.

Creating the DownloadFile() Function

The DownloadFile() function, called from OnRButtonDown(), transfers a file from the current FTP server to the user's computer, as shown here:

```
void CFTPAccessAppView::DownloadFile(CString fileName)
{
    DisplayStatusMessage("REQUESTING DOWNLOAD...");

    try
    {
        CInternetSession session;
```

```cpp
        CFtpConnection* pConnection =
            session.GetFtpConnection(m_site);
        BOOL succeeded =
            pConnection->
            SetCurrentDirectory(m_curDirectory);
        if (!succeeded)
        {
            MessageBox("Couldn't set directory.",
                "Download File",
                MB_OK | MB_ICONEXCLAMATION);
            delete pConnection;
            session.Close();
            return;
        }

        CFtpFileFind fileFind(pConnection);
        BOOL fileFound = fileFind.FindFile(fileName);
        if (!fileFound)
        {
            MessageBox("Couldn't find file.",
                "Download File",
                MB_OK | MB_ICONEXCLAMATION);
            delete pConnection;
            session.Close();
            return;
        }

        int result =
            MessageBox("Ready to download file?",
                "Download File",
                MB_OKCANCEL | MB_ICONQUESTION);
        if (result == IDOK)
        {
            DisplayStatusMessage(
                "DOWNLOADING FILE.  PLEASE WAIT...");
            pConnection->GetFile(fileName, fileName);
            MessageBox("File retrieved", "Download File",
                MB_OK | MB_ICONEXCLAMATION);
        }

        delete pConnection;
        session.Close();
    }
    catch (CInternetException* pException)
    {
        pException->ReportError();
    }
}
```

As you can see, the function first creates a `CInternetSession` object and then calls the object's `GetFtpConnection()` function to create the connection object. If this process fails, the function displays an error message box and returns.

If the program creates the session and connection successfully, it attempts to find the requested file on the server. Because the user can select only files that FTPAccessApp already found on the server, it's unlikely that this process will fail, but if it does, the user gets a message box, and the function returns.

If all goes well up to this point, the program displays a message box that asks users whether they want to download the file, giving them a chance to change their minds (maybe the right-click was accidental or on the wrong file). If the user wants to proceed, the program displays a status message and calls the connection object's GetFile() function to retrieve the file from the server. Finally, DownloadFile() displays a "File Retrieved" message box, deletes the connection object, and closes the session.

Creating the MoveToPreviousDirectory() Function

If the user clicks the MOVE TO PREVIOUS DIRECTORY command, program execution finds its way to the MoveToPreviousDirectory() function, shown as follows:

```
void CFTPAccessAppView::MoveToPreviousDirectory()
{
    if (m_curDirectory.GetLength() < 2)
        return;

    BeginWaitCursor();

    CClientDC clientDC(this);
    clientDC.SetTextColor(RGB(255,0,0));
    clientDC.TextOut(26, 100,
        "MOVE TO PREVIOUS DIRECTORY");

    int slash = m_curDirectory.ReverseFind('/');
    CString previousDir = m_curDirectory.Left(slash);
    OpenFTPDirectory(previousDir);

    EndWaitCursor();

    Invalidate();
}
```

Here, the program turns on the hourglass cursor, highlights the MOVE TO PREVIOUS DIRECTORY command in red, modifies the m_curDirectory string so that it contains the path to the previous directory, and calls OpenFTPDirectory() to do the directory change. Finally, the function returns the mouse cursor to normal and updates the window.

Creating the DisplayStatusMessage() Function

So that users don't get too antsy waiting for FTP commands to finish executing, FTPAccessApp displays status messages in the window. This way, users know that the program is at least doing something and hasn't locked up on them. Displaying a status message is as easy as calling the locally defined function `DisplayStatusMessage()`, which supplies the string to display:

```
void CFTPAccessAppView::DisplayStatusMessage(CString msg)
{
    CClientDC clientDC(this);
    clientDC.SelectStockObject(NULL_PEN);
    clientDC.Rectangle(300, 100, 800, 120);
    clientDC.SetTextColor(RGB(255,0,0));
    clientDC.TextOut(300, 100, msg);
}
```

Note

Notice that when you call `SelectStockObject()` to replace a DC's drawing object with a system-defined one, you don't have to restore the DC with the original object.

The `DisplayStatusMessage()` function creates a device context for the window, erases the old message with a white rectangle, changes the text color to red, and displays the given string. What could be easier?

Creating the InitSelection() Function

`InitSelection()` is the last function in FTPAccessApp that you'll explore:

```
BOOL CFTPAccessAppView::InitSelection(CPoint point,
    int & index, int & col, int & row)
{
    if ((point.y < 170) || (point.y > 464))
        return FALSE;

    index = (point.y - 170) / 20;
    row = 170 + index * 20;
    col = 20;

    if (point.x > 520)
    {
        index += 30;
        col = 540;
    }
    else if (point.x > 270)
    {
        index += 15;
        col = 280;
    }
```

```
        if (index >= m_fileCount)
            return FALSE;

    return TRUE;
}
```

`InitSelection()`'s task is two-fold. First, the function must verify that the user's mouse click was over a valid file name in the window. Second, the function must determine the selected item's index (its position in the file name array), as well as the item's position on the screen. Because the `index`, `col`, and `row` variables are passed to the function as integer references, the function can directly change their contents on behalf of the calling function.

Summary

As you've learned, WinInet makes creating Internet applications almost as easy as creating applications that access only local files. Whether you want to write an HTTP, FTP, or Gopher Internet program, WinInet can make the process quicker and easier. With the Internet playing such an important role in desktop computing, the WinInet classes are an invaluable part of the MFC libraries.

Also discussed in this chapter:

▶ The `CInternetSession` class represents an Internet session.

▶ The `CHttpConnection`, `CFtpConnection`, and `CGopherConnection` classes represent connections to Internet servers.

▶ The `CHttpFile` class represents HTML files on an HTTP server.

▶ The `CFtpFileFind` class enables programs to locate files on a server, as well as to obtain information about the files.

▶ To create an HTTP application with WinInet, you create a `CInternetSession` object, create a `CHttpFile` object with the session object's `OpenURL()` function, and call the file object's `ReadString()` function to read the contents of the HTML file.

▶ To create an FTP application with WinInet, you create a `CInternetSession` object, create a `CFtpConnection` object with the session object's `GetFtpConnection()` function, and access the server's directory with a `CFtpFileFind` object.

▶ Many WinInet functions throw `CInternetException` objects in response to errors.

Chapter 28

Internet Explorer

In This Chapter

▶ The Internet Explorer components
▶ Creating a simple Web browser
▶ Using HTML dialog boxes
▶ Using Dynamic HTML
▶ Distributing the browser control
▶ Running a sample Web browser

The Internet's growing popularity, especially the popularity of the World Wide Web, has triggered a few changes in software development. One of the major changes has been in the development cycle of programs. New programs are popping up everywhere, and it seems like some programs have new versions released before you finish downloading a copy of the last version. The average time it takes between developing new versions has shortened, and many programs and patches are available for download from the Internet. Another change is that almost every program that appears these days has some connection to the Internet.

Internet Explorer is an example of these changes in software development. Since its first release, Internet Explorer has undergone many changes, with new versions and patches appearing almost monthly. Some of these changes represent changes in modern programming. The main change is that Internet Explorer comprises reusable components that are well-documented. This means that you can actually make your own Web browser using these reusable parts that Microsoft is freely distributing to everyone.

Note

Programming Internet Explorer is a complex task that cannot be fully explained in a single chapter. This chapter is only an introduction to the programming techniques required to create a basic Internet Explorer application. After you master the topics in this chapter, if you want to learn more, you should pick up a book that concentrates on Internet Explorer programming.

The Internet Explorer Components

The Internet Explorer components are more than an easy way to create a Web browser. They are a complete set of reusable objects that were specifically created for dealing with HTML files, which means that you can use the Internet Explorer components as all of the following:

- A Web browser
- A rich-content viewer
- An alternative help system
- HTML dialog boxes
- A scripting host
- An HTML parser

Note: The complete documentation, with examples for the Internet Explorer components, is available in the Internet SDK. This is a free download from http://msdn.microsoft.com.

Let's first look at the capabilities of the WebBrowser component and how it uses the WebBrowser objects, as shown in Figure 28-1. At the top level is the program — Internet Explorer. Internet Explorer is the framework, or container, required in order to use the other components. This framework is a relatively small program that provides a user interface to the Internet components. It uses a toolbar and menus to receive commands from the user, such as a request to return to a previously displayed page, signaled when a user clicks on the Back button. Internet Explorer sends this command to the WebBrowser component for processing.

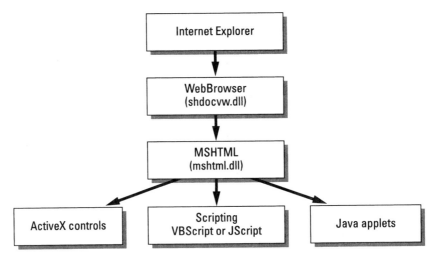

Figure 28-1: Internet Explorer uses components to display HTML pages.

The WebBrowser control—the file shdocvw.dll—makes up the next level of the component hierarchy. This object encapsulates the lower interfaces, providing a higher-level interface and several added features. For example, this control adds the functionality of in-place hyperlinking—the ability to view a link without starting a new instance of the browser object—and the Platform for Internet Content Selection (PICS). This control also maintains a history list, allowing browsers to move backward and forward through previously visited sites.

At the next level, we find MSHTML, or the mshtml.dll. This is the main HTML component, and it does all of the parsing and rendering of HTML files. MSHTML also handles HTML extensions and uses COM hosting to support Java applet hosting, plug-ins, ActiveX controls, and scripting engines, such as VBScript and JScript. When hosted by MSHTML, these COM objects also have the capability to access the Dynamic HTML object model. (The Dynamic HTML object model is described later in this chapter.)

MSHTML is an OLE Document object, or Active Document, that supports the OC96 specification, which basically means that it is a windowless control and doesn't have to be visible. This type of control can gain in performance because it doesn't have to use resources to draw itself or its components. Chapters 18 and 22 provide more information about ActiveX Controls.

Java applets and VBScript are examples of components that can be included in your program. Rather than rebuilding your program every time you want to change a feature, you can create parts of the program in Java or a scripting language. These can then be stored on a corporate Web site or another location on the Internet. Then, instead of distributing a new release of the program, you can simply update the linked Java applet or script.

You can use the same object model as MSHTML to create your own programs that access Java VM or the scripting engines in the same manner, without needing the WebBrowser control. The COM object model is covered in Chapter 18.

Creating a Skeleton Browser Application

The primary use of the WebBrowser object is to create a browser and add Internet browsing to your programs. As mentioned earlier in this chapter, all Internet functionality is built into the WebBrowser control. All that is left up to the programmer is creating the interface and tying the interface to the control. This is quite easy to do with the following steps:

1. Create a new program using AppWizard. This example is created as a dialog box-based program with context-sensitive help, and creatively named MyBrowser.

2. Open the dialog box with the ID of IDD_MYBROWSER_DIALOG and enlarge it. After all, a Web page has to fit in the dialog box, and the default size is too small.

3. Rename the default OK and Cancel buttons Load URL and Exit, respectively. Then, all the buttons can be rearranged at the top of the dialog box to leave more room for the Web Browser control.

4. Next to the buttons, insert an Edit Box for the user to insert URLs, and a label explaining what the Edit box is for. This layout can be seen in the working copy of the program shown in Figure 28-2.

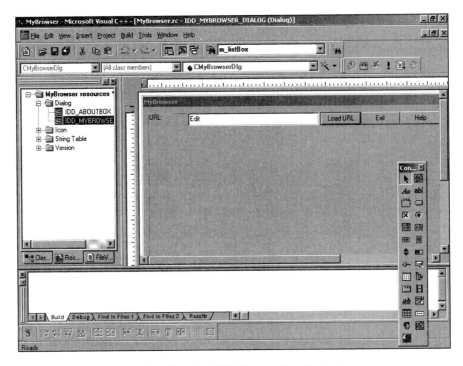

Figure 28-2: The main user interface for a Web Browser is quite simple.

5. From the Project menu, select Components and Controls in the Add to Project submenu. This opens the Components and Controls Gallery dialog box, which displays two folders, as shown in Figure 28-3.

6. Double-click the Registered ActiveX Controls folder to find a list of ActiveX controls available on the computer.

7. Double-click the Microsoft Web Browser control to add it to your program. Visual C++ will ask if you really want to add the control. Select OK.

8. The default CWebBrowser2 that is created works fine, so click OK again.

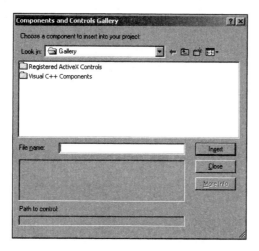

Figure 28-3: The Components and Controls Gallery dialog box lists ActiveX controls on your machine.

9. After closing the Components and Controls Gallery dialog box, select the Web Browser control from the palette and add it to the program. Enlarge the control to fill as much of the remaining space in the dialog box as possible.

10. Click the Save icon to save the work done so far.

After creating the user interface, all that is required for a working browser is a little bit of coding. The following steps outline all of the coding changes needed to make the browser work:

1. Double-click the Load URL button. `IDOK` and `BN_CLICKED` should be selected in the dialog box that pops up.

2. Select Add and Edit. Give the new function a name, such as `OnLoadURL()`, and select OK.

3. Add the following code to the function:

```
// Get a pointer to the browser
CWebBrowser2* pBrowser =
    (CWebBrowser2*)GetDlgItem(IDC_EXPLORER1);

// Get the URL from the text box
CString strURL;
GetDlgItemText(IDC_EDIT1, strURL);
COleVariant* pURL = new COleVariant(strURL);
COleVariant noArgument;

// Have the browser load the URL
pBrowser->Navigate2(pURL, &noArgument, &noArgument,
    &noArgument, &noArgument);
delete pURL;
```

4. Go to the top of the file and add the following code below the list of already included files:

```
#include "MyBrowser2.h"
#include <mshtml.h>
```

Compiling MyBrowser

MyBrowser is now ready to be compiled and run. The browser is a bit Spartan, but it does the job. Simply add a URL into the text box and click Load URL for the browser to find its first Web page. Figure 28-4 illustrates the new MyBrowser, displaying pages just as well as Internet Explorer, even though the window is a bit small.

Figure 28-4: MyBrowser displaying its first Web page

Location: `WinPrgS\Chap28\MyBrowser`

On this book's CD-ROM, you'll find the MyBrowser application. This program has a few more features than the Web browser shown in Figure 28-4. The other features of the MyBrowser application are described in the rest of this chapter.

The sample program included on the CD works fine, but you may want to modify the source and compile a new modified version. When you are ready to compile the program, you have a few variables to consider. Assuming that you have Visual C++ installed and the MyBrowser project copied on your computer, you can compile the program using the following steps:

1. Open the MyBrowser workspace into Visual C++. MyBrowser.dsw should be located in the MyBrowser folder.

2. Open the custsite.h file. This file includes some of the MFC source files, which may or may not be installed on your computer.

3. Change the line that includes the occimpl.h file. The line of code is currently set to include this header from the VC++ CD located in the G: drive.

4. Insert your VC++ CD into the computer and change the G: drive letter to your CD's drive letter. If you know that the MFC sources were installed, you can modify the statement to find the file in your installation of VC++.

5. Open MyBrowserDlg.cpp and go to line 411. This line of code loads the HTML file used in the About dialog box.

6. Change the location of the about.htm file, or modify the code to load a page from the Web. You can also use a resource, but you have to include the resource in your project before it can be used.

7. Click the Build button to compile the program.

After compiling the program, you can use the program as described in the section "Running MyBrowser." If you have any problems compiling the program, here are a couple of hints:

- An error creating the help file may mean that the Help Workshop is not installed. This will not adversely affect the program and can safely be ignored.

- Install InetSDK. This SDK includes new header files, as well as several more examples that you can explore.

One item to note is that it is possible to use Internet Explorer through OLE Automation, rather than using the WebBrowser component. This is important, because some of the properties and methods described in this chapter behave differently depending on whether you use the WebBrowser or are using Internet Explorer through OLE—accessing Internet Explorer through OLE adds functionality not available to the WebBrowser control.

Configuring the WebBrowser Control

After adding the WebBrowser control to your program, you will want to configure it to your needs. If you add the component to a dialog box, you can open the Microsoft Web Browser Property box. This allows you to change some of the basic properties listed in Table 28-1. The wrapper class provides methods to access these properties from your program.

Table 28-1 Basic WebBrowser Properties

Value	Description
AddressBar	Shows or hides the URL address bar, but is ignored by the WebBrowser component.
Offline	Sets the WebBrowser control to run in offline or online mode. In offline mode, the control will only read HTML pages from the local cache.
RegisterAsBrowser	This is generally set to false and determines if the WebBrowser should be registered as a top-level browser.
RegisterAsDropTarget	With a default value of false, this property determines if the object can receive objects through Window's drag-and-drop.
Silent	When set to the default value of false, this property allows dialog boxes to be displayed.
TheaterMode	Ignored by the WebBrowser, but allows Internet Explorer to use the full screen for displaying HTML pages.

Navigating with the WebBrowser Component

After configuring the WebBrowser component, you will need to provide a way to navigate HTML pages. Generally, you do this by adding menus, toolbars, and buttons to your application, which is explained in Part 2 of this book. The WebBrowser control includes several methods for navigation. When creating a browser, these methods are generally tied to buttons or menu commands (see Table 28-2).

Table 28-2 Important WebBrowser Methods

Value	Description
GoBack()	Navigates one item backward in the history list.
GoForward()	Navigates one item forward in the history list.
GoHome()	Navigates to the default home location. The default search page is set using the Control Panel or Internet Explorer's Options dialog box.
GoSearch()	Navigates to the default search page. The default search page is set using the Control Panel or Internet Explorer's Options dialog box.

Value	Description
Navigate()	Navigates to a target URL or path and file name locations.
Navigate2()	Extends the Navigate method to support browsing special folders, such as My Computer, along with standard URL or path and file name locations.

Each method comes with its own set of parameters. First, there is the Navigate() method:

```
HRESULT CWebBrowser2::Navigate(
    LPCTSTR URL, VARIANT* Flags,
    VARIANT* TargetFrameName, VARIANT* PostData,
    VARIANT* Headers,
);
```

As you can see, the full Navigate() method takes five parameters. Some of the parameters are optional, and you can use a COleVariant variable for those optional parameters you aren't using. A complete description of the parameters follows:

URL	A string expressing the URL, full path, or Universal Naming Convention (UNC) location and name of a resource to display.
Flags	An optional combination of constants (see Table 28-3). Some of the flags are only useful when using Internet Explorer as an OLE object instead of using the WebBrowser control.
TargetFrameName	An optional string expression representing a named HTML frame. Four reserved names can be used: _blank, _parent, _self, and _top.
PostData	An optional pointer to data to be sent to the server in a POST transaction. This parameter is ignored if the URL is not an HTTP URL.
Headers	An optional value specifying additional HTTP headers to send to the server; ignored if the URL is not an HTTP URL.

The value returned by the method will be one of S_OK, E_INVALIDARG or E_OUTOFMEMORY.

Table 28-3: Navigational Flags

Constant	Value	Description
navOpenInNewWindow	1	Opens the resource in a new window.
navNoHistory	2	Doesn't add the resource to the history list; instead, the new resource replaces the current one in the list.
navNoReadFromCache	4	Not used.
navNoWriteToCache	8	Not used.
navAllowAutoSearch	10	Only for use with IE. If the call to Navigate fails, an autosearch function will attempt to navigate to common root domains, or the URL will be passed to a search engine.
navBrowserBar	20	Only for use with IE, it attempts to have the current Explorer Bar navigate to the resource.

In most cases, you will use the Navigate() method. However, there may be times when you want to allow the user to navigate My Computer or the Desktop. These are represented as pointers to an item identifier list (PIDL). In these instances, you need to use the Navigate2() method:

```
HRESULT CWebBrowser2::Navigate2(
    VARIANT* URL, VARIANT FAR* Flags,
    VARIANT* TargetFrameName, VARIANT FAR* PostData,
    VARIANT FAR* Headers);
```

This method uses the same parameters as the Navigate() method, with the exception of URL. This variation of the URL parameter is a distinction in name only because it is also a string expressing the URL, full path, or Universal Naming Convention (UNC) location and name of a resource to display. Navigate2() also has the same return values as Navigate().

Not all of the navigation methods are appropriate for all applications. For example, the GoHome() method opens up the user's default home page. Only add the functionality that is needed for your application. The steps to adding a new button are quite similar to how the Load URL button was created earlier in this chapter. Simply add the button to the dialog box and create a function to respond to the BN_CLICKED message. The sample program included on the CD, MyBrowser, has GoHome and GoForward buttons already added to it.

PROBLEMS & SOLUTIONS

Implementing Parental Lockout

PROBLEM: *How do I implement a parental lockout for controlling what is seen on my browser?*

SOLUTION: PICS, the Platform for Internet Content Selection, defines a two-part standard used to control access to Web content. Primarily, the standard is concerned with minors accessing adult content, but a little creativity can be used with the standard to implement other uses.

PICS only presents a system for creating a rating system. It does not rate, or tell you how to rate, your content. It only provides a standard that allows content developers to tell a browser what rating system is being used and the rating of the content. The particular rating system is up to the developer. For example, the content developer could add the following META tag to an HTML page header:

```
<HEAD><HEAD>
<TITLE>Corporate Home Page</TITLE>
<META http-equiv="PICS-Label" content='(PICS=1-1
 "http://www.rsac.org/ratingsv01.html"
 l true comment "RSACi North America Server"
 for "http://www.mydomain.com/default.html"
 on "1997.12.01T22:48-0800"
 r (n 0 s 0 v 1 l 0))'>
</HEAD>
```

In this example, the content developer is using RSAC, the rating system developed by the Recreation Software Advisory Council. This rating system comprises four subsystems used to rate nudity, sex, violence, and language. Each one of these has its own value listed in the header.

The RSAC rating system is a good example of a rating system supported by Microsoft and used by Internet Explorer. You can find out more about this system by visiting www.rsac.org. You can also look at the file rsaci.rat, which is used by IE to describe the ratings. PICS does not, however, require that you use this system. You can just as easily create your own system based on the Motion Picture Association of America's rating system. Then, you could give your site a G, PG, PG-13, R, or NC-17 rating.

Because PICS is simply a standard for any type of rating, you could try to devise a system that has nothing to do with adult content. You could, for example, create a system that blocks out content if it is too cute or geeky. Suppose you have a Web site for a shareware program you are distributing. You could rate this content so that owners of the shareware copy are blocked out, while owners of the full version have complete access to your site. (Of course, there would also be those hackers who would bypass this simple security measure by using a browser that doesn't use your rating system. But the hacker would have to know where your documentation was located.)

Continued

In order to use PICS, you have to use the Internet Ratings API functions listed in Table 28-4 and add content labels. Content labels are easy to add to HTML pages using any of the HTML authoring programs available.

Table 28-4   Internet Ratings API Functions

Function	Description
`RatingAccessDeniedDialog()`	Displays a dialog box when a user has been denied access to a page, and may allow the supervisor to override the denial.
`RatingAccessDeniedDialog2()`	Displays a dialog box when a user has been denied access to a page, and may allow the supervisor to override the denial. If a modal dialog box is already displayed for the same parent, details from this function are added to the existing dialog box.
`RatingCheckUserAccess()`	Compares a PICS rating with the user-defined settings to determine whether to display the page.
`RatingEnable()`	Enables or disables ratings.
`RatingEnabledQuery()`	Determines whether ratings are being used.
`RatingFreeDetails()`	Frees the pointer of ratings information.
`RatingObtainCancel()`	Cancels a call to `RatingObtainQuery`.
`RatingObtainQuery()`	Requests and compares ratings information from various locations.
`RatingSetupUI()`	Displays a dialog box allowing a supervisor to set restriction levels.

Implementing the API functions in your program is not as simple as adding an HTML tag to a document. The first step to using the Internet Ratings API is to have the supervisor set the ratings level for the browser. Internet Explorer allows the user to set options using the Content Advisor dialog box, shown in Figure 28-5. A user can change the RSAC settings for the content ratings they want displayed. There is also an option to automatically block content that isn't rated. You may want to provide similar functionality for your program, or hard-code the settings.

Continued

Chapter 28: Internet Explorer

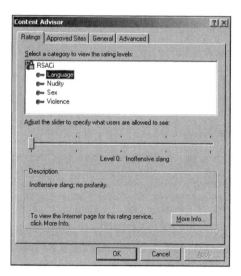

Figure 28-5: Content ratings can be changed using a dialog box.

After setting the PICS ratings, your program will need to implement the Internet Ratings API functions. The typical sequence for this is listed below:

1. The browser calls `RatingEnabledQuery()` to see if content ratings are to be used.

2. If ratings are being used, the browser calls `RatingObtainQuery()` with a URL to search for listings of ratings. `RatingCheckUserAccess()` is called if a rating is found for the URL.

3. The browser searches the downloading content for a rating to check using `Rating CheckUserAccess()`.

4. If a content label isn't found on the page, `RatingCheckUserAccess()` is called with a `NULL` value to see if the user can access unrated content.

5. After both `RatingObtainQuery()` and `RatingCheckUserAccess()` have been called, the browser should have at least one access-denied or access-allowed report. The browser should defer to the value returned by `RatingObtainQuery()`.

6. The `RatingAccessDeniedDialog()` function is called, which may allow the user to override the initial denial.

    The browser will display the content if access is allowed.

This list shows one of the benefits of using the WebBrowser control over MSHTML — it already incorporates the Internet Ratings API. For more information on PICS, check out the full documentation at www.w3.org/PICS/.

Using HTML Dialog Boxes

HTML can also be used to create dialog boxes. There are two good examples of HTML dialog boxes in Internet Explorer 5. The first example is the About dialog box shown in Figure 28-6. This dialog box uses Dynamic HTML to display copyright information if the user clicks the link.

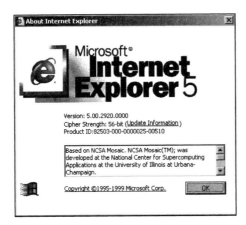

Figure 28-6: Internet Explorer presents information using HTML dialog boxes.

Another example is the Find dialog box shown in Figure 28-7. While this appears as a normal dialog box, Microsoft claims that it is also an HTML dialog box.

Figure 28-7: HTML dialog boxes can also appear as standard dialog boxes.

In order to implement HTML dialog boxes, you will need to access the `ShowHTMLDialog()` function included in MSHTML. After dynamically loading MSHTML with the `LoadLibrary()` function, calling `GetProcAddress()` acquires the address of `ShowHTMLDialog()`. MyBrowser illustrates using this call to show the HTML About dialog box shown in Figure 28-8, instead of the standard MFC dialog box. In order to test out this function, right-click the title

Chapter 28: Internet Explorer

bar. The shortcut menu that pops up includes an option for viewing the About box. The following code demonstrates these procedures:

```
void CMyBrowserDlg::OnSysCommand(UINT nID, LPARAM lParam)
{
    if ((nID & 0xFFF0) == IDM_ABOUTBOX)
    {
#if 0
        //standard call to a regular About dialog box
        CAboutDlg dlgAbout;
        dlgAbout.DoModal();
#endif
        //use an html dialog box instead
        HINSTANCE hiMSHTML = LoadLibrary(TEXT("MSHTML.DLL"));

        if(hiMSHTML)
        {
            //SHOWHTMLDIALOGFN is defined in mshtmhst.h
            SHOWHTMLDIALOGFN *pfnShowHTMLDialog;

            pfnShowHTMLDialog = (SHOWHTMLDIALOGFN*)
                GetProcAddress( hiMSHTML,
                    TEXT("ShowHTMLDialog"));

            if(pfnShowHTMLDialog)
            {
                // parameter intializiation
                IMoniker *pmk;
                TCHAR    szTemp[MAX_PATH*2];
                OLECHAR  bstr[MAX_PATH*2];

                //for a hardcoded file name
                lstrcpy(szTemp,
                    TEXT("file:D:/Chapter28/MyBrowser/about.htm"));

                LocalToBSTR(bstr, szTemp, ARRAYSIZE(bstr));

                CreateURLMoniker(NULL, bstr, &pmk);

                if(pmk)
                {
                    HRESULT  hr;
                    VARIANT  varArgs, varReturn;

                    VariantInit(&varReturn);

                    varArgs.vt = VT_BSTR;
                    //send a list of Stooges to the dialog box
                    varArgs.bstrVal SysAllocString
                        (L"Larry;Moe;Curly;Shem");
```

```cpp
            hr = (*pfnShowHTMLDialog)(NULL, pmk,
                &varArgs, NULL, &varReturn);
            VariantClear(&varArgs);
            pmk->Release();

            //display the returned information
            if(SUCCEEDED(hr))
                {
                switch(varReturn.vt)
                    {
                    case VT_BSTR:
                        {
                        //display the Stooge's name
                        TCHAR szData[MAX_PATH];
                        BSTRToLocal(szData,
                            varReturn.bstrVal,
                            ARRAYSIZE(szData));

                        wsprintf(szTemp, TEXT
                          ("The new stooge is \"%s\"."),
                          szData);

                        VariantClear(&varReturn);
                        }
                        break;

                    default:
                        lstrcpy(szTemp, TEXT
                          ("Cancel was selected."));
                        break;
                    }
                    MessageBox(szTemp, TEXT
                        ("HTML Dialog Sample"),
                        MB_OK | MB_ICONINFORMATION);
                }
            else
                MessageBox(TEXT
                  ("ShowHTMLDialog Failed."),
                  TEXT("HTML Dialog Sample"),
                  MB_OK | MB_ICONERROR);
            }
        }

        FreeLibrary(hiMSHTML);
    }
    }
    else
    {
        CDialog::OnSysCommand(nID, lParam);
    }
}
```

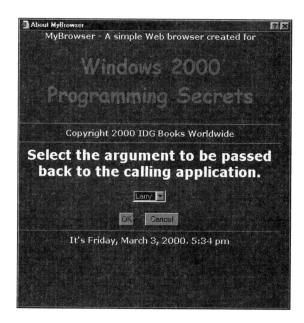

Figure 28-8: An HTML About dialog box appears for MyBrowser.

This same code can be easily added to any program to enable the addition of HTML dialog boxes. All that is required is to initialize the parameters of ShowHTMLDialog():

```
typedef HRESULT STDAPICALLTYPE SHOWHTMLDIALOGFN(
    HWND hwndParent,
    IMoniker *pmk,
    VARIANT *pvarArgIn,
    TCHAR* pchOptions,
    VARIANT *pvarArgOut
);
```

As you can see, the ShowHTMLDialog() function takes five parameters:

hwndParent	A handle for the parent window, or NULL for dialog boxes that aren't owned. NULL values are good when you don't want the calling window to be disabled.
pmk	A pointer to an IMoniker interface identifying the HTML source.
pvarArgIn	Optionally NULL, pvarArgIn points to a VARIANT filled with parameters being passed to the dialog box.

pchOptions	An optional NULL pointer to a string containing a combination of values separated by ';'. Table 28-5 lists the various features available as options.
pvarArgOut	An optional NULL pointer to the data returned from the dialog box

Table 28-5 Optional Features for HTML Dialog Boxes

Syntax	Description
`center:[yes | no | 1 | 0]`	Specifies whether to center the dialog box in the desktop. The default is yes.
`dialogHeight:number`	Sets the dialog box's height.
`dialogLeft:number`	Sets the left of the dialog box relative to the desktop.
`dialogTop:number`	Sets the top of the dialog box relative to the desktop.
`dialogWidth:number`	Sets the dialog box's width.

Including an HTML Resource

In order to access the HTML file that you use in your dialog box, you will probably want to make it a resource. This makes the HTML file easy to find and keeps the user from accidentally modifying the file. Then, the res: protocol, as opposed to http: or file:, is used to access the resource. Of course, only a few functions, such as `ShowTMLDialog()`, support the protocol. You can't navigate to a resource. Other functions such as `FindResource()` and `LocalResource()`, which are used to work with resources, can use an `lptype` of `RT_HTML` to locate an HTML resource.

You can simply include an HTML resource, such as MyProgramHomePage.htm, into your application's resource script. The resource will then be listed in your script as something similar to the following:

```
HTML_RESOURCE  23  DISCARDABLE  "MyProgramHomePage.htm"
```

`HTML_RESOURCE` is the resource identifier. Visual C++ uses the value of 23 for an HTML resource type, so you may see HTML in place of 23 for other compilers and future releases of Visual C++. Using the current version of VC++, opening the file for editing will open an editor window displaying the file's source; you may want to use another program for editing the HTML.

Working in the Dialog Box

A dialog box that displays only static information has limited usefulness. Eventually, you will want to send information or retrieve a value from the user. For example, you may want to fill a list box with values for the user to select. The following code listing is a bit of JScript from the about.htm file used in MyBrowser. It illustrates how to fill a list box, or *select element* as it is called in HTML, named `listOptions` with the values sent to the dialog box:

```
//get the arguments
var arrArgs = new Array();
arrArgs = window.dialogArguments.split(";");

//clear the list
listOptions.options.length = 0;

//add the arguments to the list
var index;
index = 0;
while(index < arrArgs.length)
{
   var tempOption = new Option(arrArgs[index]);
   listOptions.options[listOptions.options.length] =
      tempOption;
   index++;
}

//select the first argument
listOptions.options[0].selected = true;

//set a default return value
window.returnValue = 0;
```

In this example, a default `returnValue` of zero is set. This value will need to be changed when the user selects one of the items in the list. This value is then retrieved from the `pvarArgOut` parameter when the `ShowHTMLDialog()` function returns. Figure 28-9 shows a value being returned from the About box of MyBrowser.

Figure 28-9: HTML dialog boxes can return values to MyBrowser.

Using Dynamic HTML

Dynamic HTML (DHTML) is an extension to standard HTML that allows an HTML author to change a document after it has been loaded into the browser. The browser then reformats and displays the content using styles and scripts contained in the HTML page. Because the browser handles all of this, nothing is sent back to the server, and the whole process is faster than using conventional HTML.

Note

Currently, there isn't an accepted standard to Dynamic HTML. Netscape and Microsoft both have their own Dynamic HTML extensions. As this chapter is devoted to Microsoft's Internet Explorer components, it will also use Microsoft's Dynamic HTML. For more information on this topic, take a look at *Dynamic HTML* by Shelley Powers, published by IDG Books Worldwide.

Dynamic HTML uses an object model based on HTML tags. This object model gives the browser and HTML author access to virtually everything on the page. The HTML elements on the page are translated to objects with properties and methods. Other objects, such as ActiveX components, are also included in the model — to be modified by and to modify other objects. For a complete description of the object model, including all of the objects, properties, and models, check out the documentation in the Internet SDK.

Note

Dynamic HTML allows you to turn over some of your application's programming needs to Web page developers.

Introducing the DHTML Object Model

Applications can access the Dynamic HTML object model using interfaces based on `IDispatch`. `IDispatch` is an interface that allows one application to tell another application what methods are available for use. In other words, the methods available can vary from program to program, but they work in basically the same way. `IHTMLDocument2` is a wrapper class with interface maps to the document object. Essentially, this allows you to access all of the different tags that may be on an HTML page. Table 28-6 lists the dynamic HTML objects and their corresponding `IHTMLDocument2` interfaces.

Table 28-6   Dynamic HTML to IHTMLDocument2 Object Mapping

Object	Interface
A	IHTMLAnchorElement
AREA	IHTMLAreaElement
areas	IHTMLAreasCollection
BASE	IHTMLBaseElement

Object	Interface
BASEFONT	IHTMLBaseFontElement
BGSOUND	IHTMLBGsound
BODY	IHTMLBodyElement
BR	IHTMLBRElement
BUTTON	IHTMLButtonElement
CAPTION	IHTMLTableCaption
COL	IHTMLTableCol
COLGROUP	IHTMLTableCol
COMMENT	IHTMLCommentElement
DD	IHTMLDDElement
DIV	IHTMLDivElement
DL	IHTMLDListElement
document	IHTMLDocument, IHTMLDocument2
DT	IHTMLDTElement
elements	IHTMLElementCollection
EMBED	IHTMLPluginsCollection
event	IHTMLEventObj
FIELDSET	IHTMLFieldSetElement
filters	IHTMLFiltersCollection
FONT	IHTMLFontElement
FORM	IHTMLFormElement
FRAME	IHTMLFrameElement
frames	IHTMLFramesCollection2
FRAMESET	IHTMLFrameSetElement
history	IOmHistory
HR	IHTMLHRElement
IFRAME	IHTMLIFrameElement
INPUT of type file	IHTMLInputFileElement
INPUT of type hidden	IHTMLInputHiddenElement
INPUT of type image	IHTMLInputImage
INPUT of type radio	IHTMLOptionButtonElement

Continued

Table 28-6 *(continued)*

Object	Interface
INPUT of type reset	IHTMLInputButtonElement or submit
INPUT of type text	IHTMLInputTextElement
ISINDEX	IHTMLIsIndexElement
LABEL	IHTMLLabelElement
LEGEND	IHTMLLegendElement
LI	IHTMLLIElement
LINK	IHTMLLinkElement
location	IHTMLLocation
MAP	IHTMLMapElement
MARQUEE	IHTMLMarqueeElement
META	IHTMLMetaElement
navigator	IOmNavigator
NEXTID	IHTMLNextIdElement
OBJECT	IHTMLObjectElement
OL	IHTMLOListElement
OPTION	IHTMLOptionElement
P	IHTMLParaElement
screen	IHTMLScreen
SCRIPT	IHTMLScriptElement
SELECT	IHTMLSelectElement
selection	IHTMLSelectionObject
SPAN	IHTMLSpanFlow
style	IHTMLRuleStyle, IHTMLStyle
STYLE	IHTMLStyleElement
styleSheet	IHTMLStyleSheet, IHTMLStyleSheetRule, IHTMLStyleSheetRulesCollection, IHTMLStyleSheetsCollection
TABLE	IHTMLTable
TBODY	IHTMLTableSection
TD	IHTMLTableCell

Object	Interface
TEXTAREA	IHTMLTextAreaElement
TextRange	IHTMLTxtRange
TH	IHTMLTableCell
THEAD	IHTMLTableSection
TFOOT	IHTMLTableSection
TITLE	IHTMLTitleElement
TR	IHTMLTableRow
UL	IHTMLUListElement
userProfile	IHTMLOpsProfile
window	IHTMLDialog or IHTMLWindow2

The IHTMLDocument2 class, detailed in Table 28-7, also includes a few additional interfaces to make programming easier, such as the IHTMLElement interface, which is a generic interface for any HTML tags. These interfaces allow you to access a group of related elements, rather than just a specific element. An example of using ITHMLElement is found in MyBrowser.

Table 28-7 All-Purpose IHTMLDocument2 Interfaces

Interface	Applicable Elements
IHTMLElement	All element objects
IHTMLHeaderElement	Any header element (H1 to H6)
IHTMLImgElement	Common properties of IMG and INPUT of type images
IHTMLListElement	OL or UL common properties

Almost everything that can be done to the object model from your application can be done using scripts. This makes it a good idea to prototype and test what you are doing using a script.

Accessing the Document Interface

In order to access the document model, you must obtain an IHTMLDocument2 interface. This is quite easy to do, but how you do it depends on the type of application host you are using.

Using a WebBrowser control, you can obtain a pointer to the current document in two steps. First, call the control's `get_Document()` method to obtain an `IDispatch` pointer. Then call `QueryInterface()` on the pointer to request `IID_IHTMLDocument2`. The following code illustrates how to access a document's interface to change the background color of an HTML page. Simply click the Change Background button at the bottom of the page, and this function changes the color using the Dynamic HTML model:

```
void CMyBrowserDlg::OnChangeBackground()
{
// TODO: Add your control notification handler code here
    CWebBrowser2* pBrowser =
         (CWebBrowser2*)GetDlgItem( IDC_EXPLORER1 );

    IDispatch* pDisp = pBrowser->GetDocument();

    if (pDisp != NULL )
    {
       IHTMLDocument2* pHTMLDocument2;
       HRESULT hr;
       hr = pDisp->QueryInterface(IID_IHTMLDocument2,
                          (void**)&pHTMLDocument2 );
       if (hr == S_OK)
       {
          VARIANT vColor;
          vColor.vt = VT_INT;
          vColor.lVal = 0xFFF8DC;
          hr = pHTMLDocument2->put_bgColor(vColor);

          pHTMLDocument2->Release();
       }
       pDisp->Release();
    }

}
```

The process is quite similar when you are using MSHTML. However, you will need to create an object using `CoCreateInstance()` to get an object you can use to call `QueryInterface()`. The `CWebBrowser2` class already includes an object when using the WebBrowser control.

Using the Object Model

Once you have a handle on the object model, you can use it to change the content of the current document. This can be done either using a script or from your application. For example, you can change the background color of a document using the following JavaScript code:

```
document.bgColor = "#FFF8DC";
```

You can also use the following code to produce the same result:

```
VARIANT vColor;
vColor.vt = VT_INT;
vColor.lVal = 0xFFF8DC;
hr = pHTMLDocument2->put_bgColor(vColor);
```

Extending the DHTML Object Model

The WebBrowser component allows you to extend the DHTML object model. By extending HTML, you can add functionality to scripts that will be run on the browser. Any function or method that you have in your program can be accessed through the object model. This is done using the window object's external object. For example, you may be creating a statistics program and want to show a sample calculation. Because the function you want to use isn't in the VBScript or JScript library, you can add `ComplexStatisticalFunction()` to your program using an `IDispatch` interface. The script in the HTML page will call `ComplexStatisticalFunction()` using a call similar to `Variable = window.external.ComplexStatisticalFunction()`.

The best way to use the `IDispatch` interface is to create your own to extend the `IDispatch` class. The following code presents a simple `IDispatch` class that can be used to extend the Dynamic HTML object model:

```
#include "stdafx.h"
#include "idisp.h"


// Since there is only one extension, the first
// I will use constants
const    WCHAR pszFirstExtend[10]=L"first";
#define DISPID_FirstExtend 20001


/*
 * Constructors and Destructors
 */

CMyIDispatch::CMyIDispatch( void )
{
   //initialize the counter
   m_ExtensionCounter = 0;
   m_cRef = 0;
}

CMyIDispatch::~CMyIDispatch( void )
{
   ASSERT( m_cRef == 0 );
}
```

```c
/*
 * Implementation for virtual functions hanging around
 * from IUnKnown.
 */

STDMETHODIMP CMyIDispatch::QueryInterface(
              REFIID riid, void **ppv )
{
    *ppv = NULL;

    if ( IID_IDispatch == riid )
    {
        *ppv = this;
    }

    if ( NULL != *ppv )
    {
        ((LPUNKNOWN)*ppv)->AddRef();
        return NOERROR;
    }

    return E_NOINTERFACE;
}


STDMETHODIMP_(ULONG) CMyIDispatch::AddRef(void)
{
    return ++m_cRef;
}

STDMETHODIMP_(ULONG) CMyIDispatch::Release(void)
{
    return -m_cRef;
}


/*
 * Implementation for IDispatch functions
 */
STDMETHODIMP CMyIDispatch::GetTypeInfoCount(UINT*)
{
   return E_NOTIMPL;
}

STDMETHODIMP CMyIDispatch::GetTypeInfo(UINT,
              LCID, ITypeInfo**)
{
   return E_NOTIMPL;
}

/*
 * Implementation required for extending Dynamic HTML
```

Chapter 28: Internet Explorer

```c
 * the first function goes through the list of IDs
 * to find which ones are valid extensions handled by
 * the application
 */
STDMETHODIMP CMyIDispatch::GetIDsOfNames(
                REFIID riid,
                OLECHAR** rgszNames,
                UINT cNames,
                LCID lcid,
                DISPID* rgDispId)
{
   HRESULT hr;
   UINT    i;

   hr = NOERROR;    // Assume success

   // check for extension
   for ( i=0; i < cNames; i++)
   {
      if ( 2 == CompareString( lcid, NORM_IGNOREWIDTH,
         (char*)pszFirstExtend, 3,
         (char*)rgszNames[i], 3 ) )
      {
         rgDispId[i] = DISPID_FirstExtend;
      }
      else
      {
         // set return code for unknown id's
         hr = ResultFromScode(DISP_E_UNKNOWNNAME);
         rgDispId[i] = DISPID_UNKNOWN;
      }
   }
   return hr;
}

STDMETHODIMP CMyIDispatch::Invoke(
                DISPID dispIdMember,
                REFIID, LCID,
                WORD wFlags,
                DISPPARAMS* pDispParams,
                VARIANT* pVarResult,
                EXCEPINFO*,
                UINT* puArgErr)
{

   // This first extension simply returns the
   // number of times the extension was called
   if ( dispIdMember == DISPID_FirstExtend )
   {
      if ( wFlags & DISPATCH_PROPERTYGET )
      {
         if ( pVarResult != NULL )
         {
```

```
                VariantInit(pVarResult);
                pVarResult->vt = VT_UINT;
                pVarResult->lVal = ++m_ExtensionCounter;
            }
        }
    }

    return S_OK;
}
```

The `CMyIDispatch` class in this example creates a simple counter extension to the Dynamic HTML object model used by MyBrowser. Every time the extension, `first`, is called, an internal counter is incremented and returned.

In order to use this `IDispatch` extension, you must include it in your program. MyBrowser adds a new pointer, `m_pIDispatch`, for the `Idispatch`, which is initialized when the program starts up and calls `InitInstance()`. In order for the new `IDispatch` extension to work, idisp.h also has to be included in the MyBrowser source and header files. Another requirement is a class to capture events. A sample class called `CCustomOCCManager` is included with the InetSDK for just such a use.

```
BOOL MyBrowser::InitInstance()
{
    // Create a custom control manager class so we can overide the site
    CCustomOccManager *pMgr = new CCustomOccManager;

    //create a pointer to the IDispatch for use by the manager
    m_pIDispatch = new CMyIDispatch;

    //start the manager class up to catch events
    AfxEnableControlContainer(pMgr);    // The rest of your
                                        // initialization goes here
}
```

One final step is required before you can see your code in action. You will need to create an HTML file that uses the extension. Here is a sample HTML file:

```
<HTML>
<HEAD>
<TITLE>My First Dynamic HTML Extension</TITLE>

<script>
function runcounter()
{
  y=window.external.first;
  alert(y);
}
</script>
</HEAD>

Click the button to see how many times you have
used your first Dynamic HTML extension
```

```
<BR>
<input type=button
       value="extend"
       onClick="runcounter()">

</BODY>
</HTML>
```

After loading this file into MyBrowser, every time you click the button that this file displays, a function is called that uses the `first` extension. A message box then pops up displaying the number of times you have called the extension — that is, the number of times you clicked the button. Figure 28-10 shows the program with the page loaded and a dialog box on top displaying a number of clicks.

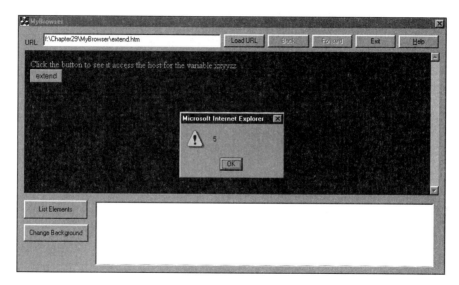

Figure 28-10: Accessing Dynamic HTML extensions

Distributing the Browser Control

When distributing your application, it is important to note that Internet Explorer must be installed on the target system in order to use the WebBrowser control. This control was first distributed with Internet Explorer version 3.0; it is available for 32-bit Windows, such as Windows 98 and Windows 2000, as well as Windows 3.1 and the Apple Macintosh.

Aside from checking to see if IE is installed, you may want to check to see if version 3.0 is already on the computer. You can develop applications that use functionality available starting with version 3.0. There are two ways of checking for a version: You can check the Registry or the version of the components installed.

Determining Versions with the Registry

Windows maintains a small database of initialization values and system settings called the Windows Registry. Information is stored hierarchically as strings and integers in multipart keys. For example, Internet Explorer has a **registry key** of `HKEY_LOCAL_MACHINE\Software\Microsoft\Internet Explorer`.

This key contains a version value, which is a string value containing the Internet Explorer 5.0 version in the following format:

`"<major version>.<minor version>.<build number>.<sub-build number>"`.

Internet Explorer 3.0*x* does not install this value, so if this value is retrieved and the major version is "5" and the minor version is "71," then Internet Explorer 5.0 is installed. To check for Internet Explorer 3.0*x*, use the Build value under this same key. For backwards compatibility, Internet Explorer 5.0 modifies or adds the Build value as well as the Version value. Internet Explorer 3.0*x*'s Build value is a string that contains a four-character build number. Internet Explorer 5.0's Build value is a larger string value in the following format:

`"4<build number>.<sub-build number>"`.

Therefore, if the Build value is the character 5 followed by a four-character build number, Internet Explorer 5.0 is installed. The following code shows a function used to determine what version of IE is installed. `GetIEMajorVersion()` returns a 5 for IE 5.*x*, a 4 for IE 4.*x*, a 3 for IE 3.*x*, and a zero for anything else:

```
int GetIEMajorVersion()
{
   long retVal;
   char *version[10];    //big enough for sub build
   int IEVersion = 0;
   HKEY hKey;

   //open the key
   retVal = RegOpenKey(HKEY_LOCAL_MACHINE,
      "Software\Microsoft\Internet Explorer", &hKey);
   if (retVal == ERROR_SUCCESS)
   {
      retVal = RegQueryValueEx(hKey, "Build", NULL,
         REG_SZ, version, sizeof(version));
      if (retVal == ERROR_SUCCESS)
      {
         select case version[0] {
         {
            case '4':
               IEVersion = 4;
               break;

            case '3':
```

Chapter 28: Internet Explorer

```
                    IEVersion = 3;
                    break;
            }
        }
        //close the key
        retVal = RegCloseKey(hKey);
    }
    return (IEVersion);
}
```

Determining Versions with shdocvw.dll

The version of the file shdocvw.dll, the WebBrowser DLL, can also be used to determine which version of Internet Explorer is installed. If this file is missing completely, you know Internet Explorer needs to be installed. You can use the following function to retrieve version information:

```
int GetBrowserVersion()
{
    HINSTANCE    hBrowser;

    int IEVersion = 0;

    //Load the DLL.
    hBrowser = LoadLibrary(TEXT("shdocvw.dll"));

    if(hBrowser)
    {
        HRESULT           hResult;
        DLLGETVERSIONPROC pDllGetVersion;

        pDllGetVersion = (DLLGETVERSIONPROC)GetProcAddress(
            hBrowser, TEXT("DllGetVersion"));
        if(pDllGetVersion)
        {
            DLLVERSIONINFO    versionInfo;

            ZeroMemory(&versionInfo sizeof(versionInfo));
            versionInfo.cbSize = sizeof(versionInfo;

            hResult = (*pDllGetVersion)(&dvi);

            if(SUCCEEDED(hResult))
            {
                if (dvi.dwMajorVersion == 4 &&
                    dvi.dwMinorVersion == 70)
                    IEVersion = 3;

                if (dvi.dwMajorVersion == 4 &&
                    dvi.dwMinorVersion == 71)
                    IEVersion = 4;
            }
```

```
        }
        FreeLibrary(hBrowser);
    }

    return IEVersion;
}
```

Using the Minimum Installation

Internet Explorer is currently designed in such a way that you can't simply install mshtml.dll or shdocvw.dll (the WebBrowser DLL files) with your program and have everything work properly. A number of system files and registry entries are required for the control to work. Simply put, you must have a full installation of the basic IE components in order to use any of them — an all-or-nothing situation. In order to distribute WebBrowser or any of the other IE technologies with your application, you must obtain a redistribution agreement from Microsoft.

This does not mean that you must have a full-blown — that is, every component included — installation of IE 5.0. Microsoft provides an Internet Explorer kit, which allows you to customize the installation. The minimum installation includes the IE 5.0 browser, Microsoft's VM for Java, and Direct Show. You can also modify the installation to run with a user interface and prompts, or to be totally automated with the rest of your installation.

This kit provides information about how to create the best installation for your needs. The easiest way to run a minimum installation of IE 5.0 is to use the command-line parameters. For example, to do a minimum installation without user interface, integrated desktop, a reboot prompt, making IE 5.0 the default browser, or adding an icon to the desktop, simply use the following command line:

```
ie5stw95.exe /Q:A /C:"ie5wzd.exe /Q:A /X /I:N /R:N /S:"#e""
```

Note A new Internet Explorer installation requires the computer to reboot in order to finish installation. You should give the user the option of rebooting or not, but IE 5.0 will not be usable until the computer reboots.

Warning Users about Uninstalling IE 5.0

Because your application requires Internet Explorer 5.0 services, you will want to add your application to the list of applications that require Internet Explorer 5.0 to be installed. This way, if the user attempts to uninstall Internet Explorer 5.0, a list will be displayed including your program, and the user will be told that your application may not function properly if Internet Explorer 5.0 is uninstalled. Users will still be able to uninstall Internet Explorer 5.0, but they will have been warned.

The Windows Registry stores the list of applications that require IE 5.0 in a string value at the following key:

`HKEY_LOCAL_MACHINE\Software\Microsoft\IE4\DependentComponents`.

The string's value will be something like `AWebApp = "Awesome New Web Browser"`, where `AWebApp` is a unique identifier in the Registry list for your program, and `"Awesome New Web Browser"` is the value that will be displayed in the list of programs requiring IE 5.0. Of course, your uninstall routine should remove this value when run.

Running MyBrowser

It's now time to look at MyBrowser in action. When you run it, it will look like Figure 28-11.

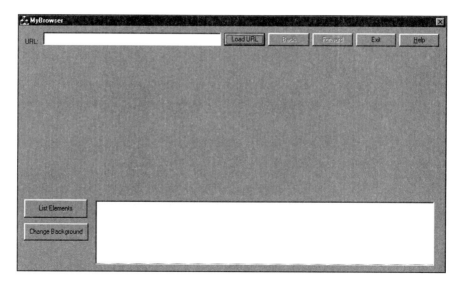

Figure 28-11: MyBrowser, a quick example of a WebBrowser

After starting up MyBrowser, you will need to enter a URL or a file location to load your first file. The program has two sample HTML files included with it, so you can begin by loading one of those files. Open the extend.htm file, and you will be able to see most of the functionality of this application, as shown in Figure 28-12.

Part VI: Internet Programming

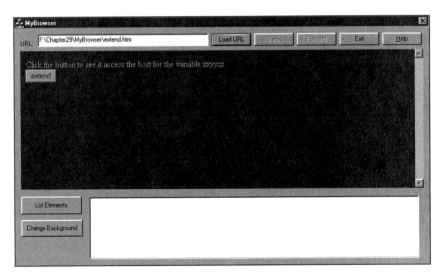

Figure 28-12: MyBrowser displaying an HTML page

At first, the Back and Forward buttons are not enabled, because there isn't a history of loaded pages to traverse. However, a few other buttons can be used. Clicking List Elements will cause a list of all the HTML elements to appear in the list box at the bottom of the program. Clicking Change Background will change the background color of the page, and your program should look like the one shown in Figure 28-13. You can also click the HTML page's Extend button to increment the program's internal counter.

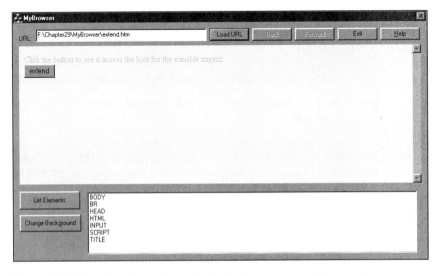

Figure 28-13: Changing the background color isn't always a good idea, as it can make your page's text unreadable.

Another thing that you can try out is loading the About dialog box by right-clicking the title bar and selecting About MyBrowser. Currently, the file location for the HTML file is hard-coded, but the source is documented with suggestions about how to change the way the file is loaded or how to use a Web page. The browser is now ready to open any of your favorite HTML pages.

Problems & Solutions

Using Robots

PROBLEM: *How do I retrieve documents using robots?*

SOLUTION: When dealing with the Internet, a *robot* is a program that automatically retrieves documents for you. These documents may be downloaded for later reference or given to another program that will index the files. Robots can also be created to simply make a backup copy of a Web site. Unlike a browser, a robot doesn't simply retrieve one document and then display it. The robot is only interested in the information on the page and does not need to waste the resources required to display the page in any particular format. A robot will look through a document and recursively traverse its hyperlinks. These programs have several uses, including the following:

*Checking for valid links in an HTML page

*Filling hard-disk drives with vast amounts of HTML

*Helping to index a Web site

*Creating a mirror of a Web site

*Acting as an example of the uses of MSHTML

The MyBrowser application can quickly be turned into a robot. Simply change the List Elements button so that it only adds a list of links. Then call a routine that will go through the list and download all of the files in it.

Summary

One of the most important things to remember when considering using Internet Explorer components in your application is not to limit your thinking to browsing the Web. The Internet has given new life to the client-server model of programming and new solutions to this style of programming. Microsoft and many other companies have spent a lot of time, energy, and money creating new avenues of application development available through the Internet.

A quick overview of the basic functions of Internet Explorer provides an introduction to what you can do with these components. At the most basic level, Internet Explorer retrieves and displays formatted text from the Internet. You no longer have to derive your own format or tools for creating your content. You can use any of the HTML authoring programs on the market to quickly create anything you would normally display on the screen. This includes online documentation, a help system, or dialog boxes — all this and networking, too.

Also discussed in this chapter:

- Web browsers are easy to create using Internet Explorer components.
- The HTML rendering system can be used to create dialog boxes and help systems.
- MSHTML can be used even without a graphical interface for creating robots and other test programs.
- Dynamic HTML allows you to change the content of a page that has already been loaded into a browser.
- The Dynamic HTML object model can be extended to add functionality to scripts run on HTML pages.
- PICS is an advanced feature that can be used with Internet Explorer components to limit access to different HTML pages and Web sites.

Appendix

About the CD-ROM

The CD-ROM that accompanies this book contains all the sample programs described in each chapter. These programs are organized into directories that are named after the chapters. That is, you can find the programs for Chapter 1 in the Chap01 folder, the programs for Chapter 2 in the Chap02 folder, and so on. (Note that not every chapter contains a sample program.) At the end of this appendix, you'll find a complete listing of the CD's contents, which will help you find the programs you want to study.

Each program on the CD-ROM includes not only the source code, but also all the project files generated by Visual C++, as well as the ready-to-run executable file. To experiment with any program under Visual C++, copy the appropriate program directory to your hard drive and then double-click the program's .dsw file to load the project into Visual C++. You can then modify the source code, compile the program, or do whatever you like with the project. Feel free to copy code from the CD-ROM into your own programs. Use the code as is or modify it to fit a specific purpose.

Please note that after you copy files from the CD-ROM to your hard drive (unless you install the entire CD-ROM by running the included batch file), you'll need to shut off the read-only attribute on any files you plan to modify. Visual C++ cannot save modified files until you do this. To turn off the read-only attribute on a set of files (after copying them to your hard drive), highlight the files in Windows Explorer and right-click the group. Then, select the Properties command from the Context menu, and turn off the Read-Only checkbox in the property sheet that appears.

CD-ROM Contents

This list of programs includes the chapter directory names, as well as the names of program directories inside each chapter directory. Each program directory contains the source code, project files, and executable file for the specific program.

File Name	Application
Chap01	BasicApp
Chap02	BasicDCApp
	BitmapBrushApp

File Name	Application
	BrushApp
	ClientDCApp
	DeviceCapsApp
	MetafileDCApp
	PatternBrushApp
	PenApp
	PenApp2
Chap03	BasicApp
	BasicApp2
	CommonDlgApp
	DialogApp
	PropSheet
	WizardApp
Chap04	CharSpaceApp
	ColorTextApp
	FontApp
	FontApp2
	HorizontalAlignApp
	TabTextApp
	TextMetricsApp
	VerticalAlignApp
Chap05	MenuApp
Chap06	ControlApp2
	DialogControlsApp
Chap07	CommonControlsApp
	CommonControlsApp2
	EditControls
	SliderApp
Chap08	BasicPrintApp
	InchApp
	PrintApp
	PrintCircleApp

Appendix : About the CD-ROM

File Name	Application
Chap09	BitmapApp
	BitmapApp2
	ColorConeApp
	ColorRecApp
Chap10	AspectRatioApp
	CartesianApp
	LineModeApp
	MagicRectApp
	MapModeApp
	PathApp
	RasterOpApp
	RegionApp
Chap11	DragDrop2
	Namespace
	Shortcut
	TrayApp
Chap12	RegistryApp
Chap14	EventThread
	ThreadApp1
	ThreadApp2
	ThreadApp3
	ThreadApp4
	ThreadApp5
	ThreadApp6
Chap15	KeyDown
	Keys
	Mouse
	NCMouse
Chap16	PersistCircleApp
	PersistCircleApp2
	String

File Name	Application
Chap17	CBCircleApp
	CBCircleApp2
	DelayedRender
Chap19	ContainerApp
Chap20	ServerApp
Chap21	AutoClientApp
	AutoServerApp
Chap22	Scramble
Chap23	DirectDrawApp
	DirectDrawApp2
Chap24	DirectSoundApp
	DirectSoundApp2
Chap25	DirectInputApp
	DirectInputApp2
Chap26	Direct3DApp
	Direct3DApp2
Chap27	FTPAccessApp
Chap28	MyBrowser

Index

Symbols
& (ampersand), 141
&attributes argument, 463
&disp argument, 478
&keyHandle2 argument, 478
&lpEnumIDList argument, 461
&lpItemIDList argument, 463
&numFetched argument, 463
&pShellLink argument, 448
&strRet argument, 464
&valSize argument, 482
&valType argument, 482
&xpos argument, 479, 482
:: (double colon), 531
"" argument, 478
+ (plus sign), 500, 506
< > (angle brackets), 743
<< operator, 574
>> operator, 574
<OBJECT> tag, 708–709

Numbers
0 argument, 477, 479, 482
1 argument, 463
1InitialCount parameter, 541
1MaxCount parameter, 541
3D. *See* Direct3D

A
Abort() function, 588, 823
AboutBox() method, code, 702–703
ABOVE_NORMAL_PRIORITY_CLASS class, 514
access level, setting DirectInput devices, 766
accessing
  automation server properties, 692
  document interfaces, 871–872
  Web sites, controlling, 859–861
Acquire() function, 767
ActivateFrame() function, 58
Active Directory, 465
ActiveX. *See also* containers; servers
  automation applications, 632–633
  automation server, 632
  COM (Component Object Model), 628
  COM+, 629
  container applications, 624, 629–630
  containers, 635
  controls, 633
  data sets, linked, 624–625
  DCOM (Distributed Component Object Model), 628
  documents, 633–634
  initializing, 689
  OLE, 626-627
  OLE 1.0, 623–626
  OLE 2.0, 626–627
  Paint, toolbars and menu bars, 631–632
  programmable objects, 626
  server applications, 624, 630–632
  view class, 662–663
ActiveX controls, 6, 850–851
  buttons, responding to, 705–706
  Calendar, 7
  Components and Controls Gallery dialog box, 853
  methods, creating, 702–705
  placing on Web pages, 708–709
  properties, creating, 702–705
  skeleton, creating, 695–697
  testing, 706–707
  user interface, creating, 697–702
ActiveX ControlWizard, 695–697
Add a Class dialog box, 210, 373, 656
Add Class button, 104
Add File Group dialog box, 498
Add Function button, 179, 216
Add Member Function dialog box, 148, 214, 215
Add Member Variable dialog box, 211, 374, 349, 639, 704
Add Method dialog box, 681
Add Property dialog box, 703
Add() function, 250
Add/Remove Programs properties window, 504
AddCircle() function, 580
adding
  applications to Start menu, 505–508
  DirectDraw files to Visual C++ project, 715–717
  DirectSound files to Visual C++ project, 742–744
  icons to system tray, 453–454
AddLight() function, 789
AddListItems() function, 276–277
AddRequestHeaders() function, 821
AddressBar property, 856
AddString() function, 191
AfxBeginThread() function, parameters, 518
AfxOleInit() function, 689
afxwin.h header file, 66
aligning text
  horizontally, 120–123
  setting, 119–127
  vertically, 123–125
Alt key, tracking, 568
ampersand (&), 141
angle brackets (< >), 743
APIs, Internet Ratings API functions, 860
Appearance property page, 101
application class, 66–67
  header file, creating, 795
  implementation file, creating, 795–796
applications. *See also* Win32 applications
  adding to Start menu, 505–508
  AspectRatioApp, 414–416
  automation, 632–633
  BasicApp2, code, 73–75
  BasicPrintApp, 298–302
  BitmapApp, creating, 345–351
  CartesianApp, 411–412
  CBCircleApp, 595–596
  CharSpaceApp, 118–119
  client resources, customizing, 684–685
  client view class, 685–689
  client-area messages, 548–549
  clipboard, 595–596
  ColorConeApp, 392–395
  ColorRecApp, 387–390

Continued

applications *(continued)*
ColorTextApp, 115–116
Common Dialog, 95–100
container, 624, 629–630
ContainerApp, 635–638
creating to install, 487–488
creating without AppWizard, 60–69
DelayedRender, 606–609
dependencies, locating, 487
Direct3DApp2, code, 809–814
DirectDraw, code to write, 736–739
DirectDrawApp2, 736–740
DirectInputApp2, code to write, 773–777
DirectSoundApp2, code, 755–760
document/view architecture, implementing, 571–578
drag-and-drop, registering as, 444
DragDrop2, 443–446
EventThread, 528–531
FontApp, 133–138
FTP, writing, 830–832
graphics, printing, 316–331
HorizontalAlignApp, 120–122
HTTP, writing, 826–829
InchApp, 325–331
initializing, 15
instances, 11
KeyDown, 562–568
Keys, 560–562
LineModeApp, 422–425
MagicRectApp, 426–428
MapModeApp, 400–403
MenuApp, 154–161
Mouse, 552–553, 556–557
MyBrowser, compiling, 854–855
NamespaceApp, 459–464
non-client-area messages, 549–552
packaging, 485–486
PathApp, 437–440
PersistCircleApp, 579–584
PersistentCircleApp2, 585
PrintApp application, 303–304
PrintCircleApp, 316–317
programmable objects, 626
PropSheet, 106–107
RasterOpApp, 417–421
RegionApp, 430–435
RegistryApp, 474–483
Scramble, 695–700
server, 624, 630–632
Shortcut, 451–452
shortcuts, placing in Programs folder, 506
SliderApp, 244

String, creating, 572–573
TabTextApp, 127
TextMetricsApp, 129–130
ThreadApp1 application, 517–518
ThreadApp2, 526–527
ThreadApp3, 531–533
ThreadApp4, 534–535
ThreadApp5, 537–540
ThreadApp6, 542–545
TrayApp, 455–457
type libraries, 685–686
VerticalAlignApp, 123–125
WizardApp, 110
applications, AutoClientApp
automation client skeleton, creating, 683–684
client application resources, customizing, 684–685
client application view class, 685–689
client application, initializing ActiveX, 689
servers, controlling from clients, 689–691
applications, AutoServerApp, automation server, 671-672
document class, 676–677
methods, defining, 678–682
properties, defining, 678–682
resources, customizing, 673–675
view class, 677–678
applications, BasicApp
afxwin.h header file, 66
application class, 66–67
code, 63–64
creating, 61–66
frame window class, 67–69
responding to mouse click, 66
applications, BitmapApp2
adding source code, 375–380
creating, 368–370
customizing resources, 370–375
running, 380–383
applications, CBCircleApp2, 610–611
copying data, 612–615
pasting data, 615–618
applications, CommonControlsApp, 227–228
progress bar, 231–233
sliders, 237–238
spinner, 248–249
applications, CommonControlsApp2, 256–259
list view, 275–279
tree view code, 291–293

applications, ControlApp2
checkboxes, 184
combo boxes, 193–194
OnCtrlColor() function, 199
pushbuttons, 181
radio buttons, 186
running, 165–169
applications, DialogControlApp
creating, 203–217
dialog box controls, 221–222
running, 220–221
applications, Direct3D
building, 790–793
writing, 808–814
applications, Direct3DApp, 802–814
application class header file, creating, 795
application class implementation file, creating, 795–796
main window class header file, creating, 796–797
running, 794
window class implementation file, code to create, 797–801
applications, DirectDrawApp, 736–740
ClearDDrawSurface() function, 726–727
CreatDDrawPal() function, 729–730
CreateDDrawSurfaces() function, 725
CreateOffScreenSurface() function, 727–728
ddraw.h header file, adding, 715
ddraw.lib file, adding, 716–717
DibToSurface() function, 730–731
InitDirectDraw() function, 724–725
InitImages() function, 728–729
InitMemberVariables() function, 723–724
OnDestroy() function, 734–735
OnInitialUpdate() function, 722–723
OnKeyDown() function, 734
OnTimer() function, 732–733
applications, DirectInputApp
code to write, 773–777
OnDestroy() function, 772–773
OnDraw() function, 771–772
OnInitialUpdate() function, 769–770
OnTimer() function, 770–771
view class constructor, 768–769
applications, DirectSoundApp

Index

CreateSoundBuffer() function, 749
CWave class, code, 750–752
  InitDirectSound() function, 748–749
  LoadWaveData() function, 753–754
  OnDestroy() function, 754–755
  OnInitialUpdate() function, 747–748
  OnLButtonDown() function, 754
  view-class constructor, 746–747
  writing, 755–760
applications, FTPAccessApp
  creating, 835–847
  DisplayStatusMessage() function, code to create, 846
  DownloadFile() function, code to create, 843–845
  InitSelection() function, code to create, 846–847
  member variables, 835–847
  MoveToPreviousDirectory() function, code to create, 845
  OnDraw() function, code to create, 837–838
  OnFtpConnection() function, code to create, 839
  OnLButtonDblClk() function, code to create, 841–842
  OnRButtonDown() function, code to create, 843
  OpenFTPDirectory() function, code to create, 840–841
  ReadFileNames() function, code to create, 841
  running, 832–835
applications, MFC non-AppWizard
  CreateLight() function, 806
  CreateMesh() function, 804–805
  CreateViewport() function, 805–806
  MakeScene() function, 804
  OnCreate() function, 802–803
  OnDestroy() function, 802
  OnPaint() function, 806–807
  OnTimer() function, 808
  writing, 795–808
applications, ServerApp, 652–654
  document class, 659–661
  resources, customizing, 655–659
  running as editor for linked items, 666–668
  running as in-place editor, 665–666
  running as stand-alone, 663–665
  running, 663–668
  server item class, 661

  view class, 662–663
applications, skeleton
  browser, creating, 851–861
  container, creating, 635–638
  creating, 572–573
  server, creating, 652–655
AppWizard
  applications, creating, 15
  applications, implementing document/view architecture, 571–578
  dialog boxes as main windows, 199–202
  DialogControlsApp application, creating, 203–206
AppWizard – Step 1 dialog box, 77
AppWizard, skeleton
  automation server, creating, 672–673
  browser application, creating, 851–861
  container application, creating, 635–638
  server application, creating, 652–655
Arc() function, 25
architectures
  DNA (Distributed interNet Application), 464–465
  document/view, 571–578
arguments
  BitBlt() function, 342
  bOpenFileDialog, 88, 89
  bPassive, 831
  cbBuf, 296
  clrInit, 95
  CLSCTX_INPROC_SERVER, 448
  CLSID_ShellLink, 448
  CoCreateInstance() function, 448
  CoInitializeEx() function, 448
  color, 42
  CPen class constructor, 42
  Create() function, 68–69
  CreateWindow() function, 12
  cx, 250
  cy, 250
  DibToSurface() function, 731
  DragQueyFile() function, 445
  dstPoint, 731
  dwContext, 828
  dwExStyle, 69
  dwFlags, 88, 89, 92, 95, 727, 828
  dwHeadersLength, 828
  dwROP, 342, 344
  dwRop, 363
  dwStyle, 69, 172, 175, 182, 189, 194
  EnumObjects() function, 461
  EnumPrinters() function, 296

  Flags, 296
  GetAttributesOf() function, 463
  GetDisplayNameOf() function, 464
  GetFtpConnection() function, 831
  GetTextExtentPoint32() function, 136
  hdc, 114, 363
  hDC, 136
  hDropInfor, 445
  hEvent, 727
  IID_IShellLink, 448
  InsertColumn() function, 268
  iUsage, 363
  KEY_ALL_ACCESS, 478
  keyHandel, 477
  keyHandle3, 479, 482
  Level, 296
  Lock() function, 727
  Lock() function, 753
  lpBits, 363
  lpBitsInfo, 363
  lpDDSurfaceDesc, 727
  lpDestRect, 727
  lpItemIDList, 464
  lplfInitial, 92
  lpszCaption, 182
  lpszClassName, 68
  lpszColumnHeading, 268
  lpszDefExt, 88, 89
  lpszFile, 445
  lpszFileName, 88, 89
  lpszFilter, 88, 89
  lpszMenuName, 69
  lpszText, 172
  lpszWindowName, 68
  "My Company", 477
  Name, 296
  nCOL, 268
  nDestHeight, 363
  nDestWidth, 363
  Next() function, 463
  nflags, 250
  nFormat, 268
  nGrow, 250
  nHeight, 342, 344
  nID, 172, 175, 182, 189, 194
  nInitial, 250
  nPort, 831
  nSrcHeight, 344, 363
  nSrcWidth, 344, 363
  nSubItem, 268
  NULL, 448, 461, 478
  numChars, 114, 136
  numTabs, 126
  nWidth, 268, 342, 343
  OpenURL() function, 828

Continued

Index

arguments *(continued)*
  pcbNeeded, 296
  pContext, 69
  pcReturned, 296
  pDC, 198
  pdcPrinter, 92
  pDib, 731
  pParentWnd, 69, 88, 89, 92, 95, 172
  pPrinterEnum, 296
  pSize, 136
  pSrcDC, 342, 344
  pstrHeaders, 828
  pstrPassword, 831
  pstrServer, 831
  pstrURL, 828
  pstrUserName, 831
  pSurface, 731
  pText, 136
  pWnd, 198
  rect, 69, 172, 175, 182, 189
  REG_DWORD, 479
  REG_OPTION_NON_VOLATILE, 478
  RegCreateKeyEx() function, 477–478
  RegQueryValueEx() function, 482
  RegSetValueEx() function, 479
  SHCONTF_FOLDERS, 461
  SHCONTF_NONFOLDERS, 461
  SHGDN_NORMAL, 464
  sizeof(DWORD), 479
  sizeof(lpszFile), 445
  srcRect, 731
  str, 126
  StretchBlt() function, 343–344
  StretchDIBits() function, 363
  string, 114
  style, 42
  TabbedTextOut() function, 126
  tabOrigin, 126
  tabs, 126
  TextOut() function, 113–114
  width, 42
  X, 114
  x, 126, 342, 343, 445
  XDest, 363
  "XPosition", 479, 482
  xSrc, 342, 344
  XSrc, 363
  Y, 114
  y, 126, 342, 343
  Ydest, 363
  ySrc, 342, 344
  YSrc, 363
arguments, numbers
  0, 477, 479, 482
  1, 463

arguments, symbols
  &attributes, 463
  &disp, 478
  &keyHandle2, 478
  &lpEnumIDList, 461
  &lpItemIDList, 463
  &numFetched, 463
  &pShellLink, 448
  &strRet, 464
  &valSize, 482
  &valType, 482
  &xpos, 479, 482
  "", 478
Arrange() function, 271
aspect ratio, 413–416
AspectRatioApp application, 414–416
ASPECTX constant, 39
ASPECTXY constant, 39
ASPECTY constant, 39
AssertValid() function, 54
atomicity (MTS attribute), 465
Attach() function, 250
attributes, MTS (Microsoft Transaction Server), 465–466
AutoClientApp application
  automation client skeleton, creating, 683–684
  client application resources, customizing, 684–685
  client application view class, 685–689
  client application, initializing ActiveX, 689
  servers, controlling from clients, 689–691
automation
  applications, 632–633
  AutoServerApp application, 671-682
  client skeleton, creating, 683–684
  OLE (object linking and embedding), 626
  skeleton automation server, creating, 672–673
Automation menu
  Display Window command, 684
  Set Diameter command, 684
  Set X command, 684
  Set Y command, 684
automation server, 632
  document class, 676–677
  resources, customizing, 673–675
  view class, 677–678
  methods, defining, 678–682
  properties, defining, 678–682
  properties, accessing, 692

AutoServerApp application
  automation server, 671
  document class, 676–677
  methods, defining, 678–682
  properties, defining, 678–682
  resources, customizing, 673–675
  skeleton, creating, 672–673
  view class, 677–678

B

back buffers, 718, 736
Back button, 107
base priority settings, 514
Basic Application window, 8
BasicApp application
  afxwin.h header file, 66
  application class, 66–67
  code, 63–64
  creating, 61–66
  frame window class, 67–69
  responding to mouse click, 66
  switch statement, 14
  window, buttons removed, 72
BasicApp2 application
  code, 73–75
  window, 76
  WS_POPUP style, 75–76
BasicPrintApp application, 298–302
BEGIN_MESSAGE_MAP() macro, 16
BeginDrag() function, 250
BeginPaint() function, 28
BELOW_NORMAL_PRIORITY_CLASS class, 514
bfOffBits (BITMAPFILEHEADER structure), 354
bfReserved1 (BITMAPFILEHEADER structure), 354
bfReserved2 (BITMAPFILEHEADER structure), 354
bfSize (BITMAPFILEHEADER structure), 354
bfType (BITMAPFILEHEADER structure), 354
biBitCount (BIMAPINFOHEADER structure), 356
biClrImportant (BIMAPINFOHEADER structure), 356
biClrUsed (BIMAPINFOHEADER structure), 356
biCompression (BIMAPINFOHEADER structure), 356
biHeight (BIMAPINFOHEADER structure), 356
BIMAPINFO structure, 355
BIMAPINFOHEADER structure, 355, 356
bInitiallyOwn parameter, 525, 537

Index

biplanes (BIMAPINFOHEADER structure), 356
biSize (BIMAPINFOHEADER structure), 356
biSizeImage (BIMAPINFOHEADER structure), 356
BitBlt() function, 25, 342, 343
Bitmap object, 24
BitmapApp application
  creating, 345–351
  running, 351–352
BitmapApp 2 application
  creating, 368–370
  resources, customizing, 370–375
  running, 380–383
  source code, adding, 375–380
BITMAPFILEHEADER structure, 354
bitmapped brushes, 48–50
bitmaps
  CDib class, 358–362
  color tables, loading, 355–358
  ColorConeApp application, 392–395
  copying and changing size, 343–344
  copying to clipboard, 596–600
  copying without changing size, 342–343
  copying, 341–342
  DDBs (device-dependent bitmaps), 335–352
  drawing on, 340–341
  functions for initializing, 337–338
  functions for manipulating, 337
  headers, loading, 355–358
  masks, 390
  memory DC, creating, 338–339
  memory DC, selecting into, 330–340
  nonrectangular, displaying, 390–395
  objects, 638
  objects, creating and initializing, 336–338
  Paint tools, 637
  pasting to clipboard, 600–603
  raster operations, 416–421
  resource editor, 370–371
  SRCAND raster operation, 391–392
  SRCCOPY raster operation, 391
  SRCPAINT raster operation, 391–392
bitmaps, DIBs (device-independent bitmaps), 335–336
  displaying, 363–364
  logical palettes, 364–366
  managing multi-images, 383–390

managing palettes, 364–368
memory storage, 385
palette changes, 366–368
programming with, 352–395
BITSPIXEL constant, 39
biWidth (BIMAPINFOHEADER structure), 356
biXPelsPerMeter (BIMAPINFOHEADER structure), 356
biYPelsPerMeter (BIMAPINFOHEADER structure), 356
BLACKNESS (bitmap raster operations), 417
bManualReset parameter, 525
bOpenFileDialog argument, 88, 89
bPassive argument, 831
Browse button, 666
browsers. *See* Internet Explorer; Web browsers
Brush object, 24
BrushApp, drawing with brush colors, 46
brushes, 47
  bitmapped, 48–50
  creating, 45
  drawing with colors, 46
BS_3STATE (button control style), 182
BS_AUTO3STATE (button control style), 182
BS_AUTOCHECKBOX (button control style), 182
BS_AUTORADIOBUTTON (button control style), 182
BS_CHECKBOX (button control style), 182
BS_DEFPUSHBUTTON (button control style), 182
BS_GROUPBOX (button control style), 182
BS_LEFTTEXT (button control style), 182
BS_OWNERDRAW (button control style), 182
BS_PUSHBUTTON (button control style), 182
BS_RADIOBUTTON (button control style), 182
buffers, secondary (DirectSound), creating, 745
Build button, 64
Build menu
  Build AutoServerApp.exe command, 682
  Media Build Wizard command, 502
  Set Active Configuration command, 792
Build Type page, 503

building Direct3D applications, 790–793
bulleted items on menus, 150–151
buttons. *See also* individual button names
  ActiveX controls, responding to, 705–706
  control styles, 182
  MFC (Microsoft Foundation Classes) control, removing, 19–20
  radio, 185–187
  removed from BasicApp window, 72
  of wizards, 107–110

C

C programming language versus MFC (Microsoft Foundation Classes), 15–17
Calendar ActiveX control, 7
calendar, OLE controls, 627
CanUndo() function, 178
Cancel button, 83
capabilities of devices, 39–41
captions, menus, 144
capturing mouse messages, 553–555
CArchive object, 578
Cartesian coordinate system, 411–412
CartesianApp application, 411–412
CAutoServerAppDoc class, 676
cbBuf argument, 296
CBCircleApp application, 595–596
CBCircleApp2 application, 610–611
  copying data, 612–615
  pasting data, 615–618
CBitmapAppView class, 347
CBN_CLOSEUP (combo box notification), 196
CBN_DBLCLK (combo box notification), 196
CBN_DROPDOWN (combo box notification), 196
CBN_EDITCHANGE (combo box notification), 196
CBN_EDITUPDATE (combo box notification), 196
CBN_KILLFOCUS (combo box notification), 197
CBN_SELCHANGE (combo box notification), 197
CBN_SELENDCANCEL (combo box notification), 197
CBN_SELENDOK (combo box notification), 197

CBN_SETFOCUS (combo box notification), 197
CBrush class, 45–48
CBS_AUTOHSCROLL (combo box control style), 195
CBS_DISABLENOSCROLL (combo box control style), 195
CBS_DROPDOWN (combo box control style), 195
CBS_DROPDOWNLIST (combo box control style), 195
CBS_HASSTRINGS (combo box control style), 195
CBS_NOINTEGRALHEIGHT (combo box control style), 195
CBS_OEMCONVERT (combo box control style), 195
CBS_OWNERDRAWFIXED (combo box control style), 195
CBS_OWNERDRAWVARIABLE (combo box control style), 195
CBS_SIMPLE (combo box control style), 195
CBS_SORT (combo box control style), 195
cbSize (NOTIFYICONDATA structure), 453
CButton class, 181, 183, 185
CChildFrame class, 78
cChildren (TV_ITEM structure), 283
cchTextMax (LV_COLUMN structure), 265
cchTextMax (LV_ITEM structure), 267
cchTextMax (TV_ITEM structure), 283
CCircleDlg class, 674
CCircles class, 579–580
CClientDC
 class, 27
 object, code to create, 32–33
CCmdTarget class, functions, 55
CCmdUI class, 148, 149
CColorDialog class, 93, 95
CComboBox class, 193
CContainerAppCntrItem class, 639
CContainerAppView class, 641
CControlDlg class
 adding code, 214–220
 header and file code, 217–220
CCriticalSection class, 533
CDC class
 device-context classes, 27
 functions, 25–26
CDC Rectangle() function, 28
CDib class, 358
 functions, 362

header file code, 359
implementation file code, 359–362
cdib.cpp file, 369
CD-ROM
 AspectRatioApp application, 414
 AutoClientApp application, 683
 AutoServerApp application, 671
 BasicPrintApp application, 298–302
 BitmapApp application, 345
 BitmapApp2 application, 368
 BrushApp folder, 45
 CartesianApp application, 411
 CBCircleApp application, 595
 CBCircleApp2 application, 610
 CharSpaceApp application, 118–119
 ColorRecApp application, 387–390
 ColorTextApp application, 115
 CommonControlsApp application, 227
 CommonControlsApp2 application, 256
 CommonDlgApp folder, 95
 ContainerApp application, 635
 ControlApp2 application, 165–169
 DelayedRender application, 606
 DeviceCapsApp folder, 40
 DialogControlsApp application, 203
 Direct3DApp application, 790, 794
 Direct3DApp2 application, 809
 DirectDrawApp application, 721
 DirectDrawApp2 application, 736–740
 DirectInputApp application, 767
 DirectInputApp2 application, writing, 773
 DirectSoundApp application, 746
 DirectSoundApp2 application, 755
 DragDrop2 application, 443
 EventThread application, 528
 FontApp application, 133–138
 FTPAccessApp application, running, 832
 HorizontalAlignApp application, 120–122
 InchApp application, 325
 KeyDown application, 562
 Keys application, 560
 LineModeApp application, 422
 MagicRectApp application, 426
 MapModeApp application, 400
 media types, selecting, 502–503

MenuApp application, 154–161
Mouse application, 552–553, 556–557
MyBrowser application, compiling, 854
NamespaceApp application, 459
PathApp application, 437
PatternBrushApp folder, 47
PenApp2 folder, 43
PersistCircleApp application, 579
PersistentCircleApp2 application, 585
PrintApp application, 303–304
PrintCircleApp application, 316–317
PropSheet application, 106
RasterOpApp application, 417
RegionApp application, 430
RegistryApp application, 474
Scramble application, 695
ServerApp application, 652–655
SliderApp application, 244
String application, creating, 572
TabTextApp application, 127
TextMetricsApp application, 129–130
ThreadApp1 application, 517
ThreadApp2 application, 526
ThreadApp3 application, 531
ThreadApp4 application, 534
ThreadApp5 application, 537
ThreadApp6 application, 542
TrayApp application, 455
VerticalAlignApp application, 123–125
WizardApp application, 110
CEdit class, 174, 177–179
center:[yes | no | 0] syntax, 866
CenterWindow() function, 56
CEvent object, 525
CF_BITMAP (clipboard constant), 594
CF_DIB (clipboard constant), 594
CF_DIBV5 (clipboard constant), 594
CF_DIF (clipboard constant), 594
CF_DSPBITMAP (clipboard constant), 594, 604
CF_DSPENHMETAFILE (clipboard constant), 594, 604
CF_DSPMETAFILEPICT (clipboard constant), 594, 604
CF_DSPTEXT (clipboard constant), 594, 604
CF_ENHMETAFILE (clipboard constant), 594
CF_GDIOBJFIRST (clipboard constant), 594

Index   895

CF_GDIOBJLAST (clipboard constant), 594
CF_HDROP (clipboard constant), 594
CF_LOCALE (clipboard constant), 594
CF_METAFILEPICT (clipboard constant), 594
CF_OEMTEXT (clipboard constant), 594
CF_OWNERDISPLAY (clipboard constant), 594
CF_PALETTE (clipboard constant), 594
CF_PENDATA (clipboard constant), 594
CF_PRIVATEFIRST (clipboard constant), 594
CF_PRIVATELAST (clipboard constant), 594
CF_SYLK (clipboard constant), 595
CF_TEXT (clipboard constant), 595
CF_TIFF (clipboard constant), 595
CF_UNICODETEXT (clipboard constant), 595
CF_WAVE (clipboard constant), 595
CFile class, 571
    file errors, detecting, 590–592
    flags, 589
    functions, 588
CFile::modeCreate (flag), 589
CFile::modeNoInherit (flag), 589
CFile::modeNoTruncate (flag), 589
CFile::modeRead (flag), 589
CFile::modeReadWrite (flag), 589
CFile::modeWrite (flag), 589
CFile::shareDenyNone (flag), 589
CFile::shareDenyRead (flag), 589
CFile::shareDenyWrite (flag), 589
CFile::shareExclusive (flag), 589
CFile::typeBinary (flag), 589
CFile::typeText (flag), 589
CFileDialog class, 86
    constructor signature, 87–88
    functions, 90–91
CFileException, 590–592
CFileFind class, 820, 824–825
CFont class, 131
CFontDialog class, 91, 92, 93
CFrameWnd class, functions, 58–59
CFtpConnection class, 820, 822–823
CFtpFileFind
    class, 820, 825–826
    object, creating, 831–832
CGopherConnection class, 820
CGopherFile class, 820
CGopherFileFind class, 820
CGopherLocator class, 820
changing window styles, 71–73

character spacing, setting, 118–119
CharFromPos() function, 178
CharSpaceApp application, 118–119
CharToItem() function, 191
checkboxes, 184–185
    checkmarks, turning on or off, 167
    control, 164
checkmarks
    for menus, 149–150
    turning on or off, 167
child
    frames, creating, 789
    windows, 77–79
CHttpConnection class, 822
CHttpFile class, 820, 824
CImageList class, 249, 250–251
CInternetConnection class, 820, 821
CInternetException class, 820, 826
CInternetFile class, 820, 823–824
CInternetSession class, 820–821
Circle menu
    Change Message command, 585
    Set Circle command, 675
circles, properties, 680
classes
    ABOVE_NORMAL_PRIORITY_CLASS, 514
    application, 66–67, 795–796
    BELOW_NORMAL_PRIORITY_CLASS, 514
    CAutoServerAppDoc, 676
    CBitmapAppView, 347
    CBrush, 45–48
    CButton, 181, 183, 185
    CChildFrame, 78
    CCircleDLg, 674
    CCircles, 579–580
    CClientDC, 27
    CCmdTarget, functions, 55
    CCmdUI, 148
    CColorDialog, 93, 95
    CComboBox, 193
    CContainerAppCntrItem, 639
    CContainerAppView, 641
    CControlDlg, adding code, 214–220
    CCriticalSection, 533
    CDC, functions, 25–26
    CDib, 358–362
    CEdit, 174, 177–179
    CFile, 571, 588–592
    CFileDialog, 86, 87–88, 90–91
    CFileFind, 820, 824–825
    CFont, 131
    CFontDialog, 91, 92, 93
    CFrameWnd, functions, 58–59

CFtpConnection, 820, 822–823
CFtpFileFind, 820, 825–826
CGopherConnection, 820
CGopherFile, 820
CGopherFileFind, 820
CGopherLocator, 820
CHttpConnection, 822
CHttpFile, 820, 824
CImageList class, 249, 250–251
CInternetConnection, 820, 821
CInternetException, 820, 826
CInternetFile, 820, 823–824
CInternetSession, 820–821
CListBox, 187–188
CListCtrl, 262, 270–272
CMDIFrameWnd, 78
CMetaFileDC, 27
CMouseView, 556
CMutex, 536, 537
CMySlider, header file code, 241–244
CObject, 54–55
COleClientItem, 661
COleDocument, 635
COleServerItem, 652, 661
CPaintDC, 27
CPen, 42–44
Cpen, constructor arguments, 42
CProgressCtrl, 229, 230, 231
CPropertyPage, 100, 109
creating with WinMain() function, 11
CRgn, functions, 429
CScrambleCtrl, 697, 705–706
CSemaphore, 541
CServerAppDoc, 659
CServerAppView, 662
CSizeDlg, 656
CSliderCtrl, 233, 236–237
CSpinButtonCtrl, 246, 247–248
CStringArray, 573
CStringDoc, 573
CTreeCtrl, 281, 282
CView, functions, 59–60
CWave, code, 750–752
CWindowDC, 27
CWinThread, 519
CWnd, 55–57
device-context, 27
Direct3DWin, constructor, 801–802
document, automation server, 676–677
document, ServerApp application, 659–661
frame window, 67–69
HIGH_PRIORITY_CLASS, 514
IAutoServerApp, 687

Continued

896 Index

classes *(continued)*
   IDLE_PRIORITY_CLASS, 514
   main window, header file, creating, 796–797
   NORMAL_PRIORITY_CLASS, 514
   priority of threads, 515
   REALTIME_PRIORITY_CLASS, 514
   server item, ServerApp application, 661
   THREAD_PRIORITY_ABOVE_NORMAL, 515
   THREAD_PRIORITY_BELOW_NORMAL, 515
   THREAD_PRIORITY_CRITICAL, 515
   THREAD_PRIORITY_HIGHEST, 515
   THREAD_PRIORITY_IDLE, 515
   THREAD_PRIORITY_LOWEST, 515
   THREAD_PRIORITY_NORMAL, 515
   window, implementation file, code to create, 797–801
   WinInet, 820
classes, view
   ActiveX, 662–663
   automation server, 677–678
   client application, 685–689
   constructor (DirectSoundApp), 746–747
   constructor, 768–769
   ServerApp application, 662–663
ClassWizard
   ActiveX control user interface, 698–699
   DeleteContents() function, overriding, 377
   dialog box, 519, 80–81
   displaying, 10, 3473
   message maps, 15, 157–158
   message-response functions for menus, 144–146
   OnCreate() function, 328, 688–689
   OnLButtonDown() message-response function, 212
   OnPrint() function, 329
   OnRectangleSize() function, 662–663
   OnSetCursor() function, 642
   PreTranslateMessage() function, overriding, 180
   property sheet, 210–211, 656
   type libraries, 685–686
   UI threads, creating, 519–522
   update command UI functions, creating, 148

Clear() function, 178
ClearDDrawSurface() function, DirectDrawApp, 726–727
ClearSel() function, 236
ClearTics() function, 236
Click Me button, 166
clicking radio buttons, results, 168
client applications
   resources, customizing, 684–685
   view class, 685–689
client-area
   device context, 29–34
   messages, 548–549
clients
   automation client skeleton, creating, 683–684
   coordinates, 398
   OLE (object linking and embedding), 626
   servers, controlling, 689–691
clipboard, 593
   application, 595–596
   bitmaps, 596–603
   CBCircleApp2 application, 610–612
   constants, 594–595
   data formats, 609–618
   delayed rendering, 605–609
   formats, 594–609
   private format, registering, 605
CLIPCAPS constant, 40
clipper object, creating, 781–782
CListBox class, 187–188, 191–193
CListCtrl class, 262, 270–272
Close() function, 588, 821, 823, 825
CloseClipboard() function, 597
CloseFigure() function, 437
closing FTP sessions, 832
clrInit argument, 95
CLSCTX_INPROC_SERVER argument, 448
CLSID_ShellLink argument, 448
CMDIFrameWnd class, 78
CMetaFileDC class, 27
CMetaFileDCCreate() function, 37
CMouseView class, 556
CMutex class, 536, 537
CMySlider class, header file code, 241–244
CObject class, functions, 54–55
CoCreateInstance() function, arguments, 448
code
   AboutBox() method, 702–703
   BasicApp application, 63–64
   BasicApp2 application, 73–75
   BitmapApp2 application, adding, 375–380

CClientDC object, creating, 32–33
CControlDlg class, 214–220
CDib class implementation file, 359–362
client-area device context, creating, 29–30
CMySlider class header file, 241–244
Color dialog box, handling, 98–99
CommonControlsApp2 application tree view, 291–293
ControlApp2 OnCreate() function, 171–172
CREATESTRUCT structure, 72
custom dialog boxes, function, 82–83
CWave class, 750–752
DeviceCapsApp, 41
DHTML (Dynamic HTML) object model, extending, 873–877
dialog box view class, 212–214
Direct3DApp2 application, 809–814
DirectDraw applications, writing, 736–739
DirectInput applications, writing, 773–777
DirectInputApp2 application, writing, 773–777
DirectSoundApp2 application, 755–760
documents, editing, 577–578
Font dialog box, handling, 98
GetBrowserVersion() function, 879–880
GetIEMajorVersions() function, 878–879
list views, creating, 269–270
Lock() function signature, 727
message maps, 157–158
MFC (Microsoft Foundation Classes) shortcuts for tree views, 287–289
OnCircleChangemesage() function, 586–587
OnCreate() function, 36–37
OnDestroy() function, 38–39, 475–476
OnDraw() function, 42–43, 46–47, 99, 116–117, 423–425
OnEditAddstring() function, 577–578
OnEditCopy() function, 597–598
OnEditPaste() function, 615–617
OnLButtonDown() function, 117–118, 451–452
OnPrint() function, 324–325

OnRButtonDown() function, 118
Open File dialog box, handling, 96–97
PreCreateWindow() function, 71, 480–481
printing from Windows program, 299–301
property sheets, managing, 105
RegSetValueEx() function, 479
RenderDisplay() function, 598–599
Save dialog box, creating and displaying, 89–90
Save File dialog box, handling, 97
ShowHTMLDialog() function, testing, 862–864
update command UI functions, 160–161
view class header file, declaring functions, 156–157
view class message-response functions, defining, 158–159
virtual key, 564–566
Win32 application, 8–10
window class implementation file, creating, 797–801
code, FTPAccessApp application
DisplayStatusMessage() function, creating, 846
DownloadFile() function, creating, 843–845
InitSelection() function, creating, 846–847
MoveToPreviousDirectory() function, creating, 845
OnDraw() function, creating, 837–838
OnFtpConnection() function, creating, 839
OnLButtonDblClk() function, creating, 841–842
OnRButtonDown() function, creating, 843
OpenFTPDirectory() function, creating, 840–841
ReadFileNames() function, creating, 841
CoInitializeEx() function, 447–448
COleClientItem class, 661
COleDocument class, 635
COleServerItem class, 652, 661
color argument, 42
Color dialog box, 86, 93–95, 98–99
color tables, loading bitmaps, 355–358
ColorConeApp application, 392–395

ColorRecApp application, 387–390
COLORRES constant, 40
colors
  brushes, drawing, 46
  standard controls, changing, 197–199
  text, setting, 114–118
ColorTextApp application, 115–116
columns, list views
  adding items, 266–267
  creating, 264–266
COM (Component Object Model), 628
  initializing, 447–448
  uninitializing, 451
COM+, 629
CombineRgn() function, 430
combining regions of screens, 430–435
combo boxes, 193–194
  control, 164
  control styles, 195
  notifications, 196–197
commands, update commandUI functions, creating, 148
common controls
  advanced, 255
  CommonControlsApp application, 227–228
  CommonControlsApp2 application, 256–259
  icons (composite), creating, 252–255
  image lists, 226, 249–251
  list views, 226, 261–279
  OnCreate() function, 228–229, 260
  progress bars, 225, 229–233
  sliders, 226, 233–245
  spinners, 226, 245–249
  status bars, 226
  toolbars, 226
common controls, tree views, 226, 279–281
  adding items, 282–285
  CommonControlsApp2 application code, 291–293
  editing items, 285–287
  functions, 289–291
  MFC (Microsoft Foundation Classes) shortcuts code, 287–289
  responding to user selections, 285
Common Dialog application, 95–100
common dialog boxes, 79, 86–100
CommonControlsApp application, 227–228

progress bar, 231–233
sliders, 237–238
spinner, 248–249
CommonControlsApp2 application, 256–259
  list view, 275–279
  tree view code, 291–293
CommonDlgApp folder, 95
CompareItem() function, 191
compiling MyBrowser application, 854–855
Component Object Model. See COM
Component-Program Files window, 495, 498
Components and Controls Gallery dialog box, 853
components
  installations, 492
  Internet Explorer, 850–851
  setting up with InstallShield, 494–499
composite icons, creating, 252–255
configuring WebBrowser control, 855–856
Confirm Classes dialog box, 686–687
Connect dialog box, 833
connections
  FTP, opening, 830–831
  HTTP servers, opening, 827–828
ConrolApp2 application, checkboxes, 184
consistency (MTS attribute), 465
console applications (Win32), 4–5
constants
  ASPECTX, 39
  ASPECTXY, 39
  ASPECTY, 39
  BITSPIXEL, 39
  clipboard, 594–595
  CLIPCAPS, 40
  COLORRES, 40
  device capabilities, 39–40
  HORZRES, 40
  HORZSIZE, 40
  LOGPIXELSY, 40
  NUMBRUSHES, 40
  NUMCOLORS, 40
  NUMFONTS, 40
  NUMPENS, 40
  NUMRESERVED, 40
  PLANES, 40
  PSWIZB_BACK, 108
  PSWIZB_DISABLEDFINISH, 108
  PSWIZB_FINISH, 108
  PSWIZB_NEXT, 108
  RASTERCAPS, 40

Continued

898 Index

constants *(continued)*
 SetWizardButtons() function, 108
 SIZEPALETTE, 40
 VERTRES, 40
 VERTSIZE, 40
 window styles, 70
 WS_BORDER, 70
 WS_CAPTION, 70
 WS_CHILD, 70
 WS_CLIPCHILDREN, 70
 WS_CLIPSIBLINGS, 70
 WS_DISABLED, 70
 WS_DLGFRAME, 70
 WS_GROUP, 70
 WS_HSCROLL, 70
 WS_MAXIMIZE, 70
 WS_MAXIMIZEBOX, 70
 WS_MINIMIZE, 70
 WS_MINIMIZEBOX, 70
 WS_OVERLAPPED, 70
 WS_OVERLAPPEDWINDOW, 70
 WS_POPUP, 70
 WS_POPUPWINDOW, 70
 WS_SYSMENU, 70
 WS_TABSTOP, 70
 WS_THICKFRAME, 70
 WS_VISIBLE, 70
 WS_VSCROLL, 70
constructor s
 CColorDialog class, signature, 95
 CFileDialog class, signature, 87–88
 CFontDialog class, signature, 92
 CPen class, arguments, 42
 Direct3DWin class, 801–802
 dwAccessType, 827
 dwContext, 827
 dwFlags, 827
 pstrAgent, 827
 pstrProxyBypass, 827
 pstrProxyName, 827
 view class, 746–747, 768–769
ContainerApp application, 635–638
containers, 635
 applications, 624, 629–630
 bitmaps, 637–638
 embedded items, deleting, 648–649
 embedded objects, 639–641, 646–647
 mouse, selecting items, 641–649
 skeleton container application, creating, 635–638
ControlApp2 application
 combo boxes, 193–194
 OnCreate() function code, 171–172
 OnCtrlColor() function, 199
 pushbuttons, 181
 radio buttons, 186
controlling servers from clients, 689–691
controls. *See also* ActiveX controls; common controls; standard controls
 buttons, MFC (Microsoft Foundation Classes), removing, 19–20
 combo boxes, styles, 195
 dialog boxes, manipulating, 202–222
 list boxes, styles, 189–190
 OLE (object linking and embedding), 627
 Scramble, 706–707
 WebBrowser control, creating skeleton browser application, 851–861, 877–881
 Windows, 164
cooperative level (device access level), 762
coordinates
 Cartesian coordinate system, 411–412
 client, 398
 logical, 397–399
 logical units, scaling, 409–410
 physical, 397–399
 screen, 398
 window, 398
 X and Y, MM_TEXT mode, 404
Copy() function, 178, 250
copying bitmaps, 341
 changing size, 343–344
 without changing size, 342–343
 clipboard, 596–600
copying data formats, CBCircleApp2 application, 612–615
CPaintDC class, 27
CPen class, 42–44
CPoint object, 556–557
CProgressCtrl class, 229, 231
CPropertyPage class, 100, 109
CreatDDrawPal() function, DirectDrawApp, 729–730
Create() function, 56, 68–69, 173, 183, 262–263
CreateBitmapIndirect() function, 338
CreateBitmapPalette() function, 378
CreateCheckbox() function, 184
CreateComboBoxes() function, 194
CreateCompatibleBitmap() function, 338
CreateCompatibleDC() function, 339
CreateDDrawSurfaces() function, DirectDrawApp, 725
CreateDevice() function, 765
CreateDeviceFromClipper() function, 782–783
CreateDirectory() function, 823
CreateDiscardableBitmap() function, 338
CreateDragImage() function, 271, 289
CreateEllipticRgn() function, 429
CreateEllipticRgnIndirect() function, 429
CreateFrame() function, 784, 786
CreateLight() function, 806
CreateLightRGB() function, 788–789
CreateListBox() function, 188
CreateListColumns() function, 276
CreateMesh() function, 804–805
CreateMeshBuilder() function, 785
CreateOffScreenSurface() function, DirectDrawApp, 727–728
CreatePalette() function, 365, 720–721
CreatePolygonRgn() function, 429
CreatePolyPolygonRgn() function, 429
CreatePushbutton() function, 181
CreateRadioButtons() function, 186
CreateRectRgn() function, 429
CreateRectRgnIndirect() function, 429
CreateRoundRectRgn() function, 429
CreateSoundBuffer() function, 745, 749
CREATESTRUCT structure, code, 72
CreateSurface() function, 718–719, 720
CreateViewport() function, 787–788, 805–806
CreateWindow() function, arguments, 12
creating
 ActiveX control methods or properties, 702–705
 ActiveX user interface, 697–702
 application class files, 795–796
 applications to install, 487–488
 applications without AppWizard, 60–69
 automation client skeleton, 683–684
 BasicApp application, 61–66
 bitmap objects, 336–338

Index   899

BitmapApp2 application, 368–370
brushes, 45
CClientDC object, code, 32–33
CFtpFileFind object, 831–832
child frames, 789
clipper object, 781–782
composite icons, 252–255
dialog boxes, 80–83, 206–211, 673–674
DialogControlsApp application, 203–217
fonts, 131–135
frames for meshes, 785–786
HTTP sessions, 829
IShellLink object, 448
light object, 788–789
list view columns, 264–267
main window class header file, 796–797
media, 502–504
memory DC, 338–339
menu resources, 139–144
meshes for objects, 785
message maps, 15
modeless dialog boxes, 84–86
paths, 436
progress bars, 230–231
regions of screens, 429–430
root frames, 784
Save dialog box, code, 89–90
sliders, 233–237
spinners, 246–248
standard controls, 170–179
String application, 572–573
tree view object, 281–282
tree view root items, 283–284
UI threads, 519–522
update commandUI functions, 148
viewport, 786–788
wizards, 107
worker threads, 516–519
creating, Direct3D
devices, 782–784
main object, 781
programs, 780
creating, DirectDraw
object, 717
offscreen surfaces, 720
palettes, 720–721
primary surface, 718–719
programs, 714
creating, DirectInput
devices, 765
object, 764–765
program, 762
creating, DirectSound
object, 742, 744

programs, 741–742
secondary buffer, 745
creating, FTPAccessApp application, 835–836
DisplayStatusMessage() function, code, 846
DownloadFile() function, code, 843–845
InitSelection() function, code, 846–847
MoveToPreviousDirectory() function, code, 845
OnDraw() function, code, 837–838
OnFtpConnection() function, code, 839
OnLButtonDblClk() function, code, 841–842
OnRButtonDown() function, code, 843
OpenFTPDirectory() function, code, 840–841
ReadFileNames() function, code, 841
creating, skeletons
ActiveX control, 695–697
applications, 572–573
automation server, 672–673
browser applications, 851–861
container application, 635–638
server application, 652–655
CRgn class, functions, 429
critical sections, 524, 533–536
CriticalThread1() function, 535
CRuntimeClass structure, 522
CScrambleCtrl class, 697, 705–706
CSemaphore class, 541
CServerAppDoc class, 659
CServerAppView class, 662
CSizeDlg class, 656
CSliderCtrl class, 233, 236–237
CSpinButtonCtrl class, 246, 247–248
CStatic control, functions, 173–174
CStringArray class, 573
CStringDoc class, 573
CTLCOLOR_BTN (WM_CTLCOLOR message), 198
CTLCOLOR_DLG (WM_CTLCOLOR message), 198
CTLCOLOR_EDIT (WM_CTLCOLOR message), 198
CTLCOLOR_LISTBOX (WM_CTLCOLOR message), 198
CTLCOLOR_MSGBOX (WM_CTLCOLOR message), 198
CTLCOLOR_SCROLLBAR (WM_CTLCOLOR message), 198

CTLCOLOR_STATIC (WM_CTLCOLOR message), 198
CTreeCtrl class, 281, 282
Ctrl key, tracking, 568
customizing
automation server resources, 673–675
client application resources, 684–685
dialog boxes, 79–86
ServerApp application, resources, 655–659
Cut() function, 178
CView class, functions, 59–60
CWave class, code, 750–752
CWindowDC class, 27
CWinThread class, 519
CWnd class, 55–57
cx (LV_COLUMN structure), 265
cx argument, 250
cy argument, 250

D

data
fields, nFlag, 560
format, DirectInput, setting, 766
formats, clipboard, 609–618
sets, linked, 624–625
types, Registry, 471
DC (device context)
classes, 27
client-area, 29–34
object, 23, 24–27
Paint, 27–39
DCOM (Distributed Component Object Model), 628
DDBs (device-dependent bitmaps), 335
bitmap objects, creating and initializing, 336–338
programming with, 336–352
ddraw.h header file, adding to DirectDrawApp, 715
ddraw.lib file, adding to DirectDrawApp, 716–717
DDSCAPS structure, 718–719
DDSURFACEDESC structure, 718–719, 720
declaring
document data objects, 573
message maps, 16
Define Custom Colors button, 94
defining
automation server methods or properties, 678–682
message-response functions, 17–18
subpaths, 437

900 Index

delayed rendering, clipboard, 605–609
DelayedRender application, 606–609
Delete() function, 648
DeleteAllCircles() function, 580
DeleteAllItems() function, 271, 289
DeleteColumn() function, 271
DeleteContents() function, 376, 377, 382, 574, 575
DeleteImageList() function, 250
DeleteItem() function, 191, 271, 289
DeleteString() function, 191
DeleteTempMap() function, 251
deleting. *See* removing
dependencies of applications, locating, 487
Depends utility, 487
DestroyWindow() function, 56
Detach() function, 251
detecting file errors, 590–592
device access levels
 cooperative level, 762
 DirectInput, setting, 766
device capabilities, 39–41
device context. *See* DC
DeviceCapsapp, code, 41
device-dependent bitmaps. *See* DDBs
device-independent bitmaps. *See* DIBs
devices. *See also* keyboards; mouse
 Direct3D, 782–784
 DirectInput, 766–767
DHTML (Dynamic HTML)
 document interfaces, accessing, 871–872
 IHTMLDocument2, 868–872
 object model, 868–877
dialog boxes, 79–86. *See also* individual dialog box names; property sheets; wizards
 Cancel button, 83
 CControlDlg class, adding code, 214–220
 ClassWizard, 80–81
 Color, 86, 93–95, 98–99
 Common Dialog application, 95–100
 common, 79, 86–100
 controls, 202–222
 creating, 206–211, 673–674
 custom, 79–86
 DoModal() function, 80
 edit boxes, 174
 File, 86–91
 Find-Replace, 86
 Font, 86, 91–93, 95, 98

HTML, 862–867
Insert Resource, 80, 101
main windows, 199–202
modeless, creating, 84–86
New Class, 104
OK button, 83
Open, 87–88, 95
Open File, code to handle, 96–97
Open, GetFileName() function, 90
Page Setup, 86
Print, 86
Save As, 87, 89–90
Save File, code to handle, 97
Save, 95
Save, code to create and display, 89–90
view class, adding code, 212–214
Dialog Properties property sheet, 102
DialogControlApp application
 creating, 203–217
 dialog box controls, 221–222
 running, 220–221
dialogHeight:number syntax, 866
dialogLeft:number syntax, 866
Dialogs menu
 Color Dialog command, 95
 Font Dialog command, 95
 Open File Dialog command, 95
 Save File Dialog command, 95
dialogTop:number syntax, 866
dialogWidth:number syntax, 866
Diameter edit box, m_diameter variable, 675
Diameter property, 680
DIBs (device-independent bitmaps), 335–336
 cdib.cpp file, 369
 DIB file, loading, 353–358
 displaying, 363–364
 logical palettes, 364–366
 memory storage, 385
 multi-image, managing, 383–390
 palettes, managing, 364–368
 programming with, 352–395
DibToSurface() function, DirectDrawApp, 730–731
dinput.h header fil, 763
dinput.lib fil, 763–764
Dir() function, 191
Direct3D, 779
 applications, building, 790–793
 applications, writing, 808–814
 clipper object, creating, 781–782
 devices, creating, 782–784
 Gouraud shading, 784
 lights, adding, 788–789
 main object, creating, 781

meshes, creating frames, 785–786
modeling skills, 794
objects, creating meshes, 785
programs, 780, 781
root frames, creating, 784
viewport, 786–788
Direct3DApp application, 790–793, 802–814
 class implementation file, creating, 795–796
 main window class header file, creating, 796–797
 running, 794
 window class implementation file, code to create, 797–801
Direct3DApp2 application, code, 809–814
Direct3DRMCreate() function, 781
Direct3DWin class, constructor, 801–802
DirectDraw, 713
 applications, code to write, 736–739
 back buffers, 718, 736
 clipper object, creating, 781–782
 files, adding to Visual C++ project, 715–717
 object, 714, 717
 offscreen surfaces, creating, 720
 page-flipping, 718
 palettes, creating, 720–721
 primary surface, creating, 718–719
 programs, creating, 714
 screen access level, setting, 717–718
DirectDrawApp application
 ClearDDrawSurface() function, 726–727
 CreatDDrawPal() function, 729–730
 CreateDDrawSurfaces() function, 725
 CreateOffScreenSurface() function, 727–728
 ddraw.h header file, adding, 715
 ddraw.lib file, adding, 716–717
 DibToSurface() function, 730–731
 InitDirectDraw() function, 724–725
 InitImages() function, 728–729
 InitMemberVariables() function, 723–724
 OnDestroy() function, 734–735
 OnInitialUpdate() function, 722–723

Index

OnKeyDown() function, 734
OnTimer() function, 732–733
DirectDrawApp2 application, 736–740
DirectDrawCreateClipper() function, 781–782
DirectInput, 761
  applications, code to write, 773–777
  data format, setting, 766
  device access levels, setting, 766
  devices, 765, 766–767
  dinput.h header file, adding, 763
  dinput.lib file, adding, 763–764
  dxguid.lib file, adding, 763–764
  files, adding to Visual C++ project, 763–764
  object, creating, 764–765
  program, creating, 762
DirectInputApp application, 767, 774–777
  OnDestroy() function, 772–773
  OnDraw() function, 771–772
  OnInitialUpdate() function, 769–770
  OnTimer() function, 770–771
  view class constructor, 768–769
DirectInputApp2 application, code to write, 773–777
DirectInputCreate() function, 765–765
directories
  Active Directory, 465
  MOVE TO PREVIOUS DIRECTORY command, 834
  reading, 831–832
  root, 831
DirectSound
  applications, writing, 755–760
  dsound.lib file, adding, 743–744
  files, adding to Visual C++ project, 742–744
  object, creating, 742, 744
  programs, creating, 741–742
  secondary buffer, creating, 745
  sound-hardware access level, setting, 744–745
DirectSoundApp application, 756–760
  CreateSoundBuffer() function, 749
  CWave class, code, 750–752
  InitDirectSound() function, 748–749
  LoadWaveData() function, 753–754
  OnDestroy() function, 754–755
  OnInitialUpdate() function, 747–748

OnLButtonDown() function, 754
  view-class constructor, 746–747
DirectSoundApp2 application, code, 755–760
DirectSoundCreate() function, 744
DirectX
  Direct3D, 779
  DirectDraw, 713–714
  DirectInput, 761
  DirectSound, 741
DirectX5.0 SDK, Microsoft Web site, 741
DirectX7.0 SDK, Microsoft Web site, 714
DirectX SDK, Microsoft Web site, 761
disabling menu items, 151–152
Disk Type page, 502
DispatchMessage() function, 13
displaying
  back buffer, 736
  ClassWizard, 103, 347
  DIBs (device-independent bitmaps), 363–364
  HTML pages, 850
  nonrectangular bitmaps, 390–395
  Save dialog box, code, 89–90
  tabbed text, 126–127
  text, 113–114
DisplayServerWindow() method, 681
DisplayStatusMessage() function, FTPAccessApp application, 846
Distributed Component Object Model (DCOM), 628
Distributed interNet Application (DNA), 464–465
distributing WebBrowser control, 877–881
DLLs (dynamic-link libraries), 5
  Shared, 496–497, 499
  Windows/System folder, 6
DNA (Distributed interNet Application), 464–465
DockControlBar() function, 59
document class
  automation server, 676–677
  ServerApp application, 659–661
document/view architecture, 571
  DeleteContents() function, overriding, 574, 575
  document data objects, declaring, 573
  editing code, 577–578
  nonpersistent objects, saving, 584–586
  OnDraw() function, 576–577

OnNewDocument() function, 573–574
  persistent objects, saving, 584–586
  Serialize() function, 574–576
  skeleton applications, creating, 572–573
documentation, Visual C++ online, function signatures, 18
documents
  ActiveX, 633–634
  ActiveX, OLE 1.0, 623–626
  ActiveX, OLE 2.0, 626–627
  clipboard, 593–594
  data objects, declaring, 573
  data sets, linked, 624–625
  interfaces, accessing, 871–872
  printing, 295–298
  retrieving with robots, 883
  Server Document, 654
DoModal() function, 80, 90, 93, 95
DoPreparePrinting() function, 59, 304–305
double colon (::), 531
DownloadFile() function, FTPAccessApp application, 843–845
DragAcceptFiles() function, 444
drag-and drop, 443
  applications, registering as, 444
  dropped file names, retrieving, 445
  operations, ending, 446
  WM_DROPFILES message, 445
DragDrop2 application, 443–446
DragEnter() function, 251
DragFinish() function, 446
DragLeave() function, 251
DragMove() function, 251
DragQueryFile() function, arguments, 445
DragShowNolock() function, 251
Draw() function, 251
Draw3dRect() function, 25
DrawDragRect() function, 25
DrawEdge() function, 25
DrawIcon() function, 25
DrawIndirect() function, 251
drawing
  on bitmaps, 340–341
  with pens, 42–44
  rectangles, 28
  regions of screens, 429–430
  shapes in MetafileDCApp, 36
DrawItem() function, 183, 191, 271
Drop Down Combo Box, 169
dropped file names, retrieving, 445
DSBUFFERDESC structure, 745

902 Index

dsound.lib file, adding to DirectSound, 743–744
DSTINVERT (bitmap raster operations), 417
dstPoint argument, 731
Dump() function, 54
Duplicate() function, 588
durability (MTS attribute), 466
dwAccessType constructor, 827
dwContext
 argument, 828
 constructor, 827
dwCreateFlags parameter, 518
dwExStyle argument, 69
dwFlags
 argument, 88, 89, 92, 95, 727
 constructor, 827
dwHeadersLength argument, 828
dwROP argument, 342, 344, 363
dwStyle argument, 69, 172, 175, 182, 189
dxguid.lib fil, 763–764
Dynamic HTML. *See* DHTML
dynamic-link libraries. *See* DLLs

E

edit boxes
 control, 164
 single-line and multiline, 174
Edit Code button, 212–213, 216, 328, 660
edit controls, 175, 178–179
 edit boxes, single-line and multiline, 174
 notifications, 177
 styles, 176
Edit menu
 Copy command, 595–596, 597, 607, 612
 Delete command, 648
 Insert New Control command, 701, 637, 653, 665, 666
 Paste command, 595–596, 600–602, 607, 615
Edit Properties dialog box, 209
editing
 code, 577–578
 list view items, 273–275
EditLabel() function, 271, 290
editors
 linked items, ServerApp, running as, 666–668
 in-place, running ServerApp as, 665–666
 Menu Editor, menu resources, creating, 139–144
 Registry Editor, 468, 471–472

resource, 370–371
Ellipse() function, 25
embedded, items, deleting, 646–649
EmptyClipboard() function, 596
EmptyUndoBuffer() function, 178
EN_CHANGE (edit control notification), 177
EN_ERRSPACE (edit control notification), 177
EN_HSCROLL (edit control notification), 177
EN_KILLFOCUS (edit control notification), 177
EN_MAXTEXT (edit control notification), 177
EN_SETFOCUS (edit control notification), 177
EN_UPDATE (edit control notification), 177
EN_VSCROLL (edit control notification), 177
Enable() function, 151
EnableDocking() function, 59
EnableStatusCallback() function, 821
EnableWindow() function, 56
enabling menu items, 151–152
EndDrag() function, 251
EndPaint() function, 28
EndRequest() function, 821
EnsureVisible() function, 271, 290
EnumObjects() function, 460, 461
EnumPrinters() function, 296
errors, detecting in files, 590–592
ES_AUTOHSCROLL (edit control style), 176
ES_AUTOVSCROLL (edit control style), 176
ES_CENTER (edit control style), 176
ES_LEFT (edit control style), 176
ES_LOWERCASE (edit control style), 176
ES_MULTILINE (edit control style), 176
ES_NOHIDESEL (edit control style), 176
ES_OEMCONVERT (edit control style), 176
ES_PASSWORD (edit control style), 176
ES_READONLY (edit control style), 176
ES_RIGHT (edit control style), 176
ES_UPPERCASE (edit control style), 176
ES_WANTRETURN (edit control style), 176

event objects
 manual, 531–533
 program and thread communication, 528–531
events, 524
 automatic, 525–528
 of icons, responding to, 454–455
 mouse, handling, 557–558
EventThread application, 528–531
EventThread() function, 527, 532–533
ExactIcon() function, 251
exception, CFileException, 590–592
ExitInstance() function, 519
Expand() function, 290
extending DHTML (Dynamic HTML) object model, code, 873–877
extents, viewport or window, 409

F

File dialog box, 86–91
File Group dialog box, 500
File Group page (Shell Objects – Shortcuts window), 508
File Groups – Program Executable Files window, 499–500
File Groups – Program Executable Files\Links window, 500–501
File menu
 New command, 61–62, 325, 637
 Open command, 381, 637
 Save All command, 653, 673
 Save command, 637
File Name dialog box, 62
files
 afxwin.h header, 66
 cdib.cpp, 369
 CFile class, 588–592
 components, 492
 ddraw.h header, adding to DirectDrawApp, 715
 ddraw.lib file, adding to DirectDrawApp, 716–717
 DIB, loading, 353–358
 dinput.h header file, 763
 dinput.lib file, 763–764
 DirectDraw, adding to Visual C++ project, 715–717
 DirectSound, adding to Visual C++ project, 742–744
 dropped, retrieving names, 445
 dsound.lib, adding to DirectSound, 743–744
 dxguid.lib file, 763–764
 errors, detecting, 590–592

Index

group setup, 499–501
header, 795–797
implementation, 795–801
.ini, 467
linked data sets, 624–625
modified, saving, 586–587
MyApplication.exe, 500–501
MyApplication.ini, 467
objects, shell namespace, 458
packaging, 486–487
persistent objects, 578–587
reading, 828
Registry, 472–473
shdocvw.dll, Internet Explorer versions, 878–879
win.ini, 467
files, DirectInput
adding to Visual C++ project, 763–764
dinput.h header file, adding, 763
dinput.lib file, adding, 763–764
dxguid.lib file, adding, 763–764
files, document/view architecture, 571
DeleteContents() function, overriding, 574, 575
document data objects, declaring, 573
editing code, 577–578
nonpersistent objects, saving, 584–586
OnDraw() function, 576–577
OnNewDocument() function, 573–574
persistent objects, saving, 584–586
Serialize() function, 574–576
skeleton applications, creating, 572–573
Files tab (New dialog box), 62
FillPath() function, 436, 438
FillRect() function, 25, 340
FillRgn() function, 25, 429
FillSolidRect() function, 25
Find dialog box, 862
FindFile() function, 825, 826
finding application dependencies, 487
FindItem() function, 271
FindNextFile() function, 825, 826
Find-Replace dialog box, 86
FindString() function, 191
FindStringExact() function, 191
Finish button, 108, 488
first edit control, 165
Flags
argument, 296
parameter, 857

flags
CFile class, 589
navigational, WebBrowser, 858
Flip() method, 736
FloatControlBar() function, 59
FloodFill() function, 25, 38
Flush() function, 588, 823
fmt (LV_COLUMN structure), 265
FmtLines() function, 178
folders
CommonDlgApp, 95
Programs, placing application shortcuts, 506
shell namespace, 458–459
virtual, shell namespace, 458
Windows/System, DLLs (dynamic-link libraries), 6
Font
dialog box, 86, 91–93, 95, 98
object, 24
FontApp application, 133–138
fonts
creating, 131–135
LOGFONT structure, 131–132
formats
clipboard, 594–609
data, 609–618
DirectInput data, setting, 766
frame window class, 67–69
frame windows, 58, 78–79
FrameRect() function, 25, 429
frames
creating, 789
creating for meshes, 785–786
root, creating, 784
for viewport, creating, 786–787
FromHandle() function, 251, 337
FromHandlePermanent() function, 251
FTP
application, writing, 830–832
connections, opening, 830–831
directories, reading, 831–832
menu@index H:Connect command, 833
root directory, 831
server, 834
session2, closing, 832
FTPAccessApp application
DisplayStatusMessage() function, code to create, 846
DownloadFile() function, code to create, 843–845
InitSelection() function, code to create, 846–847
member variables, 835–847
MoveToPreviousDirectory() function, code to create, 845

OnDraw() function, code to create, 837–838
OnFtpConnection() function, code to create, 839
OnLButtonDblClk() function, code to create, 841–842
OnRButtonDown() function, code to create, 843
OpenFTPDirectory() function, code to create, 840–841
ReadFileNames() function, code to create, 841
running, 832–835
functions
Abort(), 588, 823
Acquire(), 767
ActivateFrame(), 58
Add(), 250
AddCircle(), 580
AddLight(), 789
AddListItems(), 276–277
AddRequestHeaders(), 821
AddString(), 191
AfxBeginThread(), 518
AfxOleInit(), 689
Arc(), 25
Arrange(), 271
AssertValid(), 54
Attach(), 250
BeginDrag(), 250
BeginPaint(), 28
BitBlt(), 25, 343, 342
bitmap initialization, 337–338
CanUndo(), 178
CButton class, 183
CCircles class, 580
CCmdTarget class, 55
CColorDialog class, 95
CDC class, 25–26
CDC Rectangle(), 28
CEdit class, 177–179
CenterWindow(), 56
CFile class, 588
CFileDialog class, 90–91
CFileFind class, 825
CFontDialog class, 93
CFrameWnd class, 58–59
CFtpConnection class, 823
CFtpFileFind class, 826
CharFromPos(), 178
CharToItem(), 191
CHttpFile class, 824
CImageList class, 250–251
CInternetConnection class, 821
CInternetFile class, 823–824
CInternetSession class, 821
Clear(), 178
ClearDDrawSurface(), 726–727

Continued

functions *(continued)*
 ClearSel(), 236
 ClearTics(), 236
 CListBox class, 191–193
 CListCtrl class, 270–272
 Close(), 588, 821, 823, 825
 CloseClipboard(), 597
 CloseFigure(), 437
 CMetaFileDCCreate(), 37
 CObject class, 54–55
 CoCreateInstance(), 448
 CoInitializeEx(), 447–448
 CombineRgn(), 430
 CompareItem(), 191
 Copy(), 178, 250
 CProgressCtrl class, 231
 CPropertyPage class, 109
 CreatDDrawPal(), 729–730
 Create(), 173, 178, 183, 191, 231
 CreateBitmapIndirect(), 338
 CreateBitmapPalette(), 378
 CreateCheckbox(), 184
 CreateComboBoxes(), 194
 CreateCompatibleBitmap(), 338
 CreateCompatibleDC(), 339
 CreateDDrawSurfaces(), 725
 CreateDevice(), 765
 CreateDeviceFromClipper(), 782–783
 CreateDirectory(), 823
 CreateDiscardableBitmap(), 338
 CreateDragImage(), 271, 289
 CreateEllipticRgn(), 429
 CreateEllipticRgnIndirect(), 429
 CreateFrame(), 784, 786
 CreateLight(), 806
 CreateLightRGB(), 788–789
 CreateListBox(), 188
 CreateListColumns(), 276
 CreateMesh(), 804–805
 CreateMeshBuilder(), 785
 CreateOffScreenSurface(), 727–728
 CreatePalette(), 365, 720–721
 CreatePolygonRgn(), 429
 CreatePolyPolygonRgn(), 429
 CreatePushbutton(), 181
 CreateRadioButtons(), 186
 CreateRectRgn(), 429
 CreateRectRgnIndirect(), 429
 CreateRoundRectRgn(), 429
 CreateSoundBuffer(), 745, 749
 CreateSurface(), 718–719, 720
 CreateViewport(), 787–788, 805–806
 CreateWindow(), 12
 CRgn class, 429
 CriticalThread1(), 535
 CriticalThread2(), 535

 CSliderCtrl class, 236–237
 CSpinButtonCtrl class, 247–248
 CStatic control, 173–174
 custom dialog boxes, code, 82–83
 Cut(), 178
 CView class, 59–60
 CWnd class, 56–57
 Delete(), 648
 DeleteAllCircles(), 580
 DeleteAllItems(), 271, 289
 DeleteColumn(), 271
 DeleteContents(), 376, 382, 572, 574, 575
 DeleteImageList(), 250
 DeleteItem(), 191, 271, 289
 DeleteString(), 191
 DeleteTempMap(), 251
 DestroyWindow(), 56
 Detach(), 251
 DibToSurface(), 730–731
 Dir(), 191
 Direct3DRMCreate(), 781
 DirectDrawCreateClipper(), 781–782
 DirectInputCreate(), 765–765
 DirectSoundCreate(), 744
 DispatchMessage(), 13
 DisplayStatusMessage(), 846
 DockControlBar(), 59
 DoModal(), 80, 90, 93, 95
 DoPreparePrinting(), 59, 304–305
 DownloadFile(), 843–845
 DragAcceptFiles(), 444
 DragEnter(), 251
 DragFinish(), 446
 DragLeave(), 251
 DragMove(), 251
 DragQueryFile(), 445
 DragShowNolock(), 251
 Draw(), 251
 Draw3dRect(), 25
 DrawDragRect(), 25
 DrawEdge(), 25
 DrawIcon(), 25
 DrawIndirect(), 251
 DrawItem(), 183, 191, 271
 Dump(), 54
 Duplicate(), 588
 EditLabel(), 271, 290
 Ellipse(), 25
 EmptyClipboard(), 596
 EmptyUndoBuffer(), 178
 Enable(), 151
 EnableDocking(), 59
 EnableStatusCallback(), 821
 EnableWindow(), 56
 EndDrag(), 251
 EndPaint(), 28

 EndRequest(), 821
 EnsureVisible(), 271, 290
 EnumObjects(), 460, 461
 EnumPrinters(), 296
 EventThread(), 532–533, 527
 ExactIcon(), 251
 ExitInstance(), 519
 Expand(), 290
 FillPath(), 436, 438
 FillRect(), 25, 340
 FillRgn(), 25, 429
 FillSolidRect(), 25
 FindFile(), 825, 826
 FindItem(), 271
 FindNextFile(), 825, 826
 FindString(), 191
 FindStringExact(), 191
 FloatControlBar(), 59
 FloodFill(), 25, 38
 Flush(), 588, 823
 FmtLines(), 178
 FrameRect(), 25
 FrameRgn(), 25, 429
 FromHandle(), 251, 337
 FromHandlePermanent(), 251
 GetAccel(), 247
 GetActiveDocument(), 59
 GetActiveFrame(), 59
 GetActiveView(), 59
 GetActiveWindow(), 56
 GetAnchorIndex(), 191
 GetArguments(), 449
 GetAttachedSurface(), 719
 GetAttributesOf(), 463
 GetBase(), 247
 GetBipmap(), 173, 183, 337
 GetBitmapBits(), 337
 GetBitmapDimension(), 337
 GetBkColor(), 25, 251, 271
 GetBkMode(), 115
 GetBrowserVersion(), code, 879–880
 GetBuddy(), 236, 247
 GetButtonStyle(), 183
 GetCallbackMask(), 271
 GetCapture(), 56
 GetCaratIndex(), 191
 GetChannelRect(), 236
 GetCheck(), 183
 GetChildItem(), 290
 GetCircle(), 580
 GetCircleCount(), 580
 GetClientRect(), 56
 GetClipboardData(), 601
 GetColor(), 93, 95
 GetColumn(), 271
 GetColumnWidth(), 271
 GetContext(), 821
 GetControlBar(), 59

Index

GetCookie(), 821
GetCookieLength(), 821
GetCount(), 191, 290
GetCountPerPage(), 271
GetCreationTime(), 825
GetCurrentBitmap(), 25
GetCurrentBrush(), 25
GetCurrentDirectory(), 823
GetCurrentDirectoryAsURL(), 823
GetCurrentFont(), 25, 93
GetCurrentPalette(), 25
GetCurrentPen(), 25
GetCurrentPosition(), 25
GetCurSel(), 190, 192
GetCursor(), 173, 183
GetData(), 362
GetDC(), 31
GetDescription(), 449
GetDeviceCaps(), 26, 39, 40, 318–319, 323–324
GetDisplayNameOf(), 464
GetDlgItem(), 56
GetDockState(), 59
GetDocument(), 59
GetDragImage(), 251
GetDropHilightItem(), 290
GetEditControl(), 271, 290
GetEnhMetaFile(), 174
GetFaceName(), 93
GetFile(), 823
GetFileExt(), 90
GetFileName(), 90, 362, 588, 825
GetFilePath(), 588, 825
GetFileTitle(), 91, 588, 825
GetFileURL(), 821, 825, 826
GetFirstVisibleItem(), 290
GetFirstVisibleLine(), 178
GetFocus(), 56
GetFont(), 56
GetFtpConnection(), 821, 830, 831
GetGopherConnection(), 821
GetHandle(), 178
GetHeight(), 362
GetHitItem(), 645
GetHorizontalExtent(), 192
GetHotkey(), 449
GetHttpConnection(), 821
GetIcon(), 56, 174, 183
GetIconLocation(), 449
GetIDList(), 449
GetIEMajorVersions(), code, 878–879
GetImageCount(), 251
GetImageInfo(), 251
GetImageList(), 271, 290
GetIndent(), 290
GetInfo(), 362

GetItem(), 271, 290
GetItemCount(), 271
GetItemData(), 192, 271, 290
GetItemDataPtr(), 192
GetItemHeight(), 192
GetItemImage(), 290
GetItemPosition(), 271
GetItemRect(), 192, 271, 290
GetItemState(), 271, 290
GetItemText(), 271, 290
GetLastAccessTime(), 825
GetLastWriteTime(), 825
GetLength(), 588, 825
GetLimitText(), 178
GetLine(), 178
GetLineCount(), 178
GetLineSize(), 236
GetLocale(), 192
GetMapMode(), 26, 410
GetMargins(), 178
GetMenu(), 56
GetMessage(), 13
GetMessageBar(), 59
GetModify(), 178
GetNextItem(), 271, 290
GetNextSiblingItem(), 290
GetNextVisibleItem(), 290
GetNumberOfColors(), 362
GetNumTics(), 236
GetObject(), 821
GetOrigin(), 272
GetPageSize(), 236
GetParent(), 56
GetParentFrame(), 56
GetParentItem(), 290
GetParentOwner(), 56
GetPasswordChar(), 178
GetPath(), 449
GetPathName(), 91
GetPixel(), 26
GetPolyFillMode(), 26
GetPos(), 231, 236, 247
GetPosition(), 588
GetPrevSiblingItem(), 290
GetPrevVisibleItem(), 290
GetRange(), 231, 236, 247
GetRange32(), 247
GetRangeMax(), 236
GetRangeMin(), 236
GetReadyOnlyPref(), 91
GetRect(), 178
GetRGB(), 362
GetRoot(), 825
GetRootItem(), 290
GetRuntimeClass(), 55
GetSafeHandle(), 251
GetSafeHwnd(), 56
GetSavedCustomColors(), 95
GetSel(), 178, 192

GetSelCount(), 192
GetSelectedCount(), 272
GetSelectedItem(), 290
GetSelection(), 236
GetSelItems(), 192
GetServerName(), 821
GetSession(), 821
GetShowCmd(), 449
GetSize(), 93, 362
GetState(), 183
GetStatus(), 588
GetStringWidth(), 272
GetStyle(), 56
GetStyleName(), 93
GetSystemMenu(), 56
GetSystemMetrics(), 12
GetText(), 190, 192
GetTextBkColor(), 272
GetTextColor(), 26, 114, 272
GetTextExtent(), 26
GetTextExtentPoint32(), 136
GetTextLen(), 192
GetTextMetrics(), 26, 128, 309
GetTextWindow(), 26
GetThumbRect(), 236
GetTic(), 236
GetTicArray(), 236
GetTicPos(), 236
GetToolTips(), 236
GetTopIndex(), 192, 272
GetVerb(), 821
GetViewportExtEx(), 410
GetViewRect(), 272
GetVisibleCount(), 290
GetWeight(), 93
GetWidth(), 362
GetWindowExtEx(), 410
GetWindowRect(), 56, 477
GetWindowText(), 56, 178
GetWorkingDirectory(), 449
GrayString(), 26
HitTest(), 272, 290
InitApplication(), 15
InitDirectDraw(), 724–725
InitDirectSound(), 748–749
InitImages(), 728–729
InitInstance(), 15, 202, 519, 689
InitListView(), 275
InitMemberVariables(), 723–724
InitProgressBar(), 228, 231
InitRadioButtons(), 277–278
InitSelection(), 846–847
InitSlider(), 228, 237
InitSpinner(), 228
InitStaticText(), 228
InitStorage(), 192
InsertColumn(), 264–265, 268–269, 272

Continued

Index

functions *(continued)*
- InsertItem(), 268–269, 272, 290
- InsertString(), 192
- Internet Ratings API, 860
- Invalidate(), 56, 561, 771
- InvalidateRect(), 56
- InvertRgn(), 429
- IsArchived(), 825
- IsBold(), 93
- IsClipboardFormatAvailable(), 601
- IsCompressed(), 825
- IsDirectory(), 825
- IsDots(), 825
- IShellLink interface, 449–450
- IsHidden(), 825
- IsIconic(), 56
- IsItalic(), 93
- IsKindOF(), 55
- IsNormal(), 825
- IsPrinting(), 309
- IsReadOnly(), 825
- IsSerializable(), 55
- IsStrikeOut(), 93
- IsSystem(), 825
- IsTemporary(), 825
- IsUnderline(), 93
- IsValid(), 362
- IsWindowEnabled(), 56
- IsWindowVisible(), 56
- IsZoomed(), 56
- ItemFromPoint(), 192
- ItemHasChildren(), 290
- KillTimer(), 56
- LimitText(), 178
- LineFromChar(), 178
- LineIndex(), 178
- LineLength(), 178
- LineScroll(), 178
- LineTo(), 26, 37, 404
- LoadAccelTable(), 59
- LoadBarState(), 59
- LoadBitmap(), 337
- LoadLibrary(), 862
- LoadMappedBitmap(), 337
- LoadOEMBitmap(), 337
- LoadWaveData(), 753–754
- Lock(), 534, 541, 727, 753
- LockRange(), 588
- MakeScene(), 803, 804
- MatchesMask(), 825
- MeasureItem(), 192
- MessageBox(), 56, 531
- message-responses, 16–18, 144–146
- MessageThread(), 517
- MFC (Microsoft Foundation Classes) for printing, 304–316
- ModifyStyle(), 57
- MoveTo(), 26, 37, 404
- MoveToPreviousDirectory(), 845
- MoveWindow(), 57
- Next(), arguments, 463
- NotifyChanged(), 663
- NotifyIcon(), 453
- OffsetPos(), 231
- OnActivateFrame(), 59
- OnActivateView(), 59
- OnAutomationSetdiameter(), 687
- OnAutomationSetxposition(), 688
- OnAutomationSetyposition(), 688
- OnBeginPrinting(), 60, 306–310, 324
- OnButton1(), 216–217
- OnChangeEdit1(), 217
- OnChangeItemPosition(), 639–640
- OnChar(), 560, 561
- OnCircleChangemessage(), code, 586–587
- OnCircleSetcircle(), 677–678
- OnColorOK(), 95
- OnCreate(), 36–37, 228–229, 260, 320–321, 802–803
- OnCtrlColor(), 198, 199
- OnDestroy(), 38–39, 475–476, 734–735, 754–755, 772–773
- OnDraw(), 28, 60, 99, 771–772, 837–838
- OnEditAddstring(), code, 577–578
- OnEditChange(), 177
- OnEditCopy(), 597–598, 607–608, 612, 660–661
- OnEditPaste(), 600, 602, 615–617
- OnEndPrinting(), 60, 315–316
- OnEndPrintPreview(), 60
- OnFileNameOK(), 91
- OnFileOpen(), 376
- OnFtpConnection(), 839
- OnGetItemPosition(), 640
- OnHScroll(), 235–236
- OnInitDialog(), 214
- OnInitialUpdate(), 60, 722–723, 747–748, 769–770
- OnKeyDown(), 648–649, 734
- OnLButtonDblClk(), 841–842
- OnLButtonDown(), 31, 117–118, 212, 239–240, 451–452
- OnLButtonUp(), 239–241
- OnListViewDblClk(), 279
- OnLoadURL(), 853
- OnMouseMove(), 556
- OnNcMouseMove(), 551–552
- OnNewDocument(), 572, 573–574, 661
- OnNotify(), 274
- OnPaint(), 806–807
- OnPaletteChanged(), 367
- OnPrepareDC(), 60, 310–312
- OnPreparePrinting(), 60, 304–306, 323
- OnPrint(), 60, 313–315, 324–325, 329
- OnQueryNewPalette(), 367
- OnRButtonDown(), 118, 456, 557–558, 843
- OnRButtonUp(), 558
- OnRectangleSize(), 662–663
- OnRenderAllFormats(), 609
- OnRenderFormat(), 608–609
- OnSetCursor(), 642
- OnShareViolation(), 91
- OnSize(), 413
- OnStatusCallback(), 821
- OnTimer(), 732–733, 770–771, 803, 808
- OnTrayMessage(), 457
- OnUpdate(), 60
- OnUpdateViewToolbar(), 150
- OnWizardBack(), 109
- OnWizardFinish(), 109
- OnWizardNext(), 109
- Open(), 588
- OpenClipboard(), 57, 596
- OpenFile(), 823
- OpenFTPDirectory(), 840–841
- OpenURL(), 821, 828
- PaintRgn(), 429
- ParseCircleText(), 617–618
- Paste(), 178
- Pie(), 26
- Play(), 754
- Polygon(), 26
- Polyline(), 26
- PosFromChar(), 179
- PostMessage(), 57
- PreCreateWindow(), 57, 71, 480–481
- PreTranslateMessage(), 180
- PrintRectangle(), 301
- ProcessFolder(), 461–464
- PutFile(), 823
- QueryInfo(), 821
- QueryInfoStatusCode(), 821
- QueryInterface(), 449
- QueryOption(), 821
- RatingAccessDeniedDialog(), 860
- RatingCheckUserAccess(), 860
- RatingEnable(), 860
- RatingEnabledQuery(), 860
- RatingFreeDetails(), 860

Index

RatingObtainCancel(), 860
RatingObtainQuery(), 860
RatingSetupUI(), 860
Read(), 251, 588, 823
ReadFileNames(), 841
ReadHuge(), 588
ReadString(), 823, 828
RealizePalette(), 26
Rectangle(), 26, 37
RedrawItems(), 272
RegCloseKey(), 473, 474
RegCreateKey(), 473, 474
RegCreateKeyEx(), 477–479
RegDeleteKey(), 473, 474
RegDeleteValue(), 474
RegEnumKey(), 474
RegEnumKeyEx(), 474
RegEnumValue(), 474
RegFlushKey(), 474
RegisterClass(), 15
RegOpenKey(), 474
RegOpenKeyEx(), 474, 477
RegQueryInfoKey(), 474
RegQueryValue(), 474
RegQueryValueEx(), 474, 482
RegSetValue(), 474
RegSetValueEx(), 474, 479
Release(), 451, 734, 754
ReleaseDC(), 31
Remove(), 251, 588, 823
RemoveDirectory(), 823
Rename(), 588, 823
RenderAsBitmap(), 613
RenderAsText(), 614–615
RenderDisplay(), 598–599, 613
Replace(), 251
ReplaceSel(), 179
ResetContent(), 192
Resolve(), 449
ResumeThread(), 536
RoundRect(), 26
Save(), 450–451
SaveBarState(), 59
Scroll(), 272
Seek(), 588, 823
SeekToBegin(), 588
SeekToEnd(), 588
SelecObject(), 26
Select(), 290
SelectDropTarget(), 291
SelectItem(), 291
SelectObject(), 339
SelectPalette(), 26
SelectSetFirstVisible(), 291
SelectStockObject(), 26
SelectString(), 192
SelItemRange(), 192
SemaphoreThread(), 542–543
SendMessage(), 57

SendRequest(), 821
SendRequestEx(), 821
Serialize(), 55, 571, 574–576, 641, 660
ServiceTypeFromHandle(), 821
SetAccel(), 247
SetActiveView(), 59
SetActiveWindow(), 57
SetAnchorIndex(), 192
SetArguments(), 450
SetBase(), 247
SetBitmap(), 174, 83
SetBitmapBits(), 337
SetBitmapDimensions(), 337
SetBkColor(), 26, 251, 272
SetBkMode(), 115
SetBuddy(), 236, 247
SetButtonStyle(), 183
SetCallbackMask(), 272
SetCapture(), 57, 557–558
SetCaratIndex(), 192
SetCheck(), 149, 183
SetClipboardData(), 597, 605
SetColumn(), 272
SetColumnWidth(), 192, 272
SetCookie(), 821
SetCooperativeLevel(), 717–718, 744–745, 766
SetCurrentColor(), 95
SetCurrentDirectory(), 823
SetCurSel(), 192
SetCursor(), 174, 183
SetDataFormat(), 766
SetDescription(), 450
SetDragCursorImage(), 251
SetEnhMetaFile(), 174
SetEvent(), 530
SetFilePath(), 588
SetFocus(), 57
SetFont(), 57
SetHandle(), 179
SetHorizontalExtent(), 192
SetHotkey(), 450
SetHWnd(), 803
SetIcon(), 57, 174, 183
SetIconLocation(), 450
SetIDList(), 450
SetImageCount(), 251
SetImageList(), 272, 291
SetIndent(), 291
SetItem(), 272, 291
SetItemCount(), 272
SetItemData(), 192, 272, 291
SetItemDataPtr(), 192
SetItemHeight(), 192
SetItemImage(), 291
SetItemPosition(), 272
SetItemState(), 272, 291
SetItemText(), 272, 291

SetLength(), 588
SetLimitText(), 179
SetLineSize(), 236
SetLocale(), 192
SetMapMode(), 26
SetMargins(), 179
SetMaxPage(), 306
SetMenu(), 57
SetMessageText(), 59
SetMinPage(), 306
SetModifiedFlag(), 586
SetModify(), 179
SetObjectAsSelected(), 645–646
SetOption(), 821
SetOrientation(), 789
SetOverlayImage(), 251
SetPageSize(), 236
SetPasswordChar(), 179
SetPath(), 450
SetPixel(), 26
SetPos(), 231, 236, 247
SetPosition(), 786–787
SetQuality(), 783
SetRadio(), 150
SetRange(), 231, 236, 247
SetRange32(), 231, 247
SetRangeMax(), 236
SetRangeMin(), 236
SetReadBufferSize(), 824
SetReadOnly(), 179
SetRect(), 179, 640
SetRectNP(), 179
SetRelativePath(), 450
SetSel(), 179, 193
SetSelection(), 237
SetShowCmd(), 450
SetState(), 183
SetStatus(), 588
SetStep(), 231
SetTabStops(), 179, 193
SetTextAlign(), 120, 123
SetTextBkColor(), 272
SetTextColor(), 26, 114, 272
SetTic(), 237
SetTicFreq(), 237
SetTimer(), 57
SetTipSide(), 237
SetToolTips(), 237
SetTopIndex(), 193
SetupTracker(), 644–645
SetViewportExt(), 410
SetViewportOrg(), 310–311, 404–405
SetWindowExt(), 410
SetWindowLong(), 278–279
SetWindowOrg(), 405–406
SetWindowText(), 57, 177
SetWizardButtons(), 108

Continued

Index

functions *(continued)*
SetWorkingDirectory(), 450
SetWriteBufferSize(), 824
Shell_NotifyIcon(), 454, 455
SHGetDesktopFolder(), 460
SHGetMalloc(), 460
ShowControlBar(), 59
ShowHTMLDialog(), 862–866
ShowWindow(), 57
signatures, Visual C++ online documentation, 18
Sleep(), 536
SortChildren(), 291
SortChildrenCB(), 291
SortItems(), 272
StartDoc(), 297
StepIt(), 231
StretchBlt(), 26, 343–344
StretchDIBits(), 363, 385–386, 390–391
StrokeAndFillPath(), 436, 439
StrokePath(), 436, 438
SuspendThread(), 536
TabbedTextOut(), 126–127
TextOut(), 26, 113–114, 404
ThreadProc(), 516–517
Tick(), 808
TranslateMessage(), 13
tree views, 289–291
UI, menus, 147–154
Undo(), 179
Unlock(), 534, 541
UnlockRange(), 588
update command UI, 152–154
Update(), 272
UpdateAllViews(), 648
UpdateData(), 57
ValuetoText(), 615
VerifyPos(), 237
VKeyToItem(), 193
WaitForSingleObject(), 530–531
Win16 Registry API, 474
Win32 Registry API, 473–474
WinMain(), 10, 11, 15, 735
WndProc(), 13, 14
WriteHuge(), 588
WriteString(), 824
wspringf(), 40

G

GDI (Graphical Device Interface)
CBrush class, 45–48
CDC class, functions, 25–26
coordinates, physical and logical, 397–399
CPen class, 42–44
DC (device context) object, 23, 24–27
device capabilities, 39–41
objects, 23–24
Paint device context, 27–39
paths, 435–440
raster operations, 416–428
rectangles, drawing, 28
regions of screens, 428–435
GDI (Graphical Device Interface), mapping modes, 399
aspect ratio, 413–416
Cartesian coordinate system, 411–412
MM_TEXT mode, 403–406
physical units of measurement, 406–409
scaling logical units, 409–410
viewport origins, 400–403
window origins, 400–403
GetAccel() function, 247
GetActiveDocument() function, 59
GetActiveFrame() function, 59
GetActiveView() function, 59
GetActiveWindow() function, 56
GetAnchorIndex() function, 191
GetAnswerString() method, 704
GetArguments() function, 449
GetAttachedSurface() function, 719
GetAttributesOf() function, arguments, 463
GetBase() function, 247
GetBipmap() function, 173, 183, 337
GetBitmapBits() function, 337
GetBitmapDimension() function, 337
GetBkColor() function, 25, 251, 271
GetBkMode() function, 115
GetBrowserVersion() function, code, 879–880
GetBuddy() function, 236, 247
GetButtonStyle() function, 183
GetCallbackMask() function, 271
GetCapture() function, 56
GetCaratIndex() function, 191
GetChannelRect() function, 236
GetCheck() function, 183
GetChildItem() function, 290
GetCircle() function, 580
GetCircleCount() function, 580
GetClientRect() function, 56
GetClipboardData() function, 601
GetColor() function, 9, 953
GetColumn() function, 271
GetColumnWidth() function, 271
GetContext() function, 821
GetControlBar() function, 59
GetCookie() function, 821
GetCookieLength() function, 821
GetCount() function, 191, 290
GetCountPerPage() function, 271
GetCreationTime() function, 825
GetCurrentBitmap() function, 25
GetCurrentBrush() function, 25
GetCurrentDirectory() function, 823
GetCurrentDirectoryAsURL() function, 823
GetCurrentFont() function, 25, 93
GetCurrentPalette() function, 25
GetCurrentPen() function, 25
GetCurrentPosition() function, 25
GetCurSel() function, 190, 192
GetCursor() function, 173, 183
GetData() method, 752
GetData() function, 362
GetDC() function, 31
GetDescription() function
GetDeviceCaps() function, 26, 39, 318–319, 323–324, 449
GetDiameter() method, 680
GetDisplayNameOf() function, arguments, 464
GetDlgItem() function, 56
GetDockState() function, 59
GetDocument() function, 59
GetDragImage() function, 251
GetDropHilightItem() function, 290
GetEditControl() function, 271, 290
GetEnhMetaFile() function, 174
GetFaceName() function, 93
GetFile() function, 823
GetFileExt() function, 90
GetFilename() method, 752
GetFileName() function, 90, 362, 588, 825
GetFilePath() function, 588, 825
GetFileTitle() function, 91, 588, 825
GetFileURL() function, 821, 825, 826
GetFirstVisibleItem() function
GetFocus() function, 56
GetFont() function, 56
GetFormat() method, 752
GetFtpConnection() function, 821, 830, 831
GetGopherConnection() function, 821
GetHandle() function, 178
GetHeight() function, 362
GetHitItem() function, 645
GetHorizontalExtent() function, 192
GetHotkey() function, 449
GetHttpConnection() function, 821
GetIcon() function, 56, 174, 183
GetIconLocation() function, 449
GetIDList() function, 449
GetIEMajorVersions() function, code, 878–879
GetImageCount() function, 251

Index

GetImageInfo() function, 251
GetImageList() function, 271, 290
GetIndent() function, 290
GetInfo() function, 362
GetItem() function, 271, 290
GetItemCount() function, 271
GetItemData() function, 192, 271, 290
GetItemDataPtr() function, 192
GetItemHeight() function, 192
GetItemImage() function, 290
GetItemPosition() function, 271
GetItemRect() function, 192, 271, 290
GetItemState() function, 271, 290
GetItemText() function, 271, 290
GetLastAccessTime() function, 825
GetLastWriteTime() function, 825
GetLength() function, 588, 825
GetLimitText() function, 178
GetLine() function, 178
GetLineCount() function, 178
GetLineSize() function, 236
GetLocale() function, 192
GetMapMode() function, 26, 410
GetMargins() function, 178
GetMenu() function, 56
GetMessage() function, 13
GetMessageBar() function, 59
GetModify() function, 178
GetNextItem() function, 271, 290
GetNextSiblingItem() function, 290
GetNextVisibleItem() function, 290
GetNumberOfColors() function, 362
GetNumTics() function, 236
GetObject() function, 821
GetOrigin() function, 272
GetPageSize() function, 236
GetParent() function, 56
GetParentFrame() function, 56
GetParentItem() function, 290
GetParentOwner() function, 56
GetPasswordChar() function, 178
GetPath() function, 449
GetPathName() function, 91
GetPixel() function, 26
GetPolyFillMode() function, 26
GetPos() function, 231, 236, 247
GetPosition() function, 588
GetPrevSiblingItem() function, 290
GetPrevVisibleItem() function, 290
GetRange() function, 231, 236, 247
GetRange32() function, 247
GetRangeMax() function, 236
GetRangeMin() function, 236
GetReadyOnlyPref() function, 91
GetRect() function, 178
GetRGB() function, 362

GetRoot() function, 825
GetRootItem() function, 290
GetRuntimeClass() function, 55
GetSafeHandle() function, 251
GetSafeHwnd() function, 56
GetSavedCustomColors() function, 95
GetScrambleString() method, 704
GetSel() function, 178, 192
GetSelCount() function, 192
GetSelectedCount() function, 272
GetSelectedItem() function, 290
GetSelection() function, 236
GetSelItems() function, 192
GetServerName() function, 821
GetSession() function, 821
GetShowCmd() function, 449
GetSize() method, 752
GetSize() function, 93, 362
GetState() function, 183
GetStatus() function, 588
GetStringWidth() function, 272
GetStyle() function, 56
GetStyleName() function, 93
GetSystemMenu() function, 56
GetSystemMetrics() function, 12
GetText() function, 190, 192
GetTextBkColor() function, 272
GetTextColor() function, 26, 114, 272
GetTextExtent() function, 26
GetTextExtentPoint32() function, arguments, 136
GetTextLen() function, 192
GetTextMetrics() function, 26, 128, 309
GetTextWindow() function, 26
GetThumbRect() function, 236
GetTic() function, 236
GetTicArray() function, 236
GetTicPos() function, 236
GetToolTips() function, 236
GetTopIndex() function, 192, 272
GetVerb() function, 821
GetViewportExtEx() function, 410
GetViewRect() function, 272
GetVisibleCount() function, 290
GetWeight() function, 93
GetWidth() function, 362
GetWindowExtEx() function, 410
GetWindowRect() function, 56, 477
GetWindowText() function, 56, 178
GetWorkingDirectory() function, 449
GetXPostion() method, 682
GetYPostion() method, 682
GoBack() method, 856
GoForward() method, 856
GoHome() method, 856

GoSearch() method, 856
Gouraud shading, 784
Graphical Device Interface. *See* GDI
graphics, printing, 316–331
GrayString() function, 26
group box control, 164
group files, setting up, 499–501

H

handling messages, 15–17
hardware, sound-hardware access level (DirectSound), setting, 744–745
hCurrentInst parameter, 10
hdc argument, 114, 363
hDC argument, 136
hDropInfor argument, 445
header files
 application class, creating, 795
 main window class, creating, 796–797
Headers parameter, 857
headers, loading bitmaps, 355–358
hEvent argument, 727
hIcon (NOTIFYICONDATA structure), 453
HIGH_PRIORITY_CLASS class, 514
hItem (TV_ITEM structure), 283
HitTest() function, 272, 290
HKEY_CLASSES_ROOT (Registry key), 469
HKEY_CURRENT_CONFIG (Registry key), 469
HKEY_CURRENT_USER (Registry key), 469
HKEY_DYN_DATA (Registry key), 469
HKEY_LOCAL_MACHINE (Registry key), 469
HKEY_USERS (Registry key), 469
horizontal alignment of text, 120–123
HorizontalAlignApp application, 120–122
HORZRES constant, 40
HORZSIZE constant, 40
hPrevInstance parameter, 10
HTML (Hypertext Markup Language)
 dialog boxes, 862–867
 list boxes, 867
 <OBJECT> tag, 708–709
 pages, displaying, 850
 pages, navigating, 856–858
 select elements, 867
http pstrAgent constructor, 827

HTTP (Hypertext Transfer
        Protocol)
    applications, writing, 826–829
    servers, connections, opening,
        827–828
    sessions, creating and closing,
        829
hWnd (NOTIFYICONDATA structure), 453
hWnd parameter, 13
hwndParent parameter, 865
Hypertext Markup Language. *See*
        HTML
Hypertext Transfer Protocol. *See*
        HTTP

I

IAutoServerApp class, 687
icons
    adding to system tray, 453–454
    composite, creating, 252–255
    events, responding to, 454–455
    on system tray, manipulating,
        452–457
IDispatch interface, 868
IDLE_PRIORITY_CLASS class, 514
IDR_SRVR_EMBEDDED menu,
        657–658
IDR_SRVR_INPLACE menu, 657, 659
Ids, menus, 144
IE 5.0 (Internet Explorer 5.0), uninstalling warning, 880–881
IHTMLDocument2
    @index2:object mapping, 868–871
    DHTML (Dynamic HTML) object
        mapping, 868–871
    interfaces, 871–872
IID_IShellLink argument, 448
iImage (LV_ITEM structure), 267
iImage (TV_ITEM structure), 283
iItem (LV_ITEM structure), 266
image lists, 226, 249–251, 264
immediate mode, Direct3D programs, 781
IMPLEMENT_SERIAL macro, 582
implementation files
    application class, creating,
        795–796
    window class, code to create,
        797–801
implementing parental lockout for
    Web browsers, 859–861
Import from Type Library dialog
    box, 685
InchApp application, 325–331
inches, scaling factors for printing,
        323–331

Included File Groups page
        (Properties dialog
        box),496–497
.ini files, 467
InitApplication() function, 15
InitDirectDraw() function,
        DirectDrawApp, 724–725
InitDirectSound() function, 748–749
initial positions, progress bars, 230
initializing
    ActiveX, 689
    applications, 15
    bitmap objects, 336–338
    COM, 447–448
    COM, uninitializing, 451
    shortcuts, 449–450
InitImages() function,
        DirectDrawApp, 728–729
InitInstance() function, 15, 202,
        519, 689
InitListView() function, 275
InitMemberVariables() function,
        DirectDrawApp, 723–724
InitProgressBar() function, 228, 231
InitRadioButtons() function,
        277–278
InitSelection() function,
        FTPAccessApp application,
        846–847
InitSlider() function, 228, 237
InitSpinner() function, 228
InitStaticText() function, 228
InitStorage() function, 192
in-place editor, ServerApp, running
    as, 665–666
input devices. *See* keyboards;
        mouse
Insert Files into Project dialog box,
        791–792
Insert Control dialog box, 701, 706
Insert Files into Project dialog box,
        369, 763
Insert menu@index H:Resource
    command, 80, 101, 206,
        655, 673
Insert Object dialog box, 637,
        653–654, 665–667
Insert Resource dialog box, 80, 101,
        252, 655
InsertColumn() function, 264–265,
        268–269, 272
InsertItem() function, 268–269, 272,
        290
InsertResource dialog box, 206
InsertString() function, 192
Inset Files Into Project dialog box,
        743
installation packages, 485–486
installations, components, 492

installing
    Internet Explorer 5.0 (IE 5.0),
        uninstalling warning,
        880–881
    shortcuts, 447
InstallShield, 500–501
    applications, adding to Start
        menu, 505–508
    applications, creating to install,
        487–488
    components, setting up, 494–499
    file group setup, 499–501
    files, packaging, 486–487
    media, creating, 502–504
    project, starting, 488–494
    Properties dialog box, Included
        File Groups page, 496–497
    Shared DLLs, 496–497, 499
    window, 489
instances of applications, 11
interfaces. *See also* GDI; MDI
    documents, accessing, 871–872
    IDispatch, 868
    IHTMLDocument2, 871–872
    IPersistFile, pointer, 449
    IShellLink, functions, 449–450
    MDI (multiple-document interface), 54
    user, ActiveX control, creating,
        697–702
    user, Web browsers, 852
    user-interface shell, 443
Internet. *See also* Internet Explorer;
        WinInet
    Ratings API functions, 860
    SDK, Microsoft Web site, 850
    sessions, starting, 827
Internet Explorer, 849
    ActiveX controls, 850–851, 853
    components, 850–851
    DHTML (Dynamic HTML),
        868–877
    documents, retrieving with
        robots, 883
    GetIEMajorVersions() function,
        code, 878–879
    HTML dialog boxes, 862–867
    HTML pages, displaying, 850
    Internet Explorer 5.0 (IE 5.0),
        uninstalling warning,
        880–881
    Java applets, 850–851
    JScript, 850–851
    minimum installation, 880
    MSHTML (mshtml.dll), 850–851
    MyBrowser, 854–855, 881–883
    PICS (Platform for Internet
        Content Selection) ratings,
        setting, 859, 860

Index

skeleton browser applications, creating, 851–861
VBScript, 850–851
versions in Registry, 878–879
versions in shdocvw.dll file, 878–879
Web browsers, parental lockout, implementing, 859–861
Internet Explorer, WebBrowser control, configuring, 855–856
control, distributing, 877–881
HTML pages, navigating, 856–858
shdocvw.dll, 850–851
Invalidate() function, 56, 561, 771
InvalidateRect() function, 56
InvertRgn() function, 429
IPersistFile interface pointer, 449
IsArchived() function, 825
IsBold() function, 93
IsClipboardFormatAvailable() function, 601
IsCompressed() function, 825
IsDirectory() function, 825
IsDots() function, 825
iSelectedImage (TV_ITEM structure), 283
IShellLink
  interface, functions, 449–450
  object, creating, 448
IsHidden() function, 825
IsIconic() function, 56
IsItalic() function, 93
IsKindOF() function, 55
isolation (MTS attribute), 466
IsPrinting() function, 309
IsReadOnly() function, 825
IsSerializable() function, 55
IsStrikeOut() function, 93
IsSystem() function, 825
IsTemporary() function, 825
iSubItem (LV_COLUMN structure), 265
iSubItem (LV_ITEM structure), 266
IsUnderline() function, 93
IsValid() method, 752
IsValid() function, 362
IsWindowEnabled() function, 56
IsWindowVisible() function, 56
IsZoomed() function, 56
item identifiers, shell namespace, 458
ItemFromPoint() function, 192
ItemHasChildren() function, 290
items, embedded, deleting, 648–649
iUsage argument, 363

J
Java applets, 850–851
JScript, 850–851

K
KEY_ALL_ACCESS argument, 478
keyboard shortcuts
  Ctrl+F5 (compile and run applications), 330
  Ctrl+W (display ClassWizard), 103, 347
keyboards, 547–548
  Alt key, tracking, 568
  Ctrl key, tracking, 568
  events, handling, 557–558
  messages, 559–560
  Shift key, tracking, 568
  virtual key codes, 564–566
KeyDown application, 562–568
keyHandel argument, 477
keyHandle3 argument, 479, 482
Keys application, 560–562
keys
  Registry, 469–470
  Tab, non-dialog box windows, 179–180
  virtual key codes, 564–566
KillTimer() function, 56

L
LBN_DBLCLK (list box notification), 191
LBN_ERRSPACE (list box notification), 191
LBN_KILLFOCUS (list box notification), 191
LBN_SELCANCEL (list box notification), 191
LBN_SELCHANGE (list box notification), 191
LBN_SETFOCUS (list box notification), 191
LBS_DISABLENOSCROLL (list box control style), 189
LBS_EXTENDEDSEL (list box control style), 189
LBS_HASSTRINGS (list box control style), 189
LBS_MULTICOLUMN (list box control style), 189
LBS_MULTILESEL (list box control style), 189
LBS_NOINTEGRALHEIGHT (list box control style), 189
LBS_NOREDRAW (list box control style), 189
LBS_NOTIFY (list box control style), 189
LBS_OWNERDRAWFIXED (list box control style), 189
LBS_OWNERDRAWVARIABLE (list box control style), 190
LBS_SORT (list box control style), 190
LBS_STANDARD (list box control style), 190
LBS_USETABSTOPS (list box control style), 190
LBS_WANTKEYBOARDINPUT (list box control style), 190
Level argument, 296
lfCharSet (LOGFONT), 132
lfClipPrecision (LOGFONT), 132
lfEscapement (LOGFONT), 132
lfFaceName (LOGFONT), 132
lfHeight (LOGFONT), 132
lfItalic (LOGFONT), 132
lfOrientation (LOGFONT), 132
lfPitchAndFamily (LOGFONT), 132
lfQuality (LOGFONT), 132
lfStrikeOut (LOGFONT), 132
lfUnderline (LOGFONT), 132
lfWeight (LOGFONT), 132
lfWidth (LOGFONT), 132
libraries
  DLL (dynamic-link libraries), 5–6
  MFC (Microsoft Foundation Classes), 793
  type, 685–686
light object, creating, 788–789
lights
  child frame, creating, 789
  Direct3D, adding, 788–789
LimitText() function, 178
line drawing modes, raster operations, 421–425
LineFromChar() function, 178
LineIndex() function, 178
LineLength() function, 178
LineModeApp application, 422–425
lines of text, sizing, 135–138
LineScroll() function, 178
LineTo() function, 26, 37, 404
linked
  data sets, 624–625
  items, ServerApp application, running as editor for, 666–668
list boxes, 187–188, 191–193, 867
  control, 164
  control styles, 189–190
  notifications, 191
list views, 271–272
  code to create, 269–270

Continued

list views *(continued)*
  columns, adding items, 266–267
  columns, creating, 264–266
  CommonControlsApp2 application, 275–279
  image lists, setting, 264
  items, editing, 273–275
  MFC (Microsoft Foundation Classes) shortcuts, 268–270
  object, creating, 262–264
  styles, 263–264
  user selections, responding to, 267–268
lists, image, 226, 249–251, 264
LoadAccelTable() function, 59
LoadBarState() function, 59
LoadBitmap() function, 337
loading
  bitmap color tables, 355–358
  bitmap headers, 355–358
  DIB files, 353–358
LoadLibrary() function, 862
LoadMappedBitmap() function, 337
LoadOEMBitmap() function, 337
LoadWaveData() function, 753–754
locating application dependencies, 487
Lock() function, 534, 541, 727, 753
lockouts, parental for Web browsers, implementing, 859–861
LockRange() function, 588
LOGFONT structure, 131
logical
  coordinates, 397–399
  palettes, 364–366
  units, scaling, 409–410
LOGPIXELSX constant, 40
LOGPIXELSY constant, 40
LParam (LV_ITEM structure), 267
Lparam (TV_ITEM structure), 283
lParam parameter, 13
lpBits argument, 363
lpBitsInfo argument, 363
lpDDSurfaceDesc argument, 727
lpDestRect argument, 727
LPDIRECTDRAWSURFACE pointer, 719
lpItemIDList argument, 464
lplfInitial argument, 92
lpsaAttribute parameter, 525, 537, 541
LpSecurityAttrs parameter, 518
lpszCaption argument, 182
lpszClassName argument, 68
lpszCmdLine parameter, 10
lpszColumnHeading argument, 268
lpszDefExt argument, 88, 89
lpszFile argument, 445
lpszFileName argument, 88, 89
lpszFilter argument, 88, 89
lpszMenuName argument, 69
lpszName parameter, 525, 537
lpszText argument, 172
lpszWindowName argument, 68
LV_COLUMN structure, 265
LV_ITEM structure, 266–267
LVS_ALIGNLEFT (list view style), 263
LVS_ALIGNTOP (list view style), 263
LVS_AUTOARRANGE (list view style), 263
LVS_EDITLABELS (list view style), 263
LVS_ICON (list view style), 263
LVS_LIST (list view style), 263
LVS_NOCOLUMNHEADER (list view style), 263
LVS_NOLABELWRAP (list view style), 264
LVS_NOSCROLL (list view style), 264
LVS_NOSORTHEADER (list view style), 264
LVS_OWNERDRAWFIXED (list view style), 264
LVS_REPORT (list view style), 264
LVS_SHAREIMAGELISTS (list view style), 264
LVS_SHOWSELALWAYS (list view style), 264
LVS_SINGLESEL (list view style), 264
LVS_SMALLICON (list view style), 264
LVS_SORTASCENDING (list view style), 264
LVS_SORTDESCENDING (list view style), 264

M

m_bufSize variable, 747
m_button1 variable, 769
m_button2 variable, 769
m_button3 variable, 769
m_curDirectory variable, 836
m_diameter variable, 675
m_DIOK variable, 769
m_DSOK variable, 747
m_fileCount variable, 836
m_fileLengths[ ] variable, 836
m_fileNames[ ] variable, 836
m_mouseX variable, 769
m_mouseY variable, 769
m_mouseZ variable, 769
m_objectRect variable, 639
m_password variable, 836
m_pBuffer variable, 747
m_pDIMouse variable, 769
m_pDInput variable, 769
m_pDS variable, 747
m_pWave variable, 747
m_site variable, 836
m_username variable, 836
macros
  BEGIN_MESSAGE_MAP(), 16
  IMPLEMENT_SERIAL, 582
  for message maps, 16–17
  ON_COMMAND, 17
  ON_EN_CHANGE, 176–177
  ON_UPDATE_COMMAND_UI, 153
  ON_UPDATE_COMMAND_UI_RANGE, 153
  ON_WM_CTLCOLOR, 198
  ON_WM_LBUTTONDOWN(), 16
  RUNTIME_CLASS MFC, 522
MagicRectApp application, 426–428
main object (Direct3D), creating, 781
main window class header file, creating, 796–797
main windows, dialog boxes, 199–202
MakeScene() function, 803, 804
manual event objects, 531–533
MapModeApp application, 400–403
mapping modes, 399
  aspect ratio, 413–416
  Cartesian coordinate system, 411–412
  coordinates, scaling logical units, 409–410
  logical units, scaling, 409–410
  MM_ANISOTROPIC mode, 409–410, 415
  MM_HIENGLISH mode, 406–408
  MM_HIMETRIC mode, 408
  MM_ISOTROPIC mode, 409–410, 413–416
  MM_LOENGLISH mode, 406–408
  MM_LOMETRIC mode, 408
  MM_TEXT mode, 403–406
  MM_TWIPS mode, 409
  physical units of measurement, 406–409
  viewport extents, 409
  viewport origins, 400–403
  window extents, 409
  window origins, 400–403
maps, message
  creating, 15
  declaring, 16
  macros, 16–17

Index

mask (LV_COLUMN structure), 265
mask (LV_ITEM structure), 266
mask (TV_ITEM structure), 283
masks, 390
MatchesMask() function, 825
MDI (multiple-document interface), 54
  application, windows, 78
  windows, 77–79
MeasureItem() function, 192
Media Build Wizard
  Build Type page, 503
  media, creating, 502–504
  Summary page, 503
  window, 502
Member Variables page, 210–211
member variables, FTPAccessApp application, 835–847
memory
  DC, 338–340
  storing for DIBs (device-independent bitmaps), 385
menu bars, Paint, 631–632
Menu Editor, menu resources, creating, 139–144
menu ID, 139–140, 143
Menu Item Properties property sheet, 140–143
MenuApp application, 154–161
menus
  bulleted items, 150–151
  captions, 144
  checkmarks, 149–150
  ClassWizard, code for message maps, 157–158
  IDs, 144
  items, 146–147, 152–154
  message-response functions, 144–146
  option toggles, 149
  Options 1, 155
  Options 2, 156
  resources, creating, 139–144
  Start, adding applications, 505–508
  UI functions, 147–154
  update command UI functions, 148, 152–154, 160–161
  view class header file, code to declare functions, 156–157
  view class message-response functions, code to define, 158–159
MERGECOPY (bitmap raster operations), 417
MERGEPAINT (bitmap raster operations), 417
meshes, frames or objects, creating, 785–786

message boxes, displays, 168–169
message maps
  code, 157–158
  creating, 15
  declaring, 16
  macros, 16–17
  message-response functions, 16–17
message parameter, 13
MessageBox() function, 56, 531
message-response functions, 16
  defining, 17–18
  menus, 144–146
messages
  client-area, 548–549
  handling, 15–17
  keyboards, 559–560
  message-response functions, defining, 17–18
  mouse, 553–555
  non-client-area, 549–552
  Windows, WndProc() function, 14
  WM_CAPTURECHANGED, 549
  WM_CHAR, 559, 561
  WM_CTLCOLOR, types of, 198
  WM_DEADCHAR, 559
  WM_DESTROY, 14
  WM_DROPFILES, 445
  WM_KEYDOWN, 559
  WM_KEYUP, 559
  WM_LBUTTONBLCLK, 549
  WM_LBUTTONDOWN, 14, 549
  WM_LBUTTONYUP, 549
  WM_MBUTTONDBLCLK, 549
  WM_MBUTTONDOWN, 549
  WM_MBUTTONUP, 549
  WM_MOUSEACTIVATE, 549
  WM_MOUSEHOVER, 549
  WM_MOUSELEAVE, 549
  WM_MOUSEMOVE, 548, 549
  WM_MOUSEWHEEL, 549
  Wm_NCLBUTTONDBLCLK P, 550
  Wm_NCLBUTTONDOWN, 550
  Wm_NCLBUTTONUP, 550
  Wm_NCMBUTTONDBLCLK, 550
  Wm_NCMBUTTONDOWN, 550
  Wm_NCMBUTTONUP, 550
  Wm_NCMOUSEHOVER, 550
  Wm_NCMOUSELEAVE, 550
  Wm_NCMOUSEMOVE, 550, 551
  Wm_NCRBUTTONDBLCLK, 550
  Wm_NCRBUTTONDOWN, 550
  Wm_NCRBUTTONUP, 550
  Wm_NCXBUTTONDBLCLK P, 550
  Wm_NCXBUTTONDOWN, 550
  Wm_NCXBUTTONUP, 550
  WM_PAINT, 14, 27, 28
  WM_RBUTTONDBLCLK, 549

WM_RBUTTONDOWN, 549
WM_RBUTTONUP, 549
WM_SYSCHAR, 559
WM_XBUTTONDBLCLK, 549
WM_XBUTTONDDOWN, 549
WM_XBUTTONUP, 549
MessageThread() function, 517
MetafileDCApp, shapes, drawing, 36
methods
  AboutBox(), code, 702–703
  ActiveX control, creating, 702–705
  automation server, defining, 678–682
  CWave(), 752
  DisplayServerWindow(), 681
  Flip(), 736
  GetAnswerString(), 704
  GetData(), 752
  GetDiameter(), 680
  GetFilename(), 752
  GetFormat(), 752
  GetScrambleString(), 704
  GetSize(), 752
  GetXPostion(), 682
  GetYPostion(), 682
  GoBack(), 856
  GoForward(), 856
  GoHome(), 856
  GoSearch(), 856
  IsValid, 752
  Navigate(), parameters, 857
  Navigate2(), 857
  SetAnswerString(), 705
  SetDiameter(), 680
  SetScrambleString(), 704
  SetXPostion(), 682
  SetYPostion(), 682
  WebBrowser, 856–857
metrics, text, 128–130
MFC (Microsoft Foundation Classes), 7–8
  applications, initializing, 15
  applications, printing graphics, 316–331
  AppWizard – Step 1 dialog box, 77
  BasicApp2 application, code, 73–75
  C programming language, comparing, 15–17
  CCmdTarget class, functions, 55
  CFrameWnd class, functions, 58–59
  CObject class, 54–55
  control buttons, removing, 19–20

Continued

MFC *(continued)*
  CView class, functions, 59–60
  CWnd class, 55–57
  frame windows, 58
  functions for printing, 304–316
  libraries, 793
  list view shortcuts, 268–270
  message handling, 15–17
  text, printing, 302–316
  tree view shortcuts, code, 287–289
  view windows, 58
  window styles, modifying, 19–20
  windows, sizing, 18–19, 53–54, 60–69
MFC (Microsoft Foundation Classes), applications, non-AppWizard
  CreateLight() function, 806
  CreateMesh() function, 804–805
  CreateViewport() function, 805–806
  MakeScene() function, 804
  OnCreate() function, 802–803
  OnDestroy() function, 802
  OnPaint() function, 806–807
  OnTimer() function, 808
  writing, 795–808
MFC (Microsoft Foundation Classes), BasicApp application
  afxwin.h header file, 66
  application class, 66–67
  code, 63–64
  creating, 61–66
  frame window class, 67–69
  responding to mouse click, 66
Microsoft Transaction Server (MTS), attributes, 465–466
Microsoft Web site
  DirectX 7.0 SDK, 714
  DirectX SDK, 761
  DirectX5.0 SDK, 741
  Internet SDK, 850
minimum installation, Internet Explorer, 880
MM_ANISOTROPIC mapping mode, 399, 409–410, 415
MM_HIENGLISH mapping mode, 399, 406–408
MM_HIMETRIC mapping mode, 400, 408
MM_ISOTROPIC mapping mode, 400, 409–410, 413–416
MM_LOENGLISH mapping mode, 400, 406–408
MM_LOMETRIC mapping mode, 400, 408

MM_TEXT mapping mode, 400, 403–406
MM_TWIPS mapping mode, 400, 409
modeless dialog boxes, creating, 84–86
modeling skills, Direct3D, 794
models, object models, DHTML (Dynamic HTML), 868–877
modes
  immediate, Direct3D programs, 781
  line drawing, 421–425
  mapping, 399–416
  MM_TEXT mode, 403–406
  retained, Direct3D programs, 781
  RGN_AND, 432
  RGN_COPY, 433
  RGN_DIFF, 433
  RGN_XOR, 431–432
modified files, saving, 586–587
modifying MFC (Microsoft Foundation Classes) window styles, 19–20
ModifyStyle() function, 57
Mouse application, 552–553, 556–557
mouse, 547
  clicks, BasicApp application responding to, 66
  client-area messages, 548–549
  events, handling, 557–558
  messages, 553–555
  non-client-area messages, 549–552
  parameters, 557
  pointer, 554–555
  selecting items, 641–649
MOVE TO PREVIOUS DIRECTORY command, 834
MoveTo() function, 26, 37, 404
MoveToPreviousDirectory() function, FTPAccessApp application, 845
MoveWindow() function, 57
MSHTML (mshtml.dll), 850–851
MTS (Microsoft Transaction Server), attributes, 465–466
Mueller, John Paul, 443
multiline edit boxes, 174
multiple-document interface. *See* MDI
Mutex locked message box, 539–540
mutexes (mutually exclusive), 524, 536–540
"My Company" argument, 477
MyApplication

.exe file, 500–501
.ini file, 467
Resources pane, 505
window, 488
MyBrowser
  application, compiling, 854–855
  running, 881–883

N

Name argument, 296
names of dropped files, retrieving, 445
NamespaceApp application, OnCreate() function, 459–461
  ProcessFolder() function, 462–464
navAllowAutoSearch (navigational flag), 858
navBrowserBar (navigational flag), 858
Navigate() method, parameters, 857
Navigate2() method, 857
navigating HTML pages, 856–858
navigational flags, WebBrowser, 858
navNoHistory (navigational flag), 858
navNoReadFromCache (navigational flag), 858
navNoWriteToCache (navigational flag), 858
navOpenInNewWindow (navigational flag), 858
nCmdShow parameter, 10
nCOL argument, 268
nDestHeight argument, 363
nDestWidth argument, 363
New Class dialog box, 104, 210, 373, 519–520, 656
New dialog box
  Files tab, 62
  Projects tab, 61
New Icon Image dialog box, 254
New Project Information dialog box, 327, 347, 573
New Symbol dialog box, 700
Next button, 107–108
Next() function, arguments, 463
nFlag, data fields, 560
nflags argument, 250
nFlags parameter, 557
nFormat argument, 268
nGrow argument, 250
nHeight argument, 342, 344
nID argument, 172, 182, 198, 246, 281
NIM_ADD value, 454

Index

NIM_DELETE value, 454
NIM_MODIFY value, 454
nInitial argument, 250
non-AppWizard MFC applications
  CreateLight() function, 806
  CreateMesh() function, 804–805
  CreateViewport() function, 805–806
  MakeScene() function, 804
  OnCreate() function, 802–803
  OnDestroy() function, 802
  OnPaint() function, 806–807
  OnTimer() function, 808
  writing, 795–808
non-client-area messages, 549–552
non-dialog box windows
  placing standard controls, 164–165
  Tab key, 179–180
nonnonpersistent objects, saving, 584–586
nonrectangular bitmaps, displaying, 390–395
NORMAL_PRIORITY_CLASS class, 514
NotePad, CBCircleApp2 application, 611
notifications
  combo boxes, 196–197
  edit controls, 177
  list boxes, 191
NotifyChanged() function, 663
NotifyIcon() function, 453
NOTIFYICONDATA structure, 453–454
NOTSRCCOPY (bitmap raster operations), 417
NOTSRCERASE (bitmap raster operations), 417
nPort argument, 831
nPriority parameter, 518
nSrcHeight argument, 344, 363
nSrcWidth argument, 344, 363
nStackSize parameter, 518
nSubItem argument, 268
NULL argument, 448, 461, 478
NUMBRUSHES constant, 40
numChars argument, 114, 136
NUMCOLORS constant, 40
NUMFONTS constant, 40
NUMPENS constant, 40
NUMRESERVED constant, 40
numTabs argument, 126
nWidth argument, 268, 342, 343

O

object linking and embedding. *See* OLE
object mapping, DHTML (Dynamic HTML) to IHTMLDocument2, 868–871
object models, DHTML (Dynamic HTML), 868–877
objects. *See also* standard controls
  Bitmap, 24
  bitmaps, 336–338, 638
  Brush, 24
  CArchive, 578
  CClientDC, code to create, 32–33
  CCmdUI, 149
  CEvent, 525
  CFtpFileFind, creating, 831–832
  clipper, creating, 781–782
  CPoint, 556–557
  critical sections, 524
  critical, 533–536
  data, declaring, 573
  DC (device context), 23, 24–27
  DirectDraw, 714, 717
  DirectInput, creating, 764–765
  DirectSound, creating, 742, 744
  embedded, 639–641, 646–647
  event, manual, 531–533
  event, program and thread communication, 528–531
  events, 524–528
  Font, 24
  GDI (Graphical Device Interface), 23–24
  IShellLink, creating, 448
  light, creating, 788–789
  list view, creating, 262–264
  m_objectRect variable, 639
  main (Direct3D), creating, 781
  meshes, creating, 785
  mutexes, 524
  nonpersistent, saving, 584–586
  Palette, 24
  Pen, 24
  persistent, 578–587
  persistent, saving, 584–586
  polygons, 783
  programmable, 626
  semaphores, 524
  synchronization, 524
  tree view, creating, 281–282
Offline property, 856
offscreen surfaces, DirectDraw, creating, 720
OffsetPos() function, 231
OK button, 83
OLE (object linking and embedding)
  automation, 626
  clients, 626
  components, 626
  container applications, 624
  controls, 627
  data sets, linked, 624–625
  server applications, 624
  servers, 626
  OLE 1.0, 623–626
  OLE 2.0, 626–627
On/Off menu@index H:On command, 155
ON_COMMAND macro, 17
ON_EN_CHANGE macro, 176–177
ON_UPDATE_COMMAND_UI macro, 153
ON_UPDATE_COMMAND_UI_RANGE macro, 153
ON_WM_CTLCOLOR macro, 198
ON_WM_LBUTTONDOWN() macro, 16
OnActivateFrame() function, 59
OnActivateView() function, 59
OnAutomationSetdiameter() function, 687
OnAutomationSetxposition() function, 688
OnAutomationSetyposition() function, 688
OnBeginPrinting() function, 60, 306–310, 324
OnButton1() function, 216–217
OnChangeEdit1() function, 217
OnChangeItemPosition() function, 639–640
OnChar() function, 560, 561
OnCircleChangemesage() function, code, 586–587
OnCircleSetcircle() function, 677–678
OnColorOK() function, 95
OnCreate() function, 36–37, 320–321, 228–229, 459–461, 802–803
OnCtrlColor() function, 198, 199
OnDestroy() function, code, 38–39, 475–476, 734–735, 754–755, 772–773
OnDraw() function, code, 46–47, 116–117, 308–309, 321–322, 576–577
OnEditAddstring() function, code, 577–578
OnEditChange() function, 177
OnEditCopy function, 597–598, 607–608, 612, 660–661
OnEditPaste() function, 600, 602, 615–617
OnEndPrinting() function, 60, 315–316

916 Index

OnEndPrintPreview() function, 60
OnFileNameOK() function, 91
OnFileOpen() function, 376
OnFtpConnection() function,
    FTPAccessApp application,
    839
OnGetItemPosition() function, 640
OnHScroll() function, 235–236
OnInitDialog() function, 214
OnInitialUpdate() function, 60,
    722–723, 747–748, 769–770
OnKeyDown() function, 648–649,
    734
OnLButtonDblClk() function,
    FTPAccessApp application,
    841–842
OnLButtonDown() function, code,
    117–118, 239–240, 451–452,
    754
OnLButtonUp() function, 239–241
online documentation, Visual C++,
    function signatures, 18
OnListViewDblClk() function, 279
OnLoadURL() function, 853
OnMouseMove() function, 556
OnNcMouseMove() function,
    551–552
OnNewDocument() function,
    572–574, 661
OnNotify() function, 274
OnPaint() function, 806–807
OnPaletteChanged() function, 367
OnPrepareDC() function, 60,
    310–312
OnPreparePrinting() function, 60,
    304–306, 323
OnPrint() function, 60, 313–315,
    324–325, 329
OnQueryNewPalette() function,
    367
OnRButtonDown() function, code,
    118, 456, 557–558, 843
OnRectangleSize() function,
    662–663
OnRenderAllFormats() function,
    609
OnRenderFormat() function,
    608–609
OnSetCursor() function, 642
OnShareViolation() function, 91
OnSize() function, 413
OnStatusCallback() function, 821
OnTimer() function, 732–733,
    770–771, 803, 808
OnTrayMessage() function, 457
OnUpdate() function, 60
OnUpdateViewToolbar() function,
    150
OnWizardBack() function, 109

OnWizardFinish() function, 109
OnWizardNext() function, 109
Open() function, 588
Open dialog box, 87–88, 90, 95
Open File dialog box, code to handle, 96–97
OpenClipboard() function, 57, 596
OpenFile() function, 823
OpenFTPDirectory() function,
    FTPAccessApp application,
    840–841
opening FTP connections, 830–831
OpenURL() function, 821, 828
operators
    <<, 574
    >>, 574
option toggles for menus, 149
Options 1 menu, 155
Options 2 menu, 156
Origins menu@index H:Set Window
    Origin command, 400
origins, viewport or window,
    400–403
overriding
    DeleteContents() function, 377,
    574, 575
    PreTranslateMessage() function,
    180

P

packaging. *See also* InstallShield
    applications, 485-486
    files, 486–487
Page Setup dialog box, 86
page-flipping, 718
pages, property, 100
Paint device context, 27–28
    client-area device context, 29–34
    metafile device context, 35–39
Paint
    toolbars and menu bars,
    631–632
    tools, 637
painting with brushes, 45–48
PaintRgn() function, 429
Palette object, 24
PALETTEENTRY structure, 365
palettes
    changes, managing, 366–368
    DirectDraw, creating, 720–721
    logical, 364–366
    managing, 364–368
parameters
    lInitialCount, 541
    lMaxCount, 541
    AfxBeginThread() function, 518
    bInitiallyOwn, 525, 537

bManualReset, 525
CMutex class, 537
CSemaphore class, 541
dwCreateFlags, 518
Flags, 857
hCurrentInst, 10
Headers, 857
hPrevInstance, 10
hWnd, 13
hwndParent, 865
lParam, 13
lpsaAttribute, 525, 537, 541
LpSecurityAttrs, 518
lpszCmdLine, 10
lpszName, 525, 537
message, 13
mouse, 557
Navigate() method, 857
nCmdShow, 10
nFlags, 557
nPriority, 518
nStackSize, 518
pchOptions, 866
pfnThreadProc, 518
pmk, 865
point, 557
PostData, 857
pParam, 518
pstrName, 541
pvarArgIn, 865
pvarArgOut, 866
ShowHTMLDialog() function,
    865–866
TargetFrameName, 857
URL, 857
WinMain() function, 10
WndProc() function, 13
wParam, 13
parental lockout for Web browsers,
    implementing, 859–861
ParseCircleText() function, 617–618
Paste() function, 178
pasting
    bitmaps to clipboard, 600–603
    data formats, CBCircleApp 2
    application, 615–618
PATCOPY (bitmap raster operations), 417
PathApp application, 437–440
paths, 435–440
PATINVERT (bitmap raster operations), 417
PATPAINT (bitmap raster operations), 417
pcbNeeded argument, 296
pchOptions parameter, 866
pContext argument, 69
pcReturned argument, 296
pDC argument, 198

pdcPrinter argument, 92
pDib argument, 731
Pen object, 24
PenApp, pens, drawing, 43
PenApp2, pens, drawing, 44
pens, drawing with, 42–44
PersistCircleApp application, 579–584
persistent objects, 578–587
PersistentCircleApp2 application, 585
pfnThreadProc parameter, 518
pParam parameter, 518
physical
   coordinates, 397–399
   measurements, scaling factors for printing, 323–331
   units of measurement, mapping modes, 406–409
PICS (Platform for Internet Content Selection) ratings, setting, 859–861
PIDL, 458
Pie() function, 26
pixels, coordinates, 397–398
PLANES constant, 40
Platform for Internet Content Selection (PICS) ratings, setting, 859–861
Play() function, 754
plus sign (+), 500, 506
pmk parameter, 865
point parameter, 557
pointers
   IPersistFile interface, 449
   LPDIRECTDRAWSURFACE, 719
   mouse, 554–555
   releasing, 451
polygon objects, 783
Polygon() function, 26
Polyline() function, 26
PosFromChar() function, 179
PostData parameter, 857
PostMessage() function, 57
pParam parameter, 518
pParentWnd argument, 69, 88, 92, 95, 172
pPrinterEnum argument, 296
PreCreateWindow() function, 57, 71, 480–481
preference, users, writing for Registry, 475–480
PreTranslateMessage() function, overriding, 180
primary surface (DirectDraw), creating, 718–719
primary threads, 513
Print dialog box, 86
PrintApp application, 303–304

PrintCircleApp application, 316–317
printers and screens, scaling between, 317–320
printing
   BasicPrintApp application, 298–302
   documents, 295–298
   graphics, 316–331
   MFC (Microsoft Foundation Classes) functions, 304–316
   scaling factors, 323–331
   screens and printers, scaling between, 317–320
   text in MFC (Microsoft Foundation Classes) application, 302–316
   from Windows program, code, 299–301
PrintRectangle() function, 301
priority settings, processes and threads, 514–516
private clipboard formats, 603–609
processes. *See also* threads
   priority settings, 514–516
   threads, 513
ProcessFolder() function, 461–464
programmable objects, 626
programming
   with DDBs (device-dependent bitmaps), 336–352
   with DIBs (device-independent bitmaps), 352–395
   languages, C versus MFC (Microsoft Foundation Classes), 15–17
   progress bars, 230–231
   property sheets, 104–105
   sliders, 233–237
   spinners, 246–248
   standard controls, 170–179
   Windows, 7–14
Programs folder, applications, placing shortcuts, 506
programs
   code to print from, 299–301
   Direct3D, creating, 780, 781
   DirectDraw, creating, 714
   DirectInput, creating, 762
   DirectSound, creating, 741–742
   threads, communicating with, 523, 528–531
progress bars, 225, 229
   CommonControlsApp application, 231–233
   creating, 230–231
   initial positions, 230
   programming, 230–231

ranges, 230
step sizes, 230
Project menu
   Add To Project command, 368–369, 716, 743, 763
   Settings command, 64, 65, 793
Project Settings property sheet, 64, 65
Project Wizard – Choose Dialogs dialog box, 490
Project Wizard – Choose Target Platforms dialog box, 490
Project Wizard – Specify Components dialog box, 492
Project Wizard – Specify File Groups dialog box, 493
Project Wizard – Specify Setup Types dialog box, 491
Project Wizard – Summary dialog box, 493
Project Wizard – Welcome dialog box, 489
Projects tab (New dialog box), 61
Properties dialog box, 495–497
properties
   ActiveX control, creating, 702–705
   AddressBar, 856
   automation server, 678–682, 692
   Diameter, 680
   Offline, 856
   RegisterAsBrowser, 856
   RegisterAsDropTarget, 856
   Silent, 856
   TheaterMode, 856
   WebBrowser control, 856
   xPosition, 680
   yPosition, 680
property pages, 100
   Appearance, 101
   creating, 101–104
property sheets
   ClassWizard, 210–211, 656–657
   code to manage, 105
   creating, 101–104
   Dialog Properties, 102
   Menu Item Properties, 140–143
   pages, 100
   programming, 104–105
   Project Settings, 64, 65
   PropSheet application, 106–107
pSize argument, 136
pSrcDC argument, 342, 344
pstrAgent constructor, 827
pstrHeaders argument, 828
pstrName parameter, 541
pstrPassword argument, 831
pstrProxyBypass constructor, 827

pstrProxyName constructor, 827
pstrServer argument, 831
pstrURL argument, 828
pstrUserName argument, 831
pSurface argument, 731
PSWIZB_BACK constant, 108
PSWIZB_DISABLEDFINISH constant, 108
PSWIZB_FINISH constant, 108
PSWIZB_NEXT constant, 108
pszText (LV_COLUMN structure), 265
pszText (LV_ITEM structure), 266, 283
pText argument, 136
pushbutton control, 164
pushbuttons, 181–183
PutFile() function, 823
pvarArgIn parameter, 865
pvarArgOut parameter, 866
pWnd argument, 198

Q

QueryInfo() function, 821
QueryInfoStatusCode() function, 821
QueryInterface() function, 449
QueryOption() function, 821

R

R2_BLACK raster operation, 421
R2_COPYPEN raster operation, 421
R2_MASKNOTPEN raster operation, 422
R2_MASKPEN raster operation, 422
R2_MASKPENNOT raster operation, 421
R2_MERGENOTPEN raster operation, 422
R2_MERGEPEN raster operation, 422
R2_MERGEPENNOT raster operation, 421
R2_NOP raster operation, 421
R2_NOTCOPYPEN raster operation, 421
R2_NOTMASKPEN raster operation, 422
R2_NOTMERGEPEN raster operation, 422
R2_NOTXORPEN raster operation, 422
R2_WHITE raster operation, 421
R2_XORPEN raster operation, 422, 426–428
radio button control, 164

radio buttons, 168, 185–187
range selections, sliders, 238–245
ranges, progress bars, 230
raster operations, 426–428
    bitmap, 416–421
    line drawing modes, 421–425
RASTERCAPS constant, 40
RasterOpApp application, 417–421
rasters, 391–392
RatingAccessDeniedDialog() function, 860
RatingAccessDeniedDialog2() function, 860
RatingCheckUserAccess() function, 860
RatingEnable() function, 860
RatingEnabledQuery() function, 860
RatingFreeDetails() function, 860
RatingObtainCancel() function, 860
RatingObtainQuery() function, 860
RatingSetupUI() function, 860
Read() function, 251, 588, 823
ReadFileNames() function, FTPAccessApp application, 841
ReadHuge() function, 588
reading
    directories, 831–832
    files, 828
    user preferences for Registry, 480–483
ReadString() function, 823, 828
RealizePalette() function, 26
REALTIME_PRIORITY_CLASS class, 514
rect argument, 69, 172, 175, 182, 189
Rectangle menu@index H:Size command, 657, 664, 667
Rectangle() function, 26, 37
RedrawItems() function, 272
REG_BINARY (Registry data type), 471
REG_DWORD (Registry data type), 471, 479
REG_DWORD_BIG_ENDIAN (Registry data type), 471
REG_DWORD_LITTLE_ENDIAN (Registry data type), 471
REG_EXPAND_SZ (Registry data type), 471
REG_LINK (Registry data type), 471
REG_MULTI_SZ (Registry data type), 471
REG_NONE (Registry data type), 471
REG_OPTION_NON_VOLATILE argument, 478

REG_QWORD (Registry data type), 471
REG_RESOURCE_LIST (Registry data type), 471
REG_SZ (Registry data type), 471
RegCloseKey() function, 473, 474
RegCreateKey() function, 473, 474
RegCreateKeyEx() function, arguments, 477–479
RegDeleteKey() function, 473, 474
RegDeleteValue() function, 474
RegEnumKey() function, 474
RegEnumKeyEx() function, 474
RegEnumValue() function, 474
RegFlushKey() function, 474
RegionApp application, 430–435
regions of screens, 428
    combining, 430–435
    creating, 429–430
RegisterAsBrowser property, 856
RegisterAsDropTarget property, 856
RegisterClass() function, 15
registered clipboard formats, 603–609
registering
    drag-and-drop application, 444
    registering, private clipboard format, 605
Registry Editor, 468, 471–472
Registry
    data types, 471
    files, 472–473
    HKEY_CLASSES_ROOT (key), 469
    HKEY_CURRENT_CONFIG (key), 469
    HKEY_CURRENT_USER (key), 469
    HKEY_DYN_DATA (key), 469
    HKEY_LOCAL_MACHINE (key), 469
    HKEY_USERS (key), 469
    Internet Explorer versions, 878–879
    keys, 469–470
    organization of, 468–471
    overview, 467–468
    REG_BINARY (Registry data type), 471
    REG_DWORD (data type), 471
    REG_DWORD_BIG_ENDIAN (data type), 471
    REG_DWORD_LITTLE_ENDIAN (data type), 471
    REG_EXPAND_SZ (data type), 471
    REG_LINK (data type), 471
    REG_MULTI_SZ (data type), 471

Index

REG_NONE (data type), 471
REG_QWORD (data type), 471
REG_QWORD_LITTLE_ENDIAN (data type), 471
REG_RESOURCE_LIST (data type), 471
REG_SZ (data type), 471
  user preferences, reading, 480–483
  user preferences, writing, 475–480
  values, 470–471
  Win16 API functions, 474
  Win32 API functions, 473–474
RegistryApp application, 474
  reading user preferences, 480–483
  writing user preferences, 475–480
RegOpenKey() function, 474
RegOpenKeyEx() function, 474, 477
RegQueryInfoKey() function, 474
RegQueryValue() function, 474
RegQueryValueEx() function, 474
RegSetValue() function, 474
RegSetValueEx() function, 474, 479
relative priority settings, 514
Release() function, 451, 734, 754
ReleaseDC() function, 31
releasing pointers, 451
Remove() function, 251, 588
RemoveDirectory() function, 823
removing
  icons from system tray, 455
  MFC (Microsoft Foundation Classes) control buttons, 19–20
Rename() function, 588, 823
RenderAsBitmap() function, 613
RenderAsText() function, 614–615
RenderDisplay() function, 598–599, 613
rendering
  delayed to clipboard, 605–609
  paths, 436
  tasks, OnDraw() function, code, 99
Replace() function, 251
ReplaceSel() function, 179
ResetContent() function, 192
Resolve() function, 449
resource editor, 370–371
Resource Symbols dialog box, 700
Resources pane (MyApplication), 505
resources
  automation server, customizing, 673–675

BitmapApp2 application, customizing, 370–375
for menus, creating, 139–144
HTML dialog boxes, 866
semaphores, 541–545
ServerApp application, customizing, 655–659
ResumeThread() function, 536
retained mode, Direct3D programs, 781
RGN_AND mode, 432
RGN_COPY mode, 433
RGN_DIFF mode, 433
RGN_XOR mode, 431–432
robots, retrieving documents, 883
root
  directory, 831
  frames, creating, 784
  items of tree views, creating, 283–284
RoundRect() function, 26
running
  BitmapApp2 application, 380–383
  DialogControlApp application, 220–221
  Direct3DApp application, 794
  FTPAccessApp application, 832–835
  MyBrowser, 881–883
  ServerApp application, 663–668
RUNTIME_CLASS MFC macro, 522

S

Save As dialog box, 87, 89–90
Save dialog box, 89–90 95
Save File dialog box, code to handle, 97
Save() function, 450–451
SaveBarState() function, 59
saving
  files, modified, 586–587
  persistent and nonpersistent objects, 584–586
  shortcuts, 450–451
Scale menu@index H:Set Scaling command, 372, 380
scaling
  factors for printing, 323–331
  logical units, 409–410
  screens and printers, 317–320
Scramble
  application, 695–702
  control, 706–707
screens
  coordinates, 398
  DirectDraw, setting, 717–718

pixels, 397–398
and printers, scaling between, 317–320
regions, 428–435
sizes, obtaining, 12
Scroll() function, 272
SDI (single-document interface), 77
second edit control, 165–166
secondary
  buffer (DirectSound), creating, 745
  threads, 513, 538
Seek() function, 588, 823
SeekToEnd() function, 588
SelecObject() function, 26
select elements, 867
Select() function, 290
SelectDropTarget() function, 291
SelectItem() function, 291
SelectObject() function, 339
SelectPalette() function, 26
SelectSetFirstVisible() function, 291
SelectStockObject() function, 26
SelectString() function, 192
SelItemRange() function, 192
semaphores, 524, 541–545
SemaphoreThread() function, 542–543
SendMessage() function, 57
SendRequest() function, 821
SendRequestEx() function, 821
server applications, 624, 630–632
Server Document, 654
server item class, ServerApp application, 661
ServerApp application, 652–654
  document class, 659–661
  resources, customizing, 655–659
  running, 663–668
  server item class, 661
  view class, 662–663
servers, 651
  controlling from clients, 689–691
  FTP, 834
  HTTP, opening connections, 827–828
  OLE (object linking and embedding), 626
  skeleton automation, creating, 672–673
  skeleton server application, creating, 652–655
  type libraries, 685–686
  view class, 662–663
servers, automation, 632
  defining methods or properties, 678–682

Continued

Index

servers, automation *(continued)*
  document class, 676–677
  properties, accessing, 692
  resources, customizing, 673–675
  view class, 677–678
ServiceTypeFromHandle() function, 821
Set Circle dialog box, 675, 677
Set Scaling dialog box, 373
SetAccel() function, 247
SetActiveView() function, 59
SetActiveWindow() function, 57
SetAnchorIndex() function, 192
SetAnswerString() method, 705
SetArguments() function, 450
SetBase() function, 247
SetBitmap() function, 174, 183
SetBitmapBits() function, 337
SetBitmapDimensions() function, 337
SetBkColor() function, 26, 251, 272
SetBkMode() function, 115
SetBuddy() function, 236, 247
SetButtonStyle() function, 183
SetCallbackMask() function, 272
SetCapture() function, 57, 557–558
SetCaratIndex() function, 192
SetCheck() function, 149, 183
SetClipboardData() function, 597, 605
SetColumn() function, 272
SetColumnWidth() function, 192, 272
SetCookie() function, 821
SetCooperativeLevel() function, 717–718, 744–745, 766
SetCurrentColor() function, 95
SetCurrentDirectory() function, 823
SetCurSel() function, 192
SetCursor() function, 174, 183
SetDataFormat() function, 766
SetDescription() function, 450
SetDiameter() method, 680
SetDragCursorImage() function, 251
SetEnhMetaFile() function, 174
SetEvent() function, 530
SetFilePath() function, 588
SetFocus() function, 57
SetFont() function, 57
SetHandle() function, 179
SetHorizontalExtent() function, 192
SetHotkey() function, 450
SetHWnd() function, 803
SetIcon() function, 57, 174, 183
SetIconLocation() function, 450
SetIDList() function, 450
SetImageCount() function, 251

SetImageList() function, 272, 291
SetIndent() function, 291
SetItem() function, 272, 291
SetItemCount() function, 272
SetItemData() function, 192, 272, 291
SetItemDataPtr() function, 192
SetItemHeight() function, 192
SetItemImage() function, 291
SetItemPosition() function, 272
SetItemState() function, 272, 291
SetItemText() function, 272, 291
SetLength() function, 588
SetLimitText() function, 179
SetLineSize() function, 236
SetLocale() function, 192
SetMapMode() function, 26
SetMargins() function, 179
SetMaxPage() function, 306
SetMenu() function, 57
SetMessageText() function, 59
SetMinPage() function, 306
SetModifiedFlag() function, 586
SetModify() function, 179
SetObjectAsSelected() function, 645–646
SetOption() function, 821
SetOrientation() function, 789
SetOverlayImage() function, 251
SetPageSize() function, 236
SetPasswordChar() function, 179
SetPath() function, 450
SetPixel() function, 26
SetPos() function, 231, 236, 247
SetPosition() function, 786–787
SetQuality() function, 783
SetRadio() function, 150, 231, 236, 247
SetRange32() function, 231, 247
SetRangeMax() function, 236
SetRangeMin() function, 236
SetReadBufferSize() function, 824
SetReadOnly() function, 179
SetRect() function, 179, 640
SetRectNP() function, 179
SetRelativePath() function, 450
SetScrambleString() method, 704
SetSel() function, 179, 193
SetSelection() function, 237
SetShowCmd() function, 450
SetState() function, 183
SetStatus() function, 588
SetStep() function, 231
SetTabStops() function, 179, 193
SetTextAlign() function, 120, 123
SetTextBkColor() function, 272
SetTextColor() function, 26, 114, 272
SetTic() function, 237

SetTicFreq() function, 237
SetTimer() function, 57
Settings For dialog box, 64
SetTipSide() function, 237
SetToolTips() function, 237
SetTopIndex() function, 193
SetupTracker() function, 644–645
SetViewportExt() function, 410
SetViewportOrg() function, 310–311, 404–405
SetWindowExt() function, 410
SetWindowLong() function, 278–279
SetWindowOrg() function, 405–406
SetWindowText() function, 57, 177
SetWizardButtons() function, constants, 108
SetWorkingDirectory() function, 450
SetWriteBufferSize() function, 824
SetXPostion() method, 682
SetYPostion() method, 682
shading, Gouraud, 784
shapes, drawing in MetafileDCApp, 36
Shared DLLs, 496–497, 499
SHCONTF_FOLDERS, argument or values, 461
SHCONTF_INCLUDEHIDDEN values, 461
SHCONTF_INIT_ON_FIRST_NEXT values, 461
SHCONTF_NETPRINTERSRCH values, 461
SHCONTF_NONFOLDERS, argument or values, 461
shdocvw.dll file, Internet Explorer versions, 878–879
sheets. *See* property sheets
shell namespace, 458–464
Shell Objects – Shortcuts window, 506, 508
Shell_NotifyIcon() function, values, 454
ShellNotifyIcon() function, 455
shells, user-interfaceDragDrop2, 443
SHGDN_NORMAL argument, 464
SHGetDesktopFolder() function, 460
SHGetMalloc() function, 460
Shift key, tracking, 568
Shortcut application, 451–452
Shortcut Properties dialog box, 506–507
shortcuts. *See also* keyboard shortcuts
  applications, placing in Programs folder, 506

Index

COM, uninitializing, 451
COM, initializing, 447–448
initializing, 449–450
installing, 447
IPersistFile interface pointer, 449
IShellLink object, creating, 448
manipulating, 447–452
MFC (Microsoft Foundation Classes), 268–270, 287–289
pointers, releasing, 451
saving, 450–451
ShowControlBar() function, 59
ShowHTMLDialog() function, 862–866
ShowWindow() function, 57
signatures
   CColorDialog class constructor, 95
   CFileDialog class constructor, 87–88
   CFontDialog class constructor, 92
   CMutex class, 536
   Create() function, 172, 175, 181, 230, 262–263
   CSemaphore class, 541
   EnumPrinters() function, 296
   function, Visual C++ online documentation, 18
   Lock() function, code, 727
   OnCtlColor() function, 198
   ThreadProc() function, 516
   WndProc() function, 13
Silent property, 856
single-document interface (SDI), 77
single-line edit boxes, 174
Size dialog box, 658, 664, 667
sizeof(DWORD) argument, 479
sizeof(lpszFile) argument, 445
SIZEPALETTE constant, 40
sizes of screens, obtaining, 12
sizing
   lines of text, 135–138
   MFC (Microsoft Foundation Classes) windows, 18–19
skeleton
   ActiveX control, creating, 695–697
   applications, creating, 572–573
   automation server, creating, 672–673
   browser applications, creating, 851–861
   container application, creating, 635–638
   server application, creating, 652–655
Sleep() function, 536
sleeping threads, 536

SliderApp application, 244
sliders, 226
   CommonControlsApp application, 237–238
   creating, 233–237
   programming, 233–237
   range selections, 238–245
   styles, 234
   WM_HSCROLL messages, 235
SortChildren() function, 291
SortChildrenCB() function, 291
SortItems() function, 272
sound-hardware access level (DirectSound), setting, 744–745
source code. *See* code
spacing
   characters, setting, 118–119
   text, 128–130
spinners
   CommonControlsApp application, 248–249
   creating, 246–248
   programming, 246–248
   styles, 246–247
SRCAND raster operation, 391–392
SRCCOPY raster operation, 391, 417
SRCERASE (bitmap raster operations), 417
SRCINVERT (bitmap raster operations), 417
SRCPAINT raster operation, 391–392, 417
srcRect argument, 731
SS_BLACKFRAME (static control style), 172
SS_BLACKRECT (static control style), 172
SS_CENTER (static control style), 172
SS_GRAYFRAME (static control style), 173
SS_GRAYRECT (static control style), 173
SS_ICON (static control style), 173
SS_LEFT (static control style), 173
SS_LEFTNOWORDWRAP (static control style), 173
SS_NOPREFIX (static control style), 173
SS_RIGHT (static control style), 173
SS_SIMPLE (static control style), 173
SS_USERITEM (static control style), 173
SS_WHITEFRAME (static control style), 173

SS_WHITERECT (static control style), 173
stand-alone application, ServerApp, running as, 663–665
standard controls, 163
   button control styles, 182
   checkbox control, 164
   checkboxes, 167, 184–185
   colors, changing, 197–199
   combo box control, 164
   combo boxes, 193–197
   ControlApp2 application, 165–169, 171–172
   creating, 170–179
   CStatic control functions, 173–174
   Drop Down Combo Box, 169
   edit box control, 164
   edit boxes, single-line and multi-line, 174
   edit controls, 174–179
   first edit control, 165
   group box control, 164
   list box control, 164
   list boxes, 187–193
   message box displays, 168–169
   placing in non-dialog box windows, 164–165
   programming, 170–179
   pushbutton control, 164
   pushbuttons, 181–183
   radio button control, 164
   radio buttons, 168, 185–187
   second edit control, 165–166
   static controls, 170–174
   static text control, 164
   Windows controls, 164
Start menu, applications, adding, 505–508
StartDoc() function, 297
starting
   InstallShield project, 488–494
   Internet sessions, 827
state (LV_ITEM structure), 266
state (TV_ITEM structure), 283
stateMask (LV_ITEM structure), 266
stateMask (TV_ITEM structure), 283
statements, switch (BasicApp), 14
static controls, 170–174
static text control, 164
status bars, 226
Step 1 dialog box, 199–200
Step 2 dialog box, 200
step sizes, progress bars, 230
StepIt() function, 231
str argument, 126

StretchBlt() function, 26, 343–344
StretchDIBits() function, 363, 385–386, 390–391
String application, creating, 572–573
string argument, 114
StrokeAndFillPath() function, 436, 439
StrokePath() function, 436, 438
structures
    BIMAPINFO, 355
    BIMAPINFOHEADER, 355, 356
    BITMAPFILEHEADER, 354
    CREATESTRUCT, code, 72
    CRuntimeClass, 522
    DDSCAPS, 718–719
    DDSURFACEDESC, 718–719, 720
    DSBUFFERDESC, 745
    LOGFONT, 131–132
    NOTIFYICONDATA structure, 453–454
    PALETTEENTRY, 365
    TEXTMETRIC, members, 129
    TV_ITEM, 282
style argument, 42
styles
    button controls, 182
    combo box controls, 195
    CTreeCtrl class, 282
    edit controls, 176
    list box controls, 189–190
    list views, 263–264
    sliders, 234
    spinners, 246–247
    static control, 172–173
    windows, 69–76
    windows in non-MFC programs, 73–76
    WS_POPUP, 75–76
subkeys, Registry, 469–470
subpaths, defining, 437
Summary page, 503
surfaces, DirectDraw
    offscreen, creating, 720
    primary, creating, 718–719
suspending threads, 536
SuspendThread() function, 536
switch statement (BasicApp), 14
synchronization
    objects, 524
    synchronization, threads, 524–545
syntax, 866
system tray, icons, manipulating, 452–457
szTip (NOTIFYICONDATA structure), 453

T

Tab key, non-dialog box windows, 179–180
tabbed text, displaying, 126–127
TabbedTextOut() function, 126–127
tabOrigin argument, 126
tabs argument, 126
TabTextApp application, 127
tags, <OBJECT>, 708–709
TargetFrameName parameter, 857
taskbar, 452
TBS_AUTOTICKS (slider control style), 234
TBS_BOTH (slider control style), 234
TBS_BOTTOM (slider control style), 234
TBS_ENABLESELRANGE (slider control style), 234
TBS_HORZ (slider control style), 234
TBS_LEFT (slider control style), 234
TBS_NOTICKS (slider control style), 234
TBS_RIGHT (slider control style), 234
TBS_TOP (slider control style), 234
TBS_VERT (slider control style), 234
Test menu@index H:Property Sheet command, 106
testing
    ActiveX controls, 706–707
    ShowHTMLDialog() function, code, 862–864
text
    alignment, setting, 119–127
    character spacing, setting, 118–119
    color, setting, 114–118
    displaying, 113–114
    fonts, creating, 131–135
    horizontal alignment, 120–123
    lines, sizing, 135–138
    menu items, changing, 152
    metrics, 128–130
    printing in MFC (Microsoft Foundation Classes) application, 302–316
    spacing, 128–130
    tabbed, displaying, 126–127
    TEXTMETRIC structure members, 129
    vertical alignment, 123–125
TEXTMETRIC structure members, 129
TextMetricsApp application, 129–130

TextOut() function, 26, 113–114, 404
TheaterMode property, 856
Thread Message message box, 527
THREAD_PRIORITY_ABOVE_NORMAL class, 515
THREAD_PRIORITY_BELOW_NORMAL class, 515
THREAD_PRIORITY_CRITICAL class, 515
THREAD_PRIORITY_HIGHEST class, 515
THREAD_PRIORITY_IDLE class, 515
THREAD_PRIORITY_LOWEST class, 515
THREAD_PRIORITY_NORMAL class, 515
ThreadApp1 application, 517–518
ThreadApp2 application, 526–527
ThreadApp3 application, 531–533
ThreadApp4 application, 534–535
ThreadApp5 application, 537–540
ThreadApp6 application, 542–545
ThreadProc() function, 516–517
threads. *See also* processes
    base priority settings, 514
    primary, 513
    priority settings, 514–516
    programs, communicating with, 523, 528–531
    relative priority settings, 514
    secondary, 513, 538
    sleeping, 536
    suspending, 536
    synchronization, 524–545
    UI, creating, 519–522
    worker, creating, 516–519
Tick() function, 808
tmAscent (TEXTMETRIC), 129
tmAveCharWidth (TEXTMETRIC), 129
tmBreakChar (TEXTMETRIC), 129
tmCharSet (TEXTMETRIC), 129
tmDefaultChar (TEXTMETRIC), 129
tmDescent (TEXTMETRIC), 129
tmDigitalizedAspectX (TEXTMETRIC), 129
tmDigitalizedAspectY (TEXTMETRIC), 129
tmExternalLeading (TEXTMETRIC), 129
tmFirstChar (TEXTMETRIC), 129
tmHeight (TEXTMETRIC), 129
tmInternalLeading (TEXTMETRIC), 129
tmItalic (TEXTMETRIC), 129
tmLastChar (TEXTMETRIC), 129
tmMaxCharWidth (TEXTMETRIC), 129

Index

tmOverhang (TEXTMETRIC), 129
tmPitchAndFamily (TEXTMETRIC), 129
tmStruckOut (TEXTMETRIC), 129
tmUnderlined (TEXTMETRIC), 129
tmWeight (TEXTMETRIC), 129
toggles, options for menus, 149
toolbars, 226, 631–632
Tools menu
   ActiveX Control Test Container command, 701, 706
   Options command, 715
tracking
   Alt key, 568
   Ctrl key, 568
   Shift key, 568
traditional Win32 applications, 3–4
TranslateMessage() function, 13
TrayApp application, 455–457
tree views, 226, 279–280
   CommonControlsApp2 application code, 291–293
   functions, 289–291
   items, adding, 282–285
   items, editing, 285–287
   MFC (Microsoft Foundation Classes) shortcuts code, 287–289
   object, creating, 281–282
   root items, creating, 283–284
   user selections, responding to, 285
TV_ITEM structure, 282
TVS_DISABLEDRAGDROP (tree view style), 282
TVS_EDITLABELS (tree view style), 282
TVS_HASBUTTONS (tree view style), 282
TVS_HASLINES (tree view style), 282
TVS_LINESATROOT (tree view style), 282
TVS_NOTOOLTIPS (tree view style), 282
TVS_SHOWSELALWAYS (tree view style), 282
TVS_SINGLEEXPAND (tree view style), 282
type libraries, 685–686
Type Library dialog box, 686

U

uCallbackMessage (NOTIFYICON-DATA structure), 453
UDS_ALIGNLEFT (spinner style), 246
UDS_ALIGNRIGHT (spinner style), 246
UDS_ARROWKEYS (spinner style), 246
UDS_AUTOBUDDY (spinner style), 246
UDS_HORZ (spinner style), 246
UDS_NOTHOUSANDS (spinner style), 247
UDS_SETBUDDYINT (spinner style), 247
UDS_WRAP (spinner style), 247
uFlags (NOTIFYICONDATA structure), 453
UI
   functions, menus, 147–154
   threads, creating, 519–522
uID (NOTIFYICONDATA structure), 453
Undo() function, 179
uninitializing COM, 451
uninstalling warning, Internet Explorer 5.0 (IE 5.0), 880–881
Unlock() function, 534, 541
UnlockRange() function, 588
update command UI functions, 148, 152–154, 160–161
Update() function, 272
UpdateAllViews() function, 648
UpdateData() function, 57
URL parameter, 857
user interfaces
   ActiveX control, creating, 697–702
   Web browsers, 852
user preferences, Registry,
   reading, 480–483
   writing, 475–480
user selections
   list views, responding to, 267–268
   tree views, responding to, 285
user-interface shell, 443
utilities, Depends, 487

V

values
   EnumObjects() function, 461
   Registry, 470–471
   SHCONTF_FOLDERS, 461
   SHCONTF_INCLUDEHIDDEN, 461
   SHCONTF_INIT_ON_FIRST_NEXT, 461
   SHCONTF_NETPRINTERSRCH, 461
   SHCONTF_NONFOLDERS, 461
   Shell_NotifyIcon() function, 454
ValuetoText() function, 615
variables
   m_bufSize, 747
   m_button1, 769
   m_button2, 769
   m_button3, 769
   m_curDirectory, 836
   m_diameter, 675
   m_DIOK, 769
   m_DSOK, 747
   m_fileCount, 836
   m_fileLengths[ ], 836
   m_fileNames[ ], 836
   m_mouseX, 769
   m_mouseY, 769
   m_mouseZ, 769
   m_objectRect, 639
   m_password, 836
   m_pBuffer, 747
   m_pDIMouse, 769
   m_pDInput, 769
   m_pDS, 747
   m_pWave, 747
   m_site, 836
   m_username, 836
   member, FTPAccessApp application, 835–847
VBScript, 850–851
VerifyPos() function, 237
versions of Internet Explorer, 878–880
vertical alignment of text, 123–125
VerticalAlignApp application, 123–125
VERTRES constant, 40
VERTSIZE constant, 40
view class
   ActiveX, 662–663
   automation server, 677–678
   client application, 685–689
   constructor, 768–769
   dialog boxes, adding code, 212–214
   header file, code to declare functions, 156–157
   message-response functions, code to define, 158–159
   ServerApp application, 662–663
View menu@index H:Resource Symbols command, 700
view windows, 58
view-class constructor, DirectSoundApp, 746–747
viewport
   creating, 787–788
   extents, 409
   frame, creating, 786–787
   origins, 400–403

Index

views, document/view architecture, 571–578
virtual
　folders, shell namespace, 458
　key codes, 564–566
Visual C++
　online documentation, function signatures, 18
　project, DirectDraw files, adding, 715–717
　project, DirectInput files, adding, 763–764
　project, DirectSound files, adding, 742–744
VKeyToItem() function, 193

W

WaitForSingleObject() function, 530–531
Web Browser Property box, 855
Web browsers
　main user interface, 852
　parental lockout, implementing, 859–861
　skeleton browser applications, creating, 851–861
Web pages, ActiveX controls, placing, 708–709
Web sites, access control, 859–861
Web sites, Microsoft
　DirectX 7.0 SDK, 714
　DirectX SDK, 761
　DirectX5.0 SDK, 741
　Internet SDK, 850
WebBrowser
　control, configuring, 851–861, 877–881
　HTML pages, navigating, 856–858
　methods, 856–857
　navigational flags, 858
　shdocvw.dll, 850–851
WHITENESS (bitmap raster operations), 417
width argument, 42
win.ini file, 467
Win16 API Registry functions, 474
Win32 API Registry functions, 473–474
Win32 applications
　ActiveX controls, 6–7
　code, 8–10
　console applications, 4–5
　DLL (dynamic-link library), 5–6
　traditional, 3–4
　WordPad, 3–4
Windows 2000 Programming Bible, 443

Windows
　controls, 164
　messages, WndProc() function, 14
　programming, 7–14
Windows/System folder, DLLs (dynamic-link libraries), 6
windows, 53–54
　Add/Remove Programs properties, 504
　applications, creating without AppWizard, 60–69
　Basic Application, 8
　BasicApp, buttons removed, 72
　BasicApp2 application, 76
　child, 77–79
　class implementation file, code to create, 797–801
　Component-Program Files, 495, 498
　coordinates, 398
　extents, 409
　File Groups – Program Executable Files, 499–500
　File Groups – Program Executable Files\Links, 500–501
　frame, 58, 78–79
　InstallShield, 489
　main, dialog boxes, 199–202
　MDI (multiple-document interface), 77–79
　Media Build Wizard, 502
　MFC (Microsoft Foundation Classes), sizing, 18–19
　MyApplication, 488
　non-dialog box, placing standard controls, 164–165
　non-dialog box, Tab key, 179–180
　origins, 400–403
　Shell Objects – Shortcuts, 506, 508
　styles, 19–20, 69–76
　view, 58
WinInet, 819
　CFileFind class, 824–825
　CFtpConnection class, 822–823
　CFtpFileFind class, 825–826
　CHttpConnection class, 822
　CHttpFile class, 824
　CInternetConnection class, 821
　CInternetException class, 826
　CInternetFile class, 823–824
　classes, 820
　HTTP applications, writing, 826–829
　Internet sessions, starting, 827
WinInet
　FTP application, writing, 830–832

HTTP servers, connections, opening, 827–828
HTTP sessions, creating, 829
WinMain() function, 10, 11, 15, 735
WizardApp application, 110
wizards
　ActiveX ControlWizard, 695–696
　Back button, 107
　buttons, responding to, 109–110
　buttons, setting, 107–109
　creating, 107
　Finish button, 108
　Media Build Wizard window, 502
　Next button, 107–108
　WizardApp application, 110
wizards, AppWizard
　applications, creating, 15
　applications, implementing document/view architecture, 571–578
　DialogControlsApp application, creating, 203–206
　dialog boxes as main windows, 199–202
　skeleton automation server, creating, 672–673
　skeleton browser application, creating, 851–861
　skeleton container application, creating, 635–638
　skeleton server application, creating, 652–655
wizards, ClassWizard
　ActiveX control user interface, 698–699
　creating update commandUI functions, 148
　DeleteContents() function, overriding, 377
　dialog boxes, 80–81
　displaying, 103, 347
　message maps, 15
　message-response functions for menus, 144–146
　OnCreate() function, 328, 688–689
　OnLButtonDown() message-response function, 212
　OnPrint() function, 329
　OnRectangleSize() function, 662–663
　OnSetCursor() function, 642
　PreTranslateMessage() function, overriding, 180
　property sheet, 656–657
　type libraries, 685–686
　UI threads, creating, 519–522
WM_CAPTURECHANGED message, 549

Index   925

WM_CHAR message, 559, 561
WM_CTLCOLOR message, types of, 198
WM_DEADCHAR message, 559
WM_DESTROY message, 14
WM_DROPFILES message, 445
WM_HSCROLL messages, sliders, 235
WM_KEYDOWN message, 559
WM_KEYUP message, 559
WM_LBUTTONBLCLK message, 549
WM_LBUTTONDOWN message, 14, 549
WM_LBUTTONYUP message, 549
WM_MBUTTONDBLCLK message, 549
WM_MBUTTONDDOWN message, 549
WM_MBUTTONDUP message, 549
WM_MOUSEACTIVATE message, 549
WM_MOUSEHOVER message, 549
WM_MOUSELEAVE message, 549
WM_MOUSEMOVE message, 548, 549
WM_MOUSEWHEEL message, 549
WM_NCLBUTTONDBLCLK message, 550
WM_NCLBUTTONDOWN message, 550
WM_NCLBUTTONUP message, 550
WM_NCMBUTTONDBLCLK message, 550
WM_NCMBUTTONDOWN message, 550
WM_NCMBUTTONUP message, 550
WM_NCMOUSEHOVER message, 550
WM_NCMOUSELEAVE message, 550
WM_NCMOUSEMOVE message, 550, 551
WM_NCRBUTTONDBLCLK message, 550
WM_NCRBUTTONDOWN message, 550
WM_NCRBUTTONUP message, 550
WM_NCXBUTTONDBLCLK message, 550
WM_NCXBUTTONDOWN message, 550
WM_NCXBUTTONUP message, 550
WM_PAINT message, 14, 27, 28
WM_RBUTTONDBLCLK message, 549
WM_RBUTTONDOWN message, 549
WM_RBUTTONUP message, 549
WM_RENDERALL FORMATS message, 606
WM_RENDERFORMAT message, 606
WM_SYSCHAR message, 559
WM_XBUTTONDBLCLK message, 549
WM_XBUTTONDDOWN message, 549
WM_XBUTTONUP message, 549
WMDESTROYCLIPBOARD message, 606
WNDCLASS structure, 11
WndProc() function, 13, 14
WordPad, 3–4
worker threads, creating, 516–519
wParam parameter, 13
Write() function, 251, 588, 824
WriteHuge() function, 588
WriteString() function, 824
writing
  Direct3D applications, 808–814
  DirectDraw applications, code, 736–739
  DirectInput application, code, 773–777
  DirectSound applications, 755–760
  HTTP applications, 826–829
  MFC non-AppWizard applications, 795–808
  user preferences for Registry, 475–480
WS_BORDER constant, 70
WS_CAPTION constant, 70
WS_CHILD constant, 70
WS_CLIPCHILDREN constant, 70
WS_CLIPSIBLINGS constant, 70
WS_DISABLED constant, 70
WS_DLGFRAME constant, 70
WS_GROUP constant, 70
WS_HSCROLL constant, 70
WS_MAXIMIZE constant, 70
WS_MAXIMIZEBOX constant, 70
WS_MINIMIZE constant, 70
WS_MINIMIZEBOX constant, 70
WS_OVERLAPPED constant, 70
WS_OVERLAPPEDWINDOW constant, 70
WS_POPUP
  constant, 70
  style, 75–76
WS_POPUPWINDOW constant, 70
WS_SYSMENU constant, 70
WS_TABSTOP constant, 70
WS_THICKFRAME constant, 70
WS_VISIBLE constant, 70
WS_VSCROLL constant, 70
wsprintf() function, 40

X

X and Y coordinates, MM_TEXT mode, 404
X argument, 114
x argument, 126, 342, 343, 445
XDest argument, 363
"XPosition" argument, 479, 482
xPosition property, 680
xSrc argument, 342, 344
XSrc argument, 363

Y-Z

Y argument, 114
y argument, 126, 342, 343
Ydest argument, 363
yPosition property, 680
ySrc argument, 342, 344
YSrc argument, 363

IDG Books Worldwide, Inc. End-User License Agreement

READ THIS. You should carefully read these terms and conditions before opening the software packet(s) included with this book ("Book"). This is a license agreement ("Agreement") between you and IDG Books Worldwide, Inc. ("IDGB"). By opening the accompanying software packet(s), you acknowledge that you have read and accept the following terms and conditions. If you do not agree and do not want to be bound by such terms and conditions, promptly return the Book and the unopened software packet(s) to the place you obtained them for a full refund.

1. **License Grant.** IDGB grants to you (either an individual or entity) a nonexclusive license to use one copy of the enclosed software program(s) (collectively, the "Software") solely for your own personal or business purposes on a single computer (whether a standard computer or a workstation component of a multiuser network). The Software is in use on a computer when it is loaded into temporary memory (RAM) or installed into permanent memory (hard disk, CD-ROM, or other storage device). IDGB reserves all rights not expressly granted herein.

2. **Ownership.** IDGB is the owner of all right, title, and interest, including copyright, in and to the compilation of the Software recorded on the disk(s) or CD-ROM ("Software Media"). Copyright to the individual programs recorded on the Software Media is owned by the author or other authorized copyright owner of each program. Ownership of the Software and all proprietary rights relating thereto remain with IDGB and its licensers.

3. **Restrictions On Use and Transfer.**

    (a) You may only (i) make one copy of the Software for backup or archival purposes, or (ii) transfer the Software to a single hard disk, provided that you keep the original for backup or archival purposes. You may not (i) rent or lease the Software, (ii) copy or reproduce the Software through a LAN or other network system or through any computer subscriber system or bulletin-board system, or (iii) modify, adapt, or create derivative works based on the Software.

    (b) You may not reverse engineer, decompile, or disassemble the Software. You may transfer the Software and user documentation on a permanent basis, provided that the transferee agrees to accept the terms and conditions of this Agreement and you retain no copies. If the Software is an update or has been updated, any transfer must include the most recent update and all prior versions.

4. **Restrictions on Use of Individual Programs.** You must follow the individual requirements and restrictions detailed for each individual program in the About the CD-ROM appendix of this Book. These limitations are also contained in the individual license agreements

recorded on the Software Media. These limitations may include a requirement that after using the program for a specified period of time, the user must pay a registration fee or discontinue use. By opening the Software packet(s), you will be agreeing to abide by the licenses and restrictions for these individual programs that are detailed in the About the CD-ROM appendix and on the Software Media. None of the material on this Software Media or listed in this Book may ever be redistributed, in original or modified form, for commercial purposes.

5. **Limited Warranty.**

    (a) IDGB warrants that the Software and Software Media are free from defects in materials and workmanship under normal use for a period of sixty (60) days from the date of purchase of this Book. If IDGB receives notification within the warranty period of defects in materials or workmanship, IDGB will replace the defective Software Media.

    (b) **IDGB AND THE AUTHOR OF THE BOOK DISCLAIM ALL OTHER WARRANTIES, EXPRESS OR IMPLIED, INCLUDING WITHOUT LIMITATION IMPLIED WARRANTIES OF MERCHANTABILITY AND FITNESS FOR A PARTICULAR PURPOSE, WITH RESPECT TO THE SOFTWARE, THE PROGRAMS, THE SOURCE CODE CONTAINED THEREIN, AND/OR THE TECHNIQUES DESCRIBED IN THIS BOOK. IDGB DOES NOT WARRANT THAT THE FUNCTIONS CONTAINED IN THE SOFTWARE WILL MEET YOUR REQUIREMENTS OR THAT THE OPERATION OF THE SOFTWARE WILL BE ERROR FREE.**

    (c) This limited warranty gives you specific legal rights, and you may have other rights that vary from jurisdiction to jurisdiction.

6. **Remedies.**

    (a) IDGB's entire liability and your exclusive remedy for defects in materials and workmanship shall be limited to replacement of the Software Media, which may be returned to IDGB with a copy of your receipt at the following address: Software Media Fulfillment Department, Attn.: *Windows 2000 Programming Secrets*, IDG Books Worldwide, Inc., 10475 Crosspoint Blvd., Indianapolis, IN 46256, or call 1-800-762-2974. Please allow three to four weeks for delivery. This Limited Warranty is void if failure of the Software Media has resulted from accident, abuse, or misapplication. Any replacement Software Media will be warranted for the remainder of the original warranty period or thirty (30) days, whichever is longer.

    (b) In no event shall IDGB or the author be liable for any damages whatsoever (including without limitation damages for loss of business profits, business interruption, loss of business information, or any other pecuniary loss) arising from the use of or inability to use the Book or the Software, even if IDGB has been advised of the possibility of such damages.

(c) Because some jurisdictions do not allow the exclusion or limitation of liability for consequential or incidental damages, the above limitation or exclusion may not apply to you.

7. **U.S. Government Restricted Rights.** Use, duplication, or disclosure of the Software by the U.S. Government is subject to restrictions stated in paragraph (c)(1)(ii) of the Rights in Technical Data and Computer Software clause of DFARS 252.227-7013, and in subparagraphs (a) through (d) of the Commercial Computer — Restricted Rights clause at FAR 52.227-19, and in similar clauses in the NASA FAR supplement, when applicable.

8. **General.** This Agreement constitutes the entire understanding of the parties and revokes and supersedes all prior agreements, oral or written, between them and may not be modified or amended except in a writing signed by both parties hereto that specifically refers to this Agreement. This Agreement shall take precedence over any other documents that may be in conflict herewith. If any one or more provisions contained in this Agreement are held by any court or tribunal to be invalid, illegal, or otherwise unenforceable, each and every other provision shall remain in full force and effect.

my2cents.idgbooks.com

Register This Book — And Win!

Visit **http://my2cents.idgbooks.com** to register this book and we'll automatically enter you in our fantastic monthly prize giveaway. It's also your opportunity to give us feedback: let us know what you thought of this book and how you would like to see other topics covered.

Discover IDG Books Online!

The IDG Books Online Web site is your online resource for tackling technology — at home and at the office. Frequently updated, the IDG Books Online Web site features exclusive software, insider information, online books, and live events!

10 Productive & Career-Enhancing Things You Can Do at www.idgbooks.com

- Nab source code for your own programming projects.
- Download software.
- Read Web exclusives: special articles and book excerpts by IDG Books Worldwide authors.
- Take advantage of resources to help you advance your career as a Novell or Microsoft professional.
- Buy IDG Books Worldwide titles or find a convenient bookstore that carries them.
- Register your book and win a prize.
- Chat live online with authors.
- Sign up for regular e-mail updates about our latest books.
- Suggest a book you'd like to read or write.
- Give us your 2¢ about our books and about our Web site.

You say you're not on the Web yet? It's easy to get started with IDG Books' *Discover the Internet,* available at local retailers everywhere.

CD-ROM Installation Instructions

The CD-ROM that accompanies this book includes a batch file for transferring all the files on the CD-ROM to your hard drive. To transfer the files, perform the following steps:

1. Place the CD-ROM in your CD-ROM drive.

2. On the Windows Start menu, select the Run command. The Run dialog box appears.

3. In the dialog's Open box, type **A:\install A B**, where A is the letter for your CD-ROM drive and B is the destination drive. (Don't add colons to the drive letters.)

4. A DOS window appears, in which you can watch the batch file copy the book's files to your destination drive. (Example: If your CD-ROM drive is drive D, and you want to copy the book's files to drive C, you'd type **d:\install d c** into the Run dialog's Open box.

For more information on running the CD-ROM, please see the Appendix.